Test Item File

COST ACCOUNTING
A Managerial Emphasis

Test Item File

Karen Schoenebeck
Southwestern College, Winfield, Kansas

COST ACCOUNTING
A Managerial Emphasis
Eleventh Edition

HORNGREN   DATAR   FOSTER

Pearson Education

Upper Saddle River, New Jersey 07458

Acquisitions editor: Thomas Sigel
Assistant editor: Linda Albelli
Production editor: Carol Zaino
Manufacturer: Courier, Stoughton

ISBN 0-13-065021-8

10 9 8 7 6 5 4 3 2 1

CHAPTER 1: THE ACCOUNTANT'S ROLE IN THE ORGANIZATION

TRUE/FALSE

1. Management accounting information focuses on external reporting.

   Answer: False   *Difficulty*: 1   *Objective*: 1
   Management accounting information focuses on *internal* reporting.

2. A good cost accounting system is narrowly focused on a continuous reduction of costs.

   Answer: False   *Difficulty*: 2   *Objective*: 1
   A good cost accounting system is broadly focused to provide information that helps managers at all levels implement, monitor, and evaluate company strategies.

3. Modern cost accounting plays a significant role in management decision making.

   Answer: True   *Difficulty*: 1   *Objective*: 1

4. The balance sheet, income statement, and statement of cash flows are used for financial accounting, but not for management accounting.

   Answer: False   *Difficulty*: 1   *Objective*: 1
   The balance sheet, income statement, and statement of cash flows are used for financial accounting and also for management accounting.

5. Financial accounting is broader in scope than management accounting.

   Answer: False   *Difficulty*: 2   *Objective*: 1
   Management accounting is broader in scope than financial accounting.

6. Cost accounting measures and reports short-term, long-term, financial, and nonfinancial information.

   Answer: True   *Difficulty*: 2   *Objective*: 1

7. Cost management provides information that helps increase value for customers.

   Answer: True   *Difficulty*: 1   *Objective*: 1

8. Just-in-time production and purchasing is a strategy used to reduce inventories.

   Answer: True   *Difficulty*: 1   *Objective*: 2

9. All strategies should be evaluated regarding the resources and capabilities of the company.

   Answer: True   *Difficulty*: 1   *Objective*: 2

10. The best-designed strategies are valuable whether or not they are effectively implemented.

   Answer: False   *Difficulty*: 1   *Objective*: 2
   Implementation is essential or the strategy is useless.

11. The key to a company's success is creating value for customers while differentiating itself from its competitors.

   Answer: True   *Difficulty*: 1   *Objective*: 2

12. Developing a network of relationships with customers and suppliers is a valuable source of competitive advantage for a company.

   Answer: True   *Difficulty*: 1   *Objective*: 2

13. An important strategic decision is making the correct investments in productive assets.

   Answer: True   *Difficulty*: 1   *Objective*: 2

14. It is difficult to control activities without a budget.

   Answer: True   *Difficulty*: 1   *Objective*: 3

15. To take advantage of changing market opportunities, the annual budget should be strictly enforced.

   Answer: False   *Difficulty*: 2   *Objective*: 3
   To take advantage of changing market opportunities, the annual budget should be updated to reflect those changes.

16. A budget is a tool used to plan and express strategy.

   Answer: True   *Difficulty*: 2   *Objective*: 3

17. Linking rewards to performance is a major deterrent to good management performance.

   Answer: False   *Difficulty*: 1   *Objective*: 3
   Linking rewards to performance helps to motivate good management performance.

18. Employees pay little attention to how their performance is measured.

   Answer: False   *Difficulty*: 1   *Objective*: 3
   Employees are very aware of how their performance is measured.

19. A budget may be used as a planning tool, but not as a control tool.

   Answer: False   *Difficulty*: 1   *Objective*: 3
   A budget may be used as a planning tool and also as a control tool.

20. Financial accounting reports financial and nonfinancial information that helps managers implement company strategies.

Answer: False   *Difficulty*: 1   *Objective*: 3
Management accounting reports financial and nonfinancial information that helps managers implement company strategies.

21. Feedback links planning and control.

Answer: True   *Difficulty*: 1   *Objective*: 3

22. Control includes deciding what feedback to provide that will help with future decision making.

Answer: True   *Difficulty*: 1   *Objective*: 3

23. Attention-directing activities should focus on cost-reduction opportunities, and not on valued-adding opportunities.

Answer: False   *Difficulty*: 1   *Objective*: 4
Attention-directing activities should focus on cost-reduction opportunities and value-adding opportunities.

24. For strategic decisions, scorekeeping is the most prominent role played by management accounting.

Answer: False   *Difficulty*: 2   *Objective*: 4
For strategic decisions, *problem solving* is the most prominent role played by management accounting.

25. Management accountants often are simultaneously doing problem-solving, scorekeeping, and attention-directing activities.

Answer: True   *Difficulty*: 1   *Objective*: 4

26. Management accounting is playing an increasingly important role by helping managers develop and implement strategy.

Answer: True   *Difficulty*: 1   *Objective*: 4

27. An example of problem solving is evaluating bids from three different companies to supply a particular part used in manufacturing.

Answer: True   *Difficulty*: 2   *Objective*: 4

28. Key success factors are geared to improving customer satisfaction.

Answer: True   *Difficulty*: 2   *Objective*: 5

29. Value chain refers to its value to the employee.

   Answer: False   *Difficulty*: 1   *Objective*: 5
   Value chain refers to its value to the *customer*.

30. Companies have to follow strict guidelines when designing a management accounting system.

   Answer: False   *Difficulty*: 1   *Objective*: 5
   The design of a management accounting system should be guided by the challenges facing managers.

31. An effective way to cut costs is to eliminate activities that do not improve the product attributes that customers value.

   Answer: True   *Difficulty*: 1   *Objective*: 6

32. For optimal planning success it is best if each business function within the value chain is performed one at a time in sequence.

   Answer: False   *Difficulty*: 1   *Objective*: 6
   Optimally, success is achieved when two or more of the individual business functions work concurrently as a team.

33. For best results, cost management emphasizes independently coordinating supply chain activities within your company and not interfering with other companies.

   Answer: *False*   *Difficulty*: 2   *Objective*: 6
   Cost management emphasizes integrating and coordinating supply chain activities across all companies within the supply chain.

34. Tracking what is happening in other companies is illegal.

   Answer: False   *Difficulty*: 1   *Objective*: 6
   Tracking what is happening in other companies alerts managers to changes in their industry and can be accomplished in many legal ways such as visiting competitor's Web sites and reviewing their financial statements.

35. Customer focus is a key ingredient in new product development.

   Answer: True   *Difficulty*: 1   *Objective*: 6

36. Technological innovation has led to shorter product-life cycles and a need to bring new products to market more rapidly.

   Answer: True   *Difficulty*: 1   *Objective*: 6

37. Key success factors include cost, quality, timeliness, and innovation.

    Answer: True   *Difficulty*: 1   *Objective*: 6

38. Customers are demanding increased levels of performance in all aspects of the value chain and the supply chain.

    Answer: True   *Difficulty*: 1   *Objective*: 6

39. When a particular aspect of employee performance is measured, employees pay more attention to it.

    Answer: True   *Difficulty*: 2   *Objective*: 7

40. It is generally easy to quantify expected benefits and costs when applying the cost-benefit approach.

    Answer: False   *Difficulty*: 2   *Objective*: 7
    It is challenging and generally costly to quantify expected benefits and costs when applying the cost-benefit approach.

41. The use of teams to achieve corporate objectives is increasing.

    Answer: True   *Difficulty*: 2   *Objective*: 8

42. By reporting and interpreting relevant data, the controller exerts an influence that impels management toward making informed decisions.

    Answer: True   *Difficulty*: 2   *Objective*: 8

43. The controller (also called the chief accounting officer) is the financial executive primarily responsible for both management accounting and financial accounting.

    Answer: True   *Difficulty*: 1   *Objective*: 8

44. Management accountants have important ethical responsibilities that are related to competence, confidentiality, integrity, and objectivity.

    Answer: True   *Difficulty*: 1   *Objective*: 9

45. Management accounting
    a. focuses on estimating future revenues, costs, and other measures to forecast activities and their results.
    b. provides information about the company as a whole.
    c. reports information that has occurred in the past that is verifiable and reliable.
    d. provides information that is generally available only on a quarterly or annual basis.

    Answer: a   *Difficulty*: 2   *Objective*: 1

46. Financial accounting
    a. focuses on the future and includes activities such as preparing next year's operating budget.
    b. must comply with GAAP (generally accepted accounting principles).
    c. reports include detailed information on the various operating segments of the business such as product lines or departments.
    d. is prepared for the use of department heads and other employees.

    Answer: b   *Difficulty*: 2   *Objective*: 1

47. The person MOST likely to use ONLY financial accounting information is a
    a. factory shift supervisor.
    b. vice president of operations.
    c. current shareholder.
    d. department manager.

    Answer: c   *Difficulty*: 1   *Objective*: 1

48. The person MOST likely to use management accounting information is a(n)
    a. banker evaluating a credit application.
    b. shareholder evaluating a stock investment.
    c. governmental taxing authority.
    d. assembly department supervisor.

    Answer: d   *Difficulty*: 1   *Objective*: 1

49. Financial accounting provides the PRIMARY source of information
    a. for decision making in the finishing department.
    b. for improving customer service.
    c. for preparing the income statement for shareholders.
    d. for planning next year's operating budget.

    Answer: c   *Difficulty*: 2   *Objective*: 1

50. Which of the following descriptors refers to management accounting information?
    a. It is verifiable and reliable.
    b. It is driven by rules.
    c. It is prepared for shareholders.
    d. It provides reasonable and timely estimates.

    Answer: d   *Difficulty*: 2   *Objective*: 1

51. Which of the following statements refers to management accounting information?
    a. There are no regulations governing the reports.
    b. The reports are generally delayed and historical.
    c. The audience tends to be stockholders, creditors, and tax authorities.
    d. It primarily measures and records business transactions.

    Answer: a   *Difficulty*: 2   *Objective*: 1

52. Which of the following groups would be LEAST likely to receive detailed management accounting reports?
    a. Stockholders
    b. Sales representatives
    c. Production supervisors
    d. Managers

    Answer: a   *Difficulty*: 1   *Objective*: 1

53. Management accounting information includes
    a. tabulated results of customer satisfaction surveys.
    b. the cost of producing a product.
    c. the percentage of units produced that are defective.
    d. all of the above.

    Answer: d   *Difficulty*: 1   *Objective*: 1

54. Cost accounting
    a. provides information on the efficiency of factory labor.
    b. provides information on the cost of servicing commercial customers.
    c. provides information on the performance of an operating division.
    d. all of the above.

    Answer: d   *Difficulty*: 1   *Objective*: 1

55. Which of the following types of information are used in management accounting?
    a. Financial information
    b. Nonfinancial information
    c. Information focused on the long term
    d. All of the above

    Answer: d   *Difficulty*: 2   *Objective*: 1

56. Modern cost accounting plays a role in
    a.   planning new products.
    b.   evaluating operational processes.
    c.   controlling costs.
    d.   all of the above.

    Answer: d   *Difficulty:*   1   *Objective:*   1

57. A data warehouse or infobarn
    a.   is reserved for exclusive use by the CFO.
    b.   is primarily used for financial reporting purposes.
    c.   stores information used by different managers for multiple purposes.
    d.   gathers only nonfinancial information.

    Answer: c   *Difficulty:*   1   *Objective:*   1

58. Cost accounting provides all EXCEPT
    a.   information for management accounting and financial accounting.
    b.   pricing information from marketing studies.
    c.   financial information regarding the cost of acquiring resources.
    d.   nonfinancial information regarding the cost of operational efficiencies.

    Answer: b   *Difficulty:*   2   *Objective:*   1

59. Management accounting includes
    a.   implementing strategies.
    b.   developing budgets.
    c.   preparing special studies and forecasts.
    d.   all of the above.

    Answer: d   *Difficulty:*   1   *Objective:*   1

60. Financial accounting is concerned PRIMARILY with
    a.   external reporting to investors, creditors, and government authorities.
    b.   cost planning and cost controls.
    c.   profitability analysis.
    d.   providing information for strategic and tactical decisions.

    Answer: a   *Difficulty:*   2   *Objective:*   1

61. Financial accounting provides a historical perspective, whereas management accounting emphasizes
    a.   the future.
    b.   past transactions.
    c.   a current perspective.
    d.   reports to shareholders.

    Answer: a   *Difficulty:*   1   *Objective:*   1

62. Which of the following is NOT a function of a management accounting system?
    a. Budget preparation
    b. Financial reporting
    c. Operational control
    d. Product and customer costing

    Answer: b   *Difficulty:* 2   *Objective:* 2

63. Strategy specifies
    a. how an organization matches its own capabilities with the opportunities in the marketplace.
    b. standard procedures to ensure quality products.
    c. incremental changes for improved performance.
    d. the demand created for products and services.

    Answer: a   *Difficulty:* 2   *Objective:* 2

64. Strategy is formulated by answering all of the following EXCEPT
    a. Who are our most important customers?
    b. Is industry demand growing or shrinking?
    c. How can we continue to reduce production costs?
    d. How sensitive are purchasers to price, quality, and service?

    Answer: c   *Difficulty:* 3   *Objective:* 2

65. Building resources and capabilities includes
    a. reducing available cash.
    b. keeping inventory information private from suppliers.
    c. building raw-material inventory levels.
    d. building a strong distribution network.

    Answer: d   *Difficulty:* 2   *Objective:* 2

66. Well-implemented just-in-time production and purchasing techniques
    a. result in large stockpiles of inventory to keep production running.
    b. strengthen a company's ability to compete in the marketplace.
    c. increase reliance on long-term consumer forecasts.
    d. reduce a company's competitive edge.

    Answer: b   *Difficulty:* 2   *Objective:* 2

67. Long-term productive assets include
    a. cash.
    b. manufacturing equipment and buildings.
    c. patents and trademarks.
    d. brand names.

    Answer: b   *Difficulty:* 1   *Objective:* 2

68. Computer-integrated manufacturing (CIM) plants allow management to do all EXCEPT
   a. create brand recognition.
   b. diagnose the reason for a defect.
   c. access timely and accurate information regarding production costs.
   d. respond faster to changes in customer preferences.

   Answer: a   *Difficulty*: 2   *Objective*: 2

69. The Internet and the World Wide Web are PRIMARILY used to
   a. create performance reports.
   b. collect cost data.
   c. enhance contact with customers and suppliers.
   d. prepare budget information.

   Answer: c   *Difficulty*: 2   *Objective*: 2

70. Investments in long-term productive assets include all EXCEPT
   a. investments in robotics.
   b. investments in information infrastructures.
   c. investments in a high-quality parts inventory.
   d. investments in Internet applications.

   Answer: c   *Difficulty*: 2   *Objective*: 2

71. In designing strategy, a company must match the opportunities and threats in the marketplace with
   a. those of the CFO (Chief Financial Officer).
   b. its resources and capabilities.
   c. branding opportunities.
   d. capabilities of current suppliers.

   Answer: b   *Difficulty*: 2   *Objective*: 2

72. The process of preparing a budget
   a. forces coordination and communication across business functions.
   b. increases accounting efficiencies.
   c. reduces overcapacity.
   d. promotes production automation.

   Answer: a   *Difficulty*: 2   *Objective*: 3

73. Control includes
   a. implementing planning decisions.
   b. evaluating performance.
   c. providing feedback to help with future decision making.
   d. all of the above.

   Answer: d   *Difficulty*: 1   *Objective*: 3

74. A budget
    a. is a quantitative expression of a proposed management plan.
    b. helps translate strategy into actions.
    c. aids in the coordination and communication among various business functions.
    d. does all of the above.

    Answer: d   *Difficulty:* 1   *Objective:* 3

75. A budget can serve
    a. as a planning tool.
    b. as a control tool.
    c. as a basis for preparing financial statements.
    d. both (a) and (b).

    Answer: d   *Difficulty:* 1   *Objective:* 3

76. Employees _____ how their performance is measured.
    a. pay close attention to
    b. pay no attention to
    c. rarely know
    d. both (b) and (c)

    Answer: a   *Difficulty:* 1   *Objective:* 3

77. Linking rewards to performance
    a. helps to motivate managers.
    b. allows companies to charge premium prices.
    c. should only be based on financial information.
    d. does all of the above.

    Answer: a   *Difficulty:* 2   *Objective:* 3

78. Control measures should
    a. be set and not changed until the next budget cycle.
    b. be flexible to allow for employees who are slackers.
    c. be kept confidential from employees so that competitors don't have an opportunity to gain a competitive advantage.
    d. be linked by feedback to planning.

    Answer: d   *Difficulty:* 2   *Objective:* 3

79. A well-conceived plan allows managers the ability to
    a. not make decisions again until the next planning session.
    b. keep lower-level managers from implementing change.
    c. underestimate costs so that actual operating results will be favorable when comparisons are made.
    d. take advantage of unforeseen opportunities.

    Answer: d   *Difficulty:* 2   *Objective:* 3

80. For control decisions, emphasis is place on the _____ role(s) of management accounting.
    a.   problem-solving
    b.   scorekeeping
    c.   attention-directing
    d.   both (b) and (c)

    Answer: d   *Difficulty:*   2   *Objective:*   4

81. For strategic decisions, emphasis is placed on the _____ role(s) of management accounting.
    a.   problem-solving
    b.   scorekeeping
    c.   attention-directing
    d.   both (b) and (c)

    Answer: a   *Difficulty:*   1   *Objective:*   4

82. Tracking the type of product returned is a PRIMARY example of
    a.   problem solving.
    b.   scorekeeping.
    c.   attention directing.
    d.   both (a) and (b).

    Answer: c   *Difficulty:*   2   *Objective:*   4

83. A daily sales report is a PRIMARY example of
    a.   problem solving.
    b.   scorekeeping.
    c.   attention directing.
    d.   both (a) and (b).

    Answer: b   *Difficulty:*   2   *Objective:*   4

84. Making a recommendation regarding the leasing or purchasing of a fleet of vehicles is a PRIMARY example of
    a.   problem solving.
    b.   scorekeeping.
    c.   attention directing.
    d.   both (a) and (b).

    Answer: a   *Difficulty:*   2   *Objective:*   4

85. _____ means reporting and interpreting information that helps managers to focus on operating problems, imperfections, inefficiencies, and opportunities.
    a.   Scorekeeping
    b.   Attention directing
    c.   Problem solving
    d.   None of the above

    Answer: b   *Difficulty:*   1   *Objective:*   4

86. _____ identifies several available alternatives and often recommends the best course to follow.
   a.   Scorekeeping
   b.   Attention directing
   c.   Problem solving
   d.   None of the above

   Answer: c   *Difficulty:*   1   *Objective:*   4

87. Management accounting is considered successful when it
   a.   helps creditors evaluate the company's performance.
   b.   helps managers improve their decisions.
   c.   is accurate.
   d.   is relevant and reported annually.

   Answer: b   *Difficulty:*   2   *Objective:*   4

88. Strategy should focus PRIMARILY on the organization's
   a.   shareholders.
   b.   customers.
   c.   products.
   d.   employees.

   Answer: b   *Difficulty:*   2   *Objective:*   5

89. Whose perceptions of the company's products or services are the most important to the manager?
   a.   Board of directors' perception
   b.   Customers' perception
   c.   President's perception
   d.   Stockholders' perception

   Answer: b   *Difficulty:*   2   *Objective:*   5

90. To be successful, a company needs to be
   a.   customer driven.
   b.   "driven" by the board of directors.
   c.   employee driven.
   d.   management driven.

   Answer: a   *Difficulty:*   2   *Objective:*   5

91. _____ is/are when a firm compares itself with the best practice of competitors or other comparable organizations.
   a.   Value chain
   b.   Supply chain
   c.   Key success factors
   d.   Benchmarking

   Answer: d   *Difficulty:*   1   *Objective:*   6

92. Place the four business functions in the order they appear along the value chain:

   A = Customer service
   B = Design
   C = Distribution
   D = Production

   a. A B D C
   b. A C D B
   c. B D C A
   d. B A D C

   Answer: c   *Difficulty:* 2   *Objective:* 6

93. R&D, production, and customer service are business functions that are all included as part of
   a. the value chain.
   b. benchmarking.
   c. marketing.
   d. the supply chain.

   Answer: a   *Difficulty:* 1   *Objective:* 6

94. The value chain is the sequence of business functions in which
   a. value is deducted from the products or services of an organization.
   b. value is proportionately added to the products or services of an organization.
   c. products and services are evaluated with respect to their value to the supply chain.
   d. usefulness is added to the products or services of an organization.

   Answer: d   *Difficulty:* 2   *Objective:* 6

95. _____ is the generation of, and experimentation with, ideas related to new products, services, or processes.
   a. Research and development
   b. Design of products, services, or processes
   c. Production
   d. Marketing

   Answer: a   *Difficulty:* 1   *Objective:* 6

96. _____ is the detailed planning and engineering of products, services, or processes.
   a. Distribution
   b. Design of products, services, or processes
   c. Production
   d. Marketing

   Answer: b   *Difficulty:* 1   *Objective:* 6

97. _____ is the acquisition, coordination, and assembly of resources to produce a product or deliver a service.
    a.   Research and development
    b.   Customer service
    c.   Production
    d.   Marketing

    Answer: c   *Difficulty*:   1   *Objective*:   6

98. _____ is the manner by which companies promote and sell their products or services to customers or perspective customers.
    a.   Distribution
    b.   Customer service
    c.   Research and development
    d.   Marketing

    Answer: d   *Difficulty*:   1   *Objective*:   6

99. _____ is the delivery of products or services to customers.
    a.   Distribution
    b.   Customer service
    c.   Production
    d.   Design of products, services, or processes

    Answer: a   *Difficulty*:   1   *Objective*:   6

100. _____ is the after-sale support provided to customers.
    a.   Distribution
    b.   Customer service
    c.   Production
    d.   Marketing

    Answer: b   *Difficulty*:   1   *Objective*:   6

101. _____ is an operational factor that directly affects the economic viability of the organization.
    a.   Customer focus
    b.   A key success factor
    c.   Continuous improvement
    d.   Supply chain

    Answer: b   *Difficulty*:   2   *Objective*:   6

102. _____ describe(s) the flow of goods, services, and information from the purchase of materials to the delivery of products to consumers, regardless of whether those activities occur in the same organization or with other organizations.
    a. Supply chain
    b. Key success factors
    c. Continuous improvement
    d. Customer focus

    Answer: a   *Difficulty*: 1   *Objective*: 6

103. Customers are demanding improved performance related to
    a. reduced costs.
    b. both reduced costs and increased quality.
    c. lower costs, improved quality, and improved customer service.
    d. lower costs, improved quality, improved customer service, and innovative products and services.

    Answer: d   *Difficulty*: 2   *Objective*: 6

104. The act of simply measuring and reporting information
    a. focuses the attention of employees on those processes.
    b. diverts employee's attention to other activities.
    c. disproves the saying "What gets measured gets managed."
    d. has no effect on employee behavior.

    Answer: a   *Difficulty*: 2   *Objective*: 7

105. Which statement is FALSE?
    a. "What gets measured gets managed."
    b. People react to measurements.
    c. Employees spend more attention on those variables that are not getting measured.
    d. "If I can't measure it, I can't manage it."

    Answer: c   *Difficulty*: 2   *Objective*: 7

106. The PRIMARY criterion when faced with a resource allocation decision is
    a. cost minimization.
    b. reduction in the amount of time required to perform a particular job.
    c. achievement of organizational goals.
    d. how well the alternative options help achieve organizational goals in relation to the costs incurred for these systems.

    Answer: d   *Difficulty*: 3   *Objective*: 7

107. The person(s) directly responsible for the attainment of organizational objectives is/are
    a. the treasurer.
    b. line management.
    c. the controller.
    d. the chief financial officer.

    Answer: b   *Difficulty*: 1   *Objective*: 8

108. As teamwork has become more prominent in the last few years, differences between staff and line management
    a. have increased.
    b. have become more important relative to promotions.
    c. have diminished.
    d. have only been evident in the employee reward system.

    Answer: c   *Difficulty*: 2   *Objective*: 8

109. The Institute of Management Accountants (IMA)
    a. is a professional organization of management accountants.
    b. is a professional organization of financial accountants.
    c. issues standards for management accounting.
    d. issues standards for financial accounting.

    Answer: a   *Difficulty*: 2   *Objective*: 8

110. Line management includes
    a. manufacturing managers.
    b. human-resource managers.
    c. information-technology managers.
    d. management-accounting managers.

    Answer: a   *Difficulty*: 2   *Objective*: 8

111. Staff management includes
    a. manufacturing managers.
    b. human-resource managers.
    c. purchasing managers.
    d. distribution managers.

    Answer: b   *Difficulty*: 2   *Objective*: 8

112. Responsibilities of a CFO include all EXCEPT
    a. providing financial reports to shareholders.
    b. managing short-term and long-term financing.
    c. investing in new equipment.
    d. preparing federal, state, and international tax returns.

    Answer: c   *Difficulty*: 3   *Objective*: 8

113. The _____ is primarily responsible for management accounting and financial accounting.
    a.   CFO (Chief Financial Officer)
    b.   CIO (Chief Information Officer)
    c.   treasurer
    d.   controller

    Answer: d   *Difficulty:*   1   *Objective:*   8

114. All of the following report to the CFO EXCEPT the
    a.   controller.
    b.   tax department manager.
    c.   production manager.
    d.   treasurer.

    Answer: c   *Difficulty:*   1   *Objective:*   8

115. Management accounting is an integral part of the _____ function in an organization.
    a.   treasurer's
    b.   controller's
    c.   internal audit
    d.   president's

    Answer: b   *Difficulty:*   1   *Objective:*   8

116. The Standards of Ethical Conduct for management accountants include concepts related to
    a.   competence, performance, integrity, and reporting.
    b.   competence, confidentiality, integrity, and objectivity.
    c.   experience, integrity, reporting, and objectivity.
    d.   none of the above as ethical issues do not affect management accountants.

    Answer: b   *Difficulty:*   2   *Objective:*   9

117. Ethical challenges for management accountants include
    a.   whether to accept gifts from suppliers, knowing it is an effort to indirectly influence decisions.
    b.   whether to report unfavorable department information that may result in unfavorable consequences for a friend.
    c.   whether to file a tax return this year.
    d.   both (a) and (b).

    Answer: d   *Difficulty:*   2   *Objective:*   9

EXERCISES AND PROBLEMS

118. For each report listed below, identify whether the major purpose of the report is for (1) routine internal reporting, (2) nonroutine internal reporting, or for (3) external reporting to investors and other outside parties.

Required:
a. Study detailing sale information of the top-ten selling products.
b. Weekly report of total sales generated by each store in the metropolitan area.
c. Annual Report sent to shareholders.
d. Monthly report comparing budgeted sales by store to actual sales.

Answer:
a. (2) Nonroutine internal reporting
b. (1) Routine internal reporting
c. (3) External reporting to investors and other outside parties
d. (1) Routine internal reporting

Difficulty: 2   *Objective*: 1

119. For each type of report listed below, identify one planning decision and one controlling decision for which the information would be helpful. Assume you are a Walgreen Company store.

Required:
a. Annual financial statements for the past three years.
b. Report detailing sales by department by each hour of the day for the past week.
c. Special study regarding increased road traffic due to the construction of a new shopping mall at a near-by intersection.

Answer: Please note that answers will vary, but may include
a. Planning: Decision by shareholder about whether to purchase more stock in the company.
   Control: Decision by bank to determine if financial ratios maintained in the line-of-credit (LOC) agreement warrant increasing the LOC amount.

b. Planning: Decisions regarding future staffing needs.
   Control: Decision regarding whether the recent sales promotion led to an increase in revenue.

c. Planning: Decision of the store manager about whether to change the types of retail items carried.
   Control: Decision of the store manager regarding performance of the analyst that prepared the special study.

Difficulty: 3   *Objective*: 3

120. For each of the following activities, identify whether the main role of accounting is (1) problem solving, (2) scorekeeping, or (3) attention directing.

Required:
a.   Analyzing the impact of introducing a new product on production.
b.   Comparing results between actual costs and budgeted costs for each step of manufacturing a product.
c.   Preparing a report that analyzes changes in cost resulting from reducing the number of tubing sizes used during production from six down to two.
d.   Reporting sales by branch for the sales manager.

Answer:
a.   (1) Problem solving
b.   (3) Attention directing
c.   (1) Problem solving
d.   (2) Scorekeeping

Difficulty: 2   *Objective*:   4

121. Classify each cost item into one of the business functions of the value chain, either (1) R&D, (2) Design, (3) Production, (4) Marketing, (5) Distribution, or (6) Customer service.

Required:
a.   Cost of samples mailed to promote sales of a new product.
b.   Labor cost of workers in the manufacturing plant.
c.   Bonus paid to person with a 90% satisfaction rating in handling customers with complaints.
d.   Transportation costs for shipping products to retail outlets.

Answer:
a.   (4) Marketing
b.   (3) Production
c.   (6) Customer service
d.   (5) Distribution

Difficulty: 2   *Objective*:   6

122. Classify each cost item of Ripon Printers into one of the business functions of the value chain, either (1) R&D, (2) Design, (3) Production, (4) Marketing, (5) Distribution, or (6) Customer service.

Required:
a. Cost of customer order forms.
b. Cost of paper used in manufacture of books.
c. Cost of paper used in packing cartons to ship books.
d. Cost of paper used in display at national trade show.
e. Depreciation of trucks used to transport books to college bookstores.
f. Cost of the wood used to manufacture paper.
g. Salary of the scientists attempting to find another source of printing ink.
h. Cost of defining the book size so that a standard-sized box is filled to capacity.

Answer:
a. (4) Marketing
b. (3) Production
c. (5) Distribution
d. (4) Marketing
e. (5) Distribution
f. (3) Production
g. (1) Research and development
h. (2) Design

Difficulty: 2   *Objective*:   6

123. For each of the following items, identify which of the three key management guidelines applies: (1) Cost-benefit approach, (2) Behavioral and technical considerations, or (3) Different costs for different purposes.

Required:
a. Considering the desirability of hiring another production supervisor.
b. Introducing a new commission scale for salespersons.
c. Deciding between the deluxe or the standard package of a new billing software package.
d. Reporting total company sales to shareholders, but sales by store to the CFO.

Answer:
a. (1) Cost -benefit approach
b. (2) Behavioral and technical considerations
c. (1) Cost -benefit approach
d. (3) Different costs for different purposes

Difficulty: 2   *Objective*:   7

CRITICAL THINKING

124. Describe management accounting and financial accounting.

Answer:
Management accounting provides information to internal decision makers of the business such as top executives, managers, sales representatives, and production supervisors. Its purpose is to help managers predict and evaluate future results. Reports are generated often and usually broken down into smaller reporting divisions such as department or product line. There are no rules to be complied with since these reports are for internal use only. Management accounting embraces more extensively such topics as the development and implementation of strategies and policies, budgeting, special studies and forecasts, influence on employee behavior, and nonfinancial as well as financial information.

Financial accounting provides information to external decision makers such as investors and creditors. Its purpose is to present a fair picture of the financial condition of the company. Reports are generated quarterly or annually and report on the company as a whole. The financial statements must comply with GAAP (generally accepted accounting principles). A CPA audits, or verifies, that the GAAP are being followed.

Difficulty: 2   *Objective*:   1

125. Is financial accounting or management accounting more useful to an operations manager? Why?

Answer:
Management accounting is more useful to an operations manager because management accounting reports operating results by department or unit rather than for the company as a whole, it includes financial as well as nonfinancial data such as on-time deliveries and cycle times, and it includes quantitative as well as qualitative data such as the type of rework that was needed on defective units.

Difficulty: 3   *Objective*:   1

126. What is strategy? Briefly describe the two broad types of strategies that companies may choose to pursue.

Answer:
Strategy specifies how an organization matches its own capabilities with the opportunities in the marketplace to accomplish its objectives. In other words, strategy describes how a company will compete.

Companies follow one of two broad strategies. One is provide a *quality* product or service at *low* prices. The other is to compete on their ability to offer a *unique* product or service that is generally offered at a *higher* price.

Difficulty: 2   Objective: 2

127. Briefly describe how managers make use of management accounting information.

Answer:
ONE: To choose *strategy*, to communicate it, and to determine how best to implement it.

TWO: To *plan* business operations related to designing, producing, and marketing a product or service. This includes preparing budgets and determining the prices and cost of products and services. A company must know the cost of each product and service to decide which products to offer and whether to expand or discontinue product lines.

THREE: To *control* business operations that include comparing actual results to the budgeted results and taking corrective action when needed.

Difficulty: 2   *Objective*:   1,2,3

128. Briefly explain the planning and control activities in management accounting. How are these two activities linked to each other?

Answer:
Planning business operations relates to designing, producing, and marketing a product or service. This includes preparing budgets and determining the prices and cost of products and services. A company must know the cost of each product and service to decide which products to offer and whether to expand or discontinue product lines.

Controlling business operations includes comparing actual results to the budgeted results and taking corrective action when needed.

Feedback links planning and control. The control function provides information to assist in better future planning.

Difficulty: 2   *Objective*:   3

129. Explain how a budget can help management implement strategy.

Answer:
A budget is a planning tool, a quantitative expression of a plan of action. First actions are planned and then communicated to the entire organization.

The budget also helps with coordination.

Difficulty: 3   *Objective*:   3

130. Explain how a customer focus can result in increased profits for a company.

Answer:
If customers who provide a company with the most profits are attracted, satisfied, and retained, profits will increase as a result.

Difficulty: 3   *Objective*: 5

131. Describe the value chain and how it can help organizations become more effective.

Answer:
A value chain is a sequence of business functions whose objective is to provide a product to a customer or provide an intermediate good or service in a larger value chain. These business functions include R&D, design, production, marketing, distribution, and customer service.

An organization can become more effective by focusing on whether each link in the chain adds value from the customer's perspective and furthers the organization's objectives.

Difficulty: 3   *Objective*: 6

132. In most organizations, customer satisfaction is one of the top priorities. As such, attention to customers is necessary for success. Briefly describe the four types of demands customers are currently placing on organizational performance.

Answer:

Cost: Organizations are under continuous pressure to reduce the cost of the products or services they sell to their customers.

Quality: Customers are expecting higher levels of quality and are less tolerant of low quality than in the past.

Time: Time has many components: the time taken to develop and bring new products to market; the speed at which an organization responds to customer requests; and the reliability with which promised delivery dates are met. Organizations are under pressure to complete activities faster and to meet promised delivery dates more reliably than in the past in order to increase customer satisfaction.

Innovation: There is now heightened recognition that a continuing flow of innovative products or services is a prerequisite for the ongoing success of most organizations.

Difficulty: 2   *Objective*: 6

133. Management accounting helps managers focus on four key themes. Briefly describe each.

   Answer:
   1. <u>Customer focus is particularly critical</u>   This theme is central. Customers are pivotal to the success of an organization. The number of organizations aiming to be "customer-driven" is large and increasing.

   2. <u>Value-chain and supply-chain analysis</u>   This theme has two related aspects (1) treating each area of the business function as an essential and valued contributor, and (2) integrating and coordinating the efforts of all business functions in addition to developing the capabilities of each individual business function.

   3. <u>Key success factors</u>   Customers are demanding ever-improving levels of performance regarding cost, quality, time, and innovation.

   4. <u>Continuous improvement and benchmarking</u>   Continuous improvement by competitors creates a never-ending search for higher levels of performance within many organizations. Continuous improvement targets are often set by benchmarking.

   Difficulty: 3   *Objective*:   6

134. Discuss the potential behavior implications of performance evaluation.

   Answer:
   As measurements are made on operations and, especially, on individuals and groups, the behavior of the individuals and groups are affected. People react to the measurements being made. They will focus on those variables or the behavior being measured and spend less attention on variables and behavior that are not measured. In addition, if managers attempt to introduce or redesign cost and performance measurement systems, people familiar with the previous system will resist. Management accountants must understand and anticipate the reactions of individuals to information and measurements. The design and introduction of new measurements and systems must be accompanied with an analysis of the likely reactions to the innovations.

   Difficulty: 3   *Objective*:   7

135. How does a controller help "control" a company?

   Answer:
   By reporting and interpreting relevant data, the controller exerts a force or influence that impels management toward making better-informed decisions.

   The controller of Caterpillar described the job as "a business advisor to … help the team develop strategy and focus the team all the way through recommendations and implementation."

   Difficulty: 3   *Objective*:   8

CHAPTER 2: AN INTRODUCTION TO COST TERMS AND PURPOSES

TRUE/FALSE

1. Products, services, departments, and customers may be cost objects.

    Answer: True   *Difficulty*:   1   *Objective*:   1

2. Costs are accounted for in two basic stages: assignment followed by accumulation.

    Answer: False   *Difficulty*:   1   *Objective*:   1
    Costs are accounted for in two basic stages: accumulation followed by assignment.

3. Actual costs and budgeted costs are two different terms referring to the same thing.

    Answer: False   *Difficulty*:   1   *Objective*:   1
    Budgeted costs are what is planned before the beginning of the accounting period,
    while actual costs are those costs compiled at the end of the accounting period.

4. The same cost may be direct for one cost object and indirect for another cost object.

    Answer: True   *Difficulty*:   3   *Objective*:   2

5. Assigning direct costs poses more problems than assigning indirect costs.

    Answer: False   *Difficulty*:   2   *Objective*:   2
    Tracing direct costs is quite straightforward, whereas assigning indirect costs to a
    number of different cost objects can be very challenging.

6. Improvements in information-gathering technologies are making it possible to trace
    more costs as direct.

    Answer: True   *Difficulty*:   2   *Objective*:   2

7. Misallocated indirect costs may lead to promoting products that are not profitable.

    Answer: True   *Difficulty*:   2   *Objective*:   2

8. The materiality of the cost is a factor in classifying the cost as a direct or indirect cost.

    Answer: True   *Difficulty*:   2   *Objective*:   2

9. The cost of a customized machine only used in the production of a single product
    would be classified as a direct cost.

    Answer: True   *Difficulty*:   1   *Objective*:   2

10. Some fixed costs may be classified as direct manufacturing costs.

    Answer: True   *Difficulty*:   1   *Objective*:   2

11. Fixed costs have no cost driver in the short run, but may have a cost driver in the long run.

Answer: True   *Difficulty*: 2   *Objective*: 3

12. Costs that are difficult to change over the short run are always variable over the long run.

Answer: True   *Difficulty*: 2   *Objective*: 3

13. Knowing whether a cost is a period or a product cost helps to estimate total costs at a new level of activity.

Answer: False   *Difficulty*: 2   *Objective*: 3
Knowing whether a cost is a *variable* or a *fixed* cost helps to estimate total costs at a new level of activity.

14. A decision maker cannot adjust capacity over the short run.

Answer: True   *Difficulty*: 1   *Objective*: 3

15. Fixed costs vary with the level of production or sales volume.

Answer: False   *Difficulty*: 1   *Objective*: 3
Variable costs vary with the level of production or sales volume.

16. Currently, most administrative personnel costs would be classified as fixed costs.

Answer: True   *Difficulty*: 1   *Objective*: 3

17. Fixed costs depend on the resources used, not the resources acquired.

Answer: False   *Difficulty*: 2   *Objective*: 3
Fixed costs depend on the resources *acquired*, and not whether the resources are used or not.

18. When making decisions using fixed costs, the focus should be on total costs and not unit costs.

Answer: True   *Difficulty*: 2   *Objective*: 4

19. When 50,000 units are produced the fixed cost is $10 per unit. Therefore, when 100,000 units are produced fixed costs will remain at $10 per unit.

Answer: False   *Difficulty*: 3   *Objective*: 4
When 100,000 units are produced fixed costs will decrease to $5 per unit.

20. Service-sector companies provide services or intangible products to their customers.

   Answer: True   *Difficulty*: 1   *Objective*: 5

21. Inventoriable costs are reported as an asset when incurred and expensed on the income statement when the product is sold.

   Answer: True   *Difficulty*: 2   *Objective*: 6

22. Cost of goods sold refers to the products brought to completion, whether they were started before or during the current accounting period.

   Answer: False   *Difficulty*: 1   *Objective*: 6
   Cost of goods *manufactured* refers to the products brought to completion, whether they were started before or during the current accounting period.

23. Operating income is sales revenue minus cost of goods manufactured.

   Answer: False   *Difficulty*: 1   *Objective*: 6
   Operating income = sales revenue - cost of goods sold - operating expenses

24. All manufacturing costs are inventoriable costs.

   Answer: True   *Difficulty*: 2   *Objective*: 7

25. All costs reported on the income statement of a service-sector company are period costs.

   Answer: True   *Difficulty*: 1   *Objective*: 7

26. Period costs are never included as part of inventory.

   Answer: True   *Difficulty*: 1   *Objective*: 7

27. Conversion costs include all direct manufacturing costs.

   Answer: False   *Difficulty*: 1   *Objective*: 7
   Prime costs include all direct manufacturing costs.

28. Inventory of a manufacturing firm includes goods partially worked on but not yet fully completed.

   Answer: True   *Difficulty*: 1   *Objective*: 7

29. The classification of product and period costs is particularly valuable in management accounting.

Answer: False   *Difficulty*: 2   *Objective*: 7

The classification of *variable* and *fixed* costs is particularly valuable in management accounting.

30. The wages of a plant supervisor would be classified as a period cost.

Answer: False   *Difficulty*: 2   *Objective*: 7

The wages of a plant supervisor would be classified as a *product* cost.

31. For external reporting, GAAP requires that costs be classified as either variable or fixed.

Answer: False   *Difficulty*: 2   *Objective*: 7

For external reporting, GAAP requires that costs be classified as either product or period costs.

32. Overtime premium consists of the wages paid to all workers (for both direct labor and indirect labor) in excess of their straight-time wage rates.

Answer: True   *Difficulty*: 1   *Objective*: 8

33. A product cost that is useful for one decision may not be useful information for another decision.

Answer: True   *Difficulty*: 2   *Objective*: 8

34. For external reporting purposes, indirect manufacturing costs must be allocated to individual units.

Answer: True   *Difficulty*: 2   *Objective*: 8

35. The role of the cost accountant is to tailor the cost calculation to fit the current decision situation.

Answer: True   *Difficulty*: 1   *Objective*: 9

36. Cost accounting and cost management include calculating various costs, obtaining financial and nonfinancial information, and analyzing relevant information for decision-making.

Answer: True   *Difficulty*: 1   *Objective*: 9

37. Cost objects include
    a. products.
    b. customers.
    c. departments.
    d. all of the above.

    Answer: d   *Difficulty:* 2   *Objective:* 1

38. Actual costs are
    a. the costs incurred.
    b. budgeted costs.
    c. estimated costs.
    d. forecasted costs.

    Answer: a   *Difficulty:* 1   *Objective:* 1

39. The general term used to identify both the tracing and the allocation of accumulated costs to a cost object is
    a. cost accumulation.
    b. cost assignment.
    c. cost tracing.
    d. conversion costing.

    Answer: b   *Difficulty:* 1   *Objective:* 1

40. The collection of accounting data in some organized way is
    a. cost accumulation.
    b. cost assignment.
    c. cost tracing.
    d. conversion costing.

    Answer: a   *Difficulty:* 1   *Objective:* 1

41. Cost tracing is
    a. the assignment of direct costs to the chosen cost object.
    b. a function of cost allocation.
    c. the process of tracking both direct and indirect costs associated with a cost object.
    d. the process of determining the actual cost of the cost object.

    Answer: a   *Difficulty:* 2   *Objective:* 2

42. Cost allocation is
    a. the process of tracking both direct and indirect costs associated with a cost object.
    b. the process of determining the actual cost of the cost object.
    c. the assignment of indirect costs to the chosen cost object.
    d. a function of cost tracing.

    Answer: c   *Difficulty:* 2   *Objective:* 2

43. The determination of a cost as being either direct or indirect depends upon
    a. the accounting system.
    b. the allocation system.
    c. the cost tracing system.
    d. the cost object chosen.

    Answer: d   *Difficulty:* 2   *Objective:* 2

44. Classifying a cost as either direct or indirect depends upon
    a. the behavior of the cost in response to volume changes.
    b. whether the cost is expensed in the period in which it is incurred.
    c. whether the cost can be easily identified with the cost object.
    d. whether an expenditure is avoidable or not in the future.

    Answer: c   *Difficulty:* 2   *Objective:* 2

45. A manufacturing plant produces two product lines: football equipment and hockey equipment. Direct costs for the football equipment line are the
    a. beverages provided daily in the plant break room.
    b. monthly lease payments for a specialized piece of equipment needed to manufacture the football helmet.
    c. salaries of the clerical staff that work in the company administrative offices.
    d. utilities paid for the manufacturing plant.

    Answer: b   *Difficulty:* 2   *Objective:* 2

46. A manufacturing plant produces two product lines: football equipment and hockey equipment. An indirect cost for the hockey equipment line is the
    a. material used to make the hockey sticks.
    b. labor to bind the shaft to the blade of the hockey stick.
    c. shift supervisor for the hockey line.
    d. plant supervisor.

    Answer: d   *Difficulty:* 2   *Objective:* 2

47. Which one of the following items is a direct cost?
    a. Customer-service costs of a multiproduct firm; Product A is the cost object.
    b. Printing costs incurred for payroll check processing; payroll check processing is the cost object.
    c. The salary of a maintenance supervisor in a multiproduct manufacturing plant; Product B is the cost object.
    d. Utility costs of the administrative offices; the accounting department is the cost object.

    Answer: b   *Difficulty*: 2   *Objective*: 2

48. Indirect manufacturing costs
    a. can be traced to the product that created the costs.
    b. can be easily identified with the cost object.
    c. generally include the cost of material and the cost of labor.
    d. may include both variable and fixed costs.

    Answer: d   *Difficulty*: 2   *Objective*: 2

49. All of the following are true EXCEPT that indirect costs
    a. may be included in prime costs.
    b. are not easily traced to products or services.
    c. vary with the selection of the cost object.
    d. may be included in manufacturing overhead.

    Answer: a   *Difficulty*: 2   *Objective*: 2

50. Which statement is TRUE?
    a. All variable costs are direct costs.
    b. Because of a cost-benefit tradeoff, some direct costs may be treated as indirect costs.
    c. All fixed costs are indirect costs.
    d. All direct costs are variable costs.

    Answer: b   *Difficulty*: 3   *Objective*: 2

51. Cost behavior refers to
    a. how costs react to a change in the level of activity.
    b. whether a cost is incurred in a manufacturing, merchandising, or service company.
    c. classifying costs as either inventoriable or period costs.
    d. whether a particular expense has been ethically incurred.

    Answer: a   *Difficulty*: 2   *Objective*: 3

52. An understanding of the underlying behavior of costs helps in all of the following EXCEPT
    a. costs can be better estimated as volume expands and contracts.
    b. true costs can be better evaluated.
    c. process inefficiencies can be better identified and as a result improved.
    d. sales volume can be better estimated.

    Answer: d   *Difficulty:* 2   *Objective:* 3

53. At a plant where a union agreement sets annual salaries and conditions, annual labor costs usually
    a. are considered a variable cost.
    b. are considered a fixed cost.
    c. depend on the scheduling of floor workers.
    d. depend on the scheduling of production runs.

    Answer: b   *Difficulty:* 2   *Objective:* 3

54. Variable costs
    a. are always indirect costs.
    b. increase in total when the actual level of activity increases.
    c. include most personnel costs and depreciation on machinery.
    d. can always be traced directly to the cost object.

    Answer: b   *Difficulty:* 2   *Objective:* 3

55. Fixed costs
    a. may include either direct or indirect costs.
    b. vary with production or sales volumes.
    c. include parts and materials used to manufacture a product.
    d. can be adjusted in the short run to meet actual demands.

    Answer: a   *Difficulty:* 2   *Objective:* 3

56. Fixed costs depend on
    a. the amount of resources used.
    b. the amount of resources acquired.
    c. the volume of production.
    d. the volume of sales.

    Answer: b   *Difficulty:* 3   *Objective:* 3

57. Which one of the following is a variable cost in an insurance company?
    a. Rent
    b. President's salary
    c. Sales commissions
    d. Property taxes

    Answer: c   *Difficulty:* 1   *Objective:* 3

58. Which of the following is a fixed cost in an automobile manufacturing plant?
    a. Administrative salaries
    b. Electricity used by assembly-line machines
    c. Sales commissions
    d. Windows for each car produced

    Answer: a   *Difficulty:* 2   *Objective:* 3

59. If each furnace required a hose that costs $20 and 2,000 furnaces are produced for the month, the total cost for hoses is
    a. considered to be a direct fixed cost.
    b. considered to be a direct variable cost.
    c. considered to be an indirect fixed cost.
    d. considered to be an indirect variable cost.

    Answer: b   *Difficulty:* 3   *Objective:* 3

60. The MOST likely cost driver of distribution costs is
    a. the number of parts within the product.
    b. the number of miles driven.
    c. the number of products manufactured.
    d. the number of production hours.

    Answer: b   *Difficulty:* 2   *Objective:* 3

61. The MOST likely cost driver of direct material costs is
    a. the number of parts within the product.
    b. the number of miles driven.
    c. the number of products manufactured.
    d. the number of production hours.

    Answer: c   *Difficulty:* 2   *Objective:* 3

62. Which of the following statements is FALSE?
    a. There is a cause-and-effect relationship between the cost driver and the level of activity.
    b. Fixed costs have cost drivers over the short run.
    c. Over the long run all costs have cost drivers.
    d. Volume of production is a cost driver of direct manufacturing costs.

    Answer: b   *Difficulty:* 2   *Objective:* 3

63. A band of normal activity or volume in which specific cost-volume relationships are maintained is referred to as
    a.   the average range.
    b.   the cost-allocation range.
    c.   the cost driver range.
    d.   the relevant range.

    Answer: d   *Difficulty:*   1   *Objective:*   3

64. Within the relevant range, if there is a change in the level of the cost driver then
    a.   total fixed costs and total variable costs will change.
    b.   total fixed costs and total variable costs will remain the same.
    c.   total fixed costs will remain the same and total variable costs will change.
    d.   total fixed costs will change and total variable costs will remain the same.

    Answer: c   *Difficulty:*   2   *Objective:*   3

65. Within the relevant range, if there is a change in the level of the cost driver then
    a.   fixed and variable costs per unit will change.
    b.   fixed and variable costs per unit will remain the same.
    c.   fixed costs per unit will remain the same and variable costs per unit will change.
    d.   fixed costs per unit will change and variable costs per unit will remain the same.

    Answer: d   *Difficulty:*   2   *Objective:*   3

66. When 10,000 units are produced, fixed costs are $14 per unit. Therefore, when 20,000 units are produced fixed costs
    a.   will increase to $28 per unit.
    b.   will remain at $14 per unit.
    c.   will decrease to $7 per unit.
    d.   will total $280,000.

    Answer: c   *Difficulty:*   3   *Objective:*   4

67. When 10,000 units are produced, variable costs are $6 per unit. Therefore, when 20,000 units are produced
    a.   variable costs will total $120,000.
    b.   variable costs will total $60,000.
    c.   variable unit costs will increase to $12 per unit.
    d.   variable unit costs will decrease to $3 per unit.

    Answer: a   *Difficulty:*   3   *Objective:*   4

68. Christi Manufacturing provided the following information for last month.

Sales	$10,000
Variable costs	3,000
Fixed costs	5,000
Operating income	$2,000

If sales double next month, what is the projected operating income?
a. $4,000
b. $7,000
c. $9,000
d. $12,000

Answer: c   *Difficulty:* 3   *Objective:* 4
(10,000 x 2) - ($3,000 x 2) - $5,000 = $9,000

69. Kym Manufacturing provided the following information for last month.

Sales	$12,000
Variable costs	4,000
Fixed costs	1,000
Operating income	$7,000

If sales double next month, what is the projected operating income?
a. $14,000
b. $15,000
c. $18,000
d. $19,000

Answer: b   *Difficulty:* 3   *Objective:* 4
(12,000 x 2) - ($4,000 x 2) - $1,000 = $15,000

70. Wheel and Tire Manufacturing currently produces 1,000 tires per month. The following per unit data apply for sales to regular customers:

Direct materials	$20
Direct manufacturing labor	3
Variable manufacturing overhead	6
Fixed manufacturing overhead	10
Total manufacturing costs	$39

The plant has capacity for 3,000 tires and is considering expanding production to 2,000 tires. What is the total cost of producing 2,000 tires?
a. $39,000
b. $78,000
c. $68,000
d. $62,000

Answer: c   *Difficulty:* 2   *Objective:* 4
[($20 + $3 + $6) x 2,000 units] + ($10 x 1,000 units) = $68,000

71. Tire and Spoke Manufacturing currently produces 1,000 bicycles per month. The following per unit data apply for sales to regular customers:

Direct materials	$50
Direct manufacturing labor	5
Variable manufacturing overhead	14
Fixed manufacturing overhead	10
Total manufacturing costs	$79

The plant has capacity for 3,000 bicycles and is considering expanding production to 2,000 bicycles. What is the per unit cost of producing 2,000 bicycles?
a. $79 per unit
b. $158 per unit
c. $74 per unit
d. $134 per unit

Answer: c   *Difficulty*: 3   *Objective*: 4
[($50 + $5 + $14) x 2,000 units] + ($10 x 1,000 units) = $148,000 / 2,000 units = $74

THE FOLLOWING INFORMATION APPLIES TO QUESTIONS 72 AND 73.
Axle and Wheel Manufacturing currently produces 1,000 axles per month. The following per unit data apply for sales to regular customers:

Direct materials	$30
Direct manufacturing labor	5
Variable manufacturing overhead	10
Fixed manufacturing overhead	40
Total manufacturing costs	$85

72 The plant has capacity for 2,000 axles and is considering expanding production to 1,500 axles. What is the total cost of producing 1,500 axles?
a. $85,000
b. $170,000
c. $107,500
d. $102,500

Answer: c   *Difficulty*: 2   *Objective*: 4
[($30 + $5 + $10) x 1,500 units] + ($40 x 1,000 units) = $107,500

73. What is the per unit cost when producing 1,500 axles?
a. $71.67
b. $107.50
c. $85.00
d. $170.00

Answer: a   *Difficulty*: 2   *Objective*: 4
$107,500 / 1,500 = $71.67

THE FOLLOWING INFORMATION APPLIES TO QUESTIONS 74 THROUGH 76.
Pederson Company reported the following:

Manufacturing costs	$2,000,000
Units manufactured	50,000
Units sold	47,000 units sold for $75 per unit
Beginning inventory	0 units

74. What is the average manufacturing cost per unit?
   a. $40.00
   b. $42.55
   c. $00.025
   d. $75.00

   Answer: a   *Difficulty*:   1   *Objective*:   4
   $2,000,000 / 50,000 = $40.00

75. What is the amount of ending finished goods inventory?
   a. $1,880,000
   b. $120,000
   c. $225,000
   d. $105,000

   Answer: b   *Difficulty*:   2   *Objective*:   4
   (50,000 - 47,000) x $40.00 = $120,000

76. What is the amount of gross margin?
   a. $1,750,000
   b. $3,525,000
   c. $5,405,000
   d. $1,645,000

   Answer: d   *Difficulty*:   3   *Objective*:   7
   47,000 x ($75 - $40) = $1,645,000

THE FOLLOWING INFORMATION APPLIES TO QUESTIONS 77 THROUGH 79.
The following information pertains to Alleigh's Mannequins:

Manufacturing costs	$1,500,000
Units manufactured	30,000
Units sold	29,500 units sold for $85 per unit
Beginning inventory	0 units

77. What is the average manufacturing cost per unit?
   a. $50.00
   b. $50.85
   c. $17.65
   d. $85.00

   Answer: a   *Difficulty*:   1   *Objective*:   4
   $1,500,000 / 30,000 = $50.00

78. What is the amount of ending finished goods inventory?
    a. $42,500
    b. $25,424
    c. $25,000
    d. $1,475,000

    Answer: c   *Difficulty:* 2   *Objective:* 4
    (30,000 - 29,500) x $50.00 = $25,000

79. What is the amount of gross margin?
    a. $1,475,000
    b. $1,500,000
    c. $2,507,500
    d. $1,032,500

    Answer: d   *Difficulty:* 3   *Objective:* 7
    29,500 x ($85 - $50) = $1,032,500

80. Which of the following companies is part of the service sector of our economy?
    a. Wal-Mart
    b. Bank of America
    c. General Motors
    d. Amazon.com

    Answer: b   *Difficulty:* 1   *Objective:* 5

81. Which of the following companies is part of the merchandising sector of our economy?
    a. General Motors
    b. Intel
    c. The GAP
    d. Robert Meyer Accounting Firm

    Answer: c   *Difficulty:* 1   *Objective:* 5

82. Which of the following companies is part of the manufacturing sector of our economy?
    a. Nike
    b. Barnes & Noble
    c. Corvette Law Firm
    d. Sears, Roebuck, and Company

    Answer: a   *Difficulty:* 1   *Objective:* 5

83. Service-sector companies report
    a. only merchandise inventory.
    b. only finished goods inventory.
    c. direct materials inventory, work-in-process inventory, and finished goods inventory accounts.
    d. no inventory accounts.

    Answer: d   *Difficulty:* 1   *Objective:* 6

84. Manufacturing-sector companies report
    a. only merchandise inventory.
    b. only finished goods inventory.
    c. direct materials inventory, work-in-process inventory, and finished goods inventory accounts.
    d. no inventory accounts.

    Answer: c   *Difficulty:* 1   *Objective:* 6

85. For a manufacturing company, direct material costs may be included in
    a. direct materials inventory only.
    b. merchandise inventory only.
    c. both work-in-process inventory and finished goods inventory.
    d. direct materials inventory, work-in-process inventory, and finished goods inventory accounts.

    Answer: d   *Difficulty:* 3   *Objective:* 6

86. For a manufacturing company, direct labor costs may be included in
    a. direct materials inventory only.
    b. merchandise inventory only.
    c. both work-in-process inventory and finished goods inventory.
    d. direct materials inventory, work-in-process inventory, and finished goods inventory accounts.

    Answer: c   *Difficulty:* 3   *Objective:* 6

87. For a manufacturing company, indirect manufacturing costs may be included in
    a. direct materials inventory only.
    b. merchandise inventory only.
    c. both work-in-process inventory and finished goods inventory.
    d. direct materials inventory, work-in-process inventory, and finished goods inventory accounts.

    Answer: c   *Difficulty:* 3   *Objective:* 6

88. For a manufacturing-sector company, the cost of factory insurance is classified as a
    a. direct material cost.
    b. direct manufacturing labor cost.
    c. manufacturing overhead cost.
    d. period cost.

    Answer: c   *Difficulty:* 1   *Objective:* 6

89. For a printing company, the cost of paper is classified as a
    a. direct material cost.
    b. direct manufacturing labor cost.
    c. manufacturing overhead cost.
    d. period cost.

    Answer: a   *Difficulty:* 1   *Objective:* 6

90. Wages paid to machine operators on an assembly line are classified as a
    a. direct material cost.
    b. direct manufacturing labor cost.
    c. manufacturing overhead cost.
    d. period cost.

    Answer: b   *Difficulty:* 1   *Objective:* 6

91. Manufacturing overhead costs in an automobile manufacturing plant MOST likely include
    a. labor costs of the painting department.
    b. indirect material costs such as lubricants.
    c. sales commissions.
    d. steering wheel costs.

    Answer: b   *Difficulty:* 1   *Objective:* 6

92. Manufacturing overhead costs are also referred to as
    a. indirect manufacturing costs.
    b. prime costs.
    c. period costs.
    d. conversion costs.

    Answer: a   *Difficulty:* 1   *Objective:* 6

THE FOLLOWING INFORMATION APPLIES TO QUESTIONS 93 THROUGH 97.
Gilley Incorporated reported the following information:

On January 31, 20x3:
Job #101 was the only job in process with accumulated costs of $3,000.

During February the following costs were added to production:
Job #101 $10,000
Job #102 $ 8,000
Job #103 $ 7,000

On February 28, 20x3:
Job #101 was completed and sold for $18,000.
Job #102 was completed but not sold.
Job #103 remains in production.

93. What is work-in-process inventory on February 28, 20x3?
    a. $7,000
    b. $8,000
    c. $25,000
    d. $3,000

Answer: a   *Difficulty*:   1   *Objective*:   6
Job #103 $7,000

94. What is finished goods inventory on February 28, 20x3?
    a. $7,000
    b. $8,000
    c. $21,000
    d. $10,000

Answer: b   *Difficulty*:   1   *Objective*:   6
Job #102 $8,000

95. What is cost of goods manufactured for February?
    a. $10,000
    b. $8,000
    c. $13,000
    d. $21,000

Answer: d   *Difficulty*:   3   *Objective*:   7
(Job #101 $13,000)   +   (Job #102 $8,000)

96. What is cost of goods sold for February?
    a. $18,000
    b. $10,000
    c. $13,000
    d. $21,000

Answer: c   *Difficulty*:   2   *Objective*:   7
Job #101 $13,000

97. What is gross margin for February?
    a. $5,000
    b. $18,000
    c. $8,000
    d. $13,000

    Answer: a   *Difficulty:* 3   *Objective:* 7
    $18,000 - $13,000 = $5,000

98. The income statement of a manufacturing firm reports
    a. period costs only.
    b. inventoriable costs only.
    c. both period and inventoriable costs.
    d. period and inventoriable costs but at different times, the reporting varies.

    Answer: c   *Difficulty:* 2   *Objective:* 7

99. The income statement of a service-sector firm reports
    a. period costs only.
    b. inventoriable costs only.
    c. both period and inventoriable costs.
    d. period and inventoriable costs but at different times, the reporting varies.

    Answer: a   *Difficulty:* 2   *Objective:* 7

100. Manufacturing costs include all EXCEPT
    a. costs incurred inside the factory.
    b. both direct and indirect costs.
    c. both variable and fixed costs.
    d. both inventoriable and period costs.

    Answer: d   *Difficulty:* 2   *Objective:* 7

101. Inventoriable costs
    a. include administrative and marketing costs.
    b. are expensed in the accounting period sold.
    c. are particularly useful in management accounting.
    d. are also referred to as nonmanufacturing costs.

    Answer: b   *Difficulty:* 2   *Objective:* 7

102. Inventoriable costs are expensed on the income statement
    a. when direct materials for the product are purchased.
    b. after the products are manufactured.
    c. when the products are sold.
    d. not at any particular time, it varies.

    Answer: c   *Difficulty:* 2   *Objective:* 7

103. Costs that are initially recorded as assets and expensed when sold are referred to as
    a. period costs.
    b. inventoriable costs.
    c. variable costs.
    d. fixed costs.

    Answer: b   *Difficulty:* 2   *Objective:* 7

104. For merchandising companies, inventoriable costs include
    a. the cost of the goods themselves.
    b. incoming freight costs.
    c. insurance costs for the goods.
    d. all of the above.

    Answer: d   *Difficulty:* 2   *Objective:* 7

105. For manufacturing firms, inventoriable costs include
    a. plant supervisor salaries.
    b. research and development costs.
    c. costs of dealing with customers after the sale.
    d. distribution costs.

    Answer: a   *Difficulty:* 2   *Objective:* 7

106. A plant manufactures several different products. The wages of the plant supervisor can be classified as a(n)
    a. direct cost.
    b. inventoriable cost.
    c. variable cost.
    d. period cost.

    Answer: b   *Difficulty:* 2   *Objective:* 7

107. The cost of inventory reported on the balance sheet may include all of the following EXCEPT
    a. customer-service costs.
    b. wages of the plant supervisor.
    c. depreciation of the factory equipment.
    d. the cost of parts used in the manufacturing process.

    Answer: a   *Difficulty:* 2   *Objective:* 7

108. For a computer manufacturer, period costs include the cost of
    a. the keyboard.
    b. labor used for assembly and packaging.
    c. distribution.
    d. assembly-line equipment.

    Answer: c   *Difficulty:* 1   *Objective:* 7

109. Period costs
   a. include only fixed costs.
   b. seldom influence financial success or failure.
   c. include the cost of selling, delivering, and after-sales support for customers.
   d. should be treated as an indirect cost rather than as a direct manufacturing cost.

   Answer: c   *Difficulty:* 2   *Objective:* 7

110. Period costs
   a. are treated as expenses in the period they are incurred.
   b. are directly traceable to products.
   c. include direct labor.
   d. are also referred to as manufacturing overhead costs.

   Answer: a   *Difficulty:* 2   *Objective:* 7

111. Which of the following is NOT a period cost?
   a. Marketing costs
   b. General and administrative costs
   c. Research and development costs
   d. Manufacturing costs

   Answer: d   *Difficulty:* 1   *Objective:* 7

112. Costs expensed on the income statement in the accounting period incurred are referred to as
   a. direct costs.
   b. indirect costs.
   c. period costs.
   d. inventoriable costs.

   Answer: c   *Difficulty:* 1   *Objective:* 7

113. Prime costs include
   a. direct materials and direct manufacturing labor costs.
   b. direct manufacturing labor and manufacturing overhead costs.
   c. direct materials and manufacturing overhead costs.
   d. only direct materials.

   Answer: a   *Difficulty:* 1   *Objective:* 7

114. Conversion costs include
   a. direct materials and direct manufacturing labor costs.
   b. direct manufacturing labor and manufacturing overhead costs.
   c. direct materials and manufacturing overhead costs.
   d. only direct materials.

   Answer: b   *Difficulty:* 1   *Objective:* 7

115. Total manufacturing costs equal
    a.   direct materials + prime costs.
    b.   direct materials + conversion costs.
    c.   direct manufacturing labor costs + prime costs.
    d.   direct manufacturing labor costs + conversion costs.

    Answer: b   *Difficulty:*   2   *Objective:*   7

116. The cost classification system used by manufacturing firms include all of the following EXCEPT
    a.   direct materials costs and conversion costs.
    b.   direct materials costs, direct manufacturing labor costs, and manufacturing overhead costs.
    c.   indirect materials costs, indirect manufacturing labor costs, and manufacturing overhead costs.
    d.   prime costs and manufacturing overhead costs.

    Answer: c   *Difficulty:*   2   *Objective:*   7

117. Manufacturing overhead costs may include all EXCEPT
    a.   salaries of the plant janitorial staff.
    b.   labor that can be traced to individual products.
    c.   wages paid for unproductive time due to machine breakdowns.
    d.   overtime premiums paid to plant workers.

    Answer: b   *Difficulty:*   3   *Objective:*   7

118. Debated items that some companies include as direct manufacturing labor include
    a.   fringe benefits.
    b.   vacation pay.
    c.   training time.
    d.   all of the above.

    Answer: d   *Difficulty:*   2   *Objective:*   7

119. Brenda Hicks is paid $10 an hour for straight-time and $15 an hour for overtime. One week she worked 42 hours, which included 2 hours of overtime. Compensation would be reported as
    a. $400 of direct labor and $30 of manufacturing overhead.
    b. $400 of direct labor and $zero of manufacturing overhead.
    c. $420 of direct labor and $10 of manufacturing overhead.
    d. $430 of direct labor and $zero of manufacturing overhead.

    Answer: c   *Difficulty:*   2   *Objective:*   7
    Direct labor (42 hours x $10) + Overtime premium (2 hrs x $5) = $430

120. Rodney Worsham is paid $10 an hour for straight-time and $15 an hour for overtime. One week he worked 45 hours, which included 5 hours of overtime, and 3 hours of idle time caused by material shortages. Compensation would be reported as
    a. $370 of direct labor and $105 of manufacturing overhead.
    b. $420 of direct labor and $55 of manufacturing overhead.
    c. $450 of direct labor and $25 of manufacturing overhead.
    d. $445 of direct labor and $30 of manufacturing overhead.

    Answer: b   *Difficulty*: 3   *Objective*: 7
    Direct labor (42 hours x $10) + Idle time (3 hrs x $10) + Overtime premium (5 hrs x $5) = $475

121. Which of the following formulas determine cost of goods sold in a merchandising entity?
    a. Beginning inventory + Purchases + Ending inventory = Cost of goods sold
    b. Beginning inventory + Purchases - Ending inventory = Costs of goods sold
    c. Beginning inventory - Purchases + Ending inventory = Cost of goods sold
    d. Beginning inventory - Ending inventory - Purchases = Cost of goods sold

    Answer: b   *Difficulty*: 1   *Objective*: 7

122. Which of the following formulas determine cost of goods sold in a manufacturing entity?
    a. Beginning work-in-process inventory + Cost of goods manufactured - Ending work-in-process inventory = Cost of goods sold
    b. Beginning work-in-process inventory + Cost of goods manufactured + Ending work-in-process inventory = Cost of goods sold
    c. Cost of goods manufactured - Beginning finished goods inventory - Ending finished goods inventory = Cost of goods sold.
    d. Cost of goods manufactured + Beginning finished goods inventory - Ending finished goods inventory = Cost of goods sold.

    Answer: d   *Difficulty*: 2   *Objective*: 7

123. The following information pertains to the Cannady Corporation:

Beginning work-in-process inventory	$ 50,000
Ending work-in-process inventory	48,000
Beginning finished goods inventory	180,000
Ending finished goods inventory	195,000
Cost of goods manufactured	1,220,000

    What is cost of goods sold?
    a. $1,235,000
    b. $1,205,000
    c. $1,218,000
    d. $1,222,000

    Answer: b   *Difficulty*: 3   *Objective*: 7
    $180,000 + $1,220,000 - $195,000 = $1,205,000

124. The following information pertains to the Duggan Corporation:

Beginning work-in-process inventory	$ 20,000
Ending work-in-process inventory	23,000
Beginning finished goods inventory	36,000
Ending finished goods inventory	34,000
Cost of goods manufactured	246,000

What is cost of goods sold?
a. $244,000
b. $248,000
c. $243,000
d. $249,000

Answer: b   *Difficulty:*   2   *Objective:*   7
$36,000 + $246,000 - $34,000 = $248,000

THE FOLLOWING INFORMATION APPLIES TO QUESTIONS 125 THROUGH 127.
The following information pertains to Harding Company:

Beginning finished goods, 1/1/20x3	$ 80,000
Ending finished goods, 12/31/20x3	67,000
Cost of goods sold	270,000
Sales revenue	500,000
Operating expenses	145,000

125. What is cost of goods manufactured for 20x3?
a. $230,000
b. $257,000
c. $283,000
d. $355,000

Answer: b   *Difficulty:*   2   *Objective:*   7
$270,000 + $67,000 - $80,000 = $257,000

126. What is gross margin for 20x3?
a. $283,000
b. $355,000
c. $230,000
d. $257,000

Answer: c   *Difficulty:*   2   *Objective:*   7
$500,000 - $270,000 = $230,000

127. What is operating income for 20x3?
a. $85,000
b. $112,000
c. $62,000
d. $230,000

Answer: a   *Difficulty:*   2   *Objective:*   7
$500,000 - $270,000 - 145,000 = $85,000

THE FOLLOWING INFORMATION APPLIES TO QUESTIONS 128 THROUGH 130.
The following information pertains to Scott's Production Company:

Beginning finished goods, 1/1/20x3	$ 40,000
Ending finished goods, 12/31/20x3	33,000
Cost of goods sold	250,000
Sales revenue	600,000
Operating expenses	120,000

128. What is cost of goods manufactured for 20x3?
   a. $257,000
   b. $350,000
   c. $243,000
   d. $250,000

   Answer: c   *Difficulty:* 2   *Objective:* 7
   $250,000 + $33,000 - $40,000 = $243,000

129. What is gross margin for 20x3?
   a. $243,000
   b. $527,000
   c. $357,000
   d. $350,000

   Answer: d   *Difficulty:* 2   *Objective:* 7
   $600,000 - $250,000 = $350,000

130. What is operating income for 20x3?
   a. $230,000
   b. $123,000
   c. $107,000
   d. $157,000

   Answer: a   *Difficulty:* 2   *Objective:* 7
   $600,000 - $250,000 - 120,000 = $230,000

THE FOLLOWING INFORMATION APPLIES TO QUESTIONS 131 THROUGH 134.
The Singer Company manufactures several different products. Unit costs associated with Product ICT101 are as follows:

Direct materials	$ 60
Direct manufacturing labor	10
Variable manufacturing overhead	18
Fixed manufacturing overhead	32
Sales commissions (2% of sales)	4
Administrative salaries	16
Total	$140

131. What are the variable costs per unit associated with Product ICT101?
   a. $18
   b. $22
   c. $88
   d. $92

   Answer: d   *Difficulty:*   2   *Objective:*   3
   $60 + $10 + $18 + $4 = $92

132. What are the fixed costs per unit associated with Product ICT101?
   a. $102
   b. $48
   c. $52
   d. $32

   Answer: b   *Difficulty:*   2   *Objective:*   3
   $32 + 16 = $48

133. What are the inventoriable costs per unit associated with Product ICT101?
   a. $120
   b. $140
   c. $50
   d. $88

   Answer: a   *Difficulty:*   2   *Objective:*   7
   $60 + $10 + $18 + $32 = $120

134. What are the period costs per unit associated with Product ICT101?
   a. $4
   b. $16
   c. $20
   d. $52

   Answer: c   *Difficulty:*   2   *Objective:*   7
   $4 + 16 − $20

THE FOLLOWING INFORMATION APPLIES TO QUESTIONS 135 THROUGH 138.
The West Company manufactures several different products. Unit costs associated with Product ORD203 are as follows:

Direct materials	$ 40
Direct manufacturing labor	8
Variable manufacturing overhead	12
Fixed manufacturing overhead	23
Sales commissions (2% of sales)	6
Administrative salaries	9
Total	$98

135. What are the variable costs per unit associated with Product ORD203?
    a. $60
    b. $83
    c. $66
    d. $48

    Answer: c   *Difficulty*:   2   *Objective*:   3
    $40 + $8 + $12 + $6 = $66

136. What are the fixed costs per unit associated with Product ORD203?
    a. $23
    b. $32
    c. $35
    d. $44

    Answer: b   *Difficulty*:   2   *Objective*:   3
    $23 + 9 = $32

137. What are the inventoriable costs per unit associated with Product ORD203?
    a. $60
    b. $66
    c. $48
    d. $83

    Answer: d   *Difficulty*:   2   *Objective*:   7
    $40 + $8 + $12 + $23 = $83

138. What are the period costs per unit associated with Product ORD203?
    a. $15
    b. $6
    c. $9
    d. $27

    Answer: a   *Difficulty*:   2   *Objective*:   7
    $6 + 9 = $15

139. Product costs may refer to
    a.   inventoriable costs for external reporting.
    b.   design costs plus manufacturing costs for government contracts.
    c.   all costs incurred along the value chain for pricing decisions.
    d.   all of the above refer to product costs, it varies.

    Answer: d   *Difficulty:*   3   *Objective:*   8

140. Product costs used for pricing and product-mix decisions generally include
    a.   manufacturing costs only.
    b.   design costs plus manufacturing costs.
    c.   all costs incurred along the value chain.
    d.   distribution costs only.

    Answer: c   *Difficulty:*   3   *Objective:*   8

141. Product costs used for government contracts generally include
    a.   manufacturing costs only.
    b.   design costs plus manufacturing costs.
    c.   all costs incurred along the value chain.
    d.   distribution costs only.

    Answer: b   *Difficulty:*   3   *Objective:*   8

142. Product costs used for external reporting generally include
    a.   manufacturing costs only.
    b.   design costs plus manufacturing costs.
    c.   all costs incurred along the value chain.
    d.   all of the above definitions of cost, it varies.

    Answer: a   *Difficulty:*   2   *Objective:*   8

143. Inventoriable costs for external reporting purposes are also referred to as
    a.   product costs.
    b.   period costs.
    c.   variable costs.
    d.   direct manufacturing costs.

    Answer: a   *Difficulty:*   1   *Objective:*   8

144. For external reporting
    a.   costs are classified as either inventoriable or period costs.
    b.   costs reflect current values.
    c.   there are no prescribed rules since no one is exactly sure how investors and
          creditors will use these numbers.
    d.   costs include amounts that reflect both current and future benefits.

    Answer: a   *Difficulty:*   2   *Objective:*   8

145. Which of the following statements is FALSE?
    a.   Product costs and inventoriable costs are interchangeable terms.
    b.   Inventoriable costs are important for GAAP.
    c.   Inventoriable costs are a special case of product costs.
    d.   "Product costs" refers to the particular costs of a product for the purpose at hand.

    Answer: a   *Difficulty*:   3   *Objective*:   8

146. When making decisions,
    a.   it is best to use average costs.
    b.   it is best to use unit costs.
    c.   it is best to use total costs rather than unit costs.
    d.   all of the above types of costs can be used for decision making, it varies
          depending on the decision.

    Answer: d   *Difficulty*:   2   *Objective*:   9

EXERCISES AND PROBLEMS

147.   Lucas Manufacturing has three cost objects that it uses to accumulate costs for its manufacturing plants. They are:

        Cost object #1:   The physical buildings and equipment
        Cost object #2:   The use of buildings and equipment
        Cost object #3:   The availability and use of manufacturing labor

The following manufacturing overhead cost categories are found in the accounting records:

    a. Depreciation on buildings and equipment
    b. Lubricants for machines
    c. Property insurance
    d. Supervisors' salaries
    e. Fringe benefits
    f. Property taxes
    g. Utilities

Required:

Assign each of the above costs to the most appropriate cost object.

Answer:

Cost object # 1 includes categories a, c, and f.

Cost object # 2 includes categories b and g.

Cost object # 3 includes categories d and e.

Difficulty: 2   *Objective*:   1

148. Archambeau Products Company manufactures office furniture. Recently, the company decided to develop a formal cost accounting system and classify all costs into three categories. Categorize each of the following items as being appropriate for (1) cost tracing to the finished furniture, (2) cost allocation of an indirect manufacturing cost to the finished furniture, or (3) as a nonmanufacturing item.

Item	Cost Tracing	Cost Allocation	Nonmanu-facturing
Carpenter wages			
Depreciation - office building			
Glue for assembly			
Lathe department supervisor			
Lathe depreciation			
Lathe maintenance			
Lathe operator wages			
Lumber			
Samples for trade shows			
Metal brackets for drawers			
Factory washroom supplies			

Answer:

Item	Cost Tracing	Cost Allocation	Nonmanu-facturing
Carpenter wages	X		
Depreciation - office building			X
Glue for assembly		X	
Lathe department supervisor		X	
Lathe depreciation		X	
Lathe maintenance		X	
Lathe operator wages		X	
Lumber	X		
Samples for trade shows			X
Metal brackets for drawers	X		
Factory washroom supplies		X	

Difficulty: 2   *Objective*:   2

149. Butler Hospital wants to estimate the cost for each patient stay. It is a general health care facility offering only basic services and not specialized services such as organ transplants.

Required:

a. Classify each of the following costs as either direct or indirect with respect to each patient.
b. Classify each of the following costs as either fixed or variable with respect to hospital costs per day.

	Direct	Indirect	Fixed	Variable
Electronic monitoring	___	___	___	___
Meals for patients	___	___	___	___
Nurses' salaries	___	___	___	___
Parking maintenance	___	___	___	___
Security	___	___	___	___

Answer:

	Direct	Indirect	Fixed	Variable
Electronic monitoring	X			X
Meals for patients	X			X
Nurses salaries		X	X	
Parking maintenance		X	X	
Security		X	X	

Difficulty: 2   *Objectives*: 2, 3

150. Combs, Inc. reports the following information for September sales:

Sales	$15,000
Variable costs	3,000
Fixed costs	4,000
Operating income	$ 8,000

Required:

If sales double in October, what is the projected operating income?

Answer:

(15,000 x 2) - ($3,000 x 2) - $4,000 = $20,000

Difficulty: 2   *Objective*: 4

151. Axle and Wheel Manufacturing currently produces 1,000 axles per month. The following per unit data apply for sales to regular customers:

Direct materials	$200
Direct manufacturing labor	30
Variable manufacturing overhead	60
Fixed manufacturing overhead	40
Total manufacturing costs	$330

The plant has capacity for 2,000 axles.

Required:

a. What is the total cost of producing 1,000 axles?
b. What is the total cost of producing 1,500 axles?
c. What is the per unit cost when producing 1,500 axles?

Answer:

a. [($200 + $30 + $60) x 1,000 units] + ($40 x 1,000 units) = $330,000
b. [($200 + $30 + $60) x 1,500 units] + $40,000 = $475,000
c. $475,000 / 1,500 = $316.67 per unit

Difficulty: 2   *Objective*:   4

152. The following information pertains to Ball Company:

Manufacturing costs	$2,400,000
Units manufactured	40,000
Beginning inventory	0 units

39,800 units are sold during the year for $100 per unit.

Required:

a. What is the average manufacturing cost per unit?
b. What is the amount of ending finished goods inventory?
c. What is the amount of gross margin?

Answer:

a. $2,400,000 / 40,000 = $60.00
b. (40,000 – 39,800) x $60 = $12,000
c. 39,800 x ($100 - $60) = $1,592,000

Difficulty: 2   *Objectives*: 3, 4, 7

153. Cheaney Incorporated reports the following information.

On January 31, 20x1, Job #101 was the only job in process with accumulated costs of:

Direct materials	$2,000
Direct manufacturing labor	1,000
Manufacturing overhead	1,000
Total	$4,000

During February, Job #102 and Job #103 were started and the following costs were added:

	Job #101	Job #102	Job #103
Direct materials	$4,000	$5,000	$6,000
Direct manufacturing labor	1,000	2,000	3,000
Manufacturing overhead	2,000	3,000	4,000
Total	$7,000	$10,000	$13,000

On February 28, 20x1:
Job #101 was completed and sold for $20,000.
Job #102 was completed but not sold.
Job #103 remains in production.

Required:

Using the above information, determine the following amounts:

a. Work-in-process inventory on February 1, 20x1.
b. Work-in-process inventory on February 28, 20x1.
c. Finished goods inventory on February 28, 20x1.
d. Cost of goods manufactured for February.
e Cost of goods sold for February.
f. Gross margin for February.

Answer:

a. $4,000
b. Job #103 $13,000
c. Job #102 $10,000
d. (Job #101 $11,000) + (Job #102 $10,000) = $21,000
e. Job #101 $11,000
f. $20,000 - $11,000 = $9,000

Difficulty: 2   *Objectives:* 6, 7

154. Evans Inc. had the following activities during 20x1:

Direct materials:	
Beginning inventory	$ 40,000
Purchases	123,200
Ending inventory	20,800
Direct manufacturing labor	32,000
Manufacturing overhead	24,000
Beginning work-in-process inventory	1,600
Ending work-in-process inventory	8,000
Beginning finished goods inventory	48,000
Ending finished goods inventory	32,000

Required:

a. What is the cost of direct materials used during 20x1?
b. What is cost of goods manufactured for 20x1?
c. What is cost of goods sold for 20x1?
d. What amount of prime costs was added to production during 20x1?
e. What amount of conversion costs was added to production during 20x1?

Answer:

a. $40,000 + $123,200 - $20,800 = $142,400
b. $142,400 + $32,000 + $24,000 + $1,600 - $8,000 = $192,000
c. $192,000 + $48,000 - $32,000 = $208,000
d. $142,400 + $32,000 = $174,400
e. $32,000 + $24,000 = $56,000

Difficulty: 2   *Objectives*: 6, 7

155. Helmer Sporting Goods Company manufactured 100,000 units in 20x3 and reported the following costs:

Sandpaper	$ 32,000	Leasing costs - plant	$ 384,000
Materials handling	320,000	Depreciation - equipment	224,000
Coolants & lubricants	22,400	Property taxes - equipment	32,000
Indirect manufacturing labor	275,200	Fire insurance - equipment	16,000
Direct manufacturing labor	2,176,000	Direct material purchases	3,136,000
Direct materials, 1/1/x3	384,000	Direct materials, 12/31/x3	275,200
Finished goods, 1/1/x3	672,000	Sales revenue	12,800,000
Finished goods, 12/31/x3	1,280,000	Sales commissions	640,000
Work-in-process, 1/1/x3	96,000	Sales salaries	576,000
Work-in-process, 12/31/x3	64,000	Advertising costs	480,000
		Administration costs	800,000

Required:

a. What is the amount of direct materials used during 20x3?
b. What manufacturing costs were added to WIP during 20x3?
c. What is cost of goods manufactured for 20x3?
d. What is cost of goods sold for 20x3?

Answer:

a. $384,000 + $3,136,000 - $275,200 = $3,244,800

b. $3,244,800 + $2,176,000 + $32,000 + $320,000 + $22,400 + $275,200 + $384,000 + $224,000 + $32,000 + $16,000 = $6,726,400

c. $6,726,400 + $96,000 - $64,000 = $6,758,400

d. $6,758,400 + $672,000 - $1,280,000 = $6,150,400

Difficulty: 3   *Objectives*: 6, 7

156. Messinger Manufacturing Company had the following account balances for the quarter ending March 31, unless otherwise noted:

Work-in-process inventory (January 1)	$ 140,400
Work-in-process inventory (March 31)	171,000
Finished goods inventory (January 1)	540,000
Finished goods inventory (March 31)	510,000
Direct materials used	378,000
Indirect materials used	84,000
Direct manufacturing labor	480,000
Indirect manufacturing labor	186,000
Property taxes on manufacturing plant building	28,800
Salespersons' company vehicle costs	12,000
Depreciation of manufacturing equipment	264,000
Depreciation of office equipment	123,600
Miscellaneous plant overhead	135,000
Plant utilities	92,400
General office expenses	305,400
Marketing distribution costs	30,000

Required:

a. Prepare a cost of goods manufactured schedule for the quarter.
b. Prepare a cost of goods sold schedule for the quarter.

Answer:

a.

Messinger Manufacturing Company
Cost of Goods Manufactured Schedule
For quarter ending March 31

Direct materials used		$ 378,000
Direct manufacturing labor		480,000
Manufacturing overhead		
Depreciation of manufacturing equipment	$264,000	
Indirect manufacturing labor	186,000	
Indirect materials	84,000	
Miscellaneous plant overhead	135,000	
Plant utilities	92,400	
Property taxes on building	28,800	790,200
Manufacturing costs incurred		$1,648,200
Add beginning work-in-process inventory		140,400
Total manufacturing costs		$1,788,600
Less ending work-in-process inventory		171,000
Cost of goods manufactured		$1,617,600

b.

Messinger Manufacturing Company
Cost of Goods Sold Schedule
For the quarter ending March 31

Beginning finished goods inventory	$ 540,000
Cost of goods manufactured	1,617,600
Cost of goods available for sale	2,157,600
Ending finished goods inventory	510,000
Cost of goods sold	$1,647,600

Difficulty: 2   *Objectives*: 6, 7

157. Using the following information find the unknown amounts. Assume each set of information is an independent case.

a.	Merchandise Inventory	Purchases	$420,000
		Cost of goods sold	446,000
		Beginning balance	82,000
		Ending balance	?
b.	Direct Materials	Beginning balance	$ 14,000
		Ending balance	28,000
		Purchases	96,000
		Direct materials used	?
c.	Work-in-process Inventory	Ending balance	$ 44,000
		Cost of goods manufactured	42,000
		Beginning balance	16,000
		Current manufacturing costs	?
d.	Finished Goods Inventory	Cost of goods manufactured	$124,000
		Ending balance	40,000
		Cost of goods sold	122,000
		Beginning balance	?

Answer:

a. Ending balance of merchandise inventory:
   $82,000 + $420,000 - $446,000 = $56,000

b. Direct materials used:
   $14,000 + $96,000 - $28,000 = $82,000

c. Current manufacturing costs:
   $42,000 + $44,000 - $16,000 = $70,000

d. Beginning balance of finished goods inventory:
   $40,000 + $122,000 - $124,000 = $38,000

Difficulty: 2   *Objectives*: 6, 7

158. Cynthia Evans is paid $20 an hour for straight-time and $30 an hour for overtime. One week she worked 43 hours, which included 3 hours of overtime.

Required:

a. What is Cynthia's total compensation for the week?
b. What amount of compensation would be reported as direct manufacturing labor?
c. What amount of compensation would be reported as manufacturing overhead?

Answer:

a. Direct labor (43 hours x $20) + Overtime premium (3 hrs x $10) = $890
b. Direct manufacturing labor (43 hours x $20) = $860
c. Manufacturing overhead costs = Overtime premium (3 hrs x $10) = $30

Difficulty: 2   *Objective*:   7

159. Leslie Grant is paid $20 an hour for straight-time and $30 an hour for overtime. One week she worked 46 hours, which included 6 hours of overtime, and 4 hours of idle time caused by material shortages.

Required:

a. What is Leslie's total compensation for the week?
b. What amount of compensation would be reported as direct manufacturing labor?
c. What amount of compensation would be reported as manufacturing overhead?

Answer:

a. Direct manufacturing labor (42 hours x $20) + Idle time (4 hrs x $20) + Overtime premium (6 hrs x $10) = $980
b. Direct manufacturing labor (42 hours x $20) = $840
c. Manufacturing overhead costs = Idle time (4 hrs x $20) + Overtime premium (6 hrs x $10) = $140

Difficulty: 2   *Objective*:   7

160. What are the differences between direct costs and indirect costs? Give an example of each.

    Answer:
    Direct costs are costs that can be traced easily to the product manufactured or the service rendered. Examples of direct costs include direct materials and direct manufacturing labor used in a product. *Indirect* costs cannot be easily identified with individual products or services rendered, and are usually assigned using allocation formulas. In a plant that manufactures multiple products, examples of indirect costs include the plant supervisor's salary and the cost of machines used to produce more than one type of product.

    Difficulty: 2   *Objective*: 2

161. Describe a variable cost. Describe a fixed cost. Explain why the distinction between variable and fixed costs is important in cost accounting.

    Answer:
    Total variable costs increase with increased production or sales volumes.
    Fixed costs are not influenced by fluctuations in production or sales volumes. Without the knowledge of cost behaviors, budgets and other forecasting tools will be inaccurate and unreliable. Understanding whether a cost behaves as a variable or a fixed cost is essential to estimating and planning for business success.

    Difficulty: 2   *Objective*: 3

162. When should the overtime premium of direct manufacturing labor be considered an indirect manufacturing cost? A direct manufacturing cost?

    Answer:
    The overtime premium of direct manufacturing labor should be considered an indirect manufacturing cost when it is attributable to the overall volume of work, and a direct manufacturing cost when a "rush job" is the sole source of the overtime.

    Difficulty: 2   *Objective*: 7

CHAPTER 3: COST-VOLUME-PROFIT ANALYSIS

TRUE/FALSE

1. In order to perform cost-volume-profit analysis, a company must be able to separate costs into fixed and variable components.

    Answer: True   *Difficulty*: 1   *Objective*: 1

2. Cost-volume-profit analysis may be used for multi-product analysis when the proportion of different products remains constant.

    Answer: True   *Difficulty*: 1   *Objective*: 1

3. It is assumed in CVP analysis that the unit selling price, unit variable costs, and unit fixed costs are known and constant.

    Answer: False   *Difficulty*: 2   *Objective*: 1
    It is assumed in CVP analysis that the unit selling price, unit variable costs, and *total* fixed costs are known and constant.

4. In CVP analysis, the number of output units is the only revenue driver.

    Answer: True   *Difficulty*: 2   *Objective*: 1

5. Many companies find even the simplest CVP analysis helps with strategic and long-range planning.

    Answer: True   *Difficulty*: 1   *Objective*: 1

6. If the selling price per unit is $20 and the contribution margin percentage is 30%, then the variable cost per unit must be $6.

    Answer: False   *Difficulty*: 2   *Objective*: 2
    Then the variable cost per unit must be $14.

7. Total revenues less total fixed costs equal the contribution margin.

    Answer: False   *Difficulty*: 1   *Objective*: 2
    Total revenues less total variable costs equal the *contribution margin*.

8. Gross margin is reported on the contribution income statement.

    Answer: True   *Difficulty*: 1   *Objective*: 2

9. Selling price per unit $30, variable cost per unit $20, and fixed cost per unit $3. When this company operates above the breakeven point, the sale of one more unit will increase net income by $7.

Answer: False   *Difficulty*: 2   *Objective*: 3
The sale of one more unit will increase net income by $10.

10. A company with sales of $100,000; variable costs of $70,000; and fixed costs of $50,000 will reach its breakeven point if sales are increased by $20,000.

Answer: False   *Difficulty*: 2   *Objective*: 3
$50,000 / 0.30 = $166,667of total sales are needed to break even.

11. Breakeven point is not a good planning tool since the goal of business is to make a profit.

Answer: False   *Difficulty*: 2   *Objective*: 3
Breakeven point is an important planning tool that helps managers determine volume of sales/production needed to be profitable.

12. Breakeven point is that quantity of output where total revenues equal total costs.

Answer: True   *Difficulty*: 1   *Objective*: 3

13. In the graph method of CVP analysis, the breakeven point is the quantity of units sold for which the total revenues line crosses the x-axis.

Answer: True   *Difficulty*: 1   *Objective*: 3

14. A profit-volume graph shows the impact on operating income from changes in the output level.

Answer: True   *Difficulty*: 1   *Objective*: 3

15. Focusing on target net income rather than operating income will increase the breakeven point.

Answer: False   *Difficulty*: 2   *Objective*: 4
The same breakeven point will be calculated whether target operating income or target net income is used in the CVP calculation.

16. Sensitivity analysis is a "what-if" technique that managers use to examine how a result will change if the originally predicted data are not achieved or if an underlying assumption changes.

Answer: True   *Difficulty*: 1   *Objective*: 5

17. Margin of safety measures the difference between budgeted revenues and breakeven revenues.

Answer: True   *Difficulty:* 1   *Objective:* 5

18. Sensitivity analysis helps to evaluate the risk associated with decisions.

Answer: True   *Difficulty:* 1   *Objective:* 5

19. If contribution margin decreases by $1 per unit then operating profits will increase by $1 per unit.

Answer: False   *Difficulty:* 2   *Objective:* 5
If contribution margin decreases by $1 per unit then operating profits will *decrease* by $1 per unit.

20. If variable costs per unit increase, then the breakeven point will decrease.

Answer: False   *Difficulty:* 3   *Objective:* 5
If variable costs per unit increase, then the breakeven point will also *increase*.

21. Companies with a greater proportion of fixed costs have a greater risk of loss than companies with a greater proportion of variable costs.

Answer: True   *Difficulty:* 2   *Objective:* 6

22. If a company increases fixed costs, then the breakeven point will be lower.

Answer: False   *Difficulty:* 3   *Objective:* 6
If a company increases fixed costs, then the breakeven point will be *higher*.

23. Companies that are substituting fixed costs for variable costs receive a greater per unit return above the breakeven point.

Answer: True   *Difficulty:* 3   *Objective:* 6

24. A company with a high degree of operating leverage is at lesser risk during downturns in the economy.

Answer: False   *Difficulty:* 3   *Objective:* 6
A company with a high degree of operating leverage is at *greater* risk during downturns in the economy.

25. Whether the purchase cost of a machine is treated as fixed or variable depends heavily on the time horizon being considered.

Answer: True   *Difficulty:* 1   *Objective:* 6

26. Passenger-miles are a potential measure of output for the airline industry.

Answer: True   *Difficulty*: 1   *Objective*: 7

27. In multiproduct situations when sales mix shifts toward the product with the lowest contribution margin, the breakeven quantity will decrease.

Answer: False   *Difficulty*: 3   *Objective*: 7
In multiproduct situations when sales mix shifts toward the product with the lowest contribution margin, the breakeven quantity will *increase*.

28. In multiproduct situations when sales mix shifts toward the product with the highest contribution margin, operating income will be higher.

Answer: True   *Difficulty*: 3   *Objective*: 7

29. There is no unique breakeven point when there are multiple cost drivers.

Answer: True   *Difficulty*: 2   *Objective*: 8

30. When there are multiple cost drivers the simple CVP formula of $Q = (FC + OI)/CMU$ can still be used.

Answer: False   *Difficulty*: 1   *Objective*: 8
When there are multiple cost drivers the simple CVP formula no longer applies.

31. Service sector companies will never report gross margin on an income statement.

Answer: True   *Difficulty*: 2   *Objective*: 9

32. For merchandising firms, contribution margin will always be a lesser amount than gross margin.

Answer: True   *Difficulty*: 3   *Objective*: 9
True, because all variable costs are subtracted to compute contribution margin, but only COGS is subtracted to compute gross margin.

33. Contribution margin and gross margin are terms that can be used interchangeably.

Answer: False   *Difficulty*: 1   *Objective*: 9
Contribution margin and gross margin refer to different amounts.
Revenues - all variable costs = contribution margin; Revenues - COGS = gross margin

34. An expected value is the weighted average of the outcomes, with the probability of each outcome serving as the weight.

Answer: True   *Difficulty*: 2   *Objective*: A

35. Cost-volume-profit analysis is used PRIMARILY by management
    a. as a planning tool.
    b. for control purposes.
    c. to prepare external financial statements.
    d. to attain accurate financial results.

    Answer: a   *Difficulty:*   1   *Objective:*   1

36. Cost-volume-profit analysis assumes all EXCEPT
    a. all costs are variable or fixed.
    b. units manufactured equal units sold.
    c. total variable costs remain the same over the relevant range.
    d. total fixed costs remain the same over the relevant range.

    Answer: c   *Difficulty:*   2   *Objective:*   1

37. Which of the following is NOT an assumption of CVP analysis?
    a. Total costs can be divided into a fixed component and a component that is variable with respect to the level of output.
    b. When graphed, total costs curve upward.
    c. The unit-selling price is known and constant.
    d. All revenues and costs can be added and compared without taking into account the time value of money.

    Answer: b   *Difficulty:*   3   *Objective:*   1

38. Which of the following is NOT an assumption of CVP analysis?
    a. Costs may be separated into separate fixed and variable components.
    b. Total revenues and total costs are linear in relation to output units.
    c. Unit selling price, unit variable costs, and unit fixed costs are known and remain constant.
    d. Proportion of different products will remain constant when multiple products are sold.

    Answer: c   *Difficulty:*   3   *Objective:*   1

39. A revenue driver is defined as
    a. any factor that affects costs and revenues.
    b. any factor that affects revenues.
    c. only factors that can influence a change in selling price.
    d. only factors that can influence a change in demand.

    Answer: b   *Difficulty:*   1   *Objective:*   1

40. Cost-volume-profit analysis examines
    a.   changes in fixed costs.
    b.   changes in output level.
    c.   changes in selling price per unit.
    d.   changes in variable costs per unit.

    Answer: b   *Difficulty:*   1   *Objective:*   1

41. Operating income calculations use
    a.   net income.
    b.   income tax expense.
    c.   cost of goods sold and operating costs.
    d.   nonoperating revenues and nonoperating expenses.

    Answer: c   *Difficulty:*   2   *Objective:*   1

42. Which of the following statements about net income (NI) is TRUE?
    a.   NI = operating income plus nonoperating revenue.
    b.   NI = operating income plus operating costs.
    c.   NI = operating income less income taxes.
    d.   NI = operating income less cost of goods sold.

    Answer: c   *Difficulty:*   1   *Objective:*   1

43. The contribution income statement
    a.   reports gross margin.
    b.   is allowed for external reporting to shareholders.
    c.   categorizes costs as either direct or indirect.
    d.   can be used to predict future profits at different levels of activity.

    Answer: d   *Difficulty:*   1   *Objective:*   2

44. Contribution margin equals
    a.   revenues minus period costs.
    b.   revenues minus product costs.
    c.   revenues minus variable costs.
    d.   revenues minus fixed costs.

    Answer: c   *Difficulty:*   1   *Objective:*   2

45. The selling price per unit less the variable cost per unit is the
    a.   fixed cost per unit.
    b.   gross margin.
    c.   margin of safety.
    d.   contribution margin per unit.

    Answer: d   *Difficulty:*   1   *Objective:*   2

THE FOLLOWING INFORMATION APPLIES TO QUESTIONS 46 THROUGH 49.
Kaiser's Kraft Korner sells a single product. 7,000 units were sold resulting in $70,000 of sales revenue; $28,000 of variable costs; and $12,000 of fixed costs.

46. Contribution margin per unit is
   a. $4.00.
   b. $4.29.
   c. $6.00.
   d. none of the above.

   Answer: c   *Difficulty*: 2   *Objective*: 2
   ($70,000 - $28,000) / 7,000 units = $6 per unit

47. Breakeven point in units is
   a. 2,000 units.
   b. 3,000 units.
   c. 5,000 units.
   d. none of the above.

   Answer: a   *Difficulty*: 2   *Objective*: 3
   $10X - 4X - 12,000 = 0; X = 2000$ units

48. The number of units that must be sold to achieve $60,000 of operating income is
   a. 10,000 units.
   b. 11,666 units.
   c. 12,000 units.
   d. none of the above.

   Answer: c   *Difficulty*: 2   *Objective*: 3
   $10X - 4X - 12,000 = 60,000; X = 12,000$ units

49. If sales increase by $25,000, operating income will increase by
   a. $10,000.
   b. $15,000.
   c. $22,200.
   d. impossible to compute.

   Answer: b   *Difficulty*: 2   *Objective*: 2
   [($70,000 - $28,000) / $70,000] x $25,000 = $15,000

50. Schuppener Company sells its only product for $18 per unit, variable production costs are $6 per unit, and selling and administrative costs are $3 per unit. Fixed costs for 10,000 units are $10,000. The contribution margin is
   a. $12 per unit.
   b. $9 per unit.
   c. $11 per unit.
   d. $8 per unit.

   Answer: b   *Difficulty:* 2   *Objective:* 2
   $18 - $6 - $3 = $9

51. The contribution income statement highlights
   a. gross margin.
   b. products costs and period costs.
   c. different product lines.
   d. variable and fixed costs.

   Answer: d   *Difficulty:* 2   *Objective:* 2

52. At the breakeven point of 200 units, variable costs total $400 and fixed costs total $600. The 201st unit sold will contribute _____ to profits.
   a. $1
   b. $2
   c. $3
   d. $5

   Answer: c   *Difficulty:* 3   *Objective:* 3
   $1,000 - $400 - $600 = 0; Sales ($1,000 / 200) – Variable costs ($400 / 200) = $3 CM

53. The breakeven point is the activity level where
   a. revenues equal fixed costs.
   b. revenues equal variable costs.
   c. contribution margin equals variable costs.
   d. revenues equal the sum of variable and fixed costs.

   Answer: d   *Difficulty:* 3   *Objective:* 3

54. Breakeven point is
   a. total costs divided by variable costs per unit.
   b. contribution margin per unit divided by revenue per unit.
   c. fixed costs divided by contribution margin per unit.
   d. the sum of fixed and variable costs divided by contribution margin per unit.

   Answer: c   *Difficulty:* 2   *Objective:* 3

55. Sales total $200,000 when variable costs total $150,000 and fixed costs total $30,000. The breakeven point in sales dollars is
    a. $200,000.
    b. $120,000.
    c. $ 40,000.
    d. $ 30,000.

    Answer: b   *Difficulty:* 3   *Objective:* 3
    ($200,000- 150,000) / $200,000 = 25% CM%; $30,000 / 0.25 = $120,000 BE sales

56. The breakeven point in CVP analysis is defined as
    a. when fixed costs equal total revenues.
    b. fixed costs divided by the contribution margin per unit.
    c. revenues less variable costs equal operating income.
    d. when the contribution margin percentage equals total revenues divided by variable costs.

    Answer: b   *Difficulty:* 2   *Objective:* 3

57. Which of the following statements about determining the breakeven point is FALSE?
    a. Operating income is equal to zero.
    b. Contribution margin - fixed costs is equal to zero.
    c. Revenues equal fixed costs plus variable costs.
    d. Breakeven revenues equal fixed costs divided by the variable cost per unit.

    Answer: d   *Difficulty:* 3   *Objective:* 3

58. What is the breakeven point in units, assuming a product's selling price is $100, fixed costs are $8,000, unit variable costs are $20, and operating income is $32,000?
    a. 100 units
    b. 300 units
    c. 400 units
    d. 500 units

    Answer: a   *Difficulty:* 2   *Objective:* 3
    $100N - $20N - $8,000 = 0; $80N = $8,000; N = 100 units;

59. If unit outputs exceed the breakeven point
    a. there is a loss.
    b. total sales revenue exceeds total costs.
    c. there is a profit.
    d. then both (b) and (c) are correct.

    Answer: d   *Difficulty:* 2   *Objective:* 3

60. Fixed costs equal $12,000, unit contribution margin equals $20, and the number of units sold equal 1,600. Operating income is
    a. $12,000.
    b. $20,000.
    c. $32,000.
    d. $40,000.

    Answer: b   *Difficulty:* 3   *Objective:* 3
    (1,600 x $20) - $12,000 = $20,000

61. How many units would have to be sold to yield a target operating income of $22,000, assuming variable costs are $15 per unit, total fixed costs are $2,000, and the unit selling price is $20?
    a. 4,800 units
    b. 4,400 units
    c. 4,000 units
    d. 3,600 units

    Answer: a   *Difficulty:* 3   *Objective:* 3
    ($2,000 + $22,000) / ($20 - $15) = 4,800 units

62. If breakeven point is 100 units and each unit sells for $50, then
    a. selling 125 units will result in a profit.
    b. sales of $4,000 will result in a loss.
    c. sales of $5,000 will result in zero profit.
    d. all of the above are true.

    Answer: d   *Difficulty:* 2   *Objective:* 3
    100 x $50 - $5,000 of BE sales

63. If breakeven point is 100 units, each unit sells for $30, and fixed costs are $1,000, then on a graph
    a. the total revenue line and the total cost line will intersect at $3,000 of revenue.
    b. the total cost line will be zero at zero units sold.
    c. the revenue line will start at $1,000.
    d. all of the above are true.

    Answer: a   *Difficulty:* 2   *Objective:* 3

64. When fixed costs are $100,000 and variable costs are 20% of the selling price, then breakeven sales are
    a. $100,000.
    b. $125,000.
    c. $500,000.
    d. unable to be determined.

    Answer: b   *Difficulty:* 2   *Objective:* 3
    $100,000 / (1- 0.20) = $125,000 in BE sales

THE FOLLOWING INFORMATION APPLIES TO QUESTIONS 65 THROUGH 68.
Ruben intends to sell his customers a special round-trip airline ticket package. He is able to purchase the package from the airline carrier for $150 each. The round-trip tickets will be sold for $200 each and the airline intends to reimburse Ruben for any unsold ticket packages. Fixed costs include $5,000 in advertising costs.

65. What is the contribution margin per ticket package?
    a. $50
    b. $100
    c. $150
    d. $200

    Answer: a   *Difficulty:*   1   *Objective:*   3
    $200 - $150 = $50

66. How many ticket packages will Ruben need to sell in order to break even?
    a.   34 packages
    b.   50 packages
    c.   100 packages
    d.   150 packages

    Answer: c   *Difficulty:*   2   *Objective:*   3
    $200X – 150X – 5,000 = 0; X = 100$

67. How many ticket packages will Ruben need to sell in order to achieve $60,000 of operating income?
    a.   367 packages
    b.   434 packages
    c.   1,100 packages
    d.   1,300 packages
    Answer: d   *Difficulty:*   2   *Objective:*   3
    $200X – 150X – 5,000 = 60,000; X = 1,300$

68. For every $25,000 of ticket packages sold, operating income will increase by
    a. $6,250.
    b. $12,500.
    c. $18,750.
    d.   impossible to compute.

    Answer: a   *Difficulty:*   3   *Objective:*   3
    $25,000 x ($50 / $200) = $6,250

THE FOLLOWING INFORMATION APPLIES TO QUESTIONS 69 THROUGH 72.

Northenscold Company sells several products. Information of average revenue and costs are as follows:

Selling price per unit	$20.00
Variable costs per unit:	
Direct material	$4.00
Direct manufacturing labor	$1.60
Manufacturing overhead	$0.40
Selling costs	$2.00
Annual fixed costs	$96,000

69. The contribution margin per unit is
    a. $6.
    b. $8.
    c. $12.
    d. $14.

Answer: c   *Difficulty:*   2   *Objective:*   2
$20 - $4 - $1.60 - $0.40 - $2 = $12

70. The number of units that Northenscold's must sell each year to break even is
    a.   8,000 units.
    b.   12,000 units.
    c.   16,000 units.
    d.   unable to be determined.

Answer: a   *Difficulty:*   2   *Objective:*   3
20X - 8X - 96,000 = 0; X = 8,000 units

71. The number of units that Northenscold's must sell annually to make a profit of $144,000 is
    a.   12,000 units.
    b.   18,000 units.
    c.   20,000 units.
    d.   30,000 units.

Answer: c   *Difficulty:*   2   *Objective:*   3
20X – 8X – 96,000 = $144,000; X = 20,000 units

72. All of the following are assumed in the above analysis EXCEPT
    a.   a constant product mix.
    b.   fixed costs increase when activity increases.
    c.   cost and revenue relationships are reflected accurately.
    d.   all costs can be classified as either fixed or variable.

Answer: b   *Difficulty:*   2   *Objective:*   1

THE FOLLOWING INFORMATION APPLIES TO QUESTIONS 73 AND 74.
The following information is for Nichols Company:

Selling price	$150 per unit
Variable costs	$90 per unit
Total fixed costs	$300,000

73. The number of units that Nichols Company must sell to reach targeted operating income of $90,000 is
    a. 5,000 units.
    b. 6,500 units.
    c. 3,334 units.
    d. 4,334 units.

    Answer: b   *Difficulty:* 2   *Objective:* 3
    ($300,000 + $90,000)/($150 - $90) = 6,500 units

74. If targeted operating income is $120,000, then targeted sales revenue is
    a. $1,050,000.
    b. $700,000.
    c. $500,000.
    d. $750,000.

    Answer: a   *Difficulty:* 2   *Objective:* 3
    ($300,000 + $120,000) / [($150 - $90) / $150] = $1,050,000

THE FOLLOWING INFORMATION APPLIES TO QUESTIONS 75 THROUGH 77.
Stephanie's Bridal Shoppe sells wedding dresses. The average selling price of each dress is $1,000, variable costs $400, and fixed costs $90,000.

75. What is the Bridal Shoppe's operating income when 200 dresses are sold?
    a. $30,000
    b. $80,000
    c. $200,000
    d. $100,000

    Answer: a   *Difficulty:* 2   *Objective:* 3
    200($1,000) - 200($400) - $90,000 = $30,000

76. How many dresses are sold when operating income is zero?
    a. 225 dresses
    b. 150 dresses
    c. 100 dresses
    d. 90 dresses

    Answer: b   *Difficulty:* 2   *Objective:* 3
    $1,000N - $400N - $90,000 = 0; $600N = $90,000; N = 150 dresses

77. How many dresses must the Bridal Shoppe sell in order to yield after-tax net income of $18,000, assuming the tax rate is 40%?
    a.   200 dresses
    b.   170 dresses
    c.   150 dresses
    d.   145 dresses

    Answer: a   *Difficulty:*   3   *Objective:*   4
    $1,000N - $400N - $90,000 = $18,000/(1 - 0.4)$; $600N - $90,000 = $30,000$;   N = 200 units

THE FOLLOWING INFORMATION APPLIES TO QUESTIONS 78 AND 79.
Assume the following cost information for Fernandez Company:

Selling price	$120 per unit
Variable costs	$80 per unit
Total fixed costs	$80,000
Tax rate	40%

78. What volume of sales dollars is required to earn an after-tax net income of $30,000?
    a. $465,000
    b. $330,000
    c. $390,000
    d. $165,000

    Answer: c   *Difficulty:*   3   *Objective:*   4
    $[\$80,000 + (\$30,000/0.6)] / [(\$120 - \$80) / \$120] = \$390,000$

79. What is the number of units that must be sold to earn an after-tax net income of $42,000?
    a.   3,750 units
    b.   4,625 units
    c.   3,050 units
    d.   1,875 units

    Answer: a   *Difficulty:*   3   *Objective:*   4
    $[\$80,000 + (\$42,000 / 0.6)] / (\$120 - \$80) = 3,750$ units

80. In CVP analysis, focusing on target net income rather than operating income
    a.   will increase the breakeven point.
    b.   will decrease the breakeven point.
    c.   will not change the breakeven point.
    d.   does not allow calculation of breakeven point.

    Answer: c   *Difficulty:*   2   *Objective:*   4

81. To determine the effect of income tax on a decision, managers should evaluate
    a.   target operating income.
    b.   contribution margin.
    c.   target net income.
    d.   selling price.

    Answer: c   *Difficulty:*   1   *Objective:*   4

82. Assume only the specified parameters change in a cost-volume-profit analysis. If the contribution margin increases by $2 per unit then operating profits will
    a.   also increase by $2 per unit.
    b.   increase by less than $2 per unit.
    c.   decrease by $2 per unit.
    d.   not be determined.

    Answer: a   *Difficulty:*   2   *Objective:*   5

83. The Tessmer Company has fixed costs of $400,000 and variable costs are 75% of the selling price. To realize profits of $100,000 from sales of 500,000 units, the selling price per unit
    a.   must be $1.00.
    b.   must be $1.33.
    c.   must be $4.00.
    d.   cannot be determined.

    Answer: c   *Difficulty:*   3   *Objective:*   5
    ($400,000 + $100,000) / .25 = $2,000,000 in sales / 500,000 units = $4 per unit

84. The breakeven point decreases if
    a.   variable cost per unit increases.
    b.   total fixed costs decrease.
    c.   contribution margin per unit decreases.
    d.   selling price per unit decreases.

    Answer: b   *Difficulty:*   3   *Objective:*   5

85. (CPA adapted, November 1992) The strategy MOST likely to reduce the breakeven point would be to
    a.   increase both the fixed costs and the contribution margin.
    b.   decrease both the fixed costs and the contribution margin.
    c.   decrease the fixed costs and increase the contribution margin.
    d.   increase the fixed costs and decrease the contribution margin.

    Answer: c   *Difficulty:*   3   *Objective:*   5

86.   _____ is the process of varying key estimates to identify those estimates that are the most critical to a decision.
   a.   The graph method
   b.   A sensitivity analysis
   c.   The degree of operating leverage
   d.   Sales mix

   Answer: b   *Difficulty:*   1   *Objective:*   5

87.   Assume only the specified parameters change in a CVP analysis. The contribution margin percentage increases when
   a.   total fixed costs increase.
   b.   total fixed costs decrease.
   c.   variable costs per unit increase.
   d.   variable costs per unit decrease.

   Answer: d   *Difficulty:*   3   *Objective:*   5

88.   Which of the following will increase a company's breakeven point?
   a.   Increasing variable cost per unit
   b.   Increasing contribution margin per unit
   c.   Reducing its total fixed costs
   d.   Increasing the selling price per unit

   Answer: a   *Difficulty:*   3   *Objective:*   5

89.   Assume there is a reduction in the selling price and all other CVP parameters remain constant. This change will
   a.   increase contribution margin.
   b.   reduce fixed costs.
   c.   increase variable costs.
   d.   reduce operating income.

   Answer: d   *Difficulty:*   3   *Objective:*   5

90.   Assume there is an increase in advertising expenditures and all other CVP parameters remain constant. This change will
   a.   reduce operating income.
   b.   reduce contribution margin.
   c.   increase variable costs.
   d.   increase selling price.

   Answer: a   *Difficulty:*   3   *Objective:*   5

91.   The margin of safety is the difference between
   a.   budgeted expenses and breakeven expenses.
   b.   budgeted revenues and breakeven revenues.
   c.   actual operating income and budgeted operating income.
   d.   actual contribution margin and budgeted contribution margin.

   Answer: b   *Difficulty:*   1   *Objective:*   5

THE FOLLOWING INFORMATION APPLIES TO QUESTIONS 92 THROUGH 95.
Dr. Charles Hunter, MD, performs a certain outpatient procedure for $1,000. His fixed costs are $20,000, while his variable costs are $500 per procedure. Dr. Hunter currently plans to perform 200 procedures this month.

92. What is the budgeted revenue for the month assuming that Dr. Hunter plans to perform this procedure 200 times?
   a. $100,000
   b. $200,000
   c. $300,000
   d. $400,000

   Answer: b   *Difficulty:* 1   *Objective:* 5
   200 x $1,000 = $200,000

93. What is the budgeted operating income for the month assuming that Dr. Hunter plans to perform the procedure 200 times?
   a. $200,000
   b. $100,000
   c. $80,000
   d. $40,000

   Answer: c   *Difficulty:* 1   *Objective:* 3
   $200,000 - [(200 x $500) + $20,000]; $200,000 - $120,000 = $80,000

94. What is the breakeven point for the month assuming that Dr. Hunter plans to perform the procedure 200 times?
   a. 40 times
   b. 30 times
   c. 20 times
   d. 10 times

   Answer: a   *Difficulty:* 2   *Objective:* 5
   $1,000N - $500N - $20,000 = 0; $500N = $20,000; N = 40 times

95. What is the margin of safety assuming 100 procedures are budgeted?
   a. $40,000 or 40 times
   b. $50,000 or 50 times
   c. $60,000 or 60 times
   d. $100,000 or 100 times

   Answer: c   *Difficulty:* 3   *Objective:* 5
   Breakeven in number of procedures = $20,000/($1,000 - $500) = 40 times

Actual sales	100 times	x $1,000 =	$100,000
Breakeven sales	40 times	x $1,000 =	$40,000
Margin of safety	60 times		$60,000

THE FOLLOWING INFORMATION APPLIES TO QUESTIONS 96 THROUGH 100.
Nancy's Niche sells a single product. 8,000 units were sold resulting in $80,000 of sales
revenue; $20,000 of variable costs; and $10,000 of fixed costs.

96. The contribution margin percentage is
    a.   12.5%
    b.   25.0%
    c.   37.5%
    d.   75.0%

    Answer: d   *Difficulty*:   2   *Objective*:   2
    ($80,000 - $20,000) / $80,000 = 75%

97. Breakeven point in total sales dollars is
    a. $40,000.
    b. $13,334.
    c. $100,000.
    d.   none of the above.

    Answer: b   *Difficulty*:   2   *Objective*:   3
    $10,000 / 0.75 = $13,334

98. To achieve $100,000 in operating income, sales must total
    a. $440,000.
    b. $160,000.
    c. $130,000.
    d.   none of the above.

    Answer: d   *Difficulty*:   2   *Objective*:   2
    ($100,000 + 10,000) / 75% = $146,667 in sales

99. If variable costs decrease by $1 per unit, the new breakeven point is
    a.   1,539 units.
    b.   492 units.
    c. $11,765 in total sales dollars.
    d.   none of the above.

    Answer: c   *Difficulty*:   3   *Objective*:   5
    [$10 – ($2.50 – 1.00)] / $10 = 85%; $10,000 / 0.85 = $11,765

100. The question immediately above is an example of
    a.   sensitivity analysis.
    b.   incremental budgeting.
    c.   operating leverage.
    d.   multiple cost drivers

    Answer: a   *Difficulty*:   1   *Objective*:   5

THE FOLLOWING INFORMATION APPLIES TO QUESTIONS 101 THROUGH 103.
Martha Manufacturing produces a single product that sells for $80. Variable costs per unit
equal $32. The company expects total fixed costs to be $72,000 for the next month at the
projected sales level of 2,000 units. In an attempt to improve performance, management is
considering a number of alternative actions. Each situation is to be evaluated separately.

101. What is the current breakeven point in terms of number of units?
      a. 1,500 units
      b. 2,250 units
      c. 3,333 units
      d. none of the above

      Answer: a   *Difficulty*:   2   *Objective*:   3
      80X – 32X – 72,000 = 0; X = 1500 units

102. Suppose management believes that a $16,000 increase in the monthly advertising
      expense will result in a considerable increase in sales. Sales must increase by how
      much to justify this additional expenditure?
      a. 200 units
      b. 334 units
      c. 500 units
      d. none of the above

      Answer: b   *Difficulty*:   2   *Objective*:   5
      80X - 32X - 16,000 = 0; X = 334 units to cover the expenditures

103. Suppose that management believes that a 10% reduction in the selling price will result
      in a 10% increase in sales. If this proposed reduction in selling price is implemented,
      a. operating income will decrease by $8,000.
      b. operating income will increase by $8,000.
      c. operating income will decrease by $16,000.
      d. operating income will increase by $16,000.

      Answer: a   *Difficulty*:   3   *Objective*:   5
      $80 x 10% = $8 x 2,000 units =   ($16,000)
      2000 units x 10% = 200 units x ($72 - $32) =   8,000
            Change in operating income   ($8,000)

THE FOLLOWING INFORMATION APPLIES TO QUESTIONS 104 THROUGH 106.
Cheaney Manufacturing produces a single product that sells for $200. Variable costs per unit equal $50. The company expects total fixed costs to be $120,000 for the next month at the projected sales level of 2,000 units. In an attempt to improve performance, management is considering a number of alternative actions. Each situation is to be evaluated separately.

104. What is the current breakeven point in terms of number of units?
    a. 800 units
    b. 900 units
    c. 2,400 units
    d. none of the above

    Answer: a   *Difficulty*: 2   *Objective*: 3
    200X - 50X - 120,000 = 0; X = 800 units

105. Suppose that management believes that a $24,000 increase in the monthly advertising expense will result in a considerable increase in sales. Sales must increase by how much to justify this additional expenditure?
    a. 320 units
    b. 480 units
    c. 160 units
    d. none of the above

    Answer: c   *Difficulty*: 2   *Objective*: 5
    200X – 50X – 24,000 = 0; X = 160 units to cover the expenditures

106. Suppose that management believes that a 20% reduction in the selling price will result in a 20% increase in sales. If this proposed reduction in selling price is implemented,
    a. operating income will decrease by $36,000.
    b. operating income will increase by $36,000.
    c. operating income will decrease by $80,000.
    d. operating income will increase by $44,000.

    Answer: a   *Difficulty*: 3   *Objective*: 5

$200 x 20% = $40 x 2,000 units =	($80,000)
2000 units x 20% = 400 units x ($160 - $50) =	44,000
Change in operating income	($36,000)

THE FOLLOWING INFORMATION APPLIES TO QUESTIONS 107 THROUGH 110.
Southwestern College is planning to hold a fundraising banquet at one of the local country clubs. It has two options for the banquet:

OPTION 1: *Crestview Country Club*
  a. Fixed rental cost of $1,000.
  b. $12 per person for food.

OPTION 2: *Tallgrass Country Club*
  a. Fixed rental cost of $3,000.
  b. A caterer who charges $8.00 per person for food.

Southwestern College has budgeted $1,800 for administrative and marketing expenses. It plans to hire a band, which will cost another $800. Tickets are expected to be $30 per person. Local business supporters will donate any other items required for the event.

107. Which option provides the least amount of risk?
  a. Option one
  b. Option two
  c. Both options provide the same amount of risk.
  d. Neither option has risks.

Answer: a   *Difficulty:* 1   *Objective:* 6

108. Which option has the lowest breakeven point?
  a. Option one
  b. Option two
  c. Both options have the same breakeven point.
  d. This cannot be determined.

Answer: a   *Difficulty:* 2   *Objective:* 6
Option 1: 30x - 12x - 1,000 - 1,800 - 800 = 0; X = 200
Option 2: 30x - 8x - 3,000 - 1,800 - 800 = 0; X = 255

109. Which option provides the greatest operating income if 600 people attend?
  a. Option one
  b. Option two
  c. Operating incomes are identical.
  d. This cannot be determined.

Answer: b   *Difficulty:* 2   *Objective:* 6
Option 1: 18 (600) – 3,600 = 7,200; Option 2: 22 (600) - 5,600 = 7,600

110. Which option provides the greatest degree of operating leverage if 600 people attend?
  a. Option one
  b. Option two
  c. Both options provide equal degrees of operating leverage.
  d. This cannot be determined.

Answer: b   *Difficulty:* 3   *Objective:* 6
Option 1: 18 (600) / 7,200 = 1.50; Option 2: 22 (600) / 7,600 = 1.74

111. Option 1: Fixed costs of $10,000 and a breakeven point of 500 units.
Option 2: Fixed costs of $20,000 and a breakeven point of 700 units.
Which option should you choose if you are expecting to produce 600 units?
a. Option one
b. Option two
c. Both options are equally desirable.
d. This cannot be determined.

Answer: a *Difficulty:* 2 *Objective:* 6
Option 1 will result in operating income while Option 2 will result in an operating loss.

112. Mrs. Granberry is going to sell Christmas tree lights for $20 a box. The lights cost
Marsha $5 a unit and any unsold lights can be returned for a full refund. She is
planning to rent a booth at the upcoming Happy Holidays Convention, which offers
three options:
1. paying a fixed fee of $1,500,
2. paying a $500 fee plus 10% of revenues made at the convention, or
3. paying 25% of revenues made at the convention.

Which of the following statements is FALSE?
a. Her decision will determine the risk she faces.
b. Contribution margin will vary, depending upon the option chosen.
c. One of the options will allow Marsha to break even, even if she doesn't sell any
lights.
d. Operating income will be the greatest for Option 3.

Answer: d *Difficulty:* 3 *Objective:* 6

113. In a company with low operating leverage
a. fixed costs are high and variable costs are low.
b. large changes in sales volume result in small changes in net income.
c. there is a higher possibility of net loss than a higher-leveraged firm.
d. less risk is assumed than in a highly leveraged firm.

Answer: d *Difficulty:* 3 *Objective:* 6

114. If the contribution-margin ratio is 0.30, targeted net income is $76,800, and targeted
sales volume in dollars is $480,000, then total fixed costs are
a. $23,000.
b. $44,160.
c. $67,200.
d. $144,000.

Answer: c *Difficulty:* 3 *Objective:* 6
$(X + \$76,800)/0.30 = \$480,000;\ X = \$67,200$

115. Fixed costs
   a.   are considered variable costs over the long run.
   b.   provide less operating leverage.
   c.   reduce the risk of loss.
   d.   are graphed as a steeply sloped line.

   Answer: a   *Difficulty:*   2   *Objective:*   6

116. When a greater proportion of costs are fixed costs, then
   a.   a small increase in sales results in a small decrease in operating income.
   b.   when demand is low the risk of loss is high.
   c.   when demand is high the breakeven point is increased.
   d.   a decrease in sales reduces the cost per unit.

   Answer: b   *Difficulty:*   2   *Objective:*   6

117. A nonprofit organization aids the unemployed by supplementing their incomes by
   $3,200 annually, while they seek new employment skills. The organization has fixed
   costs of $240,000 and the budgeted appropriation for the year totals $800,000. How
   many individuals can receive financial assistance this year?
   a.   175 people
   b.   130 people
   c.   100 people
   d.   75 people

   Answer: a   *Difficulty:*   2   *Objective:*   7
   $800,000 - $3,200N - $240,000 = 0; $560,000 = $3,200N; N = 175 people

118. Helping Hands is a nonprofit organization that supplies electric fans during the summer
   for individuals in need. Fixed costs are $200,000. The fans cost $20.00 each. The
   organization has a budgeted appropriation of $480,000. How many people can receive
   a fan during the summer?
   a.   12,000 people
   b.   14,000 people
   c.   24,000 people
   d.   34,000 people

   Answer: b   *Difficulty:*   2   *Objective:*   7
   $480,000 - $20N - $200,000 = 0; $280,000 = $20N; N = 14,000 people

THE FOLLOWING INFORMATION APPLIES TO QUESTIONS 119 THROUGH 122.
The following information is for Barnett Corporation:

Product X:	Revenue	$10.00
	Variable Cost	$2.50
Product Y:	Revenue	$15.00
	Variable Cost	$5.00
Total fixed costs		$50,000

119. What is the breakeven point, assuming the sales mix consists of two units of Product X
and one unit of Product Y?
a.   1,000 units of Y and 2,000 units of X
b.   1012.5 units of Y and 2,025 units of X
c.   2012.5 units of Y and 4,025 units of X
d.   2,000 units of Y and 4,000 units of X

Answer: d   *Difficulty*: 3   *Objective*: 7

N = units of product Y; and 2N = units of product X;
    ($10.00 - $2.50)2N + ($15.00 - $5.00)N - $50,000 = 0
    $15N + $10N = $50,000
    $25N = $50,000
    N = 2,000 units
Product Y = 2,000 units; Product X = 4,000 units

120. What is the operating income, assuming actual sales total 150,000 units, and the sales
mix is two units of Product X and one unit of Product Y?
a. $1,200,000
b. $1,250,000
c. $1,750,000
d.   none of the above

Answer: a   *Difficulty*:   3   *Objective*:   7

	Product X	Product Y	Total
Sales units	100,000	50,000	150,000
Revenue	$1,000,000	$750,000	$1,750,000
Variable costs	250,000	250,000	500,000
Contribution margin	$750,000	$500,000	$1,250,000
Fixed costs			50,000
			$1,200,000

121. If the sales mix shifts to one unit of Product X and two units of Product Y, then the weighted-average contribution margin will
    a.   increase per unit.
    b.   stay the same.
    c.   decrease per unit.
    d.   not be determined.

Answer: a   *Difficulty:*   2   *Objective:*   7

122. If the sales mix shifts to one unit of Product X and two units of Product Y, then the breakeven point will
    a.   increase.
    b.   stay the same.
    c.   decrease.
    d.   not be determined.

Answer: c   *Difficulty:*   2   *Objective:*   7

123. Assuming a constant mix of 3 units of Small for every 1 unit of Large.

	Small	Large	Total
Sales	$20	$30	
Variable cost per unit	14	18	
Total fixed costs			$48,000

The breakeven point in units would be
    a.   4,800 units of Small and 1,600 units of Large.
    b.   1,200 units of Small and 400 units of Large.
    c.   1,600 units of Small and 4,800 units of Large.
    d.   400 units of Small and 1,200 units of Large.

Answer: a   *Difficulty:*   3   *Objective:*   7

	Small	Large
Sales	$20	$30
Variable costs	14	18
Contribution margin	$6	$12
Sales mix	x 3	x 1
Contribution margin per mix	$18	$12

Total contribution margin per mix = $18 + $12 = $30

Breakeven point in composite units = $48,000/$30 = 1,600

Small: 1,600 x 3 = 4,800 units
Large: 1,600 x 1 = 1,600 units

124. In multiproduct situations, when sales mix shifts toward the product with the highest contribution margin then
    a. total revenues will decrease.
    b. breakeven quantity will increase.
    c. total contribution margin will decrease.
    d. operating income will increase.

    Answer: d   *Difficulty*: 3   *Objective*: 7

125. Multiple cost drivers
    a. have only one revenue driver.
    b. can utilize the simple CVP formula.
    c. have no unique breakeven point.
    d. are the result of multiple products.

    Answer: c   *Difficulty*: 2   *Objective*: 8

126. Gross margin is
    a. sales revenue less variable costs.
    b. sales revenue less cost of goods sold.
    c. contribution margin less fixed costs.
    d. contribution margin less variable costs.

    Answer: b   *Difficulty*: 1   *Objective*: 9

127. In the merchandising sector
    a. only variable costs are subtracted to determine gross margin.
    b. fixed overhead costs are subtracted to determine gross margin.
    c. fixed overhead costs are subtracted to determine contribution margin.
    d. all operating costs are subtracted to determine contribution margin.

    Answer: a   *Difficulty*: 2   *Objective*: 9

128. In the manufacturing sector
    a. only variable costs are subtracted to determine gross margin.
    b. fixed overhead costs are subtracted to determine gross margin.
    c. fixed overhead costs are subtracted to determine contribution margin.
    d. all operating costs are subtracted to determine contribution margin.

    Answer: b   *Difficulty*: 2   *Objective*: 9

129. To determine contribution margin use
    a. only variable manufacturing costs.
    b. only fixed manufacturing costs.
    c. both variable and fixed manufacturing costs.
    d. both variable manufacturing costs and variable nonmanufacturing costs.

    Answer: d   *Difficulty*: 2   *Objective*: 9

130. "Uncertainty" may be defined as
   a. the possibility that an actual amount will be the same as an expected amount.
   b. the possibility that an actual amount will be either higher or lower than the expected amount.
   c. the possibility that a budgeted amount will be higher than the estimated amount.
   d. the possibility that the budgeted amount will be lower than the estimated amount.

   Answer: b   *Difficulty:* 1   *Objective:* A

131. Events, as distinguished from actions, would include
   a. personnel policy options.
   b. decisions on time schedules.
   c. decisions on direct material vendors.
   d. a financial recession.

   Answer: d   *Difficulty:* 3   *Objective:* A

132. Expected monetary value may be defined as
   a. the probability that each outcome will occur.
   b. the probability that each outcome will not occur.
   c. the weighted average of the outcomes with the probability of each outcome serving as the weight.
   d. the average of all possible outcomes.

   Answer: c   *Difficulty:* 1   *Objective:* A

133. What would be the expected monetary value for the following data using the probability method?

Probability	Cash Inflows
0.20	$100,000
0.30	$80,000
0.15	$60,000
0.35	$0

   a. $20,000
   b. $94,000
   c. $53,000
   d. $30,000

   Answer: c   *Difficulty:* 2   *Objective:* A
   $0.20(\$100,000) + 0.30(\$80,000) + 0.15(\$60,000) = \$53,000$.

THE FOLLOWING INFORMATION APPLIES TO QUESTIONS 134 AND 135.
Patrick Ross has three booth rental options at the county fair where he plans to sell his new product. The booth rental options are:

Option 1: $1,000 fixed fee
Option 2: $750 fixed fee + 5% of all revenues generated at the fair
Option 3: 20% of all revenues generated at the fair.

The product sells for $37.50 per unit. He is able to purchase the units for $12.50 each.

134. How many actions and events will a decision table contain?
    a. 1 action and 3 events
    b. 1 action and 6 events
    c. 2 actions and 3 events
    d. 3 actions and 6 events

    Answer: d   *Difficulty*: 2   *Objective*: A

135. Which option should Patrick choose in order to maximize income, assuming there is a 40% probability that 70 units will be sold and a 60% probability that 40 units will be sold?
    a. Option one
    b. Option two
    c. Option three
    d. All options maximize income equally.

    Answer: c   *Difficulty*: 3   *Objective*: A
    Expected revenues = 0.4(70 x $37.50) + 0.6(40 x $37.50) = $1,950
    Expected CM before options = 0.4(70 x $25) + 0.6(40 x $25) = $1,300

    Option 1: $1,300 - $1,000 = $300
    Option 2: $1,300 - $750 - 0.05($1,950) = $452.50
    Option 3: $1,300 - 0.2($1,950) = $910*

    * = maximization of income

EXERCISES AND PROBLEMS

136. Gilley, Inc., sells a single product. The company's most recent income statement is given below.

Sales (4,000 units)	$120,000
Less variable expenses	(68,000)
Contribution margin	52,000
Less fixed expenses	(40,000)
Net income	$ 12,000

Required:

a. Contribution margin per unit is $ _____ per unit

b. If sales are doubled to $240,000, total variable costs will equal $ _____

c. If sales are doubled to $240,000, total fixed costs will equal $ _____

d. If 10 more units are sold, profits will increase by $ _____

e. Compute how many units must be sold to break even.   # _____

f. Compute how many units must be sold to achieve profits of $20,000.   # _____

Answer:

a. Contribution margin per unit is $13 = $30 - $17
b. $136,000 = $68,000 x 2
c. $40,000
d. $130 = Contribution margin $13 x 10 units
e. 3,077 units = Fixed costs $40,000 / Contribution margin per unit $13
f. 4,616 units = (Fixed costs $40,000 + Profits $20,000) / CM per unit $13

Difficulty: 2   *Objectives*: 2, 3

137. Blankinship, Inc., sells a single product. The company's most recent income statement is given below.

Sales	$200,000
Less variable expenses	(120,000)
Contribution margin	80,000
Less fixed expenses	(50,000)
Net income	$ 30,000

Required:

a. Contribution margin ratio is _____ %

b. Breakeven point in total sales dollars is $ _____

c. To achieve $40,000 in net income, sales must total $ _____

d. If sales increase by $50,000, net income will increase by $ _____

Answer:

a. Contribution margin ratio is 40% = $80,000 / $200,000
b. $125,000 in sales = Fixed (fixed) costs $50,000 / 0.40 CM%
c. $225,000 in sales =
    [Fixed (fixed) costs $50,000 + Net income $40,000] / 0.40 CM%
d. Net income will increase by $20,000 = $50,000 x 0.40 CM%

Difficulty: 2   *Objectives*: 2, 3

138. In 2002, Grant Company has sales of $800,000, variable costs of $200,000, and fixed costs of $300,000. In 2003, the company expects annual property taxes to decrease by $15,000.

Required:
a. Calculate operating income and breakeven point for 2002.
b. Calculate breakeven point for 2003.

Answer:
a. In 2002, operating income equals $300,000 = $800,000 sales revenue - $200,000 variable costs - $300,000 fixed costs.

   The breakeven point for 2002 is $400,000 in total sales dollars. $600,000 CM / $800,000 sales revenue = 0.75 CM ratio. $300,000 total fixed costs / 0.75 CM ratio = $400,000 in total sales to break even.

b. The breakeven point for 2003 is $380,000 in total sales dollars.

   $300,000 - $15,000 reduction in property taxes = $285,000 estimated fixed costs for 2003. $285,000 total fixed costs / 75% CM ratio = $380,000 in total sales to break even.

Difficulty: 2   *Objectives*: 2, 3, 5

139. Berhannan's Cellular sells phones for $100. The unit variable cost per phone is $50 plus a selling commission of 10%. Fixed manufacturing costs total $1,250 per month, while fixed selling and administrative costs total $2,500.

Required:
a. What is the contribution margin per phone?
b. What is the breakeven point in phones?
c. How many phones must be sold to earn pretax income of $7,500?

Answer:
a. CM per phone = $100 - $50 - 0.1($100) = $40

b. N = Breakeven in phones
   $100N - $50N - $10N - $1,250 - $2,500 = 0
   $40N - $3,750 = 0
   N = $3,750 / $40 = 93.75 phones
   Breakeven is 94 phones

c. N = Phones to be sold
   $100N - $50N - $10N - $1,250 - $2,500 = $7,500
   $40N = $11,250
   N = $11,250 / $40 = 281.25 phones
   282 phones must be sold

Difficulty: 2   *Objective*: 3

140. The Holiday Card Company, a producer of specialty cards, has asked you to complete several calculations based upon the following information:

Income tax rate	30%
Selling price per unit	$6.60
Variable cost per unit	$5.28
Total fixed costs	$46,200.00

Required:

a. What is the breakeven point in cards?
b. What sales volume is needed to earn an after-tax net income of $13,028.40?
c. How many cards must be sold to earn an after-tax net income of $18,480?

Answer:

a. $46,200/($6.60 - $5.28) = 35,000 units

b. $13,028.40/0.70 = $18,612
$18,612 + $46,200 = $64,812
$64,812/$1.32 = 49,100 units
49,100 units x $6.60 = $324,060

c. $18,480/0.70 = $26,400
$26,400 + $46,200 = $72,600
$72,600/$1.32 = 55,000 units

Difficulty: 2   *Objectives*: 3, 4

141. Royer Corporation gathered the following information:

Variable costs	$945,000
Income tax rate	40%
Contribution-margin ratio	30%

Required:

a. Compute total fixed costs assuming a breakeven volume in dollars of $1,350,000.
b. Compute sales volume in dollars to produce an after-tax net income of $108,000.

Answer:

a. $1,350,000 x 0.30 = $405,000

b. $108,000/0.60 = $180,000
($180,000 + $405,000) / 0.3 = $1,950,000

Difficulty: 3   *Objectives*: 3, 4

142. Alex Miller, Inc., sells car batteries to service stations for an average of $30 each. The variable cost of each battery is $20 and monthly fixed manufacturing costs total $10,000. Other monthly fixed costs of the company total $8,000.

Required:

a. What is the breakeven point in batteries?
b. What is the margin of safety, assuming sales total $60,000?
c. What is the breakeven level in batteries, assuming variable costs increase by 20%?
d. What is the breakeven level in batteries, assuming the selling price goes up by 10%, fixed manufacturing costs decline by 10%, and other fixed costs decline by $100?

Answer:

a. N = Breakeven units
    $30N - $20N - $10,000 - $8,000 = 0
    $10N - $18,000 = 0
    N = $18,000/$10 = 1,800 batteries

b. Margin of safety = $60,000 - ($30 x 1,800) = $6,000

c. N = Breakeven units
    $30N - $24N - $10,000 - $8,000 = 0
    $6N - $18,000 = 0
    N = $18,000/$6 = 3,000 batteries

d. N = Breakeven units
    $33N - $20N - $9,000 - $7,900 = 0
    $13N - $16,900 = 0
    N = $16,900/$13 = 1,300 batteries

Difficulty: 2   *Objectives*: 3, 4, 5

143. Furniture, Inc., sells lamps for $30. The unit variable cost per lamp is $22. Fixed costs total $9,600.

Required:

a. What is the contribution margin per lamp?
b. What is the breakeven point in lamps?
c. How many lamps must be sold to earn a pretax income of $8,000?
d. What is the margin of safety, assuming 1,500 lamps are sold?

Answer:

a. Contribution margin per lamp = $30 - $22 = $8

b. N = Breakeven point in lamps
   $30N - $22N - $9,600 = 0
   $8N - $9,600 = 0
   N = $9,600/$8 = 1,200 lamps

c. N = Target sales in lamps
   $30N - $22N - $9,600 - $8,000 = 0
   $8N - $17,600 = 0
   N = $17,600/$8 = 2,200 lamps

d. Margin of safety = Sales - Breakeven sales
                     = ($30.00 x 1,500) - $36,000 = $9,000

Difficulty: 3   *Objectives*: 3, 5

144. Query Company sells pillows for $25.00 each. The manufacturing cost, all variable, is $10 per pillow. The company is planning on renting an exhibition booth for both display and selling purposes at the annual crafts and art convention. The convention coordinator allows three options for each participating company. They are:

    1. paying a fixed booth fee of $5,010, or
    2. paying an $4,000 fee plus 10% of revenue made at the convention, or
    3. paying 20% of revenue made at the convention.

Required:

a. Compute the breakeven sales in pillows of each option.
b. Which option should Query Company choose, assuming sales are expected to be 800 pillows?

Answer:

a. Option 1 N = Breakeven in pillows
    $25N - $10N - $5,010 = 0
    $15N - $5,010 = 0
    N = $5,010/$15 = 334 pillows

   Option 2 N = Breakeven in pillows
    $25N - $10N - 0.10($25N) - $4,000 = 0
    $12.5N - $4,000 = 0
    N = $4,000/$12.5 = 320 pillows

   Option 3 N = Breakeven in pillows
    $25N - $10N - 0.20($25N) = 0
    $10N - $0 = 0
    N = $0/$10 = 0 pillows

b. Option 1 profit for 800 pillows = $15 x 800 - $5,010 = $6,990
   Option 2 profit for 800 pillows = $12.5 x 800 - $4,000 = $6,000
   Option 3 profit for 800 pillows = $10 x 800 = $8,000
   Option 3 is the best choice.

Difficulty: 3   *Objectives*: 3, 6

145. Karen Hefner, a florist, operates retail stores in several shopping malls. The average selling price of an arrangement is $30 and the average cost of each sale is $18. A new mall is opening where Karen wants to locate a store, but the location manager is not sure about the rent method to accept. The mall operator offers the following three options for its retail store rentals:
1. paying a fixed rent of $15,000 a month,
2. paying a base rent of $9,000 plus 10% of revenue received, or
3. paying a base rent of $4,800 plus 20% of revenue received up to a maximum rent of $25,000.

Required:
a. For each option, compute the breakeven sales and the monthly rent paid at break-even.
b. Beginning at zero sales, show the sales levels at which each option is preferable up to 5,000 units.

Answer:
a. Option 1 N = Breakeven units
   $30N - $18N - $15,000 = 0
   $12N - $15,000 = 0
   N = $15,000/$12 = 1,250 units
Rent at breakeven = $15,000

Option 2 N = Breakeven units
   $30N - $18N - 0.10($30N) - $9,000 = 0
   $9N - $9,000 = 0
   N = $9,000/$9 = 1,000 units
Rent at breakeven = $9,000 + (0.10 x $30 x 1,000) = $12,000

Option 3 N = Breakeven units
   $30N - $18N - 0.20($30N) - $4,800 = 0
   $6N - $4,800 = 0
   N = $4,800/$6 = 800 units
Rent at breakeven = $4,800 + (0.20 x $30 x 800) = $9,600

b. Option 3 from 0 to 1,400 units for $4,800 plus $6 per unit.
   Option 2 from 1,401 to 2,000 for $9,000 plus $3 per unit.
   Option 1 above 2,000 for $15,000.

   Option 1 equals Option 2 when sales are 2,000 and favors Option 1 above 2,000 units.
   $15,000 = $9,000 + 0.10($30N); $6,000 = $3N; N = 2,000

   Option 1 equals Option 3 when sales are 1,700 and favors Option 1 above 1,700 units.
   $15,000 = $4,800 + 0.20($30N); $10,200 = $6N; N = 1,700 units

Difficulty: 3   *Objectives*: 3, 6

146. Yurus Manufacturing Company produces two products, X and Y. The following information is presented for both products:

	X	Y
Selling price per unit	$36	$24
Variable cost per unit	28	12

Total fixed costs are $234,000.

Required:

a. Calculate the contribution margin for each product.
b. Calculate breakeven point in units of both X and Y if the sales mix is 3 units of X for every unit of Y.
c. Calculate breakeven volume in total dollars if the sales mix is 2 units of X for every 3 units of Y.

Answer:

a. X: $36 - $28 = $8
   Y: $24 - $12 = $12

b. (3 x $8) + (1 x $12) = $36
   $234,000/$36 = 6,500 units
   X: 6,500 x 3 = 19,500 units
   Y: 6,500 x 1 = 6,500 units

c. (2 x $8) + (3 x $12) = $52
   $234,000/$52 = 4,500 units
   X: 4,500 x 2 = 9,000 x $36 = $324,000
   Y: 4,500 x 3 = 13,500 x $24 = $324,000
   Total dollar sales = $648,000

Difficulty: 3   *Objectives*: 3, 7

147. Bob's Textile Company sells shirts for men and boys. The average selling price and variable cost for each product are as follows:

Men's		Boys	
Selling Price	$28.80	Selling Price	$24.00
Variable Cost	$20.40	Variable Cost	$16.80

Fixed costs are $38,400.

Required:

a. What is the breakeven point in units for each type of shirt, assuming the sales mix is 2:1 in favor of men's shirts?
b. What is the operating income, assuming the sales mix is 2:1 in favor of men's shirts, and sales total 9,000 shirts?

Answer:

a. N = breakeven in boys shirts $2N$ = breakeven in men's shirts

$24N + $28.80(2N) - $16.80N - $20.40(2N) - $38,400 = 0$
$81.6N - $57.6N - $38,400 = 0$
$24N - $38,400 = 0$
$N = $38,400/$24 = 1,600$ shirts

Therefore, to break even, 1,600 boy's shirts and 3,200 men's shirts need to be sold.

b.

	Boys	Men	Total
Sales in units	3,000	6,000	9,000
Revenue	$72,000	$172,800	$244,800
Variable costs	50,400	122,400	172,800
Contribution margin	$21,600	$50,400	$72,000
Fixed costs			38,400
Operating income			$33,600

Difficulty: 3   *Objective*:   7

148. Ballpark Concessions currently sells hot dogs. During a typical month, the stand reports a profit of $9,000 with sales of $50,000, fixed costs of $21,000, and variable costs of $0.64 per hot dog.

Next year, the company plans to start selling nachos for $3 per unit. Nachos will have a variable cost of $0.72 and new equipment and personnel to produce nachos will increase monthly fixed costs by $8,808. Initial sales of nachos should total 5,000 units. Most of the nacho sales are anticipated to come from current hot dog purchasers, therefore, monthly sales of hot dogs are expected to decline to $20,000.

After the first year of nacho sales, the company president believes that hot dog sales will increase to $33,750 a month and nacho sales will increase to 7,500 units a month.

Required:

a. Determine the monthly breakeven sales in dollars before adding nachos.
b. Determine the monthly breakeven sales during the first year of nachos sales, assuming a constant sales mix of 1 hotdog and 2 units of nachos.

Answer:

a. Contribution margin   = Fixed costs + Profit
                                       = $21,000 + $9,000 = $30,000

   Variable costs   = Sales - Contribution margin
                                         = $50,000 - $30,000
                                         = $20,000

Units sold = $20,000/$0.64 = 31,250 units
Selling price = $50,000/31,250 = $1.60 per unit
Unit Variable costs = $20,000/31,250= $0.64
N = Breakeven units

$1.60N - $0.64N - $21,000 = 0
$0.96N - $21,000 = 0
N = $21,000/$0.96 = 21,875 units

b. Ratio equal to 1 hot dog to 2 units of nachos.

N   = Breakeven number of units of hot dogs
2N = Breakeven number of units of nachos

$3(2)N + $1.60N - $0.72(2N) - $0.64N - $29,808 = 0
$7.60N - $2.08N - $29,808 = 0
N = $29,808/$5.52 = 5,400 hot dogs

Therefore, 5,400 hot dogs and 10,800 units of nachos need to be sold to break even.

Difficulty: 3   *Objectives:* 3, 7

149.   Stephanie's Stuffed Animals reported the following:

Revenues	$1,000
Variable manufacturing costs	$ 200
Variable nonmanufacturing costs	$ 230
Fixed manufacturing costs	$ 150
Fixed nonmanufacturing costs	$ 140

Required:
a. Compute contribution margin.
b. Compute gross margin.
c. Compute operating income.

Answer:
a. Contribution margin $1,000 - 200 - 230 = $570
b. Gross margin $1,000 - 200 - 150 = $650
c. Operating income $1000 - 200 - 230 - 150 - 140 = $280

Difficulty: 2   *Objective*:   9

150.   Produce Company needs to know the pounds of apples to have on hand each day. Each pound of apples costs $0.50 and can be sold for $0.80. Unsold apples are worthless at the end of the day. The following demands were found after studying the last six months' sales:

200 pounds of apples 30% of the time
300 pounds of apples 40% of the time
400 pounds of apples 30% of the time

Required:
Determine whether Produce Company should order 200, 300, or 400 pounds of apples.

Answer:

Quantity Ordered	Demand Probability			Expected Value
	200	**300**	**400**	
200	$60	$60	$60	$60.00
300	10	90	90	66.00
400	(40)	40	120	40.00
p	0.30	0.40	0.30	

Demand example: 300 units ordered; but demand is either 300 or 400 units:
   ($0.80 x 300) - ($0.50 x 300) = $90
Expected value example:
   Order 400: ($(40) x 0.30) + ($40 x 0.40) + ($120 x 0.30) = $40
Answer: Should order 300 pounds of apples to maximize profit.

Difficulty: 3   *Objective*:   A

151. Explain when a manager would use cost-volume-profit analysis and sensitivity analysis.

    Answer:
    Cost-volume-profit analysis is helpful for evaluating the profit impact of management decisions that affect production and sales volume.

    Sensitivity analysis is helpful for identifying those estimates most critical for a decision.

    Difficulty: 2   *Objectives*:   1, 5

152. What is meant by the term breakeven point? Why should a manager be concerned about the breakeven point?

    Answer:
    The breakeven point is the level of production and sales at which total revenues equal total costs. Managers should be concerned about the breakeven point because it helps determine when a business venture will be profitable. Breakeven point shows a company how far sales can decline before a net loss will be incurred. It helps to assess the risk of loss.

    Difficulty: 2   *Objective*:   3

153. Auto Tires has been in the tire business for four years. It rents a building but owns all of its equipment. All employees are paid a fixed salary except for the busy season (April - June), when temporary help is hired by the hour. Utilities and other operating charges remain fairly constant during each month except those in the busy season.

    Selling prices per tire average $75 except during the busy season. Because a large number of customers buy tires prior to winter, discounts run above average during the busy season. A 15% discount is given when two tires are purchased at one time. During the busy months, selling prices per tire average $60.

    The president of Auto Tires is somewhat displeased with the company's management accounting system because the cost behavior patterns displayed by the monthly breakeven charts are inconsistent; the busy months' charts are different from the other months of the year. The president is never sure if the company has a satisfactory margin of safety or if it is just above the breakeven point.

    Required:
    a. What is wrong with the accountant's computations?
    b. How can the information be presented in a better format for the president?

153. **Answer:**
   a. The accounting system includes some assumptions about the CVP model that does not hold for Auto Tire. The CVP model requires cost and revenue to be linear. During the busy months, the company has cost and revenue which behave differently than during the other months of the year. The revenue line turns down (less slope) with the average selling price per tire decreasing from $75 to $60. The variable costs line probably turns upward (increasing slope) with the additional hourly workers being added to the work force.

   b. The accountant may want to present two sets of information regarding the revenue and cost behaviors of the company: one for the busy season and one for the other months of the year. It would show that while the breakeven point actually increases during the busy months (a negative), the marginal income increases because of increased sales (a positive).

   Difficulty: 2   *Objectives*: 3, 6

154. Dolph and Evan started the DE Restaurant in 20x3. They rented a building, bought equipment, and hired two employees to work full time at a fixed monthly salary. Utilities and other operating charges remain fairly constant during each month.

   During the past two years, the business has grown with average sales increasing 1% a month. This situation pleases both Dolph and Evan, but they do not understand how sales can grow by 1% a month while profits are increasing at an even faster pace. They are afraid that one day they will wake up to increasing sales but decreasing profits.

   Required:
   Explain why the profits have increased at a faster rate than sales. Use the terms variable costs and fixed costs in your response.

   Answer:
   The fixed cost per meal served is decreasing with increased volumes, while the contribution margin per meal served remains constant. Apparently, most of the restaurant's expenses are fixed. Therefore, as sales pass the breakeven point the profit will increase even faster because the fixed expenses have already been covered. This allows sales to cover only variable expenses before contributing to the profit margin, thereby causing it to increase at a faster rate.

   Difficulty: 2   *Objectives*: 3, 6

155. Freddie's company has mostly fixed costs and Valerie's company has mostly variable costs. Which company has the greatest risk of a net loss? Explain why

   Answer:
   Freddie's company has the greatest risk of net loss because more units are required to reach breakeven point than for Valerie.

   Difficulty: 2   *Objective*: 6

CHAPTER 4: JOB COSTING

TRUE/FALSE

1. Direct costs are allocated to the cost object using a cost-allocation method.

    Answer: False   *Difficulty*: 1   *Objective*: 1
    Indirect costs are allocated to the cost object using a cost-allocation method.

2. Quality control costs may be a direct cost of the Manufacturing Department, but an indirect cost of an individual job.

    Answer: True   *Difficulty*: 2   *Objective*: 1

3. Cost objects may be jobs, products, or customers.

    Answer: True   *Difficulty*: 1   *Objective*: 1

4. The cost driver of an indirect cost is often used as the cost-allocation base.

    Answer: True   *Difficulty*: 1   *Objective*: 1

5. A company may use job costing to assign costs to different product lines and then use process costing to calculate unit costs within each product line.

    Answer: True   *Difficulty*: 2   *Objective*: 2

6. Job costing is commonly used to estimate costs in beverage production.

    Answer: False   *Difficulty*: 1   *Objective*: 2
    Process costing is commonly used to estimate costs in beverage production.

7. In a job-costing system the cost object is an individual unit, batch, or lot of a distinct product or service.

    Answer: True   *Difficulty*: 1   *Objective*: 2

8. Actual costing is a method of job costing that allocates an indirect cost based on the actual indirect-cost rate times the actual quantity of the cost-allocation base.

    Answer: True   *Difficulty*: 1   *Objective*: 2

9. Process costing is used to assign manufacturing costs to unique batches of a product.

    Answer: False   *Difficulty*: 1   *Objective*: 2
    Job costing is used to assign manufacturing costs to unique batches of a product.

10. Job costing and process costing systems share the same objective of estimating product costs.

Answer: True   *Difficulty*: 1   *Objective*: 2

11. While costs are measured for individual jobs in a job cost system, they are measured for individual process stages in a process costing system.

Answer: True   *Difficulty*: 1   *Objective*: 2

12. If indirect cost rates were based on actual short-term usage, periods of lower demand would result in higher costs per unit.

Answer: True   *Difficulty*: 3   *Objective*: 3

13. In job costing, only direct costs are used to determine the cost of a job.

Answer: False   *Difficulty*: 1   *Objective*: 3
Both direct and indirect costs are used to determine the cost of a job.

14. Indirect manufacturing costs should be allocated equally to each job.

Answer: False   *Difficulty*: 2   *Objective*: 3
Not equally to each job, but according to the use of indirect resources by individual jobs.

15. Each cost pool may have multiple cost allocation bases.

Answer: False   *Difficulty*: 2   *Objective*: 3
There is only one cost-allocation base for each cost pool.

16. Gross margin percentage can be used to compare the profitability of different jobs.

Answer: True   *Difficulty*: 1   *Objective*: 3

17. A job-cost record is a source document, but individual items of the job-cost record may also have source documents.

Answer: True   *Difficulty*: 2   *Objective*: 3

18. The reliability of the job-cost records depends on the reliability of the inputs.

Answer: True   *Difficulty*: 1   *Objective*: 3

19. To smooth fluctuating levels of output, separate indirect-cost rates should be calculated for each month.

Answer: False   *Difficulty*: 2   *Objective*: 3
To smooth seasonal costs and fluctuating levels of output, indirect-cost rates should be calculated on an *annual* basis.

20. Grounds-maintenance costs incurred during the summer months will distort indirect-cost rates that are computed monthly.

Answer: True   *Difficulty*: 2   *Objective*: 3

21. One reason for using longer time periods to calculate indirect-cost rates is seasonal cost fluctuations.

Answer: True   *Difficulty*: 2   *Objective*: 3

22. Companies typically wait for accurate information regarding actual manufacturing overhead costs before pricing a job.

Answer: False   *Difficulty*: 2   *Objective*: 4
Companies typically use allocated manufacturing overhead costs to estimate the costs for pricing a job.

23. Direct costs are traced the same way for actual costing and normal costing.

Answer: True   *Difficulty*: 2   *Objective*: 4

24. Normal costing assigns indirect costs based on an actual indirect-cost rate.

Answer: False   *Difficulty*: 1   *Objective*: 4
Normal costing assigns indirect costs based on a *budgeted* rate.

25. A budgeted indirect-cost rate is computed for each cost pool using budgeted indirect costs and the budgeted quantity of the cost-allocation base.

Answer: True   *Difficulty*: 1   *Objective*: 4

26. For normal costing even though the budgeted indirect-cost rate is based on estimates, indirect costs are allocated to products based on actual levels of the cost-allocation base.

Answer: True   *Difficulty*: 1   *Objective*: 4

27. Work-in-Process Control will be decreased (credited) for the amount of direct-labor costs incurred.

   Answer: False   *Difficulty*: 1   *Objective*: 5
   Work-in-Process Control will be increased (debited) for the amount of direct-labor costs incurred.

28. The Work-in-Process Control account tracks job costs from the time jobs are started until they are completed.

   Answer: True   *Difficulty*: 2   *Objective*: 5

29. The Materials Control account is typically found in a subsidiary ledger.

   Answer: False   *Difficulty*: 1   *Objective*: 5
   The Materials Control account is typically found in the *general* ledger.

30. The Salaries Payable Control account has underlying subsidiary ledgers.

   Answer: True   *Difficulty*: 1   *Objective*: 5

31. Indirect materials that are requisitioned increase the Work-in-Process Control account.

   Answer: False   *Difficulty*: 1   *Objective*: 5
   Indirect materials that are requisitioned increase the Manufacturing Overhead Control account.

32. In a job-cost system, each indirect-cost pool has its own account in the general ledger.

   Answer: True   *Difficulty*: 2   *Objective*: 5

33. Manufacturing overhead costs are allocated to individual job-cost records with the use of indirect-cost rates.

   Answer: True   *Difficulty*: 1   *Objective*: 5

34. The Finished Goods Control account consists of actual manufacturing overhead costs rather than allocated manufacturing overhead costs.

   Answer: False   *Difficulty*: 2   *Objective*: 5
   The Finished Goods Control account consists of *allocated* manufacturing overhead costs rather than actual manufacturing overhead costs.

35. The ending balance in Work-in-Process Control represents the total costs of all jobs that have not yet been completed.

   Answer: True   *Difficulty*: 1   *Objective*: 5

36. For external reporting purposes, it is acceptable to allocate marketing costs to individual jobs.

Answer: False   *Difficulty:* 2   *Objective:* 5
Management may choose to allocate marketing costs to individual jobs for internal *pricing, product-mix, and cost-management decisions.*

37. Overhead costs allocated each month are expected to equal actual overhead costs incurred each month.

Answer: False   *Difficulty:* 2   *Objective:* 6
Seasonal fluctuations and lump-sum payments for items such as property taxes are not expected to be incurred evenly throughout the year.

38. When actual indirect costs exceed allocated indirect costs indirect costs have been overapplied.

Answer: False   *Difficulty:* 1   *Objective:* 6
Indirect costs have been *underapplied* when actual indirect costs exceed allocated indirect costs.

39. One reason indirect costs may be underapplied is if actual indirect costs exceed budgeted indirect costs.

Answer: True   *Difficulty:* 3   *Objective:* 6

40. The proration approach to allocating overapplied or underapplied overhead adjusts individual job-cost records.

Answer: False   *Difficulty:* 2   *Objective:* 6
The proration approach to allocating overapplied or underapplied overhead adjusts only general ledger accounts and not subsidiary ledgers or individual job-cost records.

41. The overhead accounts are closed or become zero at the end of each year.

Answer: True   *Difficulty:* 1   *Objective:* 6

42. Underallocated indirect costs occur when the allocated amount of indirect costs is greater than the amount incurred for that period.

Answer: False   *Difficulty:* 2   *Objective:* 6
Overallocated indirect costs occur when the allocated amount of indirect costs is greater than the amount incurred for that period.

43. The actual costs of all individual overhead categories are recorded in the Manufacturing Overhead Control account.

Answer: True   *Difficulty*: 1   *Objective*: 6

44. Proration is the spreading of underallocated or overallocated overhead among ending work in process, finished goods, and costs of goods sold.

Answer: True   *Difficulty*: 1   *Objective*: 6

45. A company may choose to use budgeted rates to allocate direct labor accounts if direct labor costs are difficult to trace to jobs as they are completed.

Answer: True   *Difficulty*: 1   *Objective*: 7

46. It is inappropriate for service organizations such as public accounting firms to use job costing.

Answer: False   *Difficulty*: 1   *Objective*: 7
Accounting firms, law firms, and other firms in the service industry can use Job costing.

47. In some variations of normal costing, organizations use budgeted rates to assign direct costs as well as indirect costs to jobs.

Answer: True   *Difficulty*: 2   *Objective*: 7

48. Job costing information is used
    a. to develop strategies.
    b. to make pricing decisions.
    c. for external financial reporting.
    d. for all of the above.

    Answer: d   *Difficulty*: 1   *Objective*: 1

49. Product costing information is used by managers
    a. to make decisions and strategy.
    b. for planning and control.
    c. for cost management.
    d. for all of the above.

    Answer: d   *Difficulty*: 1   *Objective*: 1

50. Each indirect-cost pool of a manufacturing firm
    a. utilizes a separate cost-allocation rate.
    b. is a subset of total indirect costs.
    c. relates to one cost object.
    d. is all of the above.

    Answer: d   *Difficulty*: 1   *Objective*: 1

51. An updated costing system should
    a. be installed even if the costs outweigh the additional benefits.
    b. be tailored to fit the underlying operations rather than the current cost system.
    c. focus specifically on the costing needs of the CFO.
    d. provide all information for management decision needs.

    Answer: b   *Difficulty*: 2   *Objective*: 1

52. In a costing system
    a. cost tracing allocates indirect costs.
    b. cost allocation assigns direct costs.
    c. a cost-allocation base can be either financial or nonfinancial.
    d. a cost object should be a product and not a department or a geographic territory.

    Answer: c   *Difficulty*: 2   *Objective*: 1

53. Assigning direct costs to a cost object is called
    a. cost allocation.
    b. cost assignment.
    c. cost pooling.
    d. cost tracing.

    Answer: d   *Difficulty:* 1   *Objective:* 1

54. _____ is the process of distributing indirect costs to products.
    a. Cost allocation
    b. Job cost recording
    c. Cost pooling
    d. Cost tracing

    Answer: a   *Difficulty:* 1   *Objective:* 1

55. A _____ links an indirect cost to a cost object.
    a. cost-allocation base
    b. cost pool
    c. cost assignment
    d. cost tracing

    Answer: a   *Difficulty:* 1   *Objective:* 1

56. Which of the following includes both traced direct costs and allocated indirect costs?
    a. Cost tracing
    b. Cost pools
    c. Cost assignments
    d. Cost allocations

    Answer: c   *Difficulty:* 1   *Objective:* 1

57. _____ costing is a cost management system that measures the cost of products, services, and customers.
    a. Job
    b. Process
    c. Normal
    d. All of the above

    Answer: d   *Difficulty:* 2   *Objective:* 2

58. Process costing
    a. allocates all product costs, even materials and labor.
    b. results in different costs for different units produced.
    c. is commonly used by general contractors who construct custom-built homes.
    d. is used exclusively in manufacturing.

    Answer: a   *Difficulty:* 2   *Objective:* 2

59. _____ costing is used by a business to price unique products for different jobs.
    a. Actual
    b. Job
    c. Process
    d. Traditional

    Answer: b   *Difficulty:* 1   *Objective:* 2

60. Job costing
    a. can only be used in manufacturing.
    b. records the flow of costs for each customer.
    c. allocates an equal amount of cost to each unit made during a time period.
    d. is commonly used when each unit of output is identical.

    Answer: b   *Difficulty:* 2   *Objective:* 2

61. Actual costing is a costing method that allocates_____ indirect costs.
    a. actual
    b. budgeted
    c. estimated
    d. predetermined

    Answer: a   *Difficulty:* 1   *Objective:* 2

62. A job that shows low profitability may be the result of
    a. wasting direct materials.
    b. inefficient direct manufacturing labor.
    c. underpricing the job.
    d. all of the above.

    Answer: d   *Difficulty:* 2   *Objective:* 3

63. Place the following steps in the order suggested by the seven steps used to assign costs to individual jobs.

A. Identify indirect costs
B. Compute the total cost of the job
C. Select cost-allocation bases
D. Compute the indirect cost rate

a. ACDB
b. CADB
c. BACD
d. DCAB

Answer: b   *Difficulty:* 2   *Objective:* 3

64. The basic source document for direct manufacturing labor is the
a. job-cost record.
b. materials-requisition record.
c. labor-time record.
d. it varies, and could be any of the above.

Answer: c   *Difficulty:* 1   *Objective:* 3

65. *Problems* with accurate costing occur when
a. incorrect job numbers are recorded on source documents.
b. bar coding is used to record materials used on the job.
c. a computer screen requests an employee number before that employee is able to work on information related to a specific job.
d. all of the above occur.

Answer: a   *Difficulty:* 2   *Objective:* 3

66. If actual indirect-cost rates were calculated monthly rather than annually, then for the month of February with only 28 days
a. variable indirect-cost rates would be lower.
b. total indirect-cost rates would be higher.
c. fixed indirect-cost rates would be lower.
d. monthly output would be higher.

Answer: b   *Difficulty:* 3   *Objective:* 3

67. If indirect-cost rates are calculated monthly, distortions might occur because of
a. rental costs paid monthly.
b. property tax payments made in July and December.
c. routine monthly preventive-maintenance costs that benefit future months.
d. both (b) and (c).

Answer: b   *Difficulty:* 2   *Objective:* 3

68. An example of a *numerator reason* for calculating annual indirect-cost rates includes
    a. fewer production workdays in a month.
    b. payment of estimated taxes four times a year.
    c. higher snow-removal costs during the winter.
    d. both (b) and (c).

    Answer: d   *Difficulty:*   3   *Objective:*   3

69. An example of a *denominator reason* for calculating annual indirect-cost rates includes
    a. higher heating bills in the winter.
    b. semi-annual insurance payments in March and September.
    c. higher levels of output demanded during the fall months.
    d. all of the above.

    Answer: c   *Difficulty:*   3   *Objective:*   3

70. In a job-costing system, a manufacturing firm typically uses an indirect-cost rate to estimate the _____ allocated to a job.
    a. direct materials
    b. direct labor
    c. manufacturing overhead costs
    d. total costs

    Answer: c   *Difficulty:*   2   *Objective:*   3

71. A job-cost sheet details the
    a. direct materials purchased and paid for.
    b. direct labor costs incurred.
    c. indirect labor costs incurred.
    d. actual indirect overhead costs incurred.

    Answer: b   *Difficulty:*   2   *Objective:*   3

72. A job-cost record uses information from
    a. a materials requisition record to record raw material purchases from suppliers.
    b. a receiving report that indicates the type and quantity of each item received in an order from a supplier.
    c. a labor-time card to record an employee's wage rate and hours spent on a particular job.
    d. all of the above.

    Answer: c   *Difficulty:*   2   *Objective:*   3

73. Costs that are subject to short-run fluctuations for given jobs are
   a.   actual costs.
   b.   budgeted direct costs.
   c.   budgeted indirect costs.
   d.   normal costs.

   Answer: a   *Difficulty:*   1   *Objective:*   3

74. Annual cost rates are preferred over actual cost rates for all of the following reasons
   EXCEPT
   a.   budgeted costs allow managers to have cost information on a timely basis.
   b.   budgeted costs may be subject to short-run fluctuations.
   c.   budgeted indirect-cost rates are known prior to the inception of a new job.
   d.   budgeted-cost rates can be used to allocate direct or indirect costs.

   Answer: b   *Difficulty:*   2   *Objective:*   3

75. Fixed costs remain constant at $200,000 per month. During high-output months
   variable costs are $160,000, and during low-output months variable costs are $40,000.
   What are the respective high and low indirect-cost rates if budgeted professional labor-
   hours are 8,000 for high-output months and 2,000 for low-output months?
   a. $45.00 per hour, $120.00 per hour
   b. $45.00 per hour, $45.00 per hour
   c. $25.00 per hour, $20.00 per hour ·
   d. $56.20 per hour, $120.00 per hour

   Answer: a   *Difficulty:*   2   *Objective:*   3
      $200,000 / 8,000 = $25.00 $200,000 / 2,000 = $100.00
      $160,000 / 8,000 =   20.00 $40,000 / 2,000 =   20.00
         High Month = $45.00   Low Month = $120.00

76. Managers and accountants collect most of the cost information that goes into their
   systems through
   a.   an information databank.
   b.   computer programs.
   c.   source documents.
   d.   time surveys.

   Answer: c   *Difficulty:*   1   *Objective:*   3

77. Which of the following statements about normal costing is TRUE?
    a.   Direct costs and indirect costs are traced using an actual rate.
    b.   Direct costs and indirect costs are traced using budgeted rates.
    c.   Direct costs are traced using a budgeted rate, and indirect costs are allocated using an actual rate.
    d.   Direct costs are traced using an actual rate, and indirect costs are allocated using a budgeted rate.

    Answer: d   *Difficulty:*   2   *Objective:*   4

78. When using a normal costing system, manufacturing overhead is allocated using the _____ manufacturing overhead rate and the _____ quantity of the allocation base.
    a.   budgeted, actual
    b.   budgeted, budgeted
    c.   actual, budgeted
    d.   actual, actual

    Answer: a   *Difficulty:*   1   *Objective:*   4

79. In a normal costing system, the Manufacturing Overhead Control account
    a.   is increased by allocated manufacturing overhead.
    b.   is credited with amounts transferred to Work-in-Process.
    c.   is decreased by allocated manufacturing overhead.
    d.   is debited with actual overhead costs.

    Answer: d   *Difficulty:*   2   *Objective:*   4

80. The Materials Control account is increased when
    a.   direct materials are purchased.
    b.   indirect materials are purchased.
    c.   materials are requisitioned for production.
    d.   both (a) and (b) occur.

    Answer: d   *Difficulty:*   1   *Objective:*   5

81. All of the following are true of the Work-in-Process Control account EXCEPT that
    a.   it tracks all direct material purchases.
    b.   the balance equals the sum of amounts from all in-process individual job-cost records.
    c.   it is an asset account.
    d.   it tracks job costs from beginning through completion.

    Answer: a   *Difficulty:*   2   *Objective:*   5

82. All of the following are general ledger accounts EXCEPT
    a. the Salaries Payable Control account.
    b. the Prepaid Insurance Control account.
    c. the Accounts Receivable subsidiary account for Ruben Electric.
    d. the Advertising Costs account.

    Answer: c   *Difficulty:* 1   *Objective:* 5

83. All of the following increase (are debited to) the Work-in-Process Control account EXCEPT
    a. actual plant insurance costs.
    b. direct materials.
    c. allocated manufacturing overhead costs.
    d. direct manufacturing labor.

    Answer: a   *Difficulty:* 2   *Objective:* 5

84. When indirect materials are requisitioned the _____ account is increased.
    a. Manufacturing Overhead Control
    b. Work-in-Process Control
    c. Materials Control
    d. Accounts Payable Control

    Answer: a   *Difficulty:* 1   *Objective:* 5

85. Payment of the total manufacturing payroll decreases the
    a. Work-in-Process Control account.
    b. Manufacturing Overhead Control account.
    c. Wages Payable Control account.
    d. none of the above.

    Answer: c   *Difficulty:* 1   *Objective:* 5

86. All are true of plant utility costs EXCEPT
    a. the source document is the utility bill.
    b. the cost increases the Manufacturing Overhead Control account.
    c. the cost increases the Work-in-Process Control account.
    d. it is an indirect cost.

    Answer: c   *Difficulty:* 1   *Objective:* 5

87. Actual (rather than allocated) manufacturing overhead costs are included in the
    a. Work-in-Process Control account.
    b. Finished Goods Control account.
    c. Manufacturing Overhead Control account.
    d. both (a) and (b).

    Answer: c   *Difficulty:* 2   *Objective:* 5

88. The ending balance in the Finished Goods Control account represents the costs of all jobs that
   a. have not been completed.
   b. have been completed but not sold.
   c. have been completed and sold to customers.
   d. are reported on the income statement.

   Answer: b   *Difficulty:* 1   *Objective:* 5

89. For externally reported inventory costs the Work-in-Process Control account is increased (debited) by
   a. marketing costs.
   b. allocated plant utility costs.
   c. the purchase costs of direct and indirect materials.
   d. customer-service costs.

   Answer: b   *Difficulty:* 2   *Objective:* 5

90. What is the appropriate journal entry if $100,000 of materials was purchased on account for the month of August?

a.	Materials Control	100,000	
	Accounts Payable Control		100,000
b.	Work-in-Process Control	100,000	
	Accounts Payable Control		100,000
c.	Manufacturing Overhead Control	100,000	
	Accounts Receivable Control		100,000
d.	Manufacturing Allocated	100,000	
	Accounts Receivable Control		100,000

   Answer: a   *Difficulty:* 2   *Objective:* 5

91. What is the appropriate journal entry if direct materials of $50,000 and indirect materials of $3,000 are sent to the manufacturing plant floor?

a.	Work-in-Process Control	50,000	
	Materials Control		50,000
b.	Work-in-Process Control	53,000	
	Materials Control		53,000
c.	Manufacturing Overhead Control	3,000	
	Materials Control	50,000	
	Work-in-Process Control		53,000
d.	Work-in-Process Control	50,000	
	Manufacturing Overhead Control	3,000	
	Materials Control		53,000

   Answer: d   *Difficulty:* 2   *Objective:* 5

92. All of the following items are debited to Work-in-Process EXCEPT
    a.   allocated manufacturing overhead.
    b.   completed goods being transferred out of the plant.
    c.   direct labor consumed.
    d.   direct materials consumed.

    Answer: b   *Difficulty*:   2   *Objective*:   5

93. What would be the appropriate journal entry if the following labor wages were incurred in a furniture manufacturing company?

	Assembly workers	$30,000
	Janitors	$20,000

    a.   Work-in-Process Control   50,000
             Wages Payable Control   50,000
    b.   Work-in-Process Control   30,000
          Manufacturing Overhead Control   20,000
             Wages Payable Control   50,000
    c.   Manufacturing Overhead Control   50,000
             Wages Payable Control   50,000
    d.   Wages Payable Control   50,000
             Work-in-Process Control   50,000

    Answer: b   *Difficulty*:   2   *Objective*:   5

94. Manufacturing overhead costs incurred for the month are:
        Utilities $15,000
        Depreciation on equipment $25,000
        Repairs $10,000
    Which is the correct journal entry assuming utilities and repairs were on account?

    a.   Manufacturing Overhead Control   50,000
             Accounts Payable Control   25,000
             Accumulated Depreciation Control   25,000
    b.   Manufacturing Overhead Control   50,000
             Accounts Payable Control   50,000
    c.   Manufacturing Overhead Control   50,000
             Accumulated Depreciation Control   50,000
    d.   Accumulated Depreciation Control   25,000
          Accounts Payable Control   25,000
             Manufacturing Overhead Control   50,000

    Answer: a   *Difficulty*:   2   *Objective*:   5

95. Which of the following statements regarding manufacturing overhead allocation is FALSE?
    a.   It is comprised of all manufacturing costs that cannot be directly traced to a product or service.
    b.   The costs can be grouped in either a single indirect-cost pool or multiple indirect-cost pools.
    c.   Total costs are unknown at the end of the accounting period.
    d.   Allocated amounts are debited to Work-in-Process.

    Answer: c   *Difficulty:*   2   *Objective:*   5

96. When a job is complete,
    a.   Work-in-Process Control is debited.
    b.   Finished Goods Control is credited.
    c.   the cost of the job is transferred to Manufacturing Overhead Control.
    d.   actual direct materials, actual direct manufacturing labor, and allocated manufacturing overhead will comprise the total cost of the job.

    Answer: d   *Difficulty:*   2   *Objective:*   5

97. During an accounting period, job costs are computed on an ongoing basis by the use of
    a.   actual allocation rates.
    b.   budgeted indirect-cost rates.
    c.   overallocated indirect-cost rates.
    d.   underallocated indirect-cost rates.

    Answer: b   *Difficulty:*   1   *Objective:*   5

98. The spreading of underallocated or overallocated overhead among ending work-in-process, finished goods, and cost of goods sold is called
    a.   the adjusted allocation rate approach.
    b.   the proration approach.
    c.   the write-off of cost of goods sold approach.
    d.   none of the above.

    Answer: b   *Difficulty:*   1   *Objective:*   6

99. The Manufacturing Overhead Control account is the record of
    a. actual direct material and direct manufacturing labor costs.
    b. actual overhead costs.
    c. allocated overhead when using normal costing.
    d. both (a) and (b) when using normal costing.

    Answer: b   *Difficulty:* 2   *Objective:* 6

100. When the allocated amount of indirect costs are less than the actual amount, indirect costs have been
    a. overabsorbed.
    b. underapplied.
    c. underallocated.
    d. both (b) and (c).

    Answer: d   *Difficulty:* 2   *Objective:* 6

101. One reason indirect costs may be overapplied is because
    a. the actual allocation base quantity exceeds the budgeted quantity.
    b. budgeted indirect costs exceed actual indirect costs.
    c. requisitioned direct materials exceed budgeted material costs.
    d. of both (a) and (b).

    Answer: b   *Difficulty:* 3   *Objective:* 6

102. The _____ approach adjusts individual job-cost records to account for underallocated or overallocated overhead.
    a. adjusted allocation-rate
    b. proration
    c. write-off to cost of goods sold
    d. both (a) and (b)

    Answer: a   *Difficulty:* 1   *Objective:* 6

103. The simplest approach to dealing with underallocated or overallocated overhead is the _____ approach.
    a. adjusted allocation-rate
    b. proration
    c. write-off to cost of goods sold
    d. both (a) and (b)

    Answer: c   *Difficulty:* 1   *Objective:* 6

104. The _____ approach carries the underallocated or overallocated amounts to overhead accounts in the following year.
   a. adjusted allocation-rate
   b. proration
   c. write-off to cost of goods sold
   d. none of the above

   Answer: d   *Difficulty:* 2   *Objective:* 6

105. In the service sector,
   a. direct labor costs are always easy to trace to jobs.
   b. a budgeted direct-labor cost rate may be used to apply direct labor to jobs.
   c. normal costing may not be used.
   d. overhead is generally applied using an actual cost-allocation rate.

   Answer: b   *Difficulty:* 2   *Objective:* 7

106. Sara employs 25 professional cleaners.
   Budgeted costs total $900,000 of which $525,000 are direct costs.
   Budgeted indirect costs are $375,000 and actual indirect costs were $396,900.
   Budgeted professional labor-hours are 500,000 and actual hours were 504,000.
   What is the budgeted direct cost-allocation rate?
   a. $1.80 per hour
   b. $1.7857 per hour
   c. $0.75 per hour
   d. $1.05 per hour

   Answer: d   *Difficulty:* 2   *Objective:* 7
   $525,000 / 500,000 = $1.05

THE FOLLOWING INFORMATION APPLIES TO QUESTIONS 107 THROUGH 110.
For 20x5, Marcotte's Animal Supply Manufacturing uses machine-hours as the only overhead cost-allocation base. The accounting records contain the following information:

	Estimated	**Actual**
Manufacturing overhead costs	$100,000	$120,000
Machine-hours	20,000	25,000

107. Using job costing, the 20x5 budgeted manufacturing overhead rate is
   a. $4.00 per machine-hour.
   b. $4.80 per machine-hour.
   c. $5.00 per machine-hour.
   d. $6.00 per machine-hour.

   Answer: c   *Difficulty:* 2   *Objective:* 4
   $100,000 / 20,000 mh = $5

108. Using normal costing, the amount of manufacturing overhead costs allocated to jobs during 20x5 is
    a. $150,000.
    b. $125,000.
    c. $120,000.
    d. $100,000.

    Answer: b   *Difficulty:*   2   *Objective:*   4
    25,000 mh x $5 allocation rate = $125,000

109. Using job costing, the 20x5 actual indirect-cost rate is
    a. $4.00 per machine-hour.
    b. $4.80 per machine-hour.
    c. $5.00 per machine-hour.
    d. $6.00 per machine-hour.

    Answer: b   *Difficulty:*   2   *Objective:*   3
    $120,000 / 25,000 mh = $4.80

110. Using actual costing, the amount of manufacturing overhead costs allocated to jobs during 20x5 is
    a. $150,000.
    b. $125,000.
    c. $120,000.
    d. $100,000.

    Answer: c   *Difficulty:*   2   *Objective:*   3
    25,000 mh x $4.80 allocation rate = $120,000

THE FOLLOWING INFORMATION APPLIES TO QUESTIONS 111 AND 112.
Rhett Company has two departments, Machining and Assembly. The following estimates are for the coming year:

	Machining	**Assembly**
Direct manufacturing labor-hours	10,000	50,000
Machine-hours	40,000	20,000
Manufacturing overhead	$200,000	$400,000

111. A single indirect-cost rate based on direct manufacturing labor-hours for the entire plant is
    a. $ 8 per direct labor-hour.
    b. $10 per direct labor-hour.
    c. $20 per direct labor-hour.
    d.   none of the above.

    Answer: b   *Difficulty:*   2   *Objective:*   4
    $600,000 / 60,000 dlh = $10

112. The budgeted indirect-cost driver rate for the Machining Department based on the number of machine-hours in that department is
    a. $5 per machine-hour.
    b. $10 per machine-hour.
    c. $20 per machine-hour.
    d.   none of the above.

    Answer: a   *Difficulty:*   1   *Objective:*   4
    $200,000 / 40,000 mh = $5

THE FOLLOWING INFORMATION APPLIES TO QUESTIONS 113 THROUGH 115.
Joni's Kitty Supplies applies manufacturing overhead costs to products at a budgeted indirect-cost rate of $60 per direct manufacturing labor-hour. A retail outlet has requested a bid on a special order of the Toy Mouse product. Estimates for this order include: Direct materials $40,000; 500 direct manufacturing labor-hours @ $20 per hour; and a 20% markup rate on total manufacturing costs.

113. Manufacturing overhead cost estimates for this special order total
    a. $10,000.
    b. $30,000.
    c. $36,000.
    d.   none of the above.

    Answer: b   *Difficulty:*   1   *Objective:*   4
    $60 x 500 dlh = $30,000

114. Estimated total product costs for this special order equal
    a. $96,000.
    b. $50,000.
    c. $80,000.
    d.   none of the above.

    Answer: c   *Difficulty:*   2   *Objective:*   5
    DM $40,000 + DML ($500 x $20) + MOH $30,000 = $80,000

115. The bid price for this special order is
    a. $50,000.
    b. $60,000.
    c. $80,000.
    d. $96,000.

    Answer: d   *Difficulty:*   2   *Objective:*   5
    80,000 x 120% = $96,000

THE FOLLOWING INFORMATION APPLIES TO QUESTIONS 116 THROUGH 118.
Sunni Company manufactures pipes and applies manufacturing overhead costs to production at a budgeted indirect-cost rate of $15 per direct labor-hour. The following data are obtained from the accounting records for June 20x2:

Direct materials	$280,000
Direct labor (7,000 hours @ $11/hour)	$ 77,000
Indirect labor	$ 20,000
Plant facility rent	$ 60,000
Depreciation on plant machinery and equipment	$ 30,000
Sales commissions	$ 40,000
Administrative expenses	$ 50,000

116. The actual amount of manufacturing overhead costs incurred in June 20x2 total
    a. $557,000.
    b. $200,000.
    c. $110,000.
    d. $ 80,000

Answer: c   *Difficulty:* 2   *Objective:* 3
$20,000 + $60,000 + $30,000 = $110,000

117. The amount of manufacturing overhead allocated to all jobs during June 20x2 totals
    a. $77,000
    b. $105,000.
    c. $110,000.
    d. $200,000.

Answer: b   *Difficulty:* 2   *Objective:* 5
7,000 x $15 per dlh = $105,000

118. For June 20x2, manufacturing overhead was
    a.   overallocated.
    b.   underallocated.
    c.   neither overallocated nor underallocated.
    d.   unable to be determined.

Answer: b   *Difficulty:* 2   *Objective:* 6
Underallocated: Allocated only $105,000 of the $110,000 actual overhead

THE FOLLOWING INFORMATION APPLIES TO QUESTIONS 119 THROUGH 122.
Gibson Manufacturing is a small textile manufacturer using machine-hours as the single indirect-cost rate to allocate manufacturing overhead costs to the various jobs contracted during the year. The following estimates are provided for the coming year for the company and for the Winfield High School band jacket job.

	Company	Winfield High School Job
Direct materials	$40,000	$1,000
Direct labor	$10,000	$200
Manufacturing overhead costs	$30,000	
Machine-hours	100,000 mh	900 mh

119. For Gibson Manufacturing, what is the annual manufacturing overhead cost-allocation rate?
    a. $0.50
    b. $0.80
    c. $0.30
    d. $33.33

Answer: c   *Difficulty:* 2   *Objective:* 5
$30,000/100,000mh = $0.30 per mh

120. What amount of manufacturing overhead costs will be allocated to this job?
    a. $270
    b. $720
    c. $450
    d. $30,000

Answer: a   *Difficulty:* 2   *Objective:* 5
900 mh x $0.30 per mh = $270

121. What are the total manufacturing costs of this job?
    a. $1,200
    b. $1,470
    c. $1,650
    d. $1,920

Answer: b   *Difficulty:* 3   *Objective:* 5
DM $1,000 + DML $200 + MOH $270 = $1,470

122. What is the bid price for the Winfield High School job if the company uses a 40% markup of total manufacturing costs?
    a. $2,310
    b. $588
    c. $1,680
    d. $2,058

Answer: d   *Difficulty:* 3   *Objective:* 5
$1,470 x 1.40 = $2,058

THE FOLLOWING INFORMATION APPLIES TO QUESTIONS 123 THROUGH 125.
Bauer Manufacturing uses departmental cost driver rates to allocate manufacturing overhead costs to products. Manufacturing overhead costs are allocated on the basis of machine-hours in the Machining Department and on the basis of direct labor-hours in the Assembly Department. At the beginning of 20x3, the following estimates were provided for the coming year:

	Machining	**Assembly**
Direct labor-hours	30,000	60,000
Machine-hours	80,000	20,000
Direct labor cost	$500,000	$900,000
Manufacturing overhead costs	$420,000	$240,000

The accounting records of the company show the following data for Job #316:

	Machining	**Assembly**
Direct labor-hours	120	70
Machine-hours	60	5
Direct material cost	$300	$200
Direct labor cost	$100	$400

123. For Bauer Manufacturing, what is the annual manufacturing overhead cost-allocation rate for the Machining Department?
    a. $4.00
    b. $4.20
    c. $4.67
    d. $5.25

    Answer: d   *Difficulty*:   2   *Objective*:   5
    $420,000/80,000mh = $5.25 per mh

124. What amount of manufacturing overhead costs will be allocated to Job #316?
    a. $439
    b. $502
    c. $595
    d. $532

    Answer: c   *Difficulty*:   3   *Objective*:   5
    ($5.25 x 60 mh) + [($240,000/60,000) x 70dlh] = $595

125. What are the total manufacturing costs of Job #316?
    a. $715
    b. $880
    c. $1,595
    d. $1,000

    Answer: c   *Difficulty*:   3   *Objective*:   5
    DM $500 + DML $500 + MOH $595 = $1,595

THE FOLLOWING INFORMATION APPLIES TO QUESTIONS 126 THROUGH 129.
Wayland Manufacturing uses a normal cost system and had the following data available for 20x4.

Direct materials purchased on account	$ 74,000
Direct materials requisitioned	41,000
Direct labor cost incurred	65,000
Factory overhead incurred	73,000
Cost of goods completed	146,000
Cost of goods sold	128,000
Beginning direct materials inventory	13,000
Beginning WIP inventory	32,000
Beginning finished goods inventory	29,000
Overhead application rate, as a percent of direct-labor costs	125 percent

126. The journal entry to record the materials placed into production would include a
    a.   credit to Direct Materials Inventory for $41,000.
    b.   debit to Direct Materials Inventory for $74,000.
    c.   credit to WIP Inventory for $41,000.
    d.   debit to WIP Inventory for $74,000.

    Answer: a   *Difficulty*:   2   *Objective*:   5

127. The ending balance of direct materials inventory is
    a. $46,000.
    b. $87,000.
    c. $41,000.
    d. $54,000.

    Answer: a   *Difficulty*:   2   *Objective*:   5
    $13,000 + $74,000 - $41,000 = $46,000

128. The ending balance of work-in-process inventory is
    a. $219,250.
    b. $73,250.
    c. $65,000.
    d. $211,000.

    Answer: b   *Difficulty*:   3   *Objective*:   5
    $32,000 + $41,000 + $65,000 + 1.25 ($65,000) - $146,000 = $73,250

129. The ending balance of finished goods inventory is
    a. $29,000.
    b. $18,000.
    c. $47,000.
    d. $146,000.

    Answer: c   *Difficulty*:   3   *Objective*:   5
    $29,000 + $146,000 - $128,000 = $47,000

THE FOLLOWING INFORMATION APPLIES TO QUESTIONS 130 THROUGH 133.
Apple Valley Corporation uses a job cost system and has two production departments, A and B. Budgeted manufacturing costs for the year are:

	Department A	Department B
Direct materials	$700,000	$100,000
Direct manufacturing labor	$200,000	$800,000
Manufacturing overhead	$600,000	$400,000

The actual material and labor costs charged to Job #432 were as follows:

		Total
Direct materials:		$25,000
Direct labor:		
Department A	$ 8,000	
Department B	$12,000	
		$20,000

Apple Valley applies manufacturing overhead costs to jobs on the basis of direct manufacturing labor cost using departmental rates determined at the beginning of the year.

130. For Department A, the manufacturing overhead allocation rate is
    a.   33%.
    b.   66%.
    c.   300%.
    d.   100%.

Answer: c   *Difficulty*: 2   *Objective*: 4
$600,000 / $200,000 = 300%

131. For Department B, the manufacturing overhead allocation rate is
    a.   50%.
    b.   100%.
    c.   200%.
    d.   300%.

Answer: a   *Difficulty*: 2   *Objective*: 4
$400,000 / $800,000 = 50%

132. Manufacturing overhead costs allocated to Job #432 total
    a. $30,000.
    b. $12,000.
    c. $24,000.
    d. $36,000.

Answer: a   *Difficulty*: 3   *Objective*: 4
($8,000 x 300%) + ($12,000 x 50%) = $30,000

133. Manufacturing costs estimated for Job #432 total
   a. $55,000.
   b. $65,000.
   c. $70,000.
   d. $75,000.

   Answer: d   *Difficulty:*   3   *Objective:*   5
   DM $25,000 + DML $20,000 + MOH $30,000 = $75,000

THE FOLLOWING INFORMATION APPLIES TO QUESTIONS 134 AND 135.
Because the Abernathy Company used a budgeted indirect-cost rate for its manufacturing operations, the amount allocated ($200,000) was different from the actual amount incurred ($225,000).

Ending balances in the relevant accounts are:	
Work-in-Process	$ 10,000
Finished Goods	20,000
Cost of Goods Sold	170,000

134. What is the journal entry used to write off the difference between allocated and actual overhead directly to cost of goods sold?

a.	Manufacturing Overhead Allocated	200,000	
	Cost of Goods Sold	25,000	
	Manufacturing Overhead Control		225,000
b.	Manufacturing Overhead Control	200,000	
	Cost of Goods Sold	25,000	
	Manufacturing Overhead Allocated		225,000
c.	Manufacturing Overhead Allocated	200,000	
	Work-in-Process Control		30,000
	Cost of Goods Sold		170,000
d.	Manufacturing Overhead Control	225,000	
	Work-in-Process Control		55,000
	Cost of Goods Sold		170,000

   Answer: a   *Difficulty:*   2   *Objective:*   6

135. What is the journal entry used to write off the difference between allocated and actual overhead using the proration approach?

a.	Manufacturing Overhead Allocated	200,000	
	Work-in-Process Control	10,000	
	Finished Goods Control	20,000	
	Manufacturing Overhead Control		230,000
b.	Manufacturing Overhead Allocated	225,000	
	Work-in-Process Control		1,250
	Finished Goods Control		2,500
	Cost of Goods Sold		21,250
	Manufacturing Overhead Control		200,000
c.	Manufacturing Overhead Control	225,000	
	Work-in-Process Control		1,250
	Finished Goods Control		2,500
	Cost of Goods Sold		21,250
	Manufacturing Overhead Allocated		200,000
d.	Manufacturing Overhead Allocated	200,000	
	Work-in-Process Control	1,250	
	Finished Goods Control	2,500	
	Cost of Goods Sold	21,250	
	Manufacturing Overhead Control		225,000

Answer: d   *Difficulty:* 2   *Objective:* 6

Work-in-process	$ 10,000	5%	x $25,000 =	$ 1,250	
Finished goods	20,000	10%	x 25,000 =	2,500	
Cost of goods sold	170,000	85%	x 25,000 =	21,250	
	$200,000	100%		$25,000	

THE FOLLOWING INFORMATION APPLIES TO QUESTIONS 136 THROUGH 141.
Roiann and Dennett Law Office employs 12 full-time attorneys and 10 paraprofessionals. Direct and indirect costs are applied on a professional labor-hour basis that includes both attorney and paraprofessional hours. Following is information for 20x3:

	Budget	Actual
Indirect costs	$270,000	$300,000
Annual salary of each attorney	$100,000	$110,000
Annual salary of each paraprofessional	$ 29,000	$ 30,000
Total professional labor-hours	50,000 dlh	60,000 dlh

136. What are the *actual* direct-cost rate and the *actual* indirect-cost rate, respectively, per professional labor-hour?
a. $27.00; $4.17
b. $29.80; $5.40
c. $32.40; $5.00
d. 27.00; $5.00

Answer: d   *Difficulty:* 2   *Objective:* 3
[($110,000 x 12) + ($30,000 x 10)] / 60,000 = $27.00 actual direct rate
$300,000 / 60,000 = $5.00 actual indirect rate

137. What are the *budgeted* direct-cost rate and the *budgeted* indirect-cost rate, respectively, per professional labor-hour?
    a. $27.00; $4.17
    b. $29.80; $5.40
    c. $32.40; $5.00
    d.   27.00; $5.00

    Answer: b   *Difficulty*:   2   *Objective*:   4
    [($100,000 x 12) + ($29,000 x 10)] / 50,000 = $29.80 budgeted direct rate
    $270,000 / 50,000 = $5.40 budgeted indirect rate

138. How much should the client be billed in an *actual* costing system if 200 professional labor-hours are used?
    a. $5,000
    b. $6,960
    c. $7,480
    d. $6,400

    Answer: d   *Difficulty*:   3   *Objective*:   3
    ($27.00 x 200) + ($5.00 x 200) = $6,400

139. How much should a client be billed in a *normal* costing system when 1,000 professional labor-hours are used?
    a. $32,000
    b. $29,800
    c. $35,200
    d. $27,000

    Answer: c   *Difficulty*:   3   *Objective*:   4
    ($29.80 x 1,000) + ($5.40 x 1,000) = $35,200

140. When a normal costing system is used, clients using proportionately more attorney time than paraprofessional time will
    a.   be overbilled for actual resources used.
    b.   be underbilled for actual resources used.
    c.   be billed accurately for actual resources used.
    d.   result in an underallocation of direct costs.

    Answer: b   *Difficulty*:   3   *Objective*:   4

141. When using a normal costing system, year-end accounting records will show that *indirect costs* are
    a.   applied improperly.
    b.   underallocated.
    c.   overbudgeted.
    d.   overallocated.

    Answer: d   *Difficulty*:   3   *Objective*:   6
    Overallocated: Allocated $324,000 ($5.40 x 60,000 dlh) when actual is only $300,000

THE FOLLOWING INFORMATION APPLIES TO QUESTIONS 142 THROUGH 144.
A local accounting firm employs 20 full-time professionals. The budgeted annual compensation per employee is $40,500. The average chargeable time is 500 hours per client annually. All professional labor costs are included in a single direct-cost category and are allocated to jobs on a per-hour basis.

Other costs are included in a single indirect-cost pool, allocated according to professional labor-hours. Budgeted indirect costs for the year are $787,500, and the firm expects to have 90 clients during the coming year.

142. What is the budgeted direct labor cost rate per hour?
    a. $18.00 per hour
    b. $17.50 per hour
    c. $4.05 per hour
    d. $2,000 per hour

    Answer: a   *Difficulty:* 2   *Objective:* 7
    Total direct labor cost = $40,500 x 20 = $810,000
    Total hours = 500 x 90 = 45,000 hours
    Direct labor cost rate per hour = $810,000 / 45,000 = $18.00 per hour

143. What is the budgeted indirect-cost rate per hour?
    a. $1,575.00 per hour
    b. $78.75 per hour
    c. $18.00 per hour
    d. $17.50 per hour

    Answer: d   *Difficulty:* 2   *Objective:* 7
    Indirect-cost rate per hour = $787,500 / 45,000 = $17.50 per hour

144. If ten clients are lost and the workforce stays at 20 employees, then the direct labor cost rate per hour
    a. will remain the same as before.
    b. will increase.
    c. will decrease.
    d. cannot be determined.

    Answer: b   *Difficulty:* 2   *Objective:* 7
    Total direct cost = $40,500 x 20 = $810,000
    Total hours = 500 x 80 = 40,000 hours
    Direct cost rate per hour = $810,000 / 40,000 = $20.25 per hour
    The direct labor cost rate per hour increased from $18.00 per hour to $20.25 per hour

EXERCISES AND PROBLEMS

145. For each item below indicate the source documents that would most likely authorize the journal entry in a job-costing system.

Required:
a.   Direct materials purchased
b.   Direct materials used
c.   Direct manufacturing labor
d.   Indirect manufacturing labor
e.   Finished goods control
f.   Cost of goods sold

Answer:
a.   Purchase invoice
b.   Materials requisition record
c.   Labor time card/record
d.   Labor time card
e.   Job-cost record
f.   Sales invoice

Difficulty: 2   *Objective*:   1

146. Fox Manufacturing is a small textile manufacturer using machine-hours as the single indirect-cost rate to allocate manufacturing overhead costs to the various jobs contracted during the year. The following estimates are provided for the coming year for the company and for the Maize High School Science Olympiad Jacket job.

	Company	Maize High School Job
Direct materials	$50,000	$500
Direct manufacturing labor	$10,000	$100
Manufacturing overhead costs	$40,000	
Machine-hours	100,000 mh	800 mh

Required:

a.   For Fox Manufacturing, determine the annual manufacturing overhead cost-allocation rate.

b.   Determine the amount of manufacturing overhead costs allocated to the Maize High School job.

c.   Determine the estimated total manufacturing costs for the Maize High School job.

Answer:

a.   Manufacturing overhead cost-allocation rate = $0.40 per mh
= $40,000/100,000 mh

b. $320 estimated manufacturing overhead costs = 800 mh x $0.40 per mh

c.		
	Direct materials	$500
	Direct manufacturing labor	$100
	Manufacturing overhead costs	$320
	Estimated total manufacturing costs	$920

Difficulty: 2   *Objectives:* 3, 4

147. Hill Manufacturing uses departmental cost driver rates to apply manufacturing overhead costs to products. Manufacturing overhead costs are applied on the basis of machine-hours in the Machining Department and on the basis of direct labor-hours in the Assembly Department. At the beginning of 20x3, the following estimates were provided for the coming year:

	Machining	Assembly
Direct labor-hours	10,000 dlh	90,000 dlh
Machine-hours	100,000 mh	5,000 mh
Direct labor cost	$ 80,000	$720,000
Manufacturing overhead costs	$250,000	$360,000

The accounting records of the company show the following data for Job #846:

	Machining	Assembly
Direct labor-hours	50 dlh	120 dlh
Machine-hours	170 mh	10 mh
Direct material cost	$2,700	$1,600
Direct labor cost	$ 400	$ 900

Required:

a. Compute the manufacturing overhead allocation rate for each department.

b. Compute the total cost of Job #846.

c. Provide possible reasons why Hill Manufacturing uses two different cost allocation rates.

Answer:

a. Machining Department cost-allocation rate: $2.50 / mh = $250,000/100,000 mh
   Assembly Department cost-allocation rate: $4.00 / dlh = $360,000/90,000 dlh

b. Total cost of Job #846 is $6,505 = Direct materials $4,300 + Direct labor $1,300 + Manufacturing overhead costs $905 (Machining $425 + Assembly $480).

c. Ideally, the cost-allocation base should reflect the factors that cause manufacturing overhead costs to increase. Apparently, Hill regards the use of machines as the principal cause of manufacturing overhead costs (such as depreciation and repairs) in the Machining Department. In contrast, Hill regards direct labor-hours as the principal cause of manufacturing overhead costs (such as indirect labor) in the Assembly Department.

Difficulty: 2   *Objectives:* 3, 4

148. Jordan Company has two departments, X and Y. Overhead is applied based on direct labor cost in Department X and machine-hours in Department Y. The following additional information is available:

Budgeted Amounts	Department X	Department Y
Direct labor cost	$180,000	$165,000
Factory overhead	$225,000	$180,000
Machine-hours	51,000 mh	40,000 mh

Actual data for Job #10	Department X	Department Y
Direct materials requisitioned	$10,000	$16,000
Direct labor cost	$11,000	$14,000
Machine-hours	5,000 mh	3,000 mh

Required:
a.   Compute the budgeted factory overhead rate for Department X.
b.   Compute the budgeted factory overhead rate for Department Y.
c.   What is the total overhead cost of Job 10?
d.   If Job 10 consists of 50 units of product, what is the unit cost of this job?

Answer:
a. $225,000/$180,000 = 125%
b. $180,000/40,000 hrs. = $4.50 per hour
c.   ($11,000 x 125 percent) + ($4.50 x 3,000 hrs.) = $27,250
d. $10,000 + $16,000 + $11,000 + $14,000 + $27,250 = $78,250/50 units = $1,565 per unit

Difficulty: 2   *Objectives*:   3, 5

149. Job-cost records for Boucher Company contained the following data:

Job No.	Date Started	Date Finished	Date Sold	Total Cost of Job at June 30
220	May 18	June 12	June 20	$6,000
221	May 20	June 19	June 21	4,000
222	June 7	July 5	July 12	7,000
223	June 10	June 28	July 1	6,500
224	June 19	July 16	July 25	8,000

Required:
a.   Compute WIP inventory at June 30.
b.   Compute finished goods inventory at June 30.
c.   Compute cost of goods sold for June.

Answer:
a.   7,000 + $8,000 = $15,000
b. $6,500
c. $6,000 + $4,000 = $10,000

Difficulty: 2   *Objectives*:   3, 5

150. LeBlanc Company has the following balances as of the year ended December 31, 20x4.

Direct Materials Inventory	$15,000	Dr.
WIP Inventory	34,500	Dr.
Finished Goods Inventory	49,500	Dr.
Factory Department Overhead	4,000	Dr.
Cost of Goods Sold	74,500	Dr.

Additional information is as follows:

Cost of direct materials purchased during 20x4	$41,000
Cost of direct materials requisitioned in 20x4	47,000
Cost of goods completed during 20x4	102,000
Factory overhead applied (120% of direct labor)	48,000

Required:

a. Compute beginning direct materials inventory.
b. Compute beginning WIP inventory.
c. Compute beginning finished goods inventory.
d. Compute actual factory overhead incurred.

Answer:

a. $47,000 - $41,000 + $15,000 = $21,000

b. $48,000/120% = $40,000 direct labor costs incurred
$102,000 - $47,000 - $40,000 - $48,000 + $34,500 = $1,500

c. $74,500 - $102,000 + $49,500 = $22,000

d. $48,000 + $4,000 = $52,000

Difficulty: 3 *Objectives:* 3, 5

151. Cowley County Hospital uses a job-costing system for all patients who have surgery. In March, the pre-operating room (PRE-OP) and operating room (OR) had budgeted allocation bases of 4,000 nursing hours and 2,000 nursing hours, respectively. The budgeted nursing overhead charges for each department for the month were $168,000 and $132,000, respectively. The hospital floor for surgery patients had budgeted overhead costs of $1,200,000 and 15,000 nursing hours for the month. For patient Fred Adams, actual hours incurred were eight and four hours, respectively, in the PRE-OP and OR rooms. He was in the hospital for 4 days (96 hours). Other costs related to Adams were:

	PRE-OP Costs	OR Costs	In-room Costs
Patient medicine	$ 200	$ 500	$2,400
Direct nursing time	$1,000	$2,000	$3,000

The hospital uses a budgeted overhead rate for applying overhead to patient stays.

Required:

What is the total cost of the stay of patient Fred Adams?

Answer:

Nursing overhead rate PRE-OP	= $168,000/4,000 hrs. = $42 per hr.
Nursing overhead rate OR	= $132,000/2,000 hrs. = $66 per hr.
Overhead rate for surgery floor	= $1,200,000/15,000 hrs. = $80 per hr.

Patient Fred Adams:

	PRE-OP	OR	In-room	Totals
Patient medicine	$ 200	$ 500	$2,400	$3,100
Direct nursing time	1,000	2,000	3,000	6,000
Nursing overhead:				
PRE-OP ($42 x 8)	336			336
OR ($66 x 4)		264		264
In-room ($80 x 96)	0	0	7,680	7,680
Total	$1,536	$2,764	$13,080	$17,380

Difficulty: 3   *Objectives:* 3, 5

152. The Dougherty Furniture Company manufactures tables. In March, the two production departments had budgeted allocation bases of 4,000 machine-hours in Department 100 and 8,000 direct manufacturing labor-hours in Department 200. The budgeted manufacturing overheads for the month were $57,500 and $62,500, respectively. For Job A, the actual costs incurred in the two departments were as follows:

	Department 100	**Department 200**
Direct materials purchased on account	$110,000	$177,500
Direct materials used	32,500	13,500
Direct manufacturing labor	52,500	53,500
Indirect manufacturing labor	11,000	9,000
Indirect materials used	7,500	4,750
Lease on equipment	16,250	3,750
Utilities	1,000	1,250

Job A incurred 800 machine-hours in Department 100 and 300 manufacturing labor-hours in Department 200. The company uses a budgeted overhead rate for applying overhead to production.

Required:
a. Determine the budgeted manufacturing overhead rate for each department.
b. Prepare the necessary journal entries to summarize the March transactions for Department 100.
c. What is the total cost of Job A?

Answer:
a. Manufacturing overhead rate Department 100 = $57,500/4,000 hours
= $14.375 per machine-hour

Manufacturing overhead rate Department 200 = $62,500/8,000 hours
= $7.8125 per labor-hour

b.
Materials Control Department 100	110,000	
Accounts Payable Control		110,000
Work-in-Process Control Department 100	32,500	
Manufacturing Overhead Control Department 100	7,500	
Materials Control Department 100		40,000
Work-in-Process Control Department 100	52,500	
Manufacturing Overhead Control Department 100	11,000	
Wages Payable Control		63,500
Manufacturing Overhead Control Department 100	17,250	
Leaseholds Payable Control		16,250
Utilities Payable Control		1,000
Work-in-Process Control Dept. 100 ($14.375 x 800 hrs)	11,500	
Manufacturing Overhead Allocated		11,500

152. (continued)

    c.   **Job A:**

Direct materials Dept. 100	$ 32,500
Direct materials Dept. 200	13,500
Direct manufacturing labor Dept. 100	52,500
Direct manufacturing labor Dept. 200	53,500
Manufacturing overhead Dept. 100 ($14.375 x 800)	11,500
Manufacturing overhead Dept. 200 ($7.8125 x 300)	2,344
Total	$165,844

Difficulty: 3   *Objective*:   5

153. Peterson's Plastic Products Company manufactures pipes and applies manufacturing costs to production at a budgeted indirect-cost rate of $8 per direct labor-hour. The following data are obtained from the accounting records for June 20x2:

Direct materials	$400,000
Direct labor (8,000 hours @ $11/hour)	$ 88,000
Indirect labor	$ 10,000
Plant facility rent	$ 50,000
Depreciation on plant machinery and equipment	$ 20,000
Sales commissions	$ 30,000
Administrative expenses	$ 40,000

Required:
a.   What actual amount of manufacturing overhead costs was incurred during June 20x2?
b.   What amount of manufacturing overhead was allocated to all jobs during June 20x2?
c.   For June 20x2, was manufacturing overhead underallocated or overallocated? Explain.

Answer:
a. $10,000 + $50,000 + $20,000 = $80,000
b.   8,000 x $8 per dlh = $64,000
c.   Underallocated: Only allocated $64,000 of the $80,000 of actual overhead

Difficulty: 2   *Objective*:   6

154. Moira Company has just finished its first year of operations and must decide which method to use for adjusting cost of goods sold. Because the company used a budgeted indirect-cost rate for its manufacturing operations, the amount that was allocated ($435,000) to cost of goods sold was different from the actual amount incurred ($425,000).

Ending balances in the relevant accounts were:

Work-in-Process	$ 40,000
Finished Goods	80,000
Cost of Goods Sold	680,000

Required:

a. Prepare a journal entry to write off the difference between allocated and actual overhead directly to Cost of Goods Sold. Be sure your journal entry closes the related overhead accounts.

b. Prepare a journal entry that prorates the write-off of the difference between allocated and actual overhead using ending account balances. Be sure your journal entry closes the related overhead accounts.

Answer:

a.
Manufacturing Overhead Allocated	435,000	
Cost of Goods Sold		10,000
Manufacturing Overhead Control		425,000

b.
Work-in-process	$ 40,000	5 %	x $10,000	= $500	
Finished goods	80,000	10	x $10,000	= 1,000	
Cost of goods sold	680,000	85	x $10,000	= 8,500	
Total	$800,000	100 %			

Manufacturing Overhead Allocated	435,000	
Work-in-Process		500
Finished Goods		1,000
Cost of Goods Sold		8,500
Manufacturing Overhead Control		425,000

Difficulty: 3   *Objective:* 6

155. Jacobs Company manufactures refrigerators. The company uses a budgeted indirect-cost rate for its manufacturing operations and during 20x3 allocated $1,000,000 to work-in-process inventory. Actual overhead incurred was $1,100,000.

Ending balances in the following accounts are:

Work-in-Process	$ 100,000
Finished Goods	750,000
Cost of Goods Sold	4,150,000

Required:

a. Prepare a journal entry to write off the difference between allocated and actual overhead directly to Cost of Goods Sold. Be sure your journal entry closes the related overhead accounts.

b. Prepare a journal entry that prorates the write-off of the difference between allocated and actual overhead using ending account balances. Be sure your journal entry closes the related overhead accounts.

Answer:

a.

Manufacturing Overhead Allocated	1,000,000	
Cost of Goods Sold	100,000	
Manufacturing Overhead Control		1,100,000

b.

Work-in-process	$100,000	2.0 %	x $100,000 =	$2,000
Finished goods	750,000	15.0	x $100,000 =	$15,000
Cost of goods sold	4,150,000	83.0	x $100,000 =	$83,000
Total	$5,000,000	100.0 %		

Manufacturing Overhead Allocated	1,000,000	
Work-in-Process	2,000	
Finished Goods	15,000	
Cost of Goods Sold	83,000	
Manufacturing Overhead Control		1,100,000

Difficulty: 3   *Objective:*   6

156. The following information was gathered for Rogers Company for the year ended December 31, 20x4.

	Budgeted	Actual
Direct labor-hours	75,000 dlh	77,500 dlh
Factory overhead	$525,000	$558,000

Assume that direct labor-hours are the cost-allocation base.

Required:
a. Compute the budgeted factory overhead rate.
b. Compute the factory overhead applied.
c. Compute the amount of over/underapplied overhead.

Answer:
a. $525,000/75,000 hrs. = $7.00 per hour
b. $7.00 x 77,500 hrs. = $542,500
c. $558,000 - $542,500 = $15,500 underapplied

Difficulty: 2   *Objective*: 6

157. Isabelle, Inc., uses a budgeted factory overhead rate to apply overhead to production. The following data are available for the year ended December 31, 20x4.

	Budgeted	Actual
Factory overhead	$675,000	$716,000
Direct labor costs	$450,000	$432,000
Direct labor-hours	12,500 dlh	13,325 dlh

Required:
a. Determine the budgeted factory overhead rate based on direct labor-hours.
b. What is the applied overhead based on direct labor-hours?
c. Is overhead overapplied or underapplied? Explain.

Answer:
a. $675,000/12,500 hrs. = $54.00 per hour
b. $54.00 x 13,325 hrs. = $719,550
c. $716,000 - $719,550 = $3,550 overapplied

Difficulty: 2   *Objective*: 6

158. Schulz Corporation applies overhead based upon machine-hours. Budgeted factory overhead was $266,400 and budgeted machine-hours were 18,500. Actual factory overhead was $287,920 and actual machine-hours were 19,050. Before disposition of under/overapplied overhead, the cost of goods sold was $560,000 and ending inventories were as follows:

Direct materials	$ 60,000
WIP	190,000
Finished goods	250,000
Total	$500,000

Required:

a. Determine the budgeted factory overhead rate per machine-hour.
b. Compute the over/underapplied overhead.
c. Prepare the journal entry to dispose of the variance using the write-off to cost of goods sold approach.
d. Prepare the journal entry to dispose of the variance using the proration approach.

Answer:

a. $266,400/18,500 hrs. = $14.40 per hour

b. $14.40 x 19,050 hours = $274,320 - $287,920 = $13,600 underapplied overhead

c.

Cost of Goods Sold	13,600	
Factory Department Overhead Control		13,600

d. $560,000 + $190,000 + $250,000 = $1,000,000

Cost of Goods Sold:
$560,000/$1,000,000 = 56% x $13,600 = $7,616

WIP:
$190,000/$1,000,000 = 19% x $13,600 = $2,584

Finished Goods:
$250,000/$1,000,000 = 25% x $13,600 = $3,400

Cost of Goods Sold	7,616	
WIP Inventory	2,584	
Finished Goods Inventory	3,400	
Factory Department Overhead Control		13,600

Difficulty: 3   *Objective*: 6

159. A local attorney employs ten full-time professionals. The budgeted compensation per employee is $80,000. The maximum billable hours for each client are 400. Clients always receive their full amount of time. All professional labor costs are included in a single direct-cost category and are traced to jobs on a per-hour basis. Any other costs are included in a single indirect-cost pool, allocated according to professional labor-hours. Budgeted indirect costs for the year are $400,000 and the firm had 20 clients.

Required:
a. What is the direct-labor-cost rate per hour?
b. What is the indirect-cost rate per hour?

Answer:
a. Total direct cost   = $80,000 x 10 = $800,000
     Total hours   = 400 x 20 = 8,000
     Direct-cost rate per unit   = $800,000/8,000 = $100.00 per hour

b. Indirect-cost rate per unit = $400,000/8,000 = $50.00 per hour

Difficulty: 2   *Objective:* 7

160. Sedgwick County Hospital uses an indirect job-costing system for all patients. In June, the budgeted nursing care charges for each department and budgeted allocation bases of nursing days are as follows:

June	Critical Care	Special Care	General Care
Budgeted nursing costs	$2,480,000	$1,644,000	$1,280,400
Budgeted nursing days	5,000	4,000	8,000

Patient Ms. Graves spent six days in critical care and eight days in special care during June. The remainder of the 30-day month was spent in the general care area.

Required:
a. Determine the budgeted overhead rate for each department.
b. What are the total charges to Ms. Graves if she was in the facility the entire month?

Answer:
a. Overhead rate critical care   = 2,480,000/5,000 nursing days = $496.00 per day.
     Overhead rate special care   = $1,644,000/4,000 nursing days = $411 per day
     Overhead rate general   = $1,280,400/8,000 nursing days = $160.05 per day

b. Ms. Graves:
     Critical care $496.00 x 6 days = $2,976.00
     Special care $411.00 x 8 days =   3,288.00
     General care $160.05 x 16 days =   2560.80
     Total overhead charges $8,824.80

Difficulty: 2   *Objective:* 7

CRITICAL THINKING

161. Describe job-costing and process-costing systems. Explain when it would be appropriate to use each.

    Answer:
    Job costing accumulates costs for different jobs required by specific customers. Process costing computes and allocates an equal amount of cost to each product. Job costing is the logical choice when the production process has many distinct products or many heterogeneous jobs, while process costing is typically used when it is not necessary to keep separate cost records for individual jobs and the products are relatively homogeneous.

    Difficulty: 2   *Objectives*: 1, 2

162. In a job-costing system, explain why it is necessary to apply indirect costs to production through the use of a manufacturing overhead cost allocation rate.

    Answer:
    First, actual manufacturing overhead costs are not known until the end of year. In order to price and invoice jobs in a timely manner, annual manufacturing overhead costs need to be estimated and allocated to specific jobs during the accounting period.
    Secondly, manufacturing overhead costs are usually not incurred evenly throughout the year. The use of a manufacturing overhead cost allocation rate evenly distributes manufacturing overhead costs over the entire year.

    Difficulty: 2   *Objectives*: 3, 4, 5, 6

163. Explain how a budgeted indirect-cost rate is determined.

    Answer:
    Manufacturing overhead cost allocation rates are determined by dividing the cost of the resources committed to the manufacturing overhead activity by the capacity made available by the resources committed to the activity.

    Difficulty: 2   *Objective*: 4

164. Hammond and Jarrett provide tax consulting for estates and trusts. Their job-costing system has a single direct-cost category (professional labor) and a single indirect-cost pool (research support). The indirect-cost pool contains all the costs except direct personnel costs. All budgeted indirect costs are allocated to individual jobs using actual professional labor-hours.

Required:

a. Discuss the reasons a consulting firm might use a normal costing system rather than an actual costing system.
b. What might be some reasons for the firm to change from a one-pool to a multiple-pool allocation concept?

Answer:

a. Budget rates are normally used because actual costs may not be available until some time after a job is completed. Decisions about billing a client for services rendered generally must be made immediately after the job is completed. Also, actual costs may reflect short-run changes in the environment that may distort the billing process. Budgeted costs are affected by weekly or monthly fluctuations and, therefore, offer a stable comparison and assignment of costs throughout the accounting cycle.

b. Having separate professional labor-hour rates assists in assigning the personnel costs to jobs closest to their real values. This helps to maintain different costs for jobs that have the same number of hours but a different mix of professionals doing the job. Seldom is there only one cause-and-effect relationship between a job and the tasks performed on the job; therefore, it may also be a good idea to develop multiple indirect-cost assignments (i.e., one for staff support and others for such items as computer support or general administrative support).

Difficulty: 2   *Objective*: 7

CHAPTER 5: ACTIVITY-BASED COSTING AND ACTIVITY-BASED MANAGEMENT

TRUE/FALSE

1. A top-selling product might actually result in losses for the company.

   Answer: True   *Difficulty*: 2   *Objective*: 1

2. Companies that undercost products will most likely lose market share.

   Answer: False   *Difficulty*: 2   *Objective*: 1
   Companies that *overcost* products will most likely lose market share.

3. If a company undercosts one of its products, then it will overcost at least one of its other products.

   Answer: True   *Difficulty*: 2   *Objective*: 1

4. Direct costs plus indirect costs equal total costs.

   Answer: True   *Difficulty*: 1   *Objective*: 2

5. When refining a costing system, a company should classify as many costs as possible as indirect costs.

   Answer: False   *Difficulty*: 1   *Objective*: 2
   When refining a costing system, a company should classify as many costs as possible as *direct* costs.

6. In a homogeneous cost pool, all costs have a similar cause-and-effect relationship with the cost-allocation base.

   Answer: True   *Difficulty*: 1   *Objective*: 2

7. Indirect labor and distribution costs would most likely be in the same activity-cost pool.

   Answer: False   *Difficulty*: 2   *Objective*: 2
   Indirect labor and distribution costs would *not* be in the same activity-cost pool because their cost drivers are very dissimilar. A cost driver of indirect labor would include direct labor hours, while a cost driver of distribution costs would include cubic feet of cargo moved.

8. Activity-based costing helps identify various activities that explain why costs are incurred.

   Answer: True   *Difficulty*: 1   *Objective*: 2

9. Direct tracing of costs improves cost accuracy.

Answer: True   *Difficulty*: 1   *Objective*: 2

10. An activity-based costing system is necessary for costing services that are similar.

Answer: False   *Difficulty*: 1   *Objective*: 3
An activity-based costing system is only necessary when services are dissimilar and different amounts of resources are used by each service.

11. Traditional systems are likely to undercost complex products with lower production volume.

Answer: True   *Difficulty*: 2   *Objective*: 3

12. For activity-based cost systems, activity costs are assigned to products in the proportion of the demand they place on activity resources.

Answer: True   *Difficulty*: 2   *Objective*: 3

13. Unit-level measures can distort product costing because the demand for overhead resources may be driven by batch-level or product-sustaining activities.

Answer: True   *Difficulty*: 2   *Objective*: 4

14. Using multiple unit-level cost drivers generally constitutes an effective activity-based cost system.

Answer: False   *Difficulty*: 2   *Objective*: 4
In addition to unit-level cost drivers, an effective activity-based cost system usually uses batch-level, product-sustaining, and facility-sustaining cost drivers.

15. Misleading cost numbers are larger when unit-level assignments and the alternative activity-cost-driver assignments are proportionately similar to each other.

Answer: False   *Difficulty*: 2   *Objective*: 4
Misleading cost numbers are larger when unit-level assignments and the alternative activity-cost-driver assignments are proportionately *dissimilar* to each other.

16. Availability of reliable data and measures should be considered when choosing a cost-allocation base.

Answer: True   *Difficulty*: 1   *Objective*: 5

17. When designing a costing system, it is easiest to calculate total costs first, and then per-unit costs.

Answer: True   *Difficulty*: 1   *Objective*: 5

18. ABC systems attempt to trace more costs as direct costs.

   Answer: True   *Difficulty*: 1   *Objective*: 5

19. ABC systems create homogeneous cost pools linked to different activities.

   Answer: True   *Difficulty*: 1   *Objective*: 5

20. ABC systems seek a cost allocation base that has a cause-and-effect relationship with costs in the cost pool.

   Answer: True   *Difficulty*: 1   *Objective*: 5

21. For service organizations, activity-based cost systems may be used to clarify appropriate cost assignments.

   Answer: True   *Difficulty*: 1   *Objective*: 5

22. ABC reveals opportunities for improving the way work is done.

   Answer: True   *Difficulty*: 1   *Objective*: 6

23. Activity-based management refers to the use of information derived from ABC analysis to analyze and improve operations.

   Answer: True   *Difficulty*: 1   *Objective*: 6

24. Information derived from an ABC analysis might be used to eliminate nonvalue-added activities.

   Answer: True   *Difficulty*: 1   *Objective*: 6

25. Department-costing systems are a further refinement of ABC systems.

   Answer: False   *Difficulty*: 1   *Objective*: 7
   ABC systems are a further refinement of department-costing systems.

26. ABC systems are useful in manufacturing, but not in the merchandising or service industries.

   Answer: False   *Difficulty*: 1   *Objective*: 7
   ABC systems can be useful in manufacturing, merchandising, and service industries.

27. Costing systems with multiple cost pools are considered ABC systems.

   Answer: False   *Difficulty*: 2   *Objective*: 7
   The uniqueness of ABC systems is not simply multiple cost pools, but that the cost pools each relate to different activities.

28. ABC systems always provide decision-making benefits that exceed implementation costs.

Answer: False   *Difficulty*: 1   *Objective*: 8
ABC system decision-making benefits do not always exceed implementation costs. This issue needs to be evaluated and if the costs exceed the benefits, then an ABC system should not be implemented.

29. The primary costs of an ABC system are the measurements necessary to implement the system.

Answer: True   *Difficulty*: 1   *Objective*: 8

30. Simply because activity-based costing systems employ more activity-cost drivers they provide more accurate product costs than traditional systems.

Answer: False   *Difficulty*: 2   *Objective*: 8
When there are more activity-cost drivers, there is also more room for error, which may not result in more accurate products costs.

MULTIPLE CHOICE

31. If products are alike, then for costing purposes
    a. a simple costing system will yield accurate cost numbers.
    b. an activity-based costing system should be used.
    c. multiple indirect-cost rates should be used.
    d. varying demands will be placed on resources.

    Answer: a   *Difficulty*: 1   *Objective*: 1

32. Undercosting a particular product may result in
    a. loss of market share.
    b. lower profits.
    c. operating inefficiencies.
    d. understating total product costs.

    Answer: b   *Difficulty*: 2   *Objective*: 1

33. Overcosting of a product is MOST likely to result from
    a. misallocating direct labor costs.
    b. overpricing the product.
    c. undercosting another product.
    d. understating total product costs.

    Answer: c   *Difficulty*: 2   *Objective*: 1

34. A company produces three products; if one product is overcosted then
    a. one product is undercosted.
    b. one or two products are undercosted.
    c. two products are undercosted.
    d. no products are undercosted.

    Answer: b   *Difficulty:* 1   *Objective:* 1

35. Misleading cost numbers are MOST likely the result of misallocating
    a. direct material costs.
    b. direct manufacturing labor costs.
    c. indirect costs.
    d. all of the above.

    Answer: c   *Difficulty:* 2   *Objective:* 1

36. An accelerated need for refined cost systems is due to
    a. global monopolies.
    b. rising prices.
    c. intcnsc competition.
    d. a shift toward increased direct costs.

    Answer: c   *Difficulty:* 2   *Objective:* 1

37. The use of a single indirect-cost rate is more likely to
    a. undercost high-volume simple products.
    b. undercost low-volume complex products.
    c. undercost lower-priced products.
    d. both (b) and (c).

    Answer: b   *Difficulty:* 2   *Objective:* 1

38. Uniformly assigning the costs of resources to cost objects when those resources are actually used in a nonuniform way is called
    a. overcosting.
    b. undercosting.
    c. peanut-butter costing.
    d. department costing.

    Answer: c   *Difficulty:* 1   *Objective:* 1

39. Refining a cost system includes
    a. classifying as many costs as indirect costs as is feasible.
    b. creating as many cost pools as possible.
    c. identifying the activities involved in a process.
    d. seeking a lesser level of dctail.

    Answer: c   *Difficulty:* 2   *Objective:* 2

40. Greater indirect costs are associated with
    a. specialized engineering drawings.
    b. quality specifications and testing.
    c. inventoried materials and material control systems.
    d. all of the above.

    Answer: d   *Difficulty:* 1   *Objective:* 2

41. Design of an ABC system requires
    a. that the job bid process be redesigned.
    b. that a cause-and-effect relationship exists between resource costs and individual activities.
    c. an adjustment to product mix.
    d. both (b) and (c).

    Answer: b   *Difficulty:* 1   *Objective:* 2

42. ABC systems create
    a. one large cost pool.
    b. homogenous activity-related cost pools.
    c. activity-cost pools with a broad focus.
    d. activity-cost pools containing many direct costs.

    Answer: b   *Difficulty:* 1   *Objective:* 3

43. Logical cost allocation bases include
    a. cubic feet of packages moved to measure distribution activity.
    b. machine hours to measure setup activity.
    c. direct manufacturing labor hours to measure designing activity.
    d. all of the above.

    Answer: a   *Difficulty:* 1   *Objective:* 3

44. ABC systems
    a. highlight the different levels of activities.
    b. limit cost drivers to units of output.
    c. allocate costs based on the overall level of activity.
    d. generally undercost complex products.

    Answer: a   *Difficulty:* 2   *Objective:* 3

45. A single indirect-cost rate may distort product costs because
    a. there is an assumption that all support activities affect all products.
    b. it recognizes specific activities that are required to produce a product.
    c. costs are not consistently recorded.
    d. it fails to measure the correct amount of total costs.

    Answer: a   *Difficulty:* 2   *Objective:* 3

46. Traditional cost systems distort product costs because
    a. they do not know how to identify the appropriate units.
    b. competitive pricing is ignored.
    c. they emphasize financial accounting requirements.
    d. they apply average support costs to each unit of product.

    Answer: d   *Difficulty:* 2   *Objective:* 3

47. Which of the following statements about activity-based costing is NOT true?
    a. Activity-based costing is useful for allocating marketing and distribution costs.
    b. Activity-based costing is more likely to result in major differences from traditional costing systems if the firm manufactures only one product rather than multiple products.
    c. Activity-based costing seeks to distinguish batch-level, product-sustaining, and facility-sustaining costs, especially when they are not proportionate to one another.
    d. Activity-based costing differs from traditional costing systems in that products are not cross-subsidized.

    Answer: b   *Difficulty:* 2   *Objective:* 3

48. Activity-based costing (ABC) can eliminate cost distortions because ABC
    a. develops cost drivers that have a cause-and-effect relationship with the activities performed.
    b. establishes multiple cost pools.
    c. eliminates product variations.
    d. recognizes interactions between different departments in assigning support costs.

    Answer: a   *Difficulty:* 1   *Objective:* 3

49. Product lines that produce different variations (models, styles, or colors) often require specialized manufacturing activities that translate into
    a. fewer indirect costs for each product line.
    b. decisions to drop product variations.
    c. a greater number of direct manufacturing labor cost allocation rates.
    d. greater overhead costs for each product line.

    Answer: d   *Difficulty:* 2   *Objective:* 3

THE FOLLOWING INFORMATION APPLIES TO QUESTIONS 50 THROUGH 55.
Merriman Company provides the following ABC costing information:

Activities	Total Costs	Activity-cost drivers
Account inquiry hours	$400,000	10,000 hours
Account billing lines	$280,000	4,000,000 lines
Account verification accounts	$150,000	40,000 accounts
Correspondence letters	$ 50,000	4,000 letters
Total costs	$880,000	

The above activities are used by Departments A and B as follows:

	Department A	Department B
Account inquiry hours	2,000 hours	4,000 hours
Account billing lines	400,000 lines	200,000 lines
Account verification accounts	10,000 accounts	8,000 accounts
Correspondence letters	1,000 letters	1,600 letters

50. How much of the account inquiry cost will be assigned to Department A?
   a. $80,000
   b. $400,000
   c. $160,000
   d.   none of the above

   Answer: a   *Difficulty*:   2   *Objective*:   3
   ($400,000 / 10,000) x 2,000 = $80,000

51. How much of the account billing cost will be assigned to Department B?
   a. $28,000
   b. $280,000
   c. $14,000
   d.   none of the above

   Answer: c   *Difficulty*:   2   *Objective*:   3
   ($280,000 / 4,000,000) x 200,000 = $14,000

52. How much of account verification costs will be assigned to Department A?
   a. $30,000
   b. $37,500
   c. $150,000.
   d. $10,000

   Answer: b   *Difficulty*:   2   *Objective*:   3
   ($150,000 / 40,000) x 10,000 = $37,500

53. How much of correspondence costs will be assigned to Department B?
    a. $1,600
    b. $12,500
    c. $50,000
    d. $20,000

    Answer: d   *Difficulty:* 2   *Objective:* 3
    ($50,000 / 4,000) x 1,600 = $20,000

54. How much of the total costs will be assigned to Department A?
    a. $158,000
    b. $80,000
    c. $224,000
    d. $880,000

    Answer: a   *Difficulty:* 2   *Objective:* 3

($400,000 / 10,000)	x 2,000	= $80,000
($280,000 / 4,000,000)	x 400,000	= $28,000
($150,000 / 40,000)	x 10,000	= $37,500
($50,000 / 4,000)	x 1,000	= $12,500
		$158,000

55. How much of the total costs will be assigned to Department B?
    a. $158,000
    b. $80,000
    c. $224,000
    d. $880,000

    Answer: c   *Difficulty:* 3   *Objective:* 3

($400,000 / 10,000)	x 4,000	= $160,000
($280,000 / 4,000,000)	x 200,000	= $ 14,000
($150,000 / 40,000)	x 8,000	= $ 30,000
($50,000 / 4,000)	x 1,600	= $ 20,000
		$224,000

56. Dalrymple Company produces a special spray nozzle. The budgeted indirect total cost of inserting the spray nozzle is $80,000. The budgeted number of nozzles to be inserted is 40,000. What is the budgeted indirect cost allocation rate for this activity?
    a. $0.50
    b. $1.00
    c. $1.50
    d. $2.00

    Answer: d   *Difficulty:* 1   *Objective:* 3
    $80,000 / 40,000 = $2.00

57. Activity-based costing is most likely to yield benefits for companies with all of the following characteristics EXCEPT
    a. numerous products that consume different amounts of resources.
    b. operations that remain fairly consistent.
    c. a highly competitive environment, where cost control is critical.
    d. accessible accounting and information systems expertise to maintain the system.

    Answer: b   *Difficulty*: 2   *Objective*: 3

58. Each of the following statements is true EXCEPT
    a. traditional product costing systems seek to assign all manufacturing costs to products.
    b. ABC product costing systems seek to assign all manufacturing costs to products.
    c. traditional product costing systems are more refined than an ABC system.
    d. cost distortions occur when a mismatch (incorrect association) occurs between the way indirect costs are incurred and the basis for their assignment to individual products.

    Answer: c   *Difficulty*: 1   *Objective*: 3

59. The MOST likely example of an output unit-level cost is
    a. general administrative costs.
    b. paying suppliers for orders received.
    c. engineering costs.
    d. machine depreciation.

    Answer: d   *Difficulty*: 1   *Objective*: 4

60. The MOST likely example of a batch-level cost is
    a. utility costs.
    b. machine repairs.
    c. product-designing costs.
    d. setup costs.

    Answer: d   *Difficulty*: 1   *Objective*: 4

61. Design costs are an example of
    a. unit-level costs
    b. batch-level costs
    c. product-sustaining costs.
    d. facility-sustaining costs.

    Answer: c   *Difficulty*: 1   *Objective*: 4

62. _____ costs support the organization as a whole.
    a. Unit-level
    b. Batch-level
    c. Product-sustaining
    d. Facility-sustaining

    Answer: d   *Difficulty*: 1   *Objective*: 4

63. It is usually difficult to find good cause-and-effect relationships between _____ and a cost allocation base.
    a. unit-level costs
    b. batch-level costs
    c. product-sustaining costs
    d. facility-sustaining costs

    Answer: d   *Difficulty*: 1   *Objective*: 4

64. To set realistic selling prices
    a. all costs should be allocated to products.
    b. costs should only be allocated when there is a strong cause-and-effect relationship.
    c. only unit-level costs and batch-level costs should be allocated.
    d. only unit-level costs should be allocated.

    Answer: a   *Difficulty*: 2   *Objective*: 4

65. Different products consume different proportions of manufacturing overhead costs because of differences in all of the following EXCEPT
    a. selling prices.
    b. customers' customization specifications.
    c. setup times.
    d. product design.

    Answer: a   *Difficulty*: 1   *Objective*: 4

66. Unit-level cost drivers are most appropriate as an overhead assignment base when
    a. several complex products are manufactured.
    b. only one product is manufactured.
    c. direct labor costs are low.
    d. factories produce a varied mix of products.

    Answer: b   *Difficulty*: 2   *Objective*: 4

67. With traditional costing systems, products manufactured in small batches and in small annual volumes may be _____ because batch-related and product-sustaining costs are assigned using unit-related drivers.
    a. overcosted
    b. fairly costed
    c. undercosted
    d. ignored

    Answer: c   *Difficulty*: 2   *Objective*: 4

THE FOLLOWING INFORMATION APPLIES TO QUESTIONS 68 AND 69.
Products S5 and CP8 each are assigned $50.00 in indirect costs by a traditional costing system. An activity analysis revealed that although production requirements are identical, S5 requires 45 minutes less setup time than CP8.

68. According to an ABC system, CP8 is _____ under the traditional system.
    a. undercosted
    b. overcosted
    c. fairly costed
    d. accurately costed

    Answer: a   *Difficulty*: 2   *Objective*: 4

69. According to an ABC system, S5 uses a disproportionately
    a. smaller amount of unit-level costs.
    b. larger amount of unit-level costs.
    c. smaller amount of batch-level costs.
    d. larger amount of batch-level costs.

    Answer: c   *Difficulty*: 2   *Objective*: 4

70. Put the following ABC implementation steps in order:
    A Identify the products that are the cost objects.
    B Select the cost allocation bases.
    C Compute the allocation rates.
    D Compute the total cost of the products.

    a. DACB
    b. DBCA
    c. BADC
    d. ABCD

    Answer: d   *Difficulty*: 1   *Objective*: 5.

71. ABC systems identify _____ costs used by products.
    a. all
    b. short-term fixed
    c. short-term variable
    d. long-term fixed

    Answer: a   *Difficulty:* 1   *Objective:* 5

72. The focus of ABC systems is on
    a. long-term decisions.
    b. short-term decisions.
    c. make-or-buy decisions.
    d. special-pricing decisions.

    Answer: a   *Difficulty:* 2   *Objective:* 5

73. When designing a costing system, it is easiest to
    a. calculate total costs first, and then per-unit cost.
    b. calculate per-unit costs first, and then total costs.
    c. calculate long-term costs first, and then short-term costs.
    d. calculate short-term costs first, and then long-term costs.

    Answer: a   *Difficulty:* 1   *Objective:* 5

74. ABC assumes all costs are _____ because over the long run management can adjust the amount of resources employed.
    a. fixed
    b. variable
    c. committed
    d. nondiscretionary

    Answer: b   *Difficulty:* 2   *Objective:* 5

75. A manufacturing firm produces multiple families of products requiring various combinations of different types of parts. Of the following, the MOST appropriate cost driver for assigning materials handling costs to the various products is
    a. direct labor hours.
    b. number of units produced.
    c. number of parts used.
    d. number of suppliers involved.

    Answer: c   *Difficulty:* 1   *Objective:* 5

THE FOLLOWING INFORMATION APPLIES TO QUESTIONS 76 THROUGH 79.
Barnes Corporation manufactures two models of office chairs, a standard and a deluxe
model. The following activity and cost information has been compiled.

Product	Number of Setups	Number of Components	Number of Direct Labor Hours
Standard	22	8	375
Deluxe	28	12	225
Overhead costs	$20,000	$40,000	

76. Assume a traditional costing system applies the $60,000 of overhead costs based on
    direct labor hours. What is the total amount of overhead costs assigned to the standard
    model?
    a. $24,800
    b. $35,200
    c. $37,500
    d. $22,500.

    Answer: c   *Difficulty:* 2   *Objective:* 5
    ($60,000 / (375 + 225)) x 375 = $37,500

77. Assume a traditional costing system applies the $60,000 of overhead costs based on
    direct labor hours. What is the total amount of overhead costs assigned to the deluxe
    model?
    a. $24,800
    b. $35,200
    c. $37,500
    d. $22,500.

    Answer: d   *Difficulty:* 2   *Objective:* 5
    [$60,000 / (375 + 225)] x 225 = $22,500

78. Number of setups and number of components are identified as activity-cost drivers for
    overhead. Assuming an activity-based costing system is used, what is the total amount
    of overhead costs assigned to the standard model?
    a. $24,800
    b. $35,200
    c. $37,500
    d. $22,500.

    Answer: a   *Difficulty:* 2   *Objective:* 5
    Setups: $20,000 / (22 + 28) = $400
    Components: $40,000 / (8 + 12) = $2,000
    ($400 x 22) + ($2,000 x 8) = $24,800

79. Number of setups and number of components are identified as activity-cost drivers for overhead. Assuming an activity-based costing system is used, what is the total amount of overhead costs assigned to the deluxe model?
    a. $24,800
    b. $35,200
    c. $37,500
    d. $22,500.

Answer: b   *Difficulty*: 2   *Objective*: 5
($400 x 28) + ($2,000 x 12) = $35,200

THE FOLLOWING INFORMATION APPLIES TO QUESTIONS 80 THROUGH 84.
Tiger Pride produces two product lines: T-shirts and Sweatshirts. Product profitability is analyzed as follows:

	T-SHIRTS	SWEATSHIRTS
Production and sales volume	60,000 units	35,000 units
Selling price	$16.00	$29.00
Direct material	$ 2.00	$ 5.00
Direct labor	$ 4.50	$ 7.20
Manufacturing overhead	$ 2.00	$ 3.00
Gross profit	$ 7.50	$13.80
Selling and administrative	$ 4.00	$ 7.00
Operating profit	$ 3.50	$ 6.80

Tiger Pride's managers have decided to revise their current assignment of overhead costs to reflect the following ABC cost information:

Activity	Activity cost	Activity-cost driver
Supervision	$100,920	Direct labor hours (DLH)
Inspection	$124,000	Inspections

Activities demanded	
T-SHIRTS	SWEATSHIRTS
0.75 DLH/unit	1.2 DLH/unit
45,000 DLHs	42,000 DLHs
60,000 inspections	17,500 inspections

80. Under the revised ABC system, the activity-cost driver rate for the supervision activity is
    a. $2.58
    b. $2.40
    c. $2.24
    d. $1.16

Answer: d   *Difficulty*: 1   *Objective*: 5
$100,920 / 87,000 dlh = $1.16 per dlh

81. Under the revised ABC system, supervision costs allocated to Sweatshirts will be
    a. $48,720.
    b. $100,800.
    c. $100,920.
    d.   none of the above.

    Answer: a   *Difficulty*:   1   *Objective*:   5
    $100,920 / 87,000 dlh = $1.16 per dlh x 42,000 dlh = $48,720

82. Under the revised ABC system, total overhead costs allocated to Sweatshirts will be
    a. $ 48,720.
    b. $ 76,720.
    c. $224,920.
    d.   none of the above.

    Answer: b   *Difficulty*:   2   *Objective*:   5
    $124,000 / 77,500 inspections = $1.60 per inspection x 17,500 = $28,000
    $48,720 + $28,000 = $76,720

83. Under the revised ABC system, overhead costs per unit for the Sweatshirts will be
    a. $1.39 per unit.
    b. $1.60 per unit.
    c. $2.19 per unit.
    d. $2.47 per unit.

    Answer: c   *Difficulty*:   2   *Objective*:   5
    $76,720 / 35,000 sweatshirts = $2.19

84. Using an ABC system, next year's estimates show manufacturing overhead costs will total $228,300 for 52,000 T-shirts. If all other T-shirt costs and sales prices remain the same, the profitability that can be expected is
    a. $5.41 per t-shirt.
    b. $4.39 per t-shirt.
    c. $1.11 per t-shirt.
    d.   ($0.81) per t-shirt.

    Answer: c   *Difficulty*:   3   *Objective*:   5
    (52,000 ($16 - $2.00 - $4.50 - $4.00)) - $228,300 = $57,700 / 52,000 = $1.11

THE FOLLOWING INFORMATION APPLIES TO QUESTIONS 85 THROUGH 88.
Mayan Potters manufactures two sizes of ceramic paperweights, regular and jumbo. The following information applies to their expectations for the planning period.

Cost Pool	Overhead Costs	Activity-cost driver
Materials handling	$ 45,000	90,000 orders
Machine maintenance	$300,000	15,000 maintenance hours
Setups	$270,000	45,000 setups
Inspections	$105,000	21,000 inspections
Total support costs	$720,000	

Production Estimates

Production units:
Regular	= 8,000,000 units
Jumbo	= 16,000,000 units
Machine-hours	= 200,000 mh
Labor-hours	= 400,000 dlh

Mayan Potters uses an ABC system and assigns overhead costs based on the overhead activity information provided above.

85. The activity-cost driver for the materials handling activity is
    a.   orders.
    b.   maintenance hours.
    c.   production units.
    d.   setups.

    Answer: a   *Difficulty*: 1   *Objective*: 5

86. The materials handling activity-cost driver rate is
    a. $2.00.
    b. $20.00.
    c. $0.50.
    d. $5.00.

    Answer: c   *Difficulty*: 1   *Objective*: 5
    $45,000 / 90,000 orders = $0.50 per order

87. The inspections activity-cost driver rate is
    a. $0.50.
    b. $2.00.
    c. $20.00.
    d. $5.00.

    Answer: d   *Difficulty*: 1   *Objective*: 5
    $105,000 / 21,000 inspections = $5.00 per inspection

88. During October Mayan produced 700,000 regular ceramic paperweights and Mayan's production manager counted 2,000 orders; 1,000 maintenance-hours; 2,000 setups; and 2,000 inspections for the regular product line. For October, Mayan's controller assigned _____ indirect costs to the regular product line.
    a. $43,000
    b. $25,000
    c. $34,000
    d. none of the above

Answer: a   *Difficulty*: 3   *Objective*: 5
[($45,000 / 90,000) x 2,000] + [($300,000 / 15,000) x 1,000] + [($270,000 / 45,000) x 2,000] + [($105,000 / 21,000) x 2,000] = $43,000

THE FOLLOWING INFORMATION APPLIES TO QUESTIONS 89 AND 90.
Nichols Inc. manufactures remote controls. Currently the company uses a plant-wide rate for allocating manufacturing overhead. The plant manager believes it is time to refine the method of cost allocation and has the accounting department identify the primary production activities and their cost drivers:

Activities	Cost driver	Allocation Rate
Material handling	Number of parts	$2 per part
Assembly	Labor hours	$20 per hour
Inspection	Time at inspection station	$3 per minute

The current traditional cost method allocates overhead based on direct manufacturing labor hours using a rate of $200 per labor hour.

89. What are the indirect manufacturing costs per remote control assuming the traditional method is used and a batch of 500 remote controls are produced? The batch requires 1,000 parts, 10 direct manufacturing labor hours, and 15 minutes of inspection time.
    a. $2,000.00 per remote control
    b. $0.25 per remote control
    c. $2.00 per remote control
    d. $4.00 per remote control

Answer: d   *Difficulty*: 2   *Objective*: 5
10 hours x $200 = $2,000 per batch / 500 units per batch = $4.00 per unit

90. What are the indirect manufacturing costs per remote control assuming an activity-based-costing method is used and a batch of 50 remote controls are produced? The batch requires 100 parts, 6 direct manufacturing labor hours, and 2.5 minutes of inspection time.
    a. $4.00 per remote control
    b. $6.55 per remote control
    c. $24.00 per remote control
    d. $327.50 per remote control

Answer: b   *Difficulty*: 2   *Objective*: 5
($2 x 100) + ($20 x 6) + ($3 x 2.5) = $327.50 per batch / 50 units per batch = $6.55 per unit

THE FOLLOWING INFORMATION APPLIES TO QUESTIONS 91 THROUGH 95.
Gregory Enterprises has identified three cost pools to allocate overhead costs. The following estimates are provided for the coming year:

Cost Pool	Overhead Costs	Cost driver	Activity level
Supervision of direct labor	$320,000	Direct labor-hours	800,000
Machine maintenance	$120,000	Machine-hours	960,000
Facility rent	$200,000	Square feet of area	100,000
Total overhead costs	$640,000		

The accounting records show the Mossman Job consumed the following resources:

Cost driver	Actual level
Direct labor-hours	200
Machine-hours	1,600
Square feet of area	50

91. If direct labor-hours are considered the only overhead cost driver, what is the single cost driver rate for Gregory Enterprises?
   a. $0.50 per direct labor-hour
   b. $0.80 per direct labor-hour
   c. $0.40 per direct labor-hour
   d. $1.20 per direct labor-hour

Answer: b   *Difficulty:* 2   *Objective:* 3
$640,000 / 800,000 = $0.80 per dlh

92. Using direct labor-hours as the only overhead cost driver, what is the amount of overhead costs allocated to the Mossman Job?
   a. $160
   b. $120
   c. $240
   d. $125

Answer: a   *Difficulty:* 2   *Objective:* 3
200 dlh x $0.80 = $160

93. If Gregory Enterprises uses the three activity cost pools to allocate overhead costs, what are the activity-cost driver rates for supervision of direct labor, machine maintenance, and facility rent, respectively?
   a. $0.60 per dlh, $0.025 per mh, $0.80 per sq ft
   b. $1.25 per dlh, $0.25 per mh, $0.50 per sq ft
   c. $0.40 per dlh, $0.05 per mh, $0.20 per sq ft
   d. $0.40 per dlh, $0.125 per mh, $2 per sq ft

   Answer: d   *Difficulty:*   2   *Objective:*   5
   Supervision cost driver rate is $0.40 per dlh = $320,000 / 800,000 dlh
   Machine maintenance cost driver rate is $0.125 per mh = $120,000 / 960,000 mh
   Facility rent cost driver rate is $2 per sq ft = $200,000 / 100,000 sq ft

94. Using the three cost pools to allocate overhead costs, what is the total amount of overhead costs to be allocated to the Mossman Job?
   a. $200
   b. $380
   c. $675
   d. $170

   Answer: b   *Difficulty:*   2   *Objective:*   5
   $380 = (200 x $0.40 per dlh) + (1,600 x $0.125 per mh) + (50 x $2 per sq ft)

95. Which method of allocation probably best estimates actual overhead costs used? Why?
   a.   Single direct labor-hours cost driver, because it is best to allocate total costs uniformly to individual jobs.
   b.   Single direct labor-hours cost driver, because it is easiest to analyze and interpret.
   c.   Three activity-cost drivers, because it best reflects the relative consumption of resources.
   d.   Three activity-cost drivers, because product costs can be significantly cross-subsidized.

   Answer: c   *Difficulty:*   2   *Objective:*   6

THE FOLLOWING INFORMATION APPLIES TO QUESTIONS 96 THROUGH 100.
Ernsting Printers has contracts to complete weekly supplements required by forty-six customers. For the year 20x5, manufacturing overhead cost estimates total $420,000 for an annual production capacity of 12 million pages.

For 20x5 Ernsting Printers has decided to evaluate the use of additional cost pools. After analyzing manufacturing overhead costs, it was determined that number of design changes, setups, and inspections are the primary manufacturing overhead cost drivers. The following information was gathered during the analysis:

Cost pool	Manufacturing overhead costs	Activity level
Design changes	$ 60,000	300 design changes
Setups	320,000	5,000 setups
Inspections	40,000	8,000 inspections
Total manufacturing overhead costs	$420,000	

During 20x5, two customers, Wealth Managers and Health Systems, are expected to use the following printing services:

Activity	Wealth Managers	Health Systems
Pages	60,000	76,000
Design changes	10	0
Setups	20	10
Inspections	30	38

96. What is the cost driver rate if manufacturing overhead costs are considered one large cost pool and are assigned based on 12 million pages of production capacity?
   a. $0.05 per page
   b. $0.035 per page
   c. $0.35 per page
   d. $0.025 per page

   Answer: b   *Difficulty:* 2   *Objective:* 3
   $0.035 per page = ($420,000 / 12,000,000 pages)

97. Using pages printed as the only overhead cost driver, what is the manufacturing overhead cost estimate for *Wealth Managers* during 20x5?
   a. $2,500
   b. $1,750
   c. $2,100
   d. $3,000

   Answer: c   *Difficulty:* 2   *Objective:* 3
   $2,100 = (60,000 pages x $0.035/page)

98. Assuming activity-cost pools are used, what are the activity-cost driver rates for design changes, setups, and inspections cost pools?
   a. $200 per change, $64 per setup, $5 per inspection
   b. $180 per change, $160 per setup, $3.20 per inspection
   c. $84 per change, $269 per setup, $21 per inspection
   d. $143 per change, $76 per setup, $10 per inspection

   Answer: a   *Difficulty:* 2   *Objective:* 5
   Design changes: $200 per change = ($60,000 / 300 design changes)
   Setups: $64 per setup = ($320,000 / 5,000 setups)
   Inspections: $5 per inspection = ($40,000 / 8,000 inspections)

99. Using the three cost pools to allocate overhead costs, what is the total manufacturing overhead cost estimate for *Wealth Managers* during 20x5?
   a. $6,850
   b. $3,250
   c. $3,430
   d. $5,096

   Answer: c   *Difficulty:* 3   *Objective:* 5
   $3,430 = (10 x $200 per change = $2,000) + (20 x $64 per setup = $1,280) + (30 x $5 per inspection = $150)

100. When costs are assigned using the single cost driver, number of pages printed, then
   a. *Ernsting Printers* will want to retain this highly-profitable customer.
   b. *Wealth Managers* will likely seek to do business with competitors.
   c. *Wealth Managers* is unfairly over billed for its use of printing resources.
   d. *Wealth Managers* is grossly under billed for the job, while other jobs will be unfairly over billed.

   Answer: d   *Difficulty:* 3   *Objective:* 6

THE FOLLOWING INFORMATION APPLIES TO QUESTIONS 101 THROUGH 105.
Wallace Printing has contracts to complete weekly supplements required by forty-six customers. For the year 20x5, manufacturing overhead cost estimates total $420,000 for an annual production capacity of 12 million pages.

For 20x5 Wallace Printing decided to evaluate the use of additional cost pools. After analyzing manufacturing overhead costs, it was determined that number of design changes, setups, and inspections are the primary manufacturing overhead cost drivers. The following information was gathered during the analysis:

Cost pool	Manufacturing overhead costs	Activity level
Design changes	$ 60,000	200 design changes
Setups	320,000	4,000 setups
Inspections	40,000	16,000 inspections
Total manufacturing overhead costs	$420,000	

During 20x5, two customers, Wealth Managers and Health Systems, are expected to use the following printing services:

Activity	Wealth Managers	Health Systems
Pages	60,000	76,000
Design changes	10	2
Setups	20	10
Inspections	30	38

101. If manufacturing overhead costs are considered one large cost pool and are assigned based on 12 million pages of production capacity, what is the cost driver rate?
   a. $0.25 per page
   b. $0.05 per page
   c. $0.025 per page
   d. $0.035 per page

Answer: d   *Difficulty*:   2   *Objective*:   3
$0.035 per page = ($420,000 / 12,000,000 pages)

102. Using the cost driver rate determined in the previous question, what is the manufacturing overhead cost estimate for *Health Systems* during 20x5?
   a.   Manufacturing overhead costs applied to Health Systems total $2,100
   b.   Manufacturing overhead costs applied to Health Systems total $1,900
   c.   Manufacturing overhead costs applied to Health Systems total $2,660
   d.   Manufacturing overhead costs applied to Health Systems total $3,800

Answer: c   *Difficulty*:   2   *Objective*:   3
$2,660 = 76,000 pages x $0.035/page

103. Assuming activity-cost pools are used, what are the activity-cost driver rates for design changes, setups, and inspections cost pools?
    a. $300 per change, $80 per setup, $2.50 per inspection
    b. $250 per change, $200 per setup, $3.75 per inspection
    c. $210 per change, $105 per setup, $26.25 per inspection
    d. $333 per change, $125 per setup, $4.00 per inspection

Answer: a   *Difficulty:*   2   *Objective:*   5
Design changes: $300 per change = ($60,000 / 200 design changes)
Setups: $80 per setup = ($320,000 / 4,000 setups)
Inspections $2.50 per inspection = ($40,000 / 16,000 inspections)

104. Using the activity-cost driver rates determined in the previous question, what is the manufacturing overhead cost estimate for *Health Systems* during 20x5?
    a. $3,113.75
    b. $1,495.00
    c. $2,068.00
    d. $3,412.50

Answer: b   *Difficulty:*   3   *Objective:*   5
$1,495 = (2 x $300 per change) + (10 x $80 per setup) + (38 x $2.50 per inspection)

105. When costs are assigned using the single cost driver, number of pages printed, then *Health Systems*
    a.   is fairly billed because resources are allocated uniformly to all jobs.
    b.   is grossly under billed for the job, while other jobs will be unfairly over billed.
    c.   will likely seek to do business with competitors.
    d.   will contribute too little to profits, and Wallace Printing will not want to accept additional work from the company.

Answer: c   *Difficulty:*   3   *Objective:*   6

106. Activity-based-costing information
    a. should be used when services place similar demands on resources.
    b. usually results in peanut-butter costing.
    c. will yield inaccurate cost numbers when products are similar.
    d. may assist in improving product design and efficiency.

    Answer: d   *Difficulty:* 2   *Objective:* 6

107. Activity-based management (ABM) includes decisions about all EXCEPT
    a. pricing and product mix.
    b. smoothing costs.
    c. reducing costs.
    d. improving processes.

    Answer: b   *Difficulty:* 1   *Objective:* 6

108. ABC systems
    a. reveal activities that can be eliminated.
    b. help control nonfinancial items such as number of setup hours.
    c. help identify new designs to reduce costs.
    d. all of the above.

    Answer: d   *Difficulty:* 1   *Objective:* 6

109. Companies use ABC system information
    a. to analyze costs.
    b. to prepare budgets.
    c. to evaluate performance.
    d. all of the above.

    Answer: d   *Difficulty:* 1   *Objective:* 6

110. It is important that the product costs reflect as much of the diversity and complexity of the manufacturing process so that
    a. product costs will reflect their relative consumption of resources.
    b. nonvalue-added costs can be eliminated.
    c. there is less likelihood of cross subsidizing of product costs.
    d. all of the above.

    Answer: d   *Difficulty:* 1   *Objective:* 6

111. A well-designed, activity-based cost system helps managers make better decisions because information derived from an ABC analysis
    a. can be used to eliminate nonvalue-added activities.
    b. is easy to analyze and interpret.
    c. takes the choices and judgment challenges away from the managers.
    d. emphasizes how managers can achieve higher sales.

    Answer: a   *Difficulty:* 2   *Objective:* 6

112. A PRIMARY reason for assigning selling and distribution costs to products for analytical purposes is
    a.   to justify a varied product mix.
    b.   that controllers are required to assign all costs when valuing inventories.
    c.   that different processes, products, and customers require different quantities of selling and distribution activities.
    d.   that all indirect costs must be assigned.

    Answer: c   *Difficulty:*   2   *Objective:*   6

113. For service organizations that bill customers at a predetermined average rate, activity-based cost systems can help to
    a.   clarify appropriate cost assignments for various service activities.
    b.   identify the profitability of various service activities.
    c.   accomplish both (a) and (b).
    d.   accomplish none of the above.

    Answer: c   *Difficulty:*   2   *Objective:*   6

114. Products make diverse demands on resources because of differences in all of the following EXCEPT
    a.   volume.
    b.   selling price.
    c.   batch size.
    d.   complexity.

    Answer: b   *Difficulty:*   2   *Objective:*   7

115. The UNIQUE feature of an ABC system is the emphasis on
    a.   costing individual jobs.
    b.   department indirect-cost rates.
    c.   multiple-cost pools.
    d.   individual activities.

    Answer: d   *Difficulty:*   3   *Objective:*   7

116. One department indirect-cost rate is sufficient when
    a.   activities relate to more than one level of the cost hierarchy.
    b.   product costs are significantly cross-subsidized.
    c.   the same allocation base is appropriate for all departmental activities.
    d.   it is a service department.

    Answer: c   *Difficulty:*   2   *Objective:*   7

THE FOLLOWING INFORMATION APPLIES TO QUESTIONS 117 THROUGH 122.
King Corporation has two departments, Small and Large. Central costs could be allocated to the two departments in various ways.

	Small Department	Large Department
Square footage	6,000	18,000
Number of employees	1,120	480
Sales	$400,000	$2,000,000

117. If advertising expense of $300,000 is allocated on the basis of sales, the amount allocated to the Small Department would be
   a. $50,000.
   b. $75,000.
   c. $210,000.
   d. $250,000.

   Answer: a   *Difficulty:* 2   *Objective:* 7
   $300,000 x $400,000 / ($400,000 + $2,000,000) = $50,000

118. If total advertising expense of $300,000 is allocated on the basis of sales, the amount allocated to the Large Department would be
   a. $225,000.
   b. $90,000.
   c. $250,000.
   d. $50,000.

   Answer: c   *Difficulty:* 2   *Objective:* 7
   $300,000 x $2,000,000 / ($400,000 + $2,000,000) = $250,000

119. If total payroll processing costs of $96,000 are allocated on the basis of number of employees, the amount allocated to the Small Department would be
   a. $67,200.
   b. $24,000.
   c. $16,000.
   d. $28,000.

   Answer: a   *Difficulty:* 2   *Objective:* 7
   $96,000 x 1,120 / (1,120 + 480) = $67,200

120. If total payroll processing costs of $60,000 are allocated on the basis of number of employees, the amount allocated to the Large Department would be
    a. $42,000
    b. $18,000.
    c. $45,000.
    d. $50,000.

    Answer: b   *Difficulty:* 2   *Objective:* 7
    $60,000 x 480 / (1,120 + 480) = $18,000

121. If total rent expense of $120,000 is allocated on the basis of square footage, the amount allocated to the Small Department would be
    a. $20,000
    b. $30,000.
    c. $84,000
    d. $90,000.

    Answer: b   *Difficulty:* 2   *Objective:* 7
    $120,000 x 6,000 / (6,000 + 18,000) = $30,000

122. If total rent expense of $288,000 is allocated on the basis of square footage, the amount allocated to the Large Department would be
    a. $86,400
    b. $240,000.
    c. $72,000.
    d. $216,000

    Answer: d   *Difficulty:* 2   *Objective:* 7
    $288,000 x 18,000 / (6,000 + 18,000) = $216,000

123. Using activity-cost rates rather than department indirect-cost rates to allocate costs results in different product costs when
    a. a single activity accounts for a sizable portion of department costs.
    b. there are several homogeneous cost pools.
    c. different activities have the same cost-allocation base.
    d. different products use different resources in the same proportion.

    Answer: b   *Difficulty:* 2   *Objective:* 7

124. A key reason for using an ABC system rather than a department-costing system is because ABC assigns indirect costs
    a. using broader averages.
    b. more simply than a department-costing system.
    c. in a less costly manner.
    d. to reflect differences required by different processes as well as customers.

    Answer: d   *Difficulty:* 1   *Objective:* 7

125. It ONLY makes sense to implement an ABC system when
    a. ABC provides information to make better decisions.
    b. its benefits exceed implementation costs.
    c. ABC traces more costs as direct costs.
    d. there is a strong cause-and-effect relationship between costs in the cost pools and their cost-allocation bases.

    Answer: b   *Difficulty*: 1   *Objective*: 8

126. Which of the following is a sign that an ABC system may be useful?
    a. There are small amounts of indirect costs.
    b. Products make diverse demands on resources because of differences in volume, process steps, batch size, or complexity.
    c. Products a company is less suited to produce and sell show small profits.
    d. Operations staff agrees with accountants about the costs of manufacturing and marketing products and services.

    Answer: b   *Difficulty*: 2   *Objective*: 8

127. Smaller cost distortions occur when the traditional systems' single indirect-cost rate and the activity-cost-driver rates
    a. use the same total costs for computations.
    b. are similar in proportion to each other.
    c. are more different than alike.
    d. use the same cost driver units.

    Answer: b   *Difficulty*: 2   *Objective*: 8

128. Activity-based costing systems provide better product costs when they
    a. employ more activity-cost drivers.
    b. employ fewer activity-cost drivers.
    c. identify and cost more indirect cost differences among products.
    d. always yield more accurate product costs than traditional systems.

    Answer: c   *Difficulty*: 2   *Objective*: 8

129. Factories producing a more varied and complex mix of products have higher costs than factories producing only a narrow range of products because
    a. more variations and complexities require more activities.
    b. they require more engineers.
    c. they require more direct laborers.
    d. they buy more robotics.

    Answer: a   *Difficulty*: 1   *Objective*: 8

130. Which of the following is NOT a sign that a "smoothing out" costing system exists?
   a. Operations managers don't use the data originated by the cost system.
   b. Products that a company is well suited to make and sell, show large profits.
   c. New product variations have been added, but the cost system has not been upgraded.
   d. The company loses bids they believe were priced competitively.

   Answer: b   *Difficulty:* 1   *Objective:* 8

THE FOLLOWING INFORMATION APPLIES TO QUESTIONS 131 AND 132.
Cannady produces six products. Under their traditional cost system using one cost driver, SR6 costs $168.00 per unit. An analysis of the activities and their costs revealed that three cost drivers would be used under the new ABC system. The new cost of SR6 was determined to be $178.00 per unit.

131. The total amount of indirect costs assigned to product SR6 using the traditional method is _____ the total amount assigned using ABC.
   a. more than
   b. less than
   c. identical to
   d. can't tell

   Answer: b   *Difficulty:* 1   *Objective:* 8

132. Given this change in the cost,
   a. SR6 will now command a higher sales price.
   b. SR6 has benefited from the new system.
   c. SR6 is definitely more accurately costed.
   d. SR6's costing results under the new system depend on the adequacy and quality of the estimated cost drivers and costs used by the system.

   Answer: d   *Difficulty:* 2   *Objective:* 8

133. The goal of a properly constructed ABC system is to
   a. have the most accurate cost system.
   b. Identify more indirect costs.
   c. develop the best cost system for an economically reasonable cost.
   d. have separate allocation rates for each department.

   Answer: c   *Difficulty:* 1   *Objective:* 8

EXERCISES AND PROBLEMS

134. Cocoa Pet Corporation manufactures two models of grooming stations, a standard and a deluxe model. The following activity and cost information has been compiled.

Product	Number of Setups	Number of Components	Number of Direct Labor Hours
Standard	3	30	650
Deluxe	7	50	150
Overhead costs	$20,000	$60,000	

Assume a traditional costing system applies the $80,000 of overhead costs based on direct labor hours.
a. What is the total amount of overhead costs assigned to the standard model?
b. What is the total amount of overhead costs assigned to the deluxe model?

Assume an activity-based costing system is used and that number of setups and number of components are identified as the activity-cost drivers for overhead.
c. What is the total amount of overhead costs assigned to the standard model?
d. What is the total amount of overhead costs assigned to the deluxe model?

e. Explain the difference between the costs obtained from the traditional costing system and the ABC system. Which system provides a better estimate of costs? Why?

Answer:
a. ($80,000 / (650 + 150)) x 650 = **$65,000**

b. ($80,000 / (650 + 150)) x 150 = **$15,000**

c. Setups: $20,000 / (3 + 7) = $2,000
Components: $60,000 / (30 + 50) = $750
($2,000 x 3) + ($750 x 30) = **$28,500**

d. ($2,000 x 7) + ($750 x 50) = **$51,500**

e. Because the products do not all require the same proportionate shares of the overhead resources of setup hours and components, the ABC system provides different results than the traditional system which allocates overhead costs on the basis of direct labor hours. The ABC system considers some important differences in overhead resource requirements and thus provides a better picture of the costs from each grooming table style, provided the activity measures are fairly estimated.

Difficulty: 2   *Objectives:* 1, 3, 5, 8

135. Come-On-In Manufacturing produces two types of entry doors: Deluxe and Standard. The assignment basis for support costs has been direct labor dollars. For 20X1, Come-On-In compiled the following data for the two products:

	Deluxe	Standard
Sales units	#50,000	#400,000
Sales price per unit	$650.00	$475.00
Direct material and labor costs per unit	$180.00	$130.00
Manufacturing support costs per unit	$ 80.00	$120.00

Last year, Come-On-In Manufacturing purchased an expensive robotics system to allow for more decorative door products in the deluxe product line. The CFO suggested that an ABC analysis could be valuable to help evaluate a product mix and promotion strategy for the next sales campaign. She obtained the following ABC information for 20X1:

Activity	Cost Driver	Cost	Total	Deluxe	Standard
Setups	# setups	$ 500,000	500	400	100
Machine-related	# of machine hours	$44,000,000	600,000	300,000	300,000
Packing	# shipments	$ 5,000,000	250,000	50,000	200,000

Required:

a. Using the current system, what is the estimated
   1. total cost of manufacturing one unit for each type of door?
   2. profit per unit for each type of door?

b. Using the current system, estimated manufacturing overhead costs per unit are less for the deluxe door ($80 per unit) than the standard door ($120 per unit). What is a likely explanation for this?

c. Review machine-related costs above. What is a likely explanation for machine-related costs being so high? What might explain why total machining hours for the deluxe doors (300,000 hours) are the same as for the standard doors (300,000 hours)?

d. Using the activity-based costing data presented above,
   1. compute the cost-driver rate for each overhead activity.
   2. compute the revised manufacturing *overhead cost* per unit for each type of entry door.
   3. compute the revised *total cost* to manufacture one unit of each type of entry door.

e. Is the deluxe door as profitable as the original data estimated? Why or why not?

f. What considerations need to be examined when determining a sales mix strategy?

135. **Answer:**
a. Currently estimated deluxe-entry door total cost per unit is $260 = $180 + $80.
    Currently estimated standard-entry door total cost per unit is $250 = $130 + $120.

    Currently estimated deluxe-entry door profit per unit is $390 = $650 - $260.
    Currently estimated standard-entry door profit per unit is $225 = $475- $250.

b. Support manufacturing costs are currently allocated based on direct labor dollars. Because the deluxe doors are manufactured using the new robotics system, it appears that less direct labor is needed to manufacture each unit in the deluxe product line.

c. The high machine-related costs are probably a result of purchasing the new robotics equipment for the deluxe product line. Yes, the total number of machine hours is the same for each product line, but the deluxe line uses 6 machine hours per unit (300,000 mh / 50,000 units), while the standard product line only uses 0.75 machine hours per unit (300,000 mh / 400,000 units). By evaluating machine hours per unit rather than total machine hours, these numbers make more sense.

d1. Manufacturing overhead cost driver rates:
    Setup activity is $1,000/setup = $500,000/500 setups.
    Machine-related activity is $73.33/machine hour = $44,000,000/600,000 machine hours.
    Packing activity is $20/shipment = $5,000,000/250,000 shipments.

d2. Revised overhead costs per unit:
    Deluxe-entry door is $468 per unit = [($1,000 x 400) + ($73.33 x 300,000) + ($20 x 50,000)] / 50,000 units.
    Standard-entry door is $65.25 per unit = [($1,000 x 100) + ($73.33 x 300,000) + ($20 x 200,000)] / 400,000 units.

d3. Revised total cost per unit for the deluxe-entry door is $648.00 = $180.00 + $468.00.
    Revised total cost per unit for the standard-entry door is $195.25 = $130.00 + $65.25.

e. No, the deluxe door is not as profitable as originally estimated because the deluxe door requires a disproportionate share of the overhead activities (the robotics system) and thus more of the overhead costs are assigned to the deluxe door when using an ABC system.
    Revised profit per unit for the deluxe-entry door is $2.00 = $650.00 - $648.00.
    Revised profit per unit for the standard-entry door is $279.75 = $475.00- $195.25.
    Currently estimated deluxe-entry door profit per unit is $390 = $650 - $260.
    Currently estimated standard-entry door profit per unit is $225 = $475- $250.

f. First, the sales-mix strategy ought to consider the current and future market demands for the two types of entry doors. Other considerations include the capacity-related constraints of the robotics system, other equipment, and the facilities. The fact that customers may be willing to pay more for the deluxe doors should be considered when evaluating the profitability of each product line. Costs do not drive a sales-mix strategy.

Difficulty: 3   *Objectives:* 1,3,5,6

136. Brilliant Accents Company manufactures and sells three styles of kitchen faucets: Brass, Chrome, and White. Production takes 25, 25, and 10 machine hours to manufacture 1,000-unit batches of brass, chrome and white faucets, respectively. The following additional data apply:

	BRASS	CHROME	WHITE
Projected sales in units	#30,000	#50,000	#40,000

PER UNIT data:

	BRASS	CHROME	WHITE
Selling price	$40	$20	$30
Direct materials	$ 8	$ 4	$ 8
Direct labor	$15	$ 3	$ 9
Overhead cost based on direct labor hours (traditional system)	$12	$ 3	$ 9

Hours per 1000-unit batch:

	BRASS	CHROME	WHITE
Direct labor hours	40	10	30
Machine hours	25	25	10
Setup hours	1.0	0.5	1.0
Inspection hours	30	20	20

Total overhead costs and activity levels for the year are estimated as follows:

Activity	Overhead costs	Activity levels
Direct labor hours		2,900 hours
Machine hours		2,400 hours
Setups	$465,500	95 setup hours
Inspections	$405,000	2,700 inspection hours
	$870,500	

Required:

a. Using the traditional system, determine the operating profit per unit for the brass style of faucet.

b. Determine the activity-cost-driver rate for setup costs and inspection costs.

c. Using the ABC system, for the brass style of faucet
   1. compute the estimated overhead costs per unit.
   2. compute the estimated operating profit per unit.

d. Explain the difference between the profits obtained from the traditional system and the ABC system. Which system provides a better estimate of profitability? Why?

136. **Answer:**
a.   Traditional system:
   Operating profit per unit for Brass faucets is $5 = $40 - ($8 + 15 + 12).

b.   The activity-cost-driver rate for setup costs is $4,900 per setup hour = $465,500/95, and for inspection costs is $150 per inspection hour = $405,000/2700.

c.   ABC system:
   *Overhead costs per unit for **Brass faucets** are $9.40 per unit.*
   30,000 units in projected sales / 1000 units per batch = 30 batches;
   30 batches x 1 setup hour per batch = 30 setup hours;
   30 batches x 30 inspection hours per batch = 900 inspection hours.

   30 setup hours x $4,900 = $147,000/30,000 units = $4.90/unit
   900 inspection hours x $150 = $135,000/30,000 units = $4.50/unit
   Overhead costs for Brass faucets ($4.90 + $4.50) = $9.40 per unit.

   Operating profit per unit for Brass faucets is $7.60 = $40 - ($8 + 15 +9.40).

d.   Traditional system: Operating profit per unit for Brass faucets is $5.00.
   ABC system: Operating profit per unit for Brass faucets is $7.60.

   Because the products do not all require the same proportionate shares of the support resources of setup hours and inspection hours, the ABC system provides different results than the traditional system which allocates overhead costs on the basis of direct labor hours. The ABC system considers some important differences in overhead resource requirements and thus provides a better picture of the profitability from each faucet style provided that the activity measures are fairly estimated.

Difficulty: 2   *Objectives*:   1, 3, 5, 6

137. Brilliant Accents Company manufactures and sells three styles of kitchen faucets: Brass, Chrome, and White. Production takes 25, 25, and 10 machine hours to manufacture 1000-unit batches of brass, chrome and white faucets, respectively. The following additional data apply:

	BRASS	CHROME	WHITE
Projected sales in units	#30,000	#50,000	#40,000

PER UNIT data:

	BRASS	CHROME	WHITE
Selling price	$40	$20	$30
Direct materials	$ 8	$ 4	$ 8
Direct labor	$15	$ 3	$ 9
Overhead cost based on direct labor hours (traditional system)	$12	$ 3	$ 9

Hours per 1000-unit batch:

	BRASS	CHROME	WHITE
Direct labor hours	40	10	30
Machine hours	25	25	10
Setup hours	1.0	0.5	1.0
Inspection hours	30	20	20

Total overhead costs and activity levels for the year are estimated as follows:

Activity	Overhead costs	Activity levels
Direct labor hours		2,900 hours
Machine hours		2,400 hours
Setups	$465,500	95 setup hours
Inspections	$405,000	2,700 inspection hours
	$870,500	

Required:

a. Using the traditional system, determine the operating profit per unit for each style of faucet.

b. Determine the activity-cost-driver rate for setup costs and inspection costs.

c. Using the ABC system, for each style of faucet
   1. compute the estimated overhead costs per unit.
   2. compute the estimated operating profit per unit.

d. Explain the differences between the profits obtained from the traditional system and the ABC system. Which system provides a better estimate of profitability? Why?

137. **Answer:**
a.   Traditional system:

Operating profit per unit for Brass faucets is $5 = $40 - ($8 + 15 + 12).
Operating profit per unit for Chrome faucets is $10 = $20 - ($4 + 3 + 3).
Operating profit per unit for White faucets is $4 = $30 - ($8 + 9 + 9)

b.   The activity-cost-driver rate for setup costs is $4,900 per setup hour = $465,500/95, and for inspection costs is $150 per inspection hour = $405,000/2700.

c.   ABC system:

Overhead costs per unit for **Brass faucets** *are $9.40 per unit.*
30,000 units in projected sales / 1,000 units per batch = 30 batches;
30 batches x 1 setup hour per batch = 30 setup hours;
30 batches x 30 inspection hours per batch = 900 inspection hours.

30 setup hours x $4,900 = $147,000/30,000 units = $4.90/unit
900 inspection hours x $150 = $135,000/30,000 units = $4.50/unit
Overhead costs for Brass faucets ($4.90 + $4.50) = $9.40 per unit.

Operating profit per unit for Brass faucets is $7.60 = $40 - ($8 + 15 +9.40).

Overhead costs per unit for **Chrome faucets** *are $5.45 per unit.*
50,000 units in projected sales / 1,000 units per batch = 50 batches;
50 batches x .5 setup hour per batch = 25 setup hours;
50 batches x 20 inspection hours per batch = 1,000 inspection hours.

25 setup hours x $4,900 = $122,500/50,000 units = $2.45/unit
1,000 inspection hours x $150 = $150,000/50,000 units = $3.00/unit
Overhead costs for Chrome faucets ($2.45 + $3.00) = $5.45 per unit.

Operating profit per unit for Chrome faucets is $7.55 = $20 – ($4 + 3 +5.45).

Overhead costs per unit for **White faucets** *are $7.90 per unit.*
40,000 units in projected sales/ 1,000 units per batch = 40 batches;
40 batches x 1 setup hour per batch = 40 setup hours;
40 batches x 20 inspection hours per batch = 800 inspection hours.

40 setup hours x $4,900 = $196,000/40,000 units = $4.90/unit
800 inspection hours x $150 = $120,000/40,000 units = $3.00/unit
Overhead costs for Brass faucets ($4.90 + $3.00) = $7.90 per unit.

Operating profit per unit for White faucets is $5.10 = $30 - ($8 + 9 + 7.90).

137. **Answer:**
d.   Traditional system:

Operating profit per unit for Brass faucets is $5 = $40 - ($8 + 15 + 12).
Operating profit per unit for Chrome faucets is $10 = $20 - ($4 + 3 + 3).
Operating profit per unit for White faucets is $4 = $30 - ($8 + 9 + 9)

ABC system:

Operating profit per unit for Brass faucets is $7.60 = $40 - ($8 + 15 +9.40).
Operating profit per unit for Chrome faucets is $7.55 = $20 – ($4 + 3 +5.45).
Operating profit per unit for White faucets is $5.10 = $30 - ($8 + 9 + 7.90).

Because the products do not all require the same proportionate shares of the overhead resources of setup hours and inspection hours, the ABC system provides different results than the traditional system which allocates overhead costs on the basis of direct labor hours. The ABC system considers some important differences in overhead resource requirements and thus provides a better picture of the profitability from each faucet style provided that the activity measures are fairly estimated.

Difficulty: 3   *Objectives*:   1, 3, 5, 6

138. At Deutschland Electronics, product lines are charged for call center support costs based on sales revenue. Last year's summary of call center operations revealed the following:

	Surveillance Products	Specialty Products
Number of calls for information	1,000	4,000
Average call length for information	3 minutes	8 minutes
Number of calls for warranties	300	1200
Average call length for warranties	7 minutes	15 minutes
Sales revenue	$8,000,000	$5,000,000

Deutschland Electronics currently allocates call center support costs using a rate of 0.5% of sales revenue.

Required:

a. Compute the amount of call center support costs allocated to each product line under the current system.

b. Assume Deutschland decides to use the *average call length for information* to assign last year's support costs. Does this allocation method seem more appropriate than percentage of sales? Why or why not?

c. Assume Deutschland decides to use the *numbers of calls of both types* to assign last year's support costs of $65,000. Compute the amount of call center support costs assigned to each product line under this revised ABC system.

d. Deutschland Electronics assigns bonuses based on departmental profits. How might the Specialty Products manager try to obtain higher profits for next year if support costs are assigned based on the average call length for information?

e. Discuss the barriers for implementing ABC for this call center.

138. **Answer:**
   a. Call center support costs allocated to surveillance products is $40,000 = 0.005 x $8,000,000 and to specialty products is $25,000 = 0.005 x $5,000,000.

   b. Yes, average call length appears to be a more appropriate allocation method because it allocates more support costs to specialty products, which consume a greater portion of the call center's resources.

   c. $65,000 of support costs / 6,500 total calls (Surveillance 1,000 + 300 + Specialty 4,000 + 1,200) = $10 per call.
   Call center support costs allocated to surveillance products is $13,000 = 1,300 calls x $10 per call, and to specialty products is $52,000 = 5,200 calls x $10 per call.

   d. To increase profits, Specialty Product managers would want less cost allocated to their departments. Therefore, if support cost allocation was based on length of call, Specialty Products management may emphasize keeping calls for their department short and to the point, rather than emphasizing understanding and helping the caller.

   e. Poor model design or poor analytical interpretation and accountability consequences may function as barriers to using ABC assignments for the call center activities. It is also important to recognize that the call volumes from this year may be an anomaly so that in an average year, the current allocation rate on sales may not be as distortive as it appears for this year.

Difficulty: 3   *Objectives*: 1, 3, 5, 6, 8

139. For each of the following activities identify an appropriate activity-cost driver.

    a.   Machine maintenance
    b.   Machine setup
    c.   Quality control
    d.   Material ordering
    e.   Production scheduling
    f.   Warehouse expense
    g.   Engineering design

Answer: Any one of the listed cost drivers is correct.

Activity			
A. Machine Maintenance	# of machines	Machine hours	Actual times for various maintenances of various machines
B. Machine Setup	# of setups	Setup hours	Actual times for various setups for various machines
C. Quality Control	# of inspections	Inspection hours	Actual times for various inspections for various controls
D. Material Ordering	# of orders	Ordering hours	Actual times for various orders for various materials
E. Production Scheduling	# of runs	Scheduling hours	Actual times for various runs for various schedules
F. Warehousing	# of bins, aisles	Picking hours	Actual times for various parts for various warehousing activities
G. Engineering Design	# of engineers # of designs	Engineering hours	Actual times for various engineering designs

Difficulty: 2   *Objectives:*   3, 5

140. The Marionettes is noted for an exceptionally impressive line of Mardi Gras masks. Marionettes has established the following selling and distribution support activity-cost pools and their corresponding activity drivers for the year 20X3:

Activity	Cost	Cost driver
Marketing	$30,000	$500,000 of sales
Customer service	10,000	5,000 customer
Order execution	5,000	100 orders
Warehousing	5,000	50 product lines

Required:

a. Determine the activity-cost-driver rate for each of the four selling and distribution activities.

b. Under what circumstances is it appropriate to use each of the activity-cost drivers?

c. Describe at least one possible negative behavioral consequence for each of the four activity-cost drivers.

Answer:

a. Activity-cost driver rate for Marketing = 6% of sales = $30,000/$500,000.
Activity-cost driver rate for Customer Service = $2 per customer = $10,000/5,000.
Activity-cost driver rate for Order Execution = $50 per order = $5,000/100.
Activity-cost driver rate for Warehousing = $100 per order = $5,000/50.

b. For marketing, using 6% of stipulated sales is appropriate when management wants to limit marketing costs to a budgeted proportion to sales. Using the number of customers for customer service is appropriate when the customer service costs are similar enough to use the average for all customers. Using the number of orders for order execution is appropriate when all orders are sufficiently alike in terms of resources used that they can be averaged. Using the number of product lines for warehousing is appropriate when each product line requires similar proportions of the warehousing efforts.

c. For marketing, using 6% of sales limits the marketing activities to an arbitrary amount without consideration for potential opportunities. Using the number of customers for customer service can lead to customer service initiatives to limit the amount of time servicing each customer to cause the number of customers serviced to increase. Using the number of orders for order execution can result in purchasers splitting orders to increase the numbers of orders executed. Using the number of product lines for warehousing can lead warehouse personnel to designate more product line differences in the warehouse.

Difficulty: 3   *Objectives:*   3, 5, 6, 8

CRITICAL THINKING

141. Explain how a top-selling product may actually result in losses for the company.

    Answer:
    If indirect costs are not properly allocated to the products, a product may appear to cost less than it actually does cost to produce. If the selling price is based on these lower costs, the selling price may actually be lower than the costs needed to produce the product resulting in losses for the company.

    Difficulty: 1   *Objective*:   1

142. How are cost drivers selected in activity-based costing systems?

    Answer:
    First, indirect costs are divided into homogeneous cost pools and classified as output unit-level, batch-level, product-sustaining, or facility-sustaining costs. The cost pools correspond to activities. Costs are allocated to products, services, or customers using activity drivers or cost-allocation bases that have a cause-and-effect relationship with each cost pool.
         Choices about how to economize on the number of activity-cost drivers, how to isolate events (because activities triggered by the same event often can use the same activity cost driver), and which cost drivers to select are influenced by the fact that the benefit of obtaining cost driver information needs to exceed implementation costs.

    Difficulty: 2   *Objectives*: 3, 8

143. Explain how activity-based costing systems can provide more accurate product costs than traditional cost systems.

    Answer:
         A key reason for assigning indirect costs using an ABC system rather than a traditional system is that ABC cost systems reflect differences required by different processes. Activity-based costing systems provide better product costs when they identify and cost more indirect cost differences among products. Activity-based costing seeks to distinguish batch-level, product-sustaining, and facility-sustaining costs especially when they are not proportionate to one another.
         Unit-level drivers in traditional cost systems distort product costs because, effectively, these systems assume that all indirect activities affect all products. Thus, these systems assign each unit of product an average cost that fails to recognize the specific activities that are required to produce that product.
         Activity-based costing differs from traditional costing systems in that products are not cross-subsidized by support costs being shared by everyone. Activity-based costing is more likely to result in major differences from traditional costing systems if the firm manufactures multiple products rather than only one product.

    Difficulty: 2   *Objective*:   3

144. Explain how traditional cost systems, using a single unit-level cost rate, may distort product costs.

Answer:
Unit-level measures can distort product costing because the demand for indirect activities may be driven by batch-level, product-sustaining, customer-sustaining, or facility-sustaining activities. Cost distortions are larger when the traditional systems' unit-level cost drivers and the alternative activity-cost drivers differ proportionately more from each other. Traditional systems are likely to undercost products with lower production volumes (relatively fewer units of production) and overcost products with higher production volumes (relatively greater units of production).

Difficulty: 2　　　　　　　*Objective*: 4

145. Do activity-based costing systems always provide more accurate product costs than conventional cost systems? Why or why not?

Answer:
No. Traditional systems contain smaller and fewer cost distortions when the traditional systems' unit-level assignments and the alternative activity-cost drivers are relatively similar in proportion to each other. Still, the use of unit-level measures to assign indirect costs is more likely to undercost low-volume products and more complex products. Both traditional product-costing systems and ABC product-costing systems seek to assign all manufacturing costs to products. Cost distortions occur when a mismatch (incorrect association) occurs between the way support costs are incurred and the basis for their assignment to individual products.

Difficulty: 2　　　　　　　*Objective*: 8

146. How can the need for a more refined costing system be identified?

Answer:
Signs that there is a need for a more refined costing system include
a.　Significant amounts of indirect costs are allocated using only one or two cost pools.
b.　All or most indirect costs are identified as output unit-level costs rather than batch-level, product-sustaining, or facility-sustaining activities.
c.　Products make diverse demands on resources because of differences in volume, process steps, batch size, or complexity.
d.　Products that a company is well suited to make and sell, show small profits; whereas, products that a company is less suited to make and sell, show large profits.
e.　Operations staff have significant disagreements with the accounting staff about the costs of manufacturing and marketing products and services.

Difficulty: 2　　　　　　　*Objective*: 8

CHAPTER 6: MASTER BUDGET AND RESPONSIBILITY ACCOUNTING

TRUE/FALSE

1. Few businesses plan to fail, but many of those that flop have failed to plan.

   Answer: True   *Difficulty:* 1   *Objective:* 1

2. The master budget reflects the impact of operating decisions, but not financing decisions.

   Answer: False   *Difficulty:* 1   *Objective:* 1
   The master budget reflects the impact of operating decisions and financing decisions.

3. Budgeted financial statements are also referred to as pro forma statements.

   Answer: True   *Difficulty:* 1   *Objective:* 1

4. Budgeting includes only the financial aspects of the plan and not any nonfinancial aspects such as the number of physical units manufactured.

   Answer: False   *Difficulty:* 2   *Objective:* 1
   Budgeting includes both financial and nonfinancial aspects of the plan.

5. Budgeting helps management anticipate and adjust for trouble spots in advance.

   Answer: True   *Difficulty:* 1   *Objective:* 1

6. Budgets can play both planning and control roles for management.

   Answer: True   *Difficulty:* 1   *Objective:* 1

7. To create greater commitment to the budget, top-management should create the budget and then share it with lower-level managers.

   Answer: False   *Difficulty:* 3   *Objective:* 2
   To create greater commitment to the budget, lower-level managers should participate in creating the budget.

8. After a budget is agreed upon and finalized by the management team, the amounts should not be changed for any reason.

   Answer: False   *Difficulty:* 2   *Objective:* 2
   Budgets should not be administered rigidly, but rather should be adjusted for changing conditions.

9. Even in the face of changing conditions, attaining the original budget is critical.

    Answer: False   *Difficulty*: 3   *Objective*: 2
    Changing conditions usually call for a change in plans. Attaining the budget should not be an end in itself.

10. A four-quarter rolling budget encourages management to be thinking about the next 12 months.

    Answer: True   *Difficulty*: 2   *Objective*: 2

11. Research has shown that challenging budgets (rather than budgets that can be easily attained) are energizing and improve performance.

    Answer: True   *Difficulty*: 2   *Objective*: 2

12. It is best to compare this year's performance with last year's actual performance rather than this year's budget.

    Answer: False   *Difficulty*: 3   *Objective*: 2
    It is best to compare this year's performance with this year's budget because inefficiencies and different conditions may be reflected in last year's actual performance amounts.

13. Budgets have the potential to compel strategic planning and the implementation of plans.

    Answer: True   *Difficulty*: 2   *Objective*: 2

14. When administered wisely, budgets promote communication and coordination among the various subunits of the organization.

    Answer: True   *Difficulty*: 2   *Objective*: 2

15. Preparation of the budgeted income statement is the final step in preparing the operating budget.

    Answer: True   *Difficulty*: 1   *Objective*: 3

16. The sales forecast should primarily be based on statistical analysis with secondary input from sales managers and sales representatives.

    Answer: False   *Difficulty*: 3   *Objective*: 3
    The sales forecast should be primarily based on input from sales managers and sales representatives with secondary input from statistical analysis.

17. The usual starting point in budgeting is to forecast net income.

Answer: False   *Difficulty:* 2   *Objective:* 3
The usual starting point in budgeting is to forecast sales demand and revenues.

18. The revenues budget should be based on the production budget.

Answer: False   *Difficulty:* 1   *Objective:* 3
The production budget should be based on the revenues budget.

19. The operating budget is that part of the master budget that includes the capital expenditures budget, cash budget, budgeted balance sheet, and the budgeted statement of cash flows.

Answer: False   *Difficulty:* 1   *Objective:* 3
Described is the financial budget part of the master budget, not the operating budget.

20. If budgeted amounts change, the kaizen approach can be used to examine changes in the budgeted results.

Answer: False   *Difficulty:* 2   *Objective:* 4
If budgeted amounts change, *sensitivity analysis* can be used to examine changes in the budgeted results.

21. Computer-based financial planning models are mathematical statements of the interrelationships among operating activities, financial activities, and other factors that affect the budget.

Answer: True   *Difficulty:* 1   *Objective:* 4

22. Most computer-based financial planning models have difficulty incorporating sensitivity (what-if) analysis.

Answer: False   *Difficulty:* 2   *Objective:* 4
Computer-based financial planning models assist management with sensitivity (what-if) analysis.

23. Sensitivity analysis incorporates continuous improvement into budgeted amounts.

Answer: False   *Difficulty:* 1   *Objective:* 5
Kaizen budgeting incorporates continuous improvement into budgeted amounts.

24. The Japanese use kaizen to mean financing alternatives.

Answer: False   *Difficulty:* 1   *Objective:* 5
The Japanese use kaizen to mean *continuous improvement*.

25. Kaizen budgeting does not make sense for profit centers.

   Answer: False   *Difficulty*:   2   *Objective*:   5
   Kaizen budgeting can be used in any type of responsibility center.

26. Kaizen budgeting encourages small incremental changes, rather than major improvements.

   Answer: True   *Difficulty*:   1   *Objective*:   5

27. Activity-based budgeting provides better decision-making information than budgeting based solely on output-based cost drivers (units produced, units sold, or revenues).

   Answer: True   *Difficulty*:   2   *Objective*:   6

28. Activity-based costing analysis takes a long-run perspective and treats all activity costs as variable costs.

   Answer: True   *Difficulty*:   3   *Objective*:   6

29. Activity-based budgeting (ABB) focuses on the budgeting cost of activities necessary to produce and sell products and services.

   Answer: True   *Difficulty*:   1   *Objective*:   6

30. A responsibility center is a part, segment, or subunit of an organization, whose manager is accountable for a specified set of activities.

   Answer: True   *Difficulty*:   1   *Objective*:   7

31. Each manager, regardless of level, is in charge of a responsibility center.

   Answer: True   *Difficulty*:   2   *Objective*:   7

32. In a profit center, a manager is responsible for investments, revenues, and costs.

   Answer: False   *Difficulty*:   1   *Objective*:   7
   In a profit center, a manager is responsible for revenues, and costs, but not investments.

33. A packaging department is MOST likely a profit center.

   Answer: False   *Difficulty*:   2   *Objective*:   7
   A packaging department is most likely a *cost* center.

34. Variances between actual and budgeted amounts inform management about performance relative to the budget.

   Answer: True   *Difficulty*: 1   *Objective*: 7

35. An organization structure is an arrangement of lines of responsibility within the entity.

   Answer: True   *Difficulty*: 1   *Objective*: 8

36. Responsibility accounting focuses on control, not on information and knowledge.

   Answer: False   *Difficulty*: 2   *Objective*: 8
   Responsibility accounting focuses on information and knowledge, not on control.

37. The fundamental purpose of responsibility accounting is to fix blame when budgets are not achieved.

   Answer: False   *Difficulty*: 2   *Objective*: 8
   The fundamental purpose of responsibility accounting is to *gather information* when budgets are not achieved.

38. Human factors are crucial parts of budgeting

   Answer: True   *Difficulty*: 2   *Objective*: 8

39. Budgetary slack provides management with a hedge against unexpected adverse circumstances.

   Answer: True   *Difficulty*: 2   *Objective*: 8

40. Most costs can be easily controlled because they are under the sole influence of one manager.

   Answer: False   *Difficulty*: 3   *Objective*: 8
   Few costs are clearly under the sole influence of one manager.

41. Performance reports of responsibility centers may include uncontrollable items to influence behavior that is in alignment with corporate strategy.

   Answer: True   *Difficulty*: 2   *Objective*: 8

42. When the operating budget is used as a control device, managers are more likely to be motivated to budget higher sales than actually anticipated.

Answer: False   *Difficulty*: 3   *Objective*: 8

When the operating budget is used as a control device, managers are *less* likely to be motivated to budget higher sales than actually anticipated.

43. Budgeting slack is most likely to occur when a firm uses the budget only as a planning device and not for control.

Answer: False   *Difficulty*: 3   *Objective*: 8

Budgeting slack is most likely to occur when a firm uses the budget for *control*.

44. If a cost is considered controllable, it indicates that all aspects of the cost are under the control of the manager of the responsibility center to which that cost is assigned.

Answer: False   *Difficulty*: 2   *Objective*: 8

A controllable cost is any cost that is primarily subject to the *influence* of a given responsibility manager.

45. A key use of sensitivity analysis is for cash-flow budgeting.

Answer: True   *Difficulty*: 1   *Objective*: A

46. The self-liquidating cycle is the movement from cash to inventories to receivables and back to cash.

Answer: True   *Difficulty*: 1   *Objective*: A

MULTIPLE CHOICE

47. Budgeting is used to help companies
    a. plan to better satisfy customers.
    b. anticipate potential problems.
    c. focus on opportunities.
    d. do all of the above.

    Answer: d   *Difficulty:* 2   *Objective:* 1

48. A master budget
    a. includes only financial aspects of a plan and excludes nonfinancial aspects.
    b. is an aid to coordinating what needs to be done to implement a plan.
    c. includes broad expectations and visionary results.
    d. should not be altered after it has been agreed upon.

    Answer: b   *Difficulty:* 2   *Objective:* 1

49. Operating decisions PRIMARILY deal with
    a. the use of scarce resources.
    b. how to obtain funds to acquire resources.
    c. acquiring equipment and buildings.
    d. satisfying stockholders.

    Answer: a   *Difficulty:* 2   *Objective:* 1

50. Financing decisions PRIMARILY deal with
    a. the use of scarce resources.
    b. how to obtain funds to acquire resources.
    c. acquiring equipment and buildings.
    d. preparing financial statements for stockholders.

    Answer: b   *Difficulty:* 2   *Objective:* 1

51. Budgeting provides all of the following EXCEPT
    a. a means to communicate the organization's short-term goals to its members.
    b. support for the management functions of planning and coordination.
    c. a means to anticipate problems.
    d. an ethical framework for decision making.

    Answer: d   *Difficulty:* 2   *Objective:* 1

52. If initial budgets prove unacceptable, planners achieve the MOST benefit from
    a. planning again in light of feedback and current conditions.
    b. deciding not to budget this year.
    c. accepting an unbalanced budget.
    d. using last year's budget.

    Answer: a   *Difficulty:* 2   *Objective:* 1

53. Operating budgets and financial budgets
    a. combined form the master budget.
    b. are prepared before the master budget.
    c. are prepared after the master budget.
    d. have nothing to do with the master budget.

    Answer: a *Difficulty:* 1 *Objective:* 1

54. A good budgeting system forces managers to examine the business as they plan, so they can
    a. detect inaccurate historical records.
    b. set specific expectations against which actual results can be compared.
    c. complete the budgeting task on time.
    d. get promoted for doing a good job.

    Answer: b *Difficulty:* 2 *Objective:* 1

55. A budget should/can do all of the following EXCEPT
    a. be prepared by managers from different functional areas working independently of each other.
    b. be adjusted if new opportunities become available during the year.
    c. help management allocate limited resources.
    d. become the performance standard against which firms can compare the actual results.

    Answer: a *Difficulty:* 3 *Objective:* 2

56. A limitation of comparing a company's performance against actual results of last year is that
    a. it includes adjustments for future conditions.
    b. feedback is no longer a possibility.
    c. past results can contain inefficiencies of the past year.
    d. the budgeting time period is set at one year.

    Answer: c *Difficulty:* 2 *Objective:* 2

57. Challenging budgets tend to
    a. decrease line-management participation in attaining corporate goals.
    b. increase failure.
    c. increase anxiety without motivation.
    d. motivate improved performance.

    Answer: d *Difficulty:* 2 *Objective:* 2

58. A company's actual performance should be compared against budgeted amounts for the same accounting period so that
   a.   adjustments for future conditions can be included.
   b.   limited feedback is possible.
   c.   inefficiencies of the past year can be included.
   d.   a rolling budget can be implemented.

   Answer: a   *Difficulty:*   2   *Objective:*   2

59. It is advantageous to coordinate budgets with
   a.   suppliers.
   b.   customers.
   c.   the marketing and production departments.
   d.   all of the above.

   Answer: d   *Difficulty:*   3   *Objective:*   2

60. A budget can help implement
   a.   strategic planning.
   b.   long-run planning.
   c.   short-run planning.
   d.   all of the above.

   Answer: d   *Difficulty:*   2   *Objective:*   2

61. To gain the benefits of budgeting _____ must understand and support the budget.
   a.   management at all levels
   b.   customers
   c.   suppliers
   d.   all of the above

   Answer: a   *Difficulty:*   3   *Objective:*   2

62. Participation of line managers in the budgeting process helps to create
   a.   greater commitment.
   b.   greater anxiety.
   c.   better judgment.
   d.   better past performance.

   Answer: a   *Difficulty:*   2   *Objective:*   2

63. Line managers who feel that top management does not believe in the budget are MOST likely to
   a.   pick up the slack and participate in the budgeting process.
   b.   be motivated by the budget.
   c.   spend little time on the budgeting process.
   d.   convert the budget to a shorter more reasonable time period.

   Answer: c   *Difficulty:*   2   *Objective:*   2

64. The time coverage of a budget should be
    a.   one year.
    b.   guided by the purpose of the budget.
    c.   cover design through manufacture and sale of the product.
    d.   shorter rather than longer.

    Answer: b   *Difficulty:*   2   *Objective:*   2

65. Rolling budgets help management to
    a.   better review the past calendar year.
    b.   deal with a 5-year time frame.
    c.   focus on the upcoming budget period.
    d.   rigidly administer the budget.

    Answer: c   *Difficulty:*   2   *Objective:*   2

66. Budgets should
    a.   be flexible.
    b.   be administered rigidly.
    c.   be developed for short periods of time.
    d.   include only variable costs.

    Answer: a   *Difficulty:*   2   *Objective:*   2

67. Operating budgets include all EXCEPT
    a.   the revenues budget.
    b.   the budgeted income statement.
    c.   the administrative costs budget.
    d.   the budgeted balance sheet.

    Answer: d   *Difficulty:*   1   *Objective:*   3

68. Operating budgets include the
    a.   budgeted balance sheet.
    b.   budgeted income statement.
    c.   capital expenditures budget.
    d.   budgeted statement of cash flows.

    Answer: b   *Difficulty:*   1   *Objective:*   3

69. The operating budget process generally concludes with the preparation of the
    a.   production budget.
    b.   distribution budget.
    c.   research and development budget.
    d.   budgeted income statement.

    Answer: d   *Difficulty.*   1   *Objective:*   3

70. Financial budgets include the
    a. capital expenditures budget.
    b. production budget.
    c. marketing costs budget.
    d. administrative costs budget.

    Answer: a   *Difficulty*: 1   *Objective*: 3

71. _____ includes a budgeted statement of cash flows and a budgeted balance sheet.
    a. An annual report
    b. The financial budget
    c. The operating budget
    d. The capital expenditures budget

    Answer: b   *Difficulty*: 1   *Objective*: 3

72. The order to follow when preparing the operating budget is
    a. revenues budget, production budget, and direct manufacturing labor costs budget.
    b. costs of goods sold budget, production budget, and cash budget.
    c. revenues budget, manufacturing overhead costs budget, and production budget.
    d. cash expenditures budget, revenues budget, and production budget.

    Answer: a   *Difficulty*: 2   *Objective*: 3

73. In which order are the following developed? First to last:
                    A = Production budget   B = Direct materials costs budget
                    C = Budgeted income statement D = Revenues budget
    a. A, B, D, C
    b. D, A, B, C
    c. D, C, A, B
    d. C, A, B, D

    Answer: b   *Difficulty*: 2   *Objective*: 3

74. The budgeting process is MOST strongly influenced by
    a. the capital budget.
    b. the budgeted statement of cash flows.
    c. the sales forecast.
    d. the production budget.

    Answer: c   *Difficulty*: 2   *Objective*: 3

75. _____ is the usual starting point for budgeting.
    a. The revenues budget
    b. Net income
    c. The production budget
    d. The cash budget

    Answer: a   *Difficulty*: 1   *Objective*: 3

76. The sales forecast should be PRIMARILY based on
    a. statistical analysis.
    b. input from sales managers and sales representatives.
    c. production capacity.
    d. input from the board of directors.

    Answer: b   *Difficulty*: 2   *Objective*: 3

77. The sales forecast is influenced by
    a. advertising and sales promotions.
    b. competition.
    c. general economic conditions.
    d. all of the above.

    Answer: d   *Difficulty*: 2   *Objective*: 3

78. A sales forecast is
    a. often the outcome of elaborate information gathering and discussions among sales managers.
    b. developed primarily to prepare next year's marketing campaign.
    c. solely based on sales of the previous year.
    d. a summary of product costs that influence pricing decisions.

    Answer: a   *Difficulty*: 2   *Objective*: 3

79. The revenues budget identifies
    a. expected cash flows for each product.
    b. actual sales from last year for each product.
    c. the expected level of sales for the company.
    d. the variance of sales from actual for each product.

    Answer: c   *Difficulty*: 1   *Objective*: 3

80. The number of units in the sales budget and the production budget may differ because of a change in
    a. finished goods inventory levels.
    b. overhead charges.
    c. direct material inventory levels.
    d. sales returns and allowances.

    Answer: a   *Difficulty*: 3   *Objective*: 3

81. Production is primarily based on
    a. projected inventory levels.
    b. the revenues budget.
    c. the administrative costs budget.
    d. the capital expenditures budget.

    Answer: b   *Difficulty*: 2   *Objective*: 3

82. Budgeted production depends on
    a. the direct materials usage budget and direct material purchases budget.
    b. the direct manufacturing labor budget.
    c. budgeted sales and expected changes in inventory levels.
    d. the manufacturing overhead costs budget.

    Answer: c   *Difficulty*: 2   *Objective*: 3

83. The direct materials usage budget is based on
    a. the units to be produced during a period.
    b. budgeted sales dollars.
    c. the predetermined factory overhead rate.
    d. the amount of labor-hours worked.

    Answer: a   *Difficulty*: 1   *Objective*: 3

84. Direct material purchases equal
    a. production needs.
    b. production needs plus target ending inventories.
    c. production needs plus beginning inventories.
    d. production needs plus target ending inventories less beginning inventories.

    Answer: d   *Difficulty*: 1   *Objective*: 3

85. Individual budgeted amounts included in the manufacturing overhead costs budget are based on input from
    a. operating personnel.
    b. costs incurred in prior years.
    c. cost changes expected in the future.
    d. all of the above.

    Answer: d   *Difficulty*: 3   *Objective*: 3

86. The manufacturing overhead costs budget includes budgeted amounts for
    a. direct materials.
    b. direct manufacturing labor.
    c. indirect manufacturing labor.
    d. all of the above.

    Answer: c   *Difficulty*: 3   *Objective*: 3

87. Budgeted manufacturing overhead costs include all types of factory expenses EXCEPT
    a. fixed items such as depreciation of manufacturing machinery.
    b. variable items such as plant supplies.
    c. indirect labor such as the salary of the plant supervisor.
    d. direct labor and direct materials.

    Answer: d   *Difficulty*: 2   *Objective*: 3

88. Schultz Company expects to manufacture and sell 30,000 baskets in 20x4 for $6 each. There are 3,000 baskets in beginning finished goods inventory with target ending inventory of 4,000 baskets. The company keeps no work-in-process inventory. What amount of sales revenue will be reported on the 20x4 budgeted income statement?
   a. $174,000
   b. $180,000
   c. $186,000
   d. $204,000

   Answer: b   *Difficulty:*   3   *Objective:*   3
   30,000 x $6 = $180,000

89. DeArmond Corporation has budgeted sales of 18,000 units, target ending finished goods inventory of 3,000 units, and beginning finished goods inventory of 900 units. How many units should be produced next year?
   a.   21,900 units
   b.   20,100 units
   c.   15,900 units
   d.   18,000 units

   Answer: b   *Difficulty:*   2   *Objective:*   3
   18,000 + 3,000 - 900 = 20,100 units

90. For next year, Galliart, Inc., has budgeted sales of 60,000 units, target ending finished goods inventory of 3,000 units, and beginning finished goods inventory of 1,800 units. All other inventories are zero. How many units should be produced next year?
   a.   58,800 units
   b.   60,000 units
   c.   61,200 units
   d.   64,800 units

   Answer: c   *Difficulty:*   2   *Objective:*   3
   60,000 + 3,000 - 1,800 = 61,200 units

91. Wilgers Company has budgeted sales volume of 30,000 units and budgeted production of 27,000 units. 5,000 units are in beginning finished goods inventory. How many units are targeted for ending finished goods inventory?
   a.   5,000 units
   b.   8,000 units
   c.   3,000 units
   d.   2,000 units

   Answer: d   *Difficulty:*   2   *Objective:*   3
   5,000 + 27,000 - 30,000 = 2,000

THE FOLLOWING INFORMATION APPLIES TO QUESTIONS 92 THROUGH 95.
Marguerite, Inc., expects to manufacture and sell 20,000 pool cues for $12.00 each. Direct materials costs are $2.00, direct manufacturing labor is $4.00, and manufacturing overhead is $0.80 per pool cue. The following inventory levels apply to 20x4:

	Beginning inventory	Ending inventory
Direct materials	24,000 units	24,000 units
Work-in-process inventory	0 units	0 units
Finished goods inventory	2,000 units	2,500 units

92. On the 20x4 budgeted income statement, what amount will be reported for sales?
    a. $246,000
    b. $240,000
    c. $312,000
    d. $318,000

    Answer: b   *Difficulty:* 2   *Objective:* 3
    20,000 x $12 = $240,000

93. How many pool cues need to be produced in 20x4?
    a. 22,500 cues
    b. 22,000 cues
    c. 20,500 cues
    d. 19,500 cues

    Answer: c   *Difficulty:* 2   *Objective:* 3
    20,000 + 2,500 - 2,000 = 20,500 cues

94. On the 20x4 budgeted income statement, what amount will be reported for cost of goods sold?
    a. $139,400
    b. $136,000
    c. $132,600
    d. $153,000

    Answer: b   *Difficulty:* 3   *Objective:* 3
    20,000 x ($4.00 + $2.00 + $0.80) = $136,000

95. What are the 20x4 budgeted costs for direct materials, direct manufacturing labor, and manufacturing overhead, respectively?
    a. $0; $96,000; $19,200
    b. $39,000; $78,000; $15,600
    c. $80,000; $40,000; $16,000
    d. $41,000; $82,000; $16,400

    Answer: d   *Difficulty:* 3   *Objective:* 3
    20,500 x $2.00 = $41,000; 20,500 x $4.00 = $82,000; 20,500 x $0.80 = $16,400

THE FOLLOWING INFORMATION APPLIES TO QUESTIONS 96 THROUGH 99.
Daniel, Inc. expects to manufacture and sell 6,000 ceramic vases for $20 each. Direct materials costs are $2, direct manufacturing labor is $10, and manufacturing overhead is $3 per vase. The following inventory levels apply to 20x4:

	Beginning inventory	Ending inventory
Direct materials	1,000 units	1,000 units
Work-in-process inventory	0 units	0 units
Finished goods inventory	400 units	500 units

96. On the 20x4 budgeted income statement, what amount will be reported for sales?
    a. $122,000
    b. $118,000
    c. $140,000
    d. $120,000

    Answer: d   *Difficulty*:   2   *Objective*:   3
    6,000 x $20 = $120,000

97. How many ceramic vases need to be produced in 20x4?
    a.   5,900 vases
    b.   6,100 vases
    c.   7,000 vases
    d.   6,000 vases

    Answer: b   *Difficulty*:   2   *Objective*:   3
    6,000 + 500 - 400 = 6,100 vases

98. On the 20x4 budgeted income statement, what amount will be reported for cost of goods sold?
    a. $91,500
    b. $105,000
    c. $90,000
    d. $88,500

    Answer: c   *Difficulty*:   3   *Objective*:   3
    6,000 x ($2 + $10 + $3) = $90,000

99. What are the 20x4 budgeted costs for direct materials, direct manufacturing labor, and manufacturing overhead, respectively?
    a. $12,200; $61,000; $18,300
    b. $12,000; $60,000; $18,000
    c. $2,000; $10,000; $3,000
    d. $2,000; $0; $18,000

    Answer: a   *Difficulty*:   3   *Objective*:   3
    6,100 x $2 = $12,200; 6,100 x $10 = $61,000; 6,100 x $3 = $18,300

THE FOLLOWING INFORMATION APPLIES TO QUESTIONS 100 THROUGH 102.
The following information pertains to the January operating budget for Casey Corporation, a retailer:

Budgeted sales are $200,000 for January
Collections of sales are 50% in the month of sale and 50% the next month
Cost of goods sold averages 70% of sales
Merchandise purchases total $150,000 in January
Marketing costs are $3,000 each month
Distribution costs are $5,000 each month
Administrative costs are $10,000 each month

100. For January, budgeted gross margin is
    a. $100,000.
    b. $140,000.
    c. $60,000.
    d. $50,000.

    Answer: c   *Difficulty*:   3   *Objective*:   3
    $200,000 - $140,000 = $60,000

101. For January, the amount budgeted for the nonmanufacturing costs budget is
    a. $78,000.
    b. $10,000.
    c. $168,000.
    d. $18,000.

    Answer: d   *Difficulty*:   2   *Objective*:   3
    $3,000 + $5,000 + $10,000 = $18,000

102. For January, budgeted net income is
    a. $42,000.
    b. $60,000.
    c. $50,000.
    d. $52,000.

    Answer: a   *Difficulty*:   3   *Objective*:   3
    $200,000 - $140,000 - $3,000 - $5,000 - $10,000 = $42,000

THE FOLLOWING INFORMATION APPLIES TO QUESTIONS 103 THROUGH 106.
Konrade, Inc., expects to manufacture and sell 30,000 athletic uniforms for $80 each in 20x4. Direct materials costs are $20, direct manufacturing labor is $8, and manufacturing overhead is $6 for each uniform. The following inventory levels apply to 20x4:

	Beginning inventory	**Ending inventory**
Direct materials	12,000 units	9,000 units
Work-in-process inventory	0 units	0 units
Finished goods inventory	6,000 units	5,000 units

103. How many uniforms need to be produced in 20x4?
    a.   26,000 uniforms
    b.   34,000 uniforms
    c.   30,000 uniforms
    d.   29,000 uniforms

    Answer: d   *Difficulty:*   2   *Objective:*   3
    30,000 + 5,000 - 6,000 = 29,000 uniforms

104. What is the amount budgeted for direct material purchases in 20x4?
    a. $520,000
    b. $600,000
    c. $580,000
    d. $760,000

    Answer: a   *Difficulty:*   3   *Objective:*   3
    29,000 units + 9,000 - 12,000 = Purchases 26,000 x $20 = $520,000

105. What is the amount budgeted for cost of goods manufactured in 20x4?
    a. $1,020,000
    b. $986,000
    c. $1,156,000
    d. $1,190,000

    Answer: b   *Difficulty:*   3   *Objective:*   3
    29,000 x ($20 + $8 + $6) = $986,000

106. What is the amount budgeted for cost of goods sold in 20x4?
    a. $1,156,000
    b. $986,000
    c. $1,020,000
    d. $2,400,000

    Answer: c   *Difficulty:*   3   *Objective:*   3
    30,000 x ($20 + $8 + $6) = $1,020,000

THE FOLLOWING INFORMATION APPLIES TO QUESTIONS 107 AND 108.
Furniture, Inc., estimates the following number of mattress sales for the first four months of 20x4:

Month	Sales
January	5,000
February	7,000
March	6,500
April	8,000

Finished goods inventory at the end of December is 1,500 units. Target ending finished goods inventory is 30% of next month's sales.

107. How many mattresses need to be produced in January 20x4?
   a.   4,400 mattresses
   b.   5,600 mattresses
   c.   6,500 mattresses
   d.   7,100 mattresses

   Answer: b   *Difficulty*: 2   *Objective*: 3
   5,000 + (7,000 x 0.30) - $1,500 = 5,600 mattresses

108. How many mattresses need to be produced in the first quarter (January, February, March) of 20x4?
   a.   18,500 mattresses
   b.   19,400 mattresses
   c.   20,900 mattresses
   d.   22,400 mattresses

   Answer: b   *Difficulty*: 2   *Objective*: 3
   5,000 + 7,000 + 6,500 + (8,000 x 0.30) - 1,500 = 19,400 mattresses

THE FOLLOWING INFORMATION APPLIES TO QUESTIONS 109 AND 110.
Wallace Company provides the following data for next year:

Month	Budgeted Sales
January	$120,000
February	108,000
March	132,000
April	144,000

The gross profit rate is 40% of sales. Inventory at the end of December is $21,600 and target ending inventory levels are 30% of next month's sales, stated at cost.

109. Purchases budgeted for January total
   a. $130,800.
   b. $72,000.
   c. $69,840.
   d. $74,160.

   Answer: c   *Difficulty*: 3   *Objective*: 3
   ($120,000 x 0.6) + ($108,000 x 0.6 x 0.3) - $21,600 = $69,840

110. Purchases budgeted for February total
    a.　$69,120.
    b.　$60,480.
    c.　$115,200.
    d.　$64,800.

Answer:　a　　　　　　　*Difficulty*:　3　　　　　　　*Objective*:　3
($108,000 x 0.6) + ($132,000 x 0.6 x 0.3) - ($108,000 x 0.6 x 0.3) = $69,120

111. Financial planning software packages assist management with
    a.　assigning responsibility to various levels of management.
    b.　identifying the target customer.
    c.　sensitivity analysis in their planning and budgeting activities.
    d.　achieving greater commitment from lower management

Answer:　c　　　　　　　*Difficulty*:　2　　　　　　　*Objective*:　4

112. _____ utilizes a "what-if" technique that examines how results will change if the originally predicted data changes.
    a.　A sales forecast
    b.　A sensitivity analysis
    c.　A pro forma financial statement
    d.　The statement of cash flows

Answer:　b　　　　　　　*Difficulty*:　1　　　　　　　*Objective*:　4

113. When performing a sensitivity analysis, if the selling price per unit is increased, then the
    a.　per unit fixed administrative costs will increase.
    b.　per unit direct materials purchase price will increase.
    c.　total volume of sales will increase.
    d.　total costs for sales commissions and other nonmanufacturing variable costs will increase.

Answer:　d　　　　　　　*Difficulty*:　3　　　　　　　*Objective*:　4

THE FOLLOWING INFORMATION APPLIES TO QUESTIONS 114 THROUGH 116.
Ossmann Enterprises reports year-end information from 20x4 as follows:

Sales (80,000 units)	$480,000
Cost of goods sold	320,000
Gross margin	160,000
Operating expenses	130,000
Operating income	$ 30,000

Ossmann is developing the 20x5 budget. In 20x5 the company would like to increase selling prices by 8%, and as a result expects a decrease in sales volume of 10%. All other operating expenses are expected to remain constant. Assume that COGS is a variable cost and that operating expenses are a fixed cost.

114. What is budgeted sales for 20x5?
    a. $518,400
    b. $533,333
    c. $466,560
    d. $432,000

Answer: c   *Difficulty:*   3   *Objective:*   4
$480,000 x 1.08 x 0.90 = $466,560

115. What is budgeted cost of goods sold for 20x5?
    a. $311,040
    b. $288,000
    c. $345,600
    d. $320,000

Answer: b   *Difficulty:*   3   *Objective:*   4
$320,000 x 0.90 = $288,000

116. Should Ossmann increase the selling price in 20x5?
    a.   Yes, because operating income is increased for 20x5.
    b.   Yes, because sales revenue is increased for 20x5.
    c.   No, because sales volume decreases for 20x5.
    d.   No, because gross margin decreases for 20x5.

Answer: a   *Difficulty:*   3   *Objective:*   4
$466,560 - $288,000 - 130,000 = $48,560   Yes, because it would result in an increase in operating income compared to 20x4.

THE FOLLOWING INFORMATION APPLIES TO QUESTIONS 117 THROUGH 119.
Katie Enterprises reports the year-end information from 20x4 as follows:

Sales (70,000 units)	$560,000
Cost of goods sold	210,000
Gross margin	350,000
Operating expenses	200,000
Operating income	$ 150,000

Katie is developing the 20x5 budget. In 20x5 the company would like to increase selling prices by 4%, and as a result expects a decrease in sales volume of 10%. All other operating expenses are expected to remain constant. Assume that COGS is a variable cost and that operating expenses are a fixed cost.

117. What is budgeted sales for 20x5?
    a. $582,400
    b. $524,160
    c. $504,000
    d. $560,000

Answer: b   *Difficulty*:   3   *Objective*:   4
$560,000 x 1.04 x 0.90 = $524,160

118. What is budgeted cost of goods sold for 20x5?
    a. $189,000
    b. $196,560
    c. $218,400
    d. $210,000

Answer: a   *Difficulty*:   3   *Objective*:   4
$210,000 x 0.90 = $189,000

119. Should Katie increase the selling price in 20x5?
    a.   Yes, because sales revenue is increased for 20x5.
    b.   Yes, because operating income is increased for 20x5.
    c.   No, because sales volume decreases for 20x5.
    d.   No, because gross margin decreases for 20x5.

Answer: d   *Difficulty*:   3   *Objective*:   4
$524,160 - $189,000 = $335,160 gross margin - $200,000 = $135,160 operating income. No, because there would be a decrease in gross margin and operating income compared to 20x4.

120. The Japanese use the term kaizen when referring to
    a.   scarce resources.
    b.   pro forma financial statements.
    c.   continuous improvement.
    d.   the sales forecast.

Answer: c   *Difficulty*:   1   *Objective*:   5

121. Kaizen refers to incorporating cost reductions
    a.   in each successive budgeting period.
    b.   in each successive sales forecast.
    c.   in all customer service centers.
    d.   in all of the above.

    Answer: a   *Difficulty:*   2   *Objective:*   5

122. All of the following are encouraged with kaizen budgeting EXCEPT
    a.   better interactions with suppliers.
    b.   large discontinuous improvements.
    c.   cost reductions during manufacturing.
    d.   systematic monthly cost reductions.

    Answer: b   *Difficulty:*   3   *Objective:*   5

THE FOLLOWING INFORMATION APPLIES TO QUESTIONS 123 AND 124.
Dan and Donna Enterprises are using the kaizen approach to budgeting for 20x5. The budgeted income statement for January 20x5 is as follows:

Sales (84,000 units)	$500,000
Less: Cost of goods sold	300,000
Gross margin	200,000
Operating expenses (includes $50,000 of fixed costs)	150,000
Operating income	$ 50,000

Under the kaizen approach, cost of goods sold and variable operating expenses are budgeted to decline by 1% per month.

123. What is budgeted cost of goods sold for March 20x5?
    a. $294,030
    b. $294,000
    c. $300,000
    d. $297,000

    Answer: a   *Difficulty:*   3   *Objective:*   5
    $300,000 x 0.99 x 0.99 = $294,030

124. What is budgeted gross margin for March 20x5?
    a. $196,020
    b. $198,000
    c. $204,020
    d. $205,970

    Answer: d   *Difficulty:*   3   *Objective:*   5
    $500,000 - $294,030 = $205,970

125. The use of activity-based budgeting is growing because of
    a.   the increased use of activity-based costing.
    b.   the increased use of kaizen costing.
    c.   increases in work-in-process inventory.
    d.   increases in direct materials inventory.

    Answer: a   *Difficulty:*   1   *Objective:*   6

126. Activity-based budgeting would separately estimate
    a.   the cost of overhead for a department.
    b.   a plant-wide cost-driver rate.
    c.   the cost of a setup activity.
    d.   all of the above.

    Answer: c   *Difficulty:*   2   *Objective:*   6

127. Activity-based-costing analysis makes no distinction between
    a.   direct-materials inventory and work-in-process inventory.
    b.   short-run variable costs and short-run fixed costs.
    c.   parts of the supply chain.
    d.   components of the value chain.

    Answer: b   *Difficulty:*   3   *Objective:*   6

128. Activity-based budgeting makes it easier
    a.   to determine a rolling budget.
    b.   to prepare pro forma financial statements.
    c.   to determine how to reduce costs.
    d.   to execute a financial budget.

    Answer: c   *Difficulty:*   3   *Objective:*   6

129. Activity-based budgeting does NOT require
    a.   knowledge of the organization's activities.
    b.   specialized expertise in financial management and control.
    c.   knowledge about how activities affect costs.
    d.   the ability to see how the organization's different activities fit together.

    Answer: b   *Difficulty:*   3   *Objective:*   6

130. Activity-based budgeting
    a.   uses one cost driver such as direct labor-hours.
    b.   uses only output-based cost drivers such as units sold.
    c.   focuses on activities necessary to produce and sell products and services.
    d.   classifies costs by functional area within the value chain.

    Answer: c   *Difficulty:*   1   *Objective:*   6

131. Activity-based budgeting includes all the following steps EXCEPT
    a.   determining demands for activities from sales and production targets.
    b.   computing the cost of performing activities.
    c.   determining a separate cost-driver rate for each department.
    d.   describing the budget as costs of activities rather than costs of functions.

    Answer: c   *Difficulty:*   2   *Objective:*   6

132. Variances between actual and budgeted amounts can be used to
    a.   alert managers to potential problems and available opportunities.
    b.   inform managers about how well the company has implemented its strategies.
    c.   signal that company strategies are ineffective.
    d.   do all of the above.

    Answer: d   *Difficulty:*   2   *Objective:*   7

133. A maintenance manager is MOST likely responsible for
    a.   a revenue center.
    b.   an investment center.
    c.   a cost center.
    d.   a profit center.

    Answer: c   *Difficulty:*   1   *Objective:*   7

134. The regional sales office manager of a national firm is MOST likely responsible for
    a.   a revenue center.
    b.   an investment center.
    c.   a cost center.
    d.   a profit center.

    Answer: a   *Difficulty:*   1   *Objective:*   7

135. A regional manager of a restaurant chain in charge of finding additional locations for expansion is MOST likely responsible for
    a.   a revenue center.
    b.   an investment center.
    c.   a cost center.
    d.   a profit center.

    Answer: b   *Difficulty:*   1   *Objective:*   7

136. The manager of a hobby store that is part of a chain of stores is MOST likely responsible for
    a.   a revenue center.
    b.   an investment center.
    c.   a cost center.
    d.   a profit center.

    Answer: d   *Difficulty:*   1   *Objective:*   7

137. A manager of a revenue center is responsible for all of the following EXCEPT
    a.   service quality and units sold.
    b.   the acquisition cost of the product or service sold.
    c.   price, product mix, and promotional activities.
    d.   sales and marketing costs.

    Answer: b   *Difficulty:*   2   *Objective:*   7

138. A manager of a profit center is responsible for all of the following EXCEPT
    a.   sales revenue.
    b.   the cost of merchandise purchased for resale.
    c.   expanding into new geographic areas.
    d.   selling and marketing costs.

    Answer: c   *Difficulty:*   2   *Objective:*   7

139. A controllable cost is any cost that can be _____ by a responsibility center manager for a period of time.
    a.   controlled
    b.   influenced
    c.   segregated
    d.   excluded

    Answer: b   *Difficulty:*   2   *Objective:*   8

140. Controllability may be difficult to pinpoint because of all EXCEPT
    a.   some costs depend on market conditions.
    b.   current managers may have inherited inefficiencies of a previous manager.
    c.   the current use of stretch or challenge targets.
    d.   few costs are under the sole influence of one manager.

    Answer: c   *Difficulty:*   2   *Objective:*   8

141. Responsibility accounting
    a.   emphasizes controllability.
    b.   focuses on whom should be asked about the information.
    c.   attempts to assign blame for problems to a specific manager.
    d.   does all of the above.

    Answer: b   *Difficulty:*   3   *Objective:*   8

142. A PRIMARY consideration in assigning a cost to a responsibility center is
    a.   whether the cost is fixed or variable.
    b.   whether the cost is direct or indirect.
    c.   who can best explain the change in that cost.
    d.   where in the organizational structure the cost was incurred.

    Answer: c   *Difficulty:*   3   *Objective:*   8

143. Building in budgetary slack includes
    a.   overestimating budgeted revenues.
    b.   underestimating budgeted costs.
    c.   making budgeted targets more easily achievable.
    d.   all of the above.

Answer: c   *Difficulty*: 2   *Objective*: 8

144. To reduce budgetary slack management may
    a.   incorporate stretch or challenge targets.
    b.   use external benchmark performance measures.
    c.   award bonuses for achieving budgeted amounts.
    d.   reduce projected cost targets by 10% across all areas.

Answer: b   *Difficulty*: 3   *Objective*: 8

145. Financial analysts use the projected cash flow statement to do all of the following EXCEPT
    a.   plan for when excess cash is generated.
    b.   plan for short-term cash investments.
    c.   project cash shortages and plan a strategy to deal with the shortages.
    d.   project depreciation expense.

Answer: d   *Difficulty*: 2   *Objective*: A

146. The cash flow statement does NOT include
    a.   cash inflows from the collection of receivables.
    b.   cash outflows paid toward raw material purchases.
    c.   all sales revenues.
    d.   interest paid and received.

Answer: c   *Difficulty*: 2   *Objective*: A

147. The cash budget is a schedule of expected cash receipts and disbursements that
    a.   requires an aging of accounts receivable and accounts payable.
    b.   is a self-liquidating cycle.
    c.   is prepared immediately after the sales forecast.
    d.   predicts the effect on the cash position at given levels of operations.

Answer: d   *Difficulty*: 1   *Objective*: A

THE FOLLOWING INFORMATION APPLIES TO QUESTIONS 148 THROUGH 151.
The following information pertains to Tiffany Company:

Month	Sales	Purchases
January	$30,000	$16,000
February	$40,000	$20,000
March	$50,000	$28,000

- Cash is collected from customers in the following manner:
  Month of sale   30%
  Month following the sale   70%
- 40% of purchases are paid for in cash in the month of purchase, and the balance is paid the following month.
- Labor costs are 20% of sales. Other operating costs are $15,000 per month (including $4,000 of depreciation). Both of these are paid in the month incurred.
- The cash balance on March 1 is $4,000. A minimum cash balance of $3,000 is required at the end of the month. Money can be borrowed in multiples of $1,000.

148. How much cash will be collected from customers in March?
    a. $47,000
    b. $43,000
    c. $50,000
    d.   None of the above

Answer: b   *Difficulty*:   2   *Objective*:   A
($40,000 x 70%) + ($50,000 x 30%) = $43,000

149. How much cash will be paid to suppliers in March?
    a. $23,200
    b. $28,000
    c. $44,000
    d.   None of the above

Answer: a   *Difficulty*:   2   *Objective*:   A
($20,000 x 60%) + ($28,000 x 40%) = $23,200

150. How much cash will be disbursed in total in March?
    a. $21,000
    b. $25,000
    c. $44,200
    d. $48,200

Answer: c   *Difficulty*:   2   *Objective*:   A
$23,200 + ($50,000 x 20%) + ($15,000 -$4,000) = $44,200

151. What is the ending cash balance for March?
    a.   ($25,000)
    b. $3,000
    c. $3,200
    d. $3,800

Answer: d   *Difficulty:*   2   *Objective:*   A
$4,000 + $43,000 - $44,200 + $1,000 = $3,800

THE FOLLOWING INFORMATION APPLIES TO QUESTIONS 152 THROUGH 154.
Fiscal Company has the following sales budget for the last six months of 20x3:

July	$100,000	October	$ 90,000
August	80,000	November	100,000
September	110,000	December	94,000

Historically, the cash collection of sales has been as follows:
    65% of sales collected in the month of sale,
    25% of sales collected in the month following the sale,
    8% of sales collected in the second month following the sale, and
    2% of sales are uncollectible.

152. Cash collections for September are
    a. $71,500.
    b. $86,700.
    c. $99,500.
    d. $102,000.

Answer: c   *Difficulty:*   2   *Objective:*   A
($110,000 x 0.65) + ($80,000 x 0.25) + ($100,000 x 0.08) = $99,500

153. What is the ending balance of accounts receivable for September, assuming
    uncollectible balances are written off during the second month following the sale?
    a. $99,500
    b. $48,500
    c. $44,900
    d. $46,500

Answer: d   *Difficulty:*   2   *Objective:*   A
($110,000 x 0.35) + ($80,000 x 0.10) = $46,500

154. Cash collections for October are
    a. $58,500.
    b. $92,400.
    c. $99,500.
    d. $88,200.

Answer: b   *Difficulty:*   2   *Objective:*   A
($90,000 x 0.65) + ($110,000 x 0.25) + ($80,000 x 0.08) = $92,400

THE FOLLOWING INFORMATION APPLIES TO QUESTIONS 155 THROUGH 157.
Bear Company has the following information:

Month	Budgeted Purchases
January	$26,800
February	29,000
March	30,520
April	29,480
May	27,680

Purchases are paid for in the following manner:
  10% in the month of purchase
  50% in the month after purchase
  40% two months after purchase

155. What is the expected balance in Accounts Payable as of March 31?
    a. $39,068
    b. $18,312
    c. $2,900
    d. $30,520

Answer: a   *Difficulty:* 2   *Objective:* A
($30,520 x 0.9) + ($29,000 x 0.4) = $39,068

156. What is the expected balance in Accounts Payable as of April 30?
    a. $26,532
    b. $38,740
    c. $12,208
    d. $17,688

Answer: b   *Difficulty:* 2   *Objective:* A
($29,480 x 0.9) + ($30,520 x 0.4) = $38,740

157. What is the expected Accounts Payable balance as of May 31?
    a. $11,792
    b. $24,912
    c. $36,704
    d. $2,948

Answer: c   *Difficulty:* 2   *Objective:* A
($27,680 x 0.9) + ($29,480 x 0.4) = $36,704

THE FOLLOWING INFORMATION APPLIES TO QUESTIONS 158 THROUGH 163.
The following information pertains to the January operating budget for Casey Corporation.
- Budgeted sales for January $100,000 and February $200,000.
- Collections for sales are 60% in the month of sale and 40% the next month.
- Gross margin is 30% of sales.
- Administrative costs are $10,000 each month.
- Beginning accounts receivable $20,000.
- Beginning inventory $14,000.
- Beginning accounts payable $60,000. (All from inventory purchases.)
- Purchases are paid in full the following month.
- Desired ending inventory is 20% of next month's cost of goods sold (COGS).

158. For January, budgeted cash collections are
    a. $20,000.
    b. $60,000.
    c. $80,000.
    d.   none of the above.

Answer: c   *Difficulty*: 3   *Objective*: A
$20,000 + ($100,000 x 60%) = $80,000

159. At the end of January, budgeted accounts receivable is
    a. $20,000.
    b. $40,000.
    c. $60,000.
    d.   none of the above.

Answer: b   *Difficulty*: 2   *Objective*: A
$100,000 x 40% = $40,000

160. For January, budgeted cost of goods sold is
    a. $20,000.
    b. $30,000.
    c. $40,000.
    d.   none of the above.

Answer: d   *Difficulty*: 3   *Objective*: A
$100,000 x 70% = $70,000

161. For January, budgeted net income is
    a. $20,000.
    b. $30,000.
    c. $40,000.
    d.   none of the above.

Answer: a   *Difficulty*: 3   *Objective*: A
$100,000 - $70,000 - $10,000 = $20,000

162. For January, budgeted cash payments for purchases are
    a. $14,000.
    b. $70,000.
    c. $60,000
    d.   none of the above.

    Answer: c   *Difficulty*:   2   *Objective*:   A
    Accounts payable, $60,000 as stated

163. At the end of January, budgeted ending inventory is
    a. $20,000.
    b. $28,000.
    c. $40,000.
    d.   none of the above.

    Answer: b   *Difficulty*:   3   *Objective*:   A
    $200,000 x 70% x 20% = $28,000

164. Spirit Company sells three products with the following seasonal sales pattern:

| | Products | | |
Quarter	A	B	C
1	40%	30%	10%
2	30%	20%	40%
3	20%	20%	40%
4	10%	30%	10%

The annual sales budget shows forecasts for the different products and their expected selling price per unit as follows:

Product	Units	Selling Price
A	50,000	$ 4
B	125,000	10
C	62,500	6

Required:

Prepare a sales budget, in units and dollars, by quarters for the company for the coming year.

Answer:	First Quarter	Second Quarter	Third Quarter	Fourth Quarter	Total
Product A:					
Sales (units)	20,000	15,000	10,000	5,000	50,000
Price	x $4	x $4	x $4	x $4	x $4
Sales ($)	$80,000	$60,000	$40,000	$20,000	$200,000
Product B:					
Sales (units)	37,500	25,000	25,000	37,500	125,000
Price	x $10	x $10	x $10	x $10	x $10
Sales ($)	$375,000	$250,000	$250,000	$375,000	$1,250,000
Product C:					
Sales (units)	6,250	25,000	25,000	6,250	62,500
Price	x $6	x $6	x $6	x $6	x $6
Sales ($)	$37,500	$150,000	$150,000	$37,500	$375,000
Total dollars	$492,500	$460,000	$440,000	$432,500	$1,825,000

Difficulty: 2   *Objective*: 3

165. Lubriderm Corporation has the following budgeted sales for the next six-month period:

Month	Unit Sales
June	90,000
July	120,000
August	210,000
September	150,000
October	180,000
November	120,000

There were 30,000 units of finished goods in inventory at the beginning of June. Plans are to have an inventory of finished products that equal 20% of the unit sales for the next month.

Five pounds of materials are required for each unit produced. Each pound of material costs $8. Inventory levels for materials are equal to 30% of the needs for the next month. Materials inventory on June 1 was 15,000 pounds.

Required:

a.   Prepare production budgets in units for July, August, and September.
b.   Prepare a purchases budget in pounds for July, August, and September, and give total purchases in both pounds and dollars for each month.

Answer:

a.

	July	August	September
Budgeted sales	120,000	210,000	150,000
Add: Required ending inventory	42,000	30,000	36,000
Total inventory requirements	162,000	240,000	186,000
Less: Beginning inventory	24,000	42,000	30,000
Budgeted production	138,000	198,000	156,000

b.

	July	August	September
Production in units	138,000	198,000	156,000
Targeted ending inventory in lbs.*	297,000	234,000	ˮ252,000
Production needs in lbs.***	690,000	990,000	780,000
Total requirements in lbs.	987,000	1,224,000	1,032,000
Less: Beginning inventory in lbs.	****207,000	297,000	234,000
Purchases needed in lbs.	780,000	927,000	798,000
Cost ($8 per lb.)	x $8	x $8	x $8
Total material purchases	$6,240,000	$7,416,000	$6,384,000

*   0.3 times next month's needs
**   (180,000 + 24,000 - 36,000) times 5 lbs. x 0.3
*** 5 lbs. times units to be produced
**** (690,000 x .3) = 207,000 lbs.

Difficulty: 3   *Objective*: 3

166. Gerdie Company has the following information:

Month	Budgeted Sales
March	$50,000
April	53,000
May	51,000
June	54,500
July	52,500

In addition, the gross profit rate is 40% and the desired inventory level is 30% of next month's cost of sales.

Required:
Prepare a purchases budget for April through June.

Answer:	**April**	**May**	**June**	**Total**
Desired ending inventory	$ 9,180	$ 9,810	$ 9,450	$ 9,450
Plus COGS	31,800	30,600	32,700	95,100
Total needed	40,980	40,410	42,150	104,550
Less beginning inventory	9,540	9,180	9,810	9,540
Total purchases	$31,440	$31,230	$32,340	$ 95,010

Difficulty: 2   *Objective*: 3

167. Picture Pretty manufactures picture frames. Sales for August are expected to be 10,000 units of various sizes. Historically, the average frame requires four feet of framing, one square foot of glass, and two square feet of backing. Beginning inventory includes 1,500 feet of framing, 500 square feet of glass, and 500 square feet of backing. Current prices are $0.30 per foot of framing, $6.00 per square foot of glass, and $2.25 per square foot of backing. Ending inventory should be 150% of beginning inventory. Purchases are paid for in the month acquired.

Required:

a. Determine the quantity of framing, glass, and backing that is to be purchased during August.
b. Determine the total costs of direct materials for August purchases.

Answer:

a.

	Framing	Glass	Backing
Desired ending inventory*	2,250	750	750
Production needs (10,000 units)**	40,000	10,000	20,000
Total needs	42,250	10,750	20,750
Less: Beginning inventory	1,500	500	500
Purchases planned	40,750	10,250	20,250

b. *Cost of direct materials*:

Framing (40,750 x $0.30)	$12,225.00
Glass (10,250 x $6.00)	61,500.00
Backing (20,250 x $2.25)	45,562.50
Total	$119,287.50

*1,500 x 1.5 = 2,250
500 x 1.5 = 750

**10,000 x 4 = 40,000
10,000 x 1 = 10,000
10,000 x 2 = 20,000

Difficulty: 2   *Objective*: 3

168. Michelle Enterprises reports the year-end information from 20x2 as follows:

Sales (100,000 units)	$250,000
Less: Cost of goods sold	150,000
Gross profit	100,000
Operating expenses (includes $10,000 of Depreciation)	60,000
Net income	$ 40,000

Michelle is developing the 20x3 budget. In 20x3 the company would like to increase selling prices by 10%, and as a result expects a decrease in sales volume of 5%. Cost of goods sold as a percentage of sales is expected to increase to 62%. Other than depreciation, all operating costs are variable.

Required:

Prepare a budgeted income statement for 20x3.

Answer:

Michelle Enterprises
Budgeted Income Statement
For the Year 20x3

Sales (95,000 x $2.75)	$261,250
Cost of goods sold (20x3 sales x 62%)	161,975
Gross profit	99,275
Less: Operating expenses [($0.50 x 95,000] + $10,000)	57,500
Net income	$ 41,775

Difficulty: 2   *Objective*: 4

169. Brad Corporation is using the kaizen approach to budgeting for 20x5. The budgeted income statement for January 20x5 is as follows:

Sales (240,000 units)	$720,000
Less: Cost of goods sold	480,000
Gross margin	240,000
Operating expenses (includes $64,000 of fixed costs)	192,000
Net income	$ 48,000

Under the kaizen approach, cost of goods sold and variable operating expenses are budgeted to decline by 1% per month.

Required:

Prepare a kaizen-based budgeted income statement for March of 20x5.

Answer:

Sales	$720,000
Less: Cost of goods sold ($480,000 x 0.99 x 0.99)	470,448
Gross margin	249,552
Operating expenses [($128,000 x 0.99 x 0.99) + $64,000]	189,453
Net income	$ 60,099

Difficulty: 2   *Objective*: 5

170. Allscott Company is developing its budgets for 20x5 and, for the first time, will use the kaizen approach. The initial 20x5 income statement, based on static data from 20x4, is as follows:

Sales (140,000 units)	$420,000
Less: Cost of goods sold	280,000
Gross margin	140,000
Operating expenses (includes $28,000 of depreciation)	112,000
Net income	$28,000

Selling prices for 20x5 are expected to increase by 8%, and sales volume in units will decrease by 10%. The cost of goods sold as estimated by the kaizen approach will decline by 10% per unit. Other than depreciation, all other operating costs are expected to decline by 5%.

Required:

Prepare a kaizen-based budgeted income statement for 20x5.

Answer:

Sales (126,000 x $3.24)	$408,240
Less: COGS (126,000 x $1.80)	226,800
Gross margin	181,440
Operating expenses ($28,000 + $79,800)	107,800
Net income	$ 73,640

Difficulty: 2   *Objectives*: 4, 5

171. Russell Company has the following projected account balances for June 30, 20x3:

Accounts payable	$40,000	Sales	$800,000
Accounts receivable	100,000	Capital stock	400,000
Depreciation, factory	24,000	Retained earnings	?
Inventories (5/31 & 6/30)	180,000	Cash	56,000
Direct materials used	200,000	Equipment, net	240,000
Office salaries	80,000	Buildings, net	400,000
Insurance, factory	4,000	Utilities, factory	16,000
Plant wages	140,000	Selling expenses	60,000
Bonds payable	160,000	Maintenance, factory	28,000

Required:

a. Prepare a budgeted income statement for June 20x3.
b. Prepare a budgeted balance sheet as of June 30, 20x3.

Answer:

a.

Russell Company
Income Statement
For the Month of June 20x3

Sales		$800,000
Cost of goods sold:		
Materials used	$200,000	
Wages	140,000	
Depreciation	24,000	
Insurance	4,000	
Maintenance	28,000	
Utilities	16,000	412,000
Gross profit		$388,000
Operating expenses:		
Selling expenses	$60,000	
Office salaries	80,000	140,000
Net income		$248,000

b.

Russell Company
Balance Sheet
June 30, 20x3

Assets:		**Liabilities and Owners' Equity:**	
Cash	$ 56,000	Accounts payable	$ 40,000
Accounts receivable	100,000	Bonds payable	160,000
Inventories	180,000	Capital stock	400,000
Equipment, net	240,000	Retained earnings*	376,000
Buildings, net	400,000		
Total	$976,000	Total	$976,000

*$976,000 – ($40,000 + $160,000 + $400,000) = $376,000

Difficulty: 2   *Objectives*: 3, A

172. Duffy Corporation has prepared the following sales budget:

Month	Cash Sales	Credit Sales
May	$16,000	$68,000
June	20,000	80,000
July	18,000	74,000
August	24,000	92,000
September	22,000	76,000

Collections are 40% in the month of sale, 45% in the month following the sale, and 10% two months following the sale. The remaining 5% is expected to be uncollectible.

Required:

Prepare a schedule of cash collections for July through September.

Answer:

	July	August	September	Total
Cash sales	$18,000	$24,000	$22,000	$64,000
Collections of credit sales from:				
Current month	29,600	36,800	30,400	96,800
Previous month	36,000	33,300	41,400	110,700
Two months ago	6,800	8,000	7,400	22,200
Total collections	$90,400	$102,100	$101,200	$293,700

Difficulty: 2   *Objective*: A

173. The following information pertains to Amigo Corporation:

Month	Sales	Purchases
July	$30,000	$10,000
August	34,000	12,000
September	38,000	14,000
October	42,000	16,000
November	48,000	18,000
December	60,000	20,000

- Cash is collected from customers in the following manner:

Month of sale (2% cash discount)	30%
Month following sale	50%
Two months following sale	15%
Amount uncollectible	5%

- 40% of purchases are paid for in cash in the month of purchase, and the balance is paid the following month.

Required:

a. Prepare a summary of cash collections for the 4th quarter.
b. Prepare a summary of cash disbursements for the 4th quarter.

Answer:

a. Cash collections Oct $36,448 + Nov $40,812 + Dec $47,940 = $125,200

	October	November	December
August	$ 5,100		
September	19,000	5,700	
October	12,348	21,000	6,300
November		14,112	24,000
December			17,640
	--------	---------	--------
	$36,448	$40,812	$47,940

b. Cash disbursements Oct $14,800 + Nov $16,800 + Dec $18,800 = $50,400

	October	November	December
September	8,400		
October	6,400	9,600	
November		7,200	10,800
December			8,000
	--------	---------	--------
	$14,800	$16,800	$18,800

Difficulty: 2   *Objective:* A

CRITICAL THINKING

174. Describe the benefits to an organization of preparing an operating budget.

Answer:

A well-prepared operating budget should serve as a guide for a company to follow during the budgeted period. It is not "set in stone." If new information or opportunities arise, the budget should be adjusted.

A well-prepared operating budget assists management with the allocation of scarce resources. It can help management see trouble spots in advance, and decide where to allocate its limited resources.

A well-prepared operating budget fosters communication and coordination among various segments of the company. The process of preparing a budget requires managers from different functional areas to work together and communicate performance levels they both want and can attain.

A well-prepared operating budget can become the performance standard against which firms can compare the actual results.

Difficulty: 2   *Objective*:   1

175. Bob and Dale have just purchased a small honey manufacturing company that was having financial difficulties. After a brief operating period, they decided that the company's main problem was lack of any financial planning. The company made a good product and market potential was great.

Required:

Explain why a company needs a good budgeting plan. Specifically address the need for a master budget.

Answer:

The master budget is a series of interrelated budgets that quantify management's expectations about a company's revenues, expenses, net income, cash flows, and financial position. When administered wisely, a budget
1.   compels strategic planning and implementation of plans,
2.   provides a framework for judging performance,
3.   motivates managers and employees, and
4.   promotes coordination and communication among subunits within the company.

Difficulty: 2   *Objective*: 1

176. Describe operating and financial budgets and give at least two examples of each discussed in the textbook.

Answer:

Operating budgets specify the expected outcomes of any selling, manufacturing, purchasing, labor management, R&D, marketing, distribution, customer service, and administrative activities during the planning period. Operations personnel use these plans to guide and coordinate activities during the planning period.

Examples of operating budgets include the revenues budget, production budget, direct materials costs budget, direct manufacturing labor costs budget, manufacturing overhead budget, and budgets for R&D, marketing, distribution, customer service, and administrative activities.

Financial budgets are used to evaluate the financial consequences of a proposed decision.

Examples of financial budgets include the capital expenditures budget, cash budget, budgeted balance sheet, and the budgeted statement of cash flows.

Difficulty: 2   *Objective*:   3

177. Discuss the importance of the sales forecast and items that influence its accuracy.

Answer:

All other budgets are based on information from the sales forecast.

The sales forecast is a challenge to predict because its accuracy depends on the ability to forecast the state of the general economy, changes in the industry, actions of the competition, and developments in technology. Each of these items affects individual products or product lines and are quantified and aggregated to obtain the sales forecast.

Difficulty: 2   *Objective*:   3

178. Distinguish between controllable and uncontrollable aspects of revenue and costs. Can a manager totally control all revenue and costs? Why or why not?

Answer:

Although no revenue or cost can be totally controlled, a cost or revenue is a controllable item when a manager has significant influence over the amount of a cost or revenue. It is uncontrollable if this is not the case. A manager's ability to influence costs and revenues depends on two factors: (1) the manager's level of authority, and (2) the time period involved. Costs and revenue contracts, the economic costs of disposing of fixed assets, and the economy are three conditions that are likely to affect the period of time during which an item is not controllable.

Difficulty: 2   *Objective*: 7

179. Describe some of the drawbacks of using the operating budget as a control device.

Answer:

When the operating budget is used as a control device it can lead to behavior that is actually detrimental to the organization.

The major problem with the budget performance report is not the report itself, but rather the way it is used. In general, managers are rewarded for favorable variances, and disciplined for unfavorable variances. This encourages managers to set lax standards for both sales and costs so favorable variances result. It can also lead to "budget games."

Another drawback is that once the budget is established if there is any variance between budget and actual, it is assumed to be because of actual. However, as we know, the budget will never be totally accurate due to the uncertainties of predicting the future.

If used properly, however, the operating budget can be a tremendous benefit to any company.

Difficulty: 2   *Objective*:   8

180. What is budget slack? What are the pros and cons of building slack into the budget from the point of view of (a) an employee and (b) a senior manager?

Answer:

Budget slack occurs when subordinates (a) ask for excess resources above and beyond what they need to accomplish budget objectives and (b) distort information by claiming they are not as efficient or effective at what they do, thus lowering management's performance expectations of them.

Employee's point of view: There are two benefits from this point of view. First, the subordinate may be able to obtain excess resources to achieve desired goals. This may take a lot of pressure off the subordinate and reduce job anxiety. Second, the subordinate may be able to convince senior management to lower their work expectations of him or her. This may also lead to lower pressure on the subordinate to perform. Both of these types of slack building are designed to reduce job stress for the subordinate. However, if incentives are graduated in such a way that achieving higher and higher goals provides the subordinate with more and more compensation in the form of bonuses, then the subordinate may lose income by selecting lower goals.

Senior management's point of view: When subordinates build in slack, they are either using unnecessary resources to achieve a goal that they should have been able to achieve with fewer resources, or they are understating their performance capabilities. Thus, the organization is either not running as efficiently as it can, or is losing potential productivity from employees who are not working as hard as they can. In some cases, senior management may believe that subordinates build in slack to relieve job pressure. If burnout of employees has been happening in the organization, then perhaps senior management may be more forgiving and view some slack building as necessary to keep their employees from quitting.

Difficulty: 2   *Objective*:   8

CHAPTER 7: FLEXIBLE BUDGETS, VARIANCES, AND MANAGEMENT CONTROL: I

TRUE/FALSE

1. The master budget is one type of flexible budget.

   Answer: False   *Difficulty*: 1   *Objective*: 1
   The master budget is a *static* budget.

2. A flexible budget is calculated at the start of the budget period.

   Answer: False   *Difficulty*: 1   *Objective*: 1
   A flexible budget is calculated at the *end* of the budget period when actual output is known.

3. Information regarding the causes of variances is provided when the master budget is compared with actual results.

   Answer: False   *Difficulty*: 2   *Objective*: 1
   Little information regarding the causes of variances is provided when the master budget is compared with actual results because you are comparing a budget for one level of activity with actual costs for a different level of activity.

4. A favorable variance results when budgeted revenues exceed actual revenues.

   Answer: False   *Difficulty*: 2   *Objective*: 1
   An *unfavorable* variance results when budgeted revenues exceed actual revenues.

5. Management by exception is the practice of concentrating on areas not operating as anticipated (such as a cost overrun) and placing less attention on areas operating as anticipated.

   Answer: True   *Difficulty*: 1   *Objective*: 1

6. The essence of variance analysis is to capture a departure from what was expected.

   Answer: True   *Difficulty*: 1   *Objective*: 1

7. A favorable variance should be ignored by management.

   Answer: False   *Difficulty*: 1   *Objective*: 1
   Favorable variance investigation may lead to improved production methods, other discoveries for future opportunities, or not be good news at all and adversely affect other variances.

8. An unfavorable variance may be due to poor planning rather than due to inefficiency.

   Answer: True   *Difficulty*: 2   *Objective*: 1

9. If budgets contain slack, cost variances will tend to be favorable.

    Answer: True *Difficulty:* 2 *Objective:* 1

10. The only difference between the static budget and flexible budget is that the static budget is prepared using planned output.

    Answer: True *Difficulty:* 2 *Objective:* 2

11. The static-budget variance can be subdivided into the flexible-budget variance and the sales-volume variance.

    Answer: True *Difficulty:* 2 *Objective:* 2

12. The flexible-budget variance may be the result of inaccurate forecasting of units sold.

    Answer: False *Difficulty:* 3 *Objective:* 2
    The *sales-volume* variance is the result of inaccurate forecasting of units sold.

13. Decreasing demand for a product may create a favorable sales-volume variance.

    Answer: False *Difficulty:* 2 *Objective:* 2
    Decreasing demand for a product may create an *unfavorable* sales-volume variance.

14. An unfavorable variance is conclusive evidence of poor performance.

    Answer: False *Difficulty:* 2 *Objective:* 2
    An unfavorable variance suggests further investigation, not conclusive evidence of poor performance.

15. A company would not need to use a flexible budget if it had perfect foresight about actual output units.

    Answer: True *Difficulty:* 2 *Objective:* 2

16. The flexible-budget variance pertaining to revenues is often called a selling-price variance.

    Answer: True *Difficulty:* 1 *Objective:* 2

17. Cost control is the focus of the sales-volume variance.

    Answer: False *Difficulty:* 2 *Objective:* 2
    The sales-volume variance is not a measure of cost, but rather a measure of actual output units differing from budgeted output units.

18. Managers generally have more control over efficiency variances than price variances.

    Answer: True   *Difficulty*: 3   *Objective*: 3
    Efficiency variances are primarily affected by internal factors, whereas price changes may be influenced by market factors.

19. To prepare budgets based on actual data from past periods is preferred since past inefficiencies are excluded.

    Answer: False   *Difficulty*: 2   *Objective*: 3
    A deficiency of using budgeted input quantity information based on actual quantity data from past periods is that past inefficiencies are included.

20. All budgets are based on standard costs.

    Answer: False   *Difficulty*: 2   *Objective*: 3
    Budgets may be based on standard costs, actual amounts from last year, or data from other companies.

21. A standard is attainable through efficient operations but allows for normal disruptions such as machine breakdowns and defective production.

    Answer: True   *Difficulty*: 3   *Objective*: 3

22. The presumed cause of a material price variance will determine how a company responds.

    Answer: True   *Difficulty*: 1   *Objective*: 4

23. The use of high-quality raw materials is likely to result in a favorable efficiency variance and an unfavorable price variance.

    Answer: True   *Difficulty*: 2   *Objective*: 4

24. The direct manufacturing labor price variance is likely to be favorable if higher-skilled workers are put on a job.

    Answer: False   *Difficulty*: 2   *Objective*: 4
    The direct manufacturing labor variance is likely to be unfavorable if higher-skilled workers are put on a job since they are usually also higher paid.

25. Although computed separately, price variances and efficiency variances should not be analyzed separately from each other.

    Answer: True   *Difficulty*: 2   *Objective*: 4

26. A favorable variance can be automatically interpreted as "good news."

Answer: False *Difficulty*: 1 *Objective*: 5
A favorable variance may not be good news at all because it adversely affects other variances that increase total costs.

27. Variances often affect each other.

Answer: True *Difficulty*: 1 *Objective*: 5

28. If variance analysis is used for performance evaluation, managers are encouraged to meet targets using creativity and resourcefulness.

Answer: False *Difficulty*: 2 *Objective*: 5
The most common outcome when variance analysis is used for performance evaluation is that managers seek targets that are easily attainable and avoid targets that require creativity and resourcefulness.

29. For critical items such as product defects, a small variance may prompt investigation.

Answer: True *Difficulty*: 2 *Objective*: 5

30. A particular variance generally signals one particular problem.

Answer: False *Difficulty*: 1 *Objective*: 5
There are many potential causes of a single variance.

31. Continuous improvement budgeted costs target price reductions and efficiency improvements.

Answer: True *Difficulty*: 1 *Objective*: 6

32. Improvement opportunities are easier to identify when products have been on the market for a considerable period of time.

Answer: False *Difficulty*: 2 *Objective*: 6
Improvement opportunities are easier to identify when products are first produced.

33. It is best to rely totally on financial performance measures rather than using a combination of financial and nonfinancial performance measures.

Answer: False *Difficulty*: 2 *Objective*: 6
It is best to rely on a combination of financial and nonfinancial performance measures.

34. From the perspective of control, the direct materials price variance should be isolated at the time the direct materials are requisitioned for use.

   Answer: False   *Difficulty:*   2   *Objective:*   6
   From the perspective of control, the direct materials price variance should be isolated at the earliest possible time, which is at the *time of purchase* not of use.

35. Employees logging in to production floor terminals and other modern technologies greatly facilitate the use of a standard costing system.

   Answer: True   *Difficulty:*   1   *Objective:*   6

36. Performance variance analysis can be used in activity-based costing systems.

   Answer: True   *Difficulty:*   1   *Objective:*   7

37. Price variances can be calculated for batch-level costs as well as for output unit-level costs.

   Answer: True   *Difficulty:*   1   *Objective:*   7

38. Benchmarking is the continuous process of measuring products, services, and activities against the best possible levels of performance, either inside or outside the organization.

   Answer: True   *Difficulty:*   1   *Objective:*   8

39. When benchmarking, the best levels of performance are typically found in companies that are totally different.

   Answer: False   *Difficulty:*   1   *Objective:*   8
   When benchmarking, the best levels of performance are typically found in competing companies or in companies having similar processes

40. One problem with benchmarking is ensuring that numbers are comparable.

   Answer: True   *Difficulty:*   1   *Objective:*   8

41. When benchmarking it is best when management accountants simply analyze the costs and allow management to provide the insight as to why the revenues and costs differ between companies.

   Answer: False   *Difficulty:*   1   *Objective:*   8
   When benchmarking, management accountants are more valuable when they analyze the costs and also provide management with insight as to why the revenues and costs differ between companies.

42. The master budget is
    a. a flexible budget.
    b. a static budget.
    c. developed at the end of the period.
    d. based on the actual level of output.

    Answer: b   *Difficulty*: 1   *Objective*: 1

43. A flexible budget
    a. is another name for management by exception.
    b. is developed at the end of the period.
    c. is based on the budgeted level of output.
    d. provides favorable operating results.

    Answer: b   *Difficulty*: 1   *Objective*: 1

44. Management by exception is the practice of concentrating on
    a. the master budget.
    b. areas not operating as anticipated.
    c. favorable variances.
    d. unfavorable variances.

    Answer: b   Difficulty: 1   Objective: 1

45. A variance is
    a. the gap between an actual result and a benchmark amount.
    b. the required number of inputs for one standard output.
    c. the difference between an actual result and a budgeted amount.
    d. the difference between a budgeted amount and a standard amount.

    Answer: c   *Difficulty*: 1   *Objective*: 1

46. An unfavorable variance indicates that
    a. actual costs are less than budgeted costs.
    b. actual revenues exceed budgeted revenues.
    c. the actual amount decreased operating income relative to the budgeted amount.
    d. all of the above are true.

    Answer: c   *Difficulty*: 2   *Objective*: 1

47. A favorable variance indicates that
    a. budgeted costs are less than actual costs.
    b. actual revenues exceed budgeted revenues.
    c. the actual amount decreased operating income relative to the budgeted amount.
    d. all of the above are true.

    Answer: b   *Difficulty*: 2   *Objective*: 1

THE FOLLOWING INFORMATION APPLIES TO QUESTIONS 48 THROUGH 50.
Abernathy Corporation used the following data to evaluate their current operating system.
The company sells items for $10 each and used a budgeted selling price of $10 per unit.

	Actual	**Budgeted**
Units sold	92,000 units	90,000 units
Variable costs	$450,800	$432,000
Fixed costs	$ 95,000	$100,000

48. What is the static-budget variance of revenues?
    a. $20,000 favorable
    b. $20,000 unfavorable
    c. $2,000 favorable
    d. $2,000 unfavorable

Answer: a   *Difficulty*: 2   *Objective*: 1
(92,000 units x $10) - (90,000 units x $10) = $20,000 F

49. What is the static-budget variance of variable costs?
    a. $1,200 favorable
    b. $18,800 unfavorable
    c. $20,000 favorable
    d. $1,200 unfavorable

Answer: b   *Difficulty*: 2   *Objective*: 1
$450,800 - $432,000 = $18,800 U

50. What is the static-budget variance of operating income?
    a. $3,800 favorable
    b. $3,800 unfavorable
    c. $6,200 favorable
    d. $6,200 unfavorable

Answer: c   *Difficulty*: 2   *Objective*: 1

	Actual Results	**Static Budget**	**Static-budget Variance**	
Units sold	92,000	90,000		
Revenues	$920,000	$900,000	$20,000	F
Variable costs	450,800	432,000	18,800	U
Contribution margin	$469,200	$468,000	$1,200	F
Fixed costs	95,000	100,000	(5,000)	F
Operating income	$374,200	$368,000	$6,200	F

THE FOLLOWING INFORMATION APPLIES TO QUESTIONS 51 THROUGH 53.
Bates Corporation used the following data to evaluate their current operating system. The company sells items for $10 each and used a budgeted selling price of $10 per unit.

	Actual	**Budgeted**
Units sold	495,000 units	500,000 units
Variable costs	$1,250,000	$1,500,000
Fixed costs	$ 925,000	$ 900,000

51. What is the static-budget variance of revenues?
   a. $50,000 favorable
   b. $50,000 unfavorable
   c. $5,000 favorable
   d. $5,000 unfavorable

   Answer: b   *Difficulty*: 2   *Objective*: 1
   (495,000 units x $10) - (500,000 units x $10) = $50,000 U

52. What is the static-budget variance of variable costs?
   a. $200,000 favorable
   b. $50,000 unfavorable
   c. $250,000 favorable
   d. $250,000 unfavorable

   Answer: c   *Difficulty*: 2   *Objective*: 1
   $1,250,000 - $1,500,000= $250,000 F

53. What is the static-budget variance of operating income?
   a. $175,000 favorable
   b. $195,000 unfavorable
   c. $225,000 favorable
   d. $325,000 unfavorable

   Answer: a   *Difficulty*: 2   *Objective*: 1

	Actual Results	**Static Budget**	**Static-budget Variance**
Units sold	495,000	500,000	
Revenues	$4,950,000	$5,000,000	$(50,000) U
Variable costs	1,250,000	1,500,000	(250,000) F
Contribution margin	$3,700,000	$3,500,000	$200,000 F
Fixed costs	925,000	900,000	25,000 U
Operating income	$2,775,000	$2,600,000	$175,000 F

54. Regier Company had planned for operating income of $10 million in the master budget but actually achieved operating income of only $7 million.
    a.   The static-budget variance for operating income is $3 million favorable.
    b.   The static-budget variance for operating income is $3 million unfavorable.
    c.   The flexible-budget variance for operating income is $3 million favorable.
    d.   The flexible-budget variance for operating income is $3 million unfavorable.

    Answer: b   *Difficulty:*   2   *Objective:*   1

55. The flexible budget contains
    a.   budgeted amounts for actual output.
    b.   budgeted amounts for planned output.
    c.   actual costs for actual output.
    d.   actual costs for planned output.

    Answer: a   *Difficulty:*   1   *Objective:*   2

56. The following items are the same for the flexible budget and the master budget EXCEPT
    a.   the same variable cost per unit.
    b.   the same total fixed costs.
    c.   the same units sold.
    d.   the same sales price per unit.

    Answer: c   *Difficulty:*   2   *Objective:*   2

57. The sales-volume variance is due to
    a.   using a different selling price from that budgeted.
    b.   inaccurate forecasting of units sold.
    c.   poor production performance.
    d.   both (a) and (b).

    Answer: b   *Difficulty:*   2   *Objective:*   2

58. An unfavorable sales-volume variance could result from
    a.   decreased demand for the product.
    b.   competitors taking market share.
    c.   customer dissatisfaction with the product.
    d.   all of the above.

    Answer: d   *Difficulty:*   2   *Objective:*   2

59. If a sales-volume variance was caused by poor-quality products, then the _____ would be in the best position to explain the variance.
    a.   production manager
    b.   sales manager
    c.   purchasing manager
    d.   management accountant

    Answer: a   *Difficulty:*   2   *Objective:*   2

60. The variance that is BEST for measuring operating performance is the
    a. static-budget variance.
    b. flexible-budget variance.
    c. sales-volume variance.
    d. selling-price variance.

    Answer: b   *Difficulty:* 2   *Objective:* 2

61. An unfavorable flexible-budget variance for variable costs may be the result of
    a. using more input quantities than were budgeted.
    b. paying higher prices for inputs than were budgeted.
    c. selling output at a higher selling price than budgeted.
    d. both (a) and (b).

    Answer: d   *Difficulty:* 3   *Objective:* 2

62. An unfavorable variance
    a. may suggest investigation is needed.
    b. is conclusive evidence of poor performance.
    c. demands that standards be recomputed.
    d. indicates continuous improvement is needed.

    Answer: a   *Difficulty:* 2   *Objective:* 2

63. All of the following are needed to prepare a flexible budget EXCEPT
    a. determining the budgeted variable cost per output unit.
    b. determining the budgeted fixed costs.
    c. determining the actual selling price per unit.
    d. determining the actual quantity of output units.

    Answer: c   *Difficulty:* 3   *Objective:* 2

64. The variance that LEAST affects cost control is the
    a. flexible-budget variance.
    b. direct-material-price variance.
    c. sales-volume variance.
    d. direct manufacturing labor efficiency variance.

    Answer: c   *Difficulty:* 2   *Objective:* 2

65. A flexible-budget variance is $800 favorable for unit-related costs. This indicates that
    a. costs were $800 more than the master budget.
    b. costs were $800 less than for the planned level of activity.
    c. costs were $800 more than standard for the achieved level of activity.
    d. costs were $800 less than standard for the achieved level of activity.

    Answer: d   *Difficulty:* 2   *Objective:* 2

THE FOLLOWING INFORMATION APPLIES TO QUESTIONS 66 THROUGH 68.
JJ White planned to use $82 of material per unit but actually used $80 of material per unit, and planned to make 1,200 units but actually made 1,000 units.

66. The flexible-budget amount is
   a. $80,000.
   b. $82,000.
   c. $96,000.
   d. $98,400.

   Answer: b   *Difficulty*: 2   *Objective*: 2
   1,000 units x $82 = $82,000

67. The flexible-budget variance is
   a. $2,000 favorable.
   b. $14,000 unfavorable.
   c. $16,400 unfavorable.
   d. $2,400 favorable.

   Answer: a   *Difficulty*: 2   *Objective*: 2
   ($80 - $82) x 1,000 = $2,000 F

68. The sales-volume variance is
   a. $2,000 favorable.
   b. $14,000 unfavorable.
   c. $16,400 unfavorable.
   d. $2,400 favorable.

   Answer: c   *Difficulty*: 2   *Objective*: 2
   (1,000 – 1,200) x $82 = $16,400 U

69. Aebi Corporation currently produces cardboard boxes in an automated process. Expected production per month is 20,000 units, direct-material costs are $0.60 per unit, and manufacturing overhead costs are $9,000 per month. Manufacturing overhead is allocated based on units of production. What is the flexible budget for 10,000 and 20,000 units, respectively?
   a. $10,500; $16,500
   b. $10,500; $21,000
   c. $15,000; $21,000
   d. none of the above

   Answer: c   *Difficulty*: 2   *Objective*: 2

	10,000 units	20,000 units
Materials ($0.60)	$ 6,000	$12,000
Machinery	9,000	9,000
	$15,000	$21,000

THE FOLLOWING INFORMATION APPLIES TO QUESTIONS 70 THROUGH 72.
McKenna Incorporated planned to use $24 of material per unit but actually used $25 of material per unit, and planned to make 1,000 units but actually made 1,200 units.

70. The flexible-budget amount is
    a. $24,000.
    b. $25,000.
    c. $28,800.
    d. $30,000.

    Answer: c   *Difficulty*:   2   *Objective*:   2
    1,200 units x $24 = $28,800

71. The flexible-budget variance is
    a. $4,800 favorable.
    b. $1,200 unfavorable.
    c. $5,000 unfavorable.
    d. $6,000 favorable.

    Answer: b   *Difficulty*:   2   *Objective*:   2
    ($25 - $24) x 1,200 = $1,200 U

72. The sales-volume variance is
    a. $4,800 favorable.
    b. $1,200 unfavorable.
    c. $5,000 unfavorable.
    d. $6,000 favorable.

    Answer: a   *Difficulty*:   2   *Objective*:   2
    (1,200 – 1,000) x $24 = $4,800 F

73. Hemberger Corporation currently produces baseball caps in an automated process. Expected production per month is 20,000 units, direct material costs are $1.50 per unit, and manufacturing overhead costs are $23,000 per month. Manufacturing overhead is allocated based on units of production. What is the flexible budget for 10,000 and 20,000 units, respectively?
    a. $26,500; $41,500
    b. $26,500; $53,000
    c. $38,000; $53,000
    d.   none of the above

    Answer: c   *Difficulty*:   2   *Objective*:   2

	10,000 units	20,000 units
Materials ($1.50)	$15,000	$30,000
Machinery	23,000	23,000
	$38,000	$53,000

THE FOLLOWING INFORMATION APPLIES TO QUESTIONS 74 THROUGH 77.
The actual information pertains to the month of August. As part of the budgeting process
Alloway's Fencing Company developed the following static budget for August. Alloway is
in the process of preparing the flexible budget and understanding the results.

	Actual Results	Flexible Budget	Static Budget
Sales volume (in units)	# 20,000		# 25,000
		========	
Sales revenues	$1,000,000	$	$1,250,000
Variable costs	512,000	$ _____	600,000
Contribution margin	488,000	$	650,000
Fixed costs	458,000	$ _____	450,000
Operating profit	$ 30,000	$ _____	$ 200,000

74. The flexible budget will report _____ for variable costs.
    a. $512,000
    b. $600,000
    c. $480,000
    d. $640,000

    Answer: c   *Difficulty*:   2   *Objective*:   2
    20,000 units ($600,000/25,000) = $480,000

75. The flexible budget will report _____ for the fixed costs.
    a. $458,000
    b. $450,000
    c. $360,000
    d. $572,500

    Answer: b   *Difficulty*:   2   *Objective*:   2
    $450,000, given in the static budget

76. The flexible-budget variance for variable costs is
    a. $32,000 unfavorable.
    b. $120,000 unfavorable.
    c. $32,000 favorable.
    d. $120,000 favorable.

    Answer: a   *Difficulty*:   2   *Objective*:   2
    $512,000 - (20,000 x $600,000/25,000) = $32,000 U

77. The PRIMARY reason for low operating profits was
    a. the variable-cost variance.
    b. increased fixed costs.
    c. a poor management accounting system.
    d. lower sales volume than planned.

    Answer: d   *Difficulty*:   3   *Objective*:   2

THE FOLLOWING INFORMATION APPLIES TO QUESTIONS 78 THROUGH 82.
Peters' Company manufacturers tires. Some of the company's data was misplaced. Use the following information to replace the lost data:

	Actual Results	Flexible-Budget Variances	Flexible Budget	Sales-Volume Variances	Static Budget
Units sold	#225,000		#225,000		#206,250
Revenues	$84,160	$2,000 F	(A)	$2,800 U	(B)
Variable costs	(C)	$400 U	$31,720	$4,680 F	$36,400
Fixed costs	$16,560	$1,720 F	$18,280	0	$18,280
Operating income	$35,480	(D)	$32,160	(E)	$30,280

78. What amounts are reported for revenues in the flexible-budget (A) and the static-budget (B), respectively?
   a. $82,160; $79,360
   b. $82,160; $84,960
   c. $84,960; $88,960
   d. $84,960; $83,360

   Answer: b   *Difficulty:* 2   *Objective:* 2

79. What are the actual variable costs (C)?
   a. $36,400
   b. $32,120
   c. $31,320
   d. $27,040

   Answer: b   *Difficulty:* 2   *Objective:* 2

80. What is the total flexible-budget variance (D)?
   a. $120 unfavorable
   b. $0
   c. $680 favorable
   d. $3,320 favorable

   Answer: d   *Difficulty:* 2   *Objective:* 2

81. What is the total sales-volume variance (E)?
   a. $7,480 unfavorable
   b. $2,800 unfavorable
   c. $1,880 favorable
   d. $7,480 favorable

   Answer: c   *Difficulty:* 2   *Objective:* 2

82. What is the total static-budget variance?
    a. $5,200 favorable
    b. $3,320 favorable
    c. $1,880 unfavorable
    d. $1,880 favorable

    Answer: a   *Difficulty:* 2   *Objective:* 2

83. The flexible-budget variance for direct cost inputs can be further subdivided into
    a. a static-budget variance and a sales-volume variance.
    b. a sales-volume variance and an efficiency variance.
    c. a price variance and an efficiency variance.
    d. a static-budget variance and a price variance.

    Answer: c   *Difficulty:* 1   *Objective:* 3

84. Budgeted input quantity information may be obtained from
    a. actual input quantities used last period.
    b. standards developed by your company.
    c. data from other companies that have similar processes.
    d. all of the above.

    Answer: d   *Difficulty:* 1   *Objective:* 3

85. When actual input data from past periods is used to develop a budget
    a. past inefficiencies are excluded.
    b. expected future changes are incorporated.
    c. information is available at a low cost.
    d. audited financial information must be used.

    Answer: c   *Difficulty:* 2   *Objective:* 3

86. When standards are used to develop a budget
    a. past inefficiencies are excluded.
    b. benchmarking must also be used.
    c. information is available at a low cost.
    d. flexible-budget amounts are difficult to determine.

    Answer: a   *Difficulty:* 2   *Objective:* 3

87. The term budget indicates
    a. that standards have been used to develop the budget.
    b. that actual input data from past periods have been used to develop the budget.
    c. that engineering studies have been used to develop the budget.
    d. planned amounts for a future accounting period.

    Answer: d   *Difficulty:* 1   *Objective:* 3

88. A standard input
   a. is a carefully determined price, cost, or quantity.
   b. is usually expressed on a per unit basis.
   c. may be developed using engineering studies.
   d. is all of the above.

   Answer: d   *Difficulty:* 1   *Objective:* 3

89. Ideal standards
   a. assume peak operating conditions.
   b. allow for normal machine breakdowns.
   c. greatly improve employee motivation and performance.
   d. are all of the above.

   Answer: a   *Difficulty:* 1   *Objective:* 3

90. A favorable price variance for direct materials indicates that
   a. a lower price than planned was paid for materials.
   b. a higher price than planned was paid for materials.
   c. less material was used during production than planned for actual output.
   d. more material was used during production than planned for actual output.

   Answer: a   *Difficulty:* 2   *Objective:* 4

91. A favorable efficiency variance for direct manufacturing labor indicates that
   a. a lower wage rate than planned was paid for direct labor.
   b. a higher wage rate than planned was paid for direct labor.
   c. less direct manufacturing labor-hours were used during production than planned for actual output.
   d. more direct manufacturing labor-hours were used during production than planned for actual output.

   Answer: c   *Difficulty:* 2   *Objective:* 4

92. An unfavorable price variance for direct materials might indicate
   a. that the purchasing manager purchased in smaller quantities due to a change to just-in-time inventory methods.
   b. congestion due to scheduling problems.
   c. that the purchasing manager skillfully negotiated a better purchase price.
   d. that the market had an unexpected oversupply of those materials.

   Answer: a   *Difficulty:* 3   *Objective:* 4

93. A favorable efficiency variance for direct materials might indicate
   a. that lower-quality materials were purchased.
   b. an overskilled workforce.
   c. poor design of products or processes.
   d. a lower-priced supplier was used.

   Answer: b   *Difficulty:* 3   *Objective:* 4

94. A favorable price variance for direct manufacturing labor might indicate that
    a. employees were paid more than planned.
    b. budgeted price standards are too tight.
    c. underskilled employees are being hired.
    d. an efficient labor force.

    Answer: c   *Difficulty*: 3   *Objective*: 4

95. An unfavorable efficiency variance for direct manufacturing labor might indicate that
    a. work was efficiently scheduled.
    b. machines were not properly maintained.
    c. budgeted time standards are too lax.
    d. higher-skilled workers were scheduled than planned.

    Answer: b   *Difficulty*: 3   *Objective*: 4

THE FOLLOWING INFORMATION APPLIES TO QUESTIONS 96 THROUGH 100.
Robb Industries Inc. (RII) developed standard costs for direct material and direct labor. In 2004, RII estimated the following standard costs for one of their major products, the 10-gallon plastic container.

	Budgeted quantity	**Budgeted price**
Direct materials	0.10 pounds	$30 per pound
Direct labor	0.05 hours	$15 per hour

During June RII produced and sold 5,000 containers using 490 pounds of direct materials at an average cost per pound of $32 and 250 direct manufacturing labor-hours at an average wage of $15.25 per hour.

96. June's direct material flexible-budget variance is
    a. $980 unfavorable.
    b. $300 favorable.
    c. $680 unfavorable.
    d. none of the above.

    Answer: c   *Difficulty*: 2   *Objective*: 4
    (490 x $32) – (5,000 x 0.10 x $30) = 680 U

97. June's direct material price variance is
    a. $980 unfavorable.
    b. $300 favorable.
    c. $680 favorable.
    d. none of the above.

    Answer: a   *Difficulty*: 2   *Objective*: 4
    490 ($32 - $30) = 980 U

98. June's direct material efficiency variance is
    a. $980 unfavorable.
    b. $300 favorable.
    c. $680 favorable.
    d.   none of the above.

    Answer: b   *Difficulty*:   2   *Objective*:   4
    $30 (490 – 500) = 300 F

99. June's direct manufacturing labor price variance is
    a. $62.50 unfavorable.
    b. $62.50 favorable.
    c. $3,811.75 unfavorable.
    d.   none of the above.

    Answer: a   *Difficulty*:   2   *Objective*:   4
    250 dlh ($15.25 - $15.00) = $62.50 U

100. June's direct manufacturing labor efficiency variance is
    a. $62.50 unfavorable.
    b. $62.50 favorable.
    c. $3,811.75 unfavorable.
    d.   none of the above.

    Answer: d   *Difficulty*:   2   *Objective*:   4
    [250 dlh - (5,000 x 0.05)] x $15 = Zero

THE FOLLOWING INFORMATION APPLIES TO QUESTIONS 101 THROUGH 106.
Sawyer Industries Inc. (SII) developed standard costs for direct material and direct labor. In
2004, SII estimated the following standard costs for one of their major products, the 30-
gallon heavy-duty plastic container.

	Budgeted quantity	**Budgeted price**
Direct materials	0.20 pounds	$25 per pound
Direct labor	0.10 hours	$15 per hour

During July SII produced and sold 10,000 containers using 2,200 pounds of direct materials
at an average cost per pound of $24 and 1,050 direct manufacturing labor hours at an average
wage of $14.75 per hour.

101. July's direct material flexible-budget variance is
    a. $2,800 unfavorable.
    b. $2,200 favorable.
    c. $5,000 unfavorable.
    d.   none of the above.

    Answer: a   *Difficulty*:   2   *Objective*:   4
    (2200 x $24) – (10,000 x 0.20 x $25) = 2,800 U

102. July's direct material price variance is
    a. $2,800 favorable.
    b. $2,200 favorable.
    c. $5,000 unfavorable.
    d. none of the above.

    Answer: b   *Difficulty*:   2   *Objective*:   4
    2200 ($24 - $25) = 2,200 F

103. July's direct material efficiency variance is
    a. $2,800 unfavorable.
    b. $2,200 favorable.
    c. $5,000 unfavorable.
    d. none of the above.

    Answer: c   *Difficulty*:   2   *Objective*:   4
    $25 [2200 – (10,000 x 0.20)] = 5,000 U

104. July's direct manufacturing labor flexible-budget variance is
    a. $750.00 unfavorable.
    b. $262.50 favorable.
    c. $487.50 unfavorable.
    d. none of the above.

    Answer: c   *Difficulty*:   2   *Objective*:   4
    (1050 x $14.75) - (10,000 x 0.10 x $15) = $487.50 U

105. July's direct manufacturing labor price variance is
    a. $750.00 unfavorable.
    b. $262.50 favorable.
    c. $487.50 favorable.
    d. none of the above.

    Answer: b   *Difficulty*:   2   *Objective*:   4
    1050 dlh ($14.75 - $15.00) = $262.50 F

106. July's direct manufacturing labor efficiency variance is
    a. $750.00 unfavorable.
    b. $262.50 favorable.
    c. $487.50 favorable.
    d. none of the above.

    Answer: a   *Difficulty*:   2   *Objective*:   4
    [1050 dlh - (10,000 x 0.10)] x $15 = 750 U

THE FOLLOWING INFORMATION APPLIES TO QUESTIONS 107 THROUGH 110.
These questions refer to flexible-budget variance formulas with the following descriptions for the variables: A = Actual; B = Budgeted; P = Price; Q = Quantity.

107. The best label for the formula (AQ – BQ) BP is the
   a.   efficiency variance.
   b.   price variance.
   c.   total flexible-budget variance.
   e.   spending variance.

   Answer: a   *Difficulty*:   2   *Objective*:   4

108. The best label for the formula (AP – BP) AQ is the
   a.   efficiency variance.
   b.   price variance.
   c.   total flexible-budget variance.
   d.   spending variance.

   Answer: b   *Difficulty*:   2   *Objective*:   4

109. The best label for the formula [(AP)(AQ)– (BP)(AQ)] is the
   a.   efficiency variance.
   b.   price variance.
   c.   total flexible-budget variance.
   d.   spending variance.

   Answer: b   *Difficulty*:   2   *Objective*:   4

110. The best label for the formula [(AP)(AQ)– (BP)(BQ)] is the
   a.   efficiency variance.
   b.   price variance.
   c.   total flexible-budget variance.
   d.   spending variance.

   Answer: c   *Difficulty*:   2   *Objective*:   4

THE FOLLOWING INFORMATION APPLIES TO QUESTIONS 111 THROUGH 113.
Ruben's Camera Shop has prepared the following flexible budget for September and is in the process of interpreting the variances. **F** denotes a favorable variance and **U** denotes an unfavorable variance.

	Flexible Budget	Variances Price	Efficiency
Material A	$20,000	$1,000F	$3,000U
Material B	30,000	500U	1,500F
Direct manufacturing labor	40,000	500U	2,500F

111. The MOST likely explanation of the above variances for Material A is that
   a.   a lower price than expected was paid for Material A.
   b.   higher-quality raw materials were used than were planned.
   d.   the company used a higher-priced supplier.
   d.   Material A used during September was $2,000 less than expected.

   Answer: a   *Difficulty:*   3   *Objective:*   4

112. The actual amount spent for Material B was
   a. $28,000.
   b. $29,000.
   c. $30,000.
   d. $31,000.

   Answer: b   *Difficulty:*   2   *Objective:*   4
   $30,000 + 500 U – 1,500 F = $29,000

113. The MOST likely explanation of the above direct manufacturing labor variances is that
   a.   the average wage rate paid to employees was less than expected.
   b.   employees did not work as efficiently as expected to accomplish the job.
   c.   the company may have assigned more experienced employees this month than originally planned.
   d.   management may have a problem with budget slack and be using lax standards for both labor-wage rates and expected efficiency.

   Answer: c   *Difficulty:*   3   *Objective:*   4

THE FOLLOWING INFORMATION APPLIES TO QUESTIONS 114 THROUGH 116.
Hector's Camera Shop has prepared the following flexible budget for September and is in the process of interpreting the variances. **F** denotes a favorable variance and **U** denotes an unfavorable variance.

| | Flexible Budget | ------------Variances------------ | |
		Price	Efficiency
Material A	$20,000	$1,000U	$1,200F
Material B	30,000	500F	800U
Material C	40,000	1,400U	1,000F

114. The actual amount spent for Material A was
   a. $18,800.
   b. $20,200.
   c. $19,800.
   d. $21,000.

   Answer: c   *Difficulty*:   2   *Objective*:   4
   $20,000 + 1,000 U - 1,200 F = $19,800

115. The actual amount spent for Material B was
   a. $29,700.
   b. $30,800.
   c. $30,500.
   d. $30,300.

   Answer: d   *Difficulty*:   2   *Objective*:   4
   $30,000 – 500 F + 800 U = $30,300

116. The explanation that lower-quality materials were purchased is MOST likely for
   a.   Material A.
   b.   Material B.
   c.   Material C.
   d.   both Material A and C.

   Answer: b   *Difficulty*:   3   *Objective*:   4

117. A purchasing manager's performance is BEST evaluated using the
   a.   direct materials price variance.
   b.   direct materials flexible-budget variance.
   c.   direct manufacturing labor flexible-budget variance.
   d.   affect the manager's action has on total costs for the entire company.

   Answer: d   *Difficulty*:   3   *Objective*:   5

118. One of the primary reasons for using cost variances is
    a.   they diagnose the cause of a problem and what should be done to correct it.
    b.   for superiors to communicate expectations to lower-level employees.
    c.   to administer appropriate disciplinary action.
    d.   for financial control of operating activities and understanding why variances arise.

    Answer: d   *Difficulty:*   2   *Objective:*   5

119. A favorable cost variance of significant magnitude
    a.   is the result of good planning.
    b.   if investigated, may lead to improved production methods.
    c.   indicates management does not need to be concerned about lax standards.
    d.   does not need to be investigated.

    Answer: b   *Difficulty:*   3   *Objective:*   5

120. The variances that should be investigated by management include
    a.   only unfavorable variances.
    b.   only favorable variances.
    c.   all variances, both favorable and unfavorable.
    d.   both favorable and unfavorable variances considered significant in amount for the company.

    Answer: d   *Difficulty:*   1   *Objective:*   5

121. Typically, managers have the LEAST control over
    a.   the direct material price variance.
    b.   the direct material efficiency variance.
    c.   machine maintenance.
    d.   the scheduling of production.

    Answer: a   *Difficulty:*   2   *Objective:*   5

122. If manufacturing machines are breaking down more than expected, this will contribute to
    a.   a favorable direct manufacturing labor price variance.
    b.   an unfavorable direct manufacturing labor price variance.
    c.   a favorable direct manufacturing labor efficiency variance.
    d.   an unfavorable direct manufacturing labor efficiency variance.

    Answer: d   *Difficulty:*   2   *Objective:*   5

123. A single variance
    a.   signals the cause of a problem.
    b.   should be evaluated in isolation from other variances.
    c.   may be the result of many different problems.
    d.   should be used for performance evaluation.

    Answer: c   *Difficulty:*   2   *Objective:*   5

124. Variance analysis should be used
    a. to understand why variances arise.
    b. as the sole source of information for performance evaluation.
    c. to punish employees that do not meet standards.
    d. to encourage employees to focus on meeting standards.

    Answer: a   *Difficulty*: 3   *Objective*: 5

125. Variances should be investigated
    a. when they are kept below a certain amount.
    b. when there is a small variance for critical items such as product defects.
    c. even though the cost of investigation exceeds the benefit.
    d. when there is an in-control occurrence.

    Answer: b   *Difficulty*: 3   *Objective*: 5

126. When continuous improvement budgeted costing is implemented, cost reductions can result from
    a. price reductions.
    b. reducing materials waste.
    c. producing products faster and more efficiently.
    d. all of the above.

    Answer: d   *Difficulty*: 2   *Objective*: 6

127. Nonfinancial performance measures
    a. are usually used in combination with financial measures for control purposes.
    b. are used to evaluate overall cost efficiency.
    c. allow managers to make informed tradeoffs.
    d. are often the sole basis of a manager's performance evaluations.

    Answer: a   *Difficulty*: 3   *Objective*: 6

128. Unfavorable direct material price variances are
    a. always credits.
    b. always debits.
    c. credited to the Materials Control account.
    d. credited to the Accounts Payable Control account.

    Answer: b   *Difficulty*: 1   *Objective*: 6

129. Favorable direct manufacturing labor efficiency variances are
    a. always credits.
    b. always debits.
    c. debited to the Work-in-Process Control account.
    d. debited to the Wages Payable Control account.

    Answer: a   *Difficulty*: 1   *Objective*: 6

130. From the perspective of control, the direct materials efficiency variance should be isolated at the time of
    a.   purchase.
    b.   use.
    c.   completion of the entire product.
    d.   sale of the product.

    Answer: b   *Difficulty*:   2   *Objective*:   6

131. Standard costing systems are a useful tool when using
    a.   just-in-time systems.
    b.   total quality management.
    c.   computer-integrated manufacturing systems.
    d.   all of the above.

    Answer: d   *Difficulty*:   2   *Objective*:   6

132. Performance variance analysis can be calculated for
    a.   output unit-level costs.
    b.   batch-level costs.
    c.   product-sustaining costs.
    d.   all of the above.

    Answer: d   *Difficulty*:   2   *Objective*:   7

133. A favorable efficiency variance for material-handling labor-hours per batch could result from
    a.   inefficient production-floor layouts compared to those expected when preparing the budget.
    b.   materials-handling labor having to wait when picking up materials.
    c.   well-trained and experienced material-handling employees.
    d.   lower wages than planned for material-handling labor.

    Answer: c   *Difficulty*:   2   *Objective*:   7

134. The process by which a company's products or services are measured relative to the best possible levels of performance is known as
    a.   efficiency.
    b.   benchmarking.
    c.   a standard costing system.
    d.   variance analysis.

    Answer: b   *Difficulty*:   1   *Objective*:   8

135. When benchmarking,
   a. the best levels of performance are usually found in companies that are within different industries.
   b. finding appropriate benchmarks is a minor issue.
   c. comparisons can highlight areas for better future cost management.
   d. both (a) and (c) are true.

   Answer: c   *Difficulty*:   2   *Objective*:   8

136. Ensuring benchmark numbers are comparable can be difficult because differences can exist across companies with
   a. overall company strategy.
   b. depreciation methods.
   c. inventory methods.
   d. all of the above.

   Answer: d   *Difficulty*:   2   *Objective*:   8

137. When benchmarking, management accountants are MOST valuable when they
   a. present differences in the benchmarking data to management.
   b. highlight differences in the benchmarking data to management.
   c. provide insight into why costs or revenues differ across companies.
   d. provide complex mathematical analysis.

   Answer: c   *Difficulty*:   2   *Objective*:   8

EXERCISES AND PROBLEMS

138. The president of the company, Gregory Peters, has come to you for help. Use the following data to prepare a flexible budget for possible sales/production levels of 10,000, 11,000, and 12,000 units. Show the contribution margin at each activity level.

Sales price	$24 per unit
Variable costs:	
Manufacturing	$12 per unit
Administrative	$ 3 per unit
Selling	$ 1 per unit
Fixed costs:	
Manufacturing	$60,000
Administrative	$20,000

Answer:

Flexible Budget for Various Levels of Sales/Production Activity

Units	10,000	11,000	12,000
Sales	$240,000	$264,000	$288,000
Variable costs:			
Manufacturing	120,000	132,000	144,000
Administrative	30,000	33,000	36,000
Selling	10,000	11,000	12,000
Total variable costs	160,000	176,000	192,000
Contribution margin	80,000	88,000	96,000
Fixed costs:			
Manufacturing	60,000	60,000	60,000
Administrative	20,000	20,000	20,000
Operating income/(loss)	$ -0-	$ 8,000	$ 16,000

Difficulty: 2   *Objective*: 2

139. Strauss Table Company manufactures tables for schools. The 20x4 operating budget is based on sales of 20,000 units at $100 per table. Operating income is anticipated to be $120,000. Budgeted variable costs are $64 per unit, while fixed costs total $600,000.

Actual income for 20x4 was a surprising $354,000 on actual sales of 21,000 units at $104 each. Actual variable costs were $60 per unit and fixed costs totaled $570,000.

Required:
Prepare a variance analysis report with both flexible-budget and sales-volume variances.

Answer:

Strauss Table Company
Variance Analysis

	Actual Results	Flexible Variances	Flexible Budget	Sales-Volume Variances	Static Budget
Units sold	21,000		21,000		20,000
Sales	$2,184,000	$84,000 F	$2,100,000	$100,000 F	$2,000,000
Variable costs	1,260,000	84,000 F	1,344,000	64,000 U	1,280,000
Contribution margin	$924,000	$168,000 F	$756,000	$36,000 F	$720,000
Fixed costs	570,000	30,000 F	600,000	0	600,000
Operating income	$354,000	$198,000 F	$156,000	$36,000 F	$120,000

Total flexible-budget variance = $198,000 favorable.

Total sales-volume variance = $36,000 favorable.

Difficulty: 2   *Objective*: 2

140. Nicholas Company manufacturers TVs. Some of the company's data was misplaced. Use the following information to replace the lost data:

Analysis	Actual Results	Flexible Variances	Flexible Budget	Sales-Volume Variances	Static Budget
Units Sold	112,500		112,500		103,125
Revenues	$42,080	$1,000 F	(A)	$1,400 U	(B)
Variable Costs	(C)	$200 U	$15,860	$2,340 F	$18,200
Fixed Costs	$8,280	$860 F	$9,140		$9,140
Operating Income	$17,740	(D)	$16,080	(E)	$15,140

Required:

:
   a. What are the respective flexible-budget revenues?
   b. What are the static-budget revenues?
   c. What are the actual variable costs?
   d. What is the total flexible-budget variance?
   e. What is the total sales-volume variance?
   f. What is the total static-budget variance?

Answer:

a. $42,080 - 1,000 = $41,080

b. $41,080 + 1,400 = $42,480

c. $15,860 + $200 = $16,060

d. $17,740 - $16,080 = $1,660 favorable

e. $2,340 favorable + $1,400 unfavorable = $940 favorable

f. $17,740 - $15,140 = $2,600 favorable

Difficulty: 2   *Objective*: 2

141. Madzinga's Draperies manufactures curtains. A certain window requires the following:

Direct materials standard	10 square yards at $5 per yard
Direct manufacturing labor standard	5 hours at $10

During the second quarter, the company made 1,500 curtains and used 14,000 square yards of fabric costing $68,600. Direct labor totaled 7,600 hours for $79,800.

Required:
a. Compute the direct materials price and efficiency variances for the quarter.
b. Compute the direct manufacturing labor price and efficiency variances for the quarter.

Answer:

a. Direct materials variances:

Actual unit cost	= $68,600/14,000 square yard = $4.90 per square yard
Price variance	= 14,000 x ($5.00 - $4.90) = $1,400 favorable
Efficiency variance	= $5.00 x (14,000 - (1,500 x 10)) = $5,000 favorable

b. Direct manufacturing labor variances:

Actual labor rate	= $79,800/7,600 = $10.50 per hour
Price variance	= 7,600 x ($10.50 - $10.00) = $3,800 unfavorable
Efficiency variance	= $10.00 x (7,600 - 7,500) = $1,000 unfavorable

Difficulty: 2   *Objective*: 4

142. The following data for the Alma Company pertain to the production of 1,000 urns during August.

Direct Materials (all materials purchased were used):

Standard cost: $6.00 per pound of urn.
Total actual cost: $5,600.
Standard cost allowed for units produced was $6,000.
Materials efficiency variance was $120 unfavorable.

Direct Manufacturing Labor:

Standard cost is 2 urns per hour at $24.00 per hour.
Actual cost per hour was $24.50.
Labor efficiency variance was $336 favorable.

Required:

a. What is standard direct material amount per urn?
b. What is the direct material price variance?
c. What is the total actual cost of direct manufacturing labor?
d. What is the labor price variance for direct manufacturing labor?

Answer:

a. Standard cost per urn
= $6,000/1,000
= $6.00 per urn

Standard number of pounds per urn
= $6.00/$6.00
= 1.0 pound per urn

b. Materials price variance
= Total variance - efficiency variance
= ($5,600 - 6,000) - $120 unfavorable
= $520 favorable

c. Total standard labor cost of actual hours
= ((1,000/2) x $24) - $336
= $11,664
Actual hours = $11,664/24 = 486 hours
Total actual costs = 486 x $24.50 = $11,907

d. Labor price variance
= $11,907 - $11,664
= $243 unfavorable

Difficulty: 3   *Objective*: 4

143.   The following data for the telephone company pertain to the production of 450 rolls of telephone wire during June. Selected items are omitted because the costing records were lost in a windstorm.

Direct Materials (All materials purchased were used.)

Standard cost per roll: _a_ pounds at $4.00 per pound.
Total actual cost: _b_ pounds costing $9,600.
Standard cost allowed for units produced was $9,000.
Materials price variance: _c_ .
Materials efficiency variance was $80 unfavorable.

Direct Manufacturing Labor

Standard cost is 3 hours per roll at $8.00 per hour.
Actual cost per hour was $8.25.
Total actual cost: _d_ .
Labor price variance: _e_ .
Labor efficiency variance was $400 unfavorable.

Required:
Compute the missing elements in the report represented by the lettered items.

Answer:

a.   Standard cost per roll   = $9,000/450 = $20.00

Standard number of pounds per roll   = $20/$4 = 5 pounds per roll

b.   Actual pounds   = ($9,000 + $80)/$4 = 2,270 pounds

c.   Materials price variance   = $9,600 - ($9,000 + $80)
                                                            = $520 unfavorable

d.   Total standard labor cost of actual hours = (450 x 3 x $8) + $400 = $11,200
       Actual hours   = $11,200/$8 = 1,400

Total actual cost   = 1,400 x $8.25 = $11,550

e.   Labor price variance   = $11,550 - $11,200 = $350 unfavorable

Difficulty: 3   *Objective:* 4

144. Littrell Company produces chairs and has determined the following direct cost categories and budgeted amounts:

Category	Standard Inputs for 1 output	Standard Cost per input
Direct Materials	1.00	$7.50
Direct Labor	0.30	9.00
Direct Marketing	0.50	3.00

Actual performance for the company is shown below:

Actual output: (in units)	4,000
Direct Materials:	
Materials costs	$30,225
Input purchased and used	3,900
Actual price per input	$7.75
Direct Manufacturing Labor:	
Labor costs	$11,470
Labor-hours of input	1,240
Actual price per hour	$9.25
Direct Marketing Labor:	
Labor costs	$5,880
Labor-hours of input	2,100
Actual price per hour	$2.80

Required:
a. What is the combined total of the flexible-budget variances?
b. What is the price variance of the direct materials?
c. What is the price variance of the direct manufacturing labor and the direct marketing labor, respectively?
d. What is the efficiency variance for direct materials?
e. What are the efficiency variances for direct manufacturing labor and direct marketing labor, respectively?

Answer:
a.

	Actual Results	Flexible Budget	Variances
Direct materials	$30,225	$30,000	$225U
Direct manufacturing labor	11,470	10,800	670 U
Direct marketing labor	5,880	6,000	120 F
	$47,575	$46,800	$775 U

b. ($7.75 - $7.50) x (3,900) = $975 unfavorable

c. Manufacturing Labor ($9.25 - $9.00) x 1,240 = $310 unfavorable
Marketing Labor ($2.80 - $3.00) x 2,100 = $420 favorable

d. [3,900 - (4,000 units x 1.00)] x $7.50 = $750 favorable

e. Manufacturing Labor = [1,240 hours - (4,000 x 0.30 hours)] x $9.00 = $360 unfavorable
Marketing Labor = [2,100 hours - (4,000 x 0.50 hours)] x $3.00 = $300.00 unfavorable

Difficulty: 3   *Objective*: 4

145. Coffey Company maintains a very large direct materials inventory because of critical demands placed upon it for rush orders from large hospitals. Item A contains hard-to-get material Y. Currently, the standard cost of material Y is $2.00 per gram. During February, 22,000 grams were purchased for $2.10 per gram, while only 20,000 grams were used in production. There was no beginning inventory of material Y.

Required:

a. Determine the direct materials price variance, assuming that all materials costs are the responsibility of the materials purchasing manager.
b. Determine the direct materials price variance, assuming that all materials costs are the responsibility of the production manager.
c. Discuss the issues involved in determining the price variance at the point of purchase versus the point of consumption.

Answer:

a. Material price variance   = 22,000 x ($2.10 - $2.00)
                                = $2,200 unfavorable

b. Material price variance   = 20,000 x ($2.10 - $2.00)
                                = $2,000 unfavorable

c. Measuring the price variance at the time of materials purchased is desirable in situations where the amount of materials purchased varies substantially from the amount used during the period. Failure to measure the price variance based on materials purchased could result in a substantial delay in determining that a price change occurred.

   Also, if the purchasing manager is to be held accountable for his/her purchasing activities, it is appropriate to have the materials price variances computed at the time of purchase so the manager can include the variances on his/her monthly report. This encourages the purchasing manager to be more responsible for the activities under his/her control. It provides a closer relationship between responsibility and authority and becomes a relevant performance measure.

Difficulty: 2   *Objectives*: 4, 5

146. During February the Lungren Manufacturing Company's costing system reported several variances that the production manager was surprised to see. Most of the company's monthly variances are under $125, even though they may be either favorable or unfavorable. The following information is for the manufacture of garden gates, its only product:

   1. Direct materials price variance, $800 unfavorable.
   2. Direct materials efficiency variance, $1,800 favorable.
   3. Direct manufacturing labor price variance, $4,000 favorable.
   4. Direct manufacturing labor efficiency variance, $600 unfavorable.

Required:

a. Provide the manager with some ideas as to what may have caused the price variances.
b. What may have caused the efficiency variances?

Answer:

a. Direct materials' unfavorable price variance may have been caused by: (1) paying a higher price than the standard for the period, (2) changing to a new vendor, or (3) buying higher-quality materials.

   Direct manufacturing labor's favorable price variance may have been caused by: (1) changing the work force by hiring lower-paid employees, (2) changing the mix of skilled and unskilled workers, or (3) not giving pay raises as high as anticipated when the standards were set for the year.

b. Direct materials' favorable efficiency variance may have been caused by: (1) employees/machinery working more efficiency and having less scrap and waste materials, (2) buying better-quality materials, or (3) changing the production process.

   Direct manufacturing labor's unfavorable efficiency variance may have been caused by: (1) poor working conditions, (2) changes in the production process (learning something new initially takes longer), (3) different types of direct materials to work with, or (4) poor attitudes on behalf of the workers.

Difficulty: 3   *Objective*: 5

147. Mayberry Company had the following journal entries recorded for the end of June. Unfortunately, the company's only accountant quit on July 10 and the president is at a loss as to the company's performance for the month of June.

Materials Control	$150,000	
Direct Materials Price Variance		$ 5,000
Accounts Payable Control		145,000
Work-in-Process Control	60,000	
Direct Materials Efficiency Variance	4,000	
Materials Control		64,000
Work-in-Process Control	425,000	
Direct Manufacturing Labor Price Variance	7,500	
Direct Manufacturing Labor Efficiency Variance		9,000
Wages Payable Control		423,500

Required:

a. What kind of performance did the company have for June? Explain each variance.
b. Why is Direct Materials given in two entries?

Answer:

a. The first entry is for materials purchases. The credit entry indicates a favorable variance. This could be an indicator that the purchasing agent did a good job or he/she bought inferior goods.

Production was not as lucky in June. The debit entry for materials efficiency indicates that more materials were used than should have been under the operating plans for the month.

For labor, the price was unfavorable, while the efficiency was favorable. This could have been caused by using higher-priced workers who were, in fact, better workers. Of course, there are many other possible causes.

b. Recoding variances for direct materials is completed with two separate entries since the price variance is isolated at the point of purchase, while the efficiency variance is isolated at the point of use.

Difficulty: 2   *Objectives*: 5, 6

148. Waddell Productions makes separate journal entries for all cost accounting related activities. It uses a standard cost system for all manufacturing items. For the month of June, the following activities have taken place:

Direct Manufacturing Materials Purchased	$300,000	
Direct Manufacturing Materials Used	250,000	
Direct Materials Price Variance (at time of purchase)	10,000	unfavorable
Direct Materials Efficiency Variance	15,000	favorable
Direct Manufacturing Labor Price Variance	6,000	favorable
Direct Manufacturing Labor Efficiency Variance	4,000	favorable
Direct Manufacturing Labor Payable	170,000	

Required:

Record the necessary journal entries to close the accounts for the month.

Answer:

Materials Control	$300,000	
Direct Manufacturing Materials Price Variance	10,000	
Accounts Payable Control		$310,000
Work-in-Process Control	$265,000	
Direct Materials Efficiency Variance		$15,000
Materials Control		250,000
Work-in-Process Control	$180,000	
Direct Manufacturing Labor Price Variance		$6,000
Direct Manufacturing Labor Efficiency Variance		4,000
Wages Payable Control		170,000

Difficulty: 3   *Objective*: 6

149. Tyson's Hardware uses a flexible budget to develop planning information for its warehouse operations. For 20x3, the company anticipated that it would have 96,000 sales units for 664 customer shipments. Average storage bin usage for various inventories was estimated to be 200 per day. The costs and cost drivers were determined to be as follows:

Item	Fixed	Variable	Cost driver
Product handling	$10,000	$1.25	per 100 units
Storage		3.00	per storage bin
Utilities	1,000	1.50	per 100 units
Shipping clerks	1,000	1.00	per shipment
Supplies		0.50	per shipment

During the year, the warehouse processed 90,000 units for 600 customer shipments. The workers used 225 storage bins on average each day to sort, store, and process goods for shipment. The actual costs for 20x3 were:

Item	Actual costs
Product handling	$10,900
Storage	465
Utilities	2,020
Shipping clerks	1,400
Supplies	340

Required:
a. Prepare a static budget for 20x3 with static-budget variances.
b. Prepare a flexible budget for 20x3 with flexible-budget variances.

Answer:
a. Tyson's Hardware -- Static Budget with Variances -- 20x3

	Actual	Static Budget	Variances
Product handling	$10,900	$11,200	$300 F
Storage	465	600	135 F
Utilities	2,020	2,440	420 F
Shipping clerks	1,400	1,664	264 F
Supplies	340	332	8 U
Total	$15,125	$16,236	$1,111 F

b. Tyson's Hardware -- Flexible Budget with Variances -- 20x3

	Actual	Flexible Budget	Variances
Product handling	$10,900	$11,125	$225 F
Storage	465	675	210 F
Utilities	2,020	2,350	330 F
Shipping clerks	1,400	1,600	200 F
Supplies	340	300	40 U
Total	$15,125	$16,050	$925 F

Difficulty: 2   *Objective*: 7

CRITICAL THINKING

150. Describe the purpose of variance analysis.

    Answer:
    Variance analysis should help the company learn about what happened and how to perform better and should not be a tool in playing the "blame game."

    Difficulty: 2   *Objective*: 5

151. Give at least three good reasons why a favorable price variance for direct materials might be reported.

    Answer: Any three of the following:
    a. The purchasing manager skillfully negotiated a better purchase price.
    b. The purchasing manager changed to a lower-priced supplier.
    c. The purchasing manager purchased in larger quantities resulting in quantity discounts.
    d. The purchasing manager changed to lower-quality materials.
    e. An unexpected industry oversupply resulted in decreased prices for materials.
    f. Budgeted purchase prices were not carefully set.

    Difficulty: 3   *Objective*: 4

152. Give at least three good reasons why an unfavorable efficiency variance for direct manufacturing labor might be reported.

    Answer: Any three of the following.
    a. More lower-skilled workers were scheduled than planned.
    b. Work was inefficiently scheduled.
    c. Machines were not properly maintained.
    d. Budgeted time standards are too tight.

    Difficulty: 3   *Objective*: 4

CHAPTER 8: FLEXIBLE BUDGETS, VARIANCES, AND MANAGEMENT CONTROL: II

TRUE/FALSE

1. Overhead costs are a major part of costs for most companies – more than 50% of all costs for some companies.

   Answer: True   *Difficulty*: 1   *Objective*: 1

2. At the start of the budget period, management will have made most decisions regarding the level of variable costs to be incurred.

   Answer: False   *Difficulty*: 1   *Objective*: 1
   At the start of the budget period, management will have made most decisions regarding the level of *fixed* costs to be incurred.

3. One way to manage both variable and fixed overhead costs is to eliminate nonvalue-adding activities.

   Answer: True   *Difficulty*: 1   *Objective*: 1

4. In a standard costing system, the variable-overhead rate per unit is generally expressed as a standard cost per output unit.

   Answer: True   *Difficulty*: 1   *Objective*: 2

5. For calculating the cost of products and services, a standard costing system does not have to keep track of actual costs.

   Answer: True   *Difficulty*: 3   *Objective*: 2

6. The budget period for variable-overhead costs is typically less than 3 months.

   Answer: False   *Difficulty*: 1   *Objective*: 3
   The budget period for variable-overhead costs is typically 12 months.

7. A favorable variable overhead spending variance can be the result of paying lower prices than budgeted for variable overhead items such as energy.

   Answer: True   *Difficulty*: 1   *Objective*: 3

8. The variable overhead efficiency variance is computed in a different way than the efficiency variance for direct-cost items.

   Answer: False   *Difficulty*: 1   *Objective*: 3
   The variable overhead efficiency variance is computed the same way as the efficiency variance for direct-cost items.

9. The variable overhead flexible-budget variance measures the difference between standard variable overhead costs and flexible-budget variable overhead costs.

Answer: False   *Difficulty*: 1   *Objective*: 3
The variable overhead flexible-budget variance measures the difference between the *actual* variable overhead costs and the flexible-budget variable-overhead costs.

10. The variable overhead efficiency variance measures the efficiency with which the cost-allocation base is used.

Answer: True   *Difficulty*: 1   *Objective*: 3

11. The variable overhead efficiency variance can be interpreted the same way as the efficiency variance for direct-cost items.

Answer: False   *Difficulty*: 2   *Objective*: 4
The interpretations are different. The variable overhead efficiency variance focuses on the quantity of allocation-base used, while the efficiency variance for direct-cost items focuses on the quantity of materials and labor-hours used.

12. An unfavorable variable overhead efficiency variance indicates that variable overhead costs were wasted and inefficiently used.

Answer: False   *Difficulty*: 3   *Objective*: 4
An unfavorable variable overhead efficiency variance indicates that the company used more than planned of the cost-allocation base.

13. Causes of a favorable variable overhead efficiency variance might include using lower-skilled workers than expected.

Answer: False   *Difficulty*: 2   *Objective*: 4
Possible causes of a favorable variable overhead efficiency variance might include using *higher*-skilled workers that are more efficient than expected.

14. For fixed overhead costs, the flexible-budget amount is always the same as the static-budget amount.

Answer: True   *Difficulty*: 2   *Objective*: 5

15. The fixed overhead flexible-budget variance is the difference between actual fixed overhead costs and the fixed overhead costs in the flexible budget.

Answer: True   *Difficulty*: 1   *Objective*: 5

16. There is never an efficiency variance for fixed costs.

Answer: True   *Difficulty*: 2   *Objective*: 5

17. All unfavorable overhead variances decrease operating income compared to the budget.

Answer: True   *Difficulty*: 2   *Objective*: 5

18. A favorable fixed overhead flexible-budget variance indicates that actual fixed costs exceeded the lump-sum amount budgeted.

Answer: False   *Difficulty*: 1   *Objective*: 5
A favorable fixed overhead flexible-budget variance indicates that actual fixed costs were *less than* the lump-sum amount budgeted.

19. Caution is appropriate before interpreting the production-volume variance as a measure of the economic cost of unused capacity.

Answer: True   *Difficulty*: 1   *Objective*: 6

20. The production-volume variance arises whenever the actual level of the denominator differs from the level used to calculate the budgeted fixed overhead rate.

Answer: True   *Difficulty*: 1   *Objective*: 6

21. The lump sum budgeted for fixed overhead will always be the same amount for the static budget and the flexible budget.

Answer: True   *Difficulty*: 2   *Objective*: 6

22. A favorable production-volume variance arises when manufacturing capacity planned for is not used.

Answer: False   *Difficulty*: 1   *Objective*: 6
An *unfavorable* production-volume variance arises when manufacturing capacity planned for is not used.

23. Managers should use unitized fixed manufacturing overhead costs for planning and control.

Answer: False   *Difficulty*: 3   *Objective*: 7
Managers should *not* use unitized fixed manufacturing overhead costs for planning and control, but only for inventory costing purposes.

24. Both financial and nonfinancial performance measures are key inputs when evaluating the performance of managers.

Answer: True   *Difficulty*: 1   *Objective*: 7

25. In the journal entry that records overhead variances, the manufacturing overhead allocated accounts are closed.

   Answer: True   *Difficulty*: 1   *Objective*: 7

26. Variance analysis of fixed nonmanufacturing costs, such as distribution costs, can also be useful when planning for capacity.

   Answer: True   *Difficulty*: 1   *Objective*: 7

27. Variance analysis of fixed overhead costs is also useful when a company uses activity-based costing.

   Answer: True   *Difficulty*: 1   *Objective*: 8

28. An unfavorable fixed setup overhead spending variance could be due to higher lease costs of new setup equipment.

   Answer: True   *Difficulty*: 2   *Objective*: 8

29. A favorable variable setup overhead efficiency variance could be due to actual setup-hours exceeding the setup-hours planned for the units produced.

   Answer: False   *Difficulty*: 2   *Objective*: 8
   An *unfavorable* variable setup overhead efficiency variance could be due to actual setup-hours exceeding the setup-hours planned for the units produced.

30. Overhead costs have been increasing due to all of the following EXCEPT
    a. increased automation.
    b. more complexity in distribution processes.
    c. tracing more costs as direct costs with the help of technology.
    d. product proliferation.

    Answer: c   *Difficulty:* 3   *Objective:* 1

31. Effective planning of variable overhead costs means that a company performs those variable overhead costs that primarily add value
    a. for the current shareholders.
    b. for the customer using the products or services.
    c. for plant employees.
    d. for major suppliers of component parts.

    Answer: b   *Difficulty:* 2   *Objective:* 1

32. Variable overhead costs include
    a. plant-leasing costs.
    b. the plant manager's salary.
    c. depreciation on plant equipment.
    d. machine maintenance.

    Answer: d   *Difficulty:* 1   *Objective:* 1

33. Fixed overhead costs include
    a. the cost of sales commissions.
    b. property taxes paid on plant facilities.
    c. energy costs.
    d. indirect materials.

    Answer: b   *Difficulty:* 1   *Objective:* 1

34. Effective planning of fixed overhead costs includes all EXCEPT
    a. planning day-to-day operational decisions.
    b. eliminating nonvalue-added costs.
    c. planning to be efficient.
    d. choosing the appropriate level of capacity.

    Answer: a   *Difficulty:* 3   *Objective:* 1

35. Effective planning of variable overhead includes all EXCEPT
    a. choosing the appropriate level of capacity.
    b. eliminating nonvalue-adding costs.
    c. redesigning products to use fewer resources.
    d. redesigning the plant layout for more efficient processing.

    Answer: a   *Difficulty*: 2   *Objective*: 1

36. Choosing the appropriate level of capacity
    a. is a key strategic decision.
    b. may lead to loss of sales if overestimated.
    c. may lead to idle capacity if underestimated.
    d. can be all of the above.

    Answer: a   *Difficulty*: 2   *Objective*: 1

37. The MAJOR challenge when planning fixed overhead
    a. is calculating total costs.
    b. is calculating the cost-allocation rate.
    c. is choosing the appropriate level of capacity.
    d. is choosing the appropriate planning period.

    Answer: c   *Difficulty*: 3   *Objective*: 1

38. In a standard costing system, a cost-allocation base would MOST likely be
    a. actual machine-hours.
    b. normal machine-hours.
    c. standard machine-hours.
    d. any of the above.

    Answer: c   *Difficulty*: 3   *Objective*: 2

39. For calculating the costs of products and services, a standard costing system
    a. only requires a simple recording system.
    b. uses standard costs to determine the cost of products.
    c. does not have to keep track of actual costs.
    d. does all of the above.

    Answer: d   *Difficulty*: 3   *Objective*: 2

40. The variable overhead flexible-budget variance measures the difference between
    a. actual variable overhead costs and the static budget for variable overhead costs.
    b. actual variable overhead costs and the flexible budget for variable overhead costs.
    c. the static budget for variable overhead costs and the flexible budget for variable overhead costs.
    d. none of the above.

    Answer: b   *Difficulty*: 2   *Objective*: 2

41. A $5,000 unfavorable flexible-budget variance indicates that
    a. the flexible-budget amount exceeded actual variable manufacturing overhead by $5,000.
    b. actual variable manufacturing overhead exceeded the flexible-budget amount by $5,000.
    c. the flexible-budget amount exceeded standard variable manufacturing overhead by $5,000.
    d. standard variable manufacturing overhead exceeded the flexible-budget amount by $5,000.

    Answer: b   *Difficulty:* 2   *Objective:* 2

42. Which of the following is NOT a step in developing budgeted variable overhead rates?
    a. Identifying the variable overhead costs associated with each cost-allocation base.
    b. Estimating the budgeted denominator level based on expected utilization of available capacity.
    c. Selecting the cost-allocation bases to use.
    d. Choosing the period to be used for the budget.

    Answer: b   *Difficulty:* 2   *Objective:* 2

43. In flexible budgets, costs that remain the same regardless of the output levels within the relevant range are
    a. allocated costs.
    b. budgeted costs.
    c. fixed costs.
    d. variable costs.

    Answer: c   *Difficulty:* 1   *Objective:* 2

THE FOLLOWING INFORMATION APPLIES TO QUESTIONS 44 THROUGH 47.
Shimon Corporation manufactures industrial-sized water coolers and uses budgeted machine-hours to allocate variable manufacturing overhead. The following information pertains to the company's manufacturing overhead data.

Budgeted output units	15,000 units
Budgeted machine-hours	5,000 hours
Budgeted variable manufacturing overhead costs for 15,000 units	$161,250
Actual output units produced	22,000 units
Actual machine-hours used	7,200 hours
Actual variable manufacturing overhead costs	$242,000

44. What is the budgeted variable overhead cost rate per output unit?
    a. $10.75
    b. $11.00
    c. $32.25
    d. $48.40

Answer: a   *Difficulty*: 2   *Objective*: 2
$161,250/15,000 = $10.75

45. What is the flexible-budget amount for variable manufacturing overhead?
    a. $165,000
    b. $236,500
    c. $242,000
    d. none of the above

Answer: b   *Difficulty*: 3   *Objective*: 2
22,000 x ($161,250/15,000)] = $236,500

46. What is the flexible-budget variance for variable manufacturing overhead?
    a. $5,500 favorable
    b. $5,500 unfavorable
    c. $4,300 favorable
    d. none of the above

Answer: b   *Difficulty*: 3   *Objective*: 2
$242,000 – [22,000 x ($161,250/15,000)] = $5,500 unfavorable

47. Variable manufacturing overhead costs were _____ for actual output.
    a. higher than expected
    b. the same as expected
    c. lower than expected
    d. unable to be determined

Answer: a   *Difficulty*: 2   *Objective*: 2

THE FOLLOWING INFORMATION APPLIES TO QUESTIONS 48 THROUGH 51.
White Corporation manufactures football jerseys and uses budgeted machine-hours to allocate variable manufacturing overhead. The following information pertains to the company's manufacturing overhead data.

Budgeted output units	20,000 units
Budgeted machine-hours	30,000 hours
Budgeted variable manufacturing overhead costs for 20,000 units	$360,000
Actual output units produced	18,000 units
Actual machine-hours used	28,000 hours
Actual variable manufacturing overhead costs	$342,000

48. What is the budgeted variable overhead cost rate per output unit?
    a. $12.00
    b. $12.21
    c. $18.00
    d. $19.00

Answer: c   *Difficulty:* 2   *Objective:* 2
$360,000/20,000 = $18.00

49. What is the flexible-budget amount for variable manufacturing overhead?
    a. $324,000
    b. $342, 000
    c. $380,000
    d. none of the above

Answer: a   *Difficulty:* 3   *Objective:* 2
18,000 x ($360,000/20,000)] = $324,000

50. What is the flexible-budget variance for variable manufacturing overhead?
    a. $18,000 favorable
    b. $18,000 unfavorable
    c. zero
    d. none of the above

Answer: b   *Difficulty:* 3   *Objective:* 2
$342,000 – [18,000 x ($360,000/20,000)] = $18,000 unfavorable

51. Variable-manufacturing overhead costs were _____ for actual output.
    a. higher than expected
    b. the same as expected
    c. lower than expected
    d. unable to be determined

Answer: a   *Difficulty:* 2   *Objective:* 2

52. The variable overhead flexible-budget variance can be further subdivided into the
    a. price variance and the efficiency variance.
    b. static-budget variance and sales-volume variance.
    c. spending variance and the efficiency variance.
    d. sales-volume variance and the spending variance.

    Answer: c   *Difficulty:* 1   *Objective:* 3

53. An unfavorable variable overhead spending variance indicates that
    a. variable overhead items were not used efficiently.
    b. the price of variable overhead items was more than budgeted.
    c. the variable overhead cost-allocation base was not used efficiently.
    d. the denominator level was not accurately determined.

    Answer: b   *Difficulty:* 2   *Objective:* 3

54. When machine-hours are used as an overhead cost-allocation base, the MOST likely cause of a favorable variable overhead spending variance is
    a. excessive machine breakdowns.
    b. the production scheduler efficiently scheduled jobs.
    c. a decline in the cost of energy.
    d. strengthened demand for the product.

    Answer: c   *Difficulty:* 3   *Objective:* 3

55. When machine-hours are used as an overhead cost-allocation base, and the unexpected purchase of a new machine results in fewer expenditures for machine maintenance, the MOST likely result would be to report
    a. a favorable variable overhead spending variance.
    b. an unfavorable variable overhead efficiency variance.
    c. a favorable fixed overhead flexible-budget variance.
    d. an unfavorable production-volume variance.

    Answer: a   *Difficulty:* 3   *Objective:* 3

56. For variable manufacturing overhead, there is no
    a. spending variance.
    b. efficiency variance.
    c. flexible-budget variance.
    d. production-volume variance.

    Answer: d   *Difficulty:* 2   *Objective:* 3

THE FOLLOWING INFORMATION APPLIES TO QUESTIONS 57 AND 58.
Kellar Corporation manufactured 1,500 chairs during June. The following variable overhead data pertain to June.

Budgeted variable overhead cost per unit	$ 12.00
Actual variable manufacturing overhead cost	$16,800
Flexible-budget amount for variable manufacturing overhead	$18,000
Variable manufacturing overhead efficiency variance	$360 unfavorable

57. What is the variable overhead flexible-budget variance?
    a. $1,200 favorable
    b. $360 unfavorable
    c. $1,560 favorable
    d. $1,200 unfavorable

    Answer: a   *Difficulty*: 2   *Objective*: 3
    $16,800 - $18,000 = $1,200 (F)

58. What is the variable overhead spending variance?
    a. $840 unfavorable
    b. $1,200 favorable
    c. $1,200 unfavorable
    d. $1,560 favorable

    Answer: d   *Difficulty*: 2   *Objective*: 3
    $1200 (F) - $360 (U) = $1,560 (F)

THE FOLLOWING INFORMATION APPLIES TO QUESTIONS 59 AND 60.
Patel Corporation manufactured 1,000 coolers during October. The following variable overhead data pertain to October.

Budgeted variable overhead cost per unit	$ 9.00
Actual variable manufacturing overhead cost	$8,400
Flexible-budget amount for variable manufacturing overhead	$9,000
Variable manufacturing overhead efficiency variance	$180 unfavorable

59. What is the variable overhead flexible-budget variance?
   a. $600 favorable
   b. $420 unfavorable
   c. $780 favorable
   d. $600 unfavorable

   Answer: a   *Difficulty*: 2   *Objective*: 3
   $8,400 - $9,000 = $600 (F)

60. What is the variable overhead spending variance?
   a. $420 unfavorable
   b. $600 favorable
   c. $600 unfavorable
   d. $780 favorable

   Answer: d   *Difficulty*: 2   *Objective*: 3
   $600 (F) - 180 (U) = $780 (F)

THE FOLLOWING INFORMATION APPLIES TO QUESTIONS 61 THROUGH 64.
Roberts Corporation manufactured 100,000 buckets during February. The overhead cost-allocation base is $5.00 per machine-hour. The following variable overhead data pertain to February.

	Actual	Budgeted
Production	100,000 units	100,000 units
Machine-hours	9,800 hours	10,000 hours
Variable overhead cost per machine-hour	$5.25	$5.00

61. What is the actual variable overhead cost?
   a. $49,000
   b. $50,000
   c. $51,450
   d. none of the above

   Answer: c   *Difficulty:* 1   *Objective:* 3
   9,800 mh x $5.25 = $51,450

62. What is the flexible-budget amount?
   a. $49,000
   b. $50,000
   c. $51,450
   d. none of the above

   Answer: b   *Difficulty:* 2   *Objective:* 3
   10,000 mh x $5.00 = $50,000

63. What is the variable overhead spending variance?
   a. $1,000 favorable
   b. $1,450 unfavorable
   c. $2,450 unfavorable
   d. none of the above

   Answer: c   *Difficulty:* 2   *Objective:* 3
   ($5.25-$5.00) x 9,800 mh = $2,450 unfavorable

64. What is the variable overhead efficiency variance?
   a. $1,000 favorable
   b. $1,450 unfavorable
   c. $2,450 unfavorable
   d. none of the above

   Answer: a   *Difficulty:* 2   *Objective:* 3
   [9,800 – 10,000] x $5.00 = $1,000 favorable

THE FOLLOWING INFORMATION APPLIES TO QUESTIONS 65 THROUGH 68.
Roberson Corporation manufactured 30,000 ice chests during September. The overhead cost-allocation base is $11.25 per machine-hour. The following variable overhead data pertain to September.

	Actual	Budgeted
Production	30,000 units	24,000 units
Machine-hours	15,000 hours	10,800 hours
Variable overhead cost per machine-hour:	$11.00	$11.25

65. What is the actual variable overhead cost?
    a. $121,500
    b. $151,875
    c. $165,000
    d. $168,750

    Answer: c   *Difficulty*: 1   *Objective*: 3
    15,000 mh x $11.00 = $165,000

66. What is the flexible-budget amount?
    a. $121,500
    b. $151,875
    c. $165,000
    d. $168,750

    Answer: b   *Difficulty*: 3   *Objective*: 3
    [30,000 x (10,800/24,000)] x $11.25 = $151,875

67. What is the variable overhead spending variance?
    a. $3,750 favorable
    b. $16,875 unfavorable
    c. $13,125 unfavorable
    d. $30,375 unfavorable

    Answer: a   *Difficulty*: 3   *Objective*: 3
    ($11.00-$11.25) x 15,000 mh = $3,750 favorable

68. What is the variable overhead efficiency variance?
    a. $3,750 favorable
    b. $16,875 unfavorable
    c. $13,125 unfavorable
    d. $30,375 unfavorable

    Answer: b   *Difficulty*: 3   *Objective*: 3
    [15,000 - (30,000 x .45) mh] x $11.25 = $16,875 unfavorable

69. The variable overhead efficiency variance is computed _____ and interpreted _____ the direct-cost efficiency variance.
    a. the same as; the same as
    b. the same as; differently than
    c. differently than; the same as
    d. differently than; differently than

    Answer: b   *Difficulty:* 2   *Objective:* 4

70. An unfavorable variable overhead efficiency variance indicates that
    a. variable overhead items were not used efficiently.
    b. the price of variable overhead items was less than budgeted.
    c. the variable overhead cost-allocation base was not used efficiently.
    d. the denominator level was not accurately determined.

    Answer: c   *Difficulty:* 2   *Objective:* 4

71. Variable overhead costs can be managed by
    a. reducing the consumption of the cost-allocation base.
    b. eliminating nonvalue-adding variable costs.
    c. planning for appropriate capacity levels.
    d. both (a) and (b).

    Answer: d   *Difficulty:* 2   *Objective:* 4

72. When machine-hours are used as a cost-allocation base, the item MOST likely to contribute to a favorable variable overhead efficiency variance is
    a. excessive machine breakdowns.
    b. the production scheduler's impressive scheduling of machines.
    c. a decline in the cost of energy.
    d. strengthened demand for the product.

    Answer: b   *Difficulty:* 3   *Objective:* 4

73. When machine-hours are used as a cost-allocation base, the item MOST likely to contribute to an unfavorable variable overhead efficiency variance is
    a. using more machine hours than budgeted.
    b. workers wastefully using variable overhead items.
    c. unused capacity.
    d. more units being produced than planned.

    Answer: a   *Difficulty:* 3   *Objective:* 4

74. When machine-hours are used as an overhead cost-allocation base, a rush order resulting in unplanned overtime that used less-skilled workers on the machines would MOST likely contribute to reporting
    a. a favorable variable overhead spending variance.
    b. an unfavorable variable overhead efficiency variance.
    c. a favorable fixed overhead flexible-budget variance.
    b. an unfavorable production-volume variance.

    Answer: b   *Difficulty:* 3   *Objective:* 4

75. When machine-hours are used as an overhead cost-allocation base and annual leasing costs for equipment unexpectedly increase, the MOST likely result would be to report
    a. an unfavorable variable overhead spending variance.
    b. a favorable variable overhead efficiency variance.
    c. an unfavorable fixed overhead flexible-budget variance.
    b. a favorable production-volume variance.

    Answer: c   *Difficulty:* 3   *Objective:* 4,5

76. The fixed overhead cost variance can be further subdivided into the
    a. price variance and the efficiency variance.
    b. spending variance and flexible-budget variance.
    c. production-volume variance and the efficiency variance.
    d. flexible-budget variance and the production-volume variance.

    Answer: d   *Difficulty:* 1   *Objective:* 5

77. The amount reported for fixed overhead on the static budget is also reported
    a. as actual fixed costs.
    b. as allocated fixed overhead.
    c. on the flexible budget.
    d. as both (b) and (c).

    Answer: c   *Difficulty:* 1   *Objective:* 5

78. An unfavorable fixed overhead spending variance indicates that
    a. there was more excess capacity than planned.
    b. the price of fixed overhead items cost more than budgeted.
    c. the fixed overhead cost-allocation base was not used efficiently.
    d. the denominator level was more than planned.

    Answer: b   *Difficulty:* 2   *Objective:* 5

79. A favorable fixed overhead spending variance might indicate that
    a. more capacity was used than planned.
    b. the denominator level was less than planned.
    c. the fixed overhead cost-allocation base was not used efficiently.
    d. a plant expansion did not proceed as originally planned.

    Answer: d   *Difficulty*:   3   *Objective*:   5

80. For fixed manufacturing overhead, there is no
    a. spending variance.
    b. efficiency variance.
    c. flexible-budget variance.
    d. production-volume variance.

    Answer: b   *Difficulty*:   2   *Objective*:   5

THE FOLLOWING INFORMATION APPLIES TO QUESTIONS 81 THROUGH 84.
Jenny's Corporation manufactured 25,000 grooming kits for horses during March. The fixed-overhead cost-allocation rate is $20.00 per machine-hour. The following fixed overhead data pertain to March.

	Actual	Static Budget
Production	25,000 units	24,000 units
Machine-hours	6,100 hours	6,000 hours
Fixed overhead costs for March	$123,000	$120,000

81. What is the flexible-budget amount?
    a. $120,000
    b. $122,000
    c. $123,000
    d. $125,000

Answer: a *Difficulty*: 2 *Objective*: 5
$120,000, the same lump sum as the static budget

82. What is the amount of fixed overhead allocated to production?
    a. $120,000
    b. $122,000
    c. $123,000
    d. $125,000

Answer: d *Difficulty*: 3 *Objective*: 5
[25,000 x (6,000/24,000)] x $20.00 = $125,000

83. What is the fixed overhead spending variance?
    a. $1,000 unfavorable
    b. $2,000 favorable
    c. $3,000 unfavorable
    d. $5,000 favorable

Answer: c *Difficulty*: 3 *Objective*: 5
$123,000 actual costs - $120,000 budgeted cost = $3,000 unfavorable

84. What is the fixed overhead production-volume variance?
    a. $1,000 unfavorable
    b. $2,000 favorable
    c. $3,000 unfavorable
    d. $5,000 favorable

Answer: d *Difficulty*: 3 *Objective*: 5
$120,000 - [25,000 x (6,000/24,000) x $20.00] = $5,000 favorable

THE FOLLOWING INFORMATION APPLIES TO QUESTIONS 85 THROUGH 88.
Matthew's Corporation manufactured 10,000 golf bags during March. The fixed overhead cost-allocation rate is $20.00 per machine-hour. The following fixed overhead data pertain to March.

	Actual	Static Budget
Production	10,000 units	12,000 units
Machine-hours	5,100 hours	6,000 hours
Fixed overhead cost for March	$122,000	$120,000

85. What is the flexible-budget amount?
    a. $100,000
    b. $102,000
    c. $120,000
    d. $122,000

Answer: c   *Difficulty*: 2   *Objective*: 5
$120,000, the same lump sum as the static budget

86. What is the amount of fixed overhead allocated to production?
    a. $100,000
    b. $102,000
    c. $120,000
    d. $122,000

Answer: a   *Difficulty*: 3   *Objective*: 5
[10,000 x (6,000/12,000)] x $20.00 = $100,000

87. What is the fixed overhead production-volume variance?
    a. $2,000 unfavorable
    b. $18,000 favorable
    c. $20,000 unfavorable
    d. $22,000 unfavorable

Answer: c   *Difficulty*: 3   *Objective*: 5
$120,000 - [10,000 x (6,000/12,000) x $20.00] = $20,000 unfavorable

88. Fixed overhead is
    a. overallocated by $2,000.
    b. underallocated by $2,000.
    c. overallocated by $22,000.
    d. underallocated by $22,000.

Answer: d   *Difficulty*: 3   *Objective*: 5
$122,000 - [10,000 x (6,000/12,000) x $20.00] = $22,000 underallocated

89. The production-volume variance may also be referred to as the
   a. flexible-budget variance.
   b. denominator-level variance.
   c. spending variance.
   d. efficiency variance.

   Answer: b   *Difficulty:* 1   *Objective:* 6

90. A favorable production-volume variance indicates that the company
   a. has good management.
   b. has allocated more fixed overhead costs than budgeted.
   c. has a total economic gain from using excess capacity.
   d. should increase capacity.

   Answer: b   *Difficulty:* 2   *Objective:* 6

91. An unfavorable production-volume variance of $40,000 indicates that the company has
   a. unused fixed manufacturing overhead capacity.
   b. overallocated $40,000 of fixed manufacturing overhead costs.
   c. $40,000 more capacity than needed.
   d. an economic loss of $40,000 from selling fewer products than planned.

   Answer: a   *Difficulty:* 3   *Objective:* 6

92. When machine-hours are used as a cost-allocation base, the item MOST likely to contribute to a favorable production-volume variance is
   a. an increase in the selling price of the product.
   b. the purchase of a new manufacturing machine costing considerably less than expected.
   c. a decline in the cost of energy.
   d. strengthened demand for the product.

   Answer: d   *Difficulty:* 3   *Objective:* 6

93. When machine-hours are used as a cost-allocation base, the item MOST likely to contribute to an unfavorable production-volume variance is
   a. a new competitor gaining market share.
   b. a new manufacturing machine costing considerably more than expected.
   c. an increase in the cost of energy.
   d. strengthened demand for the product.

   Answer: a   *Difficulty:* 3   *Objective:* 6

94. Excess capacity is a sign
   a. that capacity should be reduced.
   b. that capacity may need to be re-evaluated.
   c. that the company is suffering a significant economic loss.
   d. of good management decisions.

   Answer: b   *Difficulty:* 2   *Objective:* 6

95. An unfavorable production-volume variance
    a. is not a good measure of a lost production opportunity.
    b. measures the total economic gain or loss due to unused capacity.
    c. measures the amount of extra fixed costs planned for but not used.
    d. takes into account the effect of additional revenues due to maintaining higher prices.

    Answer: c   *Difficulty*: 3   *Objective*: 6

96. The difference between budgeted fixed manufacturing overhead and the fixed manufacturing overhead allocated to actual output units achieved is called the fixed overhead
    a. efficiency variance.
    b. flexible-budget variance.
    c. combined-variance analysis.
    d. production-volume variance.

    Answer: d   *Difficulty*: 1   *Objective*: 6

97. Variable overhead costs
    a. never have any unused capacity.
    b. have no production-volume variance.
    c. allocated are always the same as the flexible-budget amount.
    d. are all of the above.

    Answer: d   *Difficulty*: 2   *Objective*: 7

98. Fixed overhead costs
    a. never have any unused capacity.
    b. should be unitized for planning purposes.
    c. are unaffected by the degree of operating efficiency in a given budget period.
    d. are both (a) and (b).

    Answer: c   *Difficulty*: 2   *Objective*: 7

99. Fixed overhead costs must be unitized for
    a. financial reporting purposes.
    b. planning purposes.
    c. calculating the production-volume variance.
    d. both (a) and (c).

    Answer: d   *Difficulty*: 2   *Objective*: 7

100. Generally Accepted Accounting Principles require that unitized fixed manufacturing costs be used for
    a. pricing decisions.
    b. costing decisions.
    c. external reporting.
    d. all of the above.

Answer: c   *Difficulty:*   1   *Objective:*   7

101. A nonfinancial measure of performance evaluation is
    a. increased sales.
    b. reducing distribution costs.
    c. energy used per machine-hour.
    d. all of the above.

Answer: c   *Difficulty:*   2   *Objective:*   7

102. Variance information regarding nonmanufacturing costs can be used
    a. to plan capacity in the service sector.
    b. to control distribution costs in the retail sector.
    c. to determine the most profitable services offered by a bank.
    d. for all of the above.

Answer: d   *Difficulty:*   2   *Objective:*   7

103. Tucker Company uses a standard cost system. In March, $133,000 of variable manufacturing overhead costs was incurred and the flexible-budget amount for the month was $150,000. Which of the following variable manufacturing overhead entries would have been recorded for March?

    a. Accounts Payable Control and other accounts $150,000
            Work-in-Process Control $150,000

    b. Variable Manufacturing Overhead Allocated $150,000
            Accounts Payable and other accounts $150,000

    c. Work-in-Process Control $133,000
            Accounts Payable Control and other accounts $133,000

    d. Variable Manufacturing Overhead Control $133,000
            Accounts Payable Control and other accounts $133,000

Answer: d   *Difficulty:*   2   *Objective:*   7

104. Alvarado Company made the following journal entry, therefore:

Variable Manufacturing Overhead Allocated	$100,000	
Variable Manufacturing Overhead Efficiency Variance	30,000	
Variable Manufacturing Overhead Control		$125,000
Variable Manufacturing Overhead Spending Variance		5,000

    a.   Alvarado overallocated variable manufacturing overhead.
    b.   a $5,000 favorable spending variance was recorded.
    c.   Work-in-Process is currently overstated.
    d.   this entry may be recorded yearly to provide timely feedback to managers.

Answer: b   *Difficulty:* 2   *Objective:* 7

105. John's Football Manufacturing Company reported:

Actual fixed overhead	$800,000
Fixed manufacturing overhead spending variance	$20,000 favorable
Fixed manufacturing production-volume variance	$30,000 unfavorable

To isolate these variances at the end of the accounting period, John would debit Fixed Manufacturing Overhead Allocated
    a.   for $780,000.
    b.   for $790,000.
    c.   for $800,000.
    d.   for $810,000.

Answer: b   *Difficulty:* 2   *Objective:* 7

106. Brandon's Basketball Manufacturing Company reported:

Actual fixed overhead	$1,000,000
Fixed manufacturing overhead spending variance	$60,000 unfavorable
Fixed manufacturing production-volume variance	$40,000 unfavorable

To isolate these variances at the end of the accounting period, Brandon would
    a.   debit Fixed Manufacturing Overhead Allocated for $1,000,000.
    b.   debit Fixed Manufacturing Overhead Spending Variance for $60,000.
    c.   credit Fixed Manufacturing Production-Volume Variance for $40,000
    d.   credit Fixed Manufacturing Control Allocated for $900,000

Answer: b   *Difficulty:* 2   *Objective:* 7

107. Jovana Company uses a standard cost system. In March, $117,000 of variable manufacturing overhead costs was incurred and the flexible-budget amount for the month was $120,000. Which of the following variable manufacturing overhead entries would have been recorded for March?

a. Accounts Payable Control and other accounts $120,000
    Work-in-Process Control $120,000

b. Work-in-Process Control $120,000
    Variable Manufacturing Overhead Allocated $120,000

c. Work-in-Process Control $117,000
    Accounts Payable Control and other accounts $117,000

d. Accounts Payable Control and other accounts $117,000
    Variable Manufacturing Overhead Control $117,000

Answer: b   *Difficulty:* 2   *Objective:* 7

108. Tate Company makes the following journal entry, therefore:

Variable Manufacturing Overhead Allocated	$150,000	
Variable Manufacturing Overhead Efficiency Variance	5,000	
Variable Manufacturing Overhead Control		$125,000
Variable Manufacturing Overhead Spending Variance		30,000

a. Tate underallocated variable manufacturing overhead.
b. a $30,000 unfavorable spending variance was recorded.
c. Work-in-Process is currently understated.
d. a $25,000 favorable flexible-budget variance was recorded.

Answer: d   *Difficulty:* 2   *Objective:* 7

109. Jeremy's Football Manufacturing Company reported:

Actual fixed overhead	$500,000
Fixed manufacturing overhead spending variance	$30,000 favorable
Fixed manufacturing production-volume variance	$20,000 unfavorable

To isolate these variances at the end of the accounting period, Jeremy would debit Fixed Manufacturing Overhead Allocated
a. for $480,000.
b. for $490,000.
c. for $500,000.
d. for $510,000.

Answer: d   *Difficulty:* 2   *Objective:* 7

110. Kristin's Basketball Manufacturing Company reported:

Actual fixed overhead	$800,000
Fixed manufacturing overhead spending variance	$60,000 favorable
Fixed manufacturing production-volume variance	$40,000 favorable

To isolate these variances at the end of the accounting period, Kristin would
a. debit Fixed Manufacturing Overhead Allocated for $900,000.
b. debit Fixed Manufacturing Overhead Spending Variance for $60,000.
c. debit Fixed Manufacturing Production-Volume Variance for $40,000
d. do all of the above

Answer: a   *Difficulty*: 2   *Objective*: 7

Variances	Spending	Efficiency	Production-Volume
Variable manufacturing overhead	$ 4,500 F	$15,000 U	(B)
Fixed manufacturing overhead	$10,000 U	(A)	$40,000 U

111. Above is a
   a.   4-variance analysis.
   b.   3-variance analysis.
   c.   2-variance analysis.
   d.   1-variance analysis.

   Answer: a   *Difficulty*:   1   *Objective*:   7

112. In the above chart, the amounts for (A) and (B), respectively, are
   a. $10,500 U; $55,000 U
   b. $10,500 U;   Zero
   c.   Zero; $55,000 U
   d.   Zero;   Zero

   Answer: d   *Difficulty*:   1   *Objective*:   7

113. In a 3-variance analysis the spending variance should be
   a. $ 4,500 F.
   b. $10,000 U.
   c. $ 5,500 U.
   d. $10,500 U.

   Answer: c   *Difficulty*:   1   *Objective*:   7
   $4,500 F + $10,000 U = $ 5,500 U

114. In a 2-variance analysis the flexible-budget variance and the production-volume
   variance should be _____, respectively.
   a. $5,500 U; $55,000 U
   b. $20,500 U; $40,000 U
   c. $10,500 U; $50,000 U
   d. $60,500 U;   Zero

   Answer: b   *Difficulty*:   2   *Objective*:   7
   $4,500 F + $10,000 U + $15,000 U = $20,500 U; $40,000 U

115. In a 1-variance analysis the total overhead variance should be
   a. $20,500 U.
   b. $60,500 U.
   c. $121,000 U.
   d.   none of the above.

   Answer: b   *Difficulty*:   2   *Objective*:   7
   $4,500 F + $10,000 U + $15,000 U + $40,000 U = $60,500 U

THE FOLLOWING INFORMATION APPLIES TO QUESTIONS 116 THROUGH 120.
Munoz, Inc. produces a special line of plastic toy racing cars. Munoz, Inc. produces the cars in batches. To manufacture a batch of the cars, Munoz, Inc. must set up the machines and molds. Setup costs are batch-level costs because they are associated with batches rather than individual units of products. A separate Setup Department is responsible for setting up machines and molds for different styles of car.

Setup overhead costs consist of some costs that are variable and some costs that are fixed with respect to the number of setup-hours. The following information pertains to June 2004.

	Actual Amounts	Static-budget Amounts
Units produced and sold	15,000	11,250
Batch size (number of units per batch)	250	225
Setup-hours per batch	5	5.25
Variable overhead cost per setup-hour	$40	$38
Total fixed setup overhead costs	$14,400	$14,000

116. Calculate the efficiency variance for variable setup overhead costs.
    a. $1,500 unfavorable
    b. $525 favorable
    c. $975 unfavorable
    d. $1,500 favorable

Answer: a   *Difficulty:*   3   *Objective:*   8
[(11,250 / 225) x 5.25 x $40] – [(11,250 / 250) x 5 x $40] = $1,500 (U)

117. Calculate the spending variance for variable setup overhead costs.
    a. $1,500 unfavorable
    b. $525 favorable
    c. $975 unfavorable
    d. $1,500 favorable

Answer: b   *Difficulty:*   3   *Objective:*   8
(11,250 / 225) x 5.25 x ($38 - $40) = $525 (F)

118. Calculate the flexible-budget variance for variable setup overhead costs.
    a. $1,500 unfavorable
    b. $525 favorable
    c. $975 unfavorable
    d. $1,500 favorable

Answer: c   *Difficulty:*   3   *Objective:*   8
$1,500 (U) + $525 (F) = $975 (U)

119. Calculate the spending variance for fixed setup overhead costs.
    a. $3,200 unfavorable
    b. $400 unfavorable
    c. $3,600 unfavorable
    d. $400 favorable

    Answer: b   *Difficulty*:   3   *Objective*:   8
    $14,000 - $14,400 = $400 (U)

120. Calculate the production-volume variance for fixed setup overhead costs.
    a. $3,200 unfavorable
    b. $400 unfavorable
    c. $3,600 unfavorable
    d. $400 favorable

    Answer: c   *Difficulty*:   3   *Objective*:   8
    Normal setup hours = (15,000 / 250) x 5 = 300 hours
    OH rate = $14,400 / 300 = $48 per setup hour
    $14,400 – [(11,250 / 250) x 5 x $48] = $3,600 (U)

121. Fixed and variable cost variances can _____ be applied to activity-based costing systems.
    a.   always
    b.   most times
    c.   seldom
    d.   never

    Answer: a   *Difficulty*:   1   *Objective*:   8

122.   Jael Equipment uses a flexible budget for its indirect manufacturing costs. For 20x4, the company anticipated that it would produce 18,000 units with 3,500 machine-hours and 7,200 employee days. The costs and cost drivers were to be as follows:

	Fixed	Variable	Cost driver
Product handling	$30,000	$0.40	per unit
Inspection	8,000	8.00	per 100 unit batch
Utilities	400	4.00	per 100 unit batch
Maintenance	1,000	0.20	per machine-hour
Supplies		5.00	per employee day

During the year, the company processed 20,000 units, worked 7,500 employee days, and had 4,000 machine-hours. The actual costs for 20x4 were:

	Actual costs
Product handling	$36,000
Inspection	9,000
Utilities	1,600
Maintenance	1,200
Supplies	37,500

Required:

a. Prepare the static budget using the overhead items above and then compute the static-budget variances.

b. Prepare the flexible budget using the overhead items above and then compute the flexible-budget variances.

Answer:

a.

Jael Equipment
Overhead Static Budget with Variances
20x4

	Actual	Static Budget	Variances
Product handling	$36,000	$37,200	$1,200 F
Inspection	9,000	9,440	440 F
Utilities	1,600	1,120	480 U
Maintenance	1,200	1,700	500 F
Supplies	37,500	36,000	1,500 U
Total	$85,300	$85,460	$160 F

b.

Jael Equipment
Overhead Flexible Budget with Variances
20x4

	Actual	Flexible Budget	Variances
Product handling	$36,000	$38,000	$2,000 F
Inspection	9,000	9,600	600 F
Utilities	1,600	1,200	400 U
Maintenance	1,200	1,800	600 F
Supplies	37,500	37,500	0
Total	$85,300	$88,100	$2,800 F

Difficulty: 2   *Objective*:   1

123.   Heather's Pillow Company manufactures pillows. The 20x4 operating budget is based on production of 20,000 pillows with 0.5 machine-hours allowed per pillow. Variable manufacturing overhead is anticipated to be $220,000.

Actual production for 20x4 was 18,000 pillows using 9,500 machine-hours. Actual variable costs were $20 per machine-hour.

Required:

Calculate the variable overhead spending and efficiency variances.

Answer:
Budgeted variable overhead per hour = $220,000/(20,000 x 0.5) machine-hours = $22

Spending variance = ($22 - $20) x 9,500 = $19,000 favorable

Efficiency variance = [9,500 - (20,000 x 0.5)] x $22 = $11,000 unfavorable

Difficulty: 3   *Objective*:   3

124. McKenna Company manufactured 1,000 units during April with a total overhead budget of $12,400. However, while manufacturing the 1,000 units the microcomputer that contained the month's cost information broke down. With the computer out of commission, the accountant has been unable to complete the variance analysis report. The information missing from the report is lettered in the following set of data:

Variable overhead:
    Standard cost per unit: 0.4 labor hour at $4 per hour
    Actual costs: $2,100 for 376 hours
    Flexible budget: _a
    Total flexible-budget variance: _b
    Variable overhead spending variance: _c
    Variable overhead efficiency variance: _d

Fixed overhead:
    Budgeted costs: _e
    Actual costs: _f
    Flexible-budget variance: $500 favorable

Required:
Compute the missing elements in the report represented by the lettered items.

Answer:

a. 1,000 x 0.40 x $4 = $1,600

b. $2,100 - $1,600 = $500 unfavorable

c. $2,100 - (376 x $4) = $596 unfavorable

d. $1,504 - $1,600 = $96 favorable

e. $12,400 - $1,600 = $10,800

f. $10,800 - $500 favorable = $10,300

Difficulty: 3   *Objectives:* 3-6

125. Everjoice Company develops clocks. The fixed overhead costs for 20x4total $720,000. The company uses direct labor-hours for fixed overhead allocation and anticipates 240,000 hours during the year for 480,000 units. An equal number of units are budgeted for each month.

During June, 42,000 clocks were produced and $63,000 was spent on fixed overhead.

Required:
a. Determine the fixed overhead rate for 20x4based on units of input.
b. Determine the fixed overhead static-budget variance for June.
c. Determine the production-volume overhead variance for June.

Answer:

a. Fixed overhead rate = $720,000/240,000 = $3.00 per hour

b. Fixed overhead static budget variance = $63,000 - $720,000/12 = $3,000 unfavorable

c. Budgeted fixed overhead rate per output unit = $720,000/480,000 = $1.50

 Denominator level in output units = (40,000 - 42,000) x $1.50 = $3,000 favorable

Difficulty: 3   *Objectives*: 5, 6

126.   Lungren has budgeted construction overhead for August of $260,000 for variable costs and $435,000 for fixed costs. Actual costs for the month totaled $275,000 for variable and $445,000 for fixed. Allocated fixed overhead totaled $440,000. The company tracks each item in an overhead control account before allocations are made to individual jobs. Spending variances for August were $10,000 unfavorable for variable and $10,000 unfavorable for fixed. The production-volume overhead variance was $5,000 favorable.

Required:
a. Make journal entries for the actual costs incurred.
b. Make journal entries to record the variances for August.

Answer:

a.   Variable Overhead Control $275,000
          Accounts Payable and other accounts $275,000
     To record actual variable construction overhead

     Fixed Overhead Control $445,000
          Accumulated Depreciation, etc. $445,000
     To record actual fixed construction overhead

b.   Variable Overhead Allocated $260,000
     Variable Overhead Spending Variance   10,000
     Variable Overhead Efficiency Variance*   5,000
          Variable Overhead Control $275,000
     To record variances for the period

     *Arrived at this number by default

     Fixed Overhead Allocated $440,000
     Fixed Overhead Spending Variance   10,000
          Fixed Overhead Production-Volume Variance $5,000
          Fixed Overhead Control   445,000
     To record variances for the period

Difficulty: 3   *Objective*:   7

127. Different management levels in Bates, Inc., require varying degrees of managerial accounting information. Because of the need to comply with the managers' requests, four different variances for manufacturing overhead are computed each month. The information for the September overhead expenditures is as follows:

Budgeted output units	3,200 units
Budgeted fixed manufacturing overhead	$20,000
Budgeted variable manufacturing overhead	$5 per direct labor hour
Budgeted direct manufacturing labor hours	2 hours per unit
Fixed manufacturing costs incurred	$26,000
Direct manufacturing labor hours used	7,200
Variable manufacturing costs incurred	$35,600
Actual units manufactured	3,400

Required:
a. Compute a 4-variance analysis for the plant controller.
b. Compute a 3-variance analysis for the plant manager.
c. Compute a 2-variance analysis for the corporate controller.
d. Compute the flexible-budget variance for the manufacturing vice president.

Answer:
a. *4-variance analysis*:
Variable overhead spending variance = $35,600 - (7,200 x $5) = $400 favorable
Variable overhead efficiency variance = $5 x (7,200 - 6,800*) = $2,000 unfavorable   *3,400 units x 2 hours = 6,800 hours
Fixed overhead spending variance = $26,000 - $20,000 = $6,000 unfavorable
Fixed overhead production-volume variance = $20,000 - (3,400 x 2 x $3.125*) = $1,250 favorable
*$20,000/(3,200 units x 2 hours) = $3.125

b. *3-variance analysis:*
Spending variance = $400 favorable + $6,000 unfavorable = $5,600 unfavorable
Efficiency variance = $2,000 unfavorable
Production-volume variance = $1,250 favorable

c. *2-variance analysis:*
Flexible-budget variance = $400 F + $2,000 U + $6,000 U = $7,600 unfavorable
Production-volume variance = $1,250 favorable

d. *1-variance analysis*:

	Actual	Flexible Budget	Variances
Fixed overhead	$26,000	$21,250*	$4,750 U
Variable overhead	35,600	34,000**	1,600 U
Flexible-budget variance			$6,350 U

*$3.125 x 3,400 x 2 = $21,250
**3,400 x 2 x $5 = $34,000

Difficulty: 3   *Objective:*   7

128. Casey Corporation produces a special line of basketball hoops. Casey Corporation produces the hoops in batches. To manufacture a batch of the basketball hoops, Casey Corporation must set up the machines and molds. Setup costs are batch-level costs because they are associated with batches rather than individual units of products. A separate Setup Department is responsible for setting up machines and molds for different styles of basketball hoops.

Setup overhead costs consist of some costs that are variable and some costs that are fixed with respect to the number of setup-hours. The following information pertains to January 2004.

	Static-budget Amounts	Actual Amounts
Basketball hoops produced and sold	30,000	28,000
Batch size (number of units per batch)	200	250
Setup-hours per batch	5	4
Variable overhead cost per setup hour	$10	$9
Total fixed setup overhead costs	$22,500	$21,000

Required:

a. Calculate the efficiency variance for variable setup overhead costs.
b. Calculate the spending variance for variable setup overhead costs.
c. Calculate the flexible-budget variance for variable setup overhead costs.
d. Calculate the spending variance for fixed setup overhead costs.
e. Calculate the production-volume variance for fixed setup overhead costs.

Answer:

a. $((28,000 / 250) \times 4 \times \$10) - (28,000 / 200) \times 5 \times \$10) = \$2,520$ (F)

b. $(28,000 / 250) \times 4 \times (\$9 - \$10) = \$448$ (F)

c. $\$2,520$ (F) + $\$448$ (F) = $\$2,968$ (F)

d. $\$22,500 - \$21,000 = \$1,500$ (F)

e. Normal setup-hours = $(30,000 / 200) \times 5 = 750$ hours
    OH rate = $\$22,500 / 750 = \$30$ per setup-hour
    $\$22,500 - ((28,000 / 200) \times 5 \times \$30) = \$1,500$ (U)

Difficulty: 3   *Objective:* 8

129. Can the variable overhead efficiency variance
    a.   be *computed* the same way as the efficiency variance for direct-cost items?
    b.   be *interpreted* the same way as the efficiency variance for direct-cost items?
         Explain.

Answer:
    a.   Yes, the variable overhead efficiency variance can be computed the same way as
         the efficiency variance for direct-cost items.
    b.   No, the interpretations are different.
         The variable overhead efficiency variance focuses on the quantity of allocation-
         base used, while the efficiency variance for direct-cost items focuses on the
         quantity of materials and labor-hours used.

Difficulty: 2   *Objectives*: 3, 4

130. Explain why there is no efficiency variance for fixed manufacturing overhead costs.

Answer:
There is no efficiency variance for fixed overhead costs because a given lump sum of
fixed costs will be unaffected by how efficiently machine-hours are used to produce
output in a given budget period.

Difficulty: 2   *Objective*:   5

131. Explain why there is no production-volume variance for variable manufacturing
    overhead costs.

Answer:
There is no production-volume variance for variable overhead costs because the amount
of variable overhead allocated is always the same as the flexible-budget amount.

Difficulty: 2   *Objective*:   7

132. Abby Company has just implemented a new cost accounting system that provides two variances for fixed manufacturing overhead. While the company's managers are familiar with the concept of spending variances, they are unclear as to how to interpret the production-volume overhead variances. Currently, the company has a production capacity of 54,000 units a month, although it generally produces only 46,000 units. However, in any given month the actual production is probably something other than 46,000.

Required:

a. Does the production-volume overhead variance measure the difference between the 54,000 and 46,000, or the difference between the 46,000 and the actual monthly production? Explain.

b. What advice can you provide the managers that will help them interpret the production-volume overhead variances?

Answer:

a. It is the difference between the 46,000 and the actual production level for the period. The difference between the 54,000 and the 46,000 is the unused capacity that was planned for the period. The difference between the 46,000 and the actual level was not planned.

b. When actual outputs are less than the denominator level, the production-volume variance is unfavorable. This is opposite the label given other variances that have a favorable label when costs are less than the budgeted amount; therefore, caution is needed.

The production-volume variance is favorable when actual production exceeds what was planned for the period. This actually provides for a cost per unit amount that was less than budgeted using the planned denominator.

Difficulty: 3   *Objective:*   6

CHAPTER 9: INVENTORY COSTING AND CAPACITY ANALYSIS

TRUE/FALSE

1.   Absorption costing "absorbs" only variable manufacturing costs.

    Answer: False   *Difficulty*:   1   *Objective*:   1
    Absorption costing "absorbs" all manufacturing costs, both fixed and variable.

2.   Variable costing includes all variable costs – both manufacturing and nonmanufacturing – in inventory.

    Answer: False   *Difficulty*:   1   *Objective*:   1
    Variable costing includes only manufacturing variable costs in inventory.

3.   Under both variable and absorption costing, all variable manufacturing costs are inventoriable costs.

    Answer: True   *Difficulty*:   1   *Objective*:   1

4.   Under variable costing, fixed manufacturing costs are treated as an expense of the period.

    Answer: True   *Difficulty*:   1   *Objective*:   1

5.   The contribution-margin format of the income statement is used with absorption costing.

    Answer: False   *Difficulty*:   1   *Objective*:   2
    The contribution-margin format of the income statement is used with *variable* costing.

6.   The contribution-margin format of the income statement distinguishes manufacturing costs from nonmanufacturing costs.

    Answer: False   *Difficulty*:   1   *Objective*:   2
    The contribution-margin format of the income statement distinguishes variable costs from fixed costs.

7.   The gross-margin format of the income statement highlights the lump sum of fixed manufacturing costs.

    Answer: False   *Difficulty*:   2   *Objective*:   2
    The gross-margin format of the income statement distinguishes manufacturing costs from nonmanufacturing costs, but does not highlight the lump sum of fixed manufacturing costs.

8. In absorption costing, all nonmanufacturing costs are subtracted from gross margin.

   Answer: True   *Difficulty:* 1   *Objective:* 2

9. Direct costing is a perfect way to describe the variable-costing inventory method.

   Answer: False   *Difficulty:* 2   *Objective:* 2
   Direct costing is a less than perfect way to describe this method because not all variable costs are inventoriable costs.

10. When production deviates from the denominator level, a production-volume variance always exists under absorption costing.

    Answer: True   *Difficulty:* 1   *Objective:* 3

11. Fixed manufacturing costs included in cost of goods available for sale + the production-volume variance will always = total fixed manufacturing costs under absorption costing.

    Answer: True   *Difficulty:* 1   *Objective:* 3

12. The production-volume variance only exists under absorption costing and not under variable costing.

    Answer: True   *Difficulty:* 1   *Objective:* 3

13. When the unit level of inventory increases during an accounting period, operating income is greater under variable costing than absorption costing.

    Answer: False   *Difficulty:* 3   *Objective:* 3
    Greater operating income is reported under variable costing than absorption costing when the unit level of inventory *decreases* during an accounting period.

14. The difference in operating income under absorption costing and variable costing is due solely to the timing difference of expensing fixed manufacturing costs.

    Answer: True   *Difficulty:* 2   *Objective:* 3

15. If managers report inventories of zero at the start and end of each accounting period, operating incomes under absorption costing and variable costing will be the same.

    Answer: True   *Difficulty:* 2   *Objective:* 3

16. Many companies use variable costing for internal reporting to reduce the undesirable incentive to build up inventories.

    Answer: True   *Difficulty:* 2   *Objective:* 4

17. Under variable costing, managers can increase operating income by simply producing more inventory at the end of the accounting period even if that inventory never gets sold.

Answer: False   *Difficulty:* 3   *Objective:* 4
Under *absorption* costing, managers can increase operating income by producing more inventory at the end of the accounting period.

18. Nonfinancial measures such as comparing units in ending inventory this period to units in ending inventory last period can help reduce buildup of excess inventory.

Answer: True   *Difficulty:* 1   *Objective:* 4

19. One of the most common problems reported by companies using variable costing is the difficulty of classifying costs into fixed or variable categories.

Answer: True   *Difficulty:* 2   *Objective:* 4

20. Managers can increase operating income when absorption costing is used by producing more inventory.

Answer: True   *Difficulty:* 2   *Objective:* 4

21. A manager is able to increase operating income by deferring maintenance beyond the current accounting period when absorption costing is used.

Answer: True   *Difficulty:* 2   *Objective:* 4

22. Throughput costing considers only direct materials and direct manufacturing labor to be truly variable costs.

Answer: False   *Difficulty:* 1   *Objective:* 5
Throughput costing considers *only direct materials* to be truly variable costs.

23. When production quantity exceeds sales, throughput costing results in reporting greater operating income than variable costing.

Answer: False   *Difficulty:* 3   *Objective:* 5
When production quantity exceeds sales, throughput costing results in reporting *lower* operating income than variable costing.

24. Throughput costing provides more incentive to produce for inventory than does absorption costing.

Answer: False   *Difficulty:* 1   *Objective:* 5
Throughput costing provides less incentive to produce for inventory than does absorption costing.

25. A company may use absorption costing for external reports and still choose to use throughput costing for internal reports.

   Answer: True   *Difficulty:* 2   *Objective:* 5

26. Throughput contribution equals revenues minus all product costs.

   Answer: False   *Difficulty:* 1   *Objective:* 5
   Throughput contribution equals revenues minus direct materials costs.

27. Determining the "right" level of capacity is one of the most strategic and difficult decisions managers face.

   Answer: True   *Difficulty:* 2   *Objective:* 6

28. Both theoretical and practical capacity measure capacity in terms of demand for the output.

   Answer: False   *Difficulty:* 2   *Objective:* 6
   Both theoretical and practical capacity measure capacity in terms of what a plant can supply – available capacity.

29. Normal capacity utilization is the expected level of capacity utilization for the current budget period, typically one year.

   Answer: False   *Difficulty:* 1   *Objective:* 6
   Master-budget capacity utilization is the expected level of capacity utilization for the current budget period, typically one year.

30. Theoretical capacity is generally much larger than master-budget capacity utilization.

   Answer: True   *Difficulty:* 1   *Objective:* 6

31. Theoretical capacity allows time for regular machine maintenance.

   Answer: False   *Difficulty:* 2   *Objective:* 6
   Theoretical capacity is the denominator-level concept that is based on producing at full efficiency all the time.

32. Estimates of human factors such as the increased risk of injury when machines work at faster speeds are important when estimating practical capacity.

   Answer: True   *Difficulty:* 2   *Objective:* 6

33. Theoretical capacity is unattainable in the real world.

   Answer: True   *Difficulty:* 1   *Objective:* 6

34. If a company chooses practical capacity for planning purposes, it must also use practical capacity for performance evaluation.

Answer: False   *Difficulty:* 2   *Objective:* 7
There is no requirement that one capacity-level concept has to be used for all purposes.

35. Theoretical capacity is most often used to cost a product.

Answer: False   *Difficulty:* 2   *Objective:* 7
Theoretical capacity is unattainable and therefore should not be used to cost a product. Practical capacity is generally used to cost a product.

36. Practical capacity highlights capacity acquired but currently not used.

Answer: True   *Difficulty:* 2   *Objective:* 7

37. For benchmarking purposes it is best to use master-budget capacity because all competitors utilize about the same about of capacity for production.

Answer: False   *Difficulty:* 2   *Objective:* 7
For benchmarking purposes it is best to use *practical* capacity because it best represents the long-run cost of capacity.

38. Using normal capacity for pricing decisions can lead to setting noncompetitive selling prices.

Answer: True   *Difficulty:* 3   *Objective:* 8

39. Using master-budget capacity for pricing purposes can lead to a downward demand spiral.

Answer: True   *Difficulty:* 2   *Objective:* 8

40. Using practical capacity is best for evaluating the marketing manager's performance for a particular year.

Answer: False   *Difficulty:* 3   *Objective:* 8
Using *master-budget capacity* is best for evaluating the marketing manager's performance.

41. The production-volume variance is affected by the choice of capacity concept used to determine the denominator level.

Answer: True   *Difficulty:* 2   *Objective:* 9

42. The higher the denominator level the higher the budgeted fixed manufacturing cost rate per unit.

   Answer: False   *Difficulty*:   2   *Objective*:   9
   The higher the denominator level the *lower* the budgeted fixed manufacturing cost rate per unit.

43. Master-budget capacity utilization can be more reliably estimated than normal capacity utilization.

   Answer: True   *Difficulty*:   2   *Objective*:   9

44. Unused capacity is considered wasted resources and the result of poor planning.

   Answer: False   *Difficulty*:   1   *Objective*:   9
   Unused capacity is not considered wasted resources because capacity has to be purchased in "large chunks" to accommodate future needs, not just the needs of the current period.

45. Challenges only result from estimating the denominator level, but not the costs in the numerator of the fixed manufacturing cost rate.

   Answer: False   *Difficulty*:   1   *Objective*:   9
   Challenges result from estimating both the denominator level and the costs in the numerator of the fixed manufacturing cost rate.

46. Estimating capacity costs is unique to manufacturing and not applicable to nonmanufacturing entities.

   Answer: False   *Difficulty*:   1   *Objective*:   9
   Estimating capacity costs is needed in both manufacturing and nonmanufacturing entities.

47. The breakeven points are the same under both variable costing and absorption costing.

   Answer: False   *Difficulty*:   2   *Objective*:   A
   The breakeven points are generally different under both variable costing and absorption costing.

48. Which of the following cost(s) are inventoried when using variable costing?
    a. Direct manufacturing costs
    b. Variable marketing costs
    c. Fixed manufacturing costs
    d. Both (a) and (b)

    Answer: a   *Difficulty:* 1   *Objective:* 1

49. Which of the following cost(s) are inventoried when using absorption costing?
    a. Direct manufacturing costs
    b. Variable marketing costs
    c. Fixed manufacturing costs
    d. Both (a) and (c)

    Answer: d   *Difficulty:* 1   *Objective:* 1

50. Absorption costing is required for all EXCEPT
    a. generally accepted accounting principles.
    b. determining a competitive selling price.
    c. external reporting to shareholders.
    d. income tax reporting.

    Answer: b   *Difficulty:* 2   *Objective:* 1

51. Absorption costing
    a. expenses marketing costs as cost of goods sold.
    b. treats direct manufacturing costs as a period cost.
    c. includes fixed manufacturing overhead as an inventoriable cost.
    d. is required for internal reports to managers.

    Answer: c   *Difficulty:* 3   *Objective:* 1

52. Variable costing
    a. expenses administrative costs as cost of goods sold.
    b. treats direct manufacturing costs as a product cost.
    c. includes fixed manufacturing overhead as an inventoriable cost.
    d. is required for external reporting to shareholders.

    Answer: b   *Difficulty:* 3   *Objective:* 1

53. _____ method(s) expense(s) variable marketing costs in the period incurred.
    a. Variable costing
    b. Absorption costing
    c. Throughput costing
    d. All of the above

    Answer: d   *Difficulty:* 1   *Objective:* 1

54. _____ method(s) include(s) fixed manufacturing overhead costs as inventoriable costs.
    a. Variable costing
    b. Absorption costing
    c. Throughput costing
    d. All of the above

    Answer: b   *Difficulty:* 1   *Objective:* 1

55. _____ method(s) expense(s) direct material costs as cost of goods sold.
    a. Variable costing
    b. Absorption costing
    c. Throughput costing
    d. All of the above

    Answer: d   *Difficulty:* 1   *Objective:* 1

56. _____ method(s) is required for tax reporting purposes.
    a. Variable costing
    b. Absorption costing
    c. Throughput costing
    d. All of the above

    Answer: b   *Difficulty:* 1   *Objective:* 1

57. Variable costing regards fixed manufacturing overhead as
    a. an administrative cost.
    b. an inventoriable cost.
    c. a period cost.
    d. a product cost.

    Answer: c   *Difficulty:* 1   *Objective:* 1

58. The only difference between variable and absorption costing is the expensing of
    a. direct manufacturing costs.
    b. variable marketing costs.
    c. fixed manufacturing costs.
    d. both (a) and (c).

    Answer: c   *Difficulty:* 2   *Objective:* 1

THE FOLLOWING INFORMATION APPLIES TO QUESTIONS 59 AND 60.
Marie's Decorating produces and sells a mantel clock for $100 per unit. In 20x1, 100,000 parts were produced and 80,000 units were sold. Other information for the year includes:

Direct materials	$30.00 per unit
Direct manufacturing labor	$ 2.00 per unit
Variable manufacturing costs	$ 3.00 per unit
Sales commissions	$ 5.00 per part
Fixed manufacturing costs	$25.00 per unit
Administrative expenses, all fixed	$15.00 per unit

59. What is the inventoriable cost per unit using variable costing?
  a. $32
  b. $35
  c. $40
  d. $60

  Answer: b   *Difficulty*:   2   *Objective*:   1
  $30.00 + $2.00 + $3.00 = $35.00

60. What is the inventoriable cost per unit using absorption costing?
  a. $32
  b. $35
  c. $60
  d. $80

  Answer: c   *Difficulty*:   2   *Objective*:   1
  $30 + $2 + $3 + $25 = $60

THE FOLLOWING INFORMATION APPLIES TO QUESTIONS 61 AND 62.
Gabe's Auto produces and sells an auto part for $30.00 per unit. In 20x1, 100,000 parts were produced and 75,000 units were sold. Other information for the year includes:

Direct materials	$12.00 per unit
Direct manufacturing labor	$ 2.25 per unit
Variable manufacturing costs	$ 0.75 per unit
Sales commissions	$ 3.00 per part
Fixed manufacturing costs	$375,000 per year
Administrative expenses, all fixed	$135,000 per year

61. What is the inventoriable cost per unit using variable costing?
  a. $14.25
  b. $15.00
  c. $18.00
  d. $21.75

  Answer: b   *Difficulty*:   2   *Objective*:   1
  $12.00 + $2.25 + $0.75 = $15.00

62. What is the inventoriable cost per unit using absorption costing?
    a. $15.00
    b. $18.00
    c. $18.75
    d. $21.75

    Answer: c   *Difficulty:* 2   *Objective:* 1
    $12.00 + $2.25 + $0.75 + ($375,000 / 100,000) = $18.75

63. The contribution-margin format of the income statement
    a. is used with absorption costing.
    b. highlights the lump sum of fixed manufacturing costs.
    c. distinguishes manufacturing costs from nonmanufacturing costs.
    d. calculates gross margin.

    Answer: b   *Difficulty:* 3   *Objective:* 2

64. The gross-margin format of the income statement
    a. distinguishes between manufacturing and nonmanufacturing costs.
    b. distinguishes variable costs from fixed costs.
    c. is used with variable costing.
    d. calculates contribution margin.

    Answer: a   *Difficulty:* 3   *Objective:* 2

65. _____ is(are) subtracted from sales to calculate contribution margin.
    a. Variable manufacturing costs
    b. Variable marketing costs
    c. Fixed manufacturing costs
    d. Both (a) and (b)

    Answer: d   *Difficulty:* 2   *Objective:* 2

66. _____ is(are) subtracted from sales to calculate gross margin.
    a. Variable manufacturing costs
    b. Variable marketing costs
    c. Fixed manufacturing costs
    d. Both (a) and (c)

    Answer: d   *Difficulty:* 2   *Objective:* 2

THE FOLLOWING INFORMATION APPLIES TO QUESTIONS 67 THROUGH 70.
Peggy's Pillows produces and sells a decorative pillow for $75.00 per unit. In the first month of operation, 2,000 units were produced and 1,750 units were sold. Actual fixed costs are the same as the amount budgeted for the month. Other information for the month includes:

Variable manufacturing costs	$20.00 per unit
Variable marketing costs	$ 3.00 per unit
Fixed manufacturing costs	$ 7.00 per unit
Administrative expenses, all fixed	$15.00 per unit
Ending inventories:	
Direct materials	-0-
WIP	-0-
Finished goods	250 units

67. What is cost of goods sold per unit using variable costing?
    a. $20
    b. $23
    c. $30
    d. $45

    Answer: a   *Difficulty:* 1   *Objective:* 2
    $20, only variable manufacturing costs are included when using variable costing.

68. What is cost of goods sold using variable costing?
    a. $35,000
    b. $40,000
    c. $47,250
    d. $54,000

    Answer: a   *Difficulty:* 2   *Objective:* 2
    $20 x 1,750 units = $35,000

69. What is contribution margin using variable costing?
    a. $96,250
    b. $91,000
    c. $104,000
    d. $110,000

    Answer: b   *Difficulty:* 3   *Objective:* 2
    ($75 x 1,750) - [($20 + $3) x 1,750 units] = $91,000

70. What is operating income using variable costing?
    a. $52,500
    b. $78,750
    c. $65,750
    d. $47,000

    Answer: d   *Difficulty:* 3   *Objective:* 2
    Contribution margin of $91,000 - [($7 + $15) x 2,000 units] = $47,000

THE FOLLOWING INFORMATION APPLIES TO QUESTIONS 71 THROUGH 73.
Andrea's Hobbies produces and sells a luxury animal pillow for $40.00 per unit. In the first month of operation, 3,000 units were produced and 2,250 units were sold. Actual fixed costs are the same as the amount budgeted for the month. Other information for the month includes:

Variable manufacturing costs	$19 per unit
Variable marketing costs	$ 1 per unit
Fixed manufacturing costs	$30,000 per month
Administrative expenses, all fixed	$6,000 per month
Ending inventories:	
Direct materials	-0-
WIP	-0-
Finished goods	750 units

71. What is cost of goods sold per unit when using absorption costing?
    a. $19
    b. $20
    c. $29
    d. $32

    Answer: c   *Difficulty:* 2   *Objective:* 2
    $19 + ($30,000 / 3,000 units) = $29

72. What is gross margin when using absorption costing?
    a. $45,000
    b. $54,750
    c. $77,250
    d. $24,750

    Answer: d   *Difficulty:* 2   *Objective:* 2
    [$40 - $19 - ($30,000/3,000)] x 2,250 units = $24,750

73. What is operating income when using absorption costing?
    a. $4,000
    b. $16,500
    c. ($11,750)
    d. $18,750

    Answer: b   *Difficulty:* 3   *Objective:* 2
    [$40 - $19 - ($30,000/3,000)] x 2,250 units = gross margin – ($1 x 2,250) – $6,000 = $16,500

74. An unfavorable production-volume variance occurs when
    a. production exceeds the denominator level.
    b. the denominator level exceeds production.
    c. production exceeds unit sales.
    d. unit sales exceed production.

    Answer: b   *Difficulty*: 2   *Objective*: 3

75. If the unit level of inventory increases during an accounting period, then
    a. less operating income will be reported under absorption costing than variable costing.
    b. more operating income will be reported under absorption costing than variable costing.
    c. operating income will be the same under absorption costing and variable costing.
    d. the exact effect on operating income cannot be determined.

    Answer: b   *Difficulty*: 2   *Objective*: 3

76. The difference between operating incomes under variable costing and absorption costing centers on how to account for
    a. direct materials costs.
    b. fixed manufacturing costs.
    c. variable manufacturing costs.
    d. both (b) and (c).

    Answer: b   *Difficulty*: 2   *Objective*: 3

77. One possible means of determining the difference between operating incomes for absorption costing and variable costing is
    a. by subtracting sales of the previous period from sales of this period.
    b. by subtracting fixed manufacturing overhead in beginning inventory from fixed manufacturing overhead in ending inventory.
    c. by multiplying the number of units produced by the budgeted fixed manufacturing cost rate.
    d. by adding fixed manufacturing costs to the production-volume variance.

    Answer: b   *Difficulty*: 3   *Objective*: 3

78. When comparing the operating incomes between absorption costing and variable costing and beginning finished inventory exceeds ending finished inventory, it may be assumed that
    a. sales increased during the period.
    b. variable cost per unit is less than fixed cost per unit.
    c. there is an unfavorable production-volume variance.
    d. variable costing operating income exceeds absorption costing operating income.

    Answer: d   *Difficulty*: 3   *Objective*: 3

79. Which of the following statements is FALSE?
    a. Absorption costing allocates fixed manufacturing overhead to actual units produced during the period.
    b. Nonmanufacturing costs are expensed in the future under variable costing.
    c. Fixed manufacturing costs in ending inventory are expensed in the future under absorption costing.
    d. Operating income under absorption costing is higher than operating income under variable costing when production units exceed sales units.

Answer: b   *Difficulty:* 3   *Objective:* 3

80. Helton Company has the following information for the current year.

Beginning fixed manufacturing overhead in inventory	$95,000
Fixed manufacturing overhead in production	375,000
Ending fixed manufacturing overhead in inventory	25,000
Beginning variable manufacturing overhead in inventory	$10,000
Variable manufacturing overhead in production	50,000
Ending variable manufacturing overhead in inventory	15,000

What is the difference between operating incomes under absorption costing and variable costing?
    a. $70,000
    b. $50,000
    c. $40,000
    d. $5,000

Answer: a   *Difficulty:* 3   *Objective:* 3
$95,000 - $25,000 = $70,000

81. The following information pertains to Brian Stone Corporation:

Beginning fixed manufacturing overhead in inventory	$60,000
Ending fixed manufacturing overhead in inventory	45,000
Beginning variable manufacturing overhead in inventory	$30,000
Ending variable manufacturing overhead in inventory	14,250
Fixed selling and administrative costs	$724,000
Units produced	5,000 units
Units sold	4,800 units

What is the difference between operating incomes under absorption costing and variable costing?
    a. $750
    b. $7,500
    c. $15,000
    d. $30,750

Answer: c   *Difficulty:* 3   *Objective:* 3
$60,000 - $45,000 = $15,000

THE FOLLOWING INFORMATION APPLIES TO QUESTIONS 82 THROUGH 85.
Heinrich Corporation incurred fixed manufacturing costs of $6,000 during 20x4. Other information for 20x4 includes:

   The budgeted denominator level is 1,000 units.
   Units produced total 750 units.
   Units sold total 600 units.
   Beginning inventory was zero.

The company uses ABSORPTION COSTING and the fixed manufacturing cost rate is based on the budgeted denominator level. Manufacturing variances are closed to cost of goods sold.

82. Fixed manufacturing costs expensed on the income statement (excluding adjustments for variances) total
  a. $3,600.
  b. $4,800.
  c. $6,000.
  d. zero.

  Answer: a   *Difficulty*: 3   *Objective*: 3
  $6,000 / 1,000 units = $6 x 600 = $3,600

83. Fixed manufacturing costs included in ending inventory total
  a. $1,200.
  b. $1,500.
  c. $900.
  d. zero.

  Answer: c   *Difficulty*: 3   *Objective*: 3
  $6,000 / 1,000 units = $6 x 150 = $900

84. The production-volume variance is
  a. $2,000.
  b. $1,500.
  c. $2,400.
  d. zero.

  Answer: b   *Difficulty*: 3   *Objective*: 3
  $6,000 / 1,000 units = $6 x 250 = $1,500

85. Operating income using absorption costing will be _____ than operating income if using variable costing.
  a. $2,400 higher
  b. $2,400 lower
  c. $900 higher
  d. $3,600 lower

  Answer: c   *Difficulty*: 3   *Objective*: 3
  Different operating incomes are reported because the unit level of inventory increased during the accounting period by 150 units x $6 denominator rate = $900. Therefore, operating income is $900 higher under absorption costing because $900 of fixed manufacturing costs remains in inventory.

THE FOLLOWING INFORMATION APPLIES TO QUESTIONS 86 THROUGH 89.
Veach Corporation incurred fixed manufacturing costs of $6,000 during 20x4. Other information for 20x4 includes:

> The budgeted denominator level is 1,000 units.
> Units produced total 750 units.
> Units sold total 600 units.
> Beginning inventory was zero.

The company uses VARIABLE COSTING and the fixed manufacturing cost rate is based on the budgeted denominator level. Manufacturing variances are closed to cost of goods sold.

86. Fixed manufacturing costs expensed on the income statement (excluding adjustments for variances) total
    a. $3,600.
    b. $4,800.
    c. $6,000.
    d. zero.

    Answer: c   *Difficulty*: 3   *Objective*: 3
    $6,000 of fixed manufacturing costs is expensed as a lump sum.

87. Fixed manufacturing costs included in ending inventory total
    a. $1,200.
    b. $1,500.
    c. $900.
    d. zero.

    Answer: d   *Difficulty*: 3   *Objective*: 3
    Under variable costing no fixed manufacturing costs are included in inventory, and all are expensed on the income statement as a lump sum.

88. The production-volume variance totals
    a. $2,000.
    b. $1,500.
    c. $2,400.
    d. zero.

    Answer: d   *Difficulty*: 3   *Objective*: 3
    Variable costing has no production-volume variance.

89. Operating income using variable costing will be _____ than operating income if using absorption costing.
    a. $2,400 higher
    b. $2,400 lower
    c. $3,600 higher
    d. $900 lower

    Answer: d   *Difficulty*: 3   *Objective*: 3
    Different operating incomes are reported because the unit level of inventory increased during the accounting period by 150 units x $6 denominator rate = $900. Therefore, operating income is $900 lower under variable costing because $900 of fixed manufacturing costs remains in inventory under absorption.

THE FOLLOWING INFORMATION APPLIES TO QUESTIONS 90 THROUGH 93.
Morse Corporation incurred fixed manufacturing costs of $7,200 during 20x4. Other information for 20x4 includes:

> The budgeted denominator level is 800 units.
> Units produced total 1,000 units.
> Units sold total 950 units.
> Beginning inventory was zero.

The fixed manufacturing cost rate is based on the budgeted denominator level.
Manufacturing variances are closed to cost of goods sold.

90. Under absorption costing, fixed manufacturing costs expensed on the income statement (excluding adjustments for variances) total
   a. $8,550.
   b. $9,000.
   c. $7,200.
   d. zero.

   Answer: a   *Difficulty:* 3   *Objective:* 3
   $7,200 / 800 units = $9 x 950 = $8,550

91. Under absorption costing, the production-volume variance is
   a. $450.
   b. $1,350.
   c. $1,800.
   d. zero.

   Answer: c   *Difficulty:* 3   *Objective:* 3
   $7,200 / 800 units = $9 x 200 = $1,800

92. Under variable costing, the fixed manufacturing costs expensed on the income statement (excluding adjustments for variances) total
   a. $8,550.
   b. $7,200.
   c. $9,000.
   d. zero.

   Answer: b   *Difficulty:* 2   *Objective:* 3
   $7,200 of fixed manufacturing costs is expensed as a lump sum.

93. Operating income using absorption costing will be _____ óperating income if using variable costing.
   a. $450 higher than
   b. $900 higher than
   c. $1,350 lower than
   d. the same as

   Answer: a   *Difficulty:* 3   *Objective:* 3
   Different operating incomes are reported because the unit level of inventory increased during the accounting period by 50 units x $9 denominator rate = $450. Therefore, operating income is $450 higher under absorption costing because $450 of fixed manufacturing costs remains in inventory under absorption costing.

94. At the end of the accounting period Susan Corporation reports operating income of $30,000 and the fixed overhead cost rate is $20 per unit. Under absorption costing, if this company now produces an additional 100 units of inventory, then operating income
    a.   will increase by $2,000.
    b.   will increase by $2,000 only if the additional 100 units of inventory are sold.
    c.   will not be affected.
    d.   cannot be determined using only the above information.

    Answer: a   *Difficulty:*   3   *Objective:*   3

95. At the end of the accounting period Bumsted Corporation reports operating income of $30,000 and the fixed overhead cost rate is $20 per unit. Under variable costing, if this company produces 100 more units of inventory, then operating income
    a.   will increase by $2,000.
    b.   will increase by $2,000 only if the 100 additional units of inventory are sold.
    c.   will not be affected.
    d.   cannot be determined using only the above information.

    Answer: c   *Difficulty:*   3   *Objective:*   3

96. Companies have recently been able to reduce inventory levels because
    a.   there is better sharing of information between suppliers and manufacturers.
    b.   just-in-time production strategies are being implemented.
    c.   production quotas are being implemented.
    d.   of both (a) and (b).

    Answer: d   *Difficulty:*   2   *Objective:*   4

97. Many companies have switched from absorption costing to variable costing for internal reporting
    a.   to comply with external reporting requirements.
    b.   to increase bonuses for managers.
    c.   to reduce the undesirable incentive to build up inventories.
    d.   so the denominator level is more accurate.

    Answer: c   *Difficulty:*   2   *Objective:*   4

98. Ways to "produce for inventory" that result in increasing operating income include
    a.   switching production to products that absorb the least amounts of fixed manufacturing costs.
    b.   delaying items that absorb the greatest amount of fixed manufacturing costs.
    c.   deferring maintenance to accelerate production.
    d.   all of the above.

    Answer: c   *Difficulty:*   2   *Objective:*   4

99. To discourage producing for inventory, management can
   a. evaluate nonfinancial measures such as units in ending inventory compared to units in sales.
   b. evaluate performance over a three to five year period rather than a single year.
   c. incorporate a carrying charge for inventory in the internal accounting system.
   d. all of the above.

   Answer: d   *Difficulty*: 2   *Objective*: 4

100. Under absorption costing, if a manager's bonus is tied to operating income, then increasing inventory levels compared to last year would result in
   a. increasing the manager's bonus.
   b. decreasing the manager's bonus.
   c. not affecting the manager's bonus.
   d. being unable to determine the manager's bonus using only the above information.

   Answer: a   *Difficulty*: 3   *Objective*: 4

101. Under variable costing, if a manager's bonus is tied to operating income, then increasing inventory levels compared to last year would result in
   a. increasing the manager's bonus.
   b. decreasing the manager's bonus.
   c. not affecting the manager's bonus.
   d. being unable to determine the manager's bonus using only the above information.

   Answer: c   *Difficulty*: 2   *Objective*: 4

102. Critics of absorption costing suggest to evaluate management on their ability to
   a. exceed production quotas.
   b. increase operating income.
   c. decrease inventory costs.
   d. do all of the above.

   Answer: c   *Difficulty*: 2   *Objective*: 4

103. Differences between absorption costing and variable costing are much smaller when
   a. a large part of the manufacturing process is subcontracted out.
   b. a just-in-time inventory strategy is implemented.
   c. a significant portion of manufacturing costs are fixed.
   d. both (a) and (b) are done.

   Answer: d   *Difficulty*: 2   *Objective*: 4

104. All of the following are examples of drawbacks of using absorption costing EXCEPT
    a.   management has the ability to manipulate operating income via production schedules.
    b.   manipulation of operating income may ultimately increase the company's costs incurred over the long run.
    c.   operating income solely reflects income from the sale of units and excludes the effects of manipulating production schedules.
    d.   decreasing maintenance activities and increasing production result in increased operating income.

Answer: c   *Difficulty:* 2   *Objective:* 4

105. Advocates of throughput costing argue that
    a.   only direct materials are truly variable.
    b.   direct manufacturing labor is relatively fixed.
    c.   variable manufacturing costs are a cost of the period.
    d.   all of the above are true.

Answer: d   *Difficulty:* 2   *Objective:* 5

106. If 600 units are produced and only 400 units are sold, _____ results in the greatest amount of expense reported on the income statement.
    a.   throughput costing
    b.   variable costing
    c.   absorption costing
    d.   period costing

Answer: a   *Difficulty:* 2   *Objective:* 5

107. If 400 units are produced and 600 units are sold, _____ results in the greatest amount of operating income.
    a.   throughput costing
    b.   variable costing
    c.   absorption costing
    d.   period costing

Answer: a   *Difficulty:* 2   *Objective:* 5

108. Advocates of throughput costing maintain that
    a.   both variable and fixed are necessary to produce goods; therefore, both types of costs should be inventoried.
    b.   all manufacturing costs plus some design costs should be inventoried.
    c.   fixed manufacturing costs are related to the capacity to produce rather than to the actual production of specific units.
    d.   both (a) and (c) are true.

Answer: c   *Difficulty:* 3   *Objective:* 5

THE FOLLOWING INFORMATION APPLIES TO QUESTIONS 109 AND 110.
Reusser Company produces wood statues. Management has provided the following information:

Actual sales	80,000 statues
Budgeted production	100,000 statues
Selling price	$20.00 per statue
Direct material costs	$5.00 per statue
Variable manufacturing costs	$1.50 per statue
Variable administrative costs	$2.50 per statue
Fixed manufacturing overhead	$2.00 per statue

109. What is the cost per statue if throughput costing is used?
   a. $11.00
   b. $9.50
   c. $7.50
   d. $5.00

   Answer: d   *Difficulty*: 2   *Objective*: 5
   Equal to direct materials = $5.00

110. What is the total throughput contribution?
   a. $1,500,000
   b. $2,000,000
   c. $720,000
   d. $1,200,000

   Answer: d   *Difficulty*: 3   *Objective*: 5
   80,000 x ($20.00 - $5.00) = $1,200,000

THE FOLLOWING INFORMATION APPLIES TO QUESTIONS 111 AND 112.
Stober Company produces a specialty item. Management has provided the following information:

Actual sales	60,000 units
Budgeted production	50,000 units
Selling price	$40.00 per unit
Direct material costs	$10.00 per unit
Variable manufacturing overhead	$3.00 per unit
Variable administrative costs	$5.00 per unit
Fixed manufacturing overhead	$4.00 per unit

111. What is the cost per statue if throughput costing is used?
   a. $22.00
   b. $19.00
   c. $15.00
   d. $10.00

   Answer: d   *Difficulty*: 1   *Objective*: 5
   Direct material cost of $10

112. What is the total throughput contribution?
    a. $1,500,000
    b. $1,620,000
    c. $1,380,000
    d. $1,800,000

Answer: d   *Difficulty*: 3   *Objective*: 5
60,000 x ($40.00 - $10.00) = $1,800,000

113. Practical capacity is the denominator-level concept that
    a. reduces theoretical capacity for unavoidable operating interruptions.
    b. is the maximum level of operations at maximum efficiency.
    c. is based on the level of capacity utilization that satisfies average customer demand over periods generally longer than one year.
    d. is based on anticipated levels of capacity utilization for the coming budget period.

Answer: a   *Difficulty*: 1   *Objective*: 6

114. _____ reduces theoretical capacity for unavoidable operating interruptions.
    a. Practical capacity
    b. Theoretical capacity
    c. Master-budget capacity utilization
    d. Normal capacity utilization

Answer: a   *Difficulty*: 1   *Objective*: 6

115. _____ is based on the level of capacity utilization that satisfies average customer demand over periods generally longer than one year.
    a. Practical capacity
    b. Theoretical capacity
    c. Master-budget capacity utilization
    d. Normal capacity utilization

Answer: d   *Difficulty*: 1   *Objective*: 6

116. _____ is (are) based on the demand for the output of the plant.
    a. Practical capacity
    b. Master-budget capacity utilization
    c. Normal capacity utilization
    d. Both (b) and (c)

Answer: d   *Difficulty*: 2   *Objective*: 6

117. Theoretical capacity allows for
    a. preventive machine maintenance.
    b. interruptions due to uncontrollable power failures.
    c. rework of the expected number of defective units.
    d. none of the above.

Answer: d   *Difficulty*: 2   *Objective*: 6

118. Theoretical capacity
    a.   is unattainable in the real world.
    b.   represents an ideal goal of capacity usage.
    c.   is based on engineering studies that provide information about the technical capabilities of machines used in production.
    d.   is all of the above.

    Answer: d   *Difficulty:*   2   *Objective:*   6

119. The budgeted fixed manufacturing cost rate is the lowest for
    a.   practical capacity.
    b.   theoretical capacity.
    c.   master-budget capacity utilization.
    d.   normal capacity utilization.

    Answer: b   *Difficulty:*   2   *Objective:*   6

120. _____ provides the lowest estimate of denominator-level capacity.
    a.   Practical capacity
    b.   Theoretical capacity
    c.   Master-budget capacity utilization
    d.   Normal capacity utilization

    Answer: c   *Difficulty:*   2   *Objective:*   6

THE FOLLOWING INFORMATION APPLIES TO QUESTIONS 121 AND 122.
A manufacturing firm is able to produce 1,000 pairs of shoes per hour, at maximum efficiency. There are three eight-hour shifts each day. Due to unavoidable operating interruptions, production averages 800 units per hour. The plant actually operates only 27 days per month.

121. What is the theoretical capacity for the month of April?
    a.   1,000,000 units
    b.   720,000 units
    c.   518,400 units
    d.   240,000 units

    Answer: b   *Difficulty:*   2   *Objective:*   6
    1,000 units x 24 hours x 30 days = 720,000 units

122. What is the practical capacity for the month of April?
    a.   1,000,000 units
    b.   720,000 units
    c.   518,400 units
    d.   240,000 units

    Answer: c   *Difficulty:*   2   *Objective:*   6
    800 units x 24 hours x 27 days = 518,400 units

123. Theoretical capacity
    a.   represents real capacity available to the company.
    b.   provides the best perspective of actual long-run costs.
    c.   when used for product costing results in the lowest cost estimate of the four capacity options.
    d.   replicates the cost of capacity in a competitor's cost structure.

Answer: c   *Difficulty:* 3   *Objective:* 7

124. Budgeted fixed manufacturing costs of a product using practical capacity
    a.   represents the cost per unit of supplying capacity.
    b.   can result in setting selling prices that are not competitive.
    c.   includes the cost of unused capacity.
    d.   should be used to evaluate a marketing manager's performance in the current year.

Answer: a   *Difficulty:* 3   *Objective:* 7

125. Normal capacity utilization
    a.   represents real capacity available to the company.
    b.   can result in setting selling prices that are not competitive.
    c.   when used for product costing results in the lowest cost estimate of the four capacity options.
    d.   represents the maximum units of production intended for current capacity.

Answer: b   *Difficulty:* 3   *Objective:* 7

126. Master-budget capacity utilization
    a.   hides the amount of unused capacity.
    b.   represents the maximum units of production intended for current capacity.
    c.   provides the best cost estimate for benchmarking purposes.
    d.   when used for product costing results in the lowest cost estimate of the four capacity options.

Answer: a   *Difficulty:* 3   *Objective:* 7

127. From the perspective of long-run product costing,
    a.   it is best to use master-budget capacity utilization to highlight unused capacity.
    b.   it is best to use normal capacity utilization for benchmarking purposes.
    c.   it is best to use practical capacity for pricing decisions.
    d.   it is best to use theoretical capacity for performance evaluation.

Answer: c   *Difficulty:* 3   *Objective:* 7

128. Customers expect to pay a price that includes
    a.   the cost of unused capacity.
    b.   the cost of actual capacity used.
    c.   no capacity costs.
    d.   both (a) and (b).

Answer: b   *Difficulty:* 2   *Objective:* 7

129. The marketing manager's performance evaluation is most fair when based on a denominator level using
    a. practical capacity.
    b. theoretical capacity.
    c. master-budget capacity utilization.
    d. normal capacity utilization.

    Answer: c   *Difficulty:* 2   *Objective:* 7

130. Using master-budget capacity to set selling prices
    a. avoids the recalculation of unit costs when expected demand levels change.
    b. spreads fixed costs over available capacity.
    c. can result in a downward demand spiral.
    d. uses the perspective of long-run product pricing.

    Answer: c   *Difficulty:* 2   *Objective:* 8

131. When large differences exist between practical capacity and master-budget capacity utilization, companies may
    a. classify the difference as planned unused capacity.
    b. use master-budget capacity utilization for setting selling prices.
    c. use practical capacity for meaningful feedback to the marketing manager.
    d. do all of the above.

    Answer: a   *Difficulty:* 2   *Objective:* 8

132. The effect of spreading fixed manufacturing costs over a shrinking master-budget capacity utilization amount results in
    a. greater utilization of capacity.
    b. increased unit costs.
    c. more competitive selling prices.
    d. greater demand for the product.

    Answer: b   *Difficulty:* 2   *Objective:* 8

133. The higher the denominator level
    a. the higher the budgeted fixed manufacturing cost rate.
    b. the lower the amount of fixed manufacturing costs allocated to each unit produced.
    c. the higher the favorable production-volume variance.
    d. the more likely actual output will exceed the denominator level.

    Answer: b   *Difficulty:* 2   *Objective:* 9

134. Operating income reported on the end-of-period financial statements is changed when _____ is (are) used to handle the production-volume variance at the end of the accounting period.
    a.   the adjusted allocation-rate approach
    b.   the proration approach
    c.   the write-off variances to cost of goods sold approach
    d.   all of the above

    Answer: c   *Difficulty*:   3   *Objective*:   9

135. Practical capacity may
    a.   increase over time due to improvements in plant layout.
    b.   decrease over time due to efficiencies offered by new technologies.
    c.   cannot be altered unless there is a major plant expansion.
    d.   be both (a) and (b).

    Answer: a   *Difficulty*:   2   *Objective*:   9

136. The Internal Revenue Service requires the use of _____ for calculating fixed manufacturing costs per unit.
    a.   practical capacity
    b.   theoretical capacity
    c.   master-budget capacity utilization
    d.   normal capacity utilization

    Answer: a   *Difficulty*:   2   *Objective*:   9

137. It is most difficult to estimate _____ because of the need to predict demand for the next few years.
    a.   practical capacity
    b.   theoretical capacity
    c.   master-budget capacity utilization
    d.   normal capacity utilization

    Answer: d   *Difficulty*:   2   *Objective*:   9

138. Managers face uncertainty when estimating
    a.   demand of the product.
    b.   the denominator level for practical capacity.
    c.   total fixed manufacturing costs for the next accounting period.
    d.   all of the above.

    Answer: d   *Difficulty*:   2   *Objective*:   9

139. Unused capacity
    a.   is a definite sign of wasted resources.
    b.   is intended for future use.
    c.   provides capacity for potential demand surges.
    d.   is both (b) and (c).

    Answer: d   *Difficulty*:   2   *Objective*:   9

140. Capacity costs
    a.   are difficult to estimate.
    b.   don't provide a useful planning tool for nonmanufacturing firms.
    c.   cannot be used with activity-based costing.
    d.   are all of the above.

    Answer: a   *Difficulty*:   2   *Objective*:   9

141. The breakeven point using absorption costing depends on all of the following factors,
    EXCEPT
    a.   the number of units sold during the current period.
    b.   the budgeted level of production.
    c.   the denominator level chosen for the fixed manufacturing overhead rate.
    d.   fulfillment of current production quotas.

    Answer: b   *Difficulty*:   2   *Objective*:   A

142. There is not an output-level variance for variable costing, because
    a.   the inventory level decreased during the period.
    b.   the inventory level increased during the period.
    c.   fixed manufacturing overhead is allocated to work in process.
    d.   fixed manufacturing overhead is not allocated to work in process.

    Answer: d   *Difficulty*:   2   *Objective*:   A

THE FOLLOWING INFORMATION APPLIES TO QUESTIONS 143 THROUGH 145.
Ms. Andrea Chadwick, the company president, has heard that there are multiple breakeven points for every product. She does not believe this and has asked you to provide the evidence of such a possibility. Some information about the company for 20x2 is as follows:

Total fixed manufacturing overhead	$180,000
Total other fixed expenses	$200,000
Total variable manufacturing expenses	$120,000
Total other variable expenses	$120,000
Units produced	30,000 units
Budgeted production	30,000 units
Units sold	25,000 units
Selling price	$40

143. What are breakeven sales in units using variable costing?
    a.   5,625 units
    b.   5,769 units
    c.   11,875 units
    d.   12,180 units

Answer: c   *Difficulty:*   2   *Objective:*   A
Breakeven units = ($180,000 + $200,000)/($40 - $4 - $4) = 11,875 units

144. What are breakeven sales in units using absorption costing?
    a.   5,625 units
    b.   6,667 units
    c.   7,692 units
    d.   8,000 units

Answer: c   *Difficulty:*   2   *Objective:*   A
Breakeven units N = [$380,000 + ($180,000/30,000 x (N - 30,000)]
                    ($40 - $4 - $4)

    N = ($380,000 + $6N - $180,000)/$32
    $32N = $200,000 + $6N
    $26N = $200,000
    N = 7,692 units

145. What are breakeven sales in units using absorption costing if the production units are actually 25,000?
   a. 5,625 units
   b. 6,667 units
   c. 7,667 units
   d. 8,846 units

Answer: d   *Difficulty*: 2   *Objective*: A

Breakeven units N = $\dfrac{[\$380,000 + (\$180,000/30,000 \times (N - 25,000)]}{(\$40 - \$4 - \$4)}$

   N = ($380,000 + $6N - $150,000)/$32
   $32N = $230,000 + $6N
   $26N = $230,000
   N = 8,846 units

THE FOLLOWING INFORMATION APPLIES TO QUESTIONS 146 AND 147.
The following information pertains to the Bean Company:

Selling price per unit	$123
Standard fixed manufacturing costs per unit	$60
Variable selling and administrative costs per unit	$12
Standard variable manufacturing costs per unit	$3
Fixed selling and administrative costs	$48,000
Units produced	10,000 units
Units sold	9,600 units

146. What is variable costing breakeven in units?
   a. 833 units
   b. 5,556 units
   c. 5,838 units
   d. 6,000 units

Answer: d   *Difficulty*: 2   *Objective*: A
Breakeven units = ($48,000 + (10,000 x $60)) / ($123 - $3 - $12) = 6,000 units

147. What is absorption costing breakeven in units?
   a. 917 units
   b. 1,000 units
   c. 5,838 units
   d. 6,000 units

Answer: b   *Difficulty*: 2   *Objective*: A
Breakeven units N = ($648,000 + ($60 x (N - 10,000) / ($123 - $3 - $12) = 1,000 units

THE FOLLOWING INFORMATION APPLIES TO QUESTIONS 148 THROUGH 150.
Greene Manufacturing incurred the following expenses during 20x2:

Fixed manufacturing costs	$45,000
Fixed nonmanufacturing costs	$35,000
Unit selling price	$100
Total unit cost	$40
Variable manufacturing cost rate	$20
Units produced	1,340 units

148. What will be the breakeven point if variable costing is used?
   a.   1,334 units
   b.   1,125 units
   c.   1,000 units
   d.   563 units

   Answer: c   *Difficulty*:   2   *Objective*:   A
   Breakeven units = ($45,000 + $35,000)/($100 - $20) = 1,000 units

149. What will be the breakeven point in units if absorption costing is used?
   a.   1,330 units
   b.   1,000 units
   c.   887 units
   d.   563 units

   Answer: c   *Difficulty*:   2   *Objective*:   A

   Breakeven units N = $\dfrac{[(\$45,000 + \$35,000) + [\$20 \times (N - 1,340)]}{(\$100 - \$20)}$

   N = ($80,000 + $20N - $26,800)/$80
   $80N = $53,200 + $20N
   N = 887 units

150. What is the breakeven point in units using absorption costing if the units produced are actually 2,250?
   a.   1,330 units
   b.   1,000 units
   c.   887 units
   d.   583 units

   Answer: d   *Difficulty*:   2   *Objective*:   A

   Breakeven units N = $\dfrac{[(\$45,000 + \$35,000) + [\$20 \times (N - 2,250)]}{(\$100 - \$20)}$

   N = ($80,000 + $20N - $45,000)/$80
   $80N = $35,000 + $20N
   N = 583 units

EXERCISES AND PROBLEMS

151. For 20x4, Nichols, Inc. had sales of 75,000 units and production of 100,000 units. Other information for the year included:

Direct manufacturing labor	$187,500
Variable manufacturing overhead	100,000
Direct materials	150,000
Variable selling expenses	100,000
Fixed administrative expenses	100,000
Fixed manufacturing overhead	200,000

There was no beginning inventory.

Required:

a. Compute the ending finished goods inventory under both absorption and variable costing.

b. Compute the cost of goods sold under both absorption and variable costing.

Answer:

a.

	Absorption	Variable
Direct materials	$150,000	$150,000
Direct manufacturing labor	187,500	187,500
Variable manufacturing overhead	100,000	100,000
Fixed manufacturing overhead	200,000	0
Total	$637,500	$437,500

Unit costs:

$637,500/100,000 units	$6.375	
$437,500/100,000 units		$4.375

Ending inventory:

25,000 units x $6.375	$159,375	
25,000 units x $4.375		$109,375

b. Cost of goods sold:

75,000 x $6.375	$478,125	
75,000 x $4.375		$328,125

Difficulty: 2   *Objective*: 1

152. Bruster Company sells its products for $66 each. The current production level is 25,000 units, although only 20,000 units are anticipated to be sold.

Unit manufacturing costs are:

Direct materials	$12.00
Direct manufacturing labor	$18.00
Variable manufacturing costs	$9.00
Total fixed manufacturing costs	$180,000
Marketing expenses	$6.00 per unit, plus $60,000 per year

Required:

a. Prepare an income statement using absorption costing.
b. Prepare an income statement using variable costing.

Answer:

a. *Absorption-costing income statement*:

Sales (20,000 x $66)		$1,320,000
Cost of goods sold (20,000 x $46.20*)		924,000
Gross margin		$396,000
Marketing:		
Variable (20,000 x $6)	$120,000	
Fixed	60,000	180,000
Operating income		$216,000

* $12.00 + $18.00 + $9.00 + ($180,000/25,000) = $46.20

b. *Variable-costing income statement*:

Sales (20,000 x $66)		$1,320,000
Variable costs:		
Cost of goods sold (20,000 x $39*)	$780,000	
Marketing (20,000 x $6)	120,000	900,000
Contribution margin		$420,000
Fixed costs:		
Manufacturing	$180,000	
Marketing	60,000	240,000
Operating income		$180,000

* $12.00 + $18.00 + $9.00 = $39

Difficulty: 2   *Objective*:   2

153. Ireland Corporation planned to be in operation for three years.

- During the first year, 20x1, it had no sales but incurred $120,000 in variable manufacturing expenses and $40,000 in fixed manufacturing expenses.
- In 20x2, it sold half of the finished goods inventory from 20x1 for $100,000 but it had no manufacturing costs.
- In 20x3, it sold the remainder of the inventory for $120,000, had no manufacturing expenses and went out of business.
- Marketing and administrative expenses were fixed and totaled $20,000 each year.

Required:

a. Prepare an income statement for each year using absorption costing.
b. Prepare an income statement for each year using variable costing.

Answer:

a. *Absorption-costing income statements*:

	20x1	**20x2**	**20x3**
Sales	$0	$100,000	$120,000
Cost of goods sold	0	80,000	80,000
Gross margin	$0	$20,000	$40,000
Marketing and administrative	20,000	20,000	20,000
Operating income	$(20,000)	$ 0	$20,000

b. *Variable-costing income statements*:

	20x1	**20x2**	**20x3**
Sales	$ 0	$100,000	$120,000
Variable expenses	0	60,000	60,000
Contribution margin	$ 0	$40,000	$60,000
Fixed expenses:			
Manufacturing	$40,000	$ 0	$ 0
Marketing and administrative	20,000	20,000	20,000
Total fixed	$60,000	$20,000	$20,000
Operating income	$(60,000)	$20,000	$40,000

Difficulty: 3   *Objective*:   2

154. Jarvis Golf Company sells a special putter for $20 each. In March, it sold 28,000 putters while manufacturing 30,000. There was no beginning inventory on March 1. Production information for March was:

Direct manufacturing labor per unit	15 minutes
Fixed selling and administrative costs	$ 40,000
Fixed manufacturing overhead	132,000
Direct materials cost per unit	2
Direct manufacturing labor per hour	24
Variable manufacturing overhead per unit	4
Variable selling expenses per unit	2

Required:

a. Compute the cost per unit under both absorption and variable costing.
b. Compute the ending inventories under both absorption and variable costing.
c. Compute operating income under both absorption and variable costing.

Answer:

a.

	Absorption	Variable
Direct manufacturing labor ($24/4)	$ 6.00	$ 6.00
Direct materials	2.00	2.00
Variable manufacturing overhead	4.00	4.00
Fixed manufacturing overhead ($132,000/30,000)	4.40	0
Total cost per unit	$16.40	$12.00

b.

	Absorption	Variable
Beginning inventory	$0	$0
Cost of goods manufactured:		
30,000 x $16.40	$492,000	
30,000 x $12.00		$360,000
Cost of goods available for sale	$492,000	$360,000
Cost of goods sold:		
28,000 x $16.40	$459,200	
28,000 x $12.00		$336,000
Ending inventory	$ 32,800	$ 24,000

154. (continued)

Answer:

c.   *Absorption-costing income statement*:

Sales (28,000 x $20)		$560,000
Cost of goods sold (28,000 x $16.40)		459,200
Gross margin		100,800
Less:		
Variable selling and administrative	$56,000	
Fixed selling and administrative	40,000	96,000
Operating income		$ 4,800

Variable-costing income statement:

Sales (28,000 x $20)		$560,000
Variable COGS (28,000 x $12)	$336,000	
Variable selling expenses (28,000 x $2)	56,000	392,000
Contribution margin		168,000
Fixed costs:		
Manufacturing	$132,000	
Selling and administrative	40,000	172,000
Operating income		$ (4,000)

Difficulty: 2   *Objective*:   2

155. Johnson Realty bought a 2,000-acre island for $10,000,000 and divided it into 200 equal size lots.

    As the lots are sold, they are cleared at an average cost of $5,000.
    Storm drains and driveways are installed at an average cost of $8,000 per site.
    Sales commissions are 10 % of selling price.
    Administrative costs are $850,000 per year.
The average selling price was $160,000 per lot during 20x2 when 50 lots were sold.

During 20x3, the company bought another 2,000-acre island and developed it exactly the same way. Lot sales in 20x3 totaled 300 with an average selling price of $160,000. All costs were the same as in 20x2.

Required:

Prepare income statements for both years using both absorption and variable costing methods.

155. (continued)

Answer:

Cost per site:	Absorption	Variable
Land cost $10,000,000/200 sites	$50,000	$0
Clearing costs	5,000	5,000
Improvements	8,000	8,000
Total	$63,000	$13,000

Absorption-costing income statements:	20x2	20x3
Sales	$8,000,000	$48,000,000
Cost of goods sold:		
50 x ($50,000 + $8,000 + $5,000)	3,150,000	
300 x ($50,000 + $8,000 + $5,000)		18,900,000
Gross margin	$4,850,000	$29,100,000
Variable marketing	800,000	4,800,000
Fixed administrative	850,000	850,000
Operating income	$3,200,000	$23,450,000

Variable-costing income statements:	20x2	20x3
Sales	$8,000,000	$48,000,000
Variable expenses:		
Cost of operations:		
50 x $13,000	650,000	
300 x $13,000		3,900,000
Selling expenses	800,000	4,800,000
Contribution margin	$6,550,000	$39,300,000
Fixed expenses:		
Land	10,000,000	10,000,000
Administrative	850,000	850,000
Operating income	$(4,300,000)	$28,450,000

Difficulty: 3   *Objective*:   2

156. Megredy Company prepared the following absorption-costing income statement for the year ended May 31, 20x4.

Sales (16,000 units)	$320,000
Cost of goods sold	216,000
Gross margin	$104,000
Selling and administrative expenses	46,000
Operating income	$ 58,000

Additional information follows:

Selling and administrative expenses include $1.50 of variable cost per unit sold. There was no beginning inventory, and 17,500 units were produced. Variable manufacturing costs were $11 per unit. Actual fixed costs were equal to budgeted fixed costs.

Required:

Prepare a variable-costing income statement for the same period.

Answer:

Sales		$320,000
Variable expenses:		
Manufacturing cost of goods sold[1]	$176,000	
Selling and administrative[2]	24,000	200,000
Contribution margin		$ 120,000
Fixed expenses:		
Fixed factory overhead[3]	$43,750	
Fixed selling and administrative[4]	22,000	65,750
Operating income		$ 54,250

[1] 16,000 units x $11 = $176,000
[2] 16,000 units x $1.50 = $24,000
[3] [($216,000/16,000 units) - $11] x 17,500 units = $43,750
[4] $46,000 - $24,000 = $22,000

Difficulty: 3   *Objective*: 2

157. The following data are available for Ruggles Company for the year ended September 30, 20x4.

Sales:	24,000 units at $50 each
Expected and actual production:	30,000 units
Manufacturing costs incurred:	
Variable:	$525,000
Fixed:	$372,000
Nonmanufacturing costs incurred:	
Variable:	$144,800
Fixed:	$77,400
Beginning inventories:	none

Required:

a. Determine operating income using the variable-costing approach.
b. Determine operating income using the absorption-costing approach.
c. Explain why operating income is not the same under the two approaches.

Answer:

a. 24,000 x $50 = $1,200,000 sales
    ($525,000/30,000) x 24,000 = $420,000 variable manufacturing cost
    $1,200,000 - $420,000 - $144,800 = $635,200 contribution margin
    $635,200 - $372,000 - $77,400 = $185,800 operating income

b. ($372,000/30,000) x 24,000 = $297,600 manufacturing fixed cost
    $1,200,000 - $420,000 - $297,600 = $482,400 gross margin
    $482,400 - $144,800 - $77,400 = $260,200 operating income

c. $260,200 - $185,800 = $74,400 or 6,000 units in ending inventory x $12.40 per unit of fixed manufacturing cost.

Difficulty: 3   *Objectives*: 2, 3

158. Bobby Smith and Sons Company was concerned that increased sales did not result in increased profits for 20x3. Both variable unit and total fixed manufacturing costs for 20x2 and 20x3 remained constant at $20 and $2,000,000, respectively.

In 20x2, the company produced 100,000 units and sold 80,000 units at a price of $50 per unit. There was no beginning inventory in 20x2. In 20x3, the company made 70,000 units and sold 90,000 units at a price of $50. Selling and administrative expenses were all fixed at $100,000 each year.

Required:

a. Prepare income statements for each year using absorption costing.
b. Prepare income statements for each year using variable costing.
c. Explain why the income was different each year using the two methods. Show computations.

Answer:

a. *Absorption-costing income statements:*

	20x2	20x3
Sales	$4,000,000	$4,500,000
Cost of goods sold:		
Beginning. inventory	0	800,000
Variable	2,000,000	1,400,000
Fixed	2,000,000	2,000,000
Subtotal	4,000,000	4,200,000
Ending inventory	800,000	0
Total COGS	3,200,000	4,200,000
Gross margin	800,000	300,000
Selling and administrative	100,000	100,000
Operating income	$ 700,000	$ 200,000

b. *Variable-costing income statements:*

	20x2	20x3
Sales	$4,000,000	$4,500,000
Variable expenses	1,600,000	1,800,000
Contribution margin	2,400,000	2,700,000
Fixed expenses:		
Manufacturing	2,000,000	2,000,000
Selling and administrative	100,000	100,000
Operating income	$ 300,000	$ 600,000

Answer:

   c.   Budgeted fixed manufacturing overhead rate for 20x2 = $2,000,000 / 100,000 = $20

20x2 difference of $400,000 = (100,000 - 80,000) x $20 = $400,000 (favors absorption method)

20x3 difference of $400,000 = (70,000 - 90,000) x $20 = -$400,000 (favors variable method)

Difficulty: 2   *Objectives*: 2, 3

159. Ernsting Bottling Works manufactures glass bottles. January and February operations were identical in every way except for the planned production.
January had a production denominator of 35,000 units.
February had a production denominator of 36,000 units.
Fixed manufacturing costs totaled $126,000.

Sales for both months totaled 45,000 units with variable manufacturing costs of $4 per unit. Selling and administrative costs were $0.40 per unit variable and $60,000 fixed. The selling price was $10 per unit.

Required:

Compute the operating income for both months using absorption costing.

Answer:

January manufacturing cost per unit:

Variable costs:	$4.00
Fixed costs ($126,000/35,000)	3.60
Total per unit	$7.60

February manufacturing cost per unit:

Variable costs	$4.00
Fixed costs $126,000/36,000	3.50
Total per unit	$7.50

January Income Statement

Sales (45,000 x $10)		$450,000
Cost of goods sold (45,000 x $7.60)		342,000
Gross margin		$108,000
Other costs:		
Variable selling and administrative	$18,000	
Fixed selling and administrative	60,000	78,000
Operating income		$30,000

159. (continued)

   Answer:

   February Income Statement

Sales (45,000 x $10)		$450,000
Cost of goods sold (45,000 x $7.50)		337,500
Gross margin		$112,500
Other costs:		
Variable selling and administrative	$18,000	
Fixcd selling and administrative	60,000	78,000
Operating income		$34,500

   Difficulty: 2   *Objectives*: 2, 7

160. Calvin Enterprises produces a specialty statue item. The following information has been provided by management:

Actual sales	150,000 units
Budgeted production	160,000 units
Selling price	$34 per unit
Direct manufacturing costs	$9 per unit
Fixed manufacturing costs	$5 per unit
Variable manufacturing costs	$4 per unit
Variable administrative costs	$2 per unit

   Required:

   a.   What is the cost per statue if absorption costing is used?
   b.   What is the cost per statue if "super-variable costing" is used?
   c.   What is the total throughput contribution?

   Answer:

   a. $9 + $5 + $4 = $18

   b.   Equal to direct materials = $9

   c.   150,000 x ($34 - $9) = $3,750,000

   Difficulty: 2   *Objective*: 5

161. Wallace's Wrench Company manufactures socket wrenches.
- For next month, the vice president of production plans on producing 4,400 wrenches per day.
- The company can produce as many as 5,000 wrenches per day, but are more likely to produce 4,500 per day.
- The demand for wrenches for the next three years is expected to average 4,250 wrenches per day.
- Fixed manufacturing costs per month total $336,600.
- The company works 20 days a month.
- Fixed manufacturing overhead is charged on a per wrench basis.

Required:

a. What is the theoretical fixed manufacturing overhead rate per wrench?
b. What is the practical fixed manufacturing overhead rate per wrench?
c. What is the normal fixed manufacturing overhead rate per wrench?
d. What is the master-budget fixed manufacturing overhead rate per wrench?

Answer:

a. Theoretical overhead rate = $336,600 / (5,000 x 20) = $3.366

b. Practical overhead rate = $336,600 / (4,500 x 20) = $3.74

c. Normal overhead rate = $336,600 / (4,250 x 20) = $3.96

d. Master-budget overhead rate = $336,600 / (4,400 x 20) = $3.825

Difficulty: 2   *Objective*:   6

162. Sutton Hot Dog Stand sells hot dogs for $1.35. Variable costs are $1.05 per unit with fixed production costs of $90,000 per month at a level of 400,000 units. Fixed administrative costs total $30,000. Sales average 400,000 units per month, with production of 400,000 hot dogs.

Required:

a. What are breakeven unit sales under variable costing?
b. What are breakeven unit sales under absorption costing if she sells everything she prepares?
c. What are breakeven unit sales under absorption costing if average sales are 498,000 and planned production is changed to 500,000?

Answer:

a. Breakeven units = ($90,000 + $30,000) / ($1.35 - $1.05) = 400,000

b. Breakeven units (N) = $\dfrac{(\$90{,}000 + \$30{,}000 + (\$0.225 \, (N - 400{,}000))}{\$1.35 - \$1.05}$

N = ($120,000 + $0.225N - $90,000) / $0.30
$0.30N = $30,000 + $0.225N
$0.075N = $30,000
N = 400,000 units

c. Breakeven units (N) = $\dfrac{(\$90{,}000 + \$30{,}000 \, (\$0.18 \, (N - 500{,}000))}{\$1.35 - \$1.05}$

N = ($120,000 + $0.18N - $90,000) / $0.30
$0.3N = $30,000 + $0.18N
$0.12N = $30,000
N = 250,000 units

Difficulty: 2   *Objective*:   A

163. a. Explain the difference between the variable and absorption costing methods.
     b. Which method(s) are required for external reporting? For internal reporting?

Answer:
a. Absorption costing includes both fixed and variable manufacturing costs as inventoriable costs, whereas variable costing only includes variable manufacturing costs as inventoriable costs.
b. Absorption costing is required for external reporting to shareholders and for income tax reporting. A company may use whichever method it chooses for internal reporting purposes.

Difficulty: 2   *Objective*:   1

164. Explain the difference between the gross margin format and the contribution margin format for the income statement. What information is highlighted with each?

Answer:
The gross margin format divides costs into product and period costs while the contribution format divides costs into variable and fixed costs. The gross margin format highlights cost function while the contribution format highlights cost behavior.

Difficulty: 2   *Objective*:   2

165. The manager of the manufacturing division of Iowa Windows does not understand why income went down when sales went up. Some of the information he has selected for evaluation include:

	January	**February**
Units produced	40,000	30,000
Units sold	30,000	40,000
Sales	$600,000	$800,000
Beginning inventory	0	150,000
Cost of production	600,000	550,000
Ending inventory	150,000	0
Operating income	70,000	35,000

The division operated at normal capacity during January.
Variable manufacturing cost per unit was $5, and the fixed costs were $400,000.
Selling and administrative expenses were all fixed.

Required:
Explain the profit differences. How would variable costing income statements help the manager understand the division's operating income?

165. (continued)

Answer:

The 10,000 units in inventory being assigned fixed manufacturing costs cause the operating income difference. The fixed manufacturing cost assigned to the inventory is carried into the next month. The fixed costs per unit were $10 per unit ($400,000/40,000), therefore, $100,000 (10,000 x $10) were carried into February.

Variable costing helps avoid confusion by relating variations in expenses to sales rather than to inventory fluctuations. Under variable costing, the total fixed amount ($400,000) would be expensed in January and none carried forward into February. Therefore, January's income would be $100,000 less than reported and February's $100,000 more than reported.

Difficulty: 2   *Objectives*: 1, 2, 3

166. Galliart Company has two identical divisions, East and West. Their sales, production volume, and fixed manufacturing costs have been the same for the last five years. The amounts for each division were as follows:

	20x1	**20x2**	**20x3**	**20x4**	**20x5**
Units produced	50,000	55,000	55,000	44,000	44,000
Units sold	45,000	45,000	50,000	50,000	50,000
Fixed manufacturing costs	$55,000	$55,000	$55,000	$55,000	$55,000

East Division uses absorption costing and West Division uses variable costing.
Both use FIFO inventory methods.
Variable manufacturing costs are $5 per unit.
Selling and administrative expenses were identical for each division.
There were no inventories at the beginning of 20x1.

Which division reports the highest income each year? Explain.

Answer:

East Division had the higher income during the first three years because production exceeded sales; this stored some of the fixed manufacturing costs each year in the ending inventory balances. West had the higher income during the last two years because sales exceeded production. During these years, East incurred all of the year's fixed manufacturing costs plus those costs that were in inventory from the prior years.

Difficulty: 2   *Objective*:   3

167. Kaiser Company just hired its fourth production manager in three years. All three previous managers had quit because they could not get the company above the break-even point, even though sales had increased somewhat each year. The company was operating at about 60 % of plant capacity. The flatware industry was growing, so increased sales were not out of the question.

I. R. Thinking took the job as manager of the production division with a very attractive salary package. After interviewing for the position, he proposed a salary and bonus package that would give him a very small salary but a large bonus if he took the operating income (using absorption costing) above the breakeven point during his very first year.

Required:

What do you think Mr. Thinking had in mind for increasing the company's operating income?

Answer:

Mr. Thinking realized that he could probably increase both production and sales during the coming year. If he substantially overproduced he knew that the extra costs would be hidden in unsold inventory. If the new production level could be sold by the sales force in the growing market, the profits would increase anyway and everybody would be happy.

Also, he could combine increased production with reduced fixed manufacturing costs such as maintenance. In the short run, several combinations could be undertaken by Mr. Thinking to ensure that the profit picture would improve.

Difficulty: 3   *Objective*:   4

168. a.   List the four different measures of capacity.
     b.   Which measure of capacity is best for setting prices? Why?
     c.   Which measure of capacity is best for evaluating the performance of the marketing manager for the current year? Why?

Answer:
   a.   Theoretical capacity, practical capacity, normal capacity utilization, and master-budget capacity utilization are the four measures of capacity.
   b.   Practical capacity is best to use when setting prices because only the actual cost of capacity used for production is included in the cost of a unit.
   c.   Master-budget capacity utilization is best for evaluating performance of managers over the current year because the manager should only be held accountable for budgeted sales of the current year and not production capacity, especially when there is unused capacity.

Difficulty: 2   *Objectives*: 6, 7

169. Explain how using master-budget capacity utilization for setting prices can lead to a downward demand spiral.

Answer:
If master-budget capacity utilization is used as the denominator level for determining fixed manufacturing costs per unit, the cost includes a charge for unused capacity. If prices are based on this cost, the product may be priced higher than competitor's products. With a higher selling price, volume of sales will probably decrease reducing the expected number of future sales. Lower expected sales leads to a lower denominator level, which in turn results in an even higher selling price and even lower sales volume. Etc., etc., etc.

Difficulty: 2   *Objective*:   8

CHAPTER 10: DETERMINING HOW COSTS BEHAVE

TRUE/FALSE

1. One assumption frequently made in cost behavior estimation is that changes in total costs can be explained by changes in the level of a single activity.

   Answer: True   *Difficulty*: 1   *Objective*: 1

2. All cost functions are linear.

   Answer: False   *Difficulty*: 1   *Objective*: 1
   All cost functions are not linear, but for cost-behavior estimation we assume some are within a relevant range.

3. y = a + bX represents the general form of the linear cost function.

   Answer: True   *Difficulty*: 1   *Objective*: 2

4. A linear cost function can only represent fixed cost behavior.

   Answer: False   *Difficulty*: 1   *Objective*: 2
   A linear cost function can represent fixed, mixed, or variable cost behavior.

5. In a graphical display of a cost function, the steepness of the slope represents the total amount of fixed costs.

   Answer: False   *Difficulty*: 1   *Objective*: 2
   In a graphical display of a cost function, the constant or the y-intercept represents the amount of fixed costs.

6. The longer the time horizon, the more likely that a cost will have a fixed cost behavior.

   Answer: False   *Difficulty*: 2   *Objective*: 2
   The longer the time horizon, the more likely that a cost will be *variable*.

7. Outside of the relevant range, variable and fixed cost-behavior patterns may change.

   Answer: True   *Difficulty*: 2   *Objective*: 2

8. Any linear cost function can be graphed by knowing only the slope coefficient.

   Answer: False   *Difficulty*: 1   *Objective*: 2
   A linear function can be graphed if the slope coefficient and the intercept are known.

9. Knowing the proper relevant range is essential to properly classify costs.

   Answer: True   *Difficulty*: 1   *Objective*: 2

10. It can be inferred that when there is a high correlation between two variables, one is the cause of the other.

    Answer: False   *Difficulty*: 2   *Objective*: 2

    It *cannot* be inferred that a high correlation between two variables indicates that one is the cause of the other. A high correlation simply indicates that the variables move together.

11. An example of a physical cause-and-effect relationship is when additional units of production increase total direct material costs.

    Answer: True   *Difficulty*: 2   *Objective*: 2

12. The industrial engineering method of cost estimation is based on opinions from various departments and is quick and of low cost to apply.

    Answer: False   *Difficulty*: 1   *Objective*: 3

    The *conference* method of cost estimation is based on opinions from various departments and is quick and of low cost to apply.

13. The account analysis method of cost estimation classifies account costs as fixed, mixed, or variable using qualitative judgments.

    Answer: True   *Difficulty*: 1   *Objective*: 3

14. The industrial engineering method uses a formal mathematical method to identify cause-and-effect relationships among past data observations.

    Answer: False   *Difficulty*: 1   *Objective*: 3

    Quantitative analysis methods use a formal mathematical method to identify cause-and-effect relationships among past data observations.

15. Individual cost items included in the dependent variable should have the same cost driver or more than one cost function should be estimated.

    Answer: True   *Difficulty*: 2   *Objective*: 4

16. An example of time-series data is to compile maintenance costs of twelve different manufacturing plants incurred during 20x3.

    Answer: False   *Difficulty*: 1   *Objective*: 4

    An example of *cross-sectional data* is to compile maintenance costs of twelve different manufacturing plants incurred during 20x3.

17. Evidence of relationships and extreme observations are highlighted when costs and their cost drivers are plotted graphically.

    Answer: True   *Difficulty*: 2   *Objective*: 4

18. The most common forms of quantitative analysis are the conference method and the account analysis method.

   Answer:　False　　　　　　*Difficulty*:　1　　　　　　*Objective*:　4
   The most common forms of quantitative analysis are the *high-low method* and *regression analysis*.

19. Regression analysis relies on only two observations to estimate a linear cost function.

   Answer:　False　　　　　　*Difficulty*:　1　　　　　　*Objective*:　4
   The *high-low method* relies on only two observations to estimate a linear cost function.

20. The y-intercept of a linear cost function is an accurate cost assessment of using zero machine-hours, even if zero machine-hours is outside of the relevant range.

   Answer:　False　　　　　　*Difficulty*:　2　　　　　　*Objective*:　4
   The y-intercept of a linear cost function is an accurate cost assessment of using zero machine-hours, only if zero machine-hours *are within the relevant range*.

21. A positive slope of a regression line indicates that total costs are lower for higher values of the cost driver.

   Answer:　False　　　　　　*Difficulty*:　2　　　　　　*Objective*:　4
   A positive slope of a regression line indicates that costs are *higher* for higher values of the cost driver.

22. The high-low method is more accurate than the regression method of estimating a cost function.

   Answer:　False　　　　　　*Difficulty*:　1　　　　　　*Objective*:　4
   The *regression* method is more accurate than the high-low method since it uses all available data to estimate a cost function.

23. If inaccurate cost estimates are too high, then a company may unknowingly reward a manager for poor performance.

   Answer:　True　　　　　　*Difficulty*:　3　　　　　　*Objective*:　4

24. Machine-hours is a more economically plausible cost driver of machine maintenance than number of direct manufacturing labor-hours.

   Answer:　True　　　　　　*Difficulty*:　2　　　　　　*Objective*:　5

25. The smaller the vertical difference between actual costs and predicted costs the better the goodness of fit.

   Answer:　True　　　　　　*Difficulty*:　2　　　　　　*Objective*:　5

26. Choosing an economically plausible cost driver for indirect costs is fairly simple and knowledge of operations is unnecessary.

Answer: False   *Difficulty*: 2   *Objective*: 5
Finding an economically plausible cost driver is not always simple and many times knowledge of operations is necessary.

27. A flat or slightly sloped regression line indicates a strong relationship.

Answer: False   *Difficulty*: 3   *Objective*: 5
A flat or slightly sloped regression line indicates a *weak* relationship.

28. When using an activity-based costing system, a batch-level cost must have a batch-level cost driver.

Answer: True   *Difficulty*: 2   *Objective*: 5

29. Economic plausibility is an important criterion for choosing a cost driver.

Answer: True   *Difficulty*: 1   *Objective*: 5

30. A step cost function is an example of a nonlinear cost function.

Answer: True   *Difficulty*: 1   *Objective*: 6

31. Step fixed-cost functions are variable over the long run.

Answer: True   *Difficulty*: 2   *Objective*: 6

32. An example of a step variable-cost function is the cost of material-handling labor when inputs are acquired in discrete quantities.

Answer: True   *Difficulty*: 2   *Objective*: 6

33. A learning curve measures the effect of learning on efficiency.

Answer: True   *Difficulty*: 1   *Objective*: 6

34. Plotting learning curve observations is helpful in selecting the appropriate learning curve model.

Answer: True   *Difficulty*: 1   *Objective*: 7

35. When new products are introduced, learning-curve effects can have a major influence on production scheduling.

Answer: True   *Difficulty*: 2   *Objective*: 7

36. It is appropriate to incorporate expected learning-curve efficiencies when evaluating performance.

Answer: True   *Difficulty:* 1   *Objective:* 7

37. The cumulative average-time learning model with a 90% learning curve indicates that if it takes 100 minutes to manufacture the first unit of a new model, then the second unit will take only 90 minutes to manufacture.

Answer: False   *Difficulty:* 3   *Objective:* 7
100 x .90 = 90; (100 + X)/2 = 90; X = 80 minutes

38. The incremental unit-time learning model with a 90% learning curve indicates that if it takes 100 minutes to manufacture the first unit of a new model, then the second unit will take only 90 minutes to manufacture.

Answer: True   *Difficulty:* 2   *Objective:* 7

39. Data collection problems can arise when data is recorded manually rather than electronically.

Answer: True   *Difficulty:* 1   *Objective:* 8

40. Misinterpretation of data can arise when fixed costs are reported on a per unit basis.

Answer: True   *Difficulty:* 2   *Objective:* 8

41. Inflation is a fact, and therefore its influence should not be removed from the data.

Answer: False   *Difficulty:* 2   *Objective:* 8
Inflation can distort data that are compared over time so purely inflationary effects should be removed.

42. The coefficient of determination (r^2) measures the percentage of variation in Y explained by X (the independent variable).

Answer: True   *Difficulty:* 1   *Objective:* A

43. Generally a coefficient of determination (r^2) that is less than 0.30 indicates a goodness of fit.

Answer: False   *Difficulty:* 2   *Objective:* A
Generally a coefficient of determination (r^2) that is *0.30 or higher* indicates a goodness of fit.

MULTIPLE CHOICE

44. Which of the following statements related to assumptions about estimating linear cost functions is FALSE?
    a. Variations in a single cost driver explain variations in total costs.
    b. A cost object is anything for which a separate measurement of costs is desired.
    c. A linear function approximates cost behavior within the relevant range of the cost driver.
    d. A high correlation between two variables ensures that a cause-and-effect relationship exists.

    Answer: d   *Difficulty:* 2   *Objective:* 1

45. A high correlation between two variables *s* and *t* indicates that
    a. *s* may cause *t,* or *t* may cause *s*.
    b. they both may be affected by a third variable.
    c. the correlation may be due to random chance.
    d. all of the above are true.

    Answer: d   *Difficulty:* 2   *Objective:* 2

46. Which of the following does NOT represent a cause-and-effect relationship?
    a. Material costs increase as the number of units produced increases.
    b. A company is charged 40 cents for each brochure printed and mailed.
    c. Utility costs increase at the same time that insurance costs increase.
    d. It makes sense that if a complex product has a large number of parts it will take longer to assemble than a simple product with fewer parts.

    Answer: c   *Difficulty:* 3   *Objective:* 2

47. Dougherty Company employs 20 individuals. Eight employees are paid $12 per hour and the rest are salaried employees paid $3,000 a month. How would total costs of personnel be classified?
    a. Variable
    b. Mixed
    c. A variable cost within a relevant range
    d. A fixed cost within a relevant range

    Answer: b   *Difficulty:* 2   *Objective:* 2

48. For January, the cost components of a picture frame include $0.35 for the glass, $.65 for the wooden frame, and $0.80 for assembly. The assembly desk and tools cost $400. 1,000 frames are expected to be produced in the coming year. What cost function best represents these costs?
    a. $y = 1.80 + 400X$
    b. $y = 400 + 1.80X$
    c. $y = 2.20 + 1,000X$
    d. $y = 1.00 + 400X$

    Answer: b   *Difficulty:* 2   *Objective:* 2

49. A linear cost function can represent
    a. mixed cost behaviors.
    b. fixed cost behaviors.
    c. variable cost behaviors.
    d. all of the above cost behaviors.

    Answer: d   *Difficulty*: 2   *Objective*: 2

50. The cost function $y = 1,000 + 5X$
    a. has a slope coefficient of 1,000.
    b. has an intercept of 5.
    c. is a straight line.
    d. represents a fixed cost.

    Answer: c   *Difficulty*: 2   *Objective*: 2

51. The cost function $y = 8,000 + 4X$
    a. represents a mixed cost.
    b. will intersect the y-axis at 4.
    c. has a slope coefficient of 8,000.
    d. is a curved line.

    Answer: a   *Difficulty*: 2   *Objective*: 2

52. Which of the following is an equation of a *variable* cost function?
    a. $y = b$
    b. $y = a + bX$
    c. $y = bX$
    d. $y = a$

    Answer: c   *Difficulty*: 2   *Objective*: 2

53. The industrial engineering method estimates cost functions
    a. based on analysis and opinions gathered from various departments.
    b. quickly while incurring little cost.
    c. using qualitative rather than quantitative analysis.
    d. by analyzing the relationship between inputs and outputs in physical terms.

    Answer: d   *Difficulty*: 2   *Objective*: 3

54. The conference method estimates cost functions
    a. using quantitative methods that can be very time consuming and costly.
    b. based on analysis and opinions gathered from various departments.
    c. using time-and-motion studies.
    d. by mathematically analyzing the relationship between inputs and outputs in physical terms.

    Answer: b   *Difficulty*: 2   *Objective*: 3

55. The account analysis method estimates cost functions
    a. by classifying cost accounts as variable, fixed, or mixed based on qualitative analysis.
    b. using time-and-motion studies.
    c. at a high cost, which is therefore seldom used.
    d. in a manner that cannot be usefully combined with any other cost estimation methods.

    Answer: a   *Difficulty:* 2   *Objective:* 3

56. Quantitative analysis methods estimate cost functions
    a. which depend on the experience and judgment of the analyst for accuracy.
    b. based on analysis and opinions gathered from various departments.
    c. using significant amounts of historical data.
    d. using the pooling of knowledge from each value chain function.

    Answer: c   *Difficulty:* 2   *Objective:* 3

57. Gathering cost information through observations and interviews from departments within an organization is known as
    a. the account analysis method.
    b. the conference method.
    c. the industrial engineering method.
    d. the quantitative analysis method.

    Answer: b   *Difficulty:* 1   *Objective:* 3

58. Which cost estimation method analyzes accounts in the subsidiary ledger as variable, fixed, or mixed using qualitative methods?
    a. The account analysis method
    b. The conference method
    c. The industrial engineering method
    d. The quantitative analysis method

    Answer: a   *Difficulty:* 1   *Objective:* 3

59. Which cost estimation method uses a formal mathematical method to develop cost functions based on past data?
    a. The account analysis method
    b. The conference method
    c. The industrial engineering method
    d. The quantitative analysis method

    Answer: d   *Difficulty:* 1   *Objective:* 3

60. Which cost estimation method may utilize time-and-motion studies to analyze the relationship between inputs and outputs in physical terms?
    a. The account analysis method
    b. The conference method
    c. The industrial engineering method
    d. The quantitative analysis method

Answer: c   *Difficulty:* 1   *Objective:* 3

THE FOLLOWING INFORMATION APPLIES TO QUESTIONS 61 THROUGH 63.
At the Jordan Company, the cost of the personnel department has always been charged to production departments based upon number of employees. Recently, opinions gathered from the department managers indicate that the number of new hires might be a better predictor of personnel costs.

Total personnel department costs are $160,000.

Department	**A**	**B**	**C**
Number of employees	30	270	100
The number of new hires	8	12	5

61. If number of employees is considered the cost driver, what amount of personnel costs will be allocated to Department A?
    a. $12,000
    b. $5,333
    c. $51,200
    d. $20,000

Answer: a   *Difficulty:* 2   *Objective:* 3
[30 / (30 + 270 + 100)] x $160,000 = $12,000

62. If number of new hires is considered the cost driver, what amount of personnel costs will be allocated to Department A?
    a. $12,000
    b. $5,333
    c. $51,200
    d. $20,000

Answer: c   *Difficulty:* 2   *Objective:* 3
[8 / (8 + 12 + 5)] x $160,000 = $51,200

63. Which cost estimation method is being used by Jordan Company?
    a. The industrial engineering method
    b. The conference method
    c. The account analysis method
    d. The quantitative analysis method

Answer: b   *Difficulty:* 2   *Objective:* 3

THE FOLLOWING INFORMATION APPLIES TO QUESTIONS 64 THROUGH 67.
Penny's TV and Appliance Store is a small company that has hired you to perform some
management advisory services. The following information pertains to 20x3 operations.

Sales (2,000 televisions)	$ 900,000
Cost of goods sold	400,000
Store manager's salary per year	70,000
Operating costs per year	157,000
Advertising and promotion per year	15,000
Commissions (4% of sales)	36,000

64. What was the variable cost per unit sold for 20x3?
    a. $18
    b. $218
    c. $339
    d. $200

Answer: b   *Difficulty:*   2   *Objective:*   3
($400,000 + $36,000) / 2,000 = $218 per unit

65. What were total fixed costs for 20x3?
    a. $678,000
    b. $436,000
    c. $242,000
    d. $227,000

Answer: c   *Difficulty:*   2   *Objective:*   3
$70,000 + $157,000 + $15,000 = $242,000

66. What are the estimated total costs if Penny's expects to sell 3,000 units next year?
    a. $896,000
    b. $678,000
    c. $1,017,000
    d. $799,000

Answer: a   *Difficulty:*   3   *Objective:*   3
$896,000 = $242,000 + 218 (3,000)

67. Which cost estimation method is being used by Penny's TV and Appliance Store?
    a.   The industrial engineering method
    b.   The conference method
    c.   The account analysis method
    d.   The quantitative analysis method

Answer: c   *Difficulty:*   2   *Objective:*   3

68. The cost to be predicted is referred to as the
    a. independent variable.
    b. dependent variable.
    c. cost driver.
    d. regression.

    Answer: b   *Difficulty:* 2   *Objective:* 4

69. The independent variable
    a. is also referred to as the cost driver.
    b. may also be called the cost-allocation base if referring to an indirect cost.
    c. should have an economically plausible relationship with the dependent variable.
    d. includes all of the above.

    Answer: ˙ d   *Difficulty:* 2   *Objective:* 4

70. How many separate cost pools should be formed given the following information:

Cost	**Cost driver**
Postage costs	# of brochures mailed
Printing and paper costs	# of brochures mailed
Quality control costs	# of inspections
Customer service costs	# of customers served

    a. 1 cost pool
    b. 2 cost pools
    c. 3 cost pools
    d. 4 cost pools

    Answer: c   *Difficulty:* 2   *Objective:* 4

71. Place the following steps in order for estimating a cost function using quantitative analysis:

    A = Plot the data
    B = Estimate the cost function
    C = Choose the dependent variable
    D = Identify the cost driver

    a. D C A B
    b. C D A B
    c. A D C B
    d. D C B A

    Answer: b   *Difficulty:* 2   *Objective:* 4

72. All individual cost items included in the dependent variable should
    a. have the same cost driver.
    b. have a cause-and-effect relationship with the independent variable.
    c. have an economically plausible relationship with the independent variable.
    d. include all of the above.

    Answer: d   *Difficulty:* 2   *Objective:* 4

73. Collecting data on the dependent variable and the cost driver may include
    a. interviews with managers.
    b. collecting data over a long period of time.
    c. collecting data from different entities over the same period of time.
    d. all of the above.

    Answer: d   *Difficulty:* 2   *Objective:* 4

74. A plot of data that results in bunched points with little slope generally indicates
    a. a strong relationship.
    b. a weak relationship.
    c. a positive relationship.
    d. a negative relationship.

    Answer: b   *Difficulty:* 3   *Objective:* 4

75. A plot of data that results in one extreme observation MOST likely indicates that
    a. more than one cost pool should be used.
    b. an unusual event such as a plant shutdown occurred during that month.
    c. the cost-allocation base has been incorrectly identified.
    d. individual cost items do not have the same cost driver.

    Answer: b   *Difficulty:* 2   *Objective:* 4

76. Cross-sectional data analysis includes
    a. using a variety of time periods to measure the dependent variable.
    b. using the highest and lowest observation.
    c. observing different entities during the same time period.
    d. comparing information in different cost pools.

    Answer: c   *Difficulty:* 2   *Objective:* 4

77. Time-series data analysis includes
    a. using a variety of time periods to measure the dependent variable.
    b. using the highest and lowest observation.
    c. observing different entities during the same time period.
    d. comparing information in different cost pools.

    Answer: a   *Difficulty:* 2   *Objective:* 4

78. When using the high-low method, the two observations used are the high and low observations
    a. of the cost driver.
    b. of the dependent variables.
    c. of the slope coefficient.
    b. of the residual term.

    Answer: a   *Difficulty:* 2   *Objective:* 4

79. When using the high-low method, the denominator of the equation that determines the slope is the
    a.   dependent variable.
    b.   independent variable.
    c.   difference between the high and low observations of the cost driver.
    d.   difference between the high and low observations of the dependent variables.

    Answer: c   *Difficulty:*   2   *Objective:*   4

80. The high-low method
    a.   easily handles estimating the relationship between the dependent variable and two or more independent variables.
    b.   is more accurate than the regression method.
    c.   calculates the slope coefficient using only two observed values within the relevant range.
    d.   uses the residual term to measure goodness of fit.

    Answer: c   *Difficulty:*   3   *Objective:*   4

81. Put the following steps in order for using the high-low method of estimating a cost function:
                          A = Identify the cost function
                          B = Calculate the constant
                          C = Calculate the slope coefficient
                          D = Identify the highest and lowest observed values
    a.   D C A B
    b.   C D A B
    c.   A D C B
    d.   D C B A

    Answer: d   *Difficulty:*   2   *Objective:*   4

82. Regression analysis
    a.   is simple to compute.
    b.   measures the change in a dependent variable associated with one or more independent variables.
    c.   is mathematical so it does not require an understanding of operations.
    d.   uses the constant to measure goodness of fit.

    Answer: d   *Difficulty:*   3   *Objective:*   4

83. Simple regression differs from multiple regression in that
    a. multiple regression uses all available data to estimate the cost function, whereas simple regression only uses simple data.
    b. simple regression is limited to the use of only the dependent variables and multiple regression can use both dependent and independent variables.
    c. simple regression uses only one independent variable and multiple regression uses more than one independent variable.
    d. simple regression uses only one dependent variable and multiple regression uses more than one dependent variable.

    Answer: c   *Difficulty*:   2   *Objective*:   4

84. The slope of the line of regression is
    a. the rate at which the dependent variable varies.
    b. the rate at which the independent variable varies.
    c. the level of total fixed costs.
    d. the level of total variable costs.

    Answer: a   *Difficulty*:   2   *Objective*:   4

THE FOLLOWING INFORMATION APPLIES TO QUESTIONS 85 THROUGH 87.
The Hunter Company uses the high-low method to estimate the cost function. The information for 20x3 is provided below:

	Machine-hours	**Labor Costs**
Highest observation of cost driver	400	$10,000
Lowest observation of cost driver	240	$ 6,800

85. What is the slope coefficient per machine-hour?
    a. $28.33
    b. $00.05
    c. $20.00
    d. $25.00

    Answer: c   *Difficulty*:   2   *Objective*:   4
    Slope = ($10,000 - $6,800)/(400 - 240) = $20

86. What is the constant for the estimating cost equation?
    a. $2,000
    b. $6,800
    c. $8,000
    d. $10,000

    Answer: a   *Difficulty*:   2   *Objective*:   4
    EITHER: Constant = $10,000 - ($20.00 x 400 hours) = $2,000
    OR: Constant = $6,800 - ($20.00 x 240 hours) = $2,000

87. What is the estimate of the total cost when 300 machine-hours are used?
    a. $2,000
    b. $4,000
    c. $6,000
    d. $8,000

    Answer: d   *Difficulty*: 3   *Objective*: 4
    y = $2,000 + ($20 x 300) = $8,000

THE FOLLOWING INFORMATION APPLIES TO QUESTIONS 88 THROUGH 90.
For Carroll Company, labor-hours are 12,500 and wages $47,000 at the high point of the relevant range, and labor-hours are 7,500 and wages $35,000 at the low point of the relevant range.

88. What is the slope coefficient per labor-hour?
    a. $4.67
    b. $3.76
    c. $2.40
    d. $0.42

    Answer: c   *Difficulty*: 2   *Objective*: 4
    Slope = ($47,000 - 35,000)/(12,500 – 7,500) = $2.40 per labor-hour

89. What is the constant?
    a. $17,000
    b. $12,000
    c. $5,000
    d. $41,750

    Answer: a   *Difficulty*: 2   *Objective*: 4
    Constant = $47,000 - ($2.40 x 12,500) = $17,000
    OR: Constant = $35,000 - ($2.40 x 7,500) = $17,000

90. What is the estimate of total labor costs at Carroll Company when 10,000 labor-hours are used?
    a. $17,000
    b. $41,000
    c. $21,167
    d. $27,000

    Answer: b   *Difficulty*: 3   *Objective*: 4
    y = $17,000 + ($2.40 x 10,000) = $41,000

THE FOLLOWING INFORMATION APPLIES TO QUESTIONS 91 AND 92.
The Barnett Company has assembled the following data pertaining to certain costs that cannot be easily identified as either fixed or variable. Barnett Company has heard about a method of measuring cost functions called the high-low method and has decided to use it in this situation.

Cost	Hours
$24,900	5,250
24,000	5,500
36,400	7,500
44,160	9,750
45,000	9,500

91.   What is the cost function?
       a.   y = $43,191 + $0.19X
       b.   y = $4,875 + $5.25X
       c.   y = $41,900 + $0.23X
       d.   y = $2,430 + $4.28X

Answer: d   *Difficulty*:   3   *Objective*:   4
($44,160 - $24,900) / (9,750 – 5,250) = $4.28 for the highest and lowest values of the cost driver

92.   What is the estimated total cost at an operating level of 8,000 hours?
       a. $43,740
       b. $36,670
       c. $46,875
       d. $37,125

Answer: b   *Difficulty*:   3   *Objective*:   4
$36,670 = $2,430 + ($4.28 x 8,000)

THE FOLLOWING INFORMATION APPLIES TO QUESTIONS 93 AND 94.
Presented below are the production data for the first six months of the year for the mixed costs incurred by Gallup Company.

Month	Cost	Units
January	$4,890	4,100
February	4,024	3,200
March	6,480	5,300
April	8,840	7,500
May	5,800	4,800
June	7,336	6,600

Gallup Company uses the high-low method to analyze mixed costs.

93. How would the cost function be stated?
   a. $y = \$440 + \$1.12X$
   b. $y = \$3,562.30 + \$0.144X$
   c. $y = \$107.20 + \$1.224X$
   d. $y = \$7,850 + \$0.132X$

   Answer: a   *Difficulty*: 3   *Objective*: 4
   $b = (\$8,840 - \$4,024) / (7,500 - 3,200) = \$1.12$
   $\$8,840 = a + \$1.12 (7,500)$
   $a = \$440$

94. What is the estimated total cost at an operating level of 5,000 units?
   a. $6,227.20
   b. $6,040.00
   c. $4,283.20
   d. $8,510.00

   Answer: b   *Difficulty*: 3   *Objective*: 4
   $y = \$440 + \$1.12 (5,000) = \$6,040$

THE FOLLOWING INFORMATION APPLIES TO QUESTIONS 95 AND 96.
The Gangwere Company has assembled the following data pertaining to certain costs that cannot be easily identified as either fixed or variable. Gangwere Company has heard about a method of measuring cost functions called the high-low method and has decided to use it in this situation.

Month	Cost	Hours
January	$40,000	3,500
February	24,400	2,000
March	31,280	2,450
April	36,400	3,000
May	44,160	3,900
June	42,400	3,740

95. How is the cost function stated?
   a. $y = \$26,672 + \$1.84X$
   b. $y = \$21,360 + \$1.52X$
   c. $y = \$10,112 + \$8.64X$
   d. $y = \$3,600 + \$10.40X$

   Answer: d   *Difficulty:*   3   *Objective:*   4
   $b = (\$44,160 - \$24,400) / (3,900 - 2,000) = \$10.40$
   $\$44,160 = a + \$10.40 (3,900)$
   $a = \$3,600$

96. What is the estimated total cost at an operating level of 2,850 hours?
   a. $25,692
   b. $33,240
   c. $32,016
   d. $34,736

   Answer: b   *Difficulty:*   3   *Objective:*   4
   $y = \$3,600 + \$10.40 (2,850) = \$33,240$

97. An inaccurate cost function with a slope coefficient that is estimated too low may MOST likely result in
   a.   predicting total costs that are too high.
   b.   initiating cost cutting measures when they are unnecessary.
   c.   evaluating a weak manager as having strong performance.
   d.   promoting a product that is actually more profitable than budgeted.

   Answer: b   *Difficulty:*   3   *Objective:*   5

98. An inaccurate cost function with a constant that is estimated too high may MOST likely result in
    a.   evaluating a weak manager as providing strong performance.
    b.   promoting a product that is actually less profitable than budgeted.
    c.   predicting total costs that are too low.
    d.   replicating processes that are truly cost saving.

    Answer: a   *Difficulty*:   3   *Objective*:   5

99. A cost function with a lower constant than a year ago could indicate all EXCEPT
    a.   last year's cost function was inaccurate.
    b.   a new operations manager is being effective.
    c.   the sales commission percentage has decreased.
    d.   insurance premiums have decreased.

    Answer: c   *Difficulty*:   3   *Objective*:   5

100. A cost function with a lower slope coefficient than a year ago could indicate that
    a.   total variable costs have decreased.
    b.   new cost-cutting initiatives are beneficial.
    c.   production has decreased.
    d.   rental costs have decreased.

    Answer: b   *Difficulty*:   3   *Objective*:   5

101. If machine maintenance is scheduled at a time when production is at a low level then
    a.   low production is the cost driver of high repair costs.
    b.   an understanding of operations is needed to determine an appropriate cost driver.
    c.   low production should be avoided since it is the cause of machine maintenance.
    d.   machine maintenance cannot be accurately predicted.

    Answer: b   *Difficulty*:   3   *Objective*:   5

102. Goodness-of-fit measures how well the predicted values in a cost estimating equation
    a.   match the cost driver.
    b.   determine the level of activity.
    c.   match the actual cost observations.
    d.   rely on the independent variable.

    Answer: c   *Difficulty*:   2   *Objective*:   5

103. A steeply sloped regression line indicates
    a.   a strong relationship between the cost driver and costs.
    b.   a greater proportion of fixed costs than variable costs.
    c.   an economically plausible relationship exists.
    d.   management should cut costs.

    Answer: a   *Difficulty*:   3   *Objective*:   5

104. The smaller the residual term
    a. the stronger the relationship between the cost driver and costs.
    b. the weaker the relationship between the cost driver and costs.
    c. the steeper the slope of the cost function.
    d. the gentler the slope of the cost function.

    Answer: a   *Difficulty*: 2   *Objective*: 5

105. When using activity-based costing all of the following are true EXCEPT that
    a. all cost drivers should be output unit-level cost drivers.
    b. there are a great number and variety of cost drivers and cost pools.
    c. industrial engineering, conference, and regression analysis can be used to estimate slope coefficients.
    d. the more cost pools, the greater the chance of estimation error.

    Answer: a   *Difficulty*: 2   *Objective*: 5

106. Over the short run, a nonlinear cost function would MOST likely result from all EXCEPT
    a. quantity discounts for each additional 10,000 parts purchased.
    b. purchasing another $250,000 printing machine to double production.
    c. hiring a third production supervisor.
    d. incurring greater total utility costs for each machine-hour of operation.

    Answer: d   *Difficulty*: 3   *Objective*: 6

107. Examples of nonlinear cost functions include all EXCEPT
    a. step variable-cost functions.
    b. step fixed-cost functions.
    c. learning curves.
    d. mixed cost functions.

    Answer: d   *Difficulty*: 2   *Objective*: 6

108. A step fixed-cost function
    a. is fixed over the short run, but not over the long run.
    b. is often approximated with a continuous variable-cost function.
    c. remains the same over a narrow range of activity.
    d. example includes setup costs.

    Answer: a   *Difficulty*: 2   *Objective*: 6

109. A step variable-cost function
    a. is fixed over the long run, but not over the short run.
    b. is often approximated with a continuous variable-cost function.
    c. remains the same over a wide range of activity.
    d. example includes adding additional warehouse space.

    Answer: b   *Difficulty*: 2   *Objective*: 6

110. A learning curve is a function
    a. that measures the decline in labor-hours per unit due to workers becoming better at a job.
    b. that increases at a greater rate as workers become more familiar with their tasks.
    c. where unit costs increase as productivity increases.
    d. that is linear.

    Answer: a   *Difficulty:* 2   *Objective:* 6

111. An experience curve
    a. is a narrower application of the learning curve.
    b. measures the decline in cost per unit as production decreases for various value-chain functions such as marketing as production increases.
    c. only measures the decline in labor-hours per unit as units produced increases.
    d. measures the increase in cost per unit as productivity increases.

    Answer: b   *Difficulty:* 2   *Objective:* 6

112. To complete the first setup on a new machine took an employee 200 minutes. Using an 80% cumulative average-time learning curve indicates that the second setup on the new machine is expected to take
    a. 160 minutes.
    b. 120 minutes.
    c. 80 minutes.
    d. 60 minutes.

    Answer: b   *Difficulty:* 3   *Objective:* 7
    $200 \times .80 = 160; (200 + X)/2 = 160; X = 120$ minutes

113. To complete the first setup on a new machine took an employee 200 minutes. Using an 80% incremental unit-time learning model indicates that the second setup on the new machine is expected to take
    a. 160 minutes.
    b. 120 minutes.
    c. 80 minutes.
    d. 60 minutes.

    Answer: a   *Difficulty:* 2   *Objective:* 7
    $200 \times .80 = 160$ minutes

114. Learning curve effects can be incorporated
    a. into performance evaluations.
    b. into production schedules.
    c. when using costs to price products.
    d. into all of the above.

    Answer: d   *Difficulty:* 2   *Objective:* 7

115. The learning-curve models presented in the text
    a. examine how quality increases over time.
    b. examine how efficiency increases as more units are produced.
    c. examine how setup costs decline as more workers are added.
    d. examine the change in variable costs when quantity discounts are available.

    Answer: b   *Difficulty*: 2   *Objective*: 7

116. The ideal database contains
    a. numerous cost driver observations.
    b. reliably measured observations.
    c. cost driver observations spanning a wide range.
    d. all of the above.

    Answer: d   *Difficulty*: 1   *Objective*: 8

117. Data collection problems arise when
    a. data are recorded electronically rather than manually.
    b. accrual-basis costs are used rather than cash-basis costs.
    c. fixed and variable costs are not separately identified and both are allocated to products on a per unit basis.
    d. purely inflationary price effects are removed.

    Answer: c   *Difficulty*: 3   *Objective*: 8

118. Managers that design data collection reports that regularly and routinely obtain required data are helping to ensure that
    a. inflationary effects are removed.
    b. all data are recorded.
    c. extreme values are not used to calculate cost functions.
    d. the relationship between the cost driver and the cost remains stable over time.

    Answer: b   *Difficulty*: 2   *Objective*: 8

119. Extreme values of observations may be the result of
    a. a misplaced decimal point in the recorded data.
    b. classifying a cost incorrectly.
    c. a temporary plant shutdown.
    d. all of the above.

    Answer: d   *Difficulty*: 2   *Objective*: 8

120. All of the following are cost analysis problems EXCEPT
    a. fixed costs are allocated as if they are variable costs.
    b. extreme observations are adjusted or removed.
    c. time periods differ for measuring items included in the dependent variable and the cost driver(s).
    d. homogeneous relationships between individual cost items in the dependent variable pool and cost drivers may not be present.

Answer: b   *Difficulty:* 3   *Objective:* 8

121. The coefficient of determination is important in explaining variances in estimating equations. For a certain estimating equation, the unexplained variation was given as 26,505. The total variation was given as 46,500. What is the coefficient of determination for the equation?
    a. 0.34
    b. 0.43
    c. 0.57
    d. 0.66

Answer: b   *Difficulty:* 2   *Objective:* A
$r^2 = 1 - (26,505/46,500) = 0.43$

122. The Bhaskara Corporation used regression analysis to predict the annual cost of indirect materials. The results were as follows:

Indirect Materials Cost Explained by Units Produced	
Constant	$21,890
Standard error of Y estimate	$4,560
r^2	0.7832
Number of observations	22
X coefficient(s)	11.75
Standard error of coefficient(s)	2.1876

What is the linear cost function?
    a. Y = $21,890 + $11.75X
    b. Y = $4,560 + $5.15X
    c. Y = $20,100 + $4.60X
    d. none of the above

Answer: a   *Difficulty:* 2   *Objective:* A

123. Craig's Cola was to manufacture 1,000 cases of cola next week. The accountant provided the following analysis of total manufacturing costs.

Variable	Coefficient	Standard Error	t-Value
Constant	100	71.94	1.39
Independent variable	200	91.74	2.18

$r^2 = 0.82$

What is the estimated cost of producing the 1,000 cases of cola?
a. $200,100
b. $142,071
c. $100,200
d. $9,000

Answer: a　　　　*Difficulty:* 2　　　　*Objective:* A
y = $100 + ($200 x 1,000) = $200,100

124. Pam's Stables used two different independent variables (trainer's hours and number of horses) in two different equations to evaluate the cost of training horses. The most recent results of the two regressions are as follows:

Trainer's hours:

Variable	Coefficient	Standard Error	t-Value
Constant	913.32	198.12	4.61
Independent Variable	20.90	2.94	7.11

$r^2 = 0.56$

Number of horses:

Variable	Coefficient	Standard Error	t-Value
Constant	4,764.50	1,073.09	4.44
Independent Variable	864.98	247.14	3.50

$r^2 = 0.63$

What is the estimated total cost for the coming year if 16,000 trainer hours are incurred and the stable has 400 horses to be trained, based on the best cost driver?
a. $99,929.09
b. $350,756.50
c. $335,313.32
d. $13,844,444.50

Answer: b　　　　*Difficulty:* 3　　　　*Objective:* A
y = $4,764.50 + $864.98(400) = $350,756.50 based on highest r^2, which uses # of horses as the cost driver

125. Write a linear cost function equation for each of the following conditions. Use y for estimated costs and X for activity of the cost driver.

   a. Direct manufacturing labor is $10 per hour.
   b. Direct materials cost $9.20 per cubic yard.
   c. Utilities have a minimum charge of $1,000, plus a charge of $0.05 per kilowatt-hour.
   d. Machine operating costs include $200,000 of machine depreciation per year, plus $75 of utility costs for each day the machinery is in operation.

   Answer:

   a. $y = \$10X$
   b. $y = \$9.20X$
   c. $y = \$1,000 + \$0.05X$
   d. $y = \$200,000 + \$75X$

   Difficulty: 1   *Objective*: 1

126. The cost of the personnel department at the Miller Company has always been charged to the production departments based upon number of employees. Recently, opinions gathered from the department managers indicated that the number of new hires might also be a predictor of personnel costs to be assigned. Total personnel department costs are $120,000.

Cost Driver	Department A	Department B	Department C
Number of employees	300	250	50
The number of new hires	15	25	10

   Required:
   Using the above data, prepare a report that contrasts the different amounts of personnel department cost that would be allocated to each of the production departments if the cost driver used is
   a. number of employees.
   b. the number of new hires.
   c. Which cost estimation method is being used by Miller Company?

   Answer:

	Cost Driver	Department A	Department B	Department C
a.	Number of employees	300/600	250/600	50/600
		$60,000	$50,000	$10,000
b.	The number of new hires	15/50	25/50	10/50
		$36,000	$60,000	$24,000

   c. Miller Company is using the *conference method* for cost estimation.

   Difficulty: 2   *Objective*: 3

127. The managers of the production department have decided to use the production levels of 20x2 and 20x4 as examples of the highest and lowest years of operating levels. Data for those years is as follows:

Year	Chemicals used	Overhead Costs
20x2	140,000 gallons	$115,000
20x4	120,000 gallons	$100,000

Required:

What is the cost estimating equation for the department if gallons of chemicals are used as the cost driver?

Answer:

Slope (variable cost) = ($115,000 - $100,000)/(140,000 - 120,000) = $0.75

Constant (fixed cost) = $100,000 - $0.75(120,000) = $10,000

Estimating equation = $10,000 + $0.75DM

Difficulty: 1 *Objective*: 4

128. Wimmer's Storage ran its freezer in February, a slow month, for 360 hours for a total cost of $57,600. In July, a peak month, the freezer ran for 720 hours for a total cost of $82,080.

Required:

a. What is the cost estimating equation for the department if hours of freezer use are used as the cost driver?

b. What is the estimated total cost at an operating level of 500 hours?

Answer:

a. Slope (variable costs) = ($82,080 - $57,600) / (720 - 360) = $68

   Constant (fixed cost) = $82,080 - (720 x $68) = $33,120

   Estimating equation = $33,120 + $68DLH

b. Total costs of 500 hours = $33,120 + $68(500) = $67,120

Difficulty: 2 *Objective*: 4

129. The Wildcat Company has provided the following information:

Units of Output	30,000 Units	42,000 Units
Direct materials	$ 180,000	$ 252,000
Workers' wages	1,080,000	1,512,000
Supervisors' salaries	312,000	312,000
Equipment depreciation	151,200	151,200
Maintenance	81,600	110,400
Utilities	384,000	528,000
Total	$2,188,800	$2,865,600

Using the high-low method and the information provided above,
a. identify the linear cost function equation and
b. estimate the total cost at 36,000 units of output.

Answer:
a. Variable cost = ($2,865,600 - $2,188,800)/(42,000 - 30,000)= $56.40
Fixed cost = $2,865,600 - $56.40(42,000) = $496,800
Cost function is y = $496,800 + $56.40X

b. Output level of 36,000 units = $496,800 + $56.40(36,000) =
= $2,527,200 total cost

Difficulty: 2   *Objective*: 4

130. As part of his job as cost analyst, Max Thompson collected the following information concerning the operations of the Machining Department:

Observation	Machine-hours	Total Operating Costs
January	4,000	$45,000
February	4,600	49,500
March	3,800	45,750
April	4,400	48,000
May	4,500	49,800

Required:
a. Use the high-low method to determine the estimating cost function with machine-hours as the cost driver.
b. If June's estimated machine-hours total 4,200, what are the total estimated costs of the Machining Department?

Answer:
a. Slope coefficient = ($49,500 - $45,750)/(4,600 - 3,800) = $4.6875 per machine-hour

Constant = $49,500 - ($4.6875 x 4,600) = $27,937.50
Estimating equation = $27,937.50 + $4.6875X

b. June's estimated costs = $27,937.50 + $4.6875(4,200) = $47,625

Difficulty: 2   *Objective*: 4

131. Tessmer Manufacturing Company produces inventory in a highly automated assembly plant in Olathe, Kansas. The automated system is in its first year of operation and management is still unsure of the best way to estimate the overhead costs of operations for budgetary purposes. For the first six months of operations, the following data were collected:

Observation	Machine-hours	Kilowatt-hours	Total Overhead Costs
January	3,800	4,520,000	$138,000
February	3,650	4,340,000	136,800
March	3,900	4,500,000	139,200
April	3,300	4,290,000	136,800
May	3,250	4,200,000	126,000
June	3,100	4,120,000	120,000

Required:

a. Use the high-low method to determine the estimating cost function with machine-hours as the cost driver.

b. Use the high-low method to determine the estimating cost function with kilowatt-hours as the cost driver.

c. For July, the company ran the machines for 3,000 hours and used 4,000,000 kilowatt-hours of power. The overhead costs totaled $114,000. Which cost driver was the best predictor for July?

Answer:

a. **Machine-hours:**
   Slope coefficient = ($139,200 - $120,000)/(3,900 - 3,100)
   $\qquad\qquad\qquad$ = $24.00 per machine-hour
   Constant $\qquad\quad$ = $139,200 - ($24 x 3,900) = $45,600
   Machine-hour estimating equation = $45,600 + $24X

b. **Kilowatt-hours:**
   Slope coefficient = ($138,000 - $120,000)/(4,520,000 - 4,120,000)
   $\qquad\qquad\qquad$ = $0.045 per kilowatt-hour
   Constant = $138,000 - ($0.045 x 4,520,000) = $(65,400)
   Kilowatt-hour estimating equation = -$65,400 + $0.045KWH

c. **July's estimated costs:**
   with machine-hours = $45,600 + $24(3,000) = $117,600
   with kilowatt-hours = -$65,400 + $0.045(4,000,000) = $114,600
   The best estimator for July was the kilowatt-hour cost driver.

Difficulty: 3 $\qquad\qquad\qquad\qquad\qquad$ *Objective*: 4

132. Patrick Ross, the president of Ross's Wild Game Company, has asked for information about the cost behavior of manufacturing overhead costs. Specifically, he wants to know how much overhead cost is fixed and how much is variable. The following data are the only records available.

Month	Machine-hours	Overhead Costs
February	1,700	$20,500
March	2,800	22,250
April	1,000	19,950
May	2,500	21,500
June	3,500	23,950

Required:

Using the high-low method, determine the overhead cost equation. Use machine-hours as your cost driver.

Answer:

High: June	3,500	$23,950
Low: April	1,000	19,950
Difference	2,500	$ 4,000

Variable cost per MH: $4,000/2,500 = $1.60 per MH

Fixed cost: $19,950 = a + $1.60(1,000)
    a = $18,350

Estimated cost equation: y = $18,350 + $1.60 (1,000)

Difficulty: 2   *Objective*: 4

133. Harry's Picture manufactures various picture frames. Each new employee takes 5 hours to make the first picture frame and 4 hours to make the second. The manufacturing overhead charge per hour is $20.

Required:

a. What is the learning-curve percentage, assuming the cumulative average method?
b. What is the time needed to build 8 picture frames by a new employee using the cumulative average-time method? You may use an index of -0.1520.
c. What is the time needed to produce the 16th frame by a new employee using the incremental unit-time method? You may use an index of -0.3219.
d. How much manufacturing overhead would be charged to the 16 picture frames using the average-time approach?

Answer:

a.

Job	Hours	Cumulative	Cumulative Average
1	5	5	5
2	4	9	4.5

Learning percentage = 4.5/5 = 0.90

b. $Y = p X^q$
$= 5 \times 8^{-.1520}$
$= 3.65$ hours
or   1 unit   = 5
2 units = 5 x 0.9 = 4.5
4 units = 4.5 x 0.9 = 4.05
8 units = 4.05 x 0.9 = 3.65 hours
Time to build 8 units: 8 x 3.65 = <u>29.2</u> hours

c. $Y = p X^q$
$= 5 \times 16^{-0.3219}$
$= 2.048$ hours
or   1 unit   = 5
2 units = 5 x 0.8 = 4
4 units = 4 x 0.8 = 3.2
8 units = 3.2 x 0.8 = 2.56
16 units = 2.56 x .8 = 2.048 hours

d. Total time = 2.048 x 16 = 32.768 hours
Overhead charge = 32.768 x $20 = $655.36

Difficulty: 3   *Objective*: 6

134. Each time Mayberry Nursery hires a new employee, it must wait for some period of time before the employee can meet production standards. Management is unsure of the learning curve in its operations but it knows the first job by a new employee averages 30 hours and the second job averages 24 hours. Assume all jobs to be equal in size.

Required:

a. What is the learning-curve percentage, assuming the cumulative average-time method?
b. What is the time for a new employee to build 16 units with this learning curve using the cumulative average-time method? You may use an index of -0.1520.

Answer:

a.

Job	Hours	Cumulative	Cumulative Average
1	30	30	30
2	24	54	27

Learning percentage = 27/30 = 0.90

b. $Y = p X^q$
$= 30 \times 16^{-.1520}$
$= 19.683$

or 1 unit = 30
2 units = 30 x 0.9 = 27
4 units = 27 x 0.9 = 24.3
8 units = 24.3 x 0.9 = 21.87
16 units = 21.87 x 0.9 = 19.683 hours

16 x 19.683 = 314.9 hours

Difficulty: 2   *Objective*: 6

135. The new cost analyst in your accounting department has just received a computer-generated report that contains the results of a simple regression program for cost estimation. The summary results of the report appear as follows:

Variable	Coefficient	Standard Error	t-Value
Constant	35.92	16.02	2.24
Independent variable	563.80	205.40	2.74

$r^2 = 0.75$

Required:
a. What is the cost estimation equation according to the report?
b. What is the goodness of fit? What does it tell about the estimating equation?

Answer:
a. y = $35.92 + $563.80X
b. Goodness of fit is 0.75. It measures how well the predicted values match the actual observations. In this case, the equation passes the goodness of fit test because it is substantially above 0.30, the threshold of acceptance.

Difficulty: 1   *Objective*: A

136. Newton Company used least squares regression analysis to obtain the following output:

Payroll Department Cost
Explained by Number of Employees

Constant	$5,800
Standard error of Y estimate	630
r^2	0.8924
Number of observations	20
X coefficient(s)	1.902
Standard error of coefficient(s)	0.0966

Required:
a. What is the total fixed cost?
b. What is the variable cost per employee?
c. Prepare the linear cost function.
d. What is the coefficient of determination? Comment on the goodness of fit.

Answer:
a. The constant or intercept is the total fixed cost of $5,800.
b. The variable cost per employee is the X coefficient of $1.902.
c. y = $5,800 + $1.902X
d. The coefficient of determination is the r^2 of 0.8924. This represents a very high goodness of fit. The closer to 1.0, the better the cost driver explains the cost. Therefore, the conclusion can be drawn that there is a significant relationship between the cost of the payroll department and the number of employees.

Difficulty: 2   *Objective*: A

137. Schotte Manufacturing Company uses two different independent variables (machine-hours and number of packages) in two different equations to evaluate costs of the packaging department. The most recent results of the two regressions are as follows:

Machine-hours:

Variable	Coefficient	Standard Error	t-Value
Constant	748.30	341.20	2.19
Independent Variable	52.90	35.20	1.50

$r^2 = 0.33$

Number of packages:

Variable	Coefficient	Standard Error	t-Value
Constant	242.90	75.04	3.24
Independent Variable	5.60	2.00	2.80

$r^2 = 0.73$

Required:

a. What are the estimating equations for each cost driver?
b. Which cost driver is best and why?

Answer:

a. Machine-hours   y = $748.30 + $52.90X
   Number of packages y = $242.90 + $5.60X

b. Machine-hours has a low r^2 which implies that a small proportion of the variance is explained by machine-hours, thereby making it less attractive than number of packages as a cost predictor.

Also, for the independent variable, number of packages, the t-value of 2.80 indicates that a relationship exists between the independent and dependent variables. For machine-hours, the t-value (1.50) is below 2.00, indicating that the coefficient is not significantly different from zero and that there may not be a relationship between the independent and dependent variables.

The t-values of the constant terms (g) for both drivers is greater than 2.00, therefore, there is no distinguishing characteristic between the constants.

Given the above findings, it appears that number of packages is the best predictor of costs of the packing department.

Difficulty: 2   *Objective*: A

138. Munir Hassan, controller, gathered data on overhead costs and direct labor-hours over the past 12 months. List and discuss the different approaches Munir can use to estimate a cost function for overhead costs using direct labor-hours as the cost driver.

Answer:

The four approaches to cost estimation are:

1. Industrial engineering method
2. Conference method
3. Account analysis method
4. Quantitative analysis of current or past cost relationships

The industrial engineering method, also called the work-measurement method, estimates cost functions by analyzing the relationship between inputs and outputs in physical terms.

The conference method estimates cost functions on the basis of analysis and opinions about costs and their drivers gathered from various departments of an organization (purchasing, process engineering, manufacturing, employee relations, etc.).

The account analysis method estimates cost functions by classifying cost accounts in the ledger as variable, fixed, or mixed with respect to the identified cost driver.

Quantitative analysis of cost relationships are formal methods, such as the high-low method or regression, to fit linear cost functions to past data observations.

Difficulty: 2   *Objective*: 3

139. Roger Moon has just purchased the film studio of a movie company that specializes in comedies. He found that the company did not try to estimate the cost of making a movie. Instead, it just gave the producer a budget and told him/her to make a movie within budget. Mr. Moon does not like the former movie-budget concept and desires to establish a formal cost estimation system.

Required:

What are some of the potential problems that may be encountered in changing from a budget to a cost estimation movie making system?

139. **Answer:**

One of the first problems will be the timing of matching the cost drivers with the actual movie production process. Under the former budget system, the relationships with many of the cost drivers were probably forced to meet budget, or else poorly kept because they were substantially under budget and control over them was weak.

Next will be the problem of determining which costs are fixed and which are variable under the budget system. It may be difficult to determine those that are truly variable.

Timing problems will also have to be reconciled. Some costs may be incurred monthly rather than by movie, and some type of accrual will have to be made to keep the costs allocated to the proper cost driver.

Lastly, there may be gaps in the historical data because only total costs had to be maintained within the budget. There was probably little attention paid to cost categories, thereby causing reliable cost data to be scarce.

Difficulty: 2   *Objective*: 8

140. Arfaei Company manufactures chairs. Because the efforts of manufacturing are approximately equal between labor and machinery, management is considering other possible cost drivers. By considering different cost drivers, it is anticipated that the estimating process can be improved. The following cost estimating equations with their r^2 values have been determined for 20x3:

1.	X = cutting time	y – \$19,500 + \$20X	$r^2 = 0.65$
2.	X = labor	y = \$5,000 + \$25X	$r^2 = 0.49$
3.	X = machinery	y = \$44,500 + \$5X	$r^2 = 0.55$

Required:
a. Which equation should be selected for the analysis?
b. What other factors should be included in the selection of the estimating equation?

Answer:
a. Equation 1 for cutting time is slightly better than the other two equations based on r^2 values. Generally, an r^2 above 0.30 indicates a goodness of fit that is acceptable for most situations. Therefore, all three equations are acceptable when considering only the coefficient of determination.

   However, because the values are so close together, other factors should be considered.

b. Other factors to be considered are economic plausibility, the significance of independent variables, and specification analysis. The best cost drivers of the dependent variables are those that meet all these criteria plus that of best coefficient of determination.

Difficulty: 2   *Objective*: A

CHAPTER 11: DECISION MAKING AND RELEVANT INFORMATION

TRUE/FALSE

1. A decision model is a formal method for making a choice, frequently involving both quantitative and qualitative analyses.

   Answer: True   *Difficulty*: 1   *Objective*: 1

2. Feedback from previous decisions uses historical information and, therefore, is irrelevant for making future predictions.

   Answer: False   *Difficulty*: 2   *Objective*: 1
   Historical costs may be helpful in making future predictions, but are not relevant costs for decision making.

3. The amount paid to purchase tools last month is an example of a sunk cost.

   Answer: True   *Difficulty*: 2   *Objective*: 2

4. For decision making, differential costs assist in choosing between alternatives.

   Answer: True   *Difficulty*: 1   *Objective*: 2

5. For a particular decision, differential revenues and differential costs are always relevant.

   Answer: True   *Difficulty*: 1   *Objective*: 2

6. A cost may be relevant for one decision, but not relevant for a different decision.

   Answer: True   *Difficulty*: 2   *Objective*: 2

7. Revenues that remain the same for two alternatives being examined are relevant revenues.

   Answer: False   *Difficulty*: 1   *Objective*: 2
   Revenues that remain the same between two alternatives are irrelevant for that decision since they do not differ between alternatives.

8. Sunk costs are past costs that are unavoidable.

   Answer: True   *Difficulty*: 1   *Objective*: 2

9. Quantitative factors are always expressed in numerical terms.

   Answer: True   *Difficulty*: 2   *Objective*: 3

10. Qualitative factors are outcomes that are measured in numerical terms, such as the costs of direct labor.

   Answer: False   *Difficulty*: 1   *Objective*: 3
   Quantitative factors are outcomes that are measured in numerical terms, such as the costs of direct labor.

11. If a manufacturer chooses to continue purchasing direct materials from a supplier because of the ongoing relationship that has developed over the years, the decision is based on qualitative factors.

   Answer: True   *Difficulty*: 2   *Objective*: 3

12. Relevant revenues and relevant costs are the only information managers need to select among alternatives.

   Answer: False   *Difficulty*: 3   *Objective*: 3
   Qualitative factors, as well as relevant revenues and relevant costs need to be considered when selecting among alternatives.

13. Full costs of a product are relevant for one-time-only special order pricing decisions.

   Answer: False   *Difficulty*: 2   *Objective*: 3
   Incremental costs of a product are relevant for one-time-only special order pricing decisions.

14. Full costs of a product include variable costs, but not fixed costs.

   Answer: False   *Difficulty*: 1   *Objective*: 3
   Full costs of a product include variable and fixed costs for all business functions in the value chain.

15. For one-time-only special orders, variable costs may be relevant but not fixed costs.

   Answer: True   *Difficulty*: 2   *Objective*: 3

16. The price quoted for a one-time-only special order may be less than the price for a long-term customer.

   Answer: True   *Difficulty*: 2   *Objective*: 3

17. Bid prices and costs that are relevant for regular orders are the same costs that are relevant for one-time-only special orders.

   Answer: False   *Difficulty*: 2   *Objective*: 3
   Since long-term costs are relevant for regular orders and short-term costs are relevant for one-time-only special orders, the relevant costs differ.

18. An incremental product cost is generally a fixed cost.

Answer: False   *Difficulty*: 1   *Objective*: 4
An incremental product cost is generally a *variable* cost.

19. If Option 1 costs $100 and Option 2 costs $80, then the differential cost is $180.

Answer: False   *Difficulty*: 1   *Objective*: 4
If Option 1 costs $100 and Option 2 costs $80, then the differential cost is $20.

20. Producing another 10,000 units *may* increase the fixed cost of rent.

Answer: True   *Difficulty*: 3   *Objective*: 4
True, if additional capacity must be added to accommodate the additional production needs.

21. Absorption cost per unit is the best product cost to use for one-time-only special order decisions.

Answer: False   *Difficulty*: 2   *Objective*: 4
Variable cost per unit is the best cost to use for one-time-only special order decisions.

22. Sometimes qualitative factors are the most important factors in make-or-buy decisions.

Answer: True   *Difficulty*: 2   *Objective*: 4

23. If a company is deciding whether to outsource a part, the reliability of the supplier is an important factor to consider.

Answer: True   *Difficulty*: 2   *Objective*: 4

24. Outsourcing is risk free to the manufacturer because the supplier now has the responsibility of producing the part.

Answer: False   *Difficulty*: 2   *Objective*: 4
Outsourcing has risks since the manufacturer is dependent on the supplier for a quality product, delivered in a timely manner, for a reasonable price.

25. When a firm maximizes profits it will simultaneously minimize opportunity costs.

Answer: True   *Difficulty*: 3   *Objective*: 5

26. In a make-or-buy decision when there are alternative uses for capacity, the opportunity cost of idle capacity is relevant.

Answer: True   *Difficulty*: 3   *Objective*: 5

27. When opportunity costs exist, they are always relevant.

Answer: True   *Difficulty*: 3   *Objective*: 5

28. When capacity is constrained, relevant costs equal incremental costs plus opportunity costs.

Answer: True   *Difficulty*: 2   *Objective*: 5

29. If the $17,000 spent to purchase inventory could be invested and earn interest of $1,000, then the opportunity cost of holding inventory is $17,000.

Answer: False   *Difficulty*: 2   *Objective*: 5
The opportunity cost of holding inventory is $1,000.

30. The choice is not really whether to make or buy, but rather how to best utilize available production capacity.

Answer: True   *Difficulty*: 1   *Objective*: 5

31. For short-run product-mix decisions, managers should focus on minimizing total fixed costs.

Answer: False   *Difficulty*: 2   *Objective*: 6
For short-run product mix decisions, managers should focus on *maximizing* total *contribution margin*.

32. For short-run product-mix decisions, maximizing contribution margin will also result in maximizing operating income.

Answer: True   *Difficulty*: 2   *Objective*: 6

33. Regardless of the restraining resource, to maximize profits managers should produce more of the product with the greatest contribution margin per unit.

Answer: False   *Difficulty*: 2   *Objective*: 6
To maximize profits, managers should produce more of the product with the *greatest contribution margin per unit of the constraining resource*.

34. Management should focus on per unit costs when deciding whether to discontinue a product or not.

Answer: False   *Difficulty*: 2   *Objective*: 7
Management should focus on *total costs* when deciding whether to discontinue a product or not.

35. Avoidable variable and fixed costs should be evaluated when deciding whether to discontinue a product, product line, business segment, or customer.

Answer: True   *Difficulty*: 2   *Objective*: 7

36. Depreciation allocated to a product line is a relevant cost when deciding to discontinue that product.

Answer: False   *Difficulty*: 2   *Objective*: 7
Depreciation is a sunk cost and never relevant.

37. A company is considering adding a fourth product to use available capacity. A relevant factor to consider is that corporate costs can now be allocated over four products rather than only three.

Answer: False   *Difficulty*: 3   *Objective*: 7
It appears that corporate costs will not change in total, and therefore are not relevant costs for deciding whether to add a fourth product.

38. When replacing an old machine with a new machine, the purchase price of the new machine is a relevant cost.

Answer: True   *Difficulty*: 1   *Objective*: 8

39. When replacing an old machine with a new machine, the book value of the old machine is a relevant cost.

Answer: False   *Difficulty*: 1   *Objective*: 8
The original price of the old machine is a past cost and therefore an irrelevant cost.

40. Replacing an old machine will increase operating income in the long run, but not for this year. A manager may choose not to replace the machine if performance evaluations are based on performance over a single year.

Answer: True   *Difficulty*: 2   *Objective*: 9

41. Linear programming is a tool that maximizes total contribution margin of a mix of products with multiple constraints.

Answer: True   *Difficulty*: 1   *Objective*: A

42. Feedback regarding previous actions may affect
    a.   future predictions.
    b.   implementation of the decision.
    c.   the decision model.
    d.   all of the above.

    Answer: d   *Difficulty*:   2   *Objective*:   1

43. Place the following steps from the five-step decision process in order:

    >   A = Make predictions about future costs
    >   B = Evaluate performance to provide feedback
    >   C = Implement the decision
    >   D = Choose an alternative

    a.   D C A B
    b.   C D A B
    c.   A D C B
    d.   D C B A

    Answer: c   *Difficulty*:   2   *Objective*:   1

44. The formal process of choosing between alternatives is known as
    a.   a relevant model.
    b.   a decision model.
    c.   an alternative model.
    d.   a prediction model.

    Answer: b   *Difficulty*:   1   *Objective*:   1

45. Ruggles Circuit Company manufactures circuit boards for other firms. Management is attempting to search for ways to reduce manufacturing labor costs and has received a proposal from a consulting company to rearrange the production floor next year. Using the information below regarding current operations and the new proposal, which of the following decisions should management accept?

	Currently	**Proposed**
Required machine operators	5	4.5
Materials-handling workers	1.25	1.25
Employee average pay	$8 per hour	$9 per hour
Hours worked per employee	2,100	2,000

    a.   Do not change the production floor.
    b.   Rearrange the production floor.
    c.   Either, because it makes no difference to the employees.
    d.   It doesn't matter because the costs incurred will remain the same.

    Answer: b   *Difficulty*:   2   *Objective*:   1
    Current operations: 5 workers x 2,100 hours x $8.00 = $84,000
    Proposal: 4.5 workers x 2,000 hours x $9.00 = $81,000

THE FOLLOWING INFORMATION APPLIES TO QUESTIONS 46 AND 47.
LeBlanc Lighting manufactures small flashlights and is considering raising the price by 50 cents a unit for the coming year. With a 50-cent price increase, demand is expected to fall by 3,000 units.

	Currently	Projected
Demand	20,000 units	17,000 units
Selling price	$4.50	$5.00
Incremental cost per unit	$3.00	$3.00

46. If the price increase is implemented, operating profit is projected to
   a. increase by $4,000.
   b. decrease by $4,000.
   c. increase by $6,000.
   d. decrease by $4,500.

   Answer: a   *Difficulty:* 2   *Objective:* 1
   [17,000 x ($5 - $3)] – [20,000 x ($4.50 - $3.00)] = increase of $4,000

47. Would you recommend the 50-cent price increase?
   a. No, because demand decreased.
   b. No, because the selling price increases.
   c Yes, because contribution margin per unit increases.
   d. Yes, because operating profits increase.

   Answer: d   *Difficulty:* 2   *Objective:* 1

48. For decision making, a listing of the relevant costs
   a. will help the decision maker concentrate on the pertinent data.
   b. will only include future costs.
   c. will only include costs that differ among alternatives.
   d. should include all of the above.

   Answer: d   *Difficulty:* 2   *Objective:* 2

49. Sunk costs
   a. are relevant.
   b. are differential.
   c. have future implications.
   d. are ignored when evaluating alternatives.

   Answer: d   *Difficulty:* 1   *Objective:* 2

50. A computer system installed last year is an example of
   a. a sunk cost.
   b. a relevant cost.
   c. a differential cost.
   d. an avoidable cost.

   Answer: a   *Difficulty:* 1   *Objective:* 2

51. Costs that CANNOT be changed by any decision made now or in the future are
    a.   fixed costs.
    b.   indirect costs.
    c.   avoidable costs.
    d.   sunk costs.

    Answer: d   *Difficulty:*   1   *Objective:*   2

52. In evaluating different alternatives, it is useful to concentrate on
    a.   variable costs.
    b.   fixed costs.
    c.   total costs.
    d.   relevant costs.

    Answer: d   *Difficulty:*   1   *Objective:*   2

53. Which of the following costs always differ among future alternatives?
    a.   Fixed costs
    b.   Historical costs
    c.   Relevant costs
    d.   Variable costs

    Answer: c   *Difficulty:*   1   *Objective:*   2

54. Which of the following costs are never relevant in the decision-making process?
    a.   Fixed costs
    b.   Historical costs
    c.   Relevant costs
    d.   Variable costs

    Answer: b   *Difficulty:*   1   *Objective:*   2

THE FOLLOWING INFORMATION APPLIES TO QUESTIONS 55 AND 56.
Jim's 5-year-old Geo Prizm requires repairs estimated at $3,000 to make it roadworthy again. His friend, Julie, suggested that he should buy a 5-year-old used Honda Civic instead for $3,000 cash. Julie estimated the following costs for the two cars:

	Geo Prizm	**Honda Civic**
Acquisition cost	$15,000	$3,000
Repairs	$ 3,000	---
Annual operating costs		
(Gas, maintenance, insurance)	$ 2,280	$2,100

55. The cost NOT relevant for this decision is(are)
    a.   the acquisition cost of the Geo Prizm.
    b.   the acquisition cost of the Honda Civic.
    c.   the repairs to the Geo Prizm.
    d.   the annual operating costs of the Honda Civic.

    Answer: a   *Difficulty:*   2   *Objective:*   2

56. What should Jim do? What are his savings in the first year?
    a. Buy the Honda Civic; $9,780
    b. Fix the Geo Prizm; $5,518
    c. Buy the Honda Civic; $180
    d. Fix the Geo Prizm; $5,280

    Answer: c   *Difficulty*: 2   *Objective*: 2
    Geo ($3,000 + $2,280) - Honda ($3,000 + $2,100) = $180 cost savings with the Honda option

57. Quantitative factors
    a. include financial information, but not nonfinancial information.
    b. can be expressed in monetary terms.
    c. are always relevant when making decisions.
    d. include employee morale.

    Answer: b   *Difficulty*: 2   *Objective*: 3

58. Qualitative factors
    a. generally are easily measured in quantitative terms.
    b. are generally irrelevant for decision making.
    c. may include either financial or nonfinancial information.
    d. include customer satisfaction.

    Answer: d   *Difficulty*: 2   *Objective*: 3

59. Historical costs are helpful
    a. for making future predictions.
    b. for decision making.
    c. because they are quantitative.
    d. with none of the above.

    Answer: a   *Difficulty*: 2   *Objective*: 3

60. When making decisions
    a. quantitative factors are the most important.
    b. qualitative factors are the most important.
    c. appropriate weight must be given to both quantitative and qualitative factors.
    d. both quantitative and qualitative factors are unimportant.

    Answer: c   *Difficulty*: 2   *Objective*: 3

61. Employee morale at Dos Santos, Inc., is very high. This type of information is known as
    a. a qualitative factor.
    b. a quantitative factor.
    c. a nonmeasurable factor.
    d. a financial factor.

    Answer: a   *Difficulty*: 1   *Objective*: 3

62. Roberto owns a small body shop. His major costs include labor, parts, and rent. In the decision-making process, these costs are considered to be
    a. fixed.
    b. qualitative factors.
    c. quantitative factors.
    d. variable.

    Answer: c   *Difficulty*: 1   *Objective*: 3

63. One-time-only special orders should only be accepted if
    a. incremental revenues exceed incremental costs.
    b. differential revenues exceed variable costs.
    c. incremental revenues exceed fixed costs.
    d. total revenues exceed total costs.

    Answer: a   *Difficulty*: 3   *Objective*: 3

64. When deciding to accept a one-time-only special order from a wholesaler, management should do all EXCEPT
    a. analyze product costs.
    b. consider the special order's impact on future prices of their products.
    c. determine whether excess capacity is available.
    d. verify past design costs for the product.

    Answer: d   *Difficulty*: 3   *Objective*: 3

65. When there is excess capacity, it makes sense to accept a one-time-only special order for less than the current selling price when
    a. incremental revenues exceed incremental costs.
    b. additional fixed costs must be incurred to accommodate the order.
    c. the company placing the order is in the same market segment as your current customers.
    d. it never makes sense.

    Answer: a   *Difficulty*: 3   *Objective*: 3

THE FOLLOWING INFORMATION APPLIES TO QUESTIONS 66 THROUGH 69.
Welch Manufacturing is approached by a European customer to fulfill a one-time-only special order
for a product similar to one offered to domestic customers. Welch Manufacturing has excess
capacity. The following per unit data apply for sales to regular customers:

Variable costs:

Direct materials	$40
Direct labor	20
Manufacturing support	35
Marketing costs	15
Fixed costs:	
Manufacturing support	45
Marketing costs	15
Total costs	170
Markup (50%)	85
Targeted selling price	$255

66. What is the full cost of the product per unit?
   a. $110
   b. $170
   c. $255
   d. $85

   Answer: b   *Difficulty:*   3   *Objective:*   3
   $40 + $20 + $35 + $15 + $45 + $15 = $170

67. What is the contribution margin per unit?
   a. $85
   b. $110
   c. $145
   d. $255

   Answer: c   *Difficulty:*   3   *Objective:*   3
   $255 − ($40 + $20 + $35 + $15) = $145

68. For Welch Manufacturing, what is the minimum acceptable price of this special order?
   a. $110
   b. $145
   c. $170
   d. $255

   Answer: a   *Difficulty:*   3   *Objective:*   3
   $40 + $20 + $35 + $15 = $110

69. What is the change in operating profits if the 1,000 unit one-time-only special order is
   accepted for $180 a unit by Welch?
   a. $70,000 increase in operating profits
   b. $10,000 increase in operating profits
   c. $10,000 decrease in operating profits
   d. $75,000 decrease in operating profits

   Answer: a   *Difficulty:*   3   *Objective:*   3
   $180 − ($40 + $20 + $35 + $15) = $70;   1,000 x $70 = $70,000 increase

70. Ratzlaff Company has a current production level of 20,000 units per month. Unit costs at this level are:

Direct materials	$0.25
Direct labor	0.40
Variable overhead	0.15
Fixed overhead	0.20
Marketing - fixed	0.20
Marketing/distribution - variable	0.40

Current monthly sales are 18,000 units. Jim Company has contacted Ratzlaff Company about purchasing 1,500 units at $2.00 each. Current sales would not be affected by the one-time-only special order, and variable marketing/distribution costs would not be incurred on the special order. What is Ratzlaff Company's change in operating profits if the special order is accepted?
   a. $400 increase in operating profits
   b. $400 decrease in operating profits
   c. $1,800 increase in operating profits
   d. $1,800 decrease in operating profits

Answer: c   *Difficulty*:   3   *Objective*:   3
Manufacturing cost per unit = $0.25 + $0.40 + $0.15 = $0.80
1,500 x ($2.00 - $0.80) = $1,800 increase

71. Black Tool Company has a production capacity is 1,500 units per month, but current production is only 1,250 units. The manufacturing costs are $60 per unit and marketing costs are $16 per unit. Doug Hall offers to purchase 250 units at $76 each for the next five months. Should Black accept the one-time-only special order if only absorption-costing data are available?
   a.   Yes, good customer relations are essential.
   b.   No, the company will only break even.
   c.   No, since only the employees will benefit.
   d.   Yes, since operating profits will most likely increase.

Answer: d   *Difficulty*:   3   *Objective*:   3
Since the $60 absorption cost per unit is most likely not all variable costs and since the entire $16 per unit of marketing costs may not be incurred, operating profits will most likely increase.

THE FOLLOWING INFORMATION APPLIES TO QUESTIONS 72 THROUGH 75.
Grant's Kitchens is approached by Ms. Tammy Wang, a new customer, to fulfill a large one-time-only special order for a product similar to one offered to regular customers. The following per unit data apply for sales to regular customers:

Direct materials	$455
Direct labor	300
Variable manufacturing support	45
Fixed manufacturing support	100
Total manufacturing costs	900
Markup (60%)	540
Targeted selling price	$1440

Grant's Kitchens has excess capacity. Ms. Wang wants the cabinets in cherry rather than oak, so direct material costs will increase by $30 per unit.

72. For Grant's Kitchens, what is the minimum acceptable price of this one-time-only special order?
    a. $830
    b. $930
    c. $785
    d. $1440

    Answer: a   *Difficulty:* 2   *Objective:* 3
    $455 + $300 + $45 + $30 = $830

73. Other than price, what other items should Grant's Kitchens consider before accepting this one-time-only special order?
    a. Reaction of shareholders
    b. Reaction of existing customers to the lower price offered to Ms. Wang
    c. Demand for cherry cabinets
    d. Price is the only consideration.

    Answer: b   *Difficulty:* 2   *Objective:* 3

74. If Ms. Wang wanted a long-term commitment for supplying this product, this analysis
    a. would definitely be different.
    b. may be different.
    c. would not be different.
    d. does not contain enough information to determine if there would be a difference.

    Answer: a   *Difficulty:* 2   *Objective:* 3

75. If there was limited capacity, all of the following amounts would change EXCEPT
    a. opportunity costs.
    b. differential costs.
    c. variable costs.
    d. the minimum acceptable price.

    Answer: c   *Difficulty:* 3   *Objective:* 5

THE FOLLOWING INFORMATION APPLIES TO QUESTIONS 76 AND 77.
Northwoods manufactures rustic furniture. The cost accounting system estimates manufacturing costs to be $90 per table, consisting of 80% variable costs and 20% fixed costs. The company has surplus capacity available. It is Northwoods' policy to add a 50% markup to full costs.

76. Northwoods is invited to bid on a one-time-only special order to supply 100 rustic tables. What is the lowest price Northwoods should bid on this special order?
   a. $6,300
   b. $7,200
   c. $9,000
   d. $13,500

   Answer: b   *Difficulty:* 2   *Objective:* 3
   $90 x 80% x 100 tables = $7,200

77. A large hotel chain is currently expanding and has decided to decorate all new hotels using the rustic style. Northwoods Incorporated is invited to submit a bid to the hotel chain. What is the lowest price per unit Northwoods should bid on this long-term order?
   a. $63
   b. $72
   c. $90
   d. $135

   Answer: d   *Difficulty:* 2   *Objective:* 3
   $90 + ($90 x 50%) = $135

78. Cochran Corporation has a plant capacity of 100,000 units per month. Unit costs at capacity are:

Direct materials	$4.00
Direct labor	6.00
Variable overhead	3.00
Fixed overhead	1.00
Marketing - fixed	7.00
Marketing/distribution - variable	3.60

   Current monthly sales are 95,000 units at $30.00 each. Suzie, Inc., has contacted Cochran Corporation about purchasing 2,000 units at $24.00 each. Current sales would not be affected by the one-time-only special order. What is Cochran's change in operating profits if the one-time-only special order is accepted?
   a. $14,800 increase
   b. $17,200 increase
   c. $22,000 increase
   d. $33,200 increase

   Answer: a   *Difficulty:* 3   *Objective:* 3
   ($4.00 + 6.00 + 3.00 + 3.60) = $16.60
   ($24.00 – 16.60) x 2,000 = $14,800 increase

79. The sum of all the costs incurred in a particular business function (for example, marketing) is called the
    a. business function cost.
    b. full product cost.
    c. gross product cost.
    d. multiproduct cost.

    Answer: a   *Difficulty:* 1   *Objective:* 3

80. The sum of all costs incurred in all business functions in the value chain (product design, manufacturing, marketing, and customer service, for example) is known as the
    a. business cost.
    b. full product cost.
    c. gross product cost.
    d. multiproduct cost.

    Answer: b   *Difficulty:* 1   *Objective:* 3

81. Problems that should be avoided when identifying relevant costs include all EXCEPT
    a. assuming all variable costs are relevant.
    b. assuming all fixed costs are irrelevant.
    c. using unit costs that do not separate variable and fixed components.
    d. using total costs that separate variable and fixed components.

    Answer: d   *Difficulty:* 2   *Objective:* 4

82. The BEST way to avoid misidentification of relevant costs is to focus on
    a. expected future costs that differ among the alternatives.
    b. historical costs.
    c. unit fixed costs.
    d. total unit costs.

    Answer: a   *Difficulty:* 2   *Objective:* 4

83. Factors used to decide whether to outsource a part include
    a. the supplier's cost of direct materials.
    b. if the supplier is reliable.
    c. the original cost of equipment currently used for production of that part.
    d. past design costs used to develop the current composition of the part.

    Answer: b   *Difficulty:* 2   *Objective:* 4

84. Relevant costs of a make-or-buy decision include all EXCEPT
    a. fixed salaries that will not be incurred if the part is outsourced.
    b. current direct material costs of the part.
    c. special machinery for the part that has no resale value.
    d. material-handling costs that can be eliminated.

    Answer: c   *Difficulty:* 3   *Objective:* 4

85. Which of following are risks of outsourcing the production of a part?
    a. Unpredictable quality
    b. Unreliable delivery
    c. Unscheduled price increases
    d. All of the above are risks of outsourcing.

    Answer: d   *Difficulty:* 1   *Objective:* 4

86. Which of the following minimize the risks of outsourcing?
    a. The use of short-term contracts that specify price
    b. The responsibility for on-time delivery is now the responsibility of the supplier
    c. Building close relationships with the supplier
    d. All of the above minimize the risks of outsourcing.

    Answer: c   *Difficulty:* 3   *Objective:* 4

87. The cost to produce Part A was $10 per unit in 20x3 and in 20x4 has increased to $11 per unit. In 20x4, Supplier XYZ has offered to supply Part A for $9 per unit. For the make-or-buy decision,
    a. incremental revenues are $2 per unit.
    b. incremental costs are $1 per unit.
    c. net relevant costs are $1 per unit.
    d. differential costs are $2 per unit.

    Answer: d   *Difficulty:* 2   *Objective:* 4

88. When evaluating a make-or-buy decision, which of the following does NOT need to be considered?
    a. Alternative uses of the production capacity
    b. The original cost of the production equipment
    c. The quality of the supplier's product
    d. The reliability of the supplier's delivery schedule

    Answer: b   *Difficulty:* 2   *Objective:* 4

89. For make-or-buy decisions, a supplier's ability to deliver the item on a timely basis is considered
    a. a qualitative factor.
    b. a relevant cost.
    c. a differential factor.
    d. an opportunity cost.

    Answer: a   *Difficulty:* 1   *Objective:* 4

90. The incremental costs of producing one more unit of product include all of the following EXCEPT
   a. direct materials.
   b. direct labor.
   c. variable overhead costs.
   d. fixed overhead costs.

   Answer: d   *Difficulty:* 2   *Objective:* 4

91. Direct materials $40, direct labor $10, variable overhead costs $30, and fixed overhead costs $20. In the short term, the incremental cost of one unit is
   a. $30.
   b. $50.
   c. $80.
   d. $100.

   Answer: c   *Difficulty:* 2   *Objective:* 4

92. Unit cost data can MOST mislead decisions by
   a. not computing fixed overhead costs.
   b. computing labor and materials costs only.
   c. computing administrative costs.
   d. not computing unit costs at the same output level.

   Answer: d   *Difficulty:* 1   *Objective:* 4

93. Schmidt Sewing Company incorporates the services of Deb's Sewing. Schmidt purchases pre-cut dresses from Deb's. This is primarily known as
   a. insourcing.
   b. outsourcing.
   c. relevant costing.
   d. sunk costing.

   Answer: b   *Difficulty:* 1   *Objective:* 4

94. Pearce Sign Company manufactures signs from direct materials to the finished product. This is considered
   a. insourcing.
   b. outsourcing.
   c. relevant costing.
   d. sunk costing.

   Answer: a   *Difficulty:* 1   *Objective:* 4

95. Which of the following would NOT be considered in a make-or-buy decision?
   a. Fixed costs that will no longer be incurred
   b. Variable costs of production
   c. Potential rental income from space occupied by the production area
   d. Unchanged supervisory costs

   Answer: d   *Difficulty:* 2   *Objective:* 4

THE FOLLOWING INFORMATION APPLIES TO QUESTIONS 96 THROUGH 98.
Konrade's Engine Company manufactures part TE456 used in several of its engine models.
Monthly production costs for 1,000 units are as follows:

Direct materials	$ 40,000
Direct labor	10,000
Variable overhead costs	30,000
Fixed overhead costs	20,000
Total costs	$100,000

It is estimated that 10% of the fixed overhead costs assigned to TE456 will no longer be incurred if the company purchases TE456 from the outside supplier. Konrade's Engine Company has the option of purchasing the part from an outside supplier at $85 per unit.

96. If Konrade's Engine Company accepts the offer from the outside supplier, the monthly avoidable costs (costs will no longer be incurred) total
   a. $ 82,000.
   b. $ 98,000.
   c. $ 50,000.
   d. $100,000.

   Answer: a   *Difficulty:*   2   *Objective:*   4
   $40,000 + $10,000 + $30,000 + ($20,000 x 10%) = $82,000

97. If Konrade's Engine Company purchases 1,000 TE456 parts from the outside supplier per month, then its monthly operating income will
   a.   increase by $2,000.
   b.   increase by $80,000.
   c.   decrease by $3,000.
   d.   decrease by $85,000.

   Answer: c   *Difficulty:*   2   *Objective:*   4
   Avoidable costs $82,000 − ($85 x 1,000 units) = decrease of $3,000

98. The *maximum* price that Konrade's Engine Company should be willing to pay the outside supplier is
   a. $80 per TE456 part.
   b. $82 per TE456 part.
   c. $98 per TE456 part.
   d. $100 per TE456 part.

   Answer: b   *Difficulty:*   2   *Objective:*   4
   Avoidable costs $82,000 / 1,000 units = $82 per part

THE FOLLOWING INFORMATION APPLIES TO QUESTIONS 99 AND 100.
Schmidt Corporation produces a part that is used in the manufacture of one of its products. The costs associated with the production of 10,000 units of this part are as follows:

Direct materials	$ 45,000
Direct labor	65,000
Variable factory overhead	30,000
Fixed factory overhead	70,000
Total costs	$210,000

Of the fixed factory overhead costs, $30,000 is avoidable.

99. Phil Company has offered to sell 10,000 units of the same part to Schmidt Corporation for $18 per unit. Assuming there is no other use for the facilities, Schmidt should
  a. make the part as this would save $3 per unit.
  b. buy the part as this would save $3 per unit.
  c. buy the part as this would save the company $30,000.
  d. make the part as this would save $1 per unit.

Answer: d   *Difficulty:* 3   *Objective:* 4
Avoidable costs total $170,000 = $45,000 + $65,000 + $30,000 + $30,000.
$18 - $170,000/10,000 = $1

100. Assuming no other use of their facilities, the highest price that Schmidt should be willing to pay for 10,000 units of the part is
  a. $210,000.
  b. $140,000.
  c. $170,000.
  d. $180,000.

Answer: c   *Difficulty:* 3   *Objective:* 4
$45,000 + $65,000 + $30,000 + $30,000 = $170,000

101. Relevant costs in a make-or-buy decision of a part include
  a. setup overhead for the manufacture of the product using the outsourced part.
  b. currently used manufacturing capacity that has alternative uses.
  c. annual plant insurance costs that will remain the same.
  d. corporate office costs that will be allocated differently.

Answer: b   *Difficulty:* 3   *Objective:* 5

102. If Horsley Corporation doesn't use one of its limited resources in the best possible way, the lost contribution to income could be called
  a. a variable cost.
  b. a fixed cost.
  c. an opportunity cost.
  d. a sunk cost.

Answer: c   *Difficulty:* 1   *Objective:* 5

103. When a firm has constrained capacity as opposed to surplus capacity, opportunity costs will be
    a.   lower.
    b.   the same.
    c.   greater.
    d.   it varies.

    Answer: c   *Difficulty:*   2   *Objective:*   5

104. Opportunity costs
    a.   result in a cash outlay.
    b.   only are considered when selecting among alternatives.
    c.   are recorded in the accounting records.
    d.   should be maximized for the best decision.

    Answer: b   *Difficulty:*   2   *Objective:*   5

105. Opportunity cost(s)
    a.   of a resource with excess capacity is zero.
    b.   should be maximized by organizations.
    c.   are recorded as an expense in the accounting records.
    d.   are most important to financial accountants.

    Answer: a   *Difficulty:*   2   *Objective:*   5

106. For make-or-buy decisions, relevant costs include
    a.   direct material costs plus direct labor costs.
    b.   incremental costs plus opportunity costs.
    c.   differential costs plus fixed costs.
    d.   incremental costs plus differential costs.

    Answer: b   *Difficulty:*   3   *Objective:*   5

107. The opportunity cost of holding significant inventory includes
    a.   the interest forgone on an alternative investment.
    b.   additional insurance costs.
    c.   additional storage costs.
    d.   all of the above.

    Answer: a   *Difficulty:*   2   *Objective:*   5

THE FOLLOWING INFORMATION APPLIES TO QUESTIONS 108 AND 109.
Stephans Corporation currently manufactures a subassembly for its main product. The costs per unit are as follows:

Direct materials	$ 1.00
Direct labor	10.00
Variable overhead	5.00
Fixed overhead	8.00
Total	$24.00

Bill Company has contacted Stephans with an offer to sell them 5,000 of the subassemblies for $22.00 each. Stephans will eliminate $25,000 of fixed overhead if it accepts the proposal.

108. What are the relevant costs for Stephans?
    a. $140,000
    b. $125,000
    c. $105,000
    d. $80,000

Answer: c   *Difficulty:* 2   *Objective:* 5
($1 + 10 + 5) x 5,000 + $25,000 = $105,000

109. Should Stephans make or buy the subassemblies? What is the difference between the two alternatives?
    a. Buy; savings = $20,000
    b. Buy; savings = $50,000
    c. Make; savings = $60,000
    d. Make; savings = $5,000

Answer: d   *Difficulty:* 3   *Objective:* 5
Cost to buy: 5,000 x $22 = $110,000
Cost to make: $110,000 - 105,000 = $5,000 ** make

110. A recent college graduate has the choice of buying a new auto for $20,000 or investing the money for four years with a 6% expected rate of return. If the graduate decides to purchase the auto, the BEST estimate of the opportunity cost of that decision is
    a. $1,200.
    b. $4,800.
    c. $20,000.
    d. zero since there is no opportunity cost for this decision.

Answer: b   *Difficulty:* 2   *Objective:* 5
$20,000 x 6% x 4 years = $4,800 cost of the opportunity not chosen.

111. A supplier offers to make Part A for $70. Jansen Company has relevant costs of $80 a unit to manufacture Part A. If there is excess capacity, the opportunity cost of buying Part A from the supplier
    a.   is zero.
    b.   is $10,000.
    c.   is $70,000.
    d.   cannot be determined using the above information.

    Answer: a   *Difficulty*:   2   *Objective*:   5

112. Jensen Company has relevant costs of $80 per unit to manufacture Part A. A current supplier offers to make Part A for $70 per unit. If capacity is constrained, the opportunity cost of buying Part A from the supplier
    a.   is zero.
    b.   is $10,000.
    c.   is $70,000.
    d.   cannot be determined using the above information.

    Answer: d   *Difficulty*:   2   *Objective*:   5
    Information regarding alternative uses for the capacity would determine the opportunity cost.

113. Determining which products should be produced when the plant is operating at full capacity is referred to as
    a.   an outsourcing analysis.
    b.   production scheduling analysis.
    c.   a product-mix decision.
    d.   a short-run focus decision.

    Answer: c   *Difficulty*:   1   *Objective*:   6

114. Product mix decisions
    a.   have a long-run focus.
    b.   help determine how to maximize operating profits.
    c.   focus on selling price per unit.
    d.   are all of the above.

    Answer: b   *Difficulty*:   2   *Objective*:   6

115. Constraints may include
    a.   the availability of direct materials in manufacturing.
    b.   linear square feet of display space for a retailer.
    c.   direct labor in the service industry.
    d.   all of the above.

    Answer: d   *Difficulty*:   1   *Objective*:   6

116. For determining the best mix of products, the one with the LEAST amount of influence is
    a. the market price of the products.
    b. corporate office costs allocated to each product.
    c. the use of capacity resources.
    d. contribution margins.

    Answer: b   *Difficulty:* 3   *Objective:* 6

117. In product-mix decisions,
    a. always focus on maximizing total contribution margin.
    b. focus on the product with the greatest contribution margin per machine-hour.
    c. focus on the full costs of the product.
    d. never focus on the short-term, but include only long-term considerations.

    Answer: a   *Difficulty:* 3   *Objective:* 6

Braun's Brakes manufactures three different product lines, Model X, Model Y, and Model Z. Considerable market demand exists for all models. The following per unit data apply:

	Model X	Model Y	Model Z
Selling price	$50	$60	$70
Direct materials	6	6	6
Direct labor ($12 per hour)	12	12	24
Variable support costs ($4 per machine-hour)	4	8	8
Fixed support costs	10	10	10

118. Which model has the greatest contribution margin per unit?
    a.   Model X
    b.   Model Y
    c.   Model Z
    d.   Both Models X and Y

    Answer: b   *Difficulty*:   2   *Objective*:   6
    Model X $50 - $6 - $12 - $4 = $28
    Model Y $60 - $6 - $12 - $8 = $34   **highest
    Model Z $70 - $6 - $24 - $8 = $32

119. Which model, has the greatest contribution margin per machine-hour?
    a.   Model X
    b.   Model Y
    c.   Model Z
    d.   Both Models Y and Z

    Answer: a   *Difficulty*:   2   *Objective*:   6
    Model X $50 - $6 - $12 - $4 = $28 / 1 = $28 **highest
    Model Y $60 - $6 - $12 - $8 = $34 / 2 = $17
    Model Z $70 - $6 - $24 - $8 = $32 / 2 = $16

120. If there is excess capacity, which model is the most profitable to produce?
    a.   Model X
    b.   Model Y
    c.   Model Z
    d.   Both Models X and Y

    Answer: b   *Difficulty*:   3   *Objective*:   6
    Model Y since it has the greatest contribution margin per unit

121. If there is a machine breakdown, which model is the most profitable to produce?
    a.   Model X
    b.   Model Y
    c.   Model Z
    d.   Both Models Y and Z

    Answer: a   *Difficulty*:   3   *Objective*:   6
    Model X since it has the greatest contribution margin per machine-hour

122. How can Lisa Braun encourage her salespeople to promote the more profitable model?
    a.   Put all sales persons on salary
    b.   Provide higher sales commissions for higher priced items
    c.   Provide higher sales commissions for items with the greatest contribution margin per constrained resource
    d.   Both (b) and (c)

    Answer: c   *Difficulty:*   2   *Objective:*   6

THE FOLLOWING INFORMATION APPLIES TO QUESTIONS 123 THROUGH 125.
Helmer's Rockers manufactures two models, Standard and Premium. Weekly demand is estimated to be 100 units of the Standard Model and 70 units of the Premium Model. The following per unit data apply:

	Standard	**Premium**
Contribution margin per unit	$18	$20
Number of machine-hours required	3	4

123. The contribution per machine-hour is
    a. $18 for Standard, $20 for Premium.
    b. $54 for Standard, $80 for Premium.
    c. $15 for Standard, $16 for Premium.
    d. $6 for Standard, $5 for Premium.

    Answer: d   *Difficulty:*   2   *Objective:*   6
    Standard $18 / 3 = $6; Premium $20 / 4 = 5

124. If there are 496 machine-hours available per week, how many rockers of each model should Jim Helmer produce to maximize profits?
    a.   100 units of Standard and 49 units of Premium
    b.   72 units of Standard and 70 units of Premium
    c.   100 units of Standard and 70 units of Premium
    d.   85 units of Standard and 60 units of Premium

    Answer: a   *Difficulty:*   2   *Objective:*   6
    Standard (100 units x 3mh) + Premium (49 units x 4 mh) = 496 machine-hours of the constrained resource

125. If there are 600 machine-hours available per week, how many rockers of each model should Jim Helmer produce to maximize profits?
    a.   100 units of Standard and 49 units of Premium
    b.   72 units of Standard and 70 units of Premium
    c.   100 units of Standard and 70 units of Premium
    d.   85 units of Standard and 60 units of Premium

    Answer: c   *Difficulty:*   2   *Objective:*   6
    Standard (100 units x 3mh) + Premium (70 units x 4 mh) = 580 machine-hours for the current demand

THE FOLLOWING INFORMATION APPLIES TO QUESTIONS 126 THROUGH 128.
Raines Company manufactures three sizes of kitchen appliances: small, medium, and large.
Product information is provided below.

	Small	Medium	Large
Unit selling price	$150	$250	$500
Unit costs:			
Variable manufacturing	(60)	(120)	(200)
Fixed manufacturing	(40)	(50)	(120)
Variable selling and administrative	(30)	(30)	(30)
Unit profit	$ 20	$ 50	$150
Demand in units	100	120	100
Machine-hours per unit	20	40	100

The maximum machine-hours available are 6,000 per week.

126. What is the contribution margin per machine-hour for a large chair?
   a. $5.00
   b. $3.00
   c. $2.70
   d. $1.80

Answer: c   *Difficulty:*   2   *Objective:*   6
$500 - $200 - $30 = $270
$270 / 100 = $2.70

127. Which of the three product models should be produced first if management
incorporates a short-run profit maximizing strategy?
   a.   Small chairs
   b.   Medium chairs
   c.   Large chairs
   d.   Either medium or large chairs

Answer: a   *Difficulty:*   2   *Objective:*   6
Small   ($150 - $60 - $30) = $60 / 20 = $3.00   **highest
Medium   ($250 - $120 - $30) = $100 / 40 = $2.50
Large   ($500 - $200 - $30) = $270 / 100 = $2.70

128. How many of each product should be produced per month using the short-run profit
maximizing strategy?

	Small	Medium	Large
a.	0	120	12
b.	100	0	40
c.	100	100	0
d.	100	20	40

Answer: b   *Difficulty:*   3   *Objective:*   6
Small (100 x 20) + Large (40 x 100) = 6,000 total machine-hours

129. When deciding whether to discontinue a segment of a business, managers should focus on
   a.   equipment used by that segment that could become idle.
   b.   reallocation of corporate costs.
   c.   how total costs differ among alternatives.
   d.   operating income per unit of the discontinued segment.

   Answer: c   *Difficulty:*   3   *Objective:*   7

130. When deciding whether to discontinue a segment of a business, relevant costs include all EXCEPT
   a.   fixed supervision costs that can be eliminated.
   b.   variable marketing costs per unit of product sold.
   c.   cost of goods sold.
   d.   future administrative costs that will continue.

   Answer: d   *Difficulty:*   2   *Objective:*   7

131. Discontinuing unprofitable products will increase profitability
   a.   if the resources no longer required by the discontinued product can be eliminated.
   b.   if capacity constraints are adjusted.
   c.   automatically.
   d.   when a large portion of the fixed costs are unavoidable.

   Answer: a   *Difficulty:*   2   *Objective:*   7

132. Camera Corner is considering eliminating Model AE2 from its camera line because of losses over the past quarter. The past three months of information for Model AE2 are summarized below.

Sales (1,000 units)	$300,000
Manufacturing costs:	
Direct materials	150,000
Direct labor ($15 per hour)	60,000
Overhead	100,000
Operating loss	($10,000)

Overhead costs are 70% variable and the remaining 30% is depreciation of special equipment for model AE2 that has no resale value.

If Model AE2 is dropped from the product line, operating income will
   a.   increase by $10,000.
   b.   decrease by $20,000.
   c.   increase by $30,000.
   d.   decrease by $10,000.

   Answer: b   *Difficulty:*   3   *Objective:*   7
   300,000 - $150,000 - $60,000 - $70,000 = $20,000   This product contributes $20,000 toward corporate profits, therefore, discontinuing this product will decrease operating income by $20,000.

THE FOLLOWING INFORMATION APPLIES TO QUESTIONS 133 AND 134.
The management accountant for Martha's Book Store has prepared the following income statement for the most current year.

	Cookbook	Travel Book	Classics	Total
Sales	$60,000	$100,000	$40,000	$200,000
Cost of goods sold	36,000	65,000	20,000	121,000
Contribution margin	24,000	35,000	20,000	79,000
Order and delivery processing	18,000	21,000	8,000	47,000
Rent (per sq. foot used)	2,000	1,000	3,000	6,000
Allocated corporate costs	7,000	7,000	7,000	21,000
Corporate profit	$ (3,000)	$ 6,000	$ 2,000	$ 5,000

133. If the cookbook product line had been discontinued prior to this year, the company would have reported
    a.   greater corporate profits.
    b.   the same amount of corporate profits.
    c.   less corporate profits.
    d.   resulting profits cannot be determined.

    Answer: c   *Difficulty*:   3   *Objective*:   7
    $60,000 - $36,000 - $18,000 - $2,000 = $4,000
    The cookbook product line contributed $4,000 toward corporate profits. Without the cookbooks, corporate profits would be $4,000 less than currently reported.

134. If the travel book line had been discontinued, corporate profits for the current year would have decreased by
    a. $35,000.
    b. $14,000.
    c. $13,000.
    d. $6,000.

    Answer: c   *Difficulty*:   3   *Objective*:   7
    $100,000 - $65,000 - $21,000 - $1,000 = $13,000

THE FOLLOWING INFORMATION APPLIES TO QUESTIONS 135 AND 136.
Denly Company has three products, A, B, and C. The following information is available:

	Product A	**Product B**	**Product C**
Sales	$60,000	$90,000	$24,000
Variable costs	36,000	48,000	15,000
Contribution margin	24,000	42,000	9,000
Fixed costs:			
Avoidable	9,000	18,000	6,000
Unavoidable	6,000	9,000	5,400
Operating income	$ 9,000	$15,000	$ (2,400)

135. Denly Company is thinking of dropping Product C because it is reporting a loss. Assuming Denly drops Product C and does not replace it, operating income will
    a.   increase by $2,400.
    b.   increase by $3,000.
    c.   decrease by $3,000.
    d.   decrease by $5,400.

    Answer: c   *Difficulty*:   3   *Objective*:   7
    $24,000 - $15,000 - $6,000 = $3,000. Product C contributes $3,000 toward corporate profits. Without Product C, operating income would be $3,000 less than currently reported.

136. Assuming Product C is discontinued and the space formerly used to produce Product C is rented for $12,000 per year, operating income will
    a.   increase by $6,600.
    b.   increase by $9,000.
    c.   increase by $12,000.
    d.   increase by $14,400.

    Answer: b   *Difficulty*:   3   *Objective*:   7
    $(3,000) + $12,000 = $9,000

THE FOLLOWING INFORMATION APPLIES TO QUESTIONS 137 AND 138.
Melodee's Preserves currently makes jams and jellies and a variety of decorative jars used for packaging. An outside supplier has offered to supply all of the needed decorative jars. For this make-or-buy decision, a cost analysis revealed the following avoidable unit costs for the decorative jars:

Direct materials	$0.25
Direct labor	0.03
Unit-related support costs	0.10
Batch-related support costs	0.12
Product-sustaining support costs	0.22
Facility-sustaining support costs	0.28
Total cost per jar	$1.00

137. The relevant cost per jar is
    a. $0.28 per jar.
    b. $0.38 per jar.
    c. $0.72 per jar.
    d. $1.00 per jar.

Answer: d   *Difficulty*: 2   *Objectives*: 4, 7
All avoidable costs are relevant for this decision.

138. The maximum price that Melodee's Preserves should be willing to pay for the decorative jars is
    a. $0.28 per jar.
    b. $0.38 per jar.
    c. $0.72 per jar.
    d. $1.00 per jar.

Answer: d   *Difficulty*: 2   *Objectives*: 4, 7
Considering only quantitative factors, the company should not pay more than the avoidable costs of $1.00 per jar. There may be qualitative factors that are also important.

139. Costs are relevant to a particular decision if they
    a. are variable costs.
    b. are fixed costs.
    c. differ across the alternatives being considered.
    d. remain unchanged across the alternatives being considered.

Answer: c   *Difficulty*: 2   *Objective*: 8

140. When deciding to lease a new cutting machine or continue using the old machine, the following costs are relevant EXCEPT the
    a. $50,000 cost of the old machine.
    b. $20,000 cost of the new machine.
    c. $10,000 selling price of the old machine.
    d. $3,000 annual savings in operating costs if the new machine is purchased.

    Answer: a   *Difficulty:* 2   *Objective:* 8

141. For machine-replacement decisions, depreciation is a cost that is
    a. not relevant.
    b. differential.
    c. incremental.
    d. variable.

    Answer: a   *Difficulty:* 1   *Objective:* 8

THE FOLLOWING INFORMATION APPLIES TO QUESTIONS 142 THROUGH 144.
Flowers For Everyone is considering replacing its existing delivery van with a new one. The new van can offer considerable savings in operating costs. Information about the existing van and the new van follow:

	Existing van	**New van**
Original cost	$100,000	$180,000
Annual operating cost	$ 35,000	$ 20,000
Accumulated depreciation	$ 60,000	---
Current salvage value of the existing van	$ 45,000	---
Remaining life	10 years	10 years
Salvage value in 10 years	$ 0	$ 0
Annual depreciation	$ 4,000	$ 18,000

142. Sunk costs include
    a. the original cost of the existing van.
    b. the original cost of the new van.
    c. the current salvage value of the existing van.
    d. the annual operating cost of the new van.

    Answer: a   *Difficulty:* 2   *Objective:* 8

143. Relevant costs for this decision include
    a. the original cost of the existing van.
    b. accumulated depreciation.
    c. the current salvage value.
    d. the salvage value in 10 years.

    Answer: c   *Difficulty:* 2   *Objective:* 8

144. If Flowers For Everyone replaces the existing delivery van with the new one, over the next 10 years operating income will
    a.   decrease by $180,000.
    b.   increase by $150,000.
    c.   decrease by $150,000.
    d.   none of the above.

Answer: b   *Difficulty:* 3   *Objective:* 8
New van ($20,000 x 10 years) - Existing van ($35,000 x 10 years) = $150,000 less in operating costs, which results in a $150,000 increase in operating income.

THE FOLLOWING INFORMATION APPLIES TO QUESTIONS 145 THROUGH 147.
Frederick, Inc., is considering replacing a machine. The following data are available:

	Old Machine	Replacement Machine
Original cost	$45,000	$35,000
Useful life in years	10	5
Current age in years	5	0
Book value	$25,000	-
Disposal value now	$8,000	-
Disposal value in 5 years	0	0
Annual cash operating costs	$7,000	$4,000

145. Which of the data provided in the table is a sunk cost?
    a.   The annual cash operating costs of the old machine
    b.   The annual cash operating costs of the replacement machine
    c.   The disposal value of the old machine
    d.   The original cost of the old machine

Answer: d   *Difficulty:* 2   *Objective:* 8

146. For the decision to keep the old machine, the relevant costs of keeping the old machine total
    a. $60,000.
    b. $35,000.
    c. $47,000.
    d. $72,000.

Answer: b   *Difficulty:* 3   *Objective:* 8
$7,000 x 5 = $35,000

147. The difference between keeping the old machine and replacing the old machine is
    a. $37,000 in favor of keeping the old machine.
    b. $12,000 in favor of keeping the old machine.
    c. $37,000 in favor of replacing the old machine.
    d. $12,000 in favor of replacing the old machine.

Answer: b   *Difficulty:* 3   *Objective:* 8
New [$35,000 + (5 x $4,000)] – Old [$8,000 + (5 x $7,000)] = $12,000

148. Managers tend to favor the alternative that makes their performance look best. Therefore, they tend to focus on
    a. how to implement the chosen alternative.
    b. the measures used in the decision model.
    c. the measures used in the performance evaluation model.
    d. gathering the required information.

    Answer: c   *Difficulty*: 2   *Objective*: 9

149. If management takes a multiple-year view in the decision model and judges success according to the current year's results, a problem will occur in the
    a. decision model.
    b. performance evaluation model.
    c. production evaluation model.
    d. quantitative model.

    Answer: b   *Difficulty*: 2   *Objective*: 9

150. The three steps involved in linear programming include all of the following EXCEPT
    a. determining the objective.
    b. determining the basic relationship.
    c. computing the optimal solution.
    d. determining the relevant and irrelevant costs.

    Answer: d   *Difficulty*: 2   *Objective*: A

151. In linear programming, the goals of management are expressed in
    a. an objective function.
    b. constraints.
    c. operating policies.
    d. business functions.

    Answer: a   *Difficulty*: 1   *Objective*: A

152. A mathematical inequality or equality that must be appeased is known as
    a. an objective function.
    b. a constraint.
    c. an operating policy.
    d. a business function.

    Answer: b   *Difficulty*: 2   *Objective*: A

153. Computer Products produces two keyboards, Regular and Special. Regular keyboards have a unit contribution margin of $128, and Special keyboards have a unit contribution margin of $720. The demand for Regulars exceeds Computer Product's production capacity, which is limited by available machine-hours and direct manufacturing labor-hours. The maximum demand for Special keyboards is 80 per month. Management desires a product mix that will maximize the contribution toward fixed costs and profits.

Direct manufacturing labor is limited to 1,600 hours a month and machine-hours are limited to 1,200 a month. The Regular keyboards require 20 hours of labor and 8 machine-hours. Special keyboards require 34 labor-hours and 20 machine-hours.

Let R represent Regular keyboards and S represent Special keyboards. The correct set of equations for the keyboard production process is

a. Maximize: $128R + $720S
   Constraints:
Labor-hours:	$20R + 34S \leq 1,600$
Machine-hours:	$8R + 20S \leq 1,200$
Special:	$S \leq 80$
	$S \geq 0$
Regular:	$R \geq 0$

b. Maximize: $128R + $720S
   Constraints:
Labor-hours:	$20R + 34S \geq 1,600$
Machine-hours:	$8R + 20S \geq\leq 1,200$
Special:	$S \geq 80$
	$S \geq 0$
Regular:	$R \geq 0$

c. Maximize: $720S + $128R
   Constraints:
Labor-hours:	$20R + 8S \leq 1,600$
Machine-hours:	$34R + 20S \leq 1,200$
Special:	$S \leq 80$
	$S \geq 0$
Regular:	$R \geq 0$

d. Maximize: $128R + $720S
   Constraints:
Labor-hours:	$20R + 34S \leq 1,600$
Machine-hours:	$8R + 20S \leq 1,200$
Special:	$S \geq 80$
	$S \leq 0$
Regular:	$R \leq 0$

Answer: a   *Difficulty*: 3   *Objective*: A

154. Fluty Corporation manufactures a product that has two parts, A and B. It is currently considering two alternative proposals related to these parts.

The first proposal is for buying Part A. This would free up some of the plant space for the manufacture of more of Part B and assembly of the final product. The product vice president believes the additional production of the final product can be sold at the current market price. No other changes in manufacturing would be needed.

The second proposal is for buying new equipment for the production of Part B. The new equipment requires fewer workers and uses less power to operate. The old equipment has a net disposal value of zero.

Required:

Tell whether the following items are relevant or irrelevant for each proposal. Treat each proposal independently.

a. Total variable manufacturing overhead, Part A
b. Total variable manufacturing overhead, Part B
c. Cost of old equipment for manufacturing Part B
d. Cost of new equipment for manufacturing Part B
e. Total variable selling and administrative costs
f. Sales revenue of the product
g. Total variable costs of assembling final products
h. Total direct manufacturing materials, Part A
i. Total direct manufacturing materials, Part B
j. Total direct manufacturing labor, Part A
k. Total direct manufacturing labor, Part B

Answer:	*Proposal 1*	*Proposal 2*
a.	R	I
b.	R	R
c.	I	I
d.	I	R
e.	R	I
f.	R	I
g.	R	I
h.	R	I
i.	R	I
j.	R	I
k.	R	R

Difficulty: 2   *Objective*: 2

155. Axle and Wheel Manufacturing is approached by a European customer to fulfill a one-time-only special order for a product similar to one offered to domestic customers. The following per unit data apply for sales to regular customers:

Direct materials	$33
Direct labor	15
Variable manufacturing support	24
Fixed manufacturing support	52
Total manufacturing costs	124
Markup (50%)	62
Targeted selling price	$186

Axle and Wheel Manufacturing has excess capacity.

Required:

a. What is the full cost of the product per unit?
b. What is the contribution margin per unit?
c. Which costs are relevant for making the decision regarding this one-time-only special order? Why?
d. For Axle and Wheel Manufacturing, what is the minimum acceptable price of this one-time-only special order?
e. For this one-time-only special order, should Axle and Wheel Manufacturing consider a price of $100 per unit? Why or why not?

Answer:

a. $124
b. $114 = Selling price $186 – Variable costs ($33 + $15 + $24).
c. Relevant costs for decision making are those costs that differ between alternatives, which in this situation are the incremental costs. The incremental costs total $72 = Variable costs ($33 + $15 + $24).
d. The minimum acceptable price is $72 = Variable costs ($33 + $15 + $24), the incremental costs in the short tem.
e. Yes, because this price is greater than the minimum acceptable price of this special order determined in (d).

Difficulty: 2   *Objectives*: 2, 3

156. Silver Lake Cabinets is approached by Ms. Jenny Zhang, a new customer, to fulfill a large one-time-only special order for a product similar to one offered to regular customers. The following per unit data apply for sales to regular customers:

Direct materials	$100
Direct labor	125
Variable manufacturing support	60
Fixed manufacturing support	75
Total manufacturing costs	360
Markup (60%)	216
Targeted selling price	$576

Silver Lake Cabinets has excess capacity. Ms. Zhang wants the cabinets in cherry rather than oak, so direct material costs will increase by $30 per unit.

Required:

a. For Silver Lake Cabinets, what is the minimum acceptable price of this one-time-only special order?

b. Other than price, what other items should Silver Lake Cabinets consider before accepting this one-time-only special order?

c. How would the analysis differ if there was limited capacity?

Answer:

a. $315 = Variable costs ($100 + $125 + $60) + $30 additional cost for cherry.

b. Silver Lake Cabinets should also consider the impact on current customers when these customers hear that another customer was offered a discounted price, and the impact on the competition and if they might choose to meet the discounted price.

c. Currently, the incremental costs total $315. If additional capacity is needed to process this order, these incremental costs will increase by the cost of adding capacity.

Difficulty: 3   *Objectives*: 2, 3, 4

157. Quiett Truck manufactures part WB23 used in several of its truck models. 10,000 units are produced each year with production costs as follows:

Direct materials	$ 45,000
Direct manufacturing labor	15,000
Variable support costs	35,000
Fixed support costs	25,000
Total costs	$120,000

Quiett Truck has the option of purchasing part WB23 from an outside supplier at $11.20 per unit. If WB23 is outsourced, 40% of the fixed costs cannot be immediately converted to other uses.

a. Describe avoidable costs. What amount of the WB23 production costs is avoidable?

b. Should Quiett Truck outsource WB23? Why or why not?

c. What other items should Quiett Truck consider before outsourcing any of the parts it currently manufactures?

Answer:

a. Avoidable costs are those costs eliminated when a part, product, product line, or business segmented is discontinued. Avoidable production costs for WB23 total $110,000, which are all but the $10,000 ($25,000 x 40%) of fixed costs that cannot be immediately converted to other uses.

b. Based on the financial considerations given, Quiett Truck should NOT outsource WB23 because the $112,000 (10,000 units x $11.20 per part) outsourced cost is greater than the $110,000 reduction in annual production costs. In other words, the outsourcing would cost Quiett Truck an additional $2,000 annually.

c. Other factors to consider include the supplier's ability to meet expected quality and delivery standards, and the likelihood of suppliers increasing prices of components in the future.

Difficulty: 2   *Objective*:   4

158. Southwestern Company needs 1,000 motors in its manufacture of automobiles. It can buy the motors from Jinx Motors for $1,250 each. Southwestern's plant can manufacture the motors for the following costs per unit:

Direct materials	$ 500
Direct manufacturing labor	250
Variable manufacturing overhead	200
Fixed manufacturing overhead	350
Total	$1,300

If Southwestern buys the motors from Jinx, 70% of the fixed manufacturing overhead applied will not be avoided.

Required:

a. Should the company make or buy the motors?
b. What additional factors should Southwestern consider in deciding whether or not to make or buy the motors?

Answer:

a. *Cost to buy the part*: (1,000 x $1,250) $1,250,000
   Relevant costs to make:
   Variable costs:
Direct materials (1,000 x $500)	$500,000	
Direct manufacturing. labor (1,000 x $250)	250,000	
Variable manufacturing overhead (1,000 x $200)	200,000	
Total	$950,000	
Avoidable fixed costs: ($350 x 1,000 x 0.30)	105,000	1,055,000
Savings if part is manufactured		$ 195,000

b. Management should consider several qualitative factors in deciding whether to make or buy the motors.

- *Quality controls* The company's ability to manufacture quality motors versus that of the supplier.
- *Delivery* Can they make them when needed versus Jinx delivering them when needed?
- *Reputation* What is the overall reputation of Jinx?
- *Term* Is Jinx willing to make long-term commitments for delivery of the motors?
- *Facilities* What are the opportunity costs of using the space and equipment to manufacture other items?

Difficulty: 2   *Objective*: 4

159. Kirkland Company manufactures a part for use in its production of hats. When 10,000 items are produced, the costs per unit are:

Direct materials	$0.60
Direct manufacturing labor	3.00
Variable manufacturing overhead	1.20
Fixed manufacturing overhead	1.60
Total	$6.40

Mike Company has offered to sell to Kirkland Company 10,000 units of the part for $6.00 per unit. The plant facilities could be used to manufacture another item at a savings of $9,000 if Kirkland accepts the offer. In addition, $1.00 per unit of fixed manufacturing overhead on the original item would be eliminated.

Required:

a. What is the relevant per unit cost for the original part?
b. Which alternative is best for Kirkland Company? By how much?

Answer:

a.

Direct materials	$0.60
Direct manufacturing labor	3.00
Variable manufacturing overhead	1.20
Avoidable fixed manufacturing. overhead	1.00
Total relevant per unit costs	$5.80

b.

	Make	**Buy**	**Effect of Buying**
Purchase price		$60,000	$(60,000)
Savings in space		(9,000)	9,000
Direct materials	$6,000		6,000
Direct mfg. labor	30,000		30,000
Variable overhead	12,000		12,000
Fixed overhead saved		(10,000)	10,000
Totals	$48,000	$41,000	$7,000

The best alternative is to buy the part.

Difficulty: 2   *Objectives*: 4, 5, 6

160. Lewis Auto Company manufactures a part for use in its production of automobiles. When 10,000 items are produced, the costs per unit are:

Direct materials	$ 12
Direct manufacturing labor	60
Variable manufacturing overhead	24
Fixed manufacturing overhead	32
Total	$128

Monty Company has offered to sell Lewis Auto Company 10,000 units of the part for $120 per unit. The plant facilities could be used to manufacture another part at a savings of $180,000 if Lewis Auto accepts the supplier's offer. In addition, $20 per unit of fixed manufacturing overhead on the original part would be eliminated.

Required:

a. What is the relevant per unit cost for the original part?
b. Which alternative is best for Lewis Auto Company? By how much?

Answer:

a.

Direct materials	$12
Direct manufacturing labor	60
Variable manufacturing overhead	24
Avoidable fixed manufacturing overhead	20
Total relevant per unit costs	$116

b.

	Make	**Buy**	**Effect of Buying**
Purchase price		$1,200,000	$(1,200,000)
Savings in space		(180,000)	180,000
Direct materials	$120,000		120,000
Direct manufacturing labor	600,000		600,000
Variable overhead	240,000		240,000
Fixed overhead saved		(200,000)	200,000
Totals	$960,000	$820,000	$140,000

The best alternative is to buy the part.

Difficulty: 2   *Objectives*: 4, 5, 6

161. Norton's Mufflers manufactures three different product lines, Model X, Model Y, and Model Z. Considerable market demand exists for all models. The following per unit data apply:

	Model X	Model Y	Model Z
Selling price	$80	$90	$100
Direct materials	30	30	30
Direct labor ($10 per hour)	15	15	20
Variable support costs ($5 per machine-hour)	5	10	10
Fixed support costs	20	20	20

a.   For each model, compute the contribution margin per unit.
b.   For each model, compute the contribution margin per machine-hour.
c.   If there is excess capacity, which model is the most profitable to produce? Why?
d.   If there is a machine breakdown, which model is the most profitable to produce? Why?
e.   How can Norton encourage her sales people to promote the more profitable model?

Answer:

a.   The contribution margin per unit is $30 for Model X ($80 - $30 - $15 - $5),
        $35 for Model Y ($90 - $30 - $15 - $10),
        and $40 for Model Z ($100 - $30 - $20 - $10).
b.   The contribution margin per machine-hour is
        $30 for Model X ($30 contribution margin / 1.0 machine-hours per unit),
        $17.50 for Model Y ($35 / 2.0), and
        $20 for Model Z ($40 / 2.0).
c.   When there is excess capacity, Model Y is the most profitable because it has the greatest contribution margin per unit.
d.   When there are machine-hour capacity constraints, Model X is the most profitable because it has the greatest contribution margin per constrained resource.
e.   To encourage sales persons to promote specific products, Norton may want to provide marketing incentives such as higher sales commissions for products contributing the most to profits. Norton may also want to educate salespeople about the effects of constrained resources.

Difficulty: 3   *Objective*:   6

162. Hackerott Camera is considering eliminating Model AE1 from its camera line because of losses over the past quarter. The past three months of information for model AE1 is summarized below.

Sales (1,000 units)	$250,000
Manufacturing costs:	
Direct materials	140,000
Direct labor ($15 per hour)	30,000
Support	100,000
Operating loss	($20,000)

Support costs are 70% variable and the remaining 30% is depreciation of special equipment for model AE1 that has no resale value.

Should Hackerott Camera eliminate Model AE1 from its product line? Why or why not?

Answer:

No, Hackerott Camera should not eliminate Model AE1 from its product line because it contributes $10,000 toward fixed costs and profits.

Sales (1,000 units)	$250,000
Manufacturing costs:	
Direct materials	140,000
Direct labor	30,000
Variable support ($100,000 x 70%)	70,000
Contribution margin	$10,000

Difficulty: 2   *Objective*:   7

163. The management accountant for the Chocolate S'more Company has prepared the following income statement for the most current year.

	Chocolate	Other Candy	Fudge	Total
Sales	$40,000	$25,000	$35,000	$100,000
Cost of goods sold	26,000	15,000	19,000	60,000
Contribution margin	14,000	10,000	16,000	40,000
Delivery and ordering costs	2,000	3,000	2,000	7,000
Rent (per sq. foot used)	3,000	3,000	2,000	8,000
Allocated corporate costs	5,000	5,000	5,000	15,000
Corporate profit	$4,000	$(1,000)	$7,000	$10,000

a. Do you recommend discontinuing the Other Candy product line? Why or why not?

b. If the Chocolate product line had been discontinued, corporate profits for the current year would have decreased by what amount?

Answer:

a. No, I would not recommend discontinuing the Other Candy product line because this product line contributes $4,000 towards corporate costs and profits.
$25,000 - $15,000 - $3,000 - $3,000 = $4,000
Without the Other Candy product line, corporate profits would be $4,000 less than currently reported.

b. If the Chocolate product line were discontinued, corporate profits would immediately decrease by $9,000.
$40,000 - $26,000 - $2,000 - $3,000 = $9,000

Difficulty: 3   *Objective*: 7

164. Pat, a Pizzeria manager, replaced the convection oven just six months ago. Today, Turbo Ovens Manufacturing announced the availability of a new convection oven that cooks more quickly with lower operating expenses. Pat is considering the purchase of this faster, lower-operating cost convection oven to replace the existing one they recently purchased. Selected information about the two ovens is given below:

	Existing	New Turbo Oven
Original cost	$60,000	$50,000
Accumulated depreciation	$ 5,000	---
Current salvage value	$40,000	---
Remaining life	5 years	5 years
Annual operating expenses	$10,000	$ 7,500
Disposal value in 5 years	$ 0	$ 0

Required:
a. What costs are sunk?
b. What costs are relevant?
c. What are the net cash flows over the next 5 years assuming the Pizzeria purchases the new convection oven?
d. What other items should Pat, as manager of the Pizzeria, consider when making this decision?

Answer:
a. Sunk costs include the original cost of the existing convection oven and the accompanying accumulated depreciation.

b. Relevant costs include:
> Acquisition cost of the new Turbo oven
> Current disposal value of the existing convection oven
> Annual operating expenses for the existing and the new Turbo oven

c. Net cash flows over 5 years with the new Turbo oven:

> *Cash inflow*:
>
> | | |
> |---|---|
> | Decrease in annual operating expenses ($2,500 x 5) | $ 12,500 |
> | Sale of the existing oven | 40,000 |
>
> *Cash outflow*:
>
> | | |
> |---|---|
> | Acquisition of the new Turbo oven | (50,000) |
> | *Net cash inflow (outflow)* | $ 2,500 |

d. Other items the manager should consider when making this decision include:
- The Turbo oven's reliability and efficiency is still unknown since it is a brand-new product.
- If the Turbo oven does bake faster as it claims, the Pizzeria may be able to increase sales due to the quicker baking time.
- After purchasing another oven just six months prior, top management should consider the Turbo oven option, but instead may question the decision-making ability of Pat, the current manager.

Difficulty: 2   *Objective*: 8

165. Local Steel Construction Company produces two products, steel and wood beams. Steel beams have a unit contribution margin of $200, and wood beams have a unit contribution margin of $150. The demand for steel beams exceeds Local Steel Construction Company's production capacity, which is limited by available direct labor and machine-hours. The maximum demand for wood beams is 90 per week. Management desires that the product mix should maximize the weekly contribution toward fixed costs and profits.

Direct manufacturing labor is limited to 3,000 hours a week and 1,000 hours is all that the company's outdated machines can run a week. The steel beams require 120 hours of labor and 60 machine-hours. Wood beams require 150 labor hours and 120 machine-hours.

Required:

Formulate the objective function and constraints necessary to determine the optimal product mix.

Answer:

S = steel beams   W = wood beams

Maximize: $200S + $150W

Constraints: Labor hours: $120S + 150W \leq 3{,}000$
                 Machine-hours: $60S + 120W \leq 1{,}000$
                 Wood beams: $W \leq 90$
                                   $W \geq 0$
                 Steel beams: $S \geq 0$

Difficulty: 2   *Objective*: A

CRITICAL THINKING

166. Explain what revenues and costs are relevant when choosing among alternatives.

    Answer:
    Future amounts that differ among alternatives are considered relevant. Amounts that remain the same among alternatives do not add useful information for selecting an alternative, and therefore, are not considered relevant for decision making.

    Difficulty: 2　　　　　　　*Objective*:　2

167. Explain why sunk costs are not considered relevant when choosing among alternatives.

    Answer:
    Amounts that remain the same among alternatives do not add useful information for selecting an alternative, and therefore, are not considered relevant for decision making. Sunk costs by definition are those costs that have already been committed, cannot be changed, and will never differ among alternatives.

    Difficulty: 2　　　　　　　*Objective*:　2

168. Assume you are a sophomore in college and are committed to earning an undergraduate degree. Your current decision is whether to finish college in four consecutive years or take a year off and work for some extra cash.
    a. Identify at least two revenues or costs that are relevant to making this decision. Explain why each is relevant.
    b. Identify at least two costs that would be considered sunk costs for this decision.
    c. Comment on at least one qualitative consideration for this decision.

    Answer:
    a. Relevant revenues/costs are those that differ between the alternatives of continuing with college or taking a year off from college and working. Relevant costs for continuing your college education without a break include:
        1. Earnings lost next year due to the hours you are not able to work because of classes and homework.
        2. As a result of graduating a year earlier, higher wages will be earned a year earlier as well.

    b. Sunk costs for this decision include:
        1. Amounts paid for college tuition and books during the past two years.
        2. Amounts committed for college tuition and books for the remaining two years.

    c. A qualitative consideration would include having different activities and priorities than your friends who are students, graduating later than students who started college the same time you did, and retaining information over the year off from school.

    Difficulty: 2　　　　　　　*Objectives*:　2, 3

169. A restaurant is deciding whether it wants to update its image or not. It currently has a cozy appeal with an outdated décor that is still in good condition, menus and carpet that need to be replaced anyway, and loyal customers.

Identify for the restaurant management
a.   those costs that are relevant to this decision,
b.   those costs that are not differential,
c.   and qualitative considerations.

Answer:

For the decision of whether to update the restaurant's image:
a.   Relevant costs include a one-time cost of the renovation for the updated image, and a change in future sales which includes an increase in sales due to the updated image, decrease in sales due to loss of that cozy appeal, and loss of sales due to being closed or having a limited serving area during renovation.

b.   Costs that are not differential include replacing the menus and the carpet since they need to be replaced whether the image is updated or not.

c.   Qualitative considerations include whether the restaurant will lose that cozy appeal it currently has, if the restaurant needs to be closed for renovations it may result in loss of customers, and new customers may not be the type of customer they want to attract.

Difficulty: 2   *Objectives*: 2, 3

170. Are relevant revenues and relevant costs the only information needed by managers to select among alternatives? Explain using examples.

Answer:

No, relevant revenues and costs provide a financial analysis but do not take into consideration qualitative implications. In a make-or-buy decision, examples of qualitative issues include the supplier's ability to meet expected quality and delivery standards, and the likelihood that suppliers increase prices of the components in the future.

Difficulty: 2   *Objective*:   3

171. Under what conditions might a manufacturing firm sell a product for less than its long-term price? Why?

Answer:

The price for a short-term order may be less than the price offered to a long-term customer. If a firm has excess capacity that is sitting idle, it is more profitable for the firm to accept a special order for a price below the long-run price than it is to let the capacity sit idle. In addition, the firm may use this strategy for market penetration and to obtain greater market share.

Difficulty: 2   *Objective*:   3

172. For short-term pricing decisions, what costs are relevant when there is available surplus capacity? When there is no available surplus capacity?

Answer:

For both situations the relevant costs are the future incremental costs. However, when there is limited capacity the incremental costs will be greater because they will include the costs of adding capacity or the opportunity costs of alternative manufacturing choices.

Difficulty: 2   *Objective*:   5

CHAPTER 12: PRICING DECISIONS AND COST MANAGEMENT

TRUE/FALSE

1. Companies must always examine pricing decisions through the eyes of their customers.

   Answer: True   *Difficulty*: 2   *Objective*: 1

2. Relevant costs for pricing decisions include manufacturing costs, but not costs from other value-chain functions.

   Answer: False   *Difficulty*: 2   *Objective*: 1
   Relevant costs for pricing decisions include costs from all value-chain functions, from R&D to customer service.

3. Cost information only helps the company decide how many units to produce.

   Answer: True   *Difficulty*: 3   *Objective*: 1

4. In markets with little or no competition, the key factor affecting price is costs, not customers' willingness to pay or competitors.

   Answer: False   *Difficulty*: 2   *Objective*: 1
   In markets with little or no competition, the key factor affecting price is the customers' willingness to pay, not costs or competitors.

5. When prices are set in a competitive marketplace, product costs are the most important influence on pricing decisions.

   Answer: False   *Difficulty*: 2   *Objective*: 1
   When prices are set in a competitive marketplace, companies have no control over setting prices and must accept the price determined by the market.

6. Short-run pricing decisions include adjusting product mix in a competitive environment.

   Answer: True   *Difficulty*: 2   *Objective*: 2

7. Profit margins are often set to earn a reasonable return on investment for short-term pricing decisions, but not long-term pricing decisions.

   Answer: False   *Difficulty*: 2   *Objective*: 2
   Profit margins are often set to earn a reasonable return on investment for long-term pricing decisions, but not short-term pricing decision.

8. In a one-time-only special order, existing fixed manufacturing costs are irrelevant.

   Answer: True   *Difficulty*: 2   *Objective*: 2

9. Relevant costs of a bidding decision should exclude revenues lost on lower-priced sales to existing customers.

    Answer: False   *Difficulty*: 3   *Objective*: 2
    Relevant costs of a bidding decision should *include* revenues lost on lower-priced sales to existing customers.

10. Customers prefer stable and predictable prices over a long time horizon.

    Answer: True   *Difficulty*: 2   *Objective*: 2

11. Product cost analysis is important even if market forces set prices.

    Answer: True   *Difficulty*: 3   *Objective*: 2
    True, because a company still has to decide how much of that product to supply to market to maximize operating income, and that decision is based on cost factors.

12. Target pricing is a form of cost-based pricing.

    Answer: False   *Difficulty*: 1   *Objective*: 3
    Target pricing is a form of *market-based pricing*.

13. The first step in target pricing is to determine the target cost of the product.

    Answer: False   *Difficulty*: 1   *Objective*: 3
    The first step in target pricing is to determine the *target price* of the product.

14. Value engineering has the objective of reducing costs while still satisfying customer needs.

    Answer: True   *Difficulty*: 1   *Objective*: 3

15. Rework is an example of a value-added cost.

    Answer: False   *Difficulty*: 1   *Objective*: 3
    Rework is an example of a *nonvalue-added cost.*

16. It is always clear which activities add value and which do not add value to a product.

    Answer: False   *Difficulty*: 2   *Objective*: 3
    Activities do not always fall neatly into value-added or nonvalue-added categories.

17. Value engineering seeks to reduce value-added costs as well as nonvalue-added costs.

    Answer: True   *Difficulty*: 3   *Objective*: 3
    True, value-added costs can be reduced through greater efficiencies.

18. Suppliers play a key role in the success of target costing.

   Answer: True   *Difficulty:* 2   *Objective:* 3

19. Costs may be locked in before they are incurred.

   Answer: True   *Difficulty:* 2   *Objective:* 4

20. Locked-in costs have already been incurred.

   Answer: False   *Difficulty:* 2   *Objective:* 4
   Locked-in costs are those costs that have not yet been incurred, but which, based on decisions that have already been made, will be incurred in the future.

21. For manufacturing firms, product costs are generally locked in during the manufacturing stage.

   Answer: False   *Difficulty:* 2   *Objective:* 4
   For manufacturing firms, product costs are generally locked in during the *design* stage.

22. One goal of target costing is to design costs out of products.

   Answer: True   *Difficulty:* 2   *Objective:* 4

23. Spending more on the design phase of a new product usually reduces subsequent product-related costs.

   Answer: True   *Difficulty:* 2   *Objective:* 4

24. Kaizen costing focuses on improving productivity and eliminating waste through continuous improvements.

   Answer: True   *Difficulty:* 1   *Objective:* 4

25. In cost-plus pricing, the markup is a rigid number that determines the actual selling price.

   Answer: False   *Difficulty:* 2   *Objective:* 5
   In cost-plus pricing, the markup is ultimately determined by the market.

26. The target rate of return on investment is another way of referring to the markup percentage.

   Answer: False   *Difficulty:* 2   *Objective:* 5
   The target rate of return on investment and the markup percentage are two different things.

27. Cost bases that include fewer costs also have lower markups.

Answer: False   *Difficulty*: 2   *Objective*: 5
Cost bases that include fewer costs have higher markups.

28. Markups tend to be lower in more competitive markets.

Answer: True   *Difficulty*: 2   *Objective*: 5

29. The full-cost formula for pricing is relatively simple to use because it does not require a detailed analysis of cost behavior.

Answer: True   *Difficulty*: 2   *Objective*: 5

30. A full-cost base rather than a variable-cost base is a better guide for discounting decisions that may affect long-term customers.

Answer: True   *Difficulty*: 2   *Objective*: 5

31. To be profitable, a company must generate revenues to cover costs incurred in all six business functions.

Answer: True   *Difficulty*: 2   *Objective*: 6

32. Life-cycle budgeting is particularly important when nonproduction costs are significant.

Answer: True   *Difficulty*: 2   *Objective*: 6

33. Many companies use life-cycle budgeting to determine target prices.

Answer: True   *Difficulty*: 2   *Objective*: 6

34. Customer life-cycle costs focus on total costs incurred by the customer from purchase to disposal.

Answer: True   *Difficulty*: 1   *Objective*: 6

35. When price discrimination is effective, cost is not a major factor in setting prices.

Answer: True   *Difficulty*: 2   *Objective*: 7

36. When demand is elastic, an increase in price will lead to an increase in profits.

Answer: False   *Difficulty*: 1   *Objective*: 7
When demand is *inelastic*, an increase in price will usually lead to an increase in profits.

37. Price discrimination is the illegal practice of charging some customers a higher price than is charged to other customers.

Answer: False   *Difficulty:* 1   *Objective:* 7
Price discrimination is a *legal* practice of charging some customers a higher price than is charged to other customers.

38. When demand is strong, firms usually increase markups.

Answer: True   *Difficulty:* 2   *Objective:* 7
True, when capacity is limited this is referred to as peak-load pricing.

39. Price discrimination laws apply only to manufacturers.

Answer: True   *Difficulty:* 2   *Objective:* 8

40. Price discrimination is only illegal if the intent is to destroy competition.

Answer: True   *Difficulty:* 1   *Objective:* 8

41. A business that engages in predatory pricing violates various U.S. antitrust laws.

Answer: True   *Difficulty:* 1   *Objective:* 8

42. Price dumping occurs when a domestic company is trying to get rid of out-of-style products at a substantially reduced price.

Answer: False   *Difficulty:* 1   *Objective:* 8
Price dumping occurs when a non-U.S. company sells a product in the United States at a price below the market value where it is produced and this action threatens to injure an industry in the United States.

43. Collusive pricing occurs when companies in an industry conspire in their pricing and output decisions to achieve a price above the competitive price.

Answer: True   *Difficulty:* 1   *Objective:* 8

44. Companies should ONLY produce and sell units as long as
    a. there is customer demand for the product.
    b. the competition allows it.
    c. the revenue from an additional unit exceeds the cost of producing it.
    d. there is a generous supply of low-cost direct materials.

    Answer: c   *Difficulty:* 2   *Objective:* 1

45. Too high a price may
    a. deter a customer from purchasing a product.
    b. increase demand for the product.
    c. indicate supply is too plentiful.
    d. decrease a competitor's market share.

    Answer: a   *Difficulty:* 1   *Objective:* 1

46. Companies must ALWAYS examine pricing
    a. based on the supply of the product.
    b. based on the cost of producing the product.
    c. through the eyes of their customers.
    d. through the eyes of their competitors.

    Answer: c   *Difficulty:* 3   *Objective:* 1

47. Competitors
    a. with alternative products can force a company to lower its prices.
    b. can gain a competitive pricing advantage with knowledge of your costs and operating policies.
    c. may span international borders.
    d. may be all of the above.

    Answer: d   *Difficulty:* 2   *Objective:* 1

48. Fluctuations in exchange rates between different currencies can influence
    a. the cost of products using foreign suppliers.
    b. the pricing of alternative products offered by foreign competitors.
    c. the demand for products of foreign competitors.
    d. all of the above.

    Answer: d   *Difficulty:* 2   *Objective:* 1

49. The cost of producing a product
    a. is an important influence on pricing.
    b. affects the willingness of a company to supply a product.
    c. for pricing decisions includes manufacturing costs, but not product design costs.
    d. in highly competitive markets controls pricing.

    Answer: b   *Difficulty:* 3   *Objective:* 1

50. In a noncompetitive environment, the key factor affecting pricing decisions is
    a.   the customer's willingness to pay.
    b.   the price charged for alternative products.
    c.   the cost of producing and delivering the product.
    d.   all of the above.

    Answer: a   *Difficulty:*   3   *Objective:*   1

51. In a competitive market with differentiated products like cameras, the key factor(s) affecting pricing decisions is/are
    a.   the customer's willingness to pay.
    b.   the price charged for alternative products.
    c.   the cost of producing and delivering the product.
    d.   all of the above.

    Answer: d   *Difficulty:*   2   *Objective:*   1

52. Three major influences on pricing decisions are
    a.   competition, costs, and customers.
    b.   competition, demand, and production efficiency.
    c.   continuous improvement, customer satisfaction, and supply.
    d.   variable costs, fixed costs, and mixed costs.

    Answer: a   *Difficulty:*   1   *Objective:*   1

53. Long-run pricing decisions
    a.   have a time horizon of less than one year.
    b.   include adjusting product mix in a competitive environment.
    c.   and short-run pricing decisions generally have the same relevant costs.
    d.   use prices that include a reasonable return on investment.

    Answer: d   *Difficulty:*   3   *Objective:*   2

54. Short-term pricing decisions
    a.   use costs that may be irrelevant for long-term pricing decisions.
    b.   are more opportunistic.
    c.   tend to decrease prices when demand is strong.
    d.   have a time horizon of more than one year.

    Answer: b   *Difficulty:*   3   *Objective:*   2

55. Relevant costs for pricing a special order include
    a.   existing fixed manufacturing overhead.
    b.   nonmanufacturing costs that will not change even if the special order is accepted.
    c.   additional setup costs for the special order.
    d.   all of the above costs.

    Answer: c   *Difficulty:*   2   *Objective:*   2

56. Which of the following factors should NOT be considered when pricing a special order?
   a. The likely bids of competitors
   b. The incremental cost of one unit of product
   c. Revenues that will be lost on existing sales if prices are lowered
   d. Stable pricing to earn the desired long-run return

   Answer: d   *Difficulty:* 3   *Objective:* 2

57. Long-run pricing
   a. needs to cover only incremental costs.
   b. only utilizes the market-based approach to pricing and not the cost-based approach.
   c. is a strategic decision.
   d. strives for flexible pricing that can respond to temporary changes in demand.

   Answer: c   *Difficulty:* 2   *Objective:* 2

58. For long-run pricing decisions, using stable prices has the advantage of
   a. minimizing the need to monitor competitors' prices frequently.
   b. reducing the need to change cost structures frequently.
   c. reducing competition.
   d. helping build buyer-seller relationships.

   Answer: d   *Difficulty:* 2   *Objective:* 2

59. A price-bidding decision for a one-time-only special order includes an analysis of
   a. all manufacturing costs.
   b. all cost drivers related to the product.
   c. all direct and indirect variable costs of each function in the value chain.
   d. all fixed manufacturing costs.

   Answer: c   *Difficulty:* 2   *Objective:* 2

60. For pricing decisions, full product costs
   a. include all costs that are traceable to the product.
   b. include all manufacturing and selling costs.
   c. include all direct costs plus an appropriate allocation of the indirect costs of all business functions.
   d. allow for the highest possible product prices.

   Answer: c   *Difficulty:* 2   *Objective:* 2

THE FOLLOWING INFORMATION APPLIES TO QUESTIONS 61 AND 62.
Northwoods manufactures rustic furniture. The cost accounting system estimates manufacturing costs to be $120 per table, consisting of 60% variable costs and 40% fixed costs. The company has surplus capacity available. It is Northwoods' policy to add a 50% markup to full costs.

61. Northwoods is invited to bid on a one-time-only special order to supply 200 rustic tables. What is the lowest price Northwoods should bid on this special order?
     a. $21,600
     b. $7,200
     c. $12,000
     d. $14,400

     Answer: d   *Difficulty*: 2   *Objective*: 2
     $120 x 60% x 200 tables = $14,400

62. A large hotel chain is currently expanding and has decided to decorate all new hotels using the rustic style. Northwoods is invited to submit a bid to the hotel chain. What per unit price will Northwoods MOST likely bid on this long-term order?
     a. $72 per unit
     b. $108 per unit
     c. $180 per unit
     d. $120 per unit

     Answer: c   *Difficulty*: 2   *Objectives*: 2, 5
     $120 + ($120 x 50%) = $180

THE FOLLOWING INFORMATION APPLIES TO QUESTIONS 63 THROUGH 65.
Rogers' Heaters is approached by Ms. Yukki, a new customer, to fulfill a large one-time-only special order for a product similar to one offered to regular customers. Rogers' Heaters has excess capacity. The following per unit data apply for sales to regular customers:

Direct materials	$200
Direct manufacturing labor	60
Variable manufacturing support	30
Fixed manufacturing support	100
Total manufacturing costs	390
Markup (30%)	117
Estimated selling price	$507

63. For Rogers' Heaters, what is the minimum acceptable price of this one-time-only special order?
   a. $290
   b. $390
   c. $260
   d. $507

   Answer: a   *Difficulty*: 2   *Objective*: 2
   $200 + $60 + $30 = $290

64. Before accepting this one-time-only special order, Rogers' Heaters should consider the impact on
   a. current plant capacity.
   b. long-term customers.
   c. competitors.
   d. all of the above.

   Answer: d   *Difficulty*: 2   *Objective*: 2

65. If Ms. Yukki wanted a long-term commitment for supplying this product, what price would MOST likely be quoted?
   a. $290
   b. $390
   c. $260
   d. $507

   Answer: d   *Difficulty*: 2   *Objective*: 2, 5
   The estimated selling price of $507.

THE FOLLOWING INFORMATION APPLIES TO QUESTIONS 66 THROUGH 68.
Welch Manufacturing is approached by a European customer to fulfill a one-time-only special order for a product similar to one offered to domestic customers. Welch Manufacturing has a policy of adding a 10% markup to full costs and currently has excess capacity. The following per unit data apply for sales to regular customers:

Variable costs:	
Direct materials	$30
Direct labor	10
Manufacturing overhead	15
Marketing costs	5
Fixed costs:	
Manufacturing overhead	100
Marketing costs	20
Total costs	180
Markup (10%)	18
Estimated selling price	$198

66. For Welch Manufacturing, what is the minimum acceptable price of this one-time-only special order?
    a. $40
    b. $55
    c. $60
    d. $66

    Answer: c   *Difficulty:*   2   *Objective:*   2
    $30 + $10 + $15 + $5 = $60

67. What is the full cost of the product per unit?
    a. $60
    b. $180
    c. $198
    d. $66

    Answer: b   *Difficulty:*   1   *Objective:*   2
    $30 + $10 + $15 + $5 + 100 + 20 = $180

68. If the European customer wanted a long-term commitment for supplying this product, what price would MOST likely be quoted?
    a. $66.00
    b. $180.00
    c. $198.00
    d. $217.80

    Answer: c   *Difficulty:*   2   *Objective:*   2, 5
    The estimated selling price of $198.

THE FOLLOWING INFORMATION APPLIES TO QUESTIONS 69 AND 70.
Berryman Products manufactures coffee tables. Berryman Products has a policy of adding a 20% markup to full costs and currently has excess capacity. The following information pertains to the company's normal operations per month:

Output units	30,000 tables
Machine-hours	8,000 hours
Direct manufacturing labor-hours	10,000 hours
Direct materials per unit	$50
Direct manufacturing labor per hour	$6
Variable manufacturing overhead costs	$161,250
Fixed manufacturing overhead costs	$600,000
Product and process design costs	$450,000
Marketing and distribution costs	$562,500

69. Berryman Products is approached by an overseas customer to fulfill a one-time-only special order for 2,000 units. All cost relationships remain the same except for a one-time setup charge of $20,000. No additional design, marketing, or distribution costs will be incurred. What is the minimum acceptable bid per unit on this one-time-only special order?
    a. $67.38
    b. $77.38
    c. $111.13
    d. $80.85

Answer: a   *Difficulty*:   3   *Objective*:   2

Direct materials	$50.000
Direct manufacturing labor ($6 x 10,000) / 30,000	2.000
Variable manufacturing ($161,250 / 30,000)	5.375
Setup ($20,000 / 2,000)	10.000
Minimum acceptable bid	$67.375

70. For long-run pricing of the coffee tables, what price will MOST likely be used by Berryman?
    a. $67.38
    b. $80.85
    c. $111.13
    d. $133.35

Answer: d   *Difficulty*:   3   *Objectives*:   2, 5

Direct materials	$ 50.000
Direct manufacturing labor ($6 x 10,000)/30,000	2.000
Variable manufacturing ($161,250/30,000)	5.375
Fixed manufacturing ($600,000/30,000)	20.000
Product and process design costs ($450,000/30,000)	15.000
Marketing and distribution ($562,500/30,000)	18.750
Full cost per unit	$111.125
Markup (20%)	22.225
Estimated selling price	$133.350

71. Target pricing
    a.   is used for short-term pricing decisions.
    b.   is one form of cost-based pricing.
    c.   estimate is based on customers' perceived value of the product.
    d.   relevant costs are all variable costs.

    Answer: c   *Difficulty:*   3   *Objective:*   3

72. To understand how competitors might price competing products a company
    a.   needs to understand the competitor's technologies and financial conditions.
    b.   may get information from suppliers that service the competitor.
    c.   may use reverse engineering.
    d.   may do all of the above.

    Answer: d   *Difficulty:*   2   *Objective:*   3

73. The department usually in the best position to identify customers' needs is the
    a.   production department.
    b.   sales and marketing department.
    c.   design department.
    d.   distribution department.

    Answer: b   *Difficulty:*   1   *Objective:*   3

74. Relevant costs for target pricing are
    a.   variable manufacturing costs.
    b.   variable manufacturing and variable nonmanufacturing costs.
    c.   all fixed costs.
    d.   all future costs, both variable and fixed.

    Answer: d   *Difficulty:*   2   *Objective:*   3

75. Place the following steps for the implementation of target costing in order:
    > A = Derive a target cost
    > B = Develop a target price
    > C = Perform value engineering
    > D = Determine target operating income

    a.   B D A C
    b.   B A D C
    c.   A D B C
    d.   A B C D

    Answer: a   *Difficulty:*   2   *Objective:*   3

76. Value engineering may result in all of the following EXCEPT
    a.   improved product design.
    b.   changes in materials specifications.
    c.   increases in the quantity of nonvalue-added cost drivers.
    d.   the evaluation of all business functions within the value chain.

    Answer: c   *Difficulty:*   3   *Objective:*   3

77. Value-added costs
    a.   are costs that a customer is unwilling to pay for.
    b.   include maintenance and repairs of the manufacturing equipment.
    c.   are reduced through improved efficiencies.
    d.   if eliminated increase profitability.

    Answer: c   *Difficulty:*   2   *Objective:*   3

78. To design costs out of products is a goal of
    a.   cost-plus pricing.
    b.   target costing.
    c.   kaizen costing.
    d.   peak-load costing.

    Answer: b   *Difficulty:*   1   *Objective:*   3

79. All of the following are true regarding target costing EXCEPT
    a.   improvements are implemented in small incremental amounts.
    b.   customer input is essential to the target costing process.
    c.   input is requested from suppliers and distributors.
    d.   a key goal is to minimize costs over the product's useful life.

    Answer: a   *Difficulty:*   3   *Objective:*   3

80. All of the following are associated with target costing EXCEPT
    a.   value engineering.
    b.   the markup component.
    c.   all value-chain business functions.
    d.   cross-functional teams.

    Answer: b   *Difficulty:*   2   *Objective:*   3

81. When target costing and target pricing are used together,
    a.   the target cost is established first, then the target price.
    b.   the target cost is the estimated long-run cost that enables a product or service to achieve a desired profit.
    c.   the focus of target pricing is to undercut the competition.
    d.   target costs are generally higher than current costs.

    Answer: b   *Difficulty:*   3   *Objective:*   3

82. The product strategy in which companies first determine the price at which they can sell a new product and then design a product that can be produced at a low enough cost to provide adequate operating income is referred to as
    a. cost-plus pricing.
    b. target costing.
    c. kaizen costing.
    a. full costing.

    Answer: b   *Difficulty:* 1   *Objective:* 3

THE FOLLOWING INFORMATION APPLIES TO QUESTIONS 83 THROUGH 86.
After conducting a market research study, Schultz Manufacturing decided to produce a new interior door to complement its exterior door line. It is estimated that the new interior door can be sold at a target price of $60. The annual target sales volume for interior doors is 20,000. Schultz has target operating income of 20% of sales.

83. What are target sales revenues?
    a. $960,000
    b. $2,000,000
    c. $1,200,000
    d. none of the above

    Answer: c   *Difficulty:* 1   *Objective:* 3
    $60 x 20,000 = $1,200,000

84. What is the target operating income?
    a. $240,000
    b. $300,000
    c. $192,000
    d. $180,000

    Answer: a   *Difficulty:* 2   *Objective:* 3
    $1,200,000 x 20% = $240,000

85. What is the target cost?
    a. $900,000
    b. $960,000
    c. $1,260,000
    d. $1,008,000

    Answer: b   *Difficulty:* 2   *Objective:* 3
    $1,200,000 - $240,000 = $960,000

86. What is the target cost for each interior door?
    a. $48
    b. $58
    c. $60
    d. $45

    Answer: a   *Difficulty:* 2   *Objective:* 3
    $960,000 / 20,000 = $48

THE FOLLOWING INFORMATION APPLIES TO QUESTIONS 87 THROUGH 89.
Sheltar's TV currently sells small televisions for $180. It has costs of $140. A competitor is bringing a new small television to market that will sell for $150. Management believes it must lower the price to $150 to compete in the market for small televisions. Marketing believes that the new price will cause sales to increase by 10%, even with a new competitor in the market. Sheltar's sales are currently 100,000 televisions per year.

87. What is the target cost if target operating income is 25% of sales?
    a. $37.50
    b. $45.00
    c. $112.50
    d. $135.00

    Answer: c   *Difficulty:* 2   *Objective:* 3
    $150 - $150(0.25) = $112.50

88. What is the change in operating income if marketing is correct and only the sales price is changed?
    a. $1,100,000
    b. $300,000
    c. $(1,100,000)
    d. $(2,900,000)

    Answer: d   *Difficulty:* 3   *Objective:* 3
    [100,000 x ($180 - $140)] – [110,000 x ($150 - $140)] = $(2,900,000)

89. What is the target cost if the company wants to maintain its same income level, and marketing is correct?
    a. $112.50
    b. $113.64
    c. $123.34
    d. $140.00

    Answer: b   *Difficulty:* 3   *Objective:* 3
    Current income = 100,000 x ($180 - $140) = $4,000,000
    Target cost y: $4,000,000 = (110,000 x $150) - 110,000y
    y = $12,500,000/110,000 = $113.64

THE FOLLOWING INFORMATION APPLIES TO QUESTIONS 90 THROUGH 92.
Frank's Computer Monitors, Inc., currently sells 17" monitors for $270. It has costs of $210. A competitor is bringing a new 17" monitor to market that will sell for $225. Management believes it must lower the price to $225 to compete in the market for 17" monitors. Marketing believes that the new price will cause sales to increase by 10%, even with a new competitor in the market. Frank's Computer Monitor, Inc.'s sales are currently 10,000 monitors per year.

90. What is the target cost if operating income is 25% of sales?
    a. $56.25
    b. $67.50
    c. $168.75
    d. $202.50

    Answer: c   *Difficulty*: 2   *Objective*: 3
    $225 - $225(0.25) = $168.75

91. What is the change in operating income if marketing is correct and only the sales price is changed?
    a. $165,000
    b. $45,000
    c. $(165,000)
    d. $(435,000)

    Answer: d   *Difficulty*: 3   *Objective*: 3
    [10,000 x ($270 - $210)] - [11,000 x ($225 - $210)] = ($435,000)

92. What is the target cost if the company wants to maintain its same income level, and marketing is correct (rounded to the nearest cent)?
    a. $168.75
    b. $170.45
    c. $185.00
    d. $210.00

    Answer: b   *Difficulty*: 3   *Objective*: 3
    Current income = 10,000 x ($270 - $210) = $600,000
    Target cost y: $600,000 = (11,000 x $225) – 11,000y
    y = $1,875,000/11,000 = $170.4545

93. Concerns about target costing include all EXCEPT
    a. cross-functional teams may add too many features.
    b. excessive pressure is put on suppliers.
    c. development time may decrease.
    d. burnout of design engineers.

    Answer: c   *Difficulty*: 2   *Objective*: 4

94. Direct material costs are locked in when they are
    a. designed.
    b. assembled.
    c. sold.
    d. delivered.

    Answer: a　　　　　*Difficulty:* 2　　　　　*Objective:* 4

95. Cost accounting systems focus on when costs
    a. are incurred.
    b. are locked in.
    c. are paid for.
    d. are used for setting prices for products and services.

    Answer: a　　　　　*Difficulty:* 1　　　　　*Objective:* 4

96. Most of a product's life-cycle costs are locked in by decisions made during the _____ business function of the value chain.
    a. design
    b. manufacturing
    c. customer-service
    d. marketing

    Answer: a　　　　　*Difficulty:* 1　　　　　*Objective:* 4

97. For most products, the majority of costs are incurred during the _____ business function of the value chain.
    a. design
    b. manufacturing
    c. customer-service
    d. marketing

    Answer: b　　　　　*Difficulty:* 1　　　　　*Objective:* 4

98. _____ focuses on reducing costs during the manufacturing stage.
    a. Target costing
    b. Kaizen costing
    c. Cost-plus pricing
    d. Life-cycle costing

    Answer: b　　　　　*Difficulty:* 1　　　　　*Objective:* 4

99. Cross-functional engineering teams may include
    a. marketing managers.
    b. suppliers.
    c. management accountants.
    d. all of the above.

    Answer: d　　　　　*Difficulty:* 1　　　　　*Objective:* 4

100. In some industries such as legal and consulting, most costs are locked in
   a. when they are incurred.
   b. during the design stage.
   c. during the customer-service stage.
   d. during the marketing stage.

   Answer: a   *Difficulty:* 2   *Objective:* 4

101. Value engineering can reduce all EXCEPT
   a. existing fixed manufacturing costs.
   b. value-added costs.
   c. nonvalue-added costs.
   d. rework-hours.

   Answer: a   *Difficulty:* 2   *Objective:* 4

102. A graph comparing locked-in costs with incurred costs will have
   a. locked-in costs rising much faster initially, but dropping to zero after the product is manufactured.
   b. the two cost lines running parallel until the end of the process, when they join.
   c. locked-in costs rising much faster initially than the incurred cost, but joining the incurred cost line at the completion of the value-chain functions.
   d. no differences unless the product is manufactured inefficiently.

   Answer: c   *Difficulty:* 2   *Objective:* 4

103. Graphic analysis of incurred and locked-in costs provides several insights as to how the different concepts influence decisions. Which of the following statements is FALSE?
   a. Costs are generally locked in before they are incurred.
   b. After a product's design has been approved, costs are difficult to influence.
   c. When and how costs are locked in are more important than when and how costs are incurred.
   d. Most costs are locked in during the manufacturing process.

   Answer: d   *Difficulty:* 2   *Objective:* 4

104. Value engineering can reduce costs by all EXCEPT
   a. simplifying the design and thereby decreasing the number of component parts.
   b. reducing the number of features offered.
   c. redesigning alternative options over and over until the wishes of all cross-functional team members are accommodated.
   d. building efficiencies into value-added costs.

   Answer: c   *Difficulty:* 3   *Objective:* 4

105. The cost-plus pricing approach is generally in the form:
    a. Cost base + Markup component = Prospective selling price.
    b. Prospective selling price - Cost base = Markup component.
    c. Cost base + Gross margin = Prospective selling price.
    d. Variable cost + Fixed cost + Contribution margin = Prospective selling price.

    Answer: a   *Difficulty:* 1   *Objective:* 5

106. In cost-plus pricing, the markup component
    a. is a rigid number.
    b. is ultimately determined by the market.
    c. provides a means to calculate the actual selling price.
    d. is the end rather than the start of pricing decisions.

    Answer: b   *Difficulty:* 2   *Objective:* 5

107. A product's markup percentage needs to cover nonmanufacturing variable costs when the cost base is
    a. the full cost of the product.
    b. the variable cost of the product.
    c. variable manufacturing costs.
    d. any of the above cost bases.

    Answer: c   *Difficulty:* 2   *Objective:* 5

108. A product's markup percentage needs to cover operating profits when the cost base is
    a. the full cost of the product.
    b. the variable cost of the product.
    c. variable manufacturing costs.
    d. any of the above cost bases.

    Answer: d   *Difficulty:* 2   *Objective:* 5

109. Erickson Company is considering pricing its 5,000-gallon petroleum tanks using either variable manufacturing or full product costs as the base. The variable cost base provides a prospective price of $3,000 and the full cost base provides a prospective price of $3,050. The difference between the two prices is
    a. the estimated amount of profit.
    b. that the variable cost base estimates fixed costs in the markup percentage while the full cost base includes an amount for fixed costs.
    c. known as price discrimination.
    d. caused by the inability of most companies to estimate fixed cost per unit with any degree of reliability.

    Answer: b   *Difficulty:* 2   *Objective:* 5

110. _____ starts with estimated product costs and next adds desired operating income.
    a. Cost-plus pricing
    b. Target costing
    c. Kaizen costing
    d. Life-cycle budgeting

    Answer: a   *Difficulty:* 2   *Objective:* 5

111. The amount of markup percentage is usually higher if
    a. there is idle capacity.
    b. demand is strong.
    c. competition is intense.
    d. demand is elastic.

    Answer: b   *Difficulty:* 2   *Objective:* 5

112. The markup percentage is usually higher if the cost base used is
    a. the full cost of the product.
    b. the variable cost of the product.
    c. variable manufacturing costs.
    d. total manufacturing costs.

    Answer: c   *Difficulty:* 2   *Objective:* 5

113. Which of the following statements is FALSE regarding cost-plus pricing?
    a. A company selects a cost base that it regards as reliable.
    b. A company uses a markup percentage that estimates a product price that covers full product costs and earns the required return on investment.
    c. The selling price computed is only a prospective price.
    d. The cost-plus price chosen has already been studied for customer reaction to the price.

    Answer: d   *Difficulty:* 3   *Objective:* 5

114. Advantages of using the full cost of the product as the cost base include all EXCEPT
    a. that managers are informed regarding the minimum long-run cost they need to recover to stay in business.
    b. that it limits the ability of a salesperson to cut prices.
    c. that fixed cost allocations can be arbitrary.
    d. that it does not require a detailed analysis of cost behavior for computations.

    Answer: c   *Difficulty:* 3   *Objective:* 5

THE FOLLOWING INFORMATION APPLIES TO QUESTIONS 115 THROUGH 117.
Timothy Company has invested $2,000,000 in a plant to make vending machines. The target
operating income desired from the plant is $300,000 annually. The company plans annual
sales of 1,500 vending machines at a selling price of $2,000 each.

115. What is the target rate of return on investment for Timothy Company?
    a.   15.0%
    b.   17.6%
    c.   10.0%
    d.   11.1%

Answer: a   *Difficulty:* 2   *Objective:* 5
$300,000 / $2,000,000 = 15%

116. What is the markup percentage as a percentage of cost for Timothy Company?
    a.   15.0%
    b.   17.6%
    c.   10.0%
    d.   11.1%

Answer: d   *Difficulty:* 2   *Objective:* 5
$300,000 / [(1,500 x $2,000) - $300,000] = 11.1%

117. What is the cost base of each vending machine for Timothy Company?
    a. $1,739
    b. $1,802
    c. $1,700
    d. $1,780

Answer: b   *Difficulty:* 3   *Objective:* 5
$2,000 / 1.11 = $1,802

THE FOLLOWING INFORMATION APPLIES TO QUESTIONS 118 THROUGH 120.
Grant Company has invested $1,000,000 in a plant to make commercial juicer machines.
The target operating income desired from the plant is $180,000 annually. The company
plans annual sales of 7,000 juicer machines at a selling price of $200 each.

118. What is the target rate of return on investment for Grant Company?
    a.   22.0%
    b.   18.0%
    c.   14.8%
    d.   12.9%

Answer: b   *Difficulty:* 2   *Objective:* 5
$180,000 / $1,000,000 = 18%

119. What is the markup percentage as a percentage of cost for Grant Company?
    a.   22.0%
    b.   18.0%
    c.   14.8%
    d.   12.9%

Answer: c   *Difficulty*: 2   *Objective*: 5
$180,000 / [(7,000 x $200) - $180,000] = 14.8%

120. What is the cost base of each juicer machine for Grant Company?
    a. $174
    b. $162
    c. $169
    d. $152

Answer: a   *Difficulty*: 3   *Objective*: 5
$200 / 1.148 = $174

THE FOLLOWING INFORMATION APPLIES TO QUESTIONS 121 THROUGH 124.
Meyer Corporation budgeted the following costs for the production of its one and only product for the next fiscal year:

Direct materials	$ 562,500
Direct labor	390,000
Manufacturing overhead	
Variable	420,000
Fixed	322,500
Selling and administrative	
Variable	180,000
Fixed	240,000
Total costs	$2,115,000

Meyer has an annual target operating income of $450,000.

121. The markup percentage for setting prices as a percentage of *total manufacturing costs* is
    a.   51%.
    b.   125%.
    c.   185%.
    d.   245%.

Answer: a   *Difficulty*: 3   *Objective*: 5
($450,000 + $180,000 + $240,000) /
($562,500 + $390,000 + $420,000 + $322,500) = 51.3%

122. The markup percentage for setting prices as a percentage of *variable manufacturing costs* is
    a. 54%.
    b. 87%.
    c. 169%.
    d. 122%.

    Answer: c   *Difficulty*: 3   *Objective*: 5
    ($450,000 + $420,000 + $322,500 + $180,000 + $240,000) /
    ($562,500 + $390,000) = 169.3%

123. The markup percentage for setting prices as a percentage of the *variable cost of the product* is
    a. 328%.
    b. 36%.
    c. 228%.
    d. 65%.

    Answer: d   *Difficulty*: 3   *Objective*: 5
    ($450,000 + $322,500 + $240,000) /
    ($562,500 + $390,000 + $420,000 + $180,000) = 65.2%

124. The markup percentage for setting prices as a percentage of the *full cost of the product* is
    a. 328%.
    b. 36%.
    c. 228%.
    d. 21%.

    Answer: d   *Difficulty*: 3   *Objective*: 5
    $450,000 / $2,115,000 = 21.3%

125. Life-cycle costing is the name given to
    a. a method of cost planning to reduce manufacturing costs to targeted levels.
    b. the process of examining each component of a product to determine whether its cost can be reduced.
    c. the process of managing all costs along the value chain.
    d. a system that focuses on reducing costs during the manufacturing cycle.

    Answer: c   *Difficulty*: 2   *Objective*: 6

126. An understanding of life-cycle costs can lead to
    a. additional costs during the manufacturing cycle.
    b. less need for evaluation of the competition.
    c. cost effective product designs that are easier to service.
    d. mutually beneficial relationships between buyers and sellers.

    Answer: c   *Difficulty*: 2   *Objective*: 6

127. Life-cycle budgeting is particularly important when
    a. the development period for R&D is short and inexpensive.
    b. there are significant nonproduction costs.
    c. most costs are locked in during production.
    d. a low percentage of costs are incurred before any revenues are received.

    Answer: b   *Difficulty:* 3   *Objective:* 6

128. Life-cycle budgeting and life-cycle costing help highlight
    a. an increase in customer-service costs due to using inferior materials.
    b. high production costs caused by a complex design.
    c. large ordering costs due to the great number of component parts used.
    d. an increase in annual operating income resulting from the new product.

    Answer: d   *Difficulty:* 3   *Objective:* 6

129. Life-cycle budgeting
    a. has little in common with target pricing.
    b. is most useful to companies that manufacture small items such as household plastics.
    c. helps companies estimate revenues over a multiyear horizon.
    d. gives companies more insight into total costs when manufacturing costs consume the majority of the resources.

    Answer: c   *Difficulty:* 2   *Objective:* 6

130. Customer life-cycle costs
    a. are the costs incurred by the selling company to satisfy the customer.
    b. are the costs to the customer for buying and using a product.
    c. are the same as the selling life-cycle prices.
    d. are the replacement costs of using a product or service.

    Answer: b   *Difficulty:* 1   *Objective:* 6

THE FOLLOWING INFORMATION APPLIES TO QUESTIONS 131 THROUGH 133.
Bicker, Inc., is in the process of evaluating a new product using the following information.
- A new transformer has two production runs each year, each with $10,000 in setup costs.
- The new transformer incurred $30,000 in development costs and is expected to be produced over the next three years.
- Direct costs of producing the transformers are $40,000 per run of 5,000 transformers each.
- Indirect manufacturing costs charged to each run are $45,000.
- Destination charges for each transformer average $1.00.
- Customer service expenses average $0.20 per transformer.
- The transformers are selling for $25 the first year and will increase by $3 each year thereafter.
- Sales units equal production units each year.

131. What are estimated life-cycle revenues?
    a. $250,000
    b. $280,000
    c. $310,000
    d. $840,000

    Answer: d   *Difficulty:* 2   *Objective:* 6

First year (5,000 x 2 runs x $25)	$250,000
Second year (5,000 x 2 x $28)	280,000
Third year (5,000 x 2 x $31)	310,000
Total	$840,000

132. What is the estimated life-cycle operating income for the first year?
    a. $18,000
    b. $20,000
    c. $48,000
    d. $119,000

    Answer: a   *Difficulty:* 3   *Objective:* 6

Sales (5,000 units x 2 runs x $25)		$250,000
Development costs	$30,000	
Setup costs (2 x $10,000)	20,000	
Direct manufacturing costs (2 x $40,000)	80,000	
Indirect manufacturing costs (2 x $45,000)	90,000	
Destination charges ($1.00 x 10,000)	10,000	
Customer service ($0.20 x 10,000)	2,000	232,000

Estimated life-cycle operating income for the first year $ 18,000

133. What is the estimated life-cycle operating income for the first three years?
    a. $174,000
    b. $204,000
    c. $636,000
    d. $840,000

Answer: b   *Difficulty*:   3   *Objective*:   6

	Year 1	Year 2	Year 3	Totals
Life-cycle revenue	$250,000	$280,000	$310,000	$840,000
Life-cycle costs:				
Development	30,000			30,000
Setup	20,000	20,000	20,000	60,000
Direct manufacturing costs	80,000	80,000	80,000	240,000
Indirect manufacturing	90,000	90,000	90,000	270,000
Destination charges	10,000	10,000	10,000	30,000
Customer service	2,000	2,000	2,000	6,000
Total costs	$232,000	$202,000	$202,000	636,000
Life-cycle operating income				$204,000

THE FOLLOWING INFORMATION APPLIES TO QUESTIONS 134 THROUGH 136.
Neises, White, Granberry and Associates are in the process of evaluating its new client services for the business consulting division.
- Estate Planning, a new service, incurred $600,000 in development costs and employee training.
- The direct costs of providing this service, which is all labor, averages $100 per hour.
- Other costs for this service are estimated at $2,000,000 per year.
- The current program for estate planning is expected to last for two years. At that time, a new law will be in place that will require new operating guidelines for the tax consulting.
- Customer service expenses average $400 per client, with each job lasting an average of 400 hours. The current staff expects to bill 40,000 hours for each of the two years the program is in effect. Billing averages $140 per hour.

134. What are estimated life-cycle revenues?
    a. $6,400,000
    b. $8,000,000
    c. $11,200,000
    d. $22,400,000

Answer: c   *Difficulty*:   1   *Objective*:   6

First year (40,000 x $140)	$ 5,600,000
Second year (40,000 x $140)	5,600,000
Total	$11,200,000

135. What is estimated life-cycle operating income for the first year?
    a. $(1,040,000)
    b. $(1,400,000)
    c. $5,600,000
    d. $6,640,000

Answer: a   *Difficulty:*   3   *Objective:*   6

Revenue (40,000 hours x $140)		$5,600,000
Development costs	$ 600,000	
Direct costs (40,000 x $100)	4,000,000	
Indirect costs	2,000,000	
Customer service ($400 x 100 clients)	40,000	6,640,000
Operating income (loss)		$(1,040,000)

136. What is the estimated life-cycle operating income for the first two years?
    a. $(1,480,000)
    b. $(1,400,000)
    c. $3,200,000
    d. $11,200,000

Answer: a   *Difficulty:* 3   *Objective:* 7

	Year 1	Year 2	Totals
Life-cycle revenue	$5,600,000	$5,600,000	$11,200,000
Life-cycle costs:			
Development	600,000		600,000
Direct costs	4,000,000	4,000,000	8,000,000
Indirect costs	2,000,000	2,000,000	4,000,000
Customer service	40,000	40,000	80,000
Total costs	$6,640,000	$6,040,000	$12,680,000
Life-cycle operating income			$(1,480,000)

137. Price discrimination is the practice of
    a.   setting different prices for different products.
    b.   charging different prices for quantity amounts.
    c.   using variable costing for some products and full costing for other products when setting prices.
    d.   charging different prices to different customers or clients for the same products or services.

Answer: d   *Difficulty:*   2   *Objective:*   7

138. Iowa Utility Company charges its high-usage commercial customers a lower rate per kilowatt-hour than other customers. This is an example of
    a. customer-preference pricing.
    b. high-load pricing.
    c. peak-load pricing.
    d. price discrimination.

    Answer: d   *Difficulty:* 1   *Objective:* 7

139. When demand for a product is inelastic and prices are increased, usually
    a. demand will increase, and operating profits will increase.
    b. demand will remain the same, and operating profits will increase.
    c. demand will decrease, and operating profits will decrease.
    d. demand will remain the same, and operating profits will decrease.

    Answer: b   *Difficulty:* 2   *Objective:* 7

140. When demand for a product is very elastic and prices are increased,
    a. demand will remain the same, and operating profits will increase.
    b. demand will remain the same, and operating profits may either increase or decrease.
    c. demand will decrease, and operating profits will decrease.
    d. demand will decrease, and operating profits may either increase or decrease.

    Answer: d   *Difficulty:* 3   *Objective:* 7

141. Costs are a major factor
    a. when demand is price-inelastic.
    b. when demand is price-clastic.
    c. when the opportunity for price discrimination exists.
    d. for peak-load pricing.

    Answer: b   *Difficulty:* 2   *Objective:* 7

THE FOLLOWING INFORMATION APPLIES TO QUESTIONS 142 AND 143.
LeBlanc Lighting manufactures table lamps and is considering raising the price by $10 a unit
for the coming year. With a $10 price increase, demand is expected to fall by 2,000 units.

	Currently	**Projected**
Demand	20,000 units	18,000 units
Selling price	$150	$160
Variable costs per unit	$100	$100

142. Would you recommend the $10 price increase?
    a.   No, because demand decreased.
    b.   No, because the selling price increases.
    c   Yes, because contribution margin per unit increases.
    d.   Yes, because operating income increases.

    Answer: d   *Difficulty*:   2   *Objective*:   1
    [18,000 x ($160 - $100)] – [20,000 x ($150 - $100)] = $80,000 operating income
    increase

143. The demand for this product
    a.   is greatly inelastic.
    b.   is slightly inelastic.
    c.   is elastic.
    d.   is impossible to determine.

    Answer: c   *Difficulty*:   2   *Objective*:   7

144. The Maize Eagles are evaluating ticket prices for its basketball games. Studies show that Friday and Saturday night games average more than twice the fans of games on other days. The following information pertains to the stadium's normal operations per season.

Average fans per game (all games)	2,500	fans
Average fans per Friday and Saturday night games	3,500	fans
Number of home games per season	30	games
Stadium capacity	3,500	seats
Variable operating costs per operating hour	$2,000	
Marketing costs per season for basketball	$138,750	
Customer-service costs per season for basketball	$25,000	

The stadium is open for 5 operating hours on each day a game is played. All employees work by the hour except for the administrators. A maximum of one game is played per day and each fan has only one ticket per game.

The stadium authority wants to charge more for games on Friday and Saturday. What is the minimum price that should be charged for peak attendance nights?
a. $4.40
b. $8.60
c. $6.18
d. $171.45

Answer: c   *Difficulty:* 3   *Objective:* 7

Variable operating costs (30 x 5 x $2,000)	$300,000
Marketing	138,750
Customer service	25,000
Total	$463,750

Attendance = 30 x 2,500 = 75,000 fans
Minimum price is $463,750 / 75,000 = $6.18

145. All are true regarding price discrimination EXCEPT that
a. the laws apply to service providers, but not manufacturers.
b. it is permissible if price differences can be explained.
c. it is illegal only if the intent is to destroy competition.
d. it is most likely to occur when the cost base is the full cost of the product.

Answer: d   *Difficulty:* 3   *Objective:* 8

146. Predatory pricing is a type of price discrimination that
a. allows prices to be cut to the level of variable costs.
b. is required when a company declares bankruptcy so that it can sell its remaining goods quickly.
c. is used in the food industry for perishable goods.
d. deliberately sets prices very low, sometimes even below costs, so as to minimize competition.

Answer: d   *Difficulty:* 1   *Objective:* 8

147. Hitz Video Rental is evaluating rental prices. Historical data show that Friday and Saturday have twice the rentals of other days of the week. The following information pertains to the store's normal operations per week.

Average rentals per day on Friday and Saturday	1,150
Average rentals per day on Sunday through Thursday	500
Store hours per day	12
Total units available for rent	10,000
Variable operating costs per hour	$ 40
Marketing costs per week	$1,500
Customer service costs per week	$ 250

The store manager wants to charge more for rentals on Friday and Saturday. What is the minimum price that should be charged during peak rental days?
   a. $0.60
   b. $0.83
   c. $0.90
   d. $1.06

Answer: d   *Difficulty*:   3   *Objective*:   7

Variable costs ($40 x 12 x 7)	$3,360
Marketing	1,500
Customer service	250
Total costs per week	$5,110

Average rental cost per customer $5,110/[(2 x 1,150) + (5 x 500)] = $1.06

148. To minimize the chances of violating pricing laws, a company should
   a.   keep detailed records of variable costs for all value-chain business functions.
   b.   use a variable cost-plus markup method of pricing.
   c.   underprice products on a consistent basis, rather than sporadically.
   d.   use dumping only when a product is at the end of its life cycle.

Answer: a   *Difficulty*:   3   *Objective*:   8

149. Collusive pricing occurs when
   a.   a company wants two products to sell for the same, or almost the same, amount.
   b.   a company wants a product to sell for the same as a competitor's product.
   c.   two or more companies agree to sell a product at a price higher than should be expected.
   d.   competitors are part of the same large parent organization.

Answer: c   *Difficulty*:   1   *Objective*:   8

EXERCISES AND PROBLEMS

150. Backwoods Incorporated manufactures rustic furniture. The cost accounting system estimates manufacturing costs to be $80 per table, consisting of 70% variable costs and 30% fixed costs. The company has surplus capacity available. It is Backwoods' policy to add a 50% markup to full costs.

   a. Backwoods Incorporated is invited to bid on an order to supply 100 rustic tables. What is the lowest price Backwoods should bid on this one-time-only special order?

   b. A large hotel chain is currently expanding and has decided to decorate all new hotels using the rustic style. Backwoods Incorporated is invited to submit a bid to the hotel chain. What is the lowest price per unit Backwoods should bid on this long-term order?

Answer:

   a. The lowest price Backwoods should bid on the 100 table one-time special order is $5,600 = Variable costs ($80 x .70 x 100 tables), the short-term incremental costs.

   b. The lowest price Backwoods should bid on the long-term hotel chain order is $120 per table = Full costs $80 + 50% markup, the long-term targeted price.

Difficulty: 2   *Objectives*: 2, 3

151. Schlickau Company manufactures basketball backboards. The following information pertains to the company's normal operations per month:

Output units	15,000 boards
Machine-hours	4,000 hours
Direct manufacturing labor-hours	5,000 hours
Direct manufacturing labor per hour	$12
Direct materials per unit	$100
Variable manufacturing overhead costs	$150,000
Fixed manufacturing overhead costs	$300,000
Product and process design costs	$200,000
Marketing and distribution costs	$250,000

Required:

a. For long-run pricing, what is the full-cost base per unit?
b. Schlickau Company is approached by an overseas city to fulfill a one-time-only special order for 1,000 units. All cost relationships remain the same except for an additional one-time setup charge of $40,000. No additional design, marketing, or distribution costs will be incurred. What is the minimum acceptable bid per unit on this one-time-only special order?

Answer:

a.
Direct materials	$150,000
Direct manufacturing labor ($12 x 5,000)/15,000	4,000
Variable manufacturing ($150,000/15,000)	10,000
Fixed manufacturing ($300,000/15,000)	20,000
Marketing and distribution ($250,000/15,000)	16,667
Research and development ($200,000/15,000)	13,333
Total	$214,000

b.
Direct materials	$100,000
Direct manufacturing labor	4,000
Variable manufacturing	10,000
Setup	40,000
Total	$154,000

Difficulty: 2   *Objective*:   2

152. Steven Corporation manufactures fishing poles that have a price of $21.00. It has costs of $16.32. A competitor is introducing a new fishing pole that will sell for $18.00. Management believes it must lower the price to $18.00 in order to compete in the highly cost-conscious fishing pole market. Marketing believes that the new price will maintain the current sales level. Steven Corporation's sales are currently 200,000 poles per year.

Required:

a. What is the target cost for the new price if target operating income is 20% of sales?
b. What is the change in operating income for the year if $18.00 is the new price and costs remain the same?
c. What is the target cost per unit if the selling price is reduced to $18.00 and the company wants to maintain its same income level?

Answer:

a. $18.00 - $18.00(0.20) = $14.40

b. Change = 200,000 x ($21.00 - $16.32) – [200,000 x ($18.00 - $16.32)]
   = $936,000 - $336,000
   = $600,000 reduction in income

c. Current income = 200,000 x ($21.00 - $16.32) = $936,000

   Target cost per unit:

   $936,000 = (200,000 x $18.00) - 200,000y
   200,000y = $2,664,000
   y = $13.32

Difficulty: 2   *Objective*: 3

153. Robert's Medical Equipment Company manufactures hospital beds. Its most popular model, Deluxe, sells for $5,000. It has variable costs totaling $2,800 and fixed costs of $1,000 per unit, based on an average production run of 5,000 units. It normally has four production runs a year, with $400,000 in setup costs each time. Plant capacity can handle up to six runs a year for a total of 30,000 beds.

A competitor is introducing a new hospital bed similar to Deluxe that will sell for $4,000. Management believes it must lower the price in order to compete. Marketing believes that the new price will increase sales by 25% a year. The plant manager thinks that production can increase by 25% with the same level of fixed costs. The company currently sells all the Deluxe beds it can produce.

Required:

a. What is the annual operating income from Deluxe at the current price of $5,000?
b. What is the annual operating income from Deluxe if the price is reduced to $4,000 and sales in units increase by 25%?
c. What is the target cost per unit for the new price if target operating income is 20% of sales?

Answer:

a. Sales (20,000 x $5,000) $100,000,000
    Costs:

Variable costs (20,000 x $2,800)	$56,000,000	
Fixed costs ($1,000 x 5,000 x 4)	20,000,000	
Setup costs ($400,000 x 4)	1,600,000	77,600,000

    Operating income $ 22,400,000

b. Sales (25,000 x $4,000) $100,000,000
    Costs:

Variable costs (25,000 x $2,800)	$70,000,000	
Fixed costs, same	20,000,000	
Setup costs ($400,000 x 5)	2,000,000	92,000,000

    Operating income $ 8,000,000

c. $4,000 - $4,000(0.20) = $3,200

Difficulty: 2   *Objective:* 3

154. Reuter Avionics currently sells radios for $1,800. It has costs of $1,400. A competitor is bringing a new radio to market that will sell for $1,600. Management believes it must lower the price to $1,600 to compete in the market for radios. Marketing believes that the new price will cause sales to increase by 10%, even with a new competitor in the market. Reuter's sales are currently 1,000 radios per year.

Required:

a. What is the target cost if target operating income is 25% of sales?
b. What is the change in operating income if marketing is correct and only the sales price is changed?
c. What is the target cost if the company wants to maintain its same income level, and marketing is correct?

Answer:

a. $1,600 - $1,600 (0.25) = $1,200

b. (1,000 x ($1,800 - $1,400)) - (1,100 x ($1,600 - $1,400)) = $180,000

c. Current income = 1,000 x ($1,800 - $1,400) = $400,000
Target cost y: $400,000 = (1,100 x $1,600) – 1,100y
y = $1,360,000/1,100
y = $1,236.3636

Difficulty: 3   *Objective:* 3

155. Nancy Company has budgeted sales of $300,000 with the following budgeted costs:

Direct materials	$60,000
Direct manufacturing labor	40,000
Factory overhead	
Variable	30,000
Fixed	50,000
Selling and administrative expenses	
Variable	20,000
Fixed	30,000

Compute the average markup percentage for setting prices as a percentage of:

a. The full cost of the product
b. The variable cost of the product
c. Variable manufacturing costs
d. Total manufacturing costs

Answer:

a. $60,000 + $40,000 + $30,000 + $50,000 + $20,000 + $30,000 = $230,000
   ($300,000 - $230,000)/$230,000 = 30.4%

b. $60,000 + $40,000 + $30,000 + $20,000 = $150,000
   ($300,000 - $150,000)/$150,000 = 100%

c. $60,000 + $40,000 + $30,000 = $130,000
   ($300,000 - $130,000)/$130,000 = 130.8%

d. $60,000 + $40,000 + $30,000 + $50,000 = $180,000
   ($300,000 - $180,000)/$180,000 = 66.7%

Difficulty: 2   *Objective*: 5

156. Timothy Company has budgeted sales of $780,000 with the following budgeted costs:

Direct materials	$168,000
Direct manufacturing labor	132,000
Factory overhead	
Variable	96,000
Fixed	108,000
Selling and administrative expenses	
Variable	72,000
Fixed	100,000

Compute the average markup percentage for setting prices as a percentage of:

a. Total manufacturing costs
b. The variable cost of the product
c. The full cost of the product
d. Variable manufacturing costs

Answer:

a. $168,000 + $132,000 + $96,000 + $108,000 = $504,000
($780,000 - $504,000)/$504,000 = 54.8%

b. $168,000 + $132,000 + $96,000 + $72,000 = $468,000
($780,000 - $468,000)/$468,000 = 66.7%

c. $168,000 + $132,000 + $96,000 + $108,000 + $72,000 + $100,000 = $676,000
($780,000 - $676,000)/$676,000 = 15.4%

d. $168,000 + $132,000 + $96,000 = $396,000
($780,000 - $396,000)/$396,000 = 97%

Difficulty: 2   *Objective*: 5

157. Henderson Company is in the process of evaluating a new part using the following information.
   - Part SLC2002 has one production run each month, each with $16,000 in setup costs.
   - Part SLC2002 incurred $40,000 in development costs and is expected to be produced over the next three years.
   - Direct costs of producing Part SLC2002 are $56,000 per run of 24,000 parts each.
   - Indirect manufacturing costs charged to each run are $88,000.
   - Destination charges for each run average $18,000.
   - Part SLC2002 is selling for $12.50 in the United States and $25 in all other countries. Sales are one-third domestic and two-thirds exported.
   - Sales units equal production units each year.

Required:

a. What are the estimated life-cycle revenues?
b. What is the estimated life-cycle operating income for the first year?

Answer:

a.
Domestic ($12.50 x 12 months x 24,000 x 3 yrs. x 1/3)		$ 3,600,000
Export ($25 x 12 months x 24,000 x 3 yrs. x 2/3)		14,400,000
Estimated life-cycle revenues		$18,000,000

b. Sales
Domestic ($12.50 x 12 months x 24,000 x 1/3)		$1,200,000
Export ($25 x 12 months x 24,000 x 2/3)		4,800,000
Total Sales		6,000,000

Costs:
Development costs	$ 40,000	
Setup costs (12 x $16,000)	192,000	
Direct manufacturing costs (12 x $56,000)	672,000	
Indirect manufacturing costs (12 x $88,000)	1,056,000	
Destination costs (12 x $18,000)	216,000	2,176,000
Estimated life-cycle operating income, first year		$3,824,000

Difficulty: 3   *Objective*: 6

158. Stone and Bicker are starting a new business venture and are in the process of evaluating their product lines. Information for one new product, hand-made lamps, is as follows:
   o Every six months a new lamp pattern will be put into production. Each new pattern will require $11,200 in setup costs.
   o The lamp product line incurred $48,000 in development costs and is expected to be produced over the next six years.
   o Direct costs of producing the lamps average $144 each. Each lamp requires 12 labor-hours and 2 machine-hours.
   o Indirect manufacturing costs are estimated at $160,000 per year.
   o Customer service expenses average $16 per lamp.
   o Current sales are expected to be 2,000 units of each lamp pattern. Each lamp sells for $224.
   o Sales units equal production units each year.

Required:

a. What are the estimated life-cycle revenues?
b. What is the estimated life-cycle operating income for the first year?

Answer:

a. Estimated life-cycle revenues:
   (2,000 x 2 patterns per year x $224 per lamp)

	$ 896,000
	x 6 years
	$5,376,000

b. Annual revenues (2,000 x $224 x 2) $896,000

Setup costs ($11,200 x 2)	$ 22,400	
Development costs	48,000	
Direct manufacturing costs (2,000 x $144 x 2)	576,000	
Indirect manufacturing costs	160,000	
Customer service costs ($16 x 2,000 lamps x 2)	64,000	870,400
Estimated life-cycle operating income for the first year		$ 25,600

Difficulty: 2   *Objective:* 6

159. Claudia Geer, controller, discusses the pricing of a new product with the sales manager, James Nolan. What major influences must Claudia and James consider in pricing the new product? Discuss each briefly.

Answer:

The major influences are customers, competitors, and costs.

Customers: Managers must always examine pricing problems through the eyes of their customers. A price increase may cause customers to reject a company's product and choose a competing or substitute product.

Competitors: Competitors' reactions influence pricing decisions. At one extreme, a rival's prices and products may force a business to lower its prices to be competitive. At the other extreme, a business without a rival in a given situation can set higher prices. A business with knowledge of its rivals' technology, plant capacity, and operating policies is able to estimate its rivals' costs, which is valuable information in setting competitive prices.

Costs: Companies price products to exceed the costs of making them. The study of cost-behavior patterns gives insight into the income that results from different combinations of price and output quantities sold for a particular product.

Difficulty: 2   *Objective*: 1

160. In target costing, what are at least two techniques used to achieve target costing goals?

Answer:

In target costing, techniques used to achieve target-costing goals include value engineering, cross-functional teams, and supply-chain management.

Difficulty: 2   *Objective*: 3

161. What is the primary reason a firm would adopt target costing?

Answer:

The primary reason a firm would adopt target costing is to reduce costs. Its unique approach is to design costs out of products during the design stage in the product life cycle. Many firms are adopting this approach when they cannot reduce costs further using traditional costing methods, which focus on cost reductions in manufacturing.

Difficulty: 2   *Objective*: 3

162. Compare target costing and kaizen costing.

Answer:

Target costing focuses on reducing costs for products during the design stage. Kaizen costing focuses on reducing costs for products in the manufacturing stage.

Difficulty: 2   *Objectives*: 3, 4

163. Ski Valet provides materials that let people teach themselves how to snow ski. It has six different skill-level programs. Each one includes visual and audio learning aids along with a workbook that can be submitted to the company for grading and evaluation purposes, if the person so desires.

The accounting system of Ski Valet is very traditional in its reporting functions with the calendar year being the company's fiscal year. It does include an abundance of information that can be used for various reporting purposes.

The company has found that any new idea soon runs its course with an effective life of about three years. Therefore, the company is always in the development stage of some new program. Program development requires experts in the area to provide the know-how of the item being developed and a development team that puts together the video, audio, and workbook materials. The actual costs of reproducing the packages are relatively inexpensive when compared to the development costs.

Required:

How might product life-cycle budgeting aid the company in improving its overall operations?

Answer:

Because the product life cycle for Ski Valet extends over several traditional accounting periods, it is critical for the company to consider a planning concept that evaluates each one of its products during its entire life cycle. Procedures that highlight an entire life cycle can include items for overall profitability, and which products might be repeated in a few years. With a large portion of their expenses in the development area, life-cycle budgeting can assist in predicting the sales needs for the entire life of a product.

It is probably more important to evaluate company performance on a product basis rather than year to year. Life-cycle budgeting would allow the company to compare products to each other rather than just comparing one year to the next.

Difficulty: 2   *Objective*: 6

164. What factors may influence the level of markups?

Answer:

Factors affecting the level of markups include the strength of demand, the elasticity of demand, and the intensity of competition. In addition, strategic reasons also may influence the level of markups. For instance, a firm may either choose a low markup to penetrate the market and win market share from established products of its competitors, or employ a high markup if it employs a skimming strategy for a market segment in which some customers are willing to pay higher prices for the privilege of owning the product.

Difficulty: 2   *Objectives*: 5, 7

165. A hotel in Orlando, Florida, experiences peak periods and slower times. How should prices be adjusted during peak periods? During slow times? Why?

Answer:

During peak periods the hotel can justify increased prices because of full capacity conditions, whereas in slower periods when there is excess capacity, the hotel may want to lower prices to fill the excess capacity.

Difficulty: 2   *Objective*:   7

166. Clark Manufacturing offers two product lines, IN2 and EL5. The demand of the IN2 product line is inelastic, while the demand of the EL5 product line is very elastic. If Clark initiates a price increase for both product lines, how will customer demand change? How will the price increase affect operating profits?

Answer:

For the inelastic product line, when prices are increased demand will stay approximately the same and profits would be expected to increase.
For the elastic product line, the increased price will result in decreased demand (i.e., lower sales volume). Whether a profit or a loss results from this change will depend on the amount of decreased demand and the amount of the increased contribution margin due to the increase in price.

Difficulty: 2   *Objective*:   7

CHAPTER 13: STRATEGY, BALANCED SCORECARD, AND STRATEGY PROFITABILITY ANALYSIS

TRUE/FALSE

1. Strategy describes how an organization matches its own capabilities with the opportunities in the marketplace to accomplish its overall objectives.

    Answer: True   *Difficulty*: 1   *Objective*: 1

2. A product differentiation strategy includes offering unique and superior products for increased prices.

    Answer: True   *Difficulty*: 1   *Objective*: 1

3. The cost leadership strategy is for products and services that are similar to competitor's products and services.

    Answer: True   *Difficulty*: 1   *Objective*: 1

4. The product differentiation strategy is probably best for a company if the engineering staff is more skilled at making process improvements than at creatively designing new products.

    Answer: False   *Difficulty*: 2   *Objective*: 1
    The *cost leadership* strategy is probably best for a company if the engineering staff is more skilled at making process improvements than at creatively designing new products.

5. In general, profit potential increases with greater competition, stronger potential entrants, products that are similar, and tougher customers and suppliers.

    Answer: False   *Difficulty*: 1   *Objective*: 1
    In general, profit potential *decreases* with greater competition, stronger potential entrants, products that are similar, and tougher customers and suppliers.

6. Reengineering is the fundamental rethinking and redesign of business processes to achieve improvements in critical measures of performance such as cost, quality, service, speed, and customer satisfaction.

    Answer: True   *Difficulty*: 1   *Objective*: 2

7. Reengineering benefits are most significant when they focus on one business function rather than crossing functional lines of the business process.

    Answer: False   *Difficulty*: 2   *Objective*: 2
    Reengineering benefits are most significant when they cut across functional lines to focus on the entire business process.

8. Successful reengineering efforts generally involve changing the roles and responsibilities of employees.

Answer: True   *Difficulty*: 2   *Objective*: 2

9. The primary purpose of the balanced scorecard is to obtain increased operating profits for the current year.

Answer: False   *Difficulty*: 2   *Objective*: 3
The primary purpose of the balanced scorecard is to implement both short-run and long-run strategies.

10. To achieve success, it is important to set nonfinancial objectives as well as financial objectives.

Answer: True   *Difficulty*: 2   *Objective*: 3

11. One valuable measure of the customer perspective of the balanced scorecard is market share.

Answer: True   *Difficulty*: 2   *Objective*: 3

12. The learning and growth perspective of the balanced scorecard evaluates the profitability of the strategy.

Answer: False   *Difficulty*: 1   *Objective*: 3
The *financial* perspective of the balanced scorecard evaluates the profitability of the strategy.

13. Employee satisfaction is a measure of the internal business perspective of the balanced scorecard.

Answer: False   *Difficulty*: 2   *Objective*: 3
Employee satisfaction is a measure of the learning and growth perspective.

14. An increase of operating income from one year to the next indicates a company's strategy was successful.

Answer: False   *Difficulty*: 3   *Objective*: 4
Operating income could have increased simply because the entire market expanded and have nothing to do with the implementation of a company's strategy.

15. To evaluate the success of its strategy, a company can subdivide the change in operating income into growth, price-recovery, and productivity components.

Answer: True   *Difficulty*: 2   *Objective*: 4

16. The productivity component of operating income focuses exclusively on revenues.

Answer: False   *Difficulty*: 2   *Objective*: 4
The productivity component of operating income focuses exclusively on *costs*.

17. The price-recovery component measures the increase in operating income from selling more units of a product.

Answer: False   *Difficulty*: 1   *Objective*: 4
The *growth* component measures the increase in operating income from selling more units of a product.

18. Companies that have been successful at cost leadership will show large favorable price-recovery and growth components when analyzing profitability.

Answer: False   *Difficulty*: 3   *Objective*: 4
Companies that have successfully *differentiated* their products will show large favorable price-recovery and growth components when analyzing profitability.

19. Engineered costs have no measurable cause-and-effect relationship between output and resources used.

Answer: False   *Difficulty*: 2   *Objective*: 5
Discretionary costs have no measurable cause-and-effect relationship between output and resources used.

20. Discretionary costs arise from periodic (usually yearly) decisions regarding the maximum amount to be incurred.

Answer: True   *Difficulty*: 1   *Objective*: 5

21. Engineered costs contain a higher level of uncertainty than discretionary costs.

Answer: False   *Difficulty*: 2   *Objective*: 5
Discretionary costs contain a higher level of uncertainty than engineered costs.

22. Engineered costs may be variable or fixed in the short run.

Answer: True   *Difficulty*: 2   *Objective*: 5

23. It is relatively easy to identify unused capacity for discretionary costs.

Answer: False   *Difficulty*: 2   *Objective*: 6
It is *difficult* to identify unused capacity for discretionary costs because of the lack of a cause-and-effect relationship.

24. One way to eliminate unused capacity is to downsize.

   Answer: True   *Difficulty*: 1   *Objective*: 6

25. Downsizing discretionary costs is easier than downsizing engineered costs.

   Answer: False   *Difficulty*: 2   *Objective*: 6
   Downsizing discretionary costs is more difficult because the unused capacity of discretionary costs is generally unknown.

26. Downsizing often means eliminating jobs, which can have an adverse effect on employee morale.

   Answer: True   *Difficulty*: 2   *Objective*: 6

27. Productivity measures the relationship between actual inputs used (both quantities and costs) and standard outputs produced.

   Answer: False   *Difficulty*: 1   *Objective*: A
   Productivity measures the relationship between actual inputs used (both quantities and costs) and actual outputs produced.

28. Partial productivity equals quantity of output produced divided by quantity of individual input used.

   Answer: True   *Difficulty*: 1   *Objective*: A

29. Total factor productivity (TFP) is the ratio of the quantity of output produced to the costs of all inputs used, where the inputs are combined on the basis of current period prices.

   Answer: True   *Difficulty*: 1   *Objective*: A

30. Although total factor productivity (TFP) measures are comprehensive, operations personnel find financial TFP measures more difficult to understand and less useful than physical partial productivity measures in performing their tasks.

   Answer: True   *Difficulty*: 1   *Objective*: A

MULTIPLE CHOICE

31. _____ describes how an organization matches its own capabilities with the opportunities in the marketplace to accomplish its overall objectives.
    a.   Strategy
    b.   Planning
    c.   Learning and growth perspective
    d.   Customer perspective

    Answer: a   *Difficulty*:   1   *Objective*:   1

32. Which of the following is NOT a force that shapes an organization's profit potential?
    a.   Competitors
    b.   Equivalent products
    c.   Bargaining power of input suppliers
    d.   All of the above influence profit potential.

    Answer: d   *Difficulty*:   2   *Objective*:   1

33. _____ is an organization's ability to offer products or services that are perceived by its customers as being superior and unique relative to those of its competitors.
    a.   Strategy
    b.   Product differentiation
    c.   Cost leadership
    d.   The balanced scorecard

    Answer: b   *Difficulty*:   1   *Objective*:   1

34. _____ is an organization's ability to achieve low costs relative to competitors through productivity and efficiency improvements, elimination of waste, and tight cost control.
    a.   Strategy
    b.   Product differentiation
    c.   Cost leadership
    d.   The balanced scorecard

    Answer: c   *Difficulty*:   1   *Objective*:   1

35. An organization that is using the product differentiation approach would
    a.   focus on tight cost control.
    b.   carefully cultivate their brands.
    c.   provide products that are similar to competitors.
    d.   offer products at a lower cost than competitors.

    Answer: b   *Difficulty*:   2   *Objective*:   1

36. An organization that is using the cost leadership approach would
    a.   incur costs for innovative R&D.
    b.   provide products at a higher cost than competitors.
    c.   focus on productivity through efficiency improvements.
    d.   bring products to market rapidly.

    Answer: c   *Difficulty:*   2   *Objective:*   1

37. _____ is the fundamental rethinking and redesign of business processes to achieve improvements in critical measures of performance such as cost, quality, service, speed, and customer satisfaction.
    a.   Strategy
    b.   Customer perspective
    c.   Learning and growth perspective
    d.   Reengineering

    Answer: d   *Difficulty:*   1   *Objective:*   2

38. Successful reengineering involves
    a.   cutting across functional lines to focus on the entire business process.
    b.   redefining the roles and responsibilities of employees.
    c.   using information technology.
    d.   all of the above.

    Answer: d   *Difficulty:*   2   *Objective:*   2

39. _____ translates an organization's mission and strategy into a comprehensive set of performance measures that provide the framework for implementing its strategy.
    a.   Productivity component
    b.   Product differentiation
    c.   Cost leadership
    d.   The balanced scorecard

    Answer: d   *Difficulty:*   1   *Objective:*   3

40. The purpose of the balanced scorecard is BEST described as helping an organization
    a.   develop customer relations.
    b.   mobilize employee skills for continuous improvements in processing capabilities, quality, and response times.
    c.   introduce innovative products and services desired by target customers.
    d.   translate an organization's mission and strategy into a set of performance measures that help to implement the strategy.

    Answer: d   *Difficulty:*   3   *Objective:*   3

41. The FIRST step to successful balanced scorecard implementation is clarifying
    a. the organization's vision and strategy.
    b. the elements that pertain to value-added aspects of the business.
    c. the owner's expectations about return on investment.
    d. the objectives of all four balanced scorecard measurement perspectives.

    Answer: a *Difficulty:* 3 *Objective:* 3

42. The balanced scorecard is said to be "balanced" because it measures
    a. short-term and long-term objectives.
    b. financial and nonfinancial objectives.
    c. internal and external objectives.
    d. all of the above.

    Answer: d *Difficulty:* 2 *Objective:* 3

43. Balanced scorecard objectives are in balance when
    a. debits equal credits.
    b. financial performance measurements are less than the majority of measurements.
    c. the measurements are fair.
    d. the measurements reflect an improvement over the previous year.

    Answer: b *Difficulty:* 3 *Objective:* 3

44. The internal business processes perspective of the balanced scorecard comprises three subprocesses that address all of the following EXCEPT
    a. innovative processes used to create new products, services, and processes.
    b. motivating current employees.
    c. providing service and support to the customer after the sale.
    d. delivering existing products and services to best meet the needs of customers.

    Answer: b *Difficulty:* 3 *Objective:* 3

45. Identify the BEST description of the balanced scorecard's financial perspective. To achieve our firm's vision and strategy,
    a. how can we obtain greater profits for the current year?
    b. how can we increase shareholder value?
    c. how will we obtain continuous improvements?
    d. how can we secure greater customer satisfaction?

    Answer: b *Difficulty:* 2 *Objective:* 3

46. Identify the BEST description of the balanced scorecard's internal business processes perspective. To achieve our firm's vision and strategy,
    a. how do we lower costs?
    b. how do we motivate employees?
    c. how can we obtain greater profits?
    d. what processes will increase value to customers?

    Answer: d *Difficulty:* 3 *Objective:* 3

47. All of the following relate to the balanced scorecard's learning and growth perspective EXCEPT
    a. how do we achieve greater employee satisfaction?
    b. what new products do we create?
    c. how do we provide information systems with updated technology?
    d. how will we motivate and empower our employees?

    Answer: b   *Difficulty:* 3   *Objective:* 3

48. Measures of the balanced scorecard's customer perspective include
    a. market share.
    b. number of on-time deliveries.
    c. number of process improvements.
    d. revenue growth.

    Answer: a   *Difficulty:* 3   *Objective:* 3

49. Which of the following is NOT true of a good balanced scorecard?
    a. It tells the story of a company's strategy by articulating a sequence of cause-and-effect relationships.
    b. It helps to communicate corporate strategy to all members of the organization.
    c. It identifies all measures, whether significant or small, that help to implement strategy.
    d. It uses nonfinancial measures to serve as leading indicators of future financial performance.

    Answer: c   *Difficulty:* 3   *Objective:* 3

50. Which of the following is NOT true of the balanced scorecard?
    a. Different strategies call for different scorecards.
    b. Successful implementation requires commitment and leadership from top management.
    c. Only objective measures should be used and subjective measures should be avoided.
    d. Cause-and-effect linkages may not be precise and should evolve over time.

    Answer: c   *Difficulty:* 3   *Objective:* 3

51. The return-on-investment ratio is an example of a balanced-scorecard measure of the
    a. internal business process perspective.
    b. customer perspective.
    c. learning and growth perspective.
    d. financial perspective.

    Answer: d   *Difficulty:* 2   *Objective:* 3

52. The number of complaints about a product is an example of a balanced-scorecard measure of the
    a. internal business process perspective.
    b. customer perspective.
    c. learning and growth perspective.
    d. financial perspective.

    Answer: b   *Difficulty:* 2   *Objective:* 3

53. Manufacturing cycle efficiency is an example of a balanced-scorecard measure of the
    a. internal business process perspective.
    b. customer perspective.
    c. learning and growth perspective.
    d. financial perspective.

    Answer: a   *Difficulty:* 2   *Objective:* 3

54. Surveys of employee satisfaction is an example of a balanced-scorecard measure of the
    a. internal business process perspective.
    b. customer perspective.
    c. learning and growth perspective.
    d. financial perspective.

    Answer: c   *Difficulty:* 2   *Objective:* 3

THE FOLLOWING INFORMATION APPLIES TO QUESTIONS 55 AND 56.
Stewart Corporation plans to grow by offering a sound system, the SS3000 that is superior and unique from the competition. Stewart believes that putting additional resources into R&D and staying ahead of the competition with technological innovations is critical to implementing its strategy.

55. Stewart's strategy is
    a. product differentiation.
    b. downsizing.
    c. reengineering.
    d. cost leadership.

    Answer: a   *Difficulty:* 2   *Objective:* 1

56. To further company strategy, measures on the balanced scorecard would MOST likely include
    a. number of process improvements.
    b. manufacturing quality.
    c. yield.
    d. an increase in operating income from productivity gains.

    Answer: b   *Difficulty:* 3   *Objective:* 3

THE FOLLOWING INFORMATION APPLIES TO QUESTIONS 57 AND 58.
Riter Corporation manufactures water toys. It plans to grow by producing high-quality water toys at a low cost that are delivered in a timely manner. There are a number of other manufacturers who produce similar water toys. Riter believes that continuously improving its manufacturing processes and having satisfied employees are critical to implementing its strategy.

57. Riter's strategy is
    a. product differentiation.
    b. downsizing.
    c. reengineering.
    d. cost leadership.

    Answer: d   *Difficulty*: 2   *Objective*: 1

58. To further company strategy, measures on the balanced scorecard would MOST likely include
    a. number of process improvements.
    b. price premium earned.
    c. longer cycle times.
    d. an increase in operating income from increased profit margins.

    Answer: a   *Difficulty*: 3   *Objective*: 3

59. Which component measures the changes in operating income attributed solely to an increase in the quantity of output between Year 1 and Year 2?
    a. The growth component
    b. The price-recovery component
    c. The productivity component
    d. The cost leadership component

    Answer: a   *Difficulty*: 1   *Objective*: 4

60. Which component measures the change in operating income attributable solely to changes in a company's profit margins between Year 1 and Year 2?
    a. The growth component
    b. The price-recovery component
    c. The productivity component
    d. The cost leadership component

    Answer: b   *Difficulty*: 1   *Objective*: 4

61. Which component measures the reduction in costs attributable to a reduction in the quantity of inputs used in Year 2 relative to the quantity of inputs that would have been used in Year 1 to produce the Year 2 output?
    a. The growth component
    b. The price-recovery component
    c. The productivity component
    d. The cost leadership component

    Answer: c   *Difficulty:* 1   *Objective:* 4

62. When analyzing the change in operating income, the growth component
    a. calculations are similar to the selling-price variance calculations.
    b. isolates the change attributed solely to an increase in market share.
    c. isolates the change attributed solely to an increase in industry growth.
    d. isolates the change attributed solely to an increase in the quantity of units sold.

    Answer: d   *Difficulty:* 3   *Objective:* 4

63. When analyzing the change in operating income, the price-recovery component
    a. calculations are similar to the efficiency-variance calculations.
    b. compares the change in output price with the changes in input prices.
    c. will report a large positive amount when a company has successfully pursued the cost leadership strategy.
    d. isolates the change attributed solely to an increase in production efficiencies.

    Answer: b   *Difficulty:* 3   *Objective:* 4

64. When analyzing the change in operating income, the productivity component
    a. calculations are similar to the sales-volume variance calculations.
    b. compares the change in output price with the changes in input prices.
    c. will report a large positive amount when a company has successfully pursued the cost leadership strategy.
    d. isolates the change attributed solely to an increase in the quantity of units sold.

    Answer: c   *Difficulty:* 3   *Objective:* 4

65. When analyzing the change in operating income, the growth component will increase when
    a. capacity is reduced.
    b. production efficiencies are successfully implemented.
    c. selling prices are increased.
    d. more units are sold.

    Answer: d   *Difficulty:* 3   *Objective:* 4

66. When analyzing the change in operating income, the price-recovery component will increase when
    a. capacity is reduced.
    b. production efficiencies are successfully implemented.
    c. selling prices are increased.
    d. more units are sold.

    Answer: c   *Difficulty*:   3   *Objective*:   4

67. When analyzing the change in operating income, the productivity component will increase when
    a. capacity is reduced.
    b. quality is enhanced.
    c. selling prices are increased.
    d. more units are produced and sold.

    Answer: a   *Difficulty*:   3   *Objective*:   4

68. Successful implementation of a cost leadership strategy will result in
    a. large favorable growth and price-recovery components.
    b. large favorable price-recovery and productivity components.
    c. large favorable productivity and growth components.
    d. only a large favorable growth component.

    Answer: c   *Difficulty*:   3   *Objective*:   4

69. Successful implementation of a product differentiation strategy will result in
    a. a large favorable growth and price-recovery components.
    b. a large favorable price-recovery and productivity components.
    c. a large favorable productivity and growth components.
    d. only a large favorable growth component.

    Answer: a   *Difficulty*:   3   *Objective*:   4

70. An operating income analysis of Sara McCullough Incorporated revealed the following:

Operating income for 2003	$500,000
Add growth component	25,000
Deduct price-recovery component	(15,000)
Add productivity component	60,000
Operating income for 2004	$570,000

McCullough's operating income gain is consistent with the
a. product differentiation strategy.
b. downsizing strategy.
c. reengineering strategy.
d. cost leadership strategy.

Answer: d   *Difficulty*: 2   *Objective*: 4

71. An operating income analysis of Deb Schmidt Incorporated revealed the following:

Operating income for 2003	$500,000
Add growth component	15,000
Add price-recovery component	100,000
Deduct productivity component	(8,000)
Operating income for 2004	$607,000

Schmidt's operating income gain is consistent with the
a. product differentiation strategy.
b. downsizing strategy.
c. reengineering strategy.
d. cost leadership strategy.

Answer: a   *Difficulty*: 2   *Objective*: 4

THE FOLLOWING INFORMATION APPLIES TO QUESTIONS 72 THROUGH 75.
Bugos Company makes a household appliance with model number XX300. The goal for 20x4 is to reduce direct materials usage per unit. No defective units are currently produced. Manufacturing conversion costs depend on production capacity defined in terms of XX300 units that can be produced. The industry market size for appliances increased 5% from 20x3 to 20x4. The following additional data are available for 20x3 and 20x4:

	20x3	20x4
Units of XX300 produced and sold	10,000	10,500
Selling price	$100	$95
Direct materials (square feet)	30,000	29,000
Direct material costs per square foot	$10	$11
Manufacturing capacity for XX300 (units)	12,500	12,000
Total conversion costs	$250,000	$240,000
Conversion costs per unit of capacity	$20	$20

72. What is operating income for 20x3?
   a. $450,000
   b. $1,000,000
   c. $750,000
   d. $700,000

   Answer: a   *Difficulty*: 2   *Objective*: 4
   ($100 x 10,000) - [($10 x 30,000) + ($20 x 12,500)] = $450,000

73. What is operating income for 20x4?
   a. $997,500
   b. $678,500
   c. $438,500
   d. $428,500

   Answer: c   *Difficulty*: 2   *Objective*: 4
   ($95 x 10,500) - [($11 x 29,000) + ($20 x 12,000)] = $438,500

74. Which strategy is Bugos Corporation pursuing?
   a. Product differentiation, since the units produced and sold increased.
   b. Product differentiation, since total conversion costs decreased.
   c. Cost leadership, since direct material costs per square foot increased.
   d. Cost leadership, since the selling price decreased.

   Answer: d   *Difficulty*: 2   *Objective*: 1

75. Overall, was Bugos' strategy successful in 20x4?
   a. No, because the selling price per unit decreased
   b. No, because operating income decreased
   c. Yes, because less direct materials were used
   d. Yes, because more units were produced and sold

   Answer: b   *Difficulty*: 3   *Objective*: 4
   $438,500 - $450,000 = $11,500 U

THE FOLLOWING INFORMATION APPLIES TO QUESTIONS 76 THROUGH 79.
Bugos Company makes a household appliance with model number XX300. The goal for 20x4 is to reduce direct materials usage per unit. No defective units are currently produced. Manufacturing conversion costs depend on production capacity defined in terms of XX300 units that can be produced. The industry market size for appliances increased 5% from 20x3 to 20x4. The following additional data are available for 20x3 and 20x4:

	20x3	20x4
Units of XX300 produced and sold	10,000	10,500
Selling price	$100	$95
Direct materials (square feet)	30,000	29,000
Direct material costs per square foot	$10	$11
Manufacturing capacity for XX300 (units)	12,500	12,000
Total conversion costs	$250,000	$240,000
Conversion costs per unit of capacity	$20	$20

76. What is the revenue effect of the growth component?
   a. $2,500 U
   b. $52,500 U
   c. $47,500 F
   d. $50,000 F

   Answer: d   *Difficulty:* 2   *Objective:* 4
   (10,500 – 10,000) x $100 = $50,000 F

77. What is the cost effect of the growth component for direct materials?
   a. $15,000 U
   b. $10,000 U
   c. $10,000 F
   d. $16,500 F

   Answer: a   *Difficulty:* 3   *Objective:* 4
   30,000 x 10,500/10,000 = 31,500; ($31,500 - 30,000) x $10) = $15,000 U

78. What is the cost effect of the growth component for conversion costs?
   a. $12,500 U
   b. Zero
   c. $10,000 U
   d. $10,000 F

   Answer: b   *Difficulty:* 3   *Objective:* 4
   (12,500 - 12,500) x $20 = Zero

79. What is the net effect on operating income as a result of the growth component?
   a. Operating income increased due to increased market share.
   b. Operating income decreased due to increased market share.
   c. Operating income increased due to industry growth.
   d. Operating income decreased due to industry growth.

   Answer: c   *Difficulty:* 3   *Objective:* 4
   $50,000 F + $15,000 U + Zero = $35,000 F increase due to 5% industry growth

THE FOLLOWING INFORMATION APPLIES TO QUESTIONS 80 THROUGH 83.
Bugos Company makes a household appliance with model number XX300. The goal for 20x4 is to reduce direct materials usage per unit. No defective units are currently produced. Manufacturing conversion costs depend on production capacity defined in terms of XX300 units that can be produced. The industry market size for appliances increased 5% from 20x3 to 20x4. The following additional data are available for 20x3 and 20x4:

	20x3	20x4
Units of XX300 produced and sold	10,000	10,500
Selling price	$100	$95
Direct materials (square feet)	30,000	29,000
Direct material costs per square foot	$10	$11
Manufacturing capacity for XX300 (units)	12,500	12,000
Total manufacturing conversion costs	$250,000	$240,000
Manufacturing conversion costs per unit of capacity	$20	$20

80. What is the revenue effect of the price-recovery component?
   a. $2,500 U
   b. $52,500 U
   c. $47,500 F
   d. $50,000 F

Answer: b   *Difficulty*: 2   *Objective*: 4
($95 - $100) x 10,500 = $52,500 U

81. What is the cost effect of the price-recovery component?
   a. $29,000 F
   b. $30,000 U
   c. $1,000 F
   d. $31,500 U

Answer: d   *Difficulty*: 3   *Objective*: 4
30,000 x 10,500/10,000 = 31,500;
[($11 - $10) x 31,500] + [($20 - $20) x 12,500] = $31,500 U

82. What is the net effect on operating income as a result of the price-recovery component?
   a. Decreased operating income due to decreased selling price and inability to recover increased costs
   b. Decreased operating income due to the inability to recover increased costs
   c. Increased operating income due to the increased number of units produced and sold
   d. Increased operating income due to the revenue effect of the price-recovery component

Answer: a   *Difficulty*: 3   *Objective*: 4
$52,500 U + $31,500 U = $84,000 U decrease in operating income

83. What is the net effect on operating income as a result of the productivity component?
    a.   Decreased operating income due to direct material inefficiencies only
    b.   Decreased operating income due to direct material inefficiencies and capacity reduction
    c.   Increased operating income due to direct material efficiencies and capacity reduction
    d.   Increased operating income due to direct material efficiencies only

Answer: c   *Difficulty:* 3   *Objective:* 4
30,000 x 10,500/10,000 = 31,500;
[(29,000 – 31,500) x $11] + [(12,000 - 12,500) x $20] = $37,500 F

THE FOLLOWING INFORMATION APPLIES TO QUESTIONS 84 THROUGH 93.
Following a strategy of product differentiation, Lucas Company makes a high-end Appliance, AP15. Lucas Company presents the following data for the years 20x3 and 20x4:

	20x3	20x4
Units of AP15 produced and sold	20,000	21,000
Selling price	$200	$220
Direct materials (square feet)	60,000	61,500
Direct materials costs per square foot	$20	$22
Manufacturing capacity in units of AP15	25,000	25,000
Total conversion costs	$1,000,000	$1,110,000
Conversion costs per unit of capacity	$40	$44
Selling and customer-service capacity (customers)	60	58
Total selling and customer-service costs	$360,000	$362,500
Selling and customer-service capacity cost per customer	$6,000	$6,250

Lucas Company produces no defective units but it wants to reduce direct materials usage per unit of AP15 in 20x4. Manufacturing conversion costs in each year depend on production capacity defined in terms of AP15 units that can be produced. Selling and customer-service costs depend on the number of customers that the customer and service functions are designed to support. Lucas Company has 46 customers in 20x3 and 50 customers in 20x4. The industry market size for high-end appliances increased 5% from 20x3 to 20x4.

84. What is operating income for 20x3?
    a. $364,500
    b. $1,804,500
    c. $1,440,000
    d. $200,000

Answer: c   *Difficulty:* 2   *Objective:* 4
($200 x 20,000) – [($20 x 60,000) + ($40 x 25,000) + ($6,000 x 60)] = $1,440,000

85. What is operating income in 20x4?
    a. $1,440,000
    b. $1,804,500
    c. $364,500
    d. $200,000

    Answer: b   *Difficulty:* 2   *Objective:* 4
    ($220 x 21,000) – [($22 x 61,500) + ($44 x 25,000) + ($6,250 x 58)] = $1,804,500

86. What is the change in operating income from 20x3 to 20x4?
    a. $1,440,000 F
    b. $1,804,500 F
    c. $364,500 F
    d. $200,000 F

    Answer: c   *Difficulty:* 2   *Objective:* 4
    $1,440,000 - $1,804,500 = $364,500 F

87. What is the revenue effect of the growth component?
    a. $220,000 F
    b. $420,000 F
    c. $400,000 F
    d. $200,000 F

    Answer: d   *Difficulty:* 2   *Objective:* 4
    (21,000 – 20,000) x $200 = $200,000 F

88. What is the cost effect of the growth component?
    a. $60,000 U
    b. $140,000 F
    c. $60,000 F
    d. $200,000 F

    Answer: a   *Difficulty:* 3   *Objective:* 4
    [(63,000 - 60,000) x $20] + [(25,000 - 25,000) x $40] + [(60 - 60) x $6,000]
    = $60,000 U

89. What is the net effect on operating income as a result of the growth component?
    a. $60,000 U
    b. $140,000 F
    c. $60,000 F
    d. $200,000 F

    Answer: b   *Difficulty:* 3   *Objective:* 4
    $200,000 F + $60,000 U = $140,000 F

90. What is the revenue effect of the price-recovery component?
   a. $220,000 F
   b. $420,000 F
   c. $400,000 F
   d. $200,000 F

Answer: b   *Difficulty:* 2   *Objective:* 4
($220 - $200) x 21,000 = $420,000 F

91. What is the cost effect of the price-recovery component?
   a. $179,000 F
   b. $179,000 U
   c. $241,000 U
   d. $420,000 F

Answer: c   *Difficulty:* 3   *Objective:* 4
[($22 - $20) x 63,000] + [($44 - $40) x 25,000] + [($6,250 - $6,000) x 60] = $241,000 U

92. What is the net effect on operating income as a result of the price-recovery component?
   a. $179,000 F
   b. $179,000 U
   c. $241,000 U
   d. $420,000 F

Answer: a   *Difficulty:* 3   *Objective:* 4
$420,000 F + $241,000 U = $179,000 F

93. What is the net effect on operating income as a result of the productivity component?
   a. $179,000 F
   b. $45,500 F
   c. $241,000 U
   d. $420,000 F

Answer: b   *Difficulty:* 3   *Objective:* 4
[(61,500 - 63,000) x $22] + [(25,000 - 25,000) x $40] + [(58 - 60) x $6,250]
= $45,500 F

94. Engineered costs
   a. arise from periodic (usually annual) decisions.
   b. often incur a delay between when the resource is acquired and when it is used.
   c. include R&D and human resource costs.
   d. include a high level of certainty.

Answer: d   *Difficulty:* 2   *Objective:* 5

95. Discretionary costs
    a. result from a cause-and-effect relationship between the output and the input.
    b. include advertising and executive training costs.
    c. can be variable or fixed in the short run.
    d. pertain to processes that are detailed.

    Answer: b   *Difficulty:* 2   *Objective:* 5

96. A high level of uncertainty is represented in
    a. engineered costs.
    b. discretionary costs.
    c. both engineered and discretionary costs.
    d. neither engineered nor discretionary costs.

    Answer: b   *Difficulty:* 1   *Objective:* 5

97. A high level of preciseness between resources used and output produced exists with
    a. engineered costs.
    b. discretionary costs.
    c. both engineered and discretionary costs.
    d. neither engineered nor discretionary costs.

    Answer: a   *Difficulty:* 1   *Objective:* 5

98. Discretionary costs
    a. have detailed processes.
    b. are physically observable activities.
    c. possess a high level of certainty.
    d. are usually large total amounts.

    Answer: d   *Difficulty:* 2   *Objective:* 5

99. Engineered costs
    a. possess a high of level uncertainty.
    b. are nonrepetitive.
    c. are from physically observable activities.
    d. have processes that are sketchy or unavailable.

    Answer: c   *Difficulty:* 2   *Objective:* 5

100. Unused capacity is difficult to determine for
    a. engineered costs.
    b. discretionary costs.
    c. both engineered and discretionary costs.
    d. neither engineered nor discretionary costs.

    Answer: b   *Difficulty:* 2   *Objective:* 6

101. To effectively deal with unused capacity a company
    a.   may downsize.
    b.   may retain some unused capacity for future growth.
    c.   should consider it a waste of resources and eliminate all unused capacity.
    d.   should consider both (a) and (b).

    Answer: d   *Difficulty:*   2   *Objective:*   6

102. Downsizing
    a.   may include eliminating jobs.
    b.   should be done within the context of a company's overall strategy.
    c.   is most difficult with discretionary costs.
    d.   is all of the above.

    Answer: d   *Difficulty:*   2   *Objective:*   6

103. The lower the inputs for a given set of outputs or the higher the outputs for a given set of inputs, the higher the level of
    a.   standard costs.
    b.   sales.
    c.   productivity.
    d.   labor costs.

    Answer: c   *Difficulty:*   1   *Objective:*   A

104. Yield variances
    a.   reveal the effect of substitution within a single factor of production.
    b.   address the productivity of a single component of one factor of production.
    c.   capture both substitutions between factors of production as well as within factors of production.
    d.   reveal the effect of substitution within multiple factors of production.

    Answer: b   *Difficulty:*   3   *Objective:*   A

105. Partial productivity multiplied by the quantity of input used results in
    a.   expected production.
    b.   budgeted output.
    c.   actual output.
    d.   a ratio.

    Answer: c   *Difficulty:*   3   *Objective:*   A

106. _____ measures the relationship between actual inputs used and actual outputs achieved.
    a.   Total factor productivity
    b.   Partial productivity
    c.   Productivity
    d.   Product yield variance

    Answer: c   *Difficulty:*   1   *Objective:*   A

107. _____ compares the quantity of output produced with the quantity of a single input used.
   a. Total factor productivity
   b. Partial productivity
   c. Productivity
   d. Product yield variance

Answer: b   *Difficulty:* 1   *Objective:* A

108. Frazier Company provided the following information.

Budgeted input	19,500	gallons
Actual input	17,900	gallons
Budgeted production	20,000	units
Actual production	19,000	units

What is the partial productivity ratio?
   a. 0.97 units per gallon
   b. 1.02 units per gallon
   c. 1.06 units per gallon
   d. 1.12 units per gallon

Answer: c   *Difficulty:* 2   *Objective:* A
PP = 19,000 / 17,900 = 1.06 units per gallon

109. Germaine Company provided the following information.

Budgeted input	9,750	gallons
Actual input	8,950	gallons
Budgeted production	10,000	units
Actual production	9,500	units

What is the partial productivity ratio?
   a. 0.97 units per gallon
   b. 1.02 units per gallon
   c. 1.06 units per gallon
   d. 1.12 units per gallon

Answer: c   *Difficulty:* 2   *Objective:* A
PP = 9,500 / 8,950 = 1.06 units per gallon

110. Melik Company provided the following information.

Budgeted input	12,000	pounds
Actual input	15,000	pounds
Budgeted production	5,000	units
Actual production	4,750	units

What is the partial productivity ratio?
   a. 0.32 units per pound
   b. 0.33 units per pound
   c. 0.40 units per pound
   d. 3.16 units per pound

Answer: a   *Difficulty:* 2   *Objective:* A
PP = 4,750 / 15,000 = 0.32 units per pound

111. Which of the following statements is TRUE?
    a.   The lower the partial productivity ratio, the greater the productivity.
    b.   Productivity has increased when the partial productivity is high.
    c.   Prices of inputs are incorporated in the partial productivity ratio.
    d.   The partial productivity ratio measures the number of outputs produced per multiple input.

    Answer: b   *Difficulty:* 2   *Objective:* A

112. What is the direct manufacturing labor partial productivity, assuming 20,000 widgets were produced during 20x1 and 80,000 direct manufacturing labor-hours were used?
    a.   0.25 unit per direct manufacturing labor-hour
    b.   0.50 unit per direct manufacturing labor-hour
    c.   0.75 unit per direct manufacturing labor-hour
    d.   1.00 unit per direct manufacturing labor-hour

    Answer: a   *Difficulty:* 2   *Objective:* A
    20,000 / 80,000 = 0.25

113. What is the direct manufacturing labor partial productivity, assuming 10,000 units were produced during 20x1 and 40,000 direct manufacturing labor-hours were used?
    a.   0.25 unit per direct manufacturing labor-hour
    b.   0.50 unit per direct manufacturing labor-hour
    c.   0.75 unit per direct manufacturing labor-hour
    d.   1.00 unit per direct manufacturing labor-hour

    Answer: a   *Difficulty:* 2   *Objective:* A
    10,000 / 40,000 = 0.25

114. What terms describe the relationship between different quantities of inputs consumed and the quantities of output produced?
    a.   Budgeted costs or actual costs
    b.   Production technology or production function
    c.   Static budget or flexible budget
    d.   Production technology or production setup

    Answer: b   *Difficulty:* 2   *Objective:* A

115. Total factor productivity will increase if
    a.   technical productivity occurs.
    b.   the company uses more total inputs per output.
    c.   the company incurs fewer costs per input.
    d.   current technology becomes obsolete.

    Answer: a   *Difficulty:* 3   *Objective:* A

116. One problem with total factor productivity revolves around which of the following?
    a.   The measurement of combined productivity of all inputs
    b.   The control operations personnel have over inputs
    c.   The control operations personnel have over outputs
    d.   The marketing mix determined by management

    Answer: a   *Difficulty:*   2   *Objective:*   A

117. _____ is the ratio of the quantity of output produced to the costs of all inputs used, where the inputs are combined on the basis of current period prices.
    a.   Total factor productivity
    b.   Partial productivity
    c.   Productivity
    d.   Product yield variance

    Answer: a   *Difficulty:*   1   *Objective:*   A

118. The partial productivity of overhead resources can be measured by considering the cost driver as
    a.   budgeted input.
    b.   the denominator.
    c.   the fixed input.
    d.   the numerator.

    Answer: d   *Difficulty:*   3   *Objective:*   A

119. Which of the following statements about productivity measures is FALSE?
    a.   It may be stated in terms of dollars.
    b.   It provides a convenient and easily interpreted means of aggregating across different physical outputs.
    c.   The productivity measure may not be made for companies with multiple products.
    d.   The key is the identification of cost drivers.

    Answer: c   *Difficulty:*   2   *Objective:*   A

120. The average number of student credit hours taught per faculty member is an example of
    a.   an expected performance measure.
    b.   a budgeted productivity measure.
    c.   a standard productivity measure.
    d.   a partial productivity measure.

    Answer: d   *Difficulty:*   3   *Objective:*   A

EXERCISES AND PROBLEMS

121. Buck Corporation plans to grow by offering a computer monitor, the CM3000 that is superior and unique from the competition. Buck believes that putting additional resources into R&D and staying ahead of the competition with technological innovations are critical to implementing its strategy.

Required:

a. Is Buck's strategy one of product differentiation or cost leadership? Explain briefly.

Identify at least one key element that you would expect to see included in the balanced scorecard

b. for the financial perspective.
c. for the customer perspective.
d. for the internal business process perspective.
e. for the learning and growth perspective.

Answer:

a. Buck's strategy is one of product differentiation since the company plans to offer a product that is superior and unique from the competition.

The company's balanced scorecard should describe the product differentiation strategy. Key elements should include:

b. operating income growth from charging higher margins for CM3000 for the financial perspective.
c. market share in the high-end monitor market, customer satisfaction, and new customers for the customer perspective.
d. manufacturing quality, new product features added, and order delivery time for the internal business perspective.
e. development time for new features, improvements in manufacturing technologies, employee education and skill levels, and employee satisfaction for the learning and growth perspective.

Difficulty: 2   *Objectives*: 1, 3

122. Maloney Corporation manufactures plastic water bottles. It plans to grow by producing high-quality water bottles at a low cost that are delivered in a timely manner. There are a number of other manufacturers who produce similar water bottles. Maloney believes that continuously improving its manufacturing processes and having satisfied employees are critical to implementing its strategy.

Required:

a. Is Maloney's strategy one of product differentiation or cost leadership? Explain briefly.

Identify at least one key element that you would expect to see included in the balanced scorecard

b. for the financial perspective.
c. for the customer perspective.
d. for the internal business process perspective.
e. for the learning and growth perspective.

Answer:

a. Maloney's strategy is one of cost leadership since there are a number of other manufacturers who produce similar water bottles. To succeed, Maloney will have to achieve lower costs relative to competitors through productivity and efficiency improvements, elimination of waste, and tight cost controls.

The company's balanced scorecard should describe the product differentiation strategy. Key elements should include:

b. operating income growth from productivity gains and growth for the financial perspective.
c. growth in market share, new customers, customer responsiveness, and customer satisfaction for the customer perspective.
d. yield, time to complete customer jobs, and order delivery time for the internal business perspective.
e. number of process improvements, hours of employee training, and employee satisfaction for the learning and growth perspective.

Difficulty: 2   *Objectives*: 1, 3

123. An analysis of Gardner Corporation's operating income changes between 2003 and 2004 show the following:

Operating income for 2003	$1,000,000
Add growth component	50,000
Deduct price-recovery component	(30,000)
Add productivity component	120,000
Operating income for 2004	$1,140,000

Required:

Is Gardner's operating income gain consistent with the product differentiation or cost leadership strategy? Explain briefly.

Answer:

Gardner's operating income gain is consistent with the cost leadership strategy since the increase in operating income was driven by the $120,000 gain in productivity. It appears that Gardner took advantage of its productivity gain to reduce prices and to fuel growth.

Difficulty: 2   *Objectives*: 1, 4

124. An analysis of Louis Brown Corporation's operating income changes between 2003 and 2004 show the following:

Operating income for 2003	$1,000,000
Add growth component	30,000
Add price-recovery component	200,000
Deduct productivity component	(10,000)
Operating income for 2004	$1,220,000

Required:

Is Louis Brown's operating income gain consistent with the product differentiation or cost leadership strategy? Explain briefly.

Answer:

Louis Brown's operating income gain is consistent with the product differentiation strategy since the increase in operating income was driven by the $200,000 gain in the price-recovery component. It appears that Brown's superior quality stimulated slight growth and allowed it to charge a price premium for its products.

Difficulty: 2   *Objectives*: 1, 4

125. Following a strategy of product differentiation, Ernsting Corporation makes a high-end computer monitor, CM12. Ernsting Corporation presents the following data for the years 20x3 and 20x4:

	20x3	20x4
Units of CM12 produced and sold	5,000	5,500
Selling price	$400	$440
Direct materials (pounds)	15,000	15,375
Direct materials costs per pound	$40	$44
Manufacturing capacity for CM12 (units)	10,000	10,000
Conversion costs	$1,000,000	$1,100,000
Conversion costs per unit of capacity	$100	$110
Selling and customer-service capacity (customers)	60	58
Total selling and customer-service costs	$360,000	$362,500
Selling and customer-service capacity cost per customer	$6,000	$6,250

Ernsting Corporation produces no defective units but it wants to reduce direct materials usage per unit of CM12 in 20x4. Manufacturing conversion costs in each year depend on production capacity defined in terms of CM12 units that can be produced. Selling and customer-service costs depend on the number of customers that the customer and service functions are designed to support. Ernsting Corporation has 46 customers in 20x3 and 50 customers in 20x4. The industry market size for high-end computer monitors increased 5% from 20x3 to 20x4.

Required:

a. What is operating income for 20x3?
b. What is operating income in 20x4?
c. What is the change in operating income from 20x3 to 20x4?

Answer:

a. ($400 x 5,000) - [($40 x 15,000) + ($100 x 10,000) + ($6,000 x 60)] = $40,000

b. ($440 x 5,500) – [($44 x 15,375) + ($110 x 10,000) + ($6,250 x 58)] = $281,000

c. $40,000- $281,000= $241,000 F

Difficulty: 2   *Objective*: 4

126. Following a strategy of product differentiation, Ernsting Corporation makes a high-end computer monitor, CM12. Ernsting Corporation presents the following data for the years 20x3 and 20x4:

	20x3	20x4
Units of CM12 produced and sold	5,000	5,500
Selling price	$400	$440
Direct materials (pounds)	15,000	15,375
Direct materials costs per pound	$40	$44
Manufacturing capacity for CM12 (units)	10,000	10,000
Conversion costs	$1,000,000	$1,100,000
Conversion costs per unit of capacity	$100	$110
Selling and customer-service capacity (customers)	60	58
Total selling and customer-service costs	$360,000	$362,500
Selling and customer-service capacity cost per customer	$6,000	$6,250

Ernsting Corporation produces no defective units but it wants to reduce direct materials usage per unit of CM12 in 20x4. Manufacturing conversion costs in each year depend on production capacity defined in terms of CM12 units that can be produced. Selling and customer-service costs depend on the number of customers that the customer and service functions are designed to support. Ernsting Corporation has 46 customers in 20x3 and 50 customers in 20x4. The industry market size for high-end computer monitors increased 5% from 20x3 to 20x4.

Required:

a. What is the revenue effect of the growth component?
b. What is the cost effect of the growth component?
c. What is the net effect on operating income as a result of the growth component?

Answer:

a. (5,500 - 5,000) x $400 = $200,000 F

b. 15,000 x 5,500 / 5,000 = 16,500; [(16,500 - 15,000) x $40]
   + [(10,000 - 10,000) x $100] + [(60 - 60) x $6,000] = $60,000 U

c. $200,000 F + $60,000 U = $140,000 F

Difficulty: 3   *Objective*: 4

127. Following a strategy of product differentiation, Ernsting Corporation makes a high-end computer monitor, CM12. Ernsting Corporation presents the following data for the years 20x3 and 20x4:

	20x3	20x4
Units of CM12 produced and sold	5,000	5,500
Selling price	$400	$440
Direct materials (pounds)	15,000	15,375
Direct materials costs per pound	$40	$44
Manufacturing capacity for CM12 (units)	10,000	10,000
Conversion costs	$1,000,000	$1,100,000
Conversion costs per unit of capacity	$100	$110
Selling and customer-service capacity (customers)	60	58
Total selling and customer-service costs	$360,000	$362,500
Selling and customer-service capacity cost per customer	$6,000	$6,250

Ernsting Corporation produces no defective units but it wants to reduce direct materials usage per unit of CM12 in 20x4. Manufacturing conversion costs in each year depend on production capacity defined in terms of CM12 units that can be produced. Selling and customer-service costs depend on the number of customers that the customer and service functions are designed to support. Ernsting Corporation has 46 customers in 20x3 and 50 customers in 20x4. The industry market size for high-end computer monitors increased 5% from 20x3 to 20x4.

Required:

a. What is the revenue effect of the price-recovery component?
b. What is the cost effect of the price-recovery component?
c. What is the net effect on operating income as a result of the price-recovery component?
d. What is the net effect on operating income as a result of the productivity component?

Answer:

a. ($440 - $400) x 5,500 = $220,000 F

b. 15,000 x 5,500 / 5,000 = 16,500; [($44 - $40) x 16,500] + [($110 - $100) x 10,000] + [($6,250 - $6,000) x 60] = $181,000 U

c. $220,000 F + $181,000 U = $39,000 F

d. 15,000 x 5,500 / 5,000 = 16,500; [(15,375 - 16,500) x $44]
  + [(10,000 - 10,000) x $110] + [(58 - 60) x 6,250] = $62,000 F

Difficulty: 3   *Objective*: 4

128. Power Company has been unhappy with the financial accounting variances that its cost accounting system has been producing, because its managers believe that there is more to evaluating an operation than just examining accounting numbers. Therefore, it has started gathering data to assist in the examination of nonfinancial results of operations. The following information relates to the manufacture of remote control units for televisions, radios, and stereo components:

	20x1	20x2
Remote control units produced and sold	40,000	50,000
Direct manufacture labor-hours	6,000	6,600
Direct materials used (sets)	40,300	50,250
Direct manufacture cost per hour	$18	$20
Direct materials cost per set	$31	$32

Required:

a. What is the partial productivity of direct materials for each year?
b. What is the partial productivity of direct manufacturing labor for each year?
c. Did each area improve between 20x1 and 20x2? Explain.
d. What will be the projected direct material and labor needs for 20x3 if remote control units increase by 6,000 units, assuming Power Company applies the constant returns to scale technology?

Answer:

a. 20x1 Partial productivity of direct materials = 40,000/40,300 = 0.993
   20x2 Partial productivity of direct materials = 50,000/50,250 = 0.995

b. 20x1 Partial productivity direct manufacturing labor = 40,000/6,000 = 6.67
   20x2 Partial productivity direct manufacturing labor = 50,000/6,600 = 7.58

c. Yes, both areas showed improvement because the ratios went up.

d. Production increase = 6,000/50,000 = 12 percent
   Projected direct material sets = 50,250 x 1.12 = 56,280 sets
   Projected direct manufacturing labor = 6,600 x 1.12 = 7,392 hours

Difficulty: 2   *Objective*: A

129. Grader Company manufactures road graders. Because its managers all have engineering backgrounds, they prefer nonfinancial information for their decision-making models. Therefore, they require the accountants gather data to assist in the examination of nonfinancial results of operations. The following information relates to the manufacture of a paver:

	20x1	20x2
Units produced and sold	3,400	2,800
Direct manufacture labor-hours	68,000	57,600
Direct materials used (tons)	14,500	12,200
Direct manufacture cost per hour	$21	$22
Direct materials cost per ton	$431	$443

Required:

a. What is the partial productivity for direct materials for each year?
b. What is the partial productivity for direct manufacturing labor for each year?
c. What is the total factor productivity for each year?

Answer:

a. 20x1   Partial productivity of direct materials = 3,400/14,500 = 0.234
    20x2   Partial productivity of direct materials = 2,800/12,200 = 0.230

b. 20x1   Partial productivity for direct manufacturing labor = 3,400/68,000 = 0.050
    20x2   Partial productivity for direct manufacturing labor = 2,800/57,600 = 0.049

c. 20x1   Direct materials = 14,500 x $431 = $6,249,500
         Direct manufacturing labor = 68,000 x $21 =   1,428,000
           Total $7,677,500

    20x2   Direct materials = 12,200 x $443 = $5,404,600
         Direct mfg. labor = 57,600 x $22 =   1,267,200
           Total $6,671,800

    20x1   Total factor productivity = 3,400/$7,677,500 =   0.00044

    20x2   Total factor productivity = 2,800/$6,671,800 =   0.00042

Difficulty: 3   *Objective*: A

130. Fairytale Weddings manufactures wedding dresses. The following information relates to the manufacture of gowns in its Perth plant:

	20x1	20x2
Units produced and sold	43,000	52,600
Direct manufacture labor-hours	22,000	26,000
Direct materials used (square yards)	130,000	152,000
Direct manufacture cost per hour	$16	$17
Direct materials cost per yard	$10	$11

Required:

Prepare an analysis of change in annual costs from 20x1 to 20x2 including direct materials, direct manufacturing labor, and total inputs.

Answer:

Direct materials:
Actual 20x1 costs: 130,000 x $10 =	$1,300,000
20x1 input for 20x2 output: 130,000 x 52,600/43,000 x $10 =	1,590,233
Output adjustment	$ 290,233 U

20x1 input for 20x2 output: =	$1,590,233
20x1 input with 20x2 costs: 130,000 x 52,600/43,000 x $11 =	1,749,256
Input price change	$ 159,023 U

20x1 input with 20x2 costs: =	$1,749,256
20x2 costs: 152,000 x $11 =	1,672,000
Productivity change	$ 77,256 F

Direct manufacturing labor:
Actual 20x1 costs: 22,000 x $16 =	$352,000
20x1 input for 20x2 output: 22,000 x 52,600/43,000 x $16 =	430,586
Output adjustment	$ 78,586 U

20x1 input for 20x2 output: =	$430,586
20x1 input with 20x2 costs: 22,000 x 52,600/43,000 x $17 =	457,498
Input price change	$ 26,912 U

20x1 input with 20x2 costs: =	$457,498
20x2 costs: 26,000 x $17 =	442,000
Productivity change	$ 15,498 F

All inputs:
Output adjustment: $290,233 U + $78,586 U =	$368,819 U
Input price change: $159,023 U + $26,912 U =	$185,935 U
Productivity change: $77,256 F + $15,498 F =	$ 92,754 F

Difficulty: 3 *Objective*: A

CRITICAL THINKING

131. What is the primary purpose of the balanced scorecard?

    Answer:

    The primary purpose of the balanced scorecard is to translate an organization's mission and strategy into a set of performance measures that put that strategy into action with clearly-stated objectives, measures, targets, and initiatives.

    Difficulty: 2   *Objective*:   3

132. What are the four key perspectives in the balanced scorecard?

    Answer:

    The four key perspectives in the balanced scorecard are
    a.   the financial perspective,
    b.   the customer perspective,
    c.   the internal business processes perspective, and
    d.   the learning and growth perspective.

    Difficulty: 2   *Objective*:   3

133. Describe three key components in doing a strategic analysis of operating income.

    Answer:

    The three key components in doing a strategic analysis of operating income include:
    a.   the growth component, which measures the change in operating income attributable solely to an increase in the quantity of output sold from one year to the next.

    b.   the price-recovery component, which measures the change in operating income attributable solely to changes in the prices of the inputs and the outputs from one year to the next.

    c.   the productivity component, which measures the change in costs attributable to a change in the quantity of inputs used in the current year relative to the quantity of inputs that would have been used in the previous year to produce current year output.

    Difficulty: 2   *Objective*:   4

134. Ralph Company has been very aggressive in developing various types of financial and nonfinancial measurement schemes to help with the evaluation of its manufacturing processes. It appears that some of the managers are suboptimizing in that their decision processes are geared solely for their department's benefit, sometimes to the detriment of the organization as a whole.

Required:

What changes in the evaluation system could the company implement to help minimize the suboptimization of the managers' decision-making process?

Answer:

The company could implement a total factor productivity concept. Its major advantage is that it measures the combined productivity of all inputs to produce outputs and, therefore, explicitly evaluates substitution among inputs. For example, if buying a cheap material makes the cost of materials look favorable but causes more labor-hours, therefore causing labor costs to be unfavorable, suboptimization may be occurring. The total factor productivity takes into account both the materials costs and the labor costs and if they offset each other, that is fine, but if they do not offset, then the variance will be so noted.

Difficulty: 2   *Objective*: A

135. Total factor productivity (TFP) is easy to compute for a single-product company. When dealing with a multiproduct company, one of two adjustments must be made. What are these potential adjustments?

Answer:

One of the following two adjustments must be made in the TFP calculations:

1. Convert the outputs from physical measures to a dollar value common denominator, analogous to the multiple input case.

2. Allocate the input costs to the different outputs. This is appropriate when the inputs can be reasonably allocated to the different outputs.

Difficulty: 2   *Objective*: A

CHAPTER 14: COST ALLOCATION, CUSTOMER-PROFITABILITY ANALYSIS, AND SALES-VARIANCE ANALYSIS

TRUE/FALSE

1. Indirect costs are costs that cannot be traced to cost objects in an economically feasible way.

    Answer: True   *Difficulty*:   1   *Objective*:   1

2. To motivate engineers to design simpler products, costs for production, distribution, and customer service may be included in product-cost estimates.

    Answer: True   *Difficulty*:   2   *Objective*:   1

3. For external reporting, inventoriable costs under GAAP sometimes include R&D costs.

    Answer: False   *Difficulty*:   2   *Objective*:   1

    Under GAAP, inventoriable costs include only the costs of producing and sometimes the design costs of the product.

4. Today, companies are simplifying their cost systems and moving toward less-detailed and less-complex cost allocation bases.

    Answer: False   *Difficulty*:   3   *Objective*:   2
    Companies are moving toward more-detailed and more-complex cost allocations because today technology can capture these costs in a relatively inexpensive manner.

5. When using the cause-and-effect criterion, cost drivers are selected as the cost allocation bases.

    Answer: True   *Difficulty*:   1   *Objective*:   2

6. The ability-to-bear criterion is considered superior when the purpose of cost allocation is motivation.

    Answer: False   *Difficulty*:   2   *Objective*:   2
    The *cause-and-effect* or *benefits-received* criteria is considered superior when the purpose of cost allocation is motivation.

7. The benefits of implementing a more-complex cost allocation system are relatively easy to quantify for application of the cost-benefit approach.

    Answer: False   *Difficulty*:   2   *Objective*:   2
    The benefits of implementing a more-complex cost allocation system are difficult to measure.

8. Each company must decide which corporate cost categories should be included in the indirect costs of the divisions -- all, only a subset, or none.

   Answer: True   *Difficulty:* 2   *Objective:* 3

9. Full allocation of corporate costs to divisions is justified when the notion of controllability is applied.

   Answer: False   *Difficulty:* 3   *Objective:* 3
   The controllability notion is used to justify excluding some or all corporate costs from division reports, not to justify including full costs.

10. When there is a lesser degree of homogeneity, fewer cost pools are required to accurately explain the use of company resources.

    Answer: False   *Difficulty:* 2   *Objective:* 3
    The *greater* the degree of homogeneity, the fewer the cost pools required to accurately explain the use of company resources.

11. If a cost pool is homogeneous, the cost allocations using that pool will be the same as they would be if costs of each individual activity in that pool were allocated separately.

    Answer: True   *Difficulty:* 2   *Objective:* 3

12. Facility-sustaining costs do not have a cause-and-effect relationship with individual products.

    Answer: True   *Difficulty:* 2   *Objective:* 3

13. An individual cost item can be simultaneously a direct cost of one cost object and an indirect cost of another cost object.

    Answer: True   *Difficulty:* 3   *Objective:* 3

14. All customers are equally important to a company and should receive equal levels of attention.

    Answer: False   *Difficulty:* 3   *Objective:* 4
    Customers should receive a level of attention from the company that matches their contribution to the company's profitability.

15. The purpose of price discounting is to encourage increases in customer purchases.

    Answer: True   *Difficulty:* 3   *Objective:* 4

16. There are two elements that influence customer profitability – revenues and costs.

    Answer: True   *Difficulty:* 2   *Objective:* 4

17. Companies that only record the invoice price can usually track the magnitude of price discounting.

   Answer: False   *Difficulty:* 2   *Objective:* 4
   In order to track discounting, the discount must be recorded.

18. An activity-based costing system may focus on customers rather than products.

   Answer: True   *Difficulty:* 2   *Objective:* 5

19. A customer cost hierarchy may include distribution-channel costs.

   Answer: True   *Difficulty:* 1   *Objective:* 5

20. The cost of visiting customers is an example of a customer output unit-level cost.

   Answer: False   *Difficulty:* 2   *Objective:* 5
   The cost of visiting customers is an example of a *customer-sustaining* cost.

21. In general, distribution-channel costs are more easily influenced by customer actions than customer batch-level costs.

   Answer: False   *Difficulty:* 3   *Objective:* 6
   In general, *customer batch-level costs* are more easily influenced by customer actions than distribution-channel costs.

22. If one of four distribution channels is discontinued, corporate-sustaining costs such as general administration costs will most likely be reduced by 25%.

   Answer: False   *Difficulty:* 3   *Objective:* 6
   If one of four distribution channels is discontinued, corporate-sustaining costs such as general administration costs will most likely *not be affected*.

23. To more accurately assess customer profitability, corporate-sustaining costs should be allocated.

   Answer: False   *Difficulty:* 3   *Objective:* 6
   The allocation of corporate-sustaining costs serves no useful purpose in assessing customer profitability, decision making, performance evaluation, or motivation.

24. It is common to find that a small number of customers generate a high percentage of operating income.

   Answer: True   *Difficulty:* 2   *Objective:* 6

25. The static-budget variance is the difference between an actual result and a budgeted amount in the static budget.

   Answer: True   *Difficulty:* 1   *Objective:* 7

26. The flexible-budget variance is the difference between an actual result and the flexible-budget amount based on the level of output actually achieved in the budget period.

   Answer: True   *Difficulty*: 1   *Objective*: 7

27. Additional insight can be gained by dividing the sales-mix variance into the flexible-budget variance and the sales-volume variance.

   Answer: False   *Difficulty*: 1   *Objective*: 7
   Additional insight can be gained by dividing the *static-budget variance* into the flexible-budget variance and the sales-volume variance.

28. A favorable sales-mix variance arises when the actual sales-mix percentage is less than the budgeted sales-mix percentage.

   Answer: False   *Difficulty*: 3   *Objective*: 7
   A favorable sales-mix variance arises when the actual sales-mix percentage exceeds the budgeted sales-mix percentage.

29. A composite unit is a hypothetical unit with weights based on the mix of individual units.

   Answer: True   *Difficulty*: 1   *Objective*: 7

30. The sales-mix variance can be explained in terms of the budgeted contribution margin per composite unit of the sales mix.

   Answer: True   *Difficulty*: 2   *Objective*: 7

31. The sales-quantity variance is favorable when budgeted unit sales exceed actual unit sales.

   Answer: False   *Difficulty*: 3   *Objective*: 7
   The sales-quantity variance is *unfavorable* when budgeted unit sales exceed actual unit sales.

32. The market-share variance is caused solely by the actual market share being different than the budgeted market share.

   Answer: True   *Difficulty*: 3   *Objective*: 8

33. A favorable market-size variance results with a decrease in market size.

   Answer: False   *Difficulty*: 3   *Objective*: 8
   A favorable market-size variance results with *an increase* in market size.

34. The flexible-budget variance can be further divided into the sales-mix variance and the sales-quantity variance.

Answer: False   *Difficulty*: 1   *Objective*: 8

The *sales-volume* variance can be further divided into the sales-mix variance and the sales-quantity variance.

35. The direct materials mix variance is the sum of the direct materials mix variances for each input.

Answer: True   *Difficulty*: 1   *Objective*: A

36. An unfavorable direct materials mix variance results when cheaper direct materials are substituted for more expensive direct materials.

Answer: False   *Difficulty*: 2   *Objective*: A

A *favorable* direct materials mix variance results when cheaper direct materials are substituted for more expensive direct materials.

37. A favorable direct materials yield variance results when less direct materials are used than planned.

Answer: True   *Difficulty*: 2   *Objective*: A

38. Costs which are not economically feasible to trace but are related to a cost object are known as
    a.   fixed costs.
    b.   direct costs.
    c.   indirect costs.
    d.   variable costs.

    Answer: c   *Difficulty*:   1   *Objective*:   1

39. Any item for which a separate measurement of cost is desired is known as
    a.   cost allocation.
    b.   a cost object.
    c.   a direct cost.
    d.   an indirect cost.

    Answer: b   *Difficulty*:   1   *Objective*:   1

40. Indirect costs
    a.   often comprise a large percentage of overall costs assigned to a cost object.
    b.   specifically exclude marketing costs.
    c.   cannot be used for external reporting.
    d.   are treated as period costs and not as product costs.

    Answer: a   *Difficulty*:   3   *Objective*:   1

41. All of the following illustrate purposes for allocating costs to cost objects EXCEPT
    a.   to provide information for economic decisions.
    b.   to motivate managers and employees.
    c.   to determine a selling price the market will bear.
    d.   to measure income and assets for reporting to external parties.

    Answer: c   *Difficulty*:   2   *Objective*:   1

42. The costs of all six value-chain functions should be included when determining
    a.   whether to add a new product line.
    b.   the selling price of a service.
    c.   whether to make or buy a component part from another manufacturer.
    d.   all of the above.

    Answer: d   *Difficulty*:   3   *Objective*:   1

43. R&D costs are used for which purpose of cost allocation?
    a.   To provide information for economic decisions
    b.   To report to external parties when using generally accepted accounting principles
    c.   To calculate costs of a government contract
    d.   All of the above purposes

    Answer: a   *Difficulty*:   3   *Objective*:   1

44. Which purpose of cost allocation is used to encourage sales representatives to push high-margin products or services?
 a. To provide information for economic decisions
 b. To motivate managers and other employees
 c. To justify costs or compute reimbursement
 d. To measure income and assets for reporting to external parties

 Answer: b   *Difficulty*: 2   *Objective*: 1

45. Which purpose of cost allocation is used to decide on the selling price for a customized product or service?
 a. To provide information for economic decisions
 b. To motivate managers and other employees
 c. To justify costs or compute reimbursement
 d. To measure income and assets for reporting to external parties

 Answer: a   *Difficulty*: 2   *Objective*: 1

46. To guide cost allocation decisions, the cause-and-effect criterion
 a. is used less frequently than the other criteria.
 b. is the primary criterion used in activity-based costing.
 c. is a difficult criterion on which to obtain agreement.
 d. may allocate corporate salaries to divisions based on profits.

 Answer: b   *Difficulty*: 3   *Objective*: 2

47. To guide cost allocation decisions, the benefits-received criterion
 a. generally uses the cost driver as the cost allocation base.
 b. results in subsidizing products that are not profitable.
 c. is the primarily criterion used in activity-based costing.
 d. may use an allocation base of division revenues to allocate advertising costs.

 Answer: d   *Difficulty*: 3   *Objective*: 2

48. To guide cost allocation decisions, the fairness or equity criterion
 a. is the criterion often cited in government contracts.
 b. is superior when the purpose of cost allocation is for economic decisions.
 c. is used more frequently than the other criteria.
 d. is the primary criterion used in activity-based costing.

 Answer: a   *Difficulty*: 3   *Objective*: 2

49. To guide cost allocation decisions, the ability to bear criterion
 a. is likely to be the most credible to operating personnel.
 b. allocates costs in proportion to the benefits received.
 c. results in subsidizing products that are not profitable.
 d. is the criterion often cited in government contracts.

 Answer: c   *Difficulty*: 3   *Objective*: 2

50. Which cost-allocation criterion is appropriate when making an economic decision?
    a. The fairness or equity criterion
    b. The ability to bear criterion
    c. The cause-and-effect criterion
    d. Any of the above criteria are appropriate

    Answer: d   *Difficulty:* 2   *Objective:* 2

51. Which cost-allocation criterion is MOST likely to subsidize poor performers at the expense of the best performers?
    a. The fairness or equity criterion
    b. The benefits-received criterion
    c. The ability to bear criterion
    d. The cause-and-effect criterion

    Answer: c   *Difficulty:* 2   *Objective:* 2

52. A challenge to using cost-benefit criteria for allocating costs is that
    a. the costs of designing and implementing complex cost allocations are not readily apparent.
    b. the benefits of making better-informed pricing decisions are difficult to measure.
    c. cost systems are being simplified and fewer multiple cost-allocation bases are being used.
    d. the costs of collecting and processing information keep spiraling upward.

    Answer: b   *Difficulty:* 3   *Objective:* 2

53. Corporate overhead costs can be allocated
    a. using a single cost pool.
    b. to divisions using one cost pool and then reallocating costs to products using multiple cost pools.
    c. using numerous individual corporate cost pools.
    d. using any of the above methods.

    Answer: d   *Difficulty:* 2   *Objective:* 3

54. The MOST likely reason for allocating all corporate costs to divisions include that
    a. division managers make decisions that ultimately control corporate costs.
    b. divisions receive benefits from all corporate costs.
    c. the hierarchy of costs promotes cost management.
    d. it is best to use multiple cost objects.

    Answer: b   *Difficulty:* 3   *Objective:* 3

55. The MOST likely reason for NOT allocating corporate costs to divisions include that
    a. these costs are not controllable by division managers.
    b. these costs are incurred to support division activities, not corporate activities.
    c. division resources are already used to attain corporate goals.
    d. divisions receive no benefits from corporate costs.

    Answer: a   *Difficulty:* 3   *Objective:* 3

56. Some companies only allocate corporate costs to divisions that
    a. are planned and under the control of division managers.
    b. are output unit-level costs.
    c. are perceived as causally related to division activities.
    d. are direct costs.

    Answer: c   *Difficulty:* 2   *Objective:* 3

57. Not allocating some corporate costs to divisions and products results in
    a. an increase in overall corporate profitability.
    b. the sum of individual product profitability being less than overall company profitability.
    c. the sum of individual product profitability being greater than overall company profitability.
    d. a decrease in overall corporate profitability.

    Answer: c   *Difficulty:* 3   *Objective:* 3

58. The greater the degree of homogeneity,
    a. the greater the number of needed cost pools.
    b. the fewer the number of needed cost pools.
    c. the less accurate the costs of a particular cost object.
    d. the greater the variety of cause-and-effect relationships with the cost driver.

    Answer: b   *Difficulty:* 2   *Objective:* 3

59. When individual activities within a cost pool have a similar relationship with the cost driver, those costs
    a. need to be reallocated.
    b. need multiple cost drivers.
    c. are considered a homogeneous cost pool.
    d. are considered an allocated cost pool.

    Answer: c   *Difficulty:* 2   *Objective:* 3

60. Homogeneous cost pools lead to
    a. more accurate costs of a given cost object.
    b. more resources being assigned to that cost object.
    c. the need for more cost drivers.
    d. both (a) and (c).

    Answer: a   *Difficulty:* 2   *Objective:* 3

61. Identifying homogeneous cost pools
    a. requires judgment and should be reevaluated on a regular basis.
    b. should include the input of management.
    c. should include a cost-benefit analysis.
    d. should include all of the above.

    Answer: d   *Difficulty:* 2   *Objective:* 3

62. To allocate corporate costs to divisions, the allocation base used should
    a. be an output unit-level base.
    b. have the best cause-and-effect relationship with the costs.
    c. combine administrative costs and human resource management costs.
    d. allocate the full costs.

    Answer: b   *Difficulty:* 3   *Objective:* 3

63. Corporate administrative costs allocated to a division cost pool are MOST likely
    a. output unit-level costs.
    b. facility-sustaining costs.
    c. product-sustaining costs.
    d. batch-level costs.

    Answer: b   *Difficulty:* 1   *Objective:* 3

64. To manage setup costs, a corporation might focus on
    a. the number of setup-hours.
    b. the number of units included in each production run.
    c. the batch-level costs incurred per setup-hour.
    d. both (a) and (c).

    Answer: d   *Difficulty:* 3   *Objective:* 3

THE FOLLOWING INFORMATION APPLIES TO QUESTIONS 65 THROUGH 67.
The Hassan Corporation has an Electric Mixer Division and an Electric Lamp Division. Of a
$20,000,000 bond issuance, the Electric Mixer Division utilized $14,000,000 and the Electric
Lamp Division utilized $6,000,000 for expansion. Interest costs on the bond totaled
$1,500,000 for the year.

65. What amount of interest costs should be allocated to the Electric Mixer Division?
    a. $450,000
    b. $1,050,000
    c. $4,200,000
    d. $14,000,000

    Answer: b   *Difficulty:* 2   *Objective:* 3
    $14,000,000/ $20,000,000 x $1,500,000= $1,050,000

66. What amount of interest costs should be allocated to the Electric Lamp Division?
    a. $450,000
    b. $1,050,000
    c. $4,200,000
    d. $6,000,000

    Answer: a   *Difficulty:* 2   *Objective:* 3
    $6,000,000 / $20,000,000 x $1,500,000 = $450,000

67. The above interest costs would be considered a(n)
    a. output unit-level cost.
    b. facility-sustaining cost.
    c. product-sustaining cost.
    d. batch-level cost.

    Answer: c   *Difficulty:* 2   *Objective:* · 3

68. Customers making large contributions to the profitability of the company should
    a. be treated the same as other customers since all customers are important.
    b. receive a higher level of attention from the company than less profitable customers.
    c. be charged higher prices for the same products than less profitable customers.
    d. not be offered the volume-based price discounts offered to less profitable customers.

    Answer: b   *Difficulty:* 3   *Objective:* 4

69. Price discounts are influenced by
    a. the volume of product purchased.
    b. a desire to sell to a customer in an area with high-growth potential.
    c. negotiating skills of the sales person.
    d. all of the above.

    Answer: d   *Difficulty:* 2   *Objective:* 4

70. To improve customer profitability, companies should track
    a. only the final invoice price of a sale.
    b. the volume of the products purchased by each customer.
    c. discounts taken by each customer.
    d. both (b) and (c).

    Answer: d   *Difficulty:* 2   *Objective:* 4

71. To improve customer profitability, companies should
    a. strictly enforce their volume-based price discounting policy.
    b. track discounts by customer.
    c. track discounts by sales person.
    d. both (b) and (c).

    Answer: d   *Difficulty:* 2   *Objective:* 4

72. A customer cost hierarchy categorizes costs related to customers into different cost pools on the basis of
    a. different types of cost drivers.
    b. different benefits-received relationships.
    c. different levels of cause-and-effect relationships.
    d. all of the above.

    Answer: d   *Difficulty:* 2   *Objective:* 5

73. Costs incurred to process orders would MOST likely be classified as
    a. a customer output unit-level cost.
    b. a customer batch-level cost.
    c. a customer-sustaining cost.
    d. a corporate-sustaining cost.

    Answer: b   *Difficulty*: 1   *Objective*: 5

74. Top management and general administration costs would MOST likely be classified as
    a. a customer output unit-level cost.
    b. a customer batch-level cost.
    c. a customer-sustaining cost.
    d. a corporate-sustaining cost.

    Answer: d   *Difficulty*: 1   *Objective*: 5

75. The cost of visiting customers would MOST likely be classified as
    a. a customer output unit-level cost.
    b. a customer batch-level cost.
    c. a customer-sustaining cost.
    d. a corporate-sustaining cost.

    Answer: c   *Difficulty*: 1   *Objective*: 5

76. Costs incurred to handle each unit sold would MOST likely be classified as
    a. a customer output unit-level cost.
    b. a customer batch-level cost.
    c. a customer-sustaining cost.
    d. a corporate-sustaining cost.

    Answer: a   *Difficulty*: 1   *Objective*: 5

77. _____ categorizes costs related to customers into different cost pools on the basis of either different classes of cost drivers or different degrees of difficulty in determining the cause-and-effect (or benefits-received) relationships.
    a. Customer-profitability analysis
    b. Customer revenues
    c. Customer cost hierarchy
    d. Price discounting

    Answer: c   *Difficulty*: 1   *Objective*: 5

78. An advantage of using a bar chart to visualize customer profitability is that
    a. differences in commissions paid to sales persons stand out.
    b. loss customers stand out.
    c. trends in the volume of purchases become apparent.
    d. all of the above are advantages.

    Answer: b   *Difficulty*: 3   *Objective*: 6

79. Customer actions will LEAST affect
    a. customer output unit-level costs.
    b. customer batch-level costs.
    c. customer-sustaining costs.
    d. distribution-channel costs.

    Answer: d   *Difficulty:* 2   *Objective:* 6

80. To reduce distribution-channel costs, a company could
    a. improve the efficiency of the ordering process.
    b. make fewer customer visits.
    c. eliminate distribution to retailers and only service wholesalers.
    d. do any of the above.

    Answer: c   *Difficulty:* 3   *Objective:* 6

81. Corporate-sustaining costs
    a. are common to all individual customers.
    b. have a clear cause-and-effect relationship with several cost-allocation bases.
    c. should be allocated for decisions regarding reducing customer costs.
    d. apply to all of the above.

    Answer: a   *Difficulty:* 3   *Objective:* 6

82. The allocation of corporate-sustaining costs is useful for
    a. evaluating the performance of salespersons with individual customer accounts.
    b. motivating distribution-channel management.
    c. focusing on the cause-and-effect relationships with the cost-allocation bases.
    d. none of the above.

    Answer: d   *Difficulty:* 3   *Objective:* 6

83. If deciding whether to eliminate a distribution channel, allocating corporate-sustaining costs to distribution channels
    a. helps define cost reduction possibilities.
    b. gives the misleading impression of potential cost savings.
    c. identifies administrative inefficiencies.
    d. evaluates the effectiveness of sales personnel.

    Answer: b   *Difficulty:* 3   *Objective:* 6

84. When corporate-sustaining costs are fully allocated to distribution channels then the sum of the distribution-channel operating incomes
    a. is less than company-wide operating income.
    b. is equal to company-wide operating income.
    c. is greater than company-wide operating income.
    d. cannot be determined.

    Answer: b   *Difficulty:* 3   *Objective:* 6

85. Corporate-sustaining costs should be allocated
    a. to motivate changes in customer behavior.
    b. to evaluate distribution-channel managers.
    c. to determine the selling price that will cover all costs.
    d. to identify the most profitable customers.

    Answer: c   *Difficulty:* 3   *Objective:* 6

86. A common finding in many studies is that a high percentage of operating income is
    a. contributed by a small number of customers.
    b. contributed to evenly by most customers.
    c. the result of high discounting.
    d. the result of cooperative efforts by many low-volume customers.

    Answer: a   *Difficulty:* 2   *Objective:* 6

87. Loss-causing customers
    a. should be eliminated.
    b. should be evaluated for ways to become profitable customers.
    c. should be retained because each customer adds to long-run profitability.
    d. do not exist because additional customer sales always increase profits.

    Answer: b   *Difficulty:* 3   *Objective:* 6

88. Customers are more valuable when they are all EXCEPT
    a. well known in the community.
    b. expected to continue to do business with a company.
    c. in an industry with high-growth potential.
    d. require special attention on a regular basis.

    Answer: d   *Difficulty:* 3   *Objective:* 6

89. Dropping an unprofitable customer will
    a. eliminate long-run costs assigned to that customer.
    b. eliminate most short-run costs assigned to that customer.
    c. decrease long-run profitability.
    d. increase the potential to cross-sell other products that are more desirable.

    Answer: b   *Difficulty:* 3   *Objective:* 6

90. More insight into the static-budget variance can be gained by subdividing it into
    a. the sales-mix variance and the sales-quantity variance.
    b. the market-share variance and the market-size variance.
    c. the flexible-budget variance and the sales-volume variance.
    d. a cost hierarchy.

    Answer: c   *Difficulty:* 1   *Objective:* 7

91. The static-budget variance will be favorable when
    a.   actual unit sales are less than budgeted unit sales.
    b.   the actual contribution margin is greater than the static-budget contribution margin.
    c.   the actual sales mix shifts toward the less profitable units.
    d.   the composite unit for the actual mix is greater than for the budgeted mix.

    Answer: b   *Difficulty*:   3   *Objective*:   7

92. More insight into the sales-volume variance can be gained by subdividing it into
    a.   the sales-mix variance and the sales-quantity variance.
    b.   the market-share variance and the market-size variance.
    c.   the flexible-budget variance and the market-size variance.
    d.   a cost hierarchy.

    Answer: a   *Difficulty*:   1   *Objective*:   7

93. The budgeted contribution margin per composite unit for the budgeted mix can be computed by
    a.   dividing the total budgeted contribution margin by the actual total units.
    b.   dividing the total budgeted contribution margin by the total budgeted units.
    c.   dividing the actual total contribution margin by the total actual total units
    d.   dividing the actual total contribution margin by the total budgeted units.

    Answer: b   *Difficulty*:   1   *Objective*:   7

94. The sales-mix variance results from a difference between the
    a.   actual market share and the budgeted market share.
    b.   actual contribution margin and the budgeted contribution margin.
    c.   budgeted contribution margin per composite unit for the actual mix and the budgeted contribution margin per composite unit for the budgeted mix.
    d.   actual market size in units and the budgeted market size in units.

    Answer: c   *Difficulty*:   2   *Objective*:   7

95. The sales-mix variance will be unfavorable when
    a.   the actual sales mix shifts toward the less profitable units.
    b.   the composite unit for the actual mix is greater than for the budgeted mix.
    c.   actual unit sales are less than budgeted unit sales.
    d.   the actual contribution margin is greater than the static-budget contribution margin.

    Answer: a   *Difficulty*:   3   *Objective*:   7

96. The sales-mix variance will be favorable when
   a. the actual contribution margin is greater than the static-budget contribution margin.
   b. actual unit sales are less than budgeted unit sales.
   c. the actual sales mix shifts toward the less profitable units.
   d. the composite unit for the actual mix is greater than for the budgeted mix.

   Answer: d   *Difficulty:* 3   *Objective:* 7

97. An unfavorable sales-mix variance would MOST likely be caused by
   a. a new competitor providing better service in the high-margin product sector.
   b. a competitor having distribution problems with high-margin products.
   c. the company offering low-margin products at a higher price.
   d. the company experiencing quality-control problems that get negative media coverage of low-margin products.

   Answer: a   *Difficulty:* 3   *Objective:* 7

98. A shift towards a mix of products with a lower contribution-margin per unit will MOST likely result in
   a. an unfavorable sales-mix variance.
   b. an unfavorable sales-quantity variance.
   c. a favorable sales-mix variance.
   d. a favorable sales-quantity variance.

   Answer: a   *Difficulty:* 2   *Objective:* 7

99. The sales-quantity variance will be unfavorable when
   a. the composite unit for the actual mix is greater than for the budgeted mix.
   b. actual unit sales are less than budgeted unit sales.
   c. the actual contribution margin is greater than the static-budget contribution margin.
   d. the actual sales mix shifts toward the less profitable units.

   Answer: b   *Difficulty:* 3   *Objective:* 7

100. A favorable sales-quantity variance would MOST likely be caused by
   a. a new competitor providing better service in the high-margin product sector.
   b. a competitor having distribution problems with high-margin products.
   c. the company offering low-margin products at a higher price.
   d. the company experiencing quality-control problems that get negative media coverage of low-margin products.

   Answer: b   *Difficulty:* 3   *Objective:* 7

101. (Actual sales quantity in units - Static budget sales quantity in units) x Budgeted contribution margin per unit =
    a.   the sales-volume variance.
    b.   the sales-mix variance.
    c.   the sales-quantity variance.
    d.   the market-share variance.

    Answer: a   *Difficulty:*   2   *Objective:*   7

102. The sales-quantity variance results from a difference between
    a.   the actual sales mix and the budgeted sales mix.
    b.   the actual quantity of units sold and the budgeted quantity of unit sales in the static budget.
    c.   actual contribution margin and the budgeted contribution margin.
    d.   actual market size in units and the budgeted market size in units.

    Answer: b   *Difficulty:*   2   *Objective:*   7

THE FOLLOWING INFORMATION APPLIES TO QUESTIONS 103 THROUGH 106.
Ceylon Tea Products has an exclusive contract with British Distributors. Calamine and Ceylon are two brands of teas that are imported and sold to retail outlets. The following information is provided for the month of March:

	Actual		**Budget**	
	Calamine	Ceylon	Calamine	Ceylon
Sales in pounds	1,700 lbs.	1,800 lbs.	2,000 lbs.	1,500 lbs
Price per pound	$2.50	$2.50	$2.00	$3.00
Variable cost per pound	1.00	2.00	1.00	1.50
Contribution margin	$1.50	$0.50	$1.00	$1.50

Budgeted and actual fixed corporate-sustaining costs are $1,750 and $2,000, respectively.

103. What is the actual contribution margin for the month?
    a. $3,750
    b. $4,400
    c. $4,250
    d. $3,450

    Answer: d   *Difficulty:*   2   *Objective:*   7
    (1,700 x $1.50) + (1,800 x $0.50) = $3,450

104. What is the contribution margin for the flexible budget?
    a. $3,750
    b. $4,400
    c. $4,250
    d. $3,450

    Answer: b   *Difficulty:*   2   *Objective:*   7
    (1,700 x $1.00) + (1,800 x $1.50) = $4,400

105. For the contribution margin, what is the total static-budget variance?
   a. $300 favorable
   b. $950 unfavorable
   c. $500 favorable
   d. $800 unfavorable

   Answer: d   *Difficulty:* 2   *Objective:* 7
   $800 unfavorable = $4,250 - $3,450

106. For the contribution margin, what is the total flexible-budget variance?
   a. $300 favorable
   b. $950 unfavorable
   c. $500 favorable
   d. $800 unfavorable

   Answer: b   *Difficulty:* 2   *Objective:* 7
   $950 unfavorable = $4,400 - $3,450

THE FOLLOWING INFORMATION APPLIES TO QUESTIONS 107 THROUGH 109.
Edna's Flowering Plants provides the following information for the month of May:

	Actual		**Budget**	
	Tulips	Geraniums	Tulips	Geraniums
Sales in units	1,950	1,800	2,250	1,500
Contribution margin per unit	$11	$18	$10	$20

107. What is the budgeted contribution margin per composite unit for the actual mix?
   a. $13.80
   b. $14.00
   c. $14.36
   d. $14.80

   Answer: d   *Difficulty:* 2   *Objective:* 7
   [$10 x (1,950/3,750)] + [$20 x (1,800/3,750)] = $14.80

108. What is the budgeted contribution margin per composite unit for the budgeted mix?
   a. $13.80
   b. $14.00
   c. $14.36
   d. $14.80

   Answer: b   *Difficulty:* 2   *Objective:* 7
   [$10 x (2,250/3,750)] + [$20 x (1,500/3,750)] = $14.00

109. For May, Edna will report
   a. a favorable sales-mix variance.
   b. an unfavorable sales-mix variance.
   c. a favorable sales-volume variance.
   d. an unfavorable sales-volume variance.

   Answer: a   *Difficulty:* 2   *Objective:* 7

THE FOLLOWING INFORMATION APPLIES TO QUESTIONS 110 THROUGH 112.
Edna's Flowering Plants provides the following information for the month of May:

	Actual		**Budget**	
	Fuchsia	Dogwood	Fuchsia	Dogwood
Sales in units	10,000	2,500	8,000	2,000
Contribution margin per unit	$9	$7	$10	$8

110. What is the budgeted contribution margin per composite unit for the actual mix?
    a. $8.00
    b. $8.60
    c. $9.00
    d. $9.60

Answer: d   *Difficulty*: 2   *Objective*: 7
[$10 x (10,000/12,500)] + [$8 x (2,500/12,500)] = $9.60

111. What is the budgeted contribution margin per composite unit for the budgeted mix?
    a. $8.00
    b. $8.60
    c. $9.00
    d. $9.60

Answer: d   *Difficulty*: 2   *Objective*: 7
[$10 x (8,000/10,000)] + [$8 x (2,000/10,000)] = $9.60

112. For May, Edna will report
    a. a favorable sales-mix variance.
    b. an unfavorable sales-mix variance.
    c. a favorable sales-volume variance.
    d. an unfavorable sales-volume variance.

Answer: c   *Difficulty*: 3   *Objective*: 7

THE FOLLOWING INFORMATION APPLIES TO QUESTIONS 113 THROUGH 116.
The XTRA Appliance Manufacturing Corporation manufactures two vacuum cleaners, the Standard and the Super. The following information was gathered about the two products:

	Standard	Super
Budgeted sales in units	3,200	800
Budgeted selling price	$300	$850
Budgeted contribution margin per unit	$210	$550
Actual sales in units	3,500	1,500
Actual selling price	$325	$840

113. What is the budgeted sales-mix percentage for the Standard and the Super vacuum cleaners, respectively?
   a.   0.80 and 0.20
   b.   0.70 and 0.30
   c.   0.20 and 0.80
   d.   0.30 and 0.70

   Answer: a   *Difficulty:*   1   *Objective:*   7
   3,200/(3,200 + 800) and 800/(3,200 + 800)

114. What is the total sales-volume variance in terms of the contribution margin?
   a. $108,000 unfavorable
   b. $108,000 favorable
   c. $278,000 favorable
   d. $448,000 favorable

   Answer: d   *Difficulty:*   2   *Objective:*   7
   Standard   = (3,500 - 3,200) x $210 = $ 63,000 F
   Super   = (1,500 - 800) x $550 =   385,000 F
                                                                      $448,000 F

115. What is the total sales-quantity variance in terms of the contribution margin?
   a. $110,000 favorable
   b. $170,000 favorable
   c. $278,000 favorable
   d. $448,000 favorable

   Answer: c   *Difficulty:*   2   *Objective:*   7
   Standard   = (5,000 - 4,000) x .8 x 210 = $168,000 F
   Super   = (5,000 - 4,000) x .2 x 550 =   110,000 F
                                                                      $278,000 F

116. What is the total sales-mix variance in terms of the contribution margin?
    a. $110,000 favorable
    b. $170,000 favorable
    c. $278,000 favorable
    d. $448,000 favorable

    Answer: b   *Difficulty:* 2   *Objective:* 7
    Standard   = 5,000 x (.7 - .8) x 210 = $105,000 U
    Super   = 5,000 x (.3 - .2) x 550 = $275,000 F
                                                 $170,000 F

117. More insight into the sales-quantity variance can be gained by subdividing it into
    a.   the sales-mix variance and the sales-volume variance.
    b.   the market-share variance and the market-size variance.
    c.   the flexible-budget variance and the sales-volume variance.
    d.   a cost hierarchy.

    Answer: b   *Difficulty:* 1   *Objective:* 8

118. The market-share variance results from a difference between the
    a.   actual market share and the budgeted market share.
    b.   actual contribution margin and the budgeted contribution margin.
    c.   budgeted contribution margin per composite unit for the actual mix and the budgeted contribution margin per composite unit for the budgeted mix.
    d.   actual market size in units and the budgeted market size in units.

    Answer: a   *Difficulty:* 1   *Objective:* 8

119. The market-share variance will be favorable when
    a.   the flexible-budget contribution margin is greater than the static-budget contribution margin.
    b.   the actual market share is greater than the budgeted market share.
    c.   actual market size in units is less than budgeted market size in units.
    d.   actual unit sales are less than budgeted unit sales.

    Answer: b   *Difficulty:* 2   *Objective:* 8

120. The market-share variance is MOST influenced by
    a.   economic downturns in the economy.
    b.   how well managers perform relative to their peers.
    c.   shifts in consumer preferences that are outside of the manager's control.
    d.   rates of inflation.

    Answer: b   *Difficulty:* 3   *Objective:* 8

121. An unfavorable market-share variance would MOST likely be caused by
    a. a competitor providing better service.
    b. a competitor having distribution problems.
    c. the company offering products at a lower price.
    d. the company experiencing quality-control problems that get negative media coverage.

    Answer: a   *Difficulty:* 3   *Objective:* 8

122. The market-size variance results from a difference between the
    a. actual market share and the budgeted market share.
    b. actual contribution margin and the budgeted contribution margin.
    c. budgeted contribution margin per composite unit for the actual mix and the budgeted contribution margin per composite unit for the budgeted mix.
    d. actual market size in units and the budgeted market size in units.

    Answer: d   *Difficulty:* 1   *Objective:* 8

123. The market-size variance will be unfavorable when
    a. the flexible-budget contribution margin is greater than the static-budget contribution margin.
    b. the actual market share is greater than the budgeted market share.
    c. actual market size in units is less than budgeted market size in units.
    d. actual unit sales are less than budgeted unit sales.

    Answer: c   *Difficulty:* 2   *Objective:* 8

124. A favorable market-size variance would MOST likely be caused by
    a. the company reducing the services provided to customers.
    b. an increase in overall market size.
    c. a new competitor moving into the area.
    d. a competitor providing better prices.

    Answer: b   *Difficulty:* 3   *Objective:* 8

125. Reliable information about market size and market share is available
    a. for no industries.
    b. for the management consulting and personal financial planning industries.
    c. for the automobile and television industries.
    d. for all industries.

    Answer: c   *Difficulty:* 2   *Objective:* 8

THE FOLLOWING INFORMATION APPLIES TO QUESTIONS 126 THROUGH 128.
Zorro Company manufactures remote control devices for garage doors. The following information was collected during June:

Actual market size (units)	10,000
Actual market share	32%
Actual average selling price	$10.00
Budgeted market size (units)	11,000
Budgeted market share	30%
Budgeted average selling price	$11.00
Budgeted contribution margin per composite unit for budgeted mix	$ 5.00

126. What is the market-size variance?
    a. $500 U
    b. $1,500 U
    c. $1,600 F
    d. $1,000 F

    Answer: b   *Difficulty:*   2   *Objective:*   8
    (10,000 – 11,000) x 0.30 x $5 = $1,500 U

127. What is the market-share variance?
    a. $1,000 F
    b. $1,100 F
    c. $500 U
    d. $1,500 U

    Answer: a   *Difficulty:*   2   *Objective:*   8
    10,000 x (0.32 – 0.30) x $5 = $1,000 F

128. What is the sales-quantity variance?
    a. $1,500 U
    b. $1,000 F
    c. $500 U
    d.   The variance cannot be determined.

    Answer: c   *Difficulty:*   2   *Objective:*   8
    $1,500 U + $1,000 F = $500 U

THE FOLLOWING INFORMATION APPLIES TO QUESTIONS 129 THROUGH 137.
The Sasita Corporation manufactures two types of vacuum cleaners, the ZENITH for commercial building use and the House-Helper for residences. Budgeted and actual operating data for the year 20x3 were as follows:

Static Budget	ZENITH	House-Helper	Total
Number sold	5,000	20,000	25,000
Contribution margin	$1,500,000	$3,000,000	$4,500,000

Actual Results	ZENITH	House-Helper	Total
Number sold	4,000	28,000	32,000
Contribution margin	$1,280,000	$3,920,000	$5,200,000

Prior to the beginning of the year, a consulting firm estimated the total volume for vacuum cleaners of the ZENITH and House-Helper category to be 250,000 units, but actual industry volume was 256,000 units.

129. What is the contribution margin for the flexible budget?
   a. $1,200,000
   b. $4,200,000
   c. $5,200,000
   d. $5,400,000

Answer: d   *Difficulty*:   2   *Objective*:   7
Budgeted contribution margin per unit:
ZENITH = $1,500,000/5,000 = $300   House-Helper = $3,000,000/20,000 = $150
Flexible-budget contribution margin: 4,000 x $300 = $1,200,000
                                            28,000 x $150 =   4,200,000
                                                           $5,400,000

130. What is the total static-budget variance in terms of the contribution margin?
   a. $900 favorable
   b. $700 favorable
   c. $200 unfavorable
   d. $360 unfavorable

Answer: b   *Difficulty*:   1   *Objective*:   7
$700 favorable = $4,500,000 - $5,200,000

131. What is the total flexible-budget variance in terms of the contribution margin?
   a. $900 favorable
   b. $700 favorable
   c. $200 unfavorable
   d. $360 unfavorable

Answer: c   *Difficulty*:   2   *Objective*:   7
$200 unfavorable = $5,400,000 - $5,200,000

132. What is the total sales-volume variance in terms of the contribution margin?
    a. $900 favorable
    b. $1,260 favorable
    c. $200 unfavorable
    d. $360 unfavorable

Answer: a   *Difficulty:* 2   *Objective:* 7
$900 favorable = $4,500,000 - $5,400,000

133. What is the total sales-quantity variance in terms of the contribution margin?
    a. $200 unfavorable
    b. $900 favorable
    c. $360 unfavorable
    d. $1,260 favorable

Answer: d   *Difficulty:* 3   *Objective:* 7
   Budgeted sales-mix percentage:
   ZENITH = 5,000/25,000 = 0.20   House-Helper = 20,000/25,000 = 0.80
   Actual sales-mix percentage:
   ZENITH = 4,000/32,000 = 0.125   House-Helper = 28,000/32,000 = 0.875

Sales-quantity variance	Actual units of all products sold – Budgeted units of all products sold	Budgeted sales-mix %	Budgeted CM per unit	Sales-quantity variance
ZENITH	(32,000 – 25,000) x	0.20 x	$300	= $ 420,000 F
House-Helper	(32,000 – 25,000) x	0.80 x	$150	= $ 840,000 F
Total				$1,260,000 F

134. What is the total sales-mix variance in terms of the contribution margin?
    a. $200 unfavorable
    b. $360 unfavorable
    c. $900 favorable
    d. $1,260 favorable

Answer: b   *Difficulty:* 3   *Objective:* 7

Sales-mix variance	Actual units of all products sold	Actual sales-mix % - Budgeted sales-mix %	Budgeted CM per unit	Sales-mix variance
ZENITH	32,000 x	(0.125 - 0.200) x	$300	= $720,000 F
House-Helper	32,000 x	(0.875 - 0.800) x	$150	= $360,000 U
Total				$360,000 U

135. What is the budgeted contribution margin per composite unit of the budgeted mix?
   a. $140.625
   b. $180.000
   c. $208.000
   d. $162.500

Answer: b   *Difficulty*: 2   *Objective*: 8
   ZENITH = $300 x .2 = $ 60
   House-Helper = $150 x .8 =   120
   OR $4,500,000/25,000 = $180

136. What is the market-size variance?
   a. $1,152,000 F
   b. $108,000 F
   c. $360,000 U
   d. $1,260,000 F

Answer: b   *Difficulty*: 3   *Objective*: 8
   Actual market share = 32,000/256,000 = 0.125
   Budgeted market share = 25,000/250,000 = 0.100.

Market-size variance	Actual market size in units - Budgeted market size in units	Budgeted market share	Budgeted CM per composite unit for budgeted mix	Market-size variance
Sasita Corp	(256,000 - 250,000) x	0.100 x	$180	= $108,000 F

137. What is the market-share variance?
   a. $360,000 U
   b. $1,260,000 F
   c. $1,152,000 F
   d. $108,000 F

Answer: c   *Difficulty*: 3   *Objective*: 8

Market-share variance	Actual market size in units	Actual market share – Budgeted market share	Budgeted CM per composite unit for budgeted mix	Market-share variance
Sasita Corp	256,000 x	(0.125 - 0.100) x	$180	= $1,152,000 F

138. More insight into the flexible-budget variance for direct materials can be gained by subdividing it into the direct materials
    a. mix and volume variances.
    b. market-share and market-size variances.
    c. mix and yield variances.
    d. price and efficiency variances.

    Answer: d   *Difficulty:* 2   *Objective:* A

139. More insight into the efficiency variance for direct materials can be gained by subdividing it into the direct materials
    a. mix and volume variances.
    b. market-share and market-size variances.
    c. mix and yield variances.
    d. price and efficiency variances.

    Answer: c   *Difficulty:* 2   *Objective:* A

140. The direct materials mix variance will be favorable when
    a. the flexible-budget contribution margin is greater than the actual contribution margin.
    b. the actual direct materials input mix is less expensive than the budgeted direct materials input mix.
    c. the actual quantity of total inputs used is greater than the flexible budget for total inputs.
    d. actual unit sales are less than budgeted unit sales.

    Answer: b   *Difficulty:* 2   *Objective:* A

141. The materials yield variance will be unfavorable when
    a. the flexible-budget contribution margin is greater than the actual contribution margin.
    b. the actual direct materials input mix is less expensive than the budgeted direct materials input mix.
    c. the actual quantity of total inputs used is greater than the flexible budget for total inputs.
    d. actual unit sales are less than budgeted unit sales.

    Answer: c   *Difficulty:* 2   *Objective:* A

142. The direct materials mix variance is the
    a. average of the direct materials mix variances for each input.
    b. sum of the direct materials mix variances for each input.
    c. difference between the direct materials mix variances for each input.
    d. multiple of the direct materials mix variances for each input.

    Answer: b   *Difficulty:* 2   *Objective:* A

EXERCISES AND PROBLEMS

143. For each cost pool listed select an appropriate allocation base from the list below. An allocation base may be used only once. Assume a manufacturing company.

Allocation bases for which the information system can provide data:

1. Number of employees per department
2. Employee wages and salaries per department
3. Production facility square footage
4. Hours of operation of each production department
5. Machine hours by department
6. Operations costs of each department
7. Hours of computer use per month per department
8. Indirect labor-hours per department

Cost pools:

_____   a. Vice President of Finance's office expenses
_____   b. Computer operations used in conjunction with manufacturing
_____   c. Personnel Department
_____   d. Manufacturing machinery cost
_____   e. Energy costs

Answer:

a. Operations costs of each department
b. Hours of computer use per month per department
c. Number of employees per department
d. Machine-hours by department
e. Hours of operation of each production department

Difficulty: 2   *Objective*: 3

144. Handy-Man Services is a repair-service company specializing in small household jobs. Each client pays a fixed monthly service fee based on the number of rooms in the house. Records are kept on the time and material costs used for each repair. The following profitability data apply to five customers:

	Customer Revenues	Customer Costs
Marveline Burnett	$300	$225
J Jackson	200	305
Roger Jones	80	75
Paul Saas	75	110
Becky Stephan	350	220

Required:
a. Compute the operating income for each of the five customers.
b. What options should Handy-Man Services consider in light of the customer-profitability results?
c. What problems might Handy-Man Services encounter in accurately estimating the operating costs of each customer?

Answer:
a.

	Customer Revenues	Customer Costs	Operating income
Marveline Burnett	$300	$225	$ 75
J Jackson	200	305	(105)
Roger Jones	80	75	5
Paul Saas	75	110	(35)
Becky Stephan	350	220	130

b. 1. Pay increased attention to the profitable customers Stephan and Burnett.
2. Seek ways of reducing costs and increasing revenues for the loss accounts of J Jackson and Paul Saas. Work with the customers so their behavior reduces overall costs. Reduce costs with better scheduling. Maybe a different fee schedule needs to be implemented depending on the age of the house, the distance to the home, if the repair is preventive or an emergency, etc. Determine whether the operating income pattern will probably continue or not and why.
3. As a last resort, the company may want to discontinue the Jackson account if the customer does not agree to a fee increase and the operating loss pattern is expected to continue.

c. Problems in accurately estimating operating costs of each customer include:
1. The basic underlying records may not be accurate.
2. Some repair personnel may be efficient and more experienced, others may be less experienced and slower, and still others may chit-chat more with the clients than others.
3. Costs that are allocated to more than one customer may be distorting operating income. For example, how is the cost of a trip for parts for three different customers allocated?

Difficulty: 2   *Objective*:   6

145. Aromatic Coffee, Inc., sells two types of coffee, Colombian and Blue Mountain. The monthly budget for U.S. coffee sales is based on a combination of last year's performance, a forecast of industry sales, and the company's expected share of the U.S. market. The following information is provided for March:

	Actual		**Budget**	
	Colombian	Blue Mountain	Colombian	Blue Mountain
Sales in pounds	7,000 lbs.	8,000 lbs.	6,400 lbs.	8,600 lbs
Price per pound	$25	$30	$25	$30
Variable cost per pound	11	14	12	13
Contribution margin	$14	$16	$13	$17

Budgeted and actual fixed corporate-sustaining costs are $60,000 and $72,000, respectively.

Required:

a. Calculate the actual contribution margin for the month.
b. Calculate the contribution margin for the static budget.
c. Calculate the contribution margin for the flexible budget.
d. Determine the total static-budget variance, the total flexible-budget variance, and the total sales-volume variance in terms of the contribution margin.

Answer:

a. Actual contribution margin:

$$7,000 \times \$14 = \$\ 98,000$$
$$8,000 \times \$16 = \ \underline{128,000}$$
$$\underline{\$226,000}$$

b. Static-budget contribution margin:

$$6,400 \times \$13 = \$\ 83,200$$
$$8,600 \times \$17 = \ \underline{146,200}$$
$$\underline{\$229,400}$$

c. Flexible-budget contribution margin:

$$7,000 \times \$13 = \$\ 91,000$$
$$8,000 \times \$17 = \ \underline{136,000}$$
$$\underline{\$227,000}$$

d. Static-budget variance is $3,400 unfavorable = $229,400 - $226,000
Flexible-budget variance is $1,000 unfavorable = $227,000 - $226,000
Sales-volume variance is $2,400 unfavorable = $229,400 - $227,000

Difficulty: 2   *Objective:* 7

146. Harry's Electronics manufactures TVs and VCRs. During February, the following activities occurred:

	TVs	VCRs
Budgeted units sold	17,640	66,360
Budgeted contribution margin per unit	$90	$156
Actual units sold	20,000	80,000
Actual contribution margin per unit	$100	$158

Required:

Compute the following variances in terms of the contribution margin.

a. Determine the total sales-mix variance.

b. Determine the total sales-quantity variance.

c. Determine the total sales-volume variance.

Answer:

a. TVs [(100,000 x 0.20) x $90] = $1,800,000
    [(100,000 x 0.21) x $90] = 1,890,000
    $ 90,000 unfavorable

    VCRs [(100,000 x 0.80) x $156] = $12,480,000
    (100,000 x 0.79) x $156] = 12,324,000
    $ 156,000 favorable

Total sales-mix variance = $90,000 unfavorable + $156,000 favorable = $66,000 favorable.

b. TVs {[(100,000 - 84,000) x 0.21] x $90} = $ 302,400 favorable
    VCRs {[(100,000 - 84,000) x 0.79] x $156} = 1,971,840 favorable
    Total sales-quantity variance $2,274,240 favorable

c. Total sales-volume variance = $66,000 favorable + $2,274,240 favorable = $2,340,240 favorable

Difficulty: 3   *Objective:* 7

147. Speedy Printing manufactures soft cover books. For January, the following information is available:

Budgeted market size (units)	125,000
Budgeted market share	18%
Budgeted average contribution margin per unit	$1.20
Actual market size (units)	100,000
Actual market share	19%
Actual average contribution margin per unit	$1.22

Required:

Compute the market-share variance, the market-size variance, and the sales-quantity variance in terms of the contribution margin.

Answer:

100,000 x 0.19 x $1.20	100,000 x 0.18 x $1.20	125,000 x 0.18 x $1.20
= $22,800	= $21,600	= $27,000

Market-share variance $1,200 F   Market-size variance $5,400 U

Sales-quantity variance $4,200 U

Difficulty: 2   *Objective:* 8

148. The Omega Corporation manufactures two types of vacuum cleaners, the ZENITH for commercial building use and the House-Helper for residences. Budgeted and actual operating data for the year 20x3 are as follows:

Static Budget	ZENITH	House-Helper	Total
Number sold	15,000	60,000	75,000
Contribution margin	$3,750,000	$12,000,000	$15,750,000

Actual Results	ZENITH	House-Helper	Total
Number sold	16,500	38,500	55,000
Contribution margin	$6,200,000	$10,200,000	$16,400,000

Required:

a. Calculate the contribution margin for the flexible budget.
b. Determine the total static-budget variance, the total flexible-budget variance, and the total sales-volume variance in terms of the contribution margin.

Answer:

Budgeted contribution margin per unit:
ZENITH = $3,750,000/15,000 = $250 House-Helper = $12,000,000/60,000 = $200

a. Flexible-budget contribution margin: 16,500 x $250 = $ 4,125,000
    38,500 x $200 =   7,700,000
    $11,825,000

b. Static-budget variance is $650 favorable = $15,750,000- $16,400,000
    Flexible-budget variance is $4,575 favorable = $11,825,000 - $16,400,000
    Sales-volume variance is $3,925 unfavorable = $15,750,000- $11,825,000

Difficulty: 2   *Objective:* 7

149. The Omega Corporation manufactures two types of vacuum cleaners, the ZENITH for commercial building use and the House-Helper for residences. Budgeted and actual operating data for the year 20x3 are as follows:

Static Budget	ZENITH	House-Helper	Total
Number sold	15,000	60,000	75,000
Contribution margin	$3,750,000	$12,000,000	$15,750,000

Actual Results	ZENITH	House-Helper	Total
Number sold	16,500	38,500	55,000
Contribution margin	$6,200,000	$10,200,000	$16,400,000

Required:
Compute the sales-mix variance and the sales-quantity variance by type of vacuum cleaner, and in total. (In terms of the contribution margin.)

Answer:
Budgeted sales-mix percentage:
ZENITH = 15,000/75,000 = 20%   House-Helper = 60,000/75,000 = 80%

Actual sales-mix percentage:
ZENITH = 16,500/55,000 = 30%   House-Helper = 38,500/55,000 = 70%

Budgeted contribution margin per unit:
ZENITH = $3,750,000/15,000 = $250   House-Helper = $12,000,000/60,000 = $200

Sales-mix variance	Actual units of all products sold	Actual sales-mix % - Budgeted sales-mix %	Budgeted CM per unit	Sales-mix variance
ZENITH	55,000 x	(0.3 - 0.2) x	$250	= $1,375,000 F
House-Helper	55,000 x	(0.7 -0.8) x	$200	= $1,100,000 U
Total				$ 275,000 F

Sales-quantity variance	Actual units of all products sold – Budgeted units of all products sold	Budgeted sales-mix %	Budgeted CM per unit	Sales-quantity variance
ZENITH	(55,000 – 75,000) x	0.2 x	$250	= $1,000,000 U
House-Helper	(55,000 – 75,000) x	0.8 x	$200	= $3,200,000 U
Total				$4,200,000 U

Difficulty: 3   *Objective:*   7

150. The Omega Corporation manufactures two types of vacuum cleaners, the ZENITH for commercial building use and the House-Helper for residences. Budgeted and actual operating data for the year 20x3 are as follows:

Static Budget	ZENITH	House-Helper	Total
Number sold	15,000	60,000	75,000
Contribution margin	$3,750,000	$12,000,000	$15,750,000

Actual Results	ZENITH	House-Helper	Total
Number sold	16,500	38,500	55,000
Contribution margin	$6,200,000	$10,200,000	$16,400,000

Prior to the beginning of the year, a consulting firm estimated the total volume for vacuum cleaners of the Zenith and House-Helper category to be 300,000 units, but actual industry volume was only 275,000 units.

Required:
Compute the market-share variance and market-size variance in terms of the contribution margin.

Answer:
Actual market share: =   55,000/275,000 =   0.20

Budgeted market share: =   75,000/300,000 =   0.25

Budgeted contribution margin per composite unit of budgeted mix:
       ZENITH = $250 x 0.2 = $ 50
       House-Helper = $200 x 0.8 =   160
       OR $15,750,000/75,000= $210

Market-share variance	Actual market size in units	Actual market share – Budgeted market share	Budgeted CM per composite unit for budgeted mix	Market-share variance
Omega Corp	275,000 x	(0.2 - 0.25) x	$210	= $2,887,500 U

Market-size variance	Actual market size in units - Budgeted market size in units	Budgeted market share	Budgeted CM per composite unit for budgeted mix	Market-size variance
Omega Corp	(275,000 - 300,000) x	0.25 x	$210	= $1,312,500 U

Difficulty: 3   *Objective*:   8

151. The Chair Company manufactures two modular types of chairs, one for the residential market, and the other for the office market. Budgeted and actual operating data for the year 20x3 are:

Static Budget	Residential	Office	Total
Number of chairs sold	260,000	140,000	400,000
Contribution margin	$26,000,000	$11,200,000	$37,200,000

Actual Results	Residential	Office	Total
Number of chairs sold	248,400	165,600	414,000
Contribution margin	$22,356,000	$13,248,000	$35,604,000

Prior to the beginning of the year, an office products research firm estimated the industry volume for residential and office chairs of the type sold by the Chair Company to be 2,400,000. Actual industry volume for the year 20x3 was only 2,200,000 chairs.

Required:

Compute the following variances in terms of contribution margin.
a.   Compute the total static-budget variance, the total flexible-budget variance, and the total sales-volume variance.
b.   Compute the sale-mix variance and the sales-quantity variance by type of chair, and in total.
c.   Compute the market-share variance and market-size variance.

Answer:

a.   *Budgeted contribution margin per unit*:
Residential = $26,000,000/260,000 = $100
Office = $11,200,000/140,000 = $80

Flexible-budget contribution margin:
Residential   248,400 x $100 = $24,840,000
Office   165,600 x $80 = $13,248,000
                                                   $38,088,000

Static-budget variance is $1,596,000 unfavorable
      = $37,200,000 - $35,604,000
Sales-volume variance is $888,000 favorable
      = $37,200,000 - $38,088,000
Flexible-budget variance is $2,484,000 unfavorable
      = $38,088,000 - $35,604,000

b.   *Actual sales-mix percentage*:
Residential = 248,400/414,000 = 60%
Office = 165,600/414,000 = 40%

151. **Answer:** (continued)

b. *Budgeted sales-mix percentage:*
Residential = 260,000/400,000 = 65%
Office = 140,000/400,000 = 35%

Sales-mix variance	Actual units of all products sold	Actual sales-mix % - Budgeted sales-mix %	Budgeted CM per unit	Sales-mix variance
Residential	414,000 x	(0.6 - 0.65) x	$100	= $2,070,000 U
Office	414,000 x	(0.4 - 0.35) x	$80	= $1,656,000 F
Total				$ 414,000 U

Sales-quantity variance	Actual units of all products sold – Budgeted units of all products sold	Budgeted sales-mix %	Budgeted CM per unit	Sales-quantity variance
Residential	(414,000 - 400,000) x	0.65 x	$100	= $ 910,000 F
Office	(414,000 - 400,000) x	0.35 x	$80	= $ 392,000 F
Total				$1,302,000 F

c. *Actual market share* = 414,000/ 2,200,000 = 18.81818% or 0.1881818
Budgeted market share = 400,000/ 2,400,000 = 16.66667% or 0.1666667

Budgeted contribution margin per composite unit of budgeted mix:
Residential – $100 x .65 = $65
Office = $80 x .35 = 28
OR $37,200,000/400,000 $93

Market-share variance	Actual market size in units	Actual market share – Budgeted market share	Budgeted CM per composite unit for budgeted mix	Market-share variance
Chair Company	2,200,000 x	(0.1881818- 0.1666667) x	$93	= $4,402,000 F (Answers may vary due to rounding)

Market-size variance	Actual market size in units - Budgeted market size in units	Budgeted market share	Budgeted CM per composite unit for budgeted mix	Market-size variance
Chair Company	(2,200,000 - 2,400,000) x	0.1666667 x	$93	= $3,100,000 U (Answers may vary due to rounding)

Difficulty: 3   *Objectives:* 7, 8

152. A company might choose to allocate corporate costs to various divisions within the company for what four purposes? Give an example of each.

Answer:

1. To provide information for economic decisions. For example, allocating costs from all six value-chain functions to decide on the selling price of a customized product.

2. To motivate managers and employees. For example, allocating corporate costs such as accounting support to division managers to discourage requesting a multitude of unnecessary financial reports.

3. To justify costs or compute reimbursement. For example, to allocate fixed design and production costs when arriving at a fair price for a government contract.

4. To measure income and assets for reporting to external parties. For example, allocating manufacturing overhead when costing inventories for financial statements presented in the company's annual report.

Note: Examples will vary.

Difficulty: 2   *Objective*:   1

153. An electronics manufacturer is trying to encourage its engineers to design simpler products so that overall costs are reduced.

Required:

Which of the value-chain function costs (R&D, design, production, marketing, distribution, customer service) should be included in product-cost estimates to achieve the above purpose? Why?

Answer:

All costs that are affected by the design should be included in the product cost estimate. These costs include the cost of design, production, distribution, and customer service.

Difficulty: 1   *Objective*: 1

154. List at least three different levels of costs in a customer-cost hierarchy and an example of each.

Answer:

List any three of the following:
1. Customer output unit-level costs, product-handling costs of each product sold
2. Customer batch-level costs, order processing costs incurred
3. Customer-sustaining costs, costs of visits to the customer
4. Distribution-channel costs, a particular distribution channel manager's salary
5. Corporate-sustaining costs, costs of top management

Note: Examples will vary.

Difficulty: 2   *Objective*:   5

155. Why would a manager perform customer-profitability analysis?

Answer:

Customer profitability analysis highlights how individual customers contribute to profitability. It helps managers determine whether customers who are contributing significantly to profits are receiving a comparable level of attention from the organization.

Difficulty: 2   *Objective*:   6

156.   Why would a manager want to calculate the sale-mix and the sales-quantity variances? Market-share and market-size variances?

Answer:

In order to manage effectively and make proper decisions, a manager must keep informed on whether organizational initiatives are progressing as planned. Variances help to inform managers about the reasons (whether favorable or unfavorable) for the differences between the actual result and the budgeted result.

Specifically, the sale-mix and the sales-quantity variances help to explain the sales-volume variance, and the market-share and market-size variances help to explain the sales-quantity variance.

Difficulty: 2   *Objectives*:   7, 8

CHAPTER 15: ALLOCATION OF SUPPORT DEPARTMENT COSTS, COMMON COSTS, AND REVENUES

TRUE/FALSE

1. The dual cost-allocation method classifies costs into two pools, a budgeted cost pool and an actual cost pool.

   Answer: False   *Difficulty*: 1   *Objective*: 1
   The dual cost-allocation method classifies costs into two pools, a variable cost pool and a fixed cost pool.

2. Using the single-rate method transforms the fixed costs per hour into a variable cost to users of that facility.

   Answer: True   *Difficulty*: 3   *Objective*: 1

3. The single-rate cost-allocation method provides better information for decision making than the dual-rate method.

   Answer: False   *Difficulty*: 2   *Objective*: 1
   The dual-rate cost-allocation method provides better information for decision making than the single-rate method.

4. When budgeted cost-allocation rates are used, user-division managers face uncertainty about the allocation rates for that budget period.

   Answer: False   *Difficulty*: 2   *Objective*: 2
   When budgeted cost-allocation rates are used, user-division managers face *no uncertainty* about the allocation rates for that budget period.

5. When budgeted cost-allocation rates are used, managers of the supplier division are motivated to improve efficiency.

   Answer: True   *Difficulty*: 2   *Objective*: 2

6. When budgeted cost-allocation rates are used, variations in actual usage by one division affect the costs allocated to other divisions.

   Answer: False   *Difficulty*: 2   *Objective*: 2
   When *actual* cost-allocations rates are used, variations in actual usage by one division affect the costs allocated to other divisions.

7.	The direct allocation method highlights recognition of services rendered by support departments to other support departments.

	Answer:	False	*Difficulty*:	2	*Objective*:	3
	The direct allocation method allows for no recognition of services rendered by support departments to other support departments.

8.	The reciprocal allocation method incorporates mutual services provided among all support departments.

	Answer:	True	*Difficulty*:	2	*Objective*:	3

9.	Budgeted amounts for a support department will always exceed complete reciprocated costs for that department.

	Answer:	False	*Difficulty*:	3	*Objective*:	3
	Complete reciprocated costs equal budgeted amounts for the support department plus any interdepartmental cost allocations, therefore, complete reciprocated costs always exceed budgeted amounts.

10.	The direct allocation method provides key information for outsourcing decisions regarding support services.

	Answer:	False	*Difficulty*:	3	*Objective*:	3
	Complete reciprocal costs of a support department provide key information for outsourcing decisions regarding support services. The direct allocation method does not provide this information.

11.	The incremental method of allocating common costs often creates the incentive to be the first-ranked user.

	Answer:	False	*Difficulty*:	3	*Objective*:	3
	The incremental method creates a *disincentive* to be the first-ranked user because the first-ranked user receives the greatest allocation of cost.

12.	The stand-alone method of allocating common costs emphasizes fairness and equity among users.

	Answer:	True	*Difficulty*:	2	*Objective*:	4

13.	Under the incremental method, the first incremental user usually receives the highest allocation of the common costs.

	Answer:	False	*Difficulty*:	2	*Objective*:	4
	Under the incremental method of allocating common costs, the *primary* user receives the highest allocation of the common costs.

14. All contracts with U.S. government agencies must comply with the cost accounting standards issued by the Cost Accounting Standards Board.

   Answer: True   *Difficulty*:   1   *Objective*:   5

15. Without explicit written cost-plus contracts, producer costs can be passed on to the buyer.

   Answer: True   *Difficulty*:   2   *Objective*:   5

16. An example of a bundled product is when a resort hotel charges a single price for lodging, food, and recreational activities.

   Answer: True   *Difficulty*:   1   *Objective*:   6

17. Revenue allocation is required to determine the profitability of individual items within a bundled product.

   Answer: True   *Difficulty*:   2   *Objective*:   6

18. The stand-alone method may use selling price or unit costs to allocate revenues.

   Answer: True   *Difficulty*:   2   *Objective*:   7

19. Under the incremental revenue-allocation method, there is an incentive to be the first-ranked user.

   Answer: True   *Difficulty*:   2   *Objective*:   7

20. It is most appropriate to base revenue allocation on the number of physical units when individual products in the bundle are of unequal value.

   Answer: False   *Difficulty*:   2   *Objective*:   7
   Revenue allocation based on the number of physical units is only appropriate when individual products in the bundle are of *equal* value.

21. The method that allocates costs in each cost pool using the same rate per unit is known as the
    a. incremental cost-allocation method.
    b. reciprocal cost-allocation method.
    c. single-rate cost allocation method.
    d. dual-rate cost-allocation method.

    Answer: c   *Difficulty*: 2   *Objective*: 1

22. The dual-rate cost-allocation method classifies costs in each cost pool into two pools,
    a. a budgeted-cost pool and an actual-cost pool.
    b. a variable-cost pool and a fixed-cost pool.
    c. a used-capacity-cost pool and a practical-capacity-cost pool.
    d. a direct-cost pool and a reciprocal-cost pool.

    Answer: b   *Difficulty*: 1   *Objective*: 1

23. The single-rate cost-allocation method may base the denominator choice on
    a. master-budget capacity utilization.
    b. normal capacity utilization.
    c. practical capacity.
    d. any of the above.

    Answer: d   *Difficulty*: 2   *Objective*: 1

24. When using the single-rate method, fixed cost allocation may be based on
    a. actual usage.
    b. budgeted usage.
    c. incremental cost allocation.
    d. either (a) or (b).

    Answer: d   *Difficulty*: 1   *Objective*: 1

25. Benefits of the single-rate method include
    a. the low cost of implementation.
    b. fixed costs that are transformed into variable costs for user decision making.
    c. signals regarding how variable and fixed costs behave differently.
    d. information that leads to outsourcing decisions that benefit the organization as a whole.

    Answer: a   *Difficulty*: 3   *Objective*: 1

26. Benefits of the dual-rate method include
    a.   variable costs that are transformed into fixed costs for user decision making.
    b.   the low cost of implementation.
    c.   avoidance of expensive analysis for categorizing costs as either fixed or variable.
    d.   information that leads to outsourcing decisions that benefit the organization as a whole.

    Answer: d   *Difficulty:*   3   *Objective:*   1

THE FOLLOWING INFORMATION APPLIES TO QUESTIONS 27 THROUGH 30.
The Bonawitz Corporation has a central copying facility. The copying facility has only two users, the Marketing Department and the Operations Department. The following data apply to the coming budget year.

Budgeted costs of operating the copying facility
for 200,000 to 300,000 copies:
    Fixed costs per year $30,000
    Variable costs   3 cents (.03) per copy
Budgeted long-run usage in copies per year:
    Marketing Department   60,000 copies
    Operations Department   190,000 copies

Budgeted amounts are used to calculate the allocation rates.

Actual usage for the year by the Marketing Department was 40,000 copies and by the Operations Department was 180,000 copies.

27. If a single-rate cost-allocation method is used, what amount of copying facility costs will be *budgeted* for the Marketing Department?
    a. $9,000
    b. $1,800
    c. $7,200
    d. $8,400

    Answer: a   *Difficulty:*   2   *Objective:*   1
    [(60,000/250,000) x $30,000] + (60,000 x $0.03) = $9,000

28. If a single-rate cost-allocation method is used, what amount of copying facility costs will be *allocated* to the Marketing Department? Assume actual usage is used to allocate copying costs.
    a. $8,400
    b. $9,000
    c. $6,000
    d. $4,800

    Answer: c   *Difficulty:*   3   *Objective:*   1
    [(60,000/250,000) x $30,000] + (60,000 x $0.03) = $9,000
    $9,000/60,000 copies = $0.15 per copy x 40,000 = $6,000

29. If a dual-rate cost-allocation method is used, what amount of copying facility costs will be *budgeted* for the Operations Department?
    a. $28,500
    b. $28,200
    c. $30,245
    d. $29,945

Answer: a   *Difficulty:* 2   *Objective:* 1
[(190,000/250,000) x $30,000] + (190,000 x $0.03) = $28,500

30. If a dual-rate cost-allocation method is used, what amount of copying facility costs will be *allocated* to the Operations Department? Assume budgeted usage is used to allocate fixed copying costs and actual usage is used to allocate variable copying costs.
    a. $30,245
    b. $29,945
    c. $28,500
    d. $28,200

Answer: d   *Difficulty:* 3   *Objective:* 1
[(190,000/250,000) x $30,000] + (180,000 x $0.03) = $28,200

THE FOLLOWING INFORMATION APPLIES TO QUESTIONS 31 THROUGH 34.
The Borders Corporation operates one central plant that has two divisions, the Flashlight Division and the Night Light Division. The following data apply to the coming budget year.

Budgeted costs of operating the plant for 2,000 to 3,000 hours:
    Fixed operating costs per year $900,000
    Variable operating costs $1,200 per hour
Budgeted long-run usage per year:
    Flashlight Division   2,000 hours
    Night Light Division   500 hours
Practical capacity   3,000 hours

Assume that practical capacity is used to calculate the allocation rates.

Actual usage for the year by the Flashlight Division was 1,400 hours and by the Night Light Division was 600 hours.

31. If a single-rate cost-allocation method is used, what amount of operating costs will be *budgeted* for the Flashlight Division?
    a. $3,000,000
    b. $3,120,000
    c. $2,280,000
    d. $2,820,000

Answer: a   *Difficulty:* 2   *Objective:* 1
[(2,000/3,000) x $900,000] + (2,000 x $1,200) = $3,000,000

32. If a single-rate cost-allocation method is used, what amount of cost will be *allocated* to the Flashlight Division? Assume actual usage is used to allocate operating costs.
    a. $2,280,000
    b. $2,400,000
    c. $3,000,000
    d. $2,100,000

    Answer: d   *Difficulty:* 3   *Objective:* 1
    $3,000,000/2,000 x 1,400 = $2,100,000

33. If a dual-rate cost-allocation method is used, what amount of operating costs will be *budgeted* for the Night Light Division?
    a. $780,000
    b. $900,000
    c. $750,000
    d. $870,000

    Answer: c   *Difficulty:* 2   *Objective:* 1
    [(500/3,000) x $900,000] + (500 x $1,200) = $750,000

34. If a dual-rate cost-allocation method is used, what amount of cost will be *allocated* to the Night Light Division? Assume budgeted usage is used to allocate fixed operating costs and actual usage is used to allocate variable operating costs.
    a. $750,000
    b. $870,000
    c. $780,000
    d. $900,000

    Answer: b   *Difficulty:* 3   *Objective:* 1
    [(500/3,000) x $900,000] + (600 x $1,200) = $870,000

35. When budgeted cost-allocations rates are used,
    a. variations in actual usage by one division affect the costs allocated to other divisions.
    b. the manager of the supplier division bears the risk of unfavorable cost variances.
    c. user divisions pay for costs that exceed budgeted amounts.
    d. user divisions pay for inefficiencies of the supplier department.

    Answer: b   *Difficulty:* 3   *Objective:* 2

36. When actual cost-allocations rates are used,
    a. user divisions pay for costs that exceed budgeted amounts.
    b. managers of the supplier division are motivated to improve efficiency.
    c. user divisions do not know allocated amounts until the end of the accounting period.
    d. managers of the user divisions may be tempted to underestimate planned usage.

    Answer: c   *Difficulty:* 3   *Objective:* 2

37. Under the dual-rate cost-allocation method, when fixed costs are allocated based on actual usage then
    a.   user-division managers are motivated to make accurate long-run usage forecasts.
    b.   user-division managers can better plan for the short-run and for the long-run.
    c.   the costs of unused capacity are highlighted.
    d.   variations in one division's usage affect another division's allocation.

    Answer: d   *Difficulty:*   3   *Objective:*   2

38. The costs of unused capacity are highlighted when
    a.   actual usage based allocations are used.
    b.   budgeted usage allocations are used.
    c.   practical capacity-based allocations are used.
    d.   the dual-rate cost-allocation method allocates fixed costs based on actual usage.

    Answer: c   *Difficulty:*   2   *Objective:*   2

39. To discourage unnecessary use of a support department, management might
    a.   not allocate any support department costs to user departments.
    b.   allocate support department costs based upon user department usage.
    c.   allocate a fixed amount of support department costs to each department regardless of use.
    d.   issue memos on useful services provided by the support department.

    Answer: b   *Difficulty:*   3   *Objective:*   2

40. Special cost-allocation problems arise when
    a.   support department costs exceed budgetary estimates.
    b.   practical capacity is used as the allocation base.
    c.   support departments provide reciprocal services to other support departments.
    d.   there is more than one operating department.

    Answer: c   *Difficulty:*   2   *Objective:*   3

41. Which of the following departments is NOT a support department for a boat manufacturing company?
    a.   Personnel
    b.   Molding and assembly
    c.   Data processing
    d.   Accounting

    Answer: b   *Difficulty:*   1   *Objective:*   3

42. The support department allocation method that is the most widely used because of its simplicity is the
    a. step-down method.
    b. reciprocal allocation method.
    c. direct allocation method.
    d. sequential allocation method.

    Answer: c   *Difficulty:* 1   *Objective:* 3

43. The method that allocates costs by explicitly including all the services rendered among all support departments is
    a. the direct method.
    b. the step-down method.
    c. the reciprocal method.
    d. the sequential method.

    Answer: c   *Difficulty:* 2   *Objective:* 3

44. Under which allocation method are one-way reciprocal support services recognized?
    a. The direct method
    b. The artificial cost method
    c. The reciprocal method
    d. The step-down method

    Answer: d   *Difficulty:* 2   *Objective:* 3

45. The direct allocation method
    a. partially recognizes the services provided among support departments.
    b. is also referred to as the sequential method.
    c. is conceptually the most precise method.
    d. results in allocating only the support costs used by operating departments.

    Answer: d   *Difficulty:* 3   *Objective:* 3

46. The step-down allocation method
    a. typically begins with the support department that provides the highest percentage of its total services to other support departments.
    b. recognizes the total amount of services that support departments provide to each other.
    c. allocates complete reciprocated costs.
    d. offers key input for outsourcing decisions.

    Answer: a   *Difficulty:* 3   *Objective:* 3

47. The reciprocal allocation method
    a. is the most widely used because of its simplicity.
    b. requires the ranking of support departments in the order that the allocation is to proceed.
    c. is conceptually the most precise.
    d. results in allocating more support costs to operating departments than actually incurred.

    Answer: c   *Difficulty:* 3   *Objective:* 3

48. Complete reciprocated costs
    a. are less than the support department's own costs.
    b. include the support department's costs plus any interdepartmental cost allocations.
    c. are utilized for step-down allocations.
    d. are also referred to as budgeted costs.

    Answer: b   *Difficulty:* 2   *Objective:* 3

THE FOLLOWING INFORMATION APPLIES TO QUESTIONS 49 THROUGH 51.
Jake's Battery Company has two service departments, Maintenance and Personnel.
Maintenance Department costs of $160,000 are allocated on the basis of budgeted
maintenance-hours. Personnel Department costs of $40,000 are allocated based on the
number of employees. The costs of operating departments A and B are $80,000 and
$120,000, respectively. Data on budgeted maintenance-hours and number of employees are
as follows:

	Support Departments		Production Departments	
	Maintenance Department	Personnel Department	A	B
Budgeted costs	$160,000	$40,000	$80,000	$120,000
Budgeted maintenance-hours	NA	400	480	320
Number of employees	20	NA	80	240

49. Using the direct method, what amount of Maintenance Department costs will be
allocated to Department B?
a. $48,000
b. $64,000
c. $78,000
d. $96,000

Answer: b   *Difficulty:* 2   *Objective:* 3
320/800 x $160,000 = $64,000

50. Using the direct method, what amount of Personnel Department costs will be allocated
to Department B?
a. $10,000
b. $16,000
c. $24,000
d. $30,000

Answer: d   *Difficulty:* 2   *Objective:* 3
240/320 x $40,000= $30,000

51. Using the step-down method, what amount of Maintenance Department cost will be
allocated to Department B if the service department with the highest percentage of
interdepartmental support service is allocated first? (Round up)
a. $32,000
b. $42,667
c. $57,334
d. $64,000

Answer: b   *Difficulty:* 3   *Objective:* 3
Maintenance provided to Personnel: 400/1,200= .333
Personnel provided to Maintenance: 20/340= .059
Maintenance provides the greatest amount of service to support departments, so it is
allocated first.   Dept B: 320/1,200 x $160,000 = $42,667

THE FOLLOWING INFORMATION APPLIES TO QUESTIONS 52 THROUGH 54.
Jake's Battery Company has two service departments, Maintenance and Personnel.
Maintenance Department costs of $160,000 are allocated on the basis of budgeted
maintenance-hours. Personnel Department costs of $40,000 are allocated based on the
number of employees. The costs of operating departments A and B are $80,000 and
$120,000, respectively. Data on budgeted maintenance-hours and number of employees are
as follows:

	Support Departments		Production Departments	
	Maintenance Department	**Personnel Department**	**A**	**B**
Budgeted costs	$160,000	$40,000	$80,000	$120,000
Budgeted maintenance-hours	NA	400	480	320
Number of employees	20	NA	80	240

52. Using the direct method, what amount of Maintenance Department costs will be
    allocated to Department A?
    a. $48,000
    b. $64,000
    c. $78,000
    d. $96,000

    Answer: d   *Difficulty*:   2   *Objective*:   3
    480/800 x $160,000 = $96,000

53. Using the direct method, what amount of Personnel Department costs will be allocated
    to Department A?
    a. $10,000
    b. $16,000
    c. $24,000
    d. $30,000

    Answer: a   *Difficulty*:   2   *Objective*:   3
    80/320 x $40,000= $10,000

54. Using the step-down method, what amount of Maintenance Department cost will be
    allocated to Department A if the service department with the highest percentage of
    interdepartmental support service is allocated first? (Round up)
    a. $32,000
    b. $42,667
    c. $57,334
    d. $64,000

    Answer: d   *Difficulty*:   3   *Objective*:   3
    Maintenance provided to Personnel: 400/1,200= .333
    Personnel provided to Maintenance: 20/340= .059
    Maintenance provides the greatest amount of service to support departments, so it is
    allocated first.   Dept A: 480/1,200 x $160,000 = $64,000

THE FOLLOWING INFORMATION APPLIES TO QUESTIONS 55 THROUGH 57.
Alfred, owner of Hi-Tech Fiberglass Fabricators Inc. is interested in using the reciprocal allocation method. The following data from operations were collected for analysis:

Budgeted manufacturing overhead costs:

Plant Maintenance	PM (Support Dept)	$350,000
Data Processing	DP (Support Dept)	$ 75,000
Machining	M (Operating Dept)	$225,000
Capping	C (Operating Dept)	$125,000

Services furnished:
By Plant Maintenance (budgeted labor-hours):

to Data Processing	3,500
to Machining	5,000
to Capping	8,200

By Data Processing (budgeted computer time):

to Plant Maintenance	600
to Machining	3,500
to Capping	600

55. Which of the following linear equations represents the complete reciprocated cost of the Data Processing Department?
   a. DP= $75,000 + (600/4,700) PM
   b. DP= $75,000 + (3,500/16,700) PM
   c. DP= $75,000 x (600/4,700) + $350,000 x (3,340/16,700)
   d. DP= $350,000 + (600/16,700) DP

Answer: b   *Difficulty:*   3   *Objective:*   3

56. What is the complete reciprocated cost of the Plant Maintenance Department?
   a. $393,750
   b. $369,459
   c. $365,000
   d. $375,773

Answer: b   *Difficulty:*   3   *Objective:*   3
DP = $75,000 + (3,500/16,700) PM
PM= $350,000 + (600/4,700) DP
PM= $350,000 + (600/4,700) x [$75,000 + (3,500/16,700) PM]
PM= $350,000 + $9,574 + (0.026755)PM
0.973245 PM = $359,574
PM= $369,459

57. What is the complete reciprocated cost of the Data Processing Department?
   a. $90,000
   b. $118,750
   c. $122,971
   d. $152,432

Answer: d   *Difficulty:*   3   *Objective:*   3
PM= $369,459 (see above question);   DP = $75,000 + (3,500/16,700) PM
DP= $75,000 + (3,500/16,700) $369,459 = $152,432

58. A cost of operating a facility, department, activity area, or like cost object that is shared by two or more users is called a
   a. direct cost.
   b. joint cost.
   c. fixed cost.
   d. common cost.

   Answer: d   *Difficulty*: 1   *Objective*: 4

59. Under the stand-alone method of allocating common costs
   a. a ranking is used to allocate costs among the users.
   b. disputes can arise over who is the primary user.
   c. each party bears a proportionate share of the total costs in relation to their individual stand-alone costs.
   d. an incentive is created to be the first-ranked user.

   Answer: c   *Difficulty*: 3   *Objective*: 4

60. Under the incremental method of allocating common costs
   a. the parties are interested in being viewed as primary users.
   b. each party bears a proportionate share of the total costs in relation to their individual stand-alone costs.
   c. fairness and equity are emphasized.
   d. there is a disincentive to be titled the primary user.
   Answer: d   *Difficulty*: 3   *Objective*: 4

THE FOLLOWING INFORMATION APPLIES TO QUESTIONS 61 AND 62.
The Sturgeon Bay Corporation currently utilizes a manufacturing facility costing $400,000 per year; 80% of the facility's capacity is currently being used. A start-up business has proposed a plan that would utilize the other 20% of the facility and increase the overall costs of maintaining the space by 5%.

61. If the stand-alone method were used, what amount of cost would be allocated to the start-up business?
   a. $20,000
   b. $100,000
   c. $80,000
   d. $84,000

   Answer: d   *Difficulty*: 2   *Objective*: 4
   $400,000 x 1.05 = $420,000; $420,000 x.2= $84,000

62. If the incremental method were used, what amount of cost would be allocated to the start-up business?
   a. $20,000
   b. $100,000
   c. $80,000
   d. $84,000

   Answer: a   *Difficulty*: 2   *Objective*: 4
   $400,000 x 0.05 = $20,000

THE FOLLOWING INFORMATION APPLIES TO QUESTIONS 63 AND 64.
The Egg Harbor Corporation currently leases a corporate suite in an office building for a cost of $90,000 a year. Only 70% of the corporate suite is currently being used. A start-up business has proposed a plan that would utilize the other 30% of the suite and increase the overall costs of maintaining the space by $10,000.

63. If the stand-alone method were used, what amount of cost would be allocated to the start-up business?
   a. $10,000
   b. $27,000
   c. $30,000
   d. $37,000

   Answer: c   *Difficulty:*   2   *Objective:*   4
   $100,000 x 0.30 = $30,000

64. If the incremental method were used, what amount of cost would be allocated to the start-up business?
   a. $10,000
   b. $27,000
   c. $30,000
   d. $37,000

   Answer: a   *Difficulty:*   2   *Objective:*   4
   $10,000, the increased cost of maintaining the space

65. All contracts with U.S. government agencies must comply with cost accounting standards issued by
   a. FASB.
   b. SEC.
   c. IRS.
   d. CASB.

   Answer: d   *Difficulty:*   2   *Objective:*   5

66. Contract disputes with regard to cost allocation can be reduced by
   a. defining the cost items allowed.
   b. defining the terms used, such as what constitutes direct labor.
   c. defining permissible cost-allocation bases.
   d. defining all of the above.

   Answer: d   *Difficulty:*   2   *Objective:*   5

67. Cost-based prices
   a. are one way of setting prices in a competitive market.
   b. provide an inherit incentive for the producer to control costs.
   c. pass the majority of risk to the buyer.
   d. are required in all government contracts.

   Answer: c   *Difficulty*: 3   *Objective*: 5

68. _____ is a cost that the contract parties agree to include in the costs to be reimbursed.
   a. An allowable cost
   b. An unallowable cost
   c. An incremental cost
   d. A stand-alone cost

   Answer: a   *Difficulty*: 1   *Objective*: 5

69. In certain high-cost defense contracts involving new weapons and equipment, contracts are rarely subject to competitive bidding because
   a. the government is concerned that one firm might monopolize defense contracts.
   b. there is an implicit agreement among defense contractors to "share contracts."
   c. all defense contractors have essentially the same cost structure.
   d. of none of the above.

   Answer: d   *Difficulty*: 3   *Objective*: 5

70. _____ occurs where revenues, related but not traceable to individual products, are assigned to those individual products.
   a. Revenue tracing
   b. Revenue allocation
   c. Stand-alone pricing
   d. Reciprocal pricing

   Answer: b   *Difficulty*: 1   *Objective*: 6

71. An example of a revenue object is
   a. a customer.
   b. a specific product.
   c. a division of a company.
   d. all of the above.

   Answer: d   *Difficulty*: 1   *Objective*: 6

72. AAA offers towing services, auto routing, travel brochures, and other travel services for one annual fee. This is an example of
    a. revenue tracing.
    b. revenue allocation.
    c. a bundled product.
    d. a joint product.

    Answer: c   *Difficulty:* 2   *Objective:* 6

73. Businesses offer bundled products
    a. to increase customer exposure.
    b. to increase overall company profitability.
    c. to avoid the problems of revenue allocation.
    d. both (a) and (b).

    Answer: d   *Difficulty:* 2   *Objective:* 6

74. The method LEAST likely to cause disputes among product managers is
    a. stand-alone revenue-allocation method.
    b. incremental revenue-allocation method.
    c. the direct revenue-allocation method.
    d. (a), (b), and (c) are all likely to result in the same disputes among product managers.

    Answer: a   *Difficulty:* 2   *Objective:* 7

75. The method that ranks individual products in a bundle for revenue allocation is the
    a. stand-alone revenue-allocation method.
    b. incremental revenue-allocation method.
    c. unit-cost weighting method.
    d. physical-unit weighting method.

    Answer: b   *Difficulty:* 2   *Objective:* 7

76. Approaches used to rank products for revenue allocation might include
    a. surveying customers on the importance of each product.
    b. using recent data on stand-alone sales performance.
    c. having managers use their knowledge and intuition.
    d. any of the above.

    Answer: d   *Difficulty:* 2   *Objective:* 7

77. To give more weight to the product that most likely drives the sales of the bundled product, the revenue allocation should be weighted using
    a. selling prices.
    b. unit costs.
    c. physical units.
    d. stand-alone product revenues.

    Answer: d   *Difficulty*: 2   *Objective*: 7

78. The revenue allocation may be weighted using physical units when
    a. the individual products within the bundle have approximately the same value.
    b. selling prices are unstable and unit costs are difficult to calculate.
    c. other methods cannot be used for various reasons.
    d. any of the above conditions exist.

    Answer: d   *Difficulty*: 2   *Objective*: 7

THE FOLLOWING INFORMATION APPLIES TO QUESTIONS 79 THROUGH 82.
Elmo's Educational Software Outlet sells two or more of the video games as a single package. Managers are keenly interested in individual product-profitability figures. Information pertaining to three bundled products and the stand-alone prices is as follows:

	Stand-Alone Selling Price	Cost
Reading Fun	$50	$7.20
Math Fun	$60	$8.00
Analysis	$90	$10.00

Package	Packaged Price
1. *Reading Fun & Math Fun*	$88
2. *Reading Fun & Analysis*	$112
3. *All three*	$152

79. Using the stand-alone method with selling price as the weight for revenue allocation, what amount of revenue will be allocated to Reading Fun in the first package (Reading Fun & Math Fun)?
    a. $40
    b. $44
    c. $38
    d. $50

    Answer: a   *Difficulty*: 2   *Objective*: 7
    [$50 / ($50 + $60)] x $88 = $40

80. Using the incremental method for revenue allocation, what amount of revenue will be allocated to Reading Fun in the first package (Reading Fun & Math Fun)? Assume Reading Fun is the primary product, followed by Math Fun, and then Analysis.
    a. $40
    b. $44
    c. $38
    d. $50

    Answer: d   *Difficulty*: 2   *Objective*: 7
    $50 since Reading Fun is the primary product.

81. Using the stand-alone method with selling price as the weight for revenue allocation, what amount of revenue will be allocated to Math Fun in the package that contains all three products?
    a. $48.25
    b. $60.00
    c. $45.60
    d. $50.67

    Answer: c   *Difficulty*: 2   *Objective*: 7
    [$60 / ($50 + $60 + $90)] x $152 = $45.60

82. Using the incremental method, what amount of revenue will be allocated to Math Fun in the package that contains all three products?
    a. $48.25
    b. $60.00
    c. $45.60
    d. $50.67

    Answer: b   *Difficulty*: 2   *Objective*: 7
    $152 - $50 primary product = $102 revenues remaining to be allocated to other products; $60 since there are revenues remaining to cover the selling price of Reading Fun, the first incremental product.

THE FOLLOWING INFORMATION APPLIES TO QUESTIONS 83 THROUGH 86.
The Appliance Store sells a refrigerator and a freezer as a single package for $1,000. Other data are in the chart below.

	Refrigerator	Full-size Freezer	Packaged Price
Selling price	$825	$375	$1,000
Manufacturing cost per unit	$620	$180	
Stand-alone product revenues	$1,225,000	$775,000	

83. Using the stand-alone method with selling price as the weight for revenue allocation, what amount will be allocated to the refrigerator?
   a. $500.00
   b. $825.00
   c. $687.50
   d. $625.00

   Answer: c   *Difficulty:* 2   *Objective:* 7
   Refrigerator $825/$1,200 x $1,000 = $687.50

84. Using the stand-alone method with stand-alone product revenues as the weight for revenue allocation, what amount will be allocated to the refrigerator?
   a. $687.50
   b. $612.50
   c. $625.00
   d. $825.00

   Answer: b   *Difficulty:* 2   *Objective:* 7
   Refrigerator $1,225,000/ $2,000,000 x $1,000 = $612.50

85. Using the stand-alone method with manufacturing cost per unit as the weight for revenue allocation, what amount will be allocated to the refrigerator?
   a. $500.00
   b. $612.50
   c. $620.00
   d. $775.00

   Answer: d   *Difficulty:* 2   *Objective:* 7
   Refrigerator $620/$800 x $1,000 = $775

86. Using the stand-alone method with physical units as the weight for revenue allocation, what amount will be allocated to the refrigerator?
   a. $500
   b. $20
   c. $775
   d. $825

   Answer: a   *Difficulty:* 2   *Objective:* 7
   (1 / 2) x $1,000 = $500

EXERCISES AND PROBLEMS

87. The fixed costs of operating the maintenance facility of General Hospital are $4,500,000 annually. Variable costs are incurred at the rate of $30 per maintenance-hour. The facility averages 40,000 maintenance-hours a year. Budgeted and actual hours per user for 20x3 are as follows:

	Budgeted hours	**Actual hours**
Building and grounds	10,000	12,000
Operating and emergency	8,000	8,000
Patient care	21,000	22,000
Administration	1,000	1,200
Total	40,000	43,200

Assume that budgeted maintenance-hours are used to calculate the allocation rates.

Required:
a. If a single-rate cost-allocation method is used, what amount of maintenance cost will be budgeted for each department?
b. If a single-rate cost-allocation method is used, what amount of maintenance cost will be allocated to each department based on actual usage? Based on budgeted usage?
c. If a dual-rate cost-allocation method is used, what amount of maintenance cost will be budgeted for each department?
d. If a dual-rate cost-allocation method is used, what amount of maintenance cost will be allocated to each department based on actual usage? Based on budgeted usage for fixed operating costs and actual usage for variable operating costs?

Answer:
a. Total costs + $4,500,000 + ($30 x 40,000) = $5,700,000
   Single rate = $5,700,000 / 40,000 mh = $142.50 per maintenance-hour
   Single-rate budgeted amounts:

Building and grounds	$142.50 x 10,000	= $1,425,000
Operating and emergency	$142.50 x 8,000	= $1,140,000
Patient care	$142.50 x 21,000	= $2,992,500
Administration	$142.50 x 1,000	= $ 142,500

b. Total costs + $4,500,000 + ($30 x 40,000) = $5,700,000
   Single rate = $5,700,000 / 40,000 mh = $142.50 per maintenance-hour
   Single-rate allocated amounts:

Building and grounds	$142.50 x 12,000	= $1,710,000
Operating and emergency	$142.50 x 8,000	= $1,140,000
Patient care	$142.50 x 22,000	= $3,135,000
Administration	$142.50 x 1,200	= $ 171,000

87. (continued)

c. *Dual-rate budgeted amounts*:
Building and grounds:
    Fixed ($4,500,000 x 10/40) $1,125,000
    Variable ($30 x 10,000)   300,000
    Total $1,425,000

Operating and emergency:
    Fixed ($4,500,000 x 8/40) $ 900,000
    Variable ($30 x 8,000)   240,000
    Total $1,140,000

Patient care:
    Fixed ($4,500,000 x 21/40) $2,362,500
    Variable ($30 x 21,000)   630,000
    Total $2,992,500

Administration:
    Fixed ($4,500,000 x 1/40) $ 112,500
    Variable ($30 x 1,000)   30,000
    Total $ 142,500

d. *Dual-rate allocated amounts*:
Building and grounds:
    Fixed ($4,500,000 x 10/40) $1,125,000
    Variable ($30 x 12,000)   360,000
    Total $1,485,000

Operating and emergency:
    Fixed ($4,500,000 x 8/40) $ 900,000
    Variable ($30 x 8,000)   240,000
    Total $1,140,000

Patient care:
    Fixed ($4,500,000 x 21/40) $2,362,500
    Variable ($30 x 22,000)   660,000
    Total $3,022,500

Administration:
    Fixed ($4,500,000 x 1/40) $ 112,500
    Variable ($30 x 1,200)   36,000
    Total $ 148,500

Difficulty: 2   *Objective*: 1

88. The Alex Miller Corporation operates one central plant that has two divisions, the Flashlight Division and the Night Light Division. The following data apply to the coming budget year:

Budgeted costs of the operating the plant
for 10,000 to 20,000 hours:

Fixed operating costs per year	$240,000
Variable operating costs	$10 per hour
Practical capacity	20,000 hours per year

Budgeted long-run usage per year:

Lamp Division	800 hours x 12 months	= 9,600 hours per year
Flashlight Division	450 hours x 12 months	= 5,400 hours per year

Assume that practical capacity is used to calculate the allocation rates. Further assume that actual usage of the Lamp Division was 700 hours and the Flashlight Division was 400 hours for the month of June.

Required:

a. If a single-rate cost-allocation method is used, what amount of operating costs will be budgeted for the Lamp Division each month? For the Flashlight Division each month?

b. For the month of June, if a single-rate cost-allocation method is used, what amount of cost will be allocated to the Lamp Division? To the Flashlight Division? Assume actual usage is used to allocate operating costs.

c. If a dual-rate cost-allocation method is used, what amount of operating costs will be budgeted for the Lamp Division each month? For the Flashlight Division each month?

d. For the month of June, if a dual-rate cost-allocation method is used, what amount of cost will be allocated to the Lamp Division? To the Flashlight Division? Assume budgeted usage is used to allocate fixed operating costs and actual usage is used to allocate variable operating costs.

Answer:

a. Fixed costs $240,000 / 20,000 practical capacity hours = $12 / hour
Single-rate cost-allocation = $12 + $10 = $22 per hour

Lamp Division	800 x $22 / hour	= $17,600 per month
Flashlight Division	450 x $22 / hour	= $9,900 per month

b.

Lamp Division	700 x $22 / hour	= $15,400 per month
Flashlight Division	400 x $22 / hour	= $8,800 per month

c. Fixed costs $240,000 / 20,000 practical capacity hours = $12 / hour
Budgeted costs - Lamp Division
(800 x $12 / hour) + (800 x $10/hour)   = $17,600 per month
Budgeted costs - Flashlight Division
(450 x $12 / hour) + (450 x $10/hour)   = $9,900 per month

88.   (continued)

    d.   Allocated costs for June - Lamp Division
           (800 x $12 / hour) + (700 x $10/hour)   = $16,600 per month
        Allocated costs for June - Flashlight Division
           (450 x $12 / hour) + (400 x $10/hour)   = $9,400 per month

Difficulty: 2   *Objective:*   1

89.   Blaster Drive-In is a fast-food restaurant that sells burgers and hot dogs in a 1950s environment. The fixed operating costs of the company are $5,000 per month. The controlling shareholder, interested in product profitability and pricing, wants all costs allocated to either the burgers or the hot dogs. The following information is provided for the operations of the company:

	Burgers	**Hot Dogs**
Sales for January	4,000	2,400
Sales for February	6,400	2,400

Required:
a.   What amount of fixed operating costs is assigned to the burgers and hot dogs when actual sales are used as the allocation base for January? For February?
b.   Hot dog sales for January and February remained constant. Did the amount of fixed operating costs allocated to hot dogs also remain constant for January and February? Explain why or why not. Comment on any other observations.

Answer:
a.   *January sales*:
    Burgers $5,000 x 4,000/6,400 = $3,125
    Hot dogs $5,000 x 2,400/6,400 = $1,875

    February sales:
    Burgers $5,000 x 6,400/8,800 = $3,636.36
    Hot dogs $5,000 x 2,400/8,800 = $1,363.64

b.   Even though hot dog sales remained constant for both months, the allocation of fixed operating costs decreased by more than $500. The reason is that fixed overhead costs are allocated based on actual sales. The dollar amount is fixed, and since burger sales increased, more of the fixed costs were allocated to the burgers.

    Another observation is that burger sales increased by more than 50% from January to February, while the fixed operating costs assigned to burgers increased by only 16%.

Difficulty: 2   *Objective:*   2

90. Gotham University offers only high-tech graduate-level programs. Gotham has two principal operating departments, Engineering and Computer Sciences, and two support departments, Facility and Technology Maintenance and Enrollment Services. The base used to allocate facility and technology maintenance is budgeted total maintenance hours. The base used to allocate enrollment services is number of credit hours for a department. The Facility and Technology Maintenance budget is $350,000, while the Enrollment Services budget is $950,000. The following chart summarizes budgeted amounts and allocation-base amounts used by each department.

| | | Services Provided: (Annually) | | | |
	Budget	Engineering	Computer Sciences	F&T Maintenance	Enrollment Service
F&T Maintenance (in hours)	$350,000	2,000	5,000	Zero	1,000
Enrollment Service (in credit hrs)	$950,000	24,000	36,000	2,000	Zero

Required:

Use the direct method to allocate support costs to each of the two principal operating departments, Engineering and Computer Sciences. Prepare a schedule showing the support costs allocated to each department.

Answer:

		Engineering	Computer Science
F&T Maintenance	$350,000 x 2/7 =	$100,000	
	$350,000 x 5/7 =		$250,000
Enrollment Service	$950,000 x 24/60 =	$380,000	
	$950,000 x 36/60 =		$570,000
Total		$480,000	$820,000

Difficulty: 2   *Objective*: 3

91. Gotham University offers only high-tech graduate-level programs. Gotham has two principal operating departments, Engineering and Computer Sciences, and two support departments, Facility and Technology Maintenance and Enrollment Services. The base used to allocate facility and technology maintenance is budgeted total maintenance hours. The base used to allocate enrollment services is number of credit hours for a department. The Facility and Technology Maintenance budget is $350,000, while the Enrollment Services budget is $950,000. The following chart summarizes budgeted amounts and allocation-base amounts used by each department.

| | | Services Provided: (Annually) | | | |
	Budget	Engineering	Computer Sciences	F&T Maintenance	Enrollment Service
F&T Maintenance (in hours)	$350,000	1,000	2,000	Zero	5,000
Enrollment Service (in credit hrs)	$950,000	24,000	36,000	2,000	Zero

Required:
Prepare a schedule, which allocates service department costs using the step-down method with the sequence of allocation based on the highest-percentage support concept. Compute the total amount of support costs allocated to each of the two principal operating departments, Engineering and Computer Sciences.

Answer:
F&T Maintenance provided to enrollment services = 5,000/8,000
Enrollment services provided to maintenance = 2,000/62,000
F&T Maintenance provides the greatest amount of service to support departments, so it is allocated first.

F&T Maintenance $350,000 to Enrollment Services = $350,000 x 5/8= $218,750
      to Engineering = $350,000 x 1/8= $ 43,750
      to Computer Science = $350,000 x 2/8= $ 87,500

Enrollment Service costs of $950,000 + $218,750 = $1,168,750
are allocated to Engineering and Computer Science
      to Engineering = $1,168,750 x 24/60 = $467,500
      to Computer Science = $1,168,750 x 36/60 = $701,250

F&T Maintenance	Enrollment Service	Engineering	Computer Science
$350,000	$950,000		
($350,000)	$218,750	$ 43,750	$ 87,500
$ 0	($1,168,750)	$467,500	$701,250
Totals	$ 0	$511,250	$788,750

Difficulty: 3   *Objective*: 3

92. Gotham University offers only high-tech graduate-level programs. Gotham has two principal operating departments, Engineering and Computer Sciences, and two support departments, Facility and Technology Maintenance and Enrollment Services. The base used to allocate facility and technology maintenance is budgeted total maintenance hours. The base used to allocate enrollment services is number of credit hours for a department. The Facility and Technology Maintenance budget is $350,000, while the Enrollment Services budget is $950,000. The following chart summarizes budgeted amounts and allocation-base amounts used by each department.

| | | Services Provided: (Annually) | | | |
	Budget	Engineering	Computer Sciences	F&T Maintenance	Enrollment Service
Engineering	$3,500,000				
Computer Sciences	$1,400,000				
F&T Maintenance (in hours)	$350,000	2,000	1,000	Zero	5,000
Enrollment Service (in credit hrs)	$950,000	24,000	36,000	2,000	Zero

Required:

a. Set up algebraic equations in linear equation form for each activity.

b. Determine total costs for each department by solving the equations from part (a) using the reciprocal method.
(Engineering= Eng; Computer Sciences = CS; Facility and Technical Maintenance = FTM; Enrollment Service = ES)

Answer:

a. Eng = $1,400,000 + 2/8 (FTM) + 24/62 (ES)
CS = $3,500,000 + 1/8 (FTM)+ 36/62 (ES)
FTM = $350,000 + 2/62 (ES)
ES = $950,000 + 5/8 (FTM)

b. *Enrollment Service* = $950,000 + 0.625 (FTM)
ES = $950,000 + .625 (350,000 + 2/62 ES)
ES = $950,000 + $218,750 + .02 ES
0.98 ES = $1,168,750
ES = $1,192,602

FTM = $350,000 + 2/62 ($1,192,602) = $388,471

Engineering = $1,400,000 + 2/8 ($388,471) + 24/62 ($1,192,602)
$1,400,000 + 97,118 + 461,652 = $1,958,770

CS = $3,500,000 + 1/8 ($388,471) + 36/62 ($1,192,602)
= $3,500,000 + $48,559 + $692,479
= $4,241,038

Difficulty: 3   *Objective*: 3

93. Campaign Printing has two service departments, S1 and S2, and two production departments, P1 and P2.

The data for May were as follows:

Activity	Costs	Services provided to: S1	S2	P1	P2
S1	$90,000		10%	40%	50%
S2	$60,000	20%		55%	25%
	Fixed Costs				
P1	$360,000				
P2	$520,000				

Required:

a. Set up algebraic equations in linear form for each activity.
b. Determine total costs for each department by solving the equations from part (a) using the reciprocal method.

Answer:

a. S1= $90,000 + 0.20 (S2)
   S2= $60,000 + 0.10 (S1)

   P1=$360,000 + 0.40 (S1) + 0.55 (S2)
   P2= $520,000 + 0.50 (S1) + 0.25 (S2)

b. S1 = $90,000 + 0.20 ($60,000 + 0.10 (S1))
   S1 = $90,000 + $12,000 + 0.02 (S1)
   0.98 (S1)   = $102,000
            = $104,082

   S2 = $60,000 + (0.10 X $104,082) = $70,408
   P1 = $360,000 + (0.40 x $104,082) + (0.55 x $70,408) = $440,357
   P2 = 520,000 +(0.50 x $104,082) + (0.25 x $70,408) = $589,643

Difficulty: 3   *Objective*:   3

94. The Maintenance Department has been servicing Gizmo Production for four years. Beginning next year, the company is adding a Scrap-Processing Department to recycle the materials from Gizmo Production. As a result, maintenance costs are expected to increase from $480,000 per year to $500,000 per year. The Scrap-Processing Department will utilize 25% of the maintenance efforts.

Required:
a. Using the stand-alone cost-allocation method, identify the amount of maintenance cost that will be allocated to Gizmo Production and the Scrap-Processing Department next year.

b. Using the incremental cost-allocation method, identify the amount of maintenance cost that will be allocated to Gizmo Production and the Scrap-Processing Department next year.

Answer:
a. Gizmo Production = $500,000 x 0.75 = $375,000
Scrap-Processing Department = $500,000 x 0.25 = $125,000

b. Gizmo Production would receive $480,000.
Scrap-Processing Department would receive $20,000, the incremental amount

Difficulty: 1   *Objective*: 4

95. Give examples of bundled products for each of the following industries:

a. Resort hotel
b. Bank
c. Restaurant
d. Computer store
e. Gasoline service station/convenience store
f. Software manufacturer

Answer:
a. Hotel room plus meals, free drinks, use of athletic facilities, morning newspaper
b. Checking account, safe deposit box, wire transfers, certified checks, travelers checks
c. Fixed-price meal includes a beverage, appetizer, entree, and dessert
d. Computer, keyboard, monitor, printer, software, 1-year contract for the repair and maintenance of the computer
e. Gasoline, car wash, coffee
f. Two (or more) software products

Difficulty: 2   *Objective*: 6

96. Max's Movie Store encounters revenue-allocation decisions with its bundled product sales. Here, two or more of the movie videos are sold as a single package. Managers at Max's are keenly interested in individual product-profitability figures. Information pertaining to its three bundled products and the stand-alone selling prices of its individual products is as follows:

	Stand-Alone Selling Price	Cost		Package	Packaged Price
New Releases	$15	$2.00		New & Older	$20
Older Releases	$10	$1.50		New & Classics	$17
Classics	$8	$1.25		All three	$25

Required:

a. With selling prices as the weights, allocate the $25 packaged price of "All Three" to the three videos using the stand-alone revenue-allocation method.

b. Allocate the $25 packaged price of "All Three" to the three types of videos using the incremental revenue-allocation method. Assume New Releases is the primary product, followed by Older Releases, and then Classics.

Answer:

a. New $15 + Older $10 + Classics $8   = $33.00

    New $15 / $33 x $25   = $11.36
    Old $10 / $33 x $25   = $ 7.58
    Classics $8 / $33 x $25   = $ 6.06
        Total $25.00

b.

Product	Revenue Allocated	Revenue Remaining To Be Allocated
New Releases	$15	$25-15 = $10
Older Releases	$10	$25 - $15 - $10 = $0
Classics	$ 0	none
Total revenue allocated	$25	

Difficulty: 2   *Objective*:   7

97. Software For You encounters revenue-allocation decisions with its bundled product sales. Here, two or more units of the software are sold as a single package. Managers at Software For You are keenly interested in individual product-profitability figures. Information pertaining to its three bundled products and the stand-alone selling prices of its individual products is as follows:

	Stand-Alone Selling Price	Cost		Package	Packaged Price
Word Processing (WP)	$125	$18		WP & SS	$220
Spreadsheet (SS)	$150	$20		WP & AS	$280
Accounting Software (AS)	$225	$25		All three	$380

Required:

a. Using the stand-alone revenue-allocation method, allocate the $380 packaged price of "All Three" to the three software products
   1.   with selling prices as the weights.
   2.   with individual product costs as the weights.
   3.   based on physical units.

b. Allocate the $380 packaged price of "All Three" to the three software products using the incremental revenue-allocation method. Assume Word Processing is the primary product, followed by Spreadsheet, and then Accounting Software.

Answer:

a1.   WP $125 + SS $150 + AS $225 = $500

   WP $125 / $500 x $380   = $ 95
   SS $150 / $500 x $380   = $114
   AS $225 / $500 x $380   = $171
      Total $380

a2.   WP $18 + SS $20 + AS $25 = $63

   WP $18 / $63 x $380   = $108.57
   SS $20 / $63 x $380   = $120.64
   AS $25 / $63 x $380   = $150.79
      Total $380.00

a3.   1 / (1+ 1 + 1) x $380 = $126.67 per software package

97. (continued)

b.

Product	Revenue Allocated	Revenue Remaining To Be Allocated
WP	$125	$380-125 = $255
SS	$150	$380 - $125 - $150 = $105
AS	$105	none
Total revenue allocated	$380	

Difficulty: 2   *Objective*: 7

98. The Pitt Corporation has been outsourcing data processing in the belief that such outsourcing would reduce costs and increase corporate profitability. In spite of this, there has been no meaningful increase in corporate profitability.

    Previously, Pitt used a single-rate method to allocate data processing costs. A per unit cost for data processing was computed and compared to the price of the outside supplier. The price of the outside supplier was lower, so the outside bid was accepted.

    Required:

    Formulate a possible reason why Pitt's profitability has not shown improvement in terms of the cost allocation method used.

    Answer:

    The single-rate cost allocation method groups fixed and variable costs together within each cost pool. The deficiency of this comparison is that the fixed costs included in the cost pool will continue. Therefore, Pitt may be spending more funds in total than if the work was still performed in-house.

    Difficulty: 3   *Objective*: 1

99. Van Meter Fig Company has substantial fluctuations in its production costs because of the seasonality of figs.

    Would you recommend an actual or budgeted allocation base? Why? Would you recommend calculating monthly, seasonal, or annual allocation rates? Why?

    Answer:

    The company should use a long-term budget amount for the allocation base. Neither an actual amount nor a budgeted monthly amount will provide the company with reliable allocation amounts because of the variability in the supply of figs. With long-term budgeted usage, the user departments will know their allocated costs in advance and should help them in their planning.

    Difficulty: 3   *Objective*: 1

100. Jonathan has managed a downtown store in a major metropolitan city for several years. The firm has ten stores in varying locations. In the past, senior management noticed Jonathan's work and he has received very good annual evaluations for his management of the store.

This year his store has generated steady growth in sales, but earnings have been deteriorating. After examining the monthly performance report generated by the company budgeting department, he noticed that increasing fixed costs is what is causing the decrease in earnings.

Administrative corporate costs, primarily fixed costs, are allocated to individual stores each month based on actual sales for that month. Two of these stores are currently growing at a rapid pace, while four other stores are having operating difficulties.

Required:

From the information presented, what do you think is the cause of Jonathan's reported decrease in earnings? How can this be corrected?

Answer:

The variations in reporting are probably caused by the growth fluctuations of the other branches. When fixed costs are involved in an allocation process based on actual usage, one unit receiving the allocation can have changes even when it doesn't change itself. This is caused by the other stores causing changes in the allocation base, thereby causing everyone to receive different allocation amounts, even those who don't have changes in their base. Because Jonathan's sales have been increasing, his allocation of corporate fixed costs has also increased.

To correct the problem, the corporation should change to using budgeted performance as the allocation base and use a denominator level that reflects expected performance over the long run. An allocation base other than sales may also want to be considered.

Difficulty: 3   *Objective*:   2

101. Why would businesses want to sell bundled products? What benefits, if any, are there for the consumer?

Answer:

Businesses seek to sell bundled products as a means of increasing total revenues and spreading fixed costs across a larger dollar amount of revenues. The result is usually an increase in overall corporate profitability.

In order to sell more goods, customers must believe that they are getting value for their money.

101. (continued)

Receiving additional goods or services for what is likely only a marginal increase in price over the price of the primary product could entice consumers to buy the bundled package rather than forgoing the purchase altogether. While not strictly a bundled product, an automobile provides a good example.

Car dealers sell cars that are "loaded with options." The price is less than the basic car with the options added separately. Consumers feel they are getting a benefit even though the car might have more options than they would have purchased. The manufacturer has greater revenue than would be the case without the "bundle."

A benefit for the consumer is an extra product for only a marginal increase in price that is probably less than the separate price of the products.

Difficulty: 2   *Objective*: 6

102. Describe and discuss the two methods of allocating revenues of a bundled package to the individual products in that package. Describe any special problems associated with the method.

Answer:

Method 1. The stand-alone revenue-allocation method allocates bundled revenues using product-specific information on the bundle of products as the weights to allocate the bundled revenues to the individual products. When allocating bundled revenues, the proportion of revenues is allocated on four alternative bases: (1) individual product unit selling prices, (2) individual product unit costs, (3) physical units, or (4) stand-alone product revenues. It is preferable to allocate common revenues based on unit revenues, since this best reflects customers' willingness to pay for the different products. However, if the products are never sold separately, unit-selling prices are unavailable, so revenues are allocated based on unit costs (which should be available in the firm's accounting records), or simply by the number of physical units that comprise the bundle.

Method 2. The incremental revenue-allocation method ranks the individual products in the bundled product according to criteria determined by management. This ranking is then used to allocate the bundled revenues to individual products. One problem is how to determine the ranking. Individual product managers want to ranked first so that as much of the revenue as possible is allocated to their product. This can result in disputes between managers.

Difficulty: 2   *Objective*: 7

CHAPTER 16: COST ALLOCATION: JOINT PRODUCTS AND BYPRODUCTS

TRUE/FALSE

1. Joint costs are incurred beyond the splitoff point and are assignable to individual products.

   Answer: False   *Difficulty:* 2   *Objective:* 1
   Joint costs are incurred prior to the splitoff.

2. Separable costs are assignable after the splitoff point.

   Answer: True   *Difficulty:* 2   *Objective:* 1

3. The focus of joint costing is assigning costs to individual products as assembly occurs.

   Answer: False   *Difficulty:* 2   *Objective:* 1
   The focus is accumulating costs incurred on the joint products.

4. A byproduct has a minimal sales value.

   Answer: True   *Difficulty:* 2   *Objective:* 2

5 The sales value at splitoff method is an example of allocating costs based upon the benefits-received criterion.

   Answer: True   *Difficulty:* 2   *Objective:* 4

6. A major deficiency of the sales value at splitoff method is that this method does not allow management to obtain individual product costs and gross-margin information.

   Answer: False   *Difficulty:* 2   *Objective:* 4
   The sales value at splitoff method enables the accountant to obtain individual product costs and gross margins.

7. An advantage of the physical-measure method is that obtaining physical measures for all products is an easy task.

   Answer: False   *Difficulty:* 2   *Objective:* 4
   For some products such as gas, obtaining physical measures is difficult.

8. The general guideline for using the physical-measure method is to include only joint products or main products in the physical-measure weighting computations.

   Answer: True   *Difficulty:* 2   *Objective:* 4

9. The estimated net realizable value method is used when the market selling prices at the splitoff point are not available.

Answer: True   *Difficulty:* 2   *Objective:* 4

10. Net realizable value generally means expected sales value plus expected separable costs.

Answer: False   *Difficulty:* 2   *Objective:* 4
Net realizable value is expected sales value minus expected separable costs.

11. The net realizable value method is generally used for products or services that are processed and after splitoff additional value is added to the product and a selling price can be determined.

Answer: True   *Difficulty:* 2   *Objective:* 4

12. The estimated net realizable value method allocates joint costs on the basis of the expected final sales value in the ordinary course of business less the expected separable costs of production and marketing.

Answer: True   *Difficulty:* 2   *Objective:* 4

13. The constant gross-margin percentage method differs from market-based joint-cost allocation method (sales value at splitoff and estimated net realizable value) since no account is taken of profits earned before or after the splitoff point when allocating joint costs.

Answer: False   *Difficulty:* 2   *Objective:* 4
The constant gross-margin percentage method takes account of the profits earned before or after the splitoff when allocating joint costs.

14. The sales value at splitoff method presupposes the exact number of subsequent steps undertaken for further processing.

Answer: False   *Difficulty:* 2   *Objective:* 4
The sales value at splitoff method does not presuppose the exact number of subsequent steps.

15. A criticism of the practice of carrying inventories at estimated net realizable values is that this practice recognizes income before sales are made.

Answer: True   *Difficulty:* 2   *Objective:* 4

16. Physical measures such as weight or volume are the best indicator of the benefits received for allocating joint costs.

    Answer: False   *Difficulty*: 2   *Objective*: 5
    Revenues are a better indicator of the benefits received than are physical measures.

17. Joint costs that do not differ between alternatives are particularly relevant for decision making.

    Answer: False   *Difficulty*: 2   *Objective*: 6
    Only costs that differ are relevant to a manager's decision.

18. Byproducts are recognized in the general ledger either at the time of production or at the time of sale.

    Answer: True   *Difficulty*: 2   *Objective*: 7

19. Recognition of byproducts in the financial statements at the time of sale usually occurs when the dollar amounts of the byproducts are immaterial.

    Answer: True   *Difficulty*: 2   *Objective*: 7

20. A sound reason for reporting revenue from byproducts as an income statement item at the time of sale is to lessen the chance of managers managing reported earnings.

    Answer: False   *Difficulty*: 2   *Objective*: 7
    This method makes it easier for managers to time earnings since they can time the sale of products and give earnings a boost.

21. What type of cost is the result of an event that results in more than one product or service simultaneously?
    a. Byproduct cost
    b. Joint cost
    c. Main cost
    d. Separable cost

    Answer: b   *Difficulty:* 2   *Objective:* 1

22. All costs incurred beyond the splitoff point that are assignable to one or more individual products are called
    a. byproduct costs.
    b. joint costs.
    c. main costs.
    d. separable costs.

    Answer: d   *Difficulty:* 2   *Objective:* 1

23. In joint costing
    a. costs are assigned to individual products as assembly of the product occurs.
    b. costs are assigned to individual products as disassembly of the product occurs.
    c. a single production process yields two or more products.
    d. both (b) and (c).

    Answer: d   *Difficulty:* 3   *Objective:* 1

24. When a single manufacturing process yields two products, one of which has a relatively high sales value compared to the other, the two products are respectively known as
    a. joint products and byproducts.
    b. joint products and scrap.
    c. main products and byproducts.
    d. main products and joint products.

    Answer: c   *Difficulty:* 2   *Objective:* 2

25. Byproducts and main products are differentiated by
    a. number of units per processing period.
    b. weight or volume of outputs per period.
    c. the amount of sales value per unit.
    d. none of the above.

    Answer: c   *Difficulty:* 2   *Objective:* 2

26. All of the following changes may indicate a change in product classification of a manufacturing process which has a splitoff point EXCEPT
    a. a byproduct increases in sales value due to a new application.
    b. a main product becomes a joint product.
    c. a main product becomes technologically obsolete.
    d. a byproduct loses its market due to a new invention.

    Answer: b   *Difficulty:* 2   *Objective:* 2

27. Which of the following methods of allocating costs use market-based data?
    a. Sales value at splitoff method
    b. Estimated net realizable value method
    c. The constant gross-margin percentage method
    d. All of the above use market-based methods

    Answer: d   *Difficulty:* 1   *Objective:* 2

28. Products with a relatively low sales value are known as
    a. scrap.
    b. main products.
    c. joint products.
    d. byproducts.

    Answer: d   *Difficulty:* 1   *Objective:* 2

29. Which of the following statements is true regarding main products and byproducts?
    a. Product classifications do not change over the short run.
    b. Product classifications do not change over the long run.
    c. Product classifications may change over time.
    d. The cause-and-effect criterion determines the classification.

    Answer: c   *Difficulty:* 3   *Objective:* 2

30. Outputs with zero sales value are accounted for by
    a. listing these various outputs in a footnote to the financial statements.
    b. including the items as a relatively small portion of the value assigned to the products produced during the accounting period.
    c. making journal entries to reflect an estimate of possible values.
    d. none of the above.

    Answer: d   *Difficulty:* 3   *Objective:* 2

31. Which of the following is a reason to allocate joint costs?
    a. Rate regulation requirements, if applicable
    b. Cost of goods sold computations
    c. Insurance settlement cost information requirements
    d. All of the above are reasons to allocate joint costs.

    Answer: d   *Difficulty:* 1   *Objective:* 3

32. A business which enters into a contract to purchase a product (or products), and will compensate the manufacturer under a cost reimbursement formula, should take an active part in the determination of how joint costs are allocated because
   a. the manufacturer will attempt to allocate as large a portion of its costs to these products.
   b. if the manufacturer successfully allocates a large portion of its costs to these products then it will be able to sell its other nonreimbursed products at lower prices.
   c. the FASB requires the business to participate in the cost allocation process.
   d. of both (a) and (b).

   Answer: d   *Difficulty:* 3   *Objective:* 3

33. Proper costs allocation for inventory costing and cost-of-goods-sold computations are important because
   a. inventory costing is essential for proper balance sheet presentation.
   b. most states have laws requiring proper balance sheet presentation, and recommended allocation methods.
   c. cost of goods sold is an important component in the determination of net income.
   d. of both (a) and (c).

   Answer: d   *Difficulty:* 3   *Objective:* 3

34. Which of the following is NOT a primary reason for allocating joint costs?
   a. Cost justification and insurance settlement cost information requirements
   b. Cost justification and asset measurement
   c. Income measurement and rate regulation requirements
   d. To calculate the bonus of the chief executive officer

   Answer: d   *Difficulty:* 1   *Objective:* 3

35. All of the following methods may be used to allocate joint costs EXCEPT
   a. the constant gross-margin percentage method.
   b. the estimated net realizable value method.
   c. the present value allocation method.
   d. the sales value at splitoff method.

   Answer: c   *Difficulty:* 2   *Objective:* 4

36. An example of a market-based approach to allocating joint costs is (are) allocating joint costs based on
   a. sales value at splitoff method.
   b. physical volume.
   c. constant gross-margin percentage method.
   d. both (a) and (c).

   Answer: d   *Difficulty:* 3   *Objective:* 4

37. Which of the following statements is true in regard to the cause-and-effect relationship between allocated joint costs and individual products?
    a. A high individual product value results in a high level of joint costs.
    b. A low individual product value results in a low level of joint costs.
    c. A high individual product value results in a low level of joint costs.
    d. There is no cause-and-effect relationship.

    Answer: d   *Difficulty:* 3   *Objective:* 4

38. The benefits-received criteria for allocating joint costs indicates market-based measures are preferred because
    a. physical measures such as volume are a clearer basis for allocating cost than other measures.
    b. other measures are more difficult to calculate.
    c. revenues are usually the best indicator of the benefits received.
    d. of none of the above.

    Answer: c   *Difficulty:* 1   *Objective:* 4

THE FOLLOWING INFORMATION APPLIES TO QUESTIONS 39 THROUGH 42.
Yakima Manufacturing purchases trees from Cascade Lumber and processes them up to the splitoff point where two products (paper and pencil casings) are obtained. The products are then sold to an independent company that markets and distributes them to retail outlets. The following information was collected for the month of November:

Trees processed:	50 trees (yield is 30,000 sheets of paper and 30,000 pencil casings and no scrap)	
Production:	paper	30,000 sheets
	pencil casings	30,000
Sales:	paper	29,000 at $0.04 per page
	pencil casings	30,000 at $0.10 per casing

Cost of purchasing 50 trees and processing them up to the splitoff point to yield 30,000 sheets of paper and 30,000 pencil casings is $1,500.

Yakima's accounting department reported no beginning inventories and ending inventory of 1,000 sheets of paper.

39. What is the sales value at the splitoff point for paper?
    a. $120
    b. $1,160
    c. $1,200
    d. $1,950

    Answer: c   *Difficulty:* 2   *Objective:* 4
    Paper: 30,000 sheets x $0.04 = $1,200.00

40. What is the sales value at the splitoff point of the pencil casings?
    a. $300
    b. $1,480
    c. $3,000
    d. $3,750

Answer: c   *Difficulty:* 1   *Objective:* 4
Pencils: 30,000 casings x $0.10 = $3,000.00

41. If the sales value at splitoff method is used, what are the approximate joint costs assigned to ending inventory for paper?
    a. $14.29
    b. $50.00
    c. $435.00
    d. $750.00

Answer: a   *Difficulty:* 3   *Objective:* 4
$1,200/($1,200 + $3,000) = 28.57%
28.57% x $1,500 x 1,000/30,000 = $14.29

42. If the sales value at splitoff method is used, what is the approximate production cost for each pencil casing?
    a. $0.0250
    b. $0.0255
    c. $0.0335
    d. $0.0357

Answer: d   *Difficulty:* 3   *Objective:* 4
$3,000/($1,200 + $3,000) x $1,500 = $1,071
$1,071/30,000 casings = $0.0357

43. Yakima Manufacturing purchases trees from Cascade Lumber and processes them up to the splitoff point where two products (paper and pencil casings) are obtained. The products are then sold to an independent company that markets and distributes them to retail outlets. The following information was collected for the month of May:

Trees processed: 50 trees (yield is 35,000 sheets of paper and 30,000 pencil casings and no scrap)

Production:

	paper	35,000 sheets
	pencil casings	30,000

Sales:

	paper	34,000 at $0.04 per page
	pencil casings	30,000 at $0.10 per casing

Cost of purchasing 50 trees and processing them up to the splitoff point to yield 35,000 sheets of paper and 30,000 pencil casings is $1,500.

Yakima's Manufacturing's accounting department reported no beginning inventories and ending inventory of 1,000 sheets of paper.

What are the paper's and the pencils' approximate weighted cost proportions using the sales value at splitoff method, respectively?
a.   50.00% and 50.00%
b.   33.33% and 66.67%
c.   31.82% and 68.18%
d.   none of the above

Answer: c   *Difficulty*:   2   *Objective*:   4
$1,400 + 3,000 = $4,400
$1,400/$4,400 = 31.82%
$3,000/$4,400 = 68.18%

44. The Arvid Corporation manufactures widgets, gizmos, and turnbols from a joint process. May production is 4,000 widgets; 7,000 gizmos; and 8,000 turnbols. Respective per unit selling prices at splitoff are $15, $10, and $5. Joint costs up to the splitoff point are $75,000. If joint costs are allocated based upon the sales value at splitoff, what amount of joint costs will be allocated to the widgets?
a. $30,882
b. $26,471
c. $17,647
d. $28,125

Answer: b   *Difficulty*:   2   *Objective*:   4
$15 x 4,000   = $60,000
$10 x 7,000   = $70,000
$ 5 x 8,000   = $40,000
   Total   = $170,000
$60,000/$170,000 x $75,000 = $26,471

45. Product X is sold for $8 a unit and Product Y is sold for $12 a unit. Each product can also be sold at the splitoff point. Product X can be sold for $5 and Product Y for $4. Joint costs for the two products totaled $4,000 for January for 600 units of X and 500 units of Y. What are the respective joint costs assigned each unit of products X and Y if the sales value at splitoff method is used?

    a. $2.96 and $4.44
    b. $4.00 and $4.55
    c. $4.00 and $3.20
    d. $4.55 and $4.55

    Answer: c   *Difficulty:* 2   *Objective:* 4
    Total splitoff market value = (600 x $5) + (500 x $4) = $5,000
    Product X = $3,000/$5,000 x $4,000 = $2,400/600 = $4.00
    Product Y = $2,000/$5,000 x $4,000 = $1,600/500 = $3.20

46. A reason why a physical-measure to allocate joint costs is less preferred than the sales value at splitoff is

    a. a physical measure such as volume is difficult to estimate because of shrinkage.
    b. physical volume usually has little relationship to the revenue producing power of products.
    c. a physical measure usually results in the costs being allocated to the product that weighs the most.
    d. all of the above are reasons why the sales value at splitoff method is preferred to a physical volume measure.

    Answer: d   *Difficulty:* 2   *Objective:* 4

THE FOLLOWING INFORMATION APPLIES TO QUESTIONS 47 THROUGH 49.
The Oxnard Corporation processes a liquid component up to the splitoff point where two products, Mr. DirtOut and Mr. SinkClean, are produced and sold. The following material was collected for the month of January. There was no beginning inventory.

Direct materials processed:		250,000 gallons (242,500 gallons of good product)
Production:	Mr. DirtOut	147,500 gallons
	Mr. SinkClean	95,000 gallons
Sales:	Mr. DirtOut	140,500 at $110 per gallon
	Mr. SinkClean	91,000 at $ 100 per gallon

The cost of purchasing 250,000 gallons of direct materials and processing it up to the splitoff point to yield a total of 242,500 gallons of good product was $380,000.

47. What are the physical-volume proportions to allocate joint costs for Mr. DirtOut and Mr. SinkClean, respectively?
    a.   59.00% and 41.00%
    b.   60.82% and 39.18%
    c.   39.18% and 60.82%
    d.   59.79% and 40.21%

    Answer: b   *Difficulty*:   2   *Objective*:   4
    Mr. DirtOut: 147,500/242,500 = 60.82%
    Mr. SinkClean: 95,000/242,500 = 39.18%

48. When using a physical-volume measure, what is the approximate amount of joint costs that will be allocated to Mr. DirtOut and Mr. SinkClean?
    a. $231,116 and $148,884
    b. $224,200 and $155,800
    c. $227,202 and $152,798
    d. $230,626 and $149,374

    Answer: a   *Difficulty*:   2   *Objective*:   4
    $380,000 x 0.6082 = $231,116; $380,000 x 0.3918 = $148,884

49. When using the physical-volume method, what is Mr. DirtOut's approximate production cost per unit?
    a. $1.52
    b. $1.54
    c. $1.57
    d. $1.61

    Answer: c   *Difficulty*:   3   *Objective*:   4
    $231,116/147,500 = $1.57

50. Argon Manufacturing Company processes direct materials up to the splitoff point where two products (U and V) are obtained and sold. The following information was collected for last quarter of the calendar year.

Direct materials processed:		10,000 gallons (10,000 gallons yield 9,500 gallons of good product and 500 gallons of shrinkage)
Production:	U	5,000 gallons
	V	4,500 gallons
Sales:	U	4,750 at $150 per gallon
	V	4,000 at $100 per gallon

The cost of purchasing 10,000 gallons of direct materials and processing it up to the splitoff point to yield a total of 9,500 gallons of good products was $975,000.

Beginning inventories totaled 50 gallons for U and 25 gallons for V. Ending inventory amounts reflected 300 gallons of Product U and 525 gallons of Product V. October costs per unit were the same as November.

What are the physical-volume proportions for products U and V, respectively?
a. 47.37% and 53.63%
b. 55.00% and 45.00%
c. 52.63% and 47.37%
d. 54.00% and 46.00%

Answer: c   Difficulty: 3   Objective: 4
X: 5,000 / 9,500 = 52.63%
Y: 4,500 / 9,500 = 47.37%

THE FOLLOWING INFORMATION APPLIES TO QUESTIONS 51 THROUGH 57.

The Morton Company processes unprocessed goat milk up to the splitoff point where two products, condensed goat milk and skim goat milk result. The following information was collected for the month of October:

Direct Materials processed:	65,000 gallons (shrinkage was 10%)	
Production:	condensed goat milk	26,100 gallons
	skim goat milk	32,400 gallons
Sales:	condensed goat milk	$3.50 per gallon
	skim goat milk	$2.50 per gallon

The costs of purchasing the 65,000 gallons of unprocessed goat milk and processing it up to the splitoff point to yield a total of 58,500 gallons of salable product was $72,240. There were no inventory balances of either product.

Condensed goat milk may be processed further to yield 19,500 gallons (the remainder is shrinkage) of a medicinal milk product, Xyla, for an additional processing cost of $3 per usable gallon. Xyla can be sold for $18 per gallon.

Skim goat milk can be processed further to yield 28,100 gallons of skim goat ice cream, for an additional processing cost per usable gallon of $2.50. The product can be sold for $9 per gallon.

There are no beginning and ending inventory balances.

51. What is the estimated net realizable value of Xyla at the splitoff point?
    a. $182,650
    b. $252,900
    c. $292,500
    d. $351,000

Answer: c   *Difficulty:* 3   *Objective:* 4
See computations at #53.

52. What is the estimated net realizable value of the skim goat ice cream at the splitoff point.
    a. $182,650
    b. $252,900
    c. $110,200
    d. $85,450

Answer: a   *Difficulty:* 3   *Objective:* 4
See computations at #53.

53. Using estimated net realizable value, what amount of the $72,240 of joint costs would be allocated Xyla and the skim goat ice cream?
   a. $41,971 and $30,269
   b. $44,471 and $27,769
   c. $32,796 and $39,444
   d. $36,120 and $36,120

   Answer: b   *Difficulty:*   3   *Objective:*   4

	XYLA	Skim Goat	Total
Sales	19,500 x $18 = $351,000	28,100 x $9 = $252,900	$603,900
Less: Sep cost	19,500 x $3 = $ 58,500	28,100 x $2.50 = $ 70,250	
Est. NRValue	$292,500	$182,650	$475,150
Weighting	.6156	.3844	
Jt costs allocated	$72,240 x .6156 = $44,471	$72,240 x .3844 = $27,769	

54. Using the sales value at splitoff method, what is the gross-margin percentage for condensed goat milk at the splitoff point?
   a.   21.1%
   b.   55.1%
   c.   58.1%
   d.   38.2%

   Answer: c   *Difficulty:*   3   *Objective:*   4
   See computations at #55.

55. Using the sales value at splitoff method, what is the gross-margin percentage for skim goat milk at the splitoff point?
   a.   21.1%
   b.   55.1%
   c.   58.1%
   d.   38.2%

   Answer: c   *Difficulty:*   3   *Objective:*   4

	Condensed Goat Milk	Skim Goat Milk	Total
Revenues	26,100 x $3.50 = $91,350	32,400 x $2.50 = $81,000	$172,350
Percentage	$91,350/$172,350 = 0.53	$81,000/$172,350 = 0.47	
Separable costs	$72,240 x .53 = $38,287	$72,240 x .47 = $33,953	
Gross margin	$53,063	$47,047	
GM percentage	$53,063/$91,350 = 0.581	$47,047/$81,000 = 0.581	

56. How much (if any) extra income would Morton earn if it produced and sold all of the Xyla from the condensed goat milk? Allocate joint processing costs based upon relative sales value on the splitoff. (Extra income means income in excess of what Morton would have earned from selling condensed goat milk.)
   a. $53,063
   b. $254,213
   c. $201,150
   d. $96,787

Answer: c   *Difficulty*: 3   *Objective*: 4

See computations at #57.

57. How much (if any) extra income would Morton earn if it produced and sold skim milk ice cream from goats rather than goat skim milk? Allocate joint processing costs based upon the relative sales value at the splitoff point.
   a. $47,047
   b. $117,297
   c. $101,650
   d. $70,250

Answer: c   *Difficulty*: 3   *Objective*: 4

	Condensed Goat Milk	Skim Goat Milk
Revenue	$351,000	$252,900
Joint costs (see #55)	(38,287)	(33,953)
Process costs	($3 x 19,500) = (58,500)	($2.50 x 28,100) = (70,250)
Revenue (net)	254,213	148,697
Gross margin (see #55)	(53,063)	(47,047)
Difference	$201,150	$101,650

58. Chem Manufacturing Company processes direct materials up to the splitoff point where two products (X and Y) are obtained and sold. The following information was collected for the month of November.

Direct materials processed:		10,000 gallons (10,000 gallons yield 9,500 gallons of good product and 500 gallons of shrinkage)
Production:	X	5,000 gallons
	Y	4,500 gallons
Sales:	X	4,750 at $150 per gallon
	Y	4,000 at $100 per gallon

The cost of purchasing 10,000 gallons of direct materials and processing it up to the splitoff point to yield a total of 9,500 gallons of good products was $975,000.

The beginning inventories totaled 50 gallons for X and 25 gallons for Y. Ending inventory amounts reflected 300 gallons of Product X and 525 gallons of Product Y. October costs per unit were the same as November.

Using the physical-volume method, what is Product X's approximate gross-margin percentage?
a. 32%
b. 33%
c. 35%
d. 38%

Answer: a   *Difficulty:* 2   *Objective:* 4

Sales (4,750 x $150)	$712,500
Cost of Goods Sold 4,750 x $*513,142/5,000	487,485
Gross Margin	$225,015

* 5,000/(5,000 + 4,500) = 0.5263 x $975,000 = $513,142
Gross-margin percentage $225,015/$712,500 = 0.32 rounded

59. Beverage Drink Company processes direct materials up to the splitoff point where two products, A and B, are obtained. The following information was collected for the month of July:

Direct materials processed:	2,500	liters (with 20% shrinkage)	

Production:	A	1,500 liters
	B	500 liters

Sales:	A	$15.00 per liter
	B	$10.00 per liter

Cost of purchasing 2,500 liters of direct materials and processing it up to the splitoff point to yield a total of 2,000 liters of good products was $4,500. There were no inventory balances of A and B.

Product A may be processed further to yield 1,375 liters of Product Z5 for an additional processing cost of $150. Product Z5 is sold for $25.00 per liter. There was no beginning inventory and ending inventory was 125 liters.

Product B may be processed further to yield 375 liters of Product W3 for an additional processing cost of $275. Product W3 is sold for $30.00 per liter. There was no beginning inventory and ending inventory was 25 liters.

If Product Z5 and Product W3 are produced, what are the expected sales values of production, respectively?
a. $11,250 and $34,375
b. $22,500 and $ 5,000
c. $31,250 and $10,500
d. $34,375 and $11,250

Answer: d   *Difficulty:* 2   *Objective:* 4
Z5 = 1,375 liters x $25   = $34,375
W3 = 375 liters x $30   = $11,250

60. Cola Drink Company processes direct materials up to the splitoff point where two products, A and B, are obtained. The following information was collected for the month of July:

Direct materials processed: 2,500 liters (with 20% shrinkage)

Production: A   1,500 liters
                       B   500 liters

Sales: A $15.00 per liter
                       B $10.00 per liter

Cost of purchasing 2,500 liters of direct materials and processing it up to the splitoff point to yield a total of 2,000 liters of good products was $4,500. There were no inventory balances of A and B.

Product A may be processed further to yield 1,375 liters of Product Z5 for an additional processing cost of $150. Product Z5 is sold for $25.00 per liter. There was no beginning inventory and ending inventory was 125 liters.

Product B may be processed further to yield 375 liters of Product W3 for an additional processing cost of $275. Product W3 is sold for $30.00 per liter. There was no beginning inventory and ending inventory was 25 liters.

What is Product Z5's estimated net realizable value at the splitoff point?
a. $11,100
b. $22,350
c. $34,225
d. $34,375

Answer: c   Difficulty: 3   Objective: 4
1,375 x $25 = $34,375; $34,375 - $150 = $34,225

61. Which of the following is a disadvantage of the physical-measure method of allocating joint costs?
a.   The measurement basis for each product may be different.
b.   The need for a common denominator.
c.   The physical measure may not reflect the product's ability to generate revenues.
d.   All of the above are disadvantages.

Answer: d   Difficulty: 2   Objective: 4

62. Which of the methods of allocating joint costs usually is considered the simplest to implement?
a.   Estimated net realizable value
b.   Constant gross-margin percentage NRV
c.   Sales value at splitoff
d.   All of the above can be the easiest to implement given the proper circumstances.

Answer: c   Difficulty: 2   Objective: 4

63. Industries that recognize income on each product when production is completed include
    a.   mining.
    b.   toy manufacturers.
    c.   canning.
    d.   both (a) and (c).

    Answer: d   *Difficulty:*   2   *Objective:*   4

64 Why do accountants criticize the practice of carrying inventories at estimated net realizable values?
    a.   The costs of producing the products are usually estimates.
    b.   There is usually no clearly defined realizable value for these inventories.
    c.   The effect of this practice is to recognize income before sales are made.
    d.   All of the above are well-recognized criticisms of this practice.

    Answer: c   *Difficulty:*   2   *Objective:*   4

65. When a product is the result of a joint process, the decision to process the product past the splitoff point further should be influenced by
    a.   the total amount of the joint costs.
    b.   the portion of the joint costs allocated to the individual products.
    c.   the extra revenue earned past the splitoff point.
    d.   the extra operating income earned past the splitoff point.

    Answer: d   *Difficulty:*   1   *Objective:*   6

66. If managers make sell or process further decisions using an incremental revenue/incremental cost approach, which method will show each product budgeted to have a positive (or zero) operating income on the resulting budgeted product-line income statement?
    a.   Sales value at splitoff
    b.   Estimated NRV
    c.   Constant gross-margin percentage NRV
    d.   All of the above methods

    Answer: d   *Difficulty:*   2   *Objective:*   6

67. Which method of accounting recognizes byproducts in the financial statements at the time their production is completed?
    a.   Production allocation method
    b.   Sale method
    c.   Production method
    d.   None of the above

    Answer: c   *Difficulty:*   2   *Objective:*   7

THE FOLLOWING INFORMATION APPLIES TO QUESTIONS 68 AND 69.
Sparta Company processes 15,000 gallons of direct materials to produce two products, Product X and Product Y. Product X sells for $4 per gallon and Product Y, the main product, sells for $50 per gallon. The following information is for August:

	Production	Sales	Beginning Inventory	Ending Inventory
Product X:	4,375	4,000	0	375
Product Y:	10,000	9,625	125	500

The manufacturing costs totaled $15,000.

68. What is the byproduct's net revenue reduction if byproducts are recognized in the general ledger during production and their revenues are a reduction of cost?
    a. $0
    b. $1,500
    c. $16,000
    d. $17,500

    Answer: c *Difficulty:* 3 *Objective:* 7
    4,000 gallons x $4 = $16,000

69. How much is the ending inventory reduction for the byproduct if byproducts are recognized in the general ledger at the point of sale?
    a. $0
    b. $563
    c. $1,500
    d. $17,500

    Answer: a *Difficulty:* 2 *Objective:* 7

70. A negative consequence of recording byproducts in the accounting records when the sale occurs is
    a. the revenue from the byproducts is usually fairly large, and the accounting records will be distorted.
    b. managers can time earnings by their decision when to sell byproducts.
    c. managers have an incentive to stockpile byproducts.
    d. both (b) and (c).

    Answer: d *Difficulty:* 1 *Objective:* 7

EXERCISES AND PROBLEMS

71. In each of the following industries, identify possible joint (or severable) products at the splitoff point.

   a. Coal
   b. Petroleum
   c. Dairy
   d. Lamb
   e. Lumber
   f. Cocoa Beans
   g. Christmas Trees
   h. Salt
   i. Cowhide

   Answer:

   a. Coke, Gas, Benzole, Tar, Ammonia
   b. Crude Oil, Gas, Raw LPG
   c. Milk, Butter, Cheese, Ice Cream, Skim Milk
   d. Lamb Cuts, Tripe, Hides, Bones, Fat
   e. Board, Newsprint, Shavings, Chips, etc.
   f. Cocoa Butter, Cocoa Powder, Cocoa Shells
   g. Christmas Trees, Wreaths, Decorations
   h. Hydrogen, Chlorine, Caustic Soda
   i. Leather, Suede, Chew Toys

   Difficulty: 1   *Objective*:   1

72. List three reasons why we allocate joint costs to individual products or services. Give an example of when the particular cost allocation reason would come into use.

Answer:

a. *For inventory costing, and cost of goods sold computations for financial accounting purposes.*
Example: Cost of goods sold and ending inventory valuation is necessary for reports to shareholders and for the inland revenue service.

b. *For internal costing and cost of goods sold computations for internal reporting purposes.*
Example: These computations are necessary for division profitability analysis.

c. *Reimbursement under contracts.*
Example: A firm produces multiple products or services–and uses the same resources and facilities to produce the products or services. But not all the firm's products are under the contract. The firm must allocate the cost of these shared facilities or resources to reflect the portion used by the product under the contract.

d. *Insurance settlement computations.*
Example: Where a business with multiple products or services claim losses under an insurance policy and wants to calculate the loss. The insurance company and the insured must agree on the value of the loss.

e. *Rate regulation.* When companies are subject to rate regulation, the allocation of joint costs can be a significant factor in determining the regulated rates.
Example: Crude oil and natural gas are produced out of a common well.

Difficulty: 1   *Objective:* 3

73. For each of the following methods of allocating joint costs, give a positive or a negative aspect of selecting each one to allocate joint costs.
   a. Sales value at splitoff
   b. Estimated net realizable value method
   c. The constant gross margin method
   d. A physical measure such as volume

Answer:

a. *Positive*: Costs are allocated to products in proportion to their potential revenues. This is a fairly simple method to implement.
   Negative: We use the sales value of the entire production of the accounting period.

b. *Positive*: Can be used when the market prices of the products are not known or available.
   Negative: Can be very complex in operations with multiple products and multiple splitoff points.

c. *Positive*: Account is taken of the profits earned either before or after the splitoff point when allocating the joint costs.
   Negative: The assumption that all have the same ratio of cost to sales value. This is likely not true.

d. *Positive*: Fairly simple
   Negative: Has no relationship to the revenue-producing power of individual products.

Difficulty: 2   *Objective*: 4

74. Sugar Cane Company processes sugar beets into three products. During April, the joint costs of processing were $120,000. Production and sales value information for the month were as follows:

Product	Units Produced	Sales Value at Splitoff Point	Separable costs
Sugar	6,000	40,000	12,000
Sugar Syrup	4,000	35,000	32,000
Fructose Syrup	2,000	25,000	16,000

Required:

Determine the amount of joint cost allocated to each product if the sales value at splitoff method is used.

Answer:

Product	Units	Sales Value	Percent	Joint Cost	Allocated
Sugar	6,000	$40,000	40% x	$120,000	$48,000
Sugar Syrup	4,000	35,000	35% x	120,000	42,000
Fructose Syrup	2,000	25,000	25% x	120,000	30,000
Total		$100,000	100%		$120,000

Difficulty: 2   *Objective*: 4

75. Oregon Lumber processes timber into four products. During January, the joint costs of processing were $280,000. There was no inventory at the beginning of the month. Production and sales value information for the month were as follows:

Product	Board feet	Sales Value at Splitoff Point	Ending Inventory
2 x 4's	6,000,000	$0.30 per board foot	500,000 bdft.
2 x 6's	3,000,000	0.40 per board foot	250,000 bdft.
4 x 4's	2,000,000	0.45 per board foot	100,000 bdft.
Slabs	1,000,000	0.10 per board foot	50,000 bdft.

Required:

Determine the value of ending inventory if the sales value at splitoff method is used for product costing. Round to 3 decimal places when necessary.

Answer:

Product	Board feet	Sales Value	Percent	Joint Cost	Allocated
2 x 4's	6,000,000	$1,800,000	45.0% x	$280,000	$126,000
2 x 6's	3,000,000	1,200,000	30.0 x	280,000	84,000
4 x 4's	2,000,000	900,000	22.5 x	280,000	63,000
Slabs	1,000,000	100,000	2.5 x	280,000	7,000
Totals		$4,000,000	100.0%		$280,000

Product	Fraction of Prod. in Inventory	Allocated	Inventory value
2 x 4's	500,000/6,000,000 x	$126,000 =	$10,500
2 x 6's	250,000/3,000,000 x	84,000 =	7,000
4 x 4's	100,000/2,000,000 x	63,000 =	3,150
Slabs	50,000/1,000,000 x	7,000 =	350
Total			$21,000

Difficulty: 3   *Objective*: 4

76. Zenon Chemical, Inc., processes pine rosin into three products: turpentine, paint thinner, and spot remover. During May, the joint costs of processing were $240,000. Production and sales value information for the month were as follows:

Product	Units Produced	Sales Value at Splitoff Point
Turpentine	6,000 liters	$60,000
Paint thinner	6,000 liters	50,000
Spot remover	3,000 liters	25,000

Required:

Determine the amount of joint cost allocated to each product if the physical-measure method is used.

Answer:

Product	Units Produced	Percentage	Joint Costs	Allocated
Turpentine	6,000 liters	40% x	240,000 =	$96,000
Paint thinner	6,000 liters	40% x	240,000 =	96,000
Spot remover	3,000 liters	20% x	240,000 =	48,000
Totals	15,000	100%		240,000

Difficulty: 2   *Objective*: 4

77. Red Sauce Canning Company processes tomatoes into catsup, tomato juice, and canned tomatoes. During the summer of 20x3, the joint costs of processing the tomatoes were $420,000. There was no beginning or ending inventories for the summer. Production and sales value information for the summer were as follows:

Product	Cases	Sales Value at Splitoff Point	Separable Costs	Selling Price
Catsup	100,000	$6 per case	$3.00 per case	$28 per case
Juice	150,000	8 per case	5.00 per case	25 per case
Canned	200,000	5 per case	2.50 per case	10 per case

Required:

Determine the amount allocated to each product if the estimated net realizable value method is used, and compute the cost per case for each product.

Answer:

Product	Expected Sales Value	Separable Costs	Net Realizable Value	Percentage
Catsup	$2,800,000	$300,000	$2,500,000	35.71%
Juice	3,750,000	750,000	3,000,000	42.86%
Canned	2,000,000	500,000	1,500,000	21.43%
Totals			$7,000,000	100.00%

Product	Percentage	Joint Costs	Allocated	Separable Costs	Product Costs
Catsup	35.71% x	$420,000 =	$149,982 +	$300,000 –	$449,982
Juice	42.86% x	420,000 =	180,012 +	750,000 =	930,012
Canned	21.43% x	420,000 =	90,006 +	500,000 =	590,006

Catsup cost per case = $449,982/100,000 = $4.50
Juice cost per case = $930,012/150,000 = $6.20
Canned cost per case = $590,006/200,000 = $2.95

Difficulty: 3   *Objective*: 4

78. New York Liberty Corporation makes miniature Statutes of Liberty from cast iron. Sales total 40,000 units a year. The statutes are finished either rough or polished, with an average demand of 60% rough and 40% polished. Iron ingots, the direct material, costs $6 per pound. Processing costs are $200 to convert 20 pounds into 40 statutes. Rough statutes are sold for $15 each, and polished statutes can be sold for $18 or engraved for an additional cost of $5. Polished statues can then be sold for $30.

Required:

Determine whether New York Liberty Company should sell the engraved statutes. Why?

Answer:

New York Liberty should engrave the statutes because they increase profits by $7 per statute.

		Rough		**Polished**
Sales		$15.00		$18.00
Cost of Sales:				
Materials ($6 x 20)/40	$3.00		$3.00	
Conversion $200/40	5.00	8.00	5.00	8.00
Operating Income (loss)		$7.00		$10.00

Sales, polished and engraved		$30.00
Costs:		
Materials	$3.00	
Conversion	5.00	
Additional Processing	5.00	13.00
Advantage of processing further		$17.00

Difficulty: 1   *Objective*: 6

79. The Carolina Company prepares lumber for companies who manufacture furniture. The main product is finished lumber with a byproduct of wood shavings. The byproduct is sold to plywood manufacturers. For July, the manufacturing process incurred $332,000 in total costs. Eighty thousand board feet of lumber were produced and sold along with 6,800 pounds of shavings. The finished lumber sold for $6.00 per board foot and the shavings sold for $0.60 a pound. There were no beginning or ending inventories.

Required:
Prepare an income statement showing the byproduct (1) as a cost reduction during production, and (2) as a revenue item when sold.

Answer:

	Cost reduction when produced		Revenue when sold	
Sales: Lumber	$480,000		$480,000	
Shavings			4,080	
Total Sales:		$480,000		484,080
Cost of Good Sold:				
Total manufacturing costs	$332,000		$332,000	
Byproduct	4,080		0	
Total COGS		327,920		332,000
Gross Margin		$152,080		$152,080

Difficulty: 2   *Objective*:   7

80. Distinguish between the two principal methods of accounting for byproducts, the production byproduct method and the sale byproduct method. Briefly discuss the relative merits (or lack thereof) of each.

Answer:
a.   *Production byproduct method.*
    This method recognizes byproducts in the financial statements at the time their production is completed. The estimated net realizable value from the byproduct produced is offset against the costs of the main (or joint) products, and reported in the balance sheet as inventory. Accounting entries are made and the byproducts are reported in the balance sheet at their selling price.

b.   *Sale byproduct method.*
    This method delays recognition of the byproducts until the time of their sale. Revenues could be recorded in one accounting period, while the expense in an earlier period. Companies may find it necessary to keep an inventory of the byproduct processing costs in a separate account until the byproducts are sold. This practice can be rationalized on the grounds that the dollar amounts of byproducts are immaterial. But managers can use this method to manage reported earnings by timing when they sell byproducts.

Difficulty: 2   *Objective*:   7

CRITICAL THINKING

81. Silver Company uses one raw material, silver ore, for all its products. It spends considerable time getting the silver from the ore before it starts the actual processing of the finished products, rings, lockets, etc. Traditionally, the company made one product at a time and charged the product with all costs of production, from ore to final inspection. However, in recent months, the cost accounting reports have been somewhat disturbing to management. It seems that some of the finished products are costing more than they should, even to the point of approaching their retail value. It has been noted by the accounting manager that this problem began when the company started buying ore from different parts of the world, some of which require difficult extraction methods.

Required:

Can you explain how the company might change its accounting system to better reflect the reporting problems? Are there other problems with the purchasing area?

Answer:

It appears that the company needs to start assigning all extraction costs to a joint-cost category. It is unfair that the finished products receive a high cost simply because a certain batch of ore was very expensive to run through the extraction process when the next finished products were produced from silver that was easy to extract.

If all extraction costs are considered joint, then each finished product would share in the average cost of extraction, rather than being charged with the cost of a specific batch. This should result in costs that are more reflective of the product's actual cost. Additional problems may be with the purchasing department. The accounting department may help highlight the problem but does not pinpoint the actual problem. Maybe they should buy refined silver or else hire experts in the minerals area as part of the purchasing team.

Difficulty: 2   *Objective*:   1

82. Pilgrim Corporation processes frozen turkeys. The company has not been pleased with its profit margin per product because it appears that the high value items have too few costs assigned to them, while the low value items have too many costs assigned to them. The processing results in several products, the primary one of which is frozen small turkeys. Other products include frozen parts such as wings and legs, byproducts such as skin and bones, and unused scrap items.

Required:

What may be the cost assignment problem if a key consideration is the value of the products being sold?

Answer:

First, the company needs to consider whether the byproducts are being treated as products, rather than byproducts. For the most part, byproducts should not be assigned costs. The revenue from the byproducts should be used as either minor sale categories or else as offsets to processing costs.

A second consideration is the method used to assign the costs. It is possible that some physical measure (weight) is being used, in which case the parts items and the byproducts may weigh as much as the primary product. It may be necessary to evaluate the various methods of allocation and select the one which management feels is best for decision making.

Difficulty: 2   *Objective*: 4

83. Wharf Fisheries processes many of its seafood items to the demands of its largest customers, most of which are large retail distributors. To keep the accounting system simple, it has always assigned cost by the weight of the finished product. However, with increased competition, it has had to watch its prices closely and, in recent years, several items have incurred zero profit margins. After several weeks of investigation, your consulting firm has found that, while weight is important in processing of seafood, numerous items have very distinct processing steps and some items are processed through more steps than others.

Required:

Based on the findings of your consulting firm, what changes might you recommend to the company in the way of cost allocation among its products?

Answer:

Recommendations might include, among others, some of the following:

a. Categorize the fishing expeditions as joint costs, especially if multiple items are caught.
b. Categorize all processing activities where multiple items are processed as joint costs.
c. For those processes that are unique to only one product or a set of products, use separable cost categories.
d. Choose something other than weight for allocating joint costs. Select one of the value methods of assigning the costs.
e. Carefully separate main products from byproducts in the costing system.
f. Do not allocate the joint costs for internal decisions.

Difficulty: 2   *Objective:* 4

84. Paragon University operates an extensive and an expensive registration, testing, and counseling center, through which all students are required to pass through when they enter the University. The registration effort's costs (for the most part) are almost impossible to allocate based upon which students require time, effort, etc. The cost of this center is approximately 15% of the total costs of Paragon. This department engages in no other activities than the registration of students. Paragon is interested in determining the profitability of the three technical departments it operates. Paragon has the perception that some departments are more profitable than others, and it would like to determine an appropriate method of allocating the costs of this registration center.

Required:

Recommend to Paragon University a method (or methods) of allocating the costs of registration to the three departments.

Answer:

The joint costs of the registration effort could be allocated based on physical volume or the sales (tuition) dollars of each department.

Volume Allocating on volume would be based not upon physical measures, but upon the number of credit hours each of the three departments offer each semester. If the ratio of credit hours for the three departments were 25%, 45%, and 30% then the costs would be allocated based upon these ratios.

Sales Dollars It is possible that some departments charge more per credit hour than others. In this case it might be appropriate to allocate the costs based upon the total tuition revenues of each department.

Difficulty: 3   *Objective*: 4

CHAPTER 17: PROCESS COSTING SYSTEMS

TRUE/FALSE

1. Examples of industries that would use process costing include the pharmaceutical and semiconductor industry.

    Answer: True   *Difficulty*:   1   *Objective*:   1

2. The principal difference between process costing and job costing is that in job costing an averaging process is used to compute the unit costs of products or services.

    Answer: False   *Difficulty*:   2   *Objective*:   1
    The averaging process is used to calculate unit costs in process costing.

3. Process-costing systems separate costs into cost categories according to the timing of when costs are introduced into the process.

    Answer: True   *Difficulty*:   2   *Objective*:   1

4. Estimating the degree of completion for the calculation of equivalent units is usually easier for conversion costs than it is for direct materials.

    Answer: False   *Difficulty*:   2   *Objective*:   1
    Estimating the degree of completion is easier for the calculation of direct materials since direct materials can be measured more easily than conversion costs.

5. Process-costing journal entries and job-costing journal entries are similar with respect to direct materials and conversion costs.

    Answer: True   *Difficulty*:   2   *Objective*:   4

6. The accounting (for a bakery) entry to record the transfer of rolls from the mixing department to the baking department is:

    Work in Process-Mixing Department
          Work in Process-Baking Department

    Answer: False   *Difficulty*:   2   *Objective*:   4
    The correct accounting entry is the opposite of the entry shown here.

7. The weighted-average process costing method does not distinguish between units started in the previous period but completed during the current period and units started and completed during the current period.

    Answer: True   *Difficulty*:   2   *Objective*:   5

8. Equivalent units in beginning work in process + equivalent units of work done in the current period equals equivalent units completed and transferred out in the current period minus equivalent units in ending work in process.

   Answer: False   *Difficulty:* 2   *Objective:* 5
   The second part of the equation should be: equivalent units completed and transferred out in the current period PLUS equivalent units in ending work in process.

9. In the weighted-average costing method, the costs of direct materials in beginning inventory are not included in the cost per unit calculation since direct materials are almost always added at the start of the production process.

   Answer: False   *Difficulty:* 2   *Objective:* 5
   The costs of the direct materials are included in the cost per unit calculation.

10. The FIFO process costing method merges the work and the costs of the beginning inventory with the work and the costs done during the current period.

    Answer: False   *Difficulty:* 2   *Objective:* 6
    FIFO only includes the work done during the current period.

11. The first-in, first-out process-costing method assumes that units in beginning inventory are completed during the current accounting period.

    Answer: True   *Difficulty:* 2   *Objective:* 6

12. Process costing FIFO is usually applied to both the units entering a department and the units leaving a department.

    Answer: False   *Difficulty:* 2   *Objective:* 6
    FIFO is only applied to the goods transferred out.

13. Activity-based costing has more applicability in a process-costing system than in a job-costing environment.

    Answer: False   *Difficulty:* 2   *Objective:* 6
    Activity-based costing is less applicable to process costing because the units all go through similar processes.

14. A major advantage of the weighted-average process costing is that it provides managers with information about changes in the costs per unit from one period to the next.

    Answer: False   *Difficulty:* 2   *Objective:* 6
    This is an advantage of FIFO, not the weighted-average method.

15   Standard costing is extremely useful when unique, high cost products are produced, as compared to the production of multiple products.

Answer: False   *Difficulty*:   2   *Objective*:   7
Job costing is especially useful in this situation.

16.   Under standard costing the cost per equivalent-unit calculation is more difficult than in either weighted average or FIFO.

Answer: False   *Difficulty*:   2   *Objective*:   7
The cost per equivalent-unit calculation is simpler because the cost is assumed constant during the accounting period.

17.   Transferred-out costs are incurred in previous departments that are carried forward as the product's cost as it moves to a subsequent process in the production cycle.

Answer: True   *Difficulty*:   2   *Objective*:   8

18.   Each department is regarded as a distinct accounting entity when interdepartmental transfers are present in an organization.

Answer: True   *Difficulty*:   2   *Objective*:   8

19.   Hybrid costing systems are developed to cost products that are produced in a standardized environment, but are often customized to meet the needs of some of its customers.

Answer: True   *Difficulty*:   2   *Objective*:   8

20.   An operation-costing system uses work orders that specify needed direct materials and stcp-by-stcp operations.

Answer: True   *Difficulty*:   2   *Objective*:   A

21. Costing systems that are used for the costing of like or similar units of products in mass production are called
    a.   inventory-costing systems.
    b.   job-costing systems.
    c.   process-costing systems.
    d.   weighted-average costing systems.

    Answer: c   *Difficulty:*   1   *Objective:*   1

22. Which of the following manufactured products would not use process costing?
    a.   767 jet aircraft
    b.   19-inch television sets
    c.   Custom built houses
    d.   (a) and (c) would not use process costing.

    Answer: d   *Difficulty:*   2   *Objective:*   1

23. Process costing should be used to assign costs to products when
    a.   the units produced are similar.
    b.   the units produced are dissimilar.
    c.   the calculation of unit costs requires the averaging of unit costs over all units produced.
    d.   either (a) or (c) are present.

    Answer: d   *Difficulty:*   2   *Objective:*   1

24. Which one of the following statements is true?
    a.   In a job-costing system, individual jobs use different quantities of production resources.
    b.   In a process-costing system each unit uses approximately the same amount of resources.
    c.   An averaging process is used to calculate unit costs in a job-costing system.
    d.   Both (a) and (b) are true.

    Answer: d   *Difficulty:*   2   *Objective:*   1

25. Conversion costs
    a.   include all the factors of production.
    b.   include direct materials.
    c.   in process costing are usually considered to be added evenly throughout the production process.
    d.   include both (b) and (c).

    Answer: c   *Difficulty:*   2   *Objective:*   1

26. An example of a business which would have no beginning or ending inventory but could use process costing to compute unit costs would be
    a. a clothing manufacturer.
    b. a corporation whose sole business activity is processing the customer deposits of several banks.
    c. a manufacturer of custom houses.
    d. a manufacturer of large TVs.

    Answer: b   *Difficulty*:   2   *Objective*:   1

27. Which of the following statement (s) concerning conversion costs is correct?
    a. Estimating the degree of completion of direct materials in a partially completed unit is usually easier to calculate than estimating the degree of completion for conversion costs.
    b. The calculation of equivalent units is relatively easy for the textile industry.
    c. Estimates are usually not considered acceptable.
    d. Both (b) and (c) are correct.

    Answer: a   *Difficulty*:   2   *Objective*:   1

28. The purpose of the equivalent-unit computation is
    a. to convert completed units into the amount of partially completed output units that could be made with that quantity of input.
    b. to assist the business in determining ending inventory.
    c. to convert partially completed units into the amount of completed output units that could be made with that quantity of input.
    d. both (b) and (c).

    Answer: c   *Difficulty*:   2   *Objective*:   3

29. In a process-costing system, the calculation of equivalent units is used for
    a. calculating the dollar amount of ending inventory.
    b. calculating the dollar amount of the cost of goods sold for the accounting period.
    c. calculating the dollar cost of a particular job.
    d. both (a) and (b).

    Answer: d   *Difficulty*:   1   *Objective*:   3

30. When a bakery transfers goods from the Baking Department to the Decorating Department, the accounting entry is
    a. Work in Process - Baking Department
         Work in Process - Decorating Department
    b. Work in Process - Decorating Department
         Accounts Payable
    c. Work in Process - Decorating Department
         Work in Process - Baking Department
    d. Work in Process - Baking Department
         Accounts Payable

    Answer: c   *Difficulty*:   2   *Objective*:   4

THE FOLLOWING INFORMATION APPLIES TO QUESTIONS 31 AND 32.
Injection Molding, Inc., manufactures plastic moldings for car seats. Its costing system utilizes two cost categories, direct materials and conversion costs. Each product must pass through Department A and Department B. Direct materials are added at the beginning of production. Conversion costs are allocated evenly throughout production.

Data for Department A for February 20x3 are:

Work in process, beginning inventory, 40% converted	200 units
Units started during February	600 units
Work in process, ending inventory	100 units

Costs for Department A for February 20x3 are:

Work in process, beginning inventory:	
Direct materials	$100,000
Conversion costs	$100,000
Direct materials costs added during February	$1,000,000
Conversion costs added during February	$1,250,000

31   What is the unit cost per equivalent unit in Department A?
     a. $1,000
     b. $1,750
     c. $3,500
     d. $3,750

Answer: b   *Difficulty:*   2   *Objective:*   3

Direct materials per unit ($100,000/200 units)	$ 500
Conversion costs per unit ($100,000/(200 x 0.40) units)	1,250
Total costs per unit	$1,750

32.   How many units were completed and transferred out of Department A during February?
     a.   100 units
     b.   600 units
     c.   700 units
     d.   800 units

Answer: c   *Difficulty:*   2   *Objective:*   3
200 units + 600 units - 100 units = 700 units

33. Injection Molding, Inc., manufactures plastic moldings for car seats. Its costing system utilizes two cost categories, direct materials and conversion costs. Each product must pass through Department A and Department B. Direct materials are added at the beginning of production. Conversion costs are allocated evenly throughout production.

Data for Department A for February 20x3 are:

Work in process, beginning inventory, 40% converted	200 units
Units started during February	600 units
Work in process, ending inventory:	100 units
30% complete as to conversion costs	
100% complete as to materials	

Costs for the Department A for February 20x3 are:

Work in process, beginning inventory:	
Direct materials	$100,000
Conversion costs	$100,000
Direct materials costs added during February	$1,000,000
Conversion costs added during February	$1,250,000

What were the equivalent units of direct materials and conversion costs, respectively, at the end of February? Assume Injection Molding, Inc., uses the weighted-average process costing method.
   a.   800, 730
   b.   800, 800
   c.   800, 700
   d.   600, 500

Answer: a   *Difficulty:*   2   *Objective:*   3

Equivalent units of direct materials under weighted average = units completed + equivalent units in ending inventory = 700 + 100
Conversion costs = 700 + (100 x 30%) = 730

34. The weighted-average process-costing method calculates the equivalent units by
   a.   considering only the work done during the current period.
   b.   the units started during the current period minus the units in ending inventory.
   c.   the units started during the current period plus the units in ending inventory.
   d.   the equivalent units completed during the current period plus the equivalent units in ending inventory.

Answer: d   *Difficulty:*   2   *Objective:*   5

35. In the computation of the cost per equivalent unit, the weighted-average method of process costing considers
    a.   all the costs entering work in process from the units in beginning inventory plus the costs for the work completed during the current accounting period.
    b.   all the costs that have entered work in process from the units started or transferred in during the current accounting period.
    c.   all the costs that have entered work in process during the current accounting period from the units started or transferred in minus the costs associated with ending inventory.
    d.   all the costs that have entered work in process during the current accounting period from the units started or transferred in plus the costs associated with ending inventory.

    Answer: a   *Difficulty:*   3   *Objective:*   5

36. If there was no beginning work in process and no ending work in process under the weighted-average process costing method, the number of equivalent units for direct materials, if direct materials were added at the start of the process, would be
    a.   equal to the units started or transferred in.
    b.   equal to the units completed.
    c.   less than the units completed.
    d.   both (a) and (b).

    Answer: d   *Difficulty:*   3   *Objective:*   5

37. Under the weighted-average method, the stage of completion of beginning work in process
    a.   is relevant in determining the equivalent units.
    b.   must be combined with the work done during the current period in determining the equivalent units.
    c.   is irrelevant in determining the equivalent-unit calculation.
    d.   can almost always be determined with a high degree of precision.

    Answer: c   *Difficulty:*   2   *Objective:*   5

THE FOLLOWING INFORMATION APPLIES TO QUESTIONS 38 THROUGH 43.
The Swiss Clock Shop manufactures clocks on a highly automated assembly line. Its costing
system utilizes two cost categories, direct materials and conversion costs. Each product must
pass through the Assembly Department and the Testing Department. Direct materials are
added at the beginning of the production process. Conversion costs are allocated evenly
throughout production. Swiss Clock Shop uses weighted-average costing.

Data for the Assembly Department for June 20x3 are:

Work in process, beginning inventory	250 units
Direct materials (100% complete)	
Conversion costs (50% complete)	
Units started during June	800 units
Work in process, ending inventory:	150 units
Direct materials (100% complete)	
Conversion costs (75% complete)	

Costs for June 20x3:

Work in process, beginning inventory:	
Direct materials	$180,000
Conversion costs	$270,000
Direct materials costs added during June	$1,000,000
Conversion costs added during June	$1,000,000

38. What are the equivalent units for direct materials and conversion costs, respectively, for
June?
    a. 1,200.5 units; 1,160.64 units
    b. 1,050 units; 1,012.5 units
    c. 1,050 units; 1,050 units
    d. 962 units; 990 units

    Answer: b   *Difficulty:* 2   *Objective:* 5

	Direct materials	Conversion costs
Completed and transferred out	900	900.0
Work in process, ending	150	112.5
Total equivalent units	1,050	1,012.5

39. What is the total amount debited to the Work-in-Process account during the month of
June?
    a. $450,000
    b. $2,000,000
    c. $2,270,000
    d. $2,450,000

    Answer: b   *Difficulty:* 1   *Objective:* 5
    $1,000,000 + $1,000,000 = $2,000,000

40. What is the direct materials cost per equivalent unit during June?
    a. $1,123.81
    b. $1,730.20
    c. $1,579,00
    d. $1,890.35

Answer: a   *Difficulty:* 3   *Objective:* 5
$180,000 + $1,000,000 = $1,180,000
$1,180,000/1,050 units = $1,123.81

41. What is the conversion cost per equivalent unit in June?
    a. $1,254.32
    b. $1,579.14
    c. $1,730.20
    d. $1,890.35

Answer: a   *Difficulty:* 3   *Objective:* 5
$270,000 + $1,000,000 = $1,270,000
$1,270,000/1,012.5 = $1,254.32

42. What amount of direct materials costs is assigned to the ending Work-in-Process account for June?

    a. $168,571.50
    b. $283,552.50
    c. $259,530
    d. $236,850

Answer: a   *Difficulty:* 3   *Objective:* 5
$1,180,000/1,050= $1,124 cost per equivalent unit
$1,124 x 150= $168,571.50

43. What amount of conversion costs are assigned to ending Work-in-Process account for June?
    a. $101,956.64
    b. $141,111.00
    c. $126,450.50
    d. $188,148.00

Answer: b   *Difficulty:* 3   *Objective:* 5
(150 units x 75%) x $1,254.32 = $141,111

THE FOLLOWING INFORMATION APPLIES TO QUESTIONS 44 THROUGH 47.
The Rest-a-Lot Chair Company manufacturers a standard recliner. During February, the firm's Assembly Department started production of 75,000 chairs. During the month, the firm completed 85,000 chairs and transferred them to the Finishing Department. The firm ended the month with 10,000 chairs in ending inventory. All direct materials costs are added at the beginning of the production cycle. Weighted-average costing is used by Rest-a-Lot.

44. How many chairs were in inventory at the beginning of the month? Conversion costs are incurred uniformly over the production cycle.
    a.   10,000 chairs
    b.   20,000 chairs
    c.   15,000 chairs
    d.   25,000 chairs

    Answer: b   *Difficulty:*   2   *Objective:*   5
    Beginning inventory + 75,000 - 85,000 = 10,000
    Beginning inventory = 20,000

45. What were the equivalent units for materials for February?
    a.   95,000 chairs
    b.   85,000 chairs
    c.   80,000 chairs
    d.   75,000 chairs

    Answer: a   *Difficulty:*   3   *Objective:*   5
    10,000 + 85,000 = 95,000

46. What were the equivalent units for conversion costs for February if beginning inventory was 70% complete as to conversion costs and ending inventory was 40% complete as to conversion costs?
    a.   89,000
    b.   75,000
    c.   85,000
    d.   95,000

    Answer: a   *Difficulty:*   3   *Objective:*   5
    85,000 + (0.4) (10,000) = 89,000

47. Of the 75,000 units Rest-a-Lot started during February, how many were finished during the month?
    a.   75,000
    b.   85,000
    c.   65,000
    d.   95,000

    Answer: c   *Difficulty:*   3   *Objective:*   5
    75,000 - 10,000 = 65,000

48. A distinct feature of the FIFO process-costing method is that
    a. the work done on beginning inventory before the current period is blended in with the work done during the current period in the calculation of equivalent units.
    b. the work done on beginning inventory before the current period is kept separate from the work done during the current period in the calculation of equivalent units.
    c. the work done on ending inventory is kept separate from the work done during the current period in the calculation of equivalent units and is usually not included in the calculation.
    d. the FIFO process-costing method is only minimally different from the weighted-average process-costing method.

    Answer: b   *Difficulty:*   2   *Objective:*   6

49. On occasion, the FIFO and the weighted-average methods of process costing will result in the same dollar amount of costs being transferred to the next department. Which of the following scenarios would have that result?
    a. When the beginning and ending inventories are equal in terms of unit numbers.
    b. When the beginning and ending inventories are equal in terms of the percentage of completion for both direct materials, and conversion costs.
    c. When there is no ending inventory.
    d. When there is no beginning inventory.

    Answer: d   *Difficulty:*   2   *Objective:*   6

50 An assumption of the FIFO process-costing method is that
    a. the units in beginning inventory are not necessarily assumed to be completed by the end of the period.
    b. the units in beginning inventory are assumed to be completed first.
    c. ending inventory will always be completed in the next accounting period.
    d. no calculation of conversion costs is possible.

    Answer: b   *Difficulty:*   2   *Objective:*   6

THE FOLLOWING INFORMATION APPLIES TO QUESTIONS 51 THROUGH 54.
The Rest-a-Lot chair company manufacturers a standard recliner. During February, the firm's Assembly Department started production of 75,000 chairs. During the month, the firm completed 80,000 chairs, and transferred them to the Finishing Department. The firm ended the month with 10,000 chairs in ending inventory. There were 15,000 chairs in beginning inventory. All direct materials costs are added at the beginning of the production cycle and conversion costs are added uniformly throughout the production process. The FIFO method of process costing is used by Rest-a-Lot. Beginning work in process was 30% complete as to conversion costs, while ending work in process was 80% complete as to conversion costs.

Beginning inventory:
Direct materials	$24,000
Conversion costs	$35,000

Manufacturing costs added during the accounting period:
Direct materials	$168,000
Conversion costs	$278,000

51. How many of the units that were started during February were completed during February?
    a.   85,000
    b.   80,000
    c.   75,000
    d.   65,000

Answer: d   *Difficulty:* 2   *Objective:* 6
75,000 - 10,000 = 65,000

52. What were the equivalent units for conversion costs during February?
    a.   83,500
    b.   85,000
    c.   75,000
    d.   79,500

Answer: a   *Difficulty:* 2   *Objective:* 6
(15,000 x 0.7) + 65,000 + 10,000 (0.8) = 83,500

53. What is the amount of direct materials cost assigned to ending work-in-process inventory at the end of February?
    a. $19,200
    b. $22,400
    c. $25,600
    d. $22,500

Answer: b   *Difficulty:* 3   *Objective:* 6
$168,000/75,000 = $2.24 x 10,000 = $22,400

54. What is the cost of the goods transferred out during February?
    a. $417,750
    b. $456,015
    c. $476,750
    d. $505,000

Answer: b   *Difficulty:* 3   *Objective:* 6

The costs in beginning inventory $24,000 + $35,000 =	$ 59,000
Direct materials = $2.24 x 65,000 =	145,600
Conversion costs =	
[$278,000/(10,500 + 8,000 + 65,000)] x 65,000 =	216,450
also FG beginning inventory (15,000 x 0.7 x 3.33) =	34,965
Total	$456,015

55. A reason(s) why "pure" FIFO is rarely encountered in process costing is that
    a. FIFO is usually applied within a department to compile the cost of units transferred out.
    b. the units transferred into the department during a given time period are usually carried at a single average unit cost.
    c. tracking costs on a "pure" FIFO basis is very difficult.
    d. all of the above are reasons.

Answer: d   *Difficulty:* 2   *Objective:* 6

56. Operating income can differ materially between the results for the weighted-average and FIFO methods when
    a. direct materials or conversion costs per unit vary significantly from period to period.
    b. the physical inventory levels of work in process are large in relation to the total number of units transferred out.
    c. neither (a) nor (b) are correct.
    d. both (a) and (b) are correct.

Answer: d   *Difficulty:* 2   *Objective:* 6

57. A major advantage of using the FIFO process-costing method is
    a. FIFO makes the unit cost calculations simpler.
    b. in contrast with the weighted-average method FIFO is considered GAAP.
    c. FIFO provides managers with information about changes in the costs per unit from one period to the next.
    d. all of the above are advantages of using FIFO.

Answer: c   *Difficulty:* 2   *Objective:* 6

58. A disadvantage of the weighted-average method compared to the FIFO process-costing method is that
   a. FIFO is computationally simpler.
   b. FIFO provides better management information for planning and control purposes.
   c. when unit cost per input prices fluctuate markedly from month to month, its per unit cost is less representative than FIFO.
   d. the information it provides about changes in unit prices from one period to the next is less useful than the information provided by FIFO.

   Answer: d   *Difficulty:* 2   *Objective:* 6

59. Activity-based costing has less applicability in a process-costing environment because
   a. the use of activity-based costing makes the computational process more difficult.
   b. the products tend to be similar and thus use the resources in a similar manner.
   c. cost control in process costing is achieved by controlling the cost of the various processes rather than the individual activities.
   d. of both (b) and (c).

   Answer: d   *Difficulty:* 2   *Objective:* 6

60. Standard costing is popular among companies that
   a. produce masses of similar or identical products.
   b. manufacture textiles or ceramics.
   c. produce a product that uses few direct materials items, and has relatively few operational activities.
   d. are all of the above.

   Answer: d   *Difficulty:* 2   *Objective:* 7

THE FOLLOWING INFORMATION APPLIES TO QUESTIONS 61 AND 62.
Hudson Dock Company manufactures boat docks on an assembly line. Its standard costing system utilizes two cost categories, direct materials and conversion costs. Each product must pass through the Assembly Department and the Finishing Department. Direct materials are added at the beginning of the production process. Conversion costs are allocated evenly throughout production.

Data for the Assembly Department for May 20x3 are:

Work in process, beginning inventory:	70 units
Direct materials (100% complete)	
Conversion costs (25% complete)	
Units started during May	40 units
Work in process, ending inventory:	10 units
Direct materials (100% complete)	
Conversion costs (50% complete)	

Costs for May:

Standard costs for Assembly:	
Direct materials	$4,000 per unit
Conversion costs	$16,000 per unit
Work in process, beginning inventory:	
Direct materials	$140,000
Conversion costs	$260,000

61. What is the balance in ending work-in-process inventory?
   a. $82,000
   b. $120,000
   c. $155,000
   d. $170,000

Answer: b   *Difficulty*: 3   *Objective*: 7
10 units x $4,000 = $ 40,000
10 units x 50% x $16,000 =   80,000
                                                $120,000

62. Which of the following journal entries records the Assembly Department's conversion costs for the month, assuming conversion costs are 20% higher than expected?

a. Assembly Department Conversion Cost Control $1,680,000
    Various accounts $1,680,000
b. Materials Inventory $1,680,000
    Assembly Department Conversion Cost Control $1,680,000
c. Assembly Department Conversion Cost Control $1,400,000
    Materials Inventory $1,400,000
d. Materials Inventory $1,680,000
    Work in Process - Assembly $1,680,000

Answer: a   *Difficulty:* 3   *Objective:* 7

70 units x 75% x $16,000 =	$ 840,000
(40 - 10 units) x $16,000 =	480,000
10 units x 50% x $16,000 =	80,000
Budgeted	$1,400,000

$1,400,000 x 1.20% = $1,680,000

63. Hudson Dock Company manufactures boat docks on an assembly line. Its standard costing system utilizes two cost categories, direct materials and conversion costs. Each product must pass through the Assembly Department and the Finishing Department. Direct materials are added at the beginning of the production process. Conversion costs are allocated evenly throughout production.

Data for the Assembly Department for May 20x3 are:

Work in process, beginning inventory:	70 units
Direct materials (100% complete)	
Conversion costs (25% complete)	
Units started during May	40 units
Work in process, ending inventory:	10 units
Direct materials (100% complete)	
Conversion costs (50% complete)	

Costs for May:

Standard costs for Assembly:	
Direct materials	$4,000 per unit
Conversion costs	$16,000 per unit
Work in process, beginning inventory:	
Direct materials	$140,000
Conversion costs	$260,000

Which of the following journal entries properly records the assignment of conversion costs to work-in-process inventory and the conversion-cost variances of the Assembly Department, assuming that conversion costs are 20% higher than expected?

a.　Work in Process - Assembly　　　　　　　　　　$1,680,000
　　　　Conversion-Cost Variances　　　　　　　　　　　　　$ 280,000
　　　　Assembly Department Conversion Cost Control　　　　　$1,400,000
b.　Work in Process - Assembly　　　　　　　　　　$1,680,000
　　　　Direct Materials Variances　　　　　　　　　　　　　$ 280,000
　　　　Testing Department Conversion Cost Control　　　　　$1,400,000
c.　Work in Process - Assembly　　　　　　　　　$1,400,000
　　Conversion-Cost Variances　　　　　　　　　$ 280,000
　　　　Assembly Department Conversion Cost Control　　　　　$1,680,000
d.　Work in Process - Testing　　　　　　　　　　$1,400,000
　　　　Assembly Department Conversion Cost Control　　　　　$1,400,000

Answer:　c　　　　　　　*Difficulty:*　3　　　　　　*Objective:*　7
$1,680,000 - $1,400,000 = $280,000 conversion cost variances

64. Hudson Dock Company manufactures boat docks on an assembly line. Its standard costing system utilizes two cost categories, direct materials and conversion costs. Each product must pass through the Assembly Department and the Finishing Department. Direct materials are added at the beginning of the production process. Conversion costs are allocated evenly throughout production.

Data for the Assembly Department for May 20x3 are:

Work in process, beginning inventory:	70 units
Direct materials (100% complete)	
Conversion costs (25% complete)	
Units started during May	40 units
Work in process, ending inventory:	10 units
Direct materials (100% complete)	
Conversion costs (50% complete)	

Costs for May:

Standard costs for Assembly:	
Direct materials	$ 4,000 per unit
Conversion costs	$ 16,000 per unit
Work in process, beginning inventory:	
Direct materials	$140,000
Conversion costs	$260,000

Which of the following journal entries properly records direct materials requisitions for the work-in-process inventory and direct materials variances, assuming that the Assembly Department used 10% less materials than expected?

a.	Work in Process – Assembly	$160,000	
	Assembly Department Materials Cost Control		$160,000
b.	Work in Process – Assembly	$160,000	
	Direct Materials Variance		$ 16,000
	Assembly Department Materials Cost Control		$144,000
c.	Work in Process – Assembly	$144,000	
	Assembly Department Materials Cost Control		$144,000
d.	Work in Process – Assembly	$144,000	
	Direct Materials Variances	$ 16,000	
	Assembly Department Materials Cost Control		$160,000

Answer: b   *Difficulty*: 2   *Objective*: 7
40 x $4,000 = $160,000
$160,000 x 0.9 = $144,000

65. In a process-costing system when goods move from department to department, the accounting for such transfers is relatively simple under
    a.   standard costing.
    b.   FIFO costing.
    c.   weighted-average costing.
    d.   operations costing.

    Answer: a   *Difficulty:*   1   *Objective:*   8

66. Transferred-in costs are treated as if they are
    a.   conversion costs added at the beginning of the process.
    b.   costs of beginning inventory added at the beginning of the process.
    c.   direct labor costs added at the beginning of the process.
    d.   a separate direct material added at the beginning of the process.

    Answer: d   *Difficulty:*   2   *Objective:*   8

67. Ampco Disk Company operates a computer disk manufacturing plant. Direct materials are added at the end of the process. The following data were presented for June 20x3:

    Work in process, beginning inventory   50,000 units
        Transferred-in costs (100% complete)
        Direct materials (0% complete)
        Conversion costs (90% complete)

    Transferred in during current period   150,000 units
    Completed and transferred out   175,000 units

    Work in process, ending inventory
        Transferred-in costs (100% complete)
        Direct materials (0% complete)
        Conversion costs (65% complete)

    How many units must be accounted for during the period?
    a.   225,000 units
    b.   200,000 units
    c.   179, 500 units
    d.   150,000 units

    Answer: b   *Difficulty:*   1   *Objective:*   8
    50,000 + 150,000 = 200,000

68. Ampco Disk Company operates a computer disk manufacturing plant. Direct materials are added at the end of the process. The following data were presented for August 20x3:

Work in process, beginning inventory   100,000 units
     Transferred-in costs (100% complete)
     Direct materials (0% complete)
     Conversion costs (90% complete)

Transferred in during current period   300,000 units
Completed and transferred out   250,000 units

Work in process, ending inventory   50,000
     Transferred-in costs (100% complete)
     Direct materials (0% complete)
     Conversion costs (65% complete)

Calculate equivalent units for conversion costs using the FIFO method.
a. 401,500 units
b. 350,000 units
c. 300,000 units
d. 292,500 units

Answer: d   *Difficulty:* 2   *Objective:* 8
Beginning work in process (100,000 x 0.10)   10,000 units
Completed and transferred out   250,000 units
Ending work in process (50,000 x 0.65)   32,500 units
                                      292,500 units

69. An operation costing system would be applicable to
a. batches of similar products where each batch is a variation of a single design.
b. the construction of a bridge.
c. a suit making operation.
d. both (a) and (c).

Answer: d   *Difficulty:* 2   *Objective:* A

70. Managers find operation costing useful in cost management because
a. operations costing often results in profit maximization.
b. operations costing results in cost minimization.
c. operations costing capture the financial impact of the control of physical processes.
d. of all of the above.

Answer: c   *Difficulty:* 2   *Objective:* A

EXERCISES AND PROBLEMS

71. There are basically two distinct methods of calculating product costs.

Required:

Compare and contrast the two methods.

Answer:

In job costing the job or product is a distinctly identifiable product or service. Each job requires (or can require) vastly different amounts of input. Job costing is usually associated with products that are unique or heterogeneous. Thus each job requires different amounts of input, and can require vastly different amount of costs to finish. Job-costed products tend to be high cost per unit. Thus the costs of each (unique) job are important for planning, pricing, and profitability.

In process costing, the jobs or products are similar (or homogeneous). Each job usually requires the same inputs, and results in approximately the same costs per unit. The cost of a product or service is obtained by assigning total costs to many identical or similar units. We assume each unit receives the same amount of direct material costs, direct manufacturing labor costs, and indirect manufacturing costs. Unit costs are then computed by dividing total costs by the number of units.

The principal difference between process costing and job costing is the extent of averaging used to compute unit costs. As noted above in job costing, individual jobs use different quantities of production resources. Whereas in process costing, we assume that each job uses approximately the same amount of resources.

Difficulty: 2   *Objective*:   1

72. Why do we need to accumulate and calculate unit costs in process costing (and also job costing)?

Answer:

We need to accumulate unit costs in order to:
1. Budget (planning)
2. Price
3. For accounting purposes

1. *Budgeting* - in order to operate a successful business, we should prepare budgets, review the results, and make decisions as to how well our business is doing. Our business has formulated plans for the future. The resources we need for the future (materials, conversion costs, facilities, etc.) will depend on our estimate of the resources we need to accomplish these goals. An important part of these estimates is the unit costs of the products we plan to produce. These unit costs will tell us how many dollars we must acquire in order to accomplish our plans.

2. *Price* - In order to be a profitable business, we must sell our product at a price in excess of what it costs us to produce the product. Essential for the pricing decision is the cost per unit. We will also learn whether we can sell a product at a profit.

3. *Accounting* - During the course of the accounting period, we will be accumulating costs. At the end of the accounting period, we must allocate this pool of costs between the units that were transferred out and the goods in ending inventory. Unit costs are essential for this purpose.

Difficulty: 1   *Objective*:   1

73. The Zygon Corporation was recently formed to produce a semiconductor chip that forms an essential part of the personal computer manufactured by a major corporation. The direct materials are added at the start of the production process while conversion costs are added uniformly throughout the production process. June is Zygon's first month of operations, and therefore, there was no beginning inventory. Direct materials cost for the month totaled $895,000, while conversion costs equaled $4,225,000. Accounting records indicate that 475,000 chips were started in June, and that 425,000 chips were completed.

Ending inventory was 50% complete as to conversion costs.

Required:
a.   What is the total manufacturing cost per chip for June?
b.   Allocate the total costs between the completed chips and the chips in ending inventory.

Answer:

a.

	Direct Materials	Conversion Costs	Total
Cost to account for	$895,000	$4,225,000	$5,120,000
Divided by equiv units	475,000	450,000	
Cost per equivalent units	$1.88	$9.39	$11.27

Equivalent unit for conversion costs =
425,000 completed + (50,000 x 0.5 completed) =
425,000 + 25,000 = 450,000

b.   Completed units = $11.27 x 425,000 = $4,789,750

Ending work in process = Direct materials = 50,000 x $1.88 = $ 94,000
Conversion costs = 25,000 x $9.39 =   234,750
       Total $328,750

Difficulty: 2   *Objective*:   2

74. Cedar Rapids Chemical placed 220,000 liters of direct materials into the mixing process. At the end of the month, 10,000 liters were still in process, 30% converted as to labor and factory overhead. All direct materials are placed in mixing at the beginning of the process and conversion costs occur evenly during the process. Cedar Rapids Chemical uses weighted-average costing.

Required:

a. Determine the equivalent units in process for direct materials and conversion costs, assuming there was no beginning inventory.

b. Determine the equivalent units in process for direct materials and conversion costs, assuming that 12,000 liters of chemicals were 40% complete prior to the addition of the 220,000 liters.

Answer:

a. Direct materials:

Beginning inventory	0 liters
Units started	220,000 liters
Equivalent units	220,000 liters

Conversion costs:

Beginning inventory	0 liters
Units started	220,000 liters
To account for	220,000 liters
Units transferred out	210,000 liters
Ending inventory	10,000 liters
Units transferred out	210,000 liters
Ending inventory, 30% complete	3,000 liters
Equivalent units	213,000 liters

b. Direct materials:

Completed and transferred out (210,000 + 12,000)	222,000 liters
Ending inventory, 100% complete	10,000 liters
Equivalent units	232,000 liters

Conversion costs:

Completed and transferred out	222,000 liters
Ending inventory, 30% complete	3,000 liters
Equivalent units	225,000 liters

Difficulty: 2   *Objective*: 5

75. Jordana Woolens is a manufacturer of wool cloth. The information for March is as follows:

Beginning work in process	10,000 units
Units started	20,000 units
Units completed	25,000 units
Beginning work-in-process direct materials	$ 6,000
Beginning work-in-process conversion	$ 2,600
Direct materials added during month	$30,000
Direct manufacturing labor during month	$12,000
Factory overhead	$ 5,000

Beginning work in process was half converted as to labor and overhead. Direct materials are added at the beginning of the process. All conversion costs are incurred evenly throughout the process. Ending work in process was 60% complete.

Required:

Prepare a production cost worksheet using the weighted-average method. Include any necessary supporting schedules.

Answer:

PRODUCTION COST WORKSHEET

Flow of production	**Physical Units**	**Direct Materials**	**Conversion**
Work in process, beginning	10,000		
Started during period	20,000		
To account for	30,000		
Units completed	25,000	25,000	25,000
Work in process, ending	5,000	5,000	3,000
Accounted for	30,000	30,000	28,000

Costs	**Totals**	**Direct Materials**	**Conversion**
Work in process, beginning	$ 8,600	$ 6,000	$ 2,600
Costs added during period	47,000	30,000	17,000
Total costs to account for	$55,600	$36,000	$19,600
Divided by equivalent units		30,000	28,000
Equivalent unit costs	$ 1.90	$ 1.20	$ 0.70

75. (continued)

Assignment of costs

Costs transferred out (25,000 x $1.90)	$47,500
Work in process, ending	
Direct materials (5,000 x $1.20)	6,000
Conversion (5,000 x $0.70 x 0.60)	2,100
Costs accounted for	$55,600

Difficulty: 3   *Objective*: 5

76. Four Seasons Company makes snow blowers. Materials are added at the beginning of the process and conversion costs are uniformly incurred. At the beginning of September, work in process is 40% complete and at the end of the month it is 60% complete. Other data for the month include:

Beginning work-in-process inventory	1,600 units
Units started	2,000 units
Units placed in finished goods	3,200 units
Conversion costs	$200,000
Cost of direct materials	$260,000
Beginning work-in-process costs:	
Materials	$154,000
Conversion	$ 82,080

Required:

a. Prepare a production cost worksheet with supporting schedules using the weighted-average method of process costing.

b. Prepare journal entries to record transferring of materials to processing and from processing to finished goods.

76. **Answer:**

a.

PRODUCTION COST WORKSHEET

Flow of Production	Physical Units	Direct Materials	Conversion
Work in process, beginning	1,600		
Started during period	2,000		
To account for	3,600		
Units completed	3,200	3,200	3,200
Work in process, ending	400	400	240
Accounted for	3,600	3,600	3,440

Costs	Totals	Direct Materials	Conversion
Work in process, beginning	$236,080	$154,000	$ 82,080
Costs added during period	460,000	260,000	200,000
Total costs to account for	$696,080	$414,000	$282,080
Divided by equivalent units		3,600	3,440
Equivalent-unit costs	$197	$ 115	$ 82

Assignment of costs			
Completed units (3,200 x $197)			$630,400
Work in process, ending			
Direct materials (400 x $115)		$46,000	
Conversion (400 x $82 x 0.60)		19,680	65,680
Costs accounted for			$696,080

b.

Work in Process	$260,000	
Materials Inventory		$260,000
Finished Goods	$630,400	
Work in Process		$630,400

Difficulty: 3   *Objective*: 4, 5

77. Surf Products Company uses an automated process to clean and polish its souvenir items. For March, the company had the following activities:

Beginning work in process inventory	3,000 items, 1/3 complete
Units placed in production	12,000 units
Units completed	9,000 units
Ending work in process inventory	6,000 items, 1/2 complete
Cost of beginning work in process	$2,500
Direct material costs, current	$9,000
Conversion costs, current	$7,700

Direct materials are placed into production at the beginning of the process and conversion costs are incurred evenly throughout the process.

Required:

Prepare a production cost worksheet using the FIFO method.

Answer:

PRODUCTION COST WORKSHEET

Flow of production	Physical Units	Direct Materials	Conversion
Work in process, beginning	3,000		
Started during period	12,000		
To account for	15,000		
Units Completed:			
Work in process, beginning	3,000		2,000
Started and completed	6,000	6,000	6,000
Work in process, ending	6,000	6,000	3,000
	15,000	12,000	11,000

Costs	Totals	Direct Materials	Conversion
Work in process, beginning	$ 2,500		
Costs added during period	16,700	$ 9,000	$ 7,700
Total costs to account for	$19,200	$ 9,000	$ 7,700
Divided by equivalent units		12,000	11,000
Equivalent-unit costs	$1.45	$ 0.75	$ 0.70

77. (continued)

Assignment of costs		
Work in process, beginning		$ 2,500
Completion of beginning (2,000 x $0.70)		1,400
Total beginning inventory		3,900
Started and Completed (6,000 x $1.45)		8,700
Total costs transferred out		$12,600
Work in process, ending		
Direct materials (6,000 x $0.75)	$4,500	
Conversion (6,000 x $0.70 x 0.50)	2,100	6,600
Costs accounted for		$19,200

Difficulty: 3   *Objective*: 6

78. The Laramie Factory produces expensive boots. It has two departments that process all the items. During January, the beginning work in process in the tanning department was 40% complete as to conversion and 100% complete as to direct materials. The beginning inventory included $6,000 for materials and $18,000 for conversion costs. Ending work-in-process inventory in the tanning department was 40% complete. Direct materials are added at the beginning of the process.

Beginning work in process in the finishing department was 60% complete as to conversion. Beginning inventories included $7,000 for transferred-in costs and $10,000 for conversion costs. Ending inventory was 30% complete.

Additional information about the two departments follows:

	Tanning	Finishing
Beginning work-in-process units	5,000	4,000
Units started this period	14,000	?
Units transferred this period	16,000	18,000
Ending work-in-process units	?	2,000
Material costs added	$18,000	?
Conversion costs	32,000	$19,000
Transferred-out cost	50,000	?

Required:

Prepare a production cost worksheet using weighted-average costing for the finishing department.

78. **Answer:**

Production Cost Worksheet
Finishing Department
Weighted-Average Method

Flow of production	Physical Units	Conversion	Trans-In
Work in process, beginning	4,000		
Transferred in during period	16,000		
To account for	20,000		
Units transferred out	18,000	18,000	18,000
Work in process, ending	2,000	600	2,000
Accounted for	20,000	18,600	20,000

Costs	Totals	Conversion	Trans-in
Work in process, beginning	$17,000	$10,000	$ 7,000
Costs added during period	69,000	19,000	50,000
Total costs to account for	$86,000	$29,000	$57,000
Divided by equivalent units		18,600	20,000
Equivalent-unit costs	$ 4.41	$ 1.56	$ 2.85

Assignment of costs		
Transferred out (18,000 x $4.41)		$79,380
Work in process, ending		
Transferred-in costs (2,000 x $2.85)	$5,700	
Conversion (600 x $1.56)	936	6,636
Costs accounted for		$86,016

Difficulty: 3   *Objective*:   8

79. Lexington Company produces baseball bats and cricket paddles. It has two departments that process all products. During July, the beginning work in process in the cutting department was half completed as to conversion, and complete as to direct materials. The beginning inventory included $40,000 for materials and $60,000 for conversion costs. Ending work-in-process inventory in the cutting department was 40% complete. Direct materials are added at the beginning of the process.

Beginning work in process in the finishing department was 80% complete as to conversion. Direct materials for finishing the units are added near the end of the process. Beginning inventories included $24,000 for transferred-in costs and $28,000 for conversion costs. Ending inventory was 30% complete. Additional information about the two departments follows:

	Cutting	Finishing
Beginning work-in-process units	20,000	24,000
Units started this period	60,000	
Units transferred this period	64,000	68,000
Ending work-in-process units		20,000
Material costs added	$48,000	$34,000
Conversion costs	28,000	68,500
Transferred-out cost	128,000	

Required:

Prepare a production cost worksheet, using FIFO for the finishing department.

Answer:

Production Cost Worksheet
Finishing Department
FIFO Method

Flow of Production	Physical Units	Direct Materials	Conversion	Trans-In
Work in process, beginning	24,000			
Started during period	64,000			
To account for	88,000			
Good units completed				
Beginning work in process	24,000	24,000	4,800	
Started and completed	44,000	44,000	44,000	44,000
Ending work in process	20,000	0	6,000	20,000
Accounted for	88,000	68,000	54,800	64,000

79. (continued)

Costs	Totals	DMaterials	Conversion	Trans-In
WIP, beginning	$ 52,000			
Costs added during period	230,500	$34,000	$68,500	$128,000
Total costs to account for	$282,500	$34,000	$68,500	$128,000
Divided by equivalent units		68,000	54,800	64,000
Equivalent-unit costs	$ 3.75	$ 0.50	$ 1.25	$ 2.00

Assignment of costs		DMaterials	Conversion	
Work in process, beginning			$ 52,000	
Completion of beginning:				
Direct Materials (24,000 x $0.50)		$12,000		
Conversion (4,800 x $1.25)		6,000	18,000	
Total Beginning Inventory			70,000	
Started and Completed (44,000 x $3.75)			165,000	
Total costs transferred out			235,000	
Work in process ending:				
Transferred-in (20,000 x $2.00)		$40,000		
Conversion (20,000 x $1.25 x 0.30)		7,500	47,500	
Costs accounted for			$282,500	

Difficulty: 3   *Objective*: 8

80. General Fabricators assembles its product in several departments. It has two departments that process all units. During October, the beginning work in process in the cutting department was half completed as to conversion, and complete as to direct materials. The beginning inventory included $12,000 for materials and $3,000 for conversion costs. Ending work-in-process inventory in the cutting department was 40% complete. Direct materials are added at the beginning of the process.

Beginning work in process in the finishing department was 75% complete as to conversion. Direct materials are added at the end of the process. Beginning inventories included $16,000 for transferred-in costs and $20,000 for conversion costs. Ending inventory was 25% complete. Additional information about the two departments follows:

	Cutting	Finishing
Beginning work-in-process units	20,000	20,000
Units started this period	40,000	50,000
Units transferred this period	50,000	
Ending work-in-process units	10,000	20,000
Material costs added	$48,000	$28,000
Direct manufacturing labor	$16,000	$40,000
Other conversion costs	$ 8,000	$24,000

Required:
Prepare a production cost worksheet using weighted-average for the cutting department and FIFO for the finishing department.

80. **Answer:**

Production Cost Worksheet
Cutting Department
Weighted-Average Method

Flow of Production	Physical Units	Direct Materials	Conversion
Work in process, beginning	20,000		
Started during period	40,000		
To account for	60,000		
Units transferred out	50,000	50,000	50,000
Work in process, ending	10,000	10,000	4,000
Accounted for	60,000	60,000	54,000

Costs	Totals	Direct Materials	Conversion
Work in process, beginning	$15,000	$12,000	$ 3,000
Costs added during period	72,000	48,000	24,000
Total costs to account for	87,000	60,000	27,000
Divided by equivalent units		60,000	54,000
Equivalent-unit costs	$ 1.50	$ 1.00	$ 0.50

Assignment of costs		
Transferred out (50,000 x $1.50)		$75,000
Work in process, ending		
Direct materials (10,000 x $1.00)	$10,000	
Conversion (10,000 x 0.40 x $0.50)	2,000	12,000
Costs accounted for		$87,000

80. (continued)

Production Cost Worksheet
Finishing Department
FIFO Method

Flow of Production	Physical Units	Direct Materials	Conversion	Trans-In
Work in process, beginning	20,000			
Started During Period	50,000			
To account for	70,000			
Good Units Completed:				
Beginning Work in process	20,000	20,000	5,000	
Started and Completed	30,000	30,000	30,000	30,000
Ending work in process	20,000	0	5,000	20,000
Accounted for	70,000	50,000	40,000	50,000

Costs	Totals	Direct Materials	Conversion	Trans-In
Work in process, beginning	$ 36,000			
Costs added during period	167,000	$28,000	$64,000	$75,000
Total Costs to account for	$203,000	$28,000	$64,000	$75,000
Divided by equivalent units	-	50,000	40,000	50,000
Equivalent-unit costs	$ 3.66	$ 0.56	$ 1.60	$ 1.50

Assignment of costs		
Work in process, beginning		$ 36,000
Completion of beginning:		
Direct Materials (20,000 x $0.56)	$11,200	
Conversion (20,000 x 0.25 x $1.60)	8,000	19,200
Total Beginning Inventory		55,200
Started and Completed (30,000 x $3.66)		109,800
Total costs transferred out		165,000
Work in process ending		
Transferred-in (20,000 x $1.50)	$30,000	
Conversion (20,000 x $1.60 x 0.25)	8,000	38,000
Costs accounted for		$203,000

Difficulty: 3   *Objectives*: 5-8

CRITICAL THINKING

81. Marv and Vicki own and operate a vegetable canning plant. In recent years, their business has grown tremendously and, at any point in time, they may have 30 to 35 different vegetables being processed. Also, during the peak summer months there are several thousand bushels of vegetables in some stage of processing at any one time. With the company's growth during the past few years, the owners decided to employ an accountant to provide cost estimations on each vegetable category and prepare monthly financial statements. Although the accountant is doing exactly as instructed, Marv and Vicki are confused about the monthly operating costs. Although they process an average of 50,000 canned units a month, the monthly production report fluctuates wildly.

Required:
Explain how the production report can fluctuate wildly if they process a constant amount of vegetables each month.

Answer:
It appears that the accountant may not be using equivalent units of production but is only including completed units when preparing the monthly reports. Particularly with large summer inventories, the number and value associated costs with ending work in process could cause wide fluctuations between months if the equivalent unit concept is ignored. The accountant should start using equivalent units to determine the costs to assign to finished goods and ending work in process each month.

Difficulty: 2   *Objective*:   3

82. The president of the Gulf Coast Refining Corporation wants to know why his golfing partner, who is the chief financial officer of a large construction company, calculates his costs by the job when his own corporation calculates costs by large units rather than by individual barrel of oil.

Answer:
Oil refineries use process costing to calculate their costs per barrel of oil. Each barrel of oil is essentially the same. Thus costs are accumulated for all the oil processed during a given time period, and the total costs are divided by the barrels of oil produced. An average cost is calculated. Since the costs to actually produce the oil are essentially the same, accuracy is not lost by this process.

The construction company calculates costs by each job, since each job can require substantially different amounts of the various inputs. Thus the cost of each job could be radically different from the other jobs.

Difficulty: 1   *Objective*:   1

83. Universal Industries operates a division in Brazil, a country with very high inflation rates. Traditionally, the company has used the same costing techniques in all countries so as to facilitate reporting to corporate headquarters. However, the financial accounting reports from Brazil never seem to match the actual unit results of the division. Management has studied the problem and it appears that beginning inventories may be the cause of the unmatched information. The reason for this is that the inventories have a different financial base because of the severe inflation.

Required:
How can process costing assist in addressing the problem facing Universal Industries?

Answer:
Probably the best way to address the problem of inflation is to use FIFO costing. This method keeps the cost of beginning inventories separate from production units started and completed in a given period. Therefore, the company may be able to track the cost of items that were actually produced in a given period, versus mixing the units and costs of multiple periods.

Difficulty: 2   *Objective*: 6

84. BIG Manufacturing Products has been using FIFO process costing for tracking the costs of its manufacturing activities. However, in recent months, the system has become somewhat bogged down with details. It seems that, when the company purchased Brown Electronics last year, its product lines increased six fold. This has caused both the accountants and the suppliers of the information, the line managers, great difficulty in keeping the costs of each product line separate. Likewise, the estimation of the completion of ending work-in-process inventories and the associated costs has become very cumbersome. The chief financial officer of the company is looking for ways to improve the reporting system of product costs.

Required:
What can you recommend to improve the situation?

Answer:
A beginning point would be to change to a standard costing system. Standard costing eliminates many of the problems of FIFO costing in tracking actual costs to products. With standard costing, only the equivalent units have to be determined immediately, not the actual cost of the period. A standard cost for materials and conversion is then applied to the equivalent units for the reporting period. Actual costs and variances from standard costing can be determined later. This approach is very appropriate for a company that has many products.

Difficulty: 3   *Objective*: 7

85. Ford Motor Company is said to use a hybrid costing system. What is a hybrid costing system, and what would be the advantage to Ford of such a system?

Answer:

A hybrid costing system is one that combines the elements of job costing and process costing systems. Important elements of profitability include knowing what your costs are, and controlling costs. Ford has a basic platform that they use to produce cars. Vehicles undergo essentially the same processing and are in effect manufactured in a continuous flow using standard parts and standardized manufacturing processes.

Another important part of profitability is making your product different than other vehicles so buyers will be attracted to purchase the vehicle. Vehicles that are different can command a higher price, and thus increase profitability. Costs are accumulated using process costing up to the point where the product is differentiated. Job costing is used from that point forward.

Difficulty: 2   *Objective*:   8

CHAPTER 18: SPOILAGE, REWORKED UNITS, AND SCRAP

TRUE/FALSE

1. Reducing defects helps to reduce costs, but does not make the business more competitive.

    Answer: False   *Difficulty*: 2   *Objective*: 1
    Reducing defects does make the business more competitive.

2. Reworked goods are unacceptable units of production usually not capable of being repaired or converted into a salable product.

    Answer: False   *Difficulty*: 2   *Objective*: 1
    Reworked goods are unacceptable units of production that can be repaired into a salable product.

3. The value of scrap material can have either a high or low sales value relative to the product with which it is associated.

    Answer: False   *Difficulty*: 2   *Objective*: 1
    Scrap material by definition has a low sales value.

4. Normal spoilage adds to the cost of the job to which it is attributed in a job order costing system.

    Answer: True   *Difficulty*: 2   *Objective*: 2

5. When calculating normal spoilage rates, the base should be actual units started in production.

    Answer: False   *Difficulty*: 2   *Objective*: 2
    The base should be good units started into production.

6. Abnormal spoilage is spoilage that should arise under efficient operating conditions.

    Answer: False   *Difficulty*: 2   *Objective*: 2
    Abnormal spoilage should not arise under efficient operating conditions.

7. A company whose goal is zero defects would usually treat all spoilage as abnormal.

    Answer: True   *Difficulty*: 2   *Objective*: 2

8. Counting spoiled units as part of output units in a process-costing system usually results in a higher cost per unit.

    Answer: False   *Difficulty*: 3   *Objective*: 3
    Counting spoiled units usually results in a lower cost per unit.

9. Costs in beginning inventory are pooled with costs in the current period when determining the costs of good units under the weighted-average method of process costing.

Answer: True   *Difficulty:* 2   *Objective:* 3

10. Under the weighted-average method, the costs of normal spoilage are added to the costs of their related good units. Hence, the cost per good unit completed and transferred out equals the total costs transferred out divided by the number of good units produced.

Answer: True   *Difficulty:* 3   *Objective:* 3

11. Under the FIFO method, all spoilage costs are assumed to be related to units completed during this period using the unit costs of the current period.

Answer: True   *Difficulty:* 3   *Objective:* 4

12. When spoiled goods have a disposal value, the net cost of spoilage is computed by adding the disposal value to the costs of the spoiled goods accumulated to the inspection point.

Answer: False   *Difficulty:* 2   *Objective:* 4
The net cost of spoilage is computed by subtracting the disposal value from the costs of the spoiled goods accumulated to the inspection point.

13. Normal spoilage costs are usually deducted from the costs of good units.

Answer: False   *Difficulty:* 2   *Objective:* 5
Normal spoilage is usually added to the cost of the good units.

14. Costs of abnormal spoilage are separately accounted for as losses of the period.

Answer: True   *Difficulty:* 2   *Objective:* 5

15. In job costing, costs of abnormal spoilage are not considered as inventoriable costs and are therefore written off as costs of the period in which detection occurs.

Answer: True   *Difficulty:* 3   *Objective:* 6

16. In both job costing and process costing, normal spoilage attributable to a specific job is assigned to that job.

Answer: False   *Difficulty:* 3   *Objective:* 6
In process costing, spoilage costs are not assigned to that job.

17. When rework is normal and not attributable to any specific job, the costs of rework are charged to manufacturing overhead, and spread through overhead allocation over all jobs.

Answer: True   *Difficulty*: 3   *Objective*: 7

18. Scrap is usually divided between normal and abnormal scrap.

Answer: False   *Difficulty*: 2   *Objective*: 8
There is no abnormal scrap.

19. If scrap is returned to the company's storeroom and thus inventoried, it should not have any value in the accounting records.

Answer: False   *Difficulty*: 3   *Objective*: 8
The scrap will be inventoried. It might not have a value in dollars but it will have a physical quantity value.

20. Many companies track scrap only in nonfinancial terms (liters, for example) and record its sale as another revenue item.

Answer: True   *Difficulty*: 2   *Objective*: 8

21. Managers often cite reductions in the costs of spoilage as a(n)
    a. major justification for implementing a just-in-time production system.
    b. measurement of improved output quality.
    c. immaterial item that is not to be tracked.
    d. indication of improvement in the accounting system.

    Answer: a   *Difficulty:* 2   *Objective:* 1

22. Unacceptable units of production that are discarded or are sold for reduced prices are referred to as
    a. reworked units.
    b. spoilage.
    c. scrap.
    d. defective units.

    Answer: b   *Difficulty:* 1   *Objective:* 1

23. Unacceptable units of production that are subsequently repaired and sold as acceptable finished goods are
    a. reworked units.
    b. spoilage.
    c. scrap.
    d. defective units.

    Answer: a   *Difficulty:* 1   *Objective:* 1

24. Costs of poor quality production include
    a. the opportunity cost of the plant and workers.
    b. the effect on current customers.
    c. the effect on potential customers.
    d. all of the above are costs of poor quality production.

    Answer: d   *Difficulty:* 2   *Objective:* 1

25. Material left over when making a product is referred to as
    a. reworked units.
    b. spoilage.
    c. scrap.
    d. defective units.

    Answer: c   *Difficulty:* 1   *Objective:* 1

26. A production process which involves spoilage and rework occurs in
    a. the manufacture of high precision tools.
    b. semiconductor units.
    c. the manufacture of clothing.
    d. all of the above involve spoilage and rework.

    Answer: a   *Difficulty*: 2   *Objective*: 1

27. Spoilage that is an inherent result of the particular production process and arises under efficient operating conditions is referred to as
    a. ordinary spoilage.
    b. normal spoilage.
    c. abnormal spoilage.
    d. there is no special term for this type of spoilage.

    Answer: b   *Difficulty*: 2   *Objective*: 2

28. Spoilage that should not arise under efficient operating conditions is referred to as
    a. ordinary spoilage.
    b. normal spoilage.
    c. abnormal spoilage.
    d. there is no special term for this type of spoilage.

    Answer: c   *Difficulty*: 2   *Objective*: 2

29. Costs of normal spoilage are usually accounted for as
    a. part of the cost of goods sold.
    b. part of the cost of goods manufactured.
    c. a separate line item in the income statement.
    d. an asset in the balance sheet.

    Answer: b   *Difficulty*: 2   *Objective*: 2

30. Costs of abnormal spoilage are usually accounted for as
    a. part of the cost of goods sold.
    b. part of the cost of goods manufactured.
    c. a separate line item in the income statement.
    d. an asset in the balance sheet.

    Answer: c   *Difficulty*: 2   *Objective*: 2

31. The loss from abnormal spoilage account would not appear
    a. on the balance sheet.
    b. as a detailed item in the retained earnings schedule of the balance sheet.
    c. as a detailed item on the income statement.
    d. on either (a) or (b).

    Answer: d   *Difficulty*: 2   *Objective*: 2

32. Normal spoilage should be computed using as the base
    a. total units completed.
    b. total good units completed.
    c. total actual units started into production.
    d. none of the above.

    Answer: b   *Difficulty:* 2   *Objective:* 2

33. Companies that attempt to achieve zero defects in the manufacturing process treat spoilage as
    a. scrap.
    b. reworked units.
    c. abnormal spoilage.
    d. normal spoilage.

    Answer: c   *Difficulty:* 2   *Objective:* 2

34. Which one of the following conditions usually exists when comparing normal and abnormal spoilage to controllability?

	Normal Spoilage	Abnormal Spoilage
a.	Controllable	Controllable
b.	Controllable	Uncontrollable
c.	Uncontrollable	Uncontrollable
d.	Uncontrollable	Controllable

    Answer: d   *Difficulty:* 2   *Objective:* 2

35. Not counting spoiled units in the equivalent-unit calculation results in
    a. lower cost per good unit.
    b. higher cost per good unit.
    c. better management information.
    d. both (a) and (c).

    Answer: b   *Difficulty:* 2   *Objective:* 2

36. Recognition of spoiled units when computing output units
    a. highlights the costs of normal spoilage to management.
    b. distorts the accounting data.
    c. focuses management's attention on reducing spoilage.
    d. results in both (a) and (c).

    Answer: d   *Difficulty:* 2   *Objective:* 2

THE FOLLOWING INFORMATION APPLIES TO QUESTIONS 37 THROUGH 41.
Astoria Computer Systems, Inc., manufactures printers. All direct materials are added at the inception of the production process. During January, the accounting department noted that there was no beginning inventory. Direct materials purchases totaled $100,000 during the month. Work-in-process records revealed that 4,000 cards were started in January, 2,000 cards were complete, and 1,500 units were spoiled as expected. Ending work-in-process units are complete in respect to direct materials costs. Spoilage is not detected until the process is complete.

37. What are the respective direct material costs per equivalent unit, assuming spoiled units are recognized or ignored?
    a. $20.00; $35.00
    b. $25.00; $40.00
    c. $30.00; $45.00
    d. $35.00; $50.00

    Answer: b   *Difficulty:* 2   *Objective:* 2

	Recognized	Problem #	Ignored
Cost to account for:	$100,000		$100,000
Divided by equivalent units	4,000		2,500
Cost per equivalent unit	$ 25.00	(37)	$ 40.00
Assigned to:			
Good units completed			
(2,000 x $25; $40)	$ 50,000		$ 80,000
Normal spoilage			
(1,500 x $25)	37,500		0
Costs transferred out	87,500	(38/39)	80,000
WIP ending inventory (500 x $25; $40)	12,500	(40)	20,000
Cost accounted for:	$100,000		$100,000

38. What is the direct material cost assigned to good units completed when spoilage units are recognized?
    a. $50,000
    b. $100,000
    c. $80,000
    d. $87,500

    Answer: d   *Difficulty:* 3   *Objective:* 2
    See question #37 for computations.

39. What is the cost transferred out assuming spoilage units are ignored?
    a. $87,500
    b. $80,000
    c. $50,000
    d. $77,500

    Answer: b   *Difficulty:* 3   *Objective:* 2
    See question #37 for computations.

40. What are the amounts allocated to the work-in-process ending inventory assuming spoilage units are recognized and ignored, respectively?
    a. $20,000; $24,500
    b. $30,000; $34,250
    c. $12,500; $20,000
    d. $37,500; $40,000

    Answer: c   *Difficulty:* 3   *Objective:* 2
    See question #37 for computations.

41. Spoilage costs allocated to ending work in process are larger by which method and by how much?
    a. When spoiled units are recognized by $2,500
    b. When spoiled units are recognized by $4,250
    c. When spoiled units are ignored by $7,500
    d. When spoiled units are recognized by $7,500

    Answer: c   *Difficulty:* 3   *Objective:* 2
    $20,000- $12,500 = $7,500 or $15.00 x 500 units = $7,500

THE FOLLOWING INFORMATION APPLIES TO QUESTIONS 42 THROUGH 47.
Craft Concept manufactures small tables in its Processing Department. Direct materials are added at the initiation of the production cycle and must be bundled in single kits for each unit. Conversion costs are incurred evenly throughout the production cycle. Before inspection, some units are spoiled due to nondetectible materials defects. Inspection occurs when units are 50% converted. Spoiled units generally constitute 5% of the good units. Data for December 20x3 are as follows:

WIP, beginning inventory 12/1/20x3	10,000 units
Direct materials (100% complete)	
Conversion costs (75% complete)	
Started during December	40,000 units
Completed and transferred out 12/31/20x3	38,400 units
WIP, ending inventory 12/31/20x3	8,000 units
Direct materials (100% complete)	
Conversion costs (65% complete)	

Costs for December:	
WIP, beginning Inventory:	
Direct materials	$ 50,000
Conversion costs	30,000
Direct materials added	100,000
Conversion costs added	140,000

42.   What is the number of total spoiled units?
    a.   1,600 units
    b.   2,000 units
    c.   2,700 units
    d.   3,600 units

Answer: d   *Difficulty:*   2   *Objective:*   2
Spoiled units = (10,000 units + 40,000) - (38,400 units + 8,000) = 3,600 units

43.   Normal spoilage totals
    a.   1,600 units.
    b.   2,000 units.
    c.   1,920 units.
    d.   2,700 units

Answer: c   *Difficulty:*   2   *Objective:*   2
Normal spoilage = 5% x 38,400 units = 1,920 spoiled units.

44.   Abnormal spoilage totals
    a.   1,600 units.
    b.   2,000 units.
    c.   1,680 units.
    d.   1.920 units.

Answer: c   *Difficulty:*   3   *Objective:*   2
Abnormal spoilage = 3,600 units - 1,920 units = 1,680 units

45. What is the total cost per equivalent unit using the weighted-average method of process costing?
 a. $3.00
 b. $3.60
 c. $6.60
 d. $4.60

Answer: c   *Difficulty:* 2   *Objective:* 3

	Direct Materials	Conversion Costs
WIP, beginning inventory	$ 50,000	$ 30,000
Costs added during period	100,000	140,000
Total cost to account for	150,000	170,000
Divide by equivalent units	50,000	47,200
Equivalent-unit costs	$ 3.00	$ 3.60

Total cost per equivalent unit = $3.00 + $3.60 = $6.60

46. What cost is allocated to abnormal spoilage using the weighted-average process-costing method?
 a. $ 0
 b. $ 7,360
 c. $11,088
 d. $16,400

Answer: c   *Difficulty:* 2   *Objective:* 3
1,680 units x $6.60 = $11,088

47. What are the amounts of direct materials and conversion costs assigned to ending work in process using the weighted-average process-costing method?
 a. $18,720; $24,000
 b. $22,900; $19,820
 c. $24,000; $18,720
 d. $28,560; $14,160

Answer: c   *Difficulty:* 2   *Objective:* 3
Direct materials = 8,000 units x $3.00 = $24,000
Conversion costs = 5,200 units x $3.60 = $18,720

48. The cost per good unit in the weighted-average method is equal to
 a. the total cost of direct materials and conversion costs per equivalent unit, plus a share of normal spoilage.
 b. the sum of the costs per equivalent unit of direct materials, and conversion costs.
 c. the total costs divided by total equivalent units.
 d. none of the above.

Answer: a   *Difficulty:* 2   *Objective:* 3

49. Under the FIFO method, all spoilage costs are assumed to be
    a. related to the units in beginning inventory, plus the units completed during the period.
    b. related to the units completed during the period.
    c. related to the units in ending inventory.
    d. related to the units in both beginning and ending inventory plus the units completed during the period.

Answer: b   *Difficulty*: 2   *Objective*: 4

THE FOLLOWING INFORMATION APPLIES TO QUESTIONS 50 THROUGH 53.
Cartwright Custom Carpentry manufactures chairs in its Processing Department. Direct materials are included at the inception of the production cycle and must be bundled in single kits for each unit. Conversion costs are incurred evenly throughout the production cycle. Inspection takes place as units are placed into production. After inspection, some units are spoiled due to nondetectible material defects. Spoiled units generally constitute 3% of the good units. Data provided for March 20x3 are as follows:

WIP, beginning inventory 3/1/20x3	30,000 units
Direct materials (100% complete)	
Conversion costs (89.5% complete)	
Started during March	80,000 units
Completed and transferred out	86,000 units
WIP, ending inventory 3/31/20x3	20,000 units
Direct materials (100% complete)	
Conversion costs (75% complete)	
Costs:	
WIP, beginning inventory:	
Direct materials	$ 70,000
Conversion costs	40,000
Direct materials added	160,000
Conversion costs added	120,000

50. What are the normal and abnormal spoilage units, respectively, for March when using FIFO?
    a. 2,580 units; 1,420 units
    b. 1,950 units; 1,390 units
    c. 1,690 units; 1,050 units
    d. 1,420 units; 2,000 units

Answer: a   *Difficulty*: 3   *Objective*: 4
Normal spoilage = 3% x 86,000 units = 2,580 spoiled units
Abnormal spoilage = 4,000 units - 2,580 = 1,420 units

51. What costs would be associated with normal and abnormal spoilage, respectively, using the FIFO method of process costing?
    a. $5,890.64; $9,133.20
    b. $5,890.64; $5,826.00
    c. $6,469.64; $7,690.36
    d. $9,133.20; $5,026.80

    Answer: d   *Difficulty*: 3   *Objective*: 4

	Direct Materials	Conversion Costs
WIP, beginning inventory		
Costs added during period	$160,000	$ 120,000
Total cost to account for	160,000	120,000
Divided by equivalent units	80,000*	78,150**
Equivalent-unit costs	$ 2.00	$ 1.54

    (56,000 + 2,580 + 1,420 + 20,000) = 80,000 units
    (3,150 + 56,000 + 2,580 + 1,420 + 15,000) = 78,150 units

    Normal Spoilage = 2,580 units x $3.54 = $9,133.20
    Abnormal Spoilage = 1,420 units x $3.54 = $5,026.80

52. What costs are allocated to the ending work-in-process inventory for direct materials and conversion costs, respectively, using the FIFO method of process costing?
    a. $38,250; $24,850
    b. $40,000; $23,100
    c. $40,000; $21,590
    d. $49,500; $13,600

    Answer: b   *Difficulty*: 3   *Objective*: 4
    Direct materials: 20,000 units x $2.00 = $40,000
    Conversion costs: 15,000 units x $1.54 = $23,100

53. Which of the following journal entries correctly represents the transfer of completed goods for the current period using the FIFO method of process costing?

a. Finished Goods $ 10,560.28
      Loss from Spoilage $ 10,560.28

b. Loss from Spoilage $ 5,026.80
      Finished Goods $ 5,026.80

c. Finished Goods $327,251.00
      Work in Process $327,251.00

d. Finished Goods $401,700.00
      Work in Process $401,700.00

Answer: c   *Difficulty:* 3   *Objective:* 4

Abnormal spoilage	$ 5,026.80
Beginning WIP - completed	110,000.00
Costs added	4,851.00
Started and completed	198,240.00
Normal spoilage	9,133.20
Total cost transferred out	$327,251.00

54. The standard-costing method
a. adds a layer of complexity to the calculation of equivalent-unit costs in a process-costing environment.
b. makes calculating equivalent-unit costs unnecessary.
c. requires an analysis of the spoilage costs in beginning inventory.
d. requires an analysis of the spoilage costs in ending inventory.

Answer: b   *Difficulty:* 2   *Objective:* 5

55. The inspection point is
a. the stage of the production cycle where products are checked to determine whether they are acceptable or unacceptable units.
b. the point at which costs are allocated between normal and abnormal spoilage.
c. the point at which the calculation of equivalent units is made.
d. none of the above.

Answer: a   *Difficulty:* 2   *Objective:* 5

56. When spoiled goods have a disposal value, the net cost of the spoilage is computed by
a. deducting disposal value from the costs of the spoiled goods accumulated to the inspection point.
b. adding the costs to complete a salable product to the costs accumulated to the inspection point.
c. calculating the costs incurred to the inspection point.
d. none of the above.

Answer: a   *Difficulty:* 2   *Objective:* 5

57. The costs of normal spoilage are allocated to the units in ending work-in-process inventory, in addition to completed units
    a. if the units in ending inventory have not passed the inspection point.
    b. if the units in ending work-in-process inventory have passed the inspection point.
    c. if the units in ending work in process inventory are more than 50% complete.
    d. if the units in ending work-in-process inventory are less than 50% complete.

Answer: b   *Difficulty:* 3   *Objective:* 5

58. The Harleysville Manufacturing Shop produces motorcycle parts. Typically, 10 pieces out of a job lot of 1,000 parts are spoiled. Costs are assigned at the inspection point, $50.00 per unit. Spoiled pieces may be disposed of at $10.00 per unit. The spoiled goods must be inventoried appropriately when the normal spoilage is detected. The current job requires the production of 2,500 good parts.

Which of the following journal entries properly reflects the recording of spoiled goods?
    a. Materials Control $ 200
       Manufacturing Overhead Control $ 800
           Work-in-Process Control $1,000
    b. Materials Control $ 250
       Manufacturing Overhead Control $1,000
           Work-in-Process Control $1,250
    c. Work-in-Process Control $1,250
           Materials Control $ 250
           Manufacturing Overhead Control $1,000
    d. Manufacturing Overhead Control $1,000
           Materials Control $ 200
           Work-in-Process Control $ 800

Answer: b   *Difficulty:* 2   *Objective:* 6

Materials Control: 25 pieces x $10.00 = $250
Manufacturing Overhead Control: 25 pieces x ($50.00 - $10.00) = $1,000
WIP Control: 25 pieces x $50.00 = $1,250

59. The Harleysville Manufacturing Shop produces motorcycle parts. Typically, 10 pieces out of a job lot of 1,000 parts are spoiled. Costs are assigned at the inspection point, $50.00 per unit. Spoiled pieces may be disposed of at $10.00 per unit. The spoiled goods must be inventoried appropriately when the normal spoilage is detected. Job 101 requires the production of 2,500 good parts.

   Which of the following journal entries would be correct if the spoilage occurred due to specifications required for Job 101?
   a.   Work-in-Process Control $100
            Materials Control $100
   b.   Materials Control $100
            Work-in-Process Control $100
   c.   Materials Control $250
            Work-in-Process Control $250
   d.   Work-in-Process Control $250
            Materials Control $250

   Answer: c   *Difficulty*:   2   *Objective*:   6
   25 pieces x $10.00 = $250

60. A difference between job costing and process costing is
   a.   that job-costing systems usually do not distinguish between normal spoilage attributable to all jobs and normal spoilage attributable to a specific job.
   b.   that job-costing systems usually distinguish between normal spoilage attributable to a specific job and spoilage common to all jobs.
   c.   that process costing normally does not distinguish between normal spoilage attributable to a specific job and spoilage common to all jobs.
   d.   both (b) and (c).

   Answer: d   *Difficulty*:   2   *Objective*:   6

61. Which of the following entries reflects the original cost assignment before production items are reworked?
   a.   Work-in-Process Control   XXX
            Materials Control   XXX
            Wages Payable Control   XXX
            Manufacturing Overhead Allocated   XXX
   b.   Finished Goods Control   XXX
            Work-in-Process Control   XXX
   c.   Manufacturing Overhead Allocated   XXX
        Materials Control   XXX
            Wages Payable Control   XXX
            Work-in-Process Control   XXX
   d.   Materials Control   XXX
        Wages Payable Control   XXX
            Work-in-Process Control   XXX
            Manufacturing Overhead Allocated   XXX

   Answer: a   *Difficulty*:   2   *Objective*:   7

62. Accounting for rework in a process-costing system
   a. accounts for normal rework in the same way as a job-costing system.
   b. requires abnormal rework to be distinguished from normal rework.
   c. if the rework is normal, then rework is accounted for in the same manner as accounting for normal rework common to all jobs.
   d. all of the above are correct.

   Answer: d   *Difficulty*: 2   *Objective*: 7

63. In accounting for scrap, which one of the following statements is FALSE?
   a. Normal scrap is accounted for separately from abnormal scrap.
   b. In accounting for scrap, there is no distinction between the scrap attributable to a specific job and scrap common to all jobs.
   c. Initial entries to scrap accounting records are most often made in dollar terms.
   d. All of the above are false.

   Answer: d   *Difficulty*: 3   *Objective*: 7

64. When the amount of scrap is immaterial, the easiest accounting entry when recording scrap sold for cash is
   a. Sales of Scrap
         Cash
   b. Cash
         Manufacturing Overhead Control
   c. Cash
         Sales of Scrap
   d. Accounts Receivable
         Sales of scrap

   Answer: c   *Difficulty*: 2   *Objective*: 8

65. Assume the amount of scrap is material and the scrap is sold immediately after it is produced. If the scrap attributable to a specific job is sold on account, the journal entry is:
   a. Work-in-Process Control
         Cash
   b. Work-in-Process Control
         Accounts Receivable
   c. Accounts Receivable
         Work-in-Process Control
   d. Work-in-Process Control
         Accounts Receivable

   Answer: c   *Difficulty*: 3   *Objective*: 8

66. If scrap, common to all jobs, is returned to the storeroom and the time between the scrap being inventoried and its disposal is quite lengthy, the journal entry is:
    a. Work-in-Process Control
         Materials Control
    b. Materials Control
         Work-in-Process Control
    c. Manufacturing Overhead Control
         Materials Control
    d. Materials Control
         Manufacturing Overhead Control

    Answer: d   *Difficulty*: 3   *Objective*: 8

67. The accounting for scrap under process costing is similar to
    a. the accounting under job costing when scrap is different for each job.
    b. the accounting under job costing when scrap is common to all jobs.
    c. the accounting under process costing when scrap is different for each job.
    d. the accounting under process costing when scrap is a common to all jobs.

    Answer: b   *Difficulty*: 2   *Objective*: 8

68. Which of the following is NOT a major consideration when accounting for scrap?
    a. Keeping detailed records of physical quantities of scrap at all stages of the production process
    b. Inventory costing including when and how scrap affects operating income
    c. Planning and control including physical tracking
    d. Decisions as to whether to group scrap with reworked units

    Answer: d   *Difficulty*: 2   *Objective*: 8

69. Normal spoilage is computed on the basis of
    a. the number of good units that pass inspection during the current period.
    b. the number of units that pass the inspection point during the current period.
    c. the number of units that are 100% complete as to materials.
    d. none of the above.

    Answer: a   *Difficulty*: 2   *Objective*: A

70. Which of the following INCORRECTLY reflects what units passed inspection this period? Assume beginning work in process was completed and ending work in process was started during the period.

	Inspection Point at Completion Level		
	10%	50%	100%
a. Beginning work in process (30% complete)	No	Yes	Yes
b. Started and completed	Yes	Yes	Yes
c. Ending work in process (40% complete)	Yes	No	No
d. Beginning work in process (5% complete)	Yes	No	No

    Answer: d   *Difficulty*: 3   *Objective*: A

71. Distinguish among spoilage, reworked units, and scrap. Give an example of each.

Answer:

Spoilage refers to unacceptable units of production that are discarded or are sold for reduced prices. Both partially completed or fully completed units of output can be spoiled. Examples are defective clothes sold as seconds.

Reworked units are unacceptable units of production that are subsequently repaired and sold as acceptable finished goods. Defective units of product (such as pagers, computer disk drives, computers, and telephones) detected during production or immediately after production but before units are shipped to customers, can sometimes be reworked and sold as good products.

Scrap is material left over when making a product. It has low sales value compared with the sales value of the product. Examples are shavings and short lengths from woodworking operations and edges left over from plastic molding operations.

Difficulty: 1   *Objective:*   1

72. For each of the following items identify whether it is spoilage, reworked units, or scrap.

_____	a.	Defective jeans sold as seconds
_____	b.	Shavings
_____	c.	Edges from plastic moldings
_____	d.	Carpets sold as seconds
_____	e.	Precision tools that are not built successfully to the necessary tolerance, but can be successfully converted to a saleable product
_____	f.	Rock extracted as a result of mining processing
_____	g.	Complex defective products such as semiconductors

Answer:

a. spoilage
b. scrap
c. scrap
d. spoilage
e. spoilage and rework
f. scrap
g. spoilage (usually too complex to rework)

Difficulty: 2   *Objective:*   1

73. What are the objectives in accounting for spoilage?

Answer:
The key objectives in accounting for spoilage are determining the magnitude of the costs of the spoilage and distinguishing between the costs of normal and abnormal spoilage. In order to effectively manage a company (or a division of a business), a manager needs information concerning how his business is performing. Spoilage is a cost, which should be controlled and minimized. The dimensions of the cost must be known (the dollar amount of the spoilage). The accounting system must be capable of determining the dollar amount of the spoilage costs while distinguishing between normal and abnormal spoilage. This information must be reported and available to management on a timely basis.

Difficulty: 2 *Objective:* 2

74. The Clay Shop manufactures pottery products. All direct materials are included at the inception of the production process. For April, there was no beginning inventory in the processing plant. Direct materials totaled $310,000 for the month. Work-in-process records revealed that 5,000 tons were started in April and that 3,000 tons were finished; 1,000 tons were spoiled as expected. Ending work-in-process units are complete in respect to direct materials costs. Spoilage is not detected until the process is complete.

Required:
a. What is the cost per equivalent unit if spoiled units are recognized or ignored?
b. What are the costs assigned to completed units when spoilage units are recognized or when they are not recognized?
c. What are the costs transferred out if spoilage units are recognized or ignored?
d. What are the amounts allocated to the work-in-process ending inventory when spoilage units are recognized or ignored?

Answer:

a.

	Recognized	Ignored
Cost to account for	$310,000	$310,000
Divided by equivalent units	5,000	4,000
Cost per equivalent unit	$ 62	$ 77.50

b. Assigned to good units completed:

(3,000 x $62)	$186,000	
(3,000 x $77.50)		$232,500

c.

Transferred out - Finished	$186,000	$232,500
Normal spoilage (1,000 x $62)	62,000	0
Total	$248,000	$232,500

d. Ending work-in-process inventory:

(1,000 x $62)	$ 62,000	
(1,000 x $77.50)		$ 77,500

Difficulty: 2 *Objective:* 2

75. Endicott Shoes manufactures shoes. All direct materials are included at the inception of the production process. For March, there were 1,400 units in beginning inventory with a direct material cost of $700. Direct materials totaled $15,000 for the month. Work-in-process records revealed that 35,000 shoes were started in March and that 30,000 were finished. Normal spoilage of 2% of units finished was incurred. Ending work-in-process units are complete in respect to direct materials costs. Spoilage is not detected until the process is complete. Endicott uses the weighted-average method.

Required:

a. What are the direct materials costs assigned to completed good units when spoilage units are recognized or when they are ignored?

b. What are the direct material amounts allocated to the work-in-process ending inventory when spoilage units are recognized or ignored?

Answer:

a. Equivalent units (spoilage recognized) = 1,400 + 35,000 = 36,400

Equivalent units (spoilage ignored)
= 1,400 +35,000 - (30,000 x 0.02)
= 35,800

	Recognized	Ignored
Cost to account for:		
Beginning work in process	$ 700	$ 700
Current period	15,000	15,000
Total costs to account for	$15,700	$15,700
Divided by equivalent units	36,400	35,800
Cost per equivalent unit	$ 0.431	$ 0.439
Assigned to good units:		
(29,400 x $0.431)	$12,671	
(29,400 x $0.439)		$12,907

b. Ending work in process:

	Recognized	Ignored
(6,400 x $0.431)	$ 2,758	
(6,400 x $0.439)		$ 2,810

Difficulty: 3   *Objective*: 3

76. Viking Sports is a manufacturer of sportswear. It produces all of its products in one department. The information for the current month is as follows:

Beginning work in process	20,000 units
Units started	40,000 units
Units completed	50,000 units
Ending work in process	8,000 units
Spoilage	2,000 units
Beginning work-in-process direct materials	$12,000
Beginning work-in-process conversion	$ 4,000
Direct materials added during month	$60,000
Direct manufacturing labor during month	$20,000

Beginning work in process was half complete as to conversion. Direct materials are added at the beginning of the process. Factory overhead is applied at a rate equal to 50% of direct manufacturing labor. Ending work in process was 60% complete. All spoilage is normal and is detected at end of the process.

Required:

Prepare a production cost worksheet if spoilage is recognized and the weighted-average method is used.

Answer:

PRODUCTION COST WORKSHEET

Flow of Production	Physical units	Direct materials	Conversion
Work in process, beginning	20,000		
Started during period	40,000		
To account for	60,000		
Good units completed	50,000	50,000	50,000
Normal spoilage	2,000	2,000	2,000
Work in process, ending	8,000	8,000	4,800
Accounted for	60,000	60,000	56,800

Costs	Totals	Direct Materials	Conversion
Work in process, beginning	$ 16,000	$12,000	$ 4,000
Costs added during period	90,000	60,000	30,000
Total costs to account for	106,000	72,000	34,000
Divided by equivalent units		60,000	56,800
Equivalent unit costs	$ 1.80	$ 1.20	$ 0.60

76. (continued)

<u>Assignment of costs</u>

Costs transferred out (50,000 x $1.80)	$ 90,000
Normal spoilage (2,000 x $1.80)	3,600
Work in process, ending	
Direct materials (8,000 x $1.20)	9,600
Conversion (8,000 x $0.60 x 0.60)	<u>2,880</u>
Costs accounted for	<u>$106,080</u>

(Differences may be due to rounding)

Difficulty: 2   *Objective*: 3

77. New Image Sports uses a process-costing system. For March, the company had the following activities:

Beginning work-in-process inventory (1/3 complete)	6,000 units
Units placed in production	24,000 units
Good units completed	18,000 units
Ending work-in-process inventory	10,000 units
Cost of beginning work in process	$ 5,000
Direct material costs, current	$18,000
Conversion costs, current	$13,800

Direct materials are placed into production at the beginning of the process. All spoilage is normal and is detected at the end of the process. Ending WIP is 50% completed as to conversion.

Required:

Prepare a production cost worksheet using the FIFO method.

77. **Answer**:

Normal spoilage = 6,000 + 24,000 - 18,000 - 10,000 = 2,000
Started and completed = 18,000 - 6,000 = 12,000

PRODUCTION COST WORKSHEET

Flow Of Production	Physical Units	Direct Materials	Conversion
Work in process, beginning	6,000		
Started during period	24,000		
To account for	30,000		
Good units completed:			
Beginning work in process	6,000		4,000
Started and completed	12,000	12,000	12,000
Normal spoilage	2,000	2,000	2,000
Work in process, ending	10,000	10,000	5,000
Accounted for	30,000	24,000	23,000

Costs	Totals	Direct Materials	Conversion
Work in process, beginning	$ 5,000		
Costs added during period	31,800	$18,000	$13,800
Total costs to account for	$36,800	$18,000	$13,800
Divided by equivalent units		24,000	23,000
Equivalent-unit costs	$ 1.35	$ 0.75	$ 0.60

Assignment of cost:

Work in process, beginning		$ 5,000
Completion of beginning (4,000 x $0.60)		2,400
Total beginning inventory		7,400
Started and completed (12,000 x $1.35)		16,200
Normal spoilage (2,000 x $1.35)		2,700
Total costs transferred out		26,300
Work in process, ending		
Direct materials (10,000 x $0.75)	$7,500	
Conversion (10,000 x $0.60 x 0.5)	3,000	10,500
Costs accounted for		$36,800

Difficulty: 3   *Objective*:   4

78. Weather Instruments assembles products from component parts. It has two departments that process all products. During January, the beginning work in process in the assembly department was half complete as to conversion and complete as to direct materials. The beginning inventory included $12,000 for materials and $4,000 for conversion costs. Overhead is applied at the rate of 50% of direct manufacturing labor costs. Ending work-in-process inventory in the assembly department was 40% complete. All spoilage is considered normal and is detected at the end of the process.

Beginning work in process in the finishing department was 75% complete as to conversion and ending work in process was 25% converted. Direct materials are added at the end of the process. Beginning inventories included $16,000 for transferred-in costs and $10,000 for direct manufacturing labor costs. Overhead in this department is equal to direct manufacturing labor costs. Additional information about the two departments follows:

	Assembly	Finishing
Beginning work-in-process units	20,000	24,000
Units started this period	40,000	?
Units transferred this period	50,000	54,000
Ending work-in-process units	8,000	20,000
Material costs added	$44,000	$28,000
Direct manufacturing labor	$16,000	$24,000

Required:

Prepare a production cost worksheet using weighted-average for the assembly department and FIFO for the finishing department.

78. **Answer**:

Normal spoilage in assembly = 20,000 + 40,000 - 50,000 - 8,000 = 2,000

PRODUCTION COST WORKSHEET
Assembly Department
Weighted-Average Method

Flow of production	Physical Units	Direct Materials	Conversion
Work in process, beginning	20,000		
Started during period	40,000		
To account for	60,000		
Good units completed and			
Transferred out	50,000	50,000	50,000
Normal spoilage	2,000	2,000	2,000
Work in process, ending	8,000	8,000	3,200
Accounted for	60,000	60,000	55,200

Costs	Totals	Direct materials	Conversion
Work in process, beginning	$16,000	$12,000	$ 4,000
Costs added during period	68,000	44,000	24,000
Total costs to account for	84,000	56,000	28,000
Divided by equivalent units		60,000	55,200
Equivalent-unit costs	$ 1.44	$ 0.93	$ 0.51

Assignment of costs

Transferred out (50,000 x $1.44)		$72,000
Normal spoilage (2,000 x $1.44)		2,880
Total costs transferred out		74,880
Work in process, ending		
Direct materials (8,000 x $0.93)	$7,440	
Conversion (8,000 x 0.40 x $0.51)	1,632	9,072
Costs accounted for		$83,952

(Differences may be due to rounding)

78. (continued)

PRODUCTION COST WORKSHEET
Finishing Department
FIFO Method

Flow of Production	Physical Units	Direct Materials	Conversion	Transferred In
Work in process, beginning	24,000			
Started during period	50,000			
To account for	74,000			
Good units completed:				
Beginning work in process	24,000	24,000	6,000	
Started and completed	30,000	30,000	30,000	30,000
Work in process, ending	20,000	0	5,000	20,000
Accounted for	74,000	54,000	41,000	50,000

Costs	Physical Units	Direct Materials	Conversion	Transferred In
Work in process, beginning	$ 36,000			
Costs added during period	150,880	$28,000	$48,000	$74,880
Total costs to account for	186,880	28,000	48,000	74,880
Divided by equivalent units		54,000	41,000	50,000
Equivalent-unit costs	$ 3.19	$ 0.52	$ 1.17	$ 1.50

Assignment of costs:

Work in process, beginning		$ 36,000
Completion of beginning:		
Direct materials (24,000 x $0.52)	$12,480	
Conversion costs (24,000 x 0.25 x $1.17)	7,020	19,500
Total beginning inventory		55,500
Started and completed (30,000 x $3.19)		95,700
Total costs transferred out		151,200
Work in process, ending		
Transferred in (20,000 x $1.50)	$30,000	
Conversion costs (20,000 x $1.17 x 0.25)	5,850	35,850
Costs accounted for		$187,050

(Differences may be due to rounding)

Difficulty: 3   Objective: 4

79. Valentine Florists operate a flower shop. Because most of their orders are via telephone or fax, numerous orders have to be reworked. The average cost of the reworked orders is $6: $3.75 for labor, $1.50 for more flowers, and $0.75 for overhead. This ratio of costs holds for the average original order. On a recent day, the shop reworked 48 orders out of 249. The original cost of the 48 orders totaled $720. The average cost of all orders is $18.75, including rework, with an average selling price of $30

Required:

Prepare the necessary journal entry to record the rework for the day if the shop charges such activities to Arrangement Department Overhead Control. Prepare a journal entry to transfer the finished goods to Finished Goods Inventory.

Answer:

Arrangement Department Overhead Control	$288	
Materials Control (48 x $1.50)		$ 72
Wages Payable Control (48 x $3.75)		180
Shop Overhead Control (48 x $0.75)		36
Finished Goods	$720	
Work-in-Process Control		$720

Difficulty: 2   *Objective*: 7

80. Springfield Sign Shop manufactures only specific orders. It uses a standard cost system. During one large order for the airport authority, an unusual number of signs were spoiled. The normal spoilage rate is 10% of units started. The point of first inspection is half way through the process, the second is three-fourths through the process, and the final inspection is at the end of the process. Other information about the job is as follows:

Signs started	3,000
Signs spoiled	450
Direct materials put into process at beginning	$ 60,000
Conversion costs for job	$120,000
Standard direct material costs per sign	$27
Standard conversion cost per sign	$54
Average point of spoilage is the 3/4 completion point	
Average current disposal cost per spoiled sign	$15

Required:

Make necessary journal entries to record all spoilage.

Answer:

Average cost per sign when spoiled:

Direct material cost	$27.00
Conversion ($54 x 3/4)	40.50
Total cost per spoiled sign	$67.50

Abnormal spoilage	= Total spoilage - normal spoilage	
	= 450 - 300	
	= 150	

Materials Control (450 x $15)	$ 6,750	
Loss from Abnormal Spoilage (150 x $52.50)	7,875	
Manufacturing Overhead Control (300 x $52.50)	15,750	
Work-in-Process Control, airport job (450 x 67.50)		$30,375

Difficulty: 3   *Objective*: A

CRITICAL THINKING

81. Busy Hands Craft Company is a small manufacturing company that specializes in arts and crafts items. It recently bought an old textile mill that it has refurbished to manufacture and dye special cloth to be sold in its craft shops. However, it discovered something new for its accounting system. The company never before had finished goods that did not meet standard, leftover materials from processing runs, or unacceptable outputs.

Required:
As the business consultant for the company, explain how it can handle the items mentioned. Include any potential problems with the accounting procedures.

Answer:
First, an explanation of each item is needed.

1. Rework units are those units that are defective but can be reworked and sold as acceptable finished goods.
2. Scrap is leftover material that may have a minimal sales value. Scrap may be either sold, disposed of, or reused in another job or processing run.
3. Spoilage is the production outputs that cannot be reworked. These units are discarded or sold for minimal value.

The potential problem with these areas is that they may be treated differently by the accounting system. The company should establish an acceptable and consistent method of handling each area. A consistent policy also aids the managers who are being evaluated by their department's efforts.

Difficulty: 2   *Objective:* 1

82. You are the chief financial officer of a lumber mill, and are becoming quite concerned about the spoilage, scrap, and reworked items associated with your production processes. Your firm produces mainly products for the building industry.

Required:
Discuss the problems associated with these items, and the methods your company can use to reduce spoilage, scrap, and reworked items.

Answer:
The problems associated with these items include:
1. Your company pays for the total raw material not just the portion converted into a salable product.
2. The cost of disposing of these unsalable or unused items, both the disposal costs and the costs and problems associated with finding a landfill site or other disposal site.
3. These disposed of or unused items can create an eyesore, and attract the wrath of the environmentalists.
4. Developing high-value added products that can be produced from these various items.

82. (continued)

The methods your company can use to reduce these items include:
1. Calculating the costs of these problems. An accurate assessment of the total costs should certainly provide an incentive to your firm to investigate possible actions.
2. Exploring methods of redesigning the production process to minimize these costs.
3. Investing in more sophisticated capital equipment that can be designed to reduce these costs.

Difficulty: 3   *Objective:* 1

83. Harriet has been reviewing the accounting system for her company and is very concerned about the accounting for spoilage. It appears that spoilage is accounted for only at the end of the processing cycle. While this concept is acceptable in general, Harriet believes that a better method can be found to properly account for the spoilage when it occurs. She believes that there must be something better than the weighted-average method of accounting for spoilage. She would like the company to use a method that provides closer tracking of the spoilage with the accounting for the spoilage.

Required:

Discuss the problems Harriet is having with the accounting system.

Answer:

The main problem Harriet has is that she does not understand the accounting system. The use of weighted-average or FIFO is not for addressing the problems of spoilage tracking. While the methods do differ slightly in the tracking of costs, FIFO keeps beginning inventories separate, and the point of accounting for spoilage is not affected by the accounting method. If the company can account for spoilage at different stages of completion, these stages can be converted into percentage of completion points, and the spoilage can be accounted for as the process completes each stage.

Difficulty: 3   *Objective:* 2

84. Shazam Machines produces numerous types of money change machines. All machines are made in the same production department and many use exactly the same processes. Because customers have such different demands for the machine characteristics, the company uses a job-costing system. Unfortunately, some of the production managers have been upset for the last few months when their jobs were charged with the spoilage that occurred over an entire processing run of several types of machines. Some of the best managers have even threatened to quit unless the accounting system is changed.

Required:
What recommendations can you suggest to improve the accounting for spoilage?

Answer:
Since the manufacturing process uses similar workstations for the products, it may be best to let the spoilage be considered a manufacturing problem rather than a job problem. With this assumption, the spoilage will be spread over the entire production process with each job being charged an appropriate amount of spoilage, thereby relieving some jobs of bearing the entire burden of spoilage just because they were being worked on when the machines or process malfunctioned.

Difficulty: 2 *Objective*: 6

85. For each of the following (actual real-world examples) develop products that can be sold from the listed scrap.

a. The Federal Reserve Banks destroy old money. Burning this money is usually forbidden under the environmental laws of most municipalities.
b. A manufacturer of cotton undergarments for female prisoners has much cotton left over. The manufacturer is located in a very rural area of Alabama.
c. A hog renderer that has hog bristles as a result of the slaughtering process.

Answer:
a. The Federal Reserve Banks bag up the shredded money and sell it in gift shops. This is a very efficient use of the scrap. The purchasers pay a price in excess of what the Federal Reserve would receive from any other source. Other uses might include selling for use as packaging materials.

b. The above manufacturer sells the scrap for use in the cleaning of guns. Other uses would include similar cleaning uses or dyeing the cloth and selling it for ornaments.

c. The hog bristles can be used in shaving equipment and for bristle brushes.

Difficulty: 2 *Objective*: 8

CHAPTER 19: QUALITY, TIME, AND THE THEORY OF CONSTRAINTS

TRUE/FALSE

1. Shortening delivery times is a minor part of the quality improvement process.

   Answer: False   *Difficulty*: 2   *Objective*: 1
   Shortening delivery times is a major part of the quality improvement process.

2. ISO 9000 developed by the International Organization for Standardization is a set of five international standards for quality management adopted by more than 85 countries.

   Answer: True   *Difficulty*: 2   *Objective*: 1

3. Quality of design measures how closely the characteristics of products or services meet the needs and wants of customers.

   Answer: True   *Difficulty*: 2   *Objective*: 1

4. In the banking industry, depositing a customer's check into the wrong bank account is an example of quality of design failure.

   Answer: False   *Difficulty*: 2   *Objective*: 1
   This is an example of conformance quality failure.

5. Costs of quality (COQ) reports usually do not consider opportunity costs.

   Answer: True   *Difficulty*: 2   *Objective*: 1

6. A control chart identifies potential causes of failures or defects.

   Answer: False   *Difficulty*: 2   *Objective*: 2
   This is a definition of a Pareto diagram.

7. A cause-and-effect diagram is used to help identify potential causes of defects.

   Answer: True   *Difficulty*: 2   *Objective*: 2

8. Allocated cost amounts are an important determinant of the costs of a quality improvement program.

   Answer: False   *Difficulty*: 2   *Objective*: 3
   Allocated costs are usually ignored in calculating the costs of a quality improvement program.

9. Most companies expend a substantial amount of dollars measuring the financial costs of design quality.

   Answer: False   *Difficulty*: 2   *Objective*: 3
   Most companies do not expend a substantial amount of dollars measuring the financial costs of design quality.

10. The number of defects shipped to customers as a percentage of total units shipped are a type of nonfinancial quality measure.

   Answer: True   *Difficulty*: 2   *Objective*: 4

11. Process yield is the ratio of defective units to total output.

   Answer: False   *Difficulty*: 2   *Objective*: 4
   Process yield is the ratio of good output to total output.

12. The financial cost of quality measures serves as a common denominator for evaluating trade-offs among prevention costs and failure costs.

   Answer: True   *Difficulty*: 2   *Objective*: 5

13. Nonfinancial measures of quality are often easy to quantify and easy to understand.

   Answer: True   *Difficulty*: 2   *Objective*: 5

14. Two common operational measures of time are customer-response time and manufacturing lead time.

   Answer: False   *Difficulty*: 2   *Objective*: 6
   The two are customer-response time and on-time performance.

15. Manufacturing lead time is the sum of waiting time and manufacturing time for an order.

   Answer: True   *Difficulty*: 2   *Objective*: 6

16. Two important drivers of time are limited capacity and bottlenecks.

   Answer: False   *Difficulty*: 2   *Objective*: 6
   The drivers of time are uncertainty and limited capacity (also known as bottleneck).

17. The average waiting time is the average amount of time an order will wait at the company's shipping office before it is sent to the customer.

Answer: False   *Difficulty*: 2   *Objective*: 6

The average waiting time is the average amount of time that an order will wait in line before it is set up and processed.

18. The objective of the theory of constraints is to increase throughput contribution while decreasing investments and operating costs.

Answer: True   *Difficulty*: 2   *Objective*: 7

19. Throughput contribution is equal to revenues minus direct material and direct labor costs.

Answer: False   *Difficulty*: 2   *Objective*: 7

Throughput contribution is equal to revenues minus the direct materials cost of goods sold.

20. The cost of poor quality at a nonbottleneck operation is the cost of the materials wasted.

Answer: True   *Difficulty*: 2   *Objective*: 8

21. Quality management provides an important competitive edge because it
    a.   reduces costs.
    b.   increases customer satisfaction.
    c.   often results in substantial savings and higher revenues in the short run.
    d.   does all of the above.

    Answer: d   *Difficulty:* 1   *Objective:* 1

22. Quality of design measures how closely the characteristics of products or services match the needs and wants of customers. Conformance quality
    a.   measures the same things.
    b.   is the performance of a product or service according to design and product specifications.
    c.   is making the product according to design, engineering, and manufacturing specifications.
    d.   focuses on fitness of uses from a customer perspective.

    Answer: b   *Difficulty:* 1   *Objective:* 1

23. Which of the following fail to satisfy conformance quality?
    a.   Machines that fail to meet the needs of customers
    b.   Machines that break down
    c.   Depositing a customer's check into the correct account
    d.   All of the above fail to satisfy conformance quality.

    Answer: b   *Difficulty:* 2   *Objective:* 1

24. Costs incurred in precluding the production of products that do not conform to specifications are
    a.   prevention costs.
    b.   appraisal costs.
    c.   internal failure costs.
    d.   external failure costs.

    Answer: a   *Difficulty:* 2   *Objective:* 1

25. Costs incurred in detecting which of the individual units of products do not conform to specifications are
    a.   prevention costs.
    b.   appraisal costs.
    c.   internal failure costs.
    d.   external failure costs.

    Answer b   *Difficulty* 2   *Objective:* 1

26. Costs incurred by a nonconforming product detected before it is shipped to customers are
    a. prevention costs.
    b. appraisal costs.
    c. internal failure costs.
    d. external failure.

    Answer: c   *Difficulty:* 2   *Objective:* 1

27. Preventive equipment maintenance is an example of
    a. prevention costs.
    b. appraisal costs.
    c. internal failure costs.
    d. external failure costs.

    Answer: a   *Difficulty:* 1   *Objective:* 1

28. Spoilage is an example of
    a. prevention costs.
    b. appraisal costs.
    c. internal failure costs.
    d. external failure costs.

    Answer: c   *Difficulty:* 2   *Objective:* 1

29. Liability claims is an example of
    a. prevention costs.
    b. appraisal costs.
    c. internal failure costs.
    d. external failure costs.

    Answer: d   *Difficulty:* 2   *Objective:* 1

30. Mount Vernon Furniture manufactures expensive tables. Its varnishing department is fully automated and requires substantial inspection to keep the machines operating properly. An improperly varnished table is very expensive to correct. Inspection hours for the 10,000 tables varnished in September totaled 2,500 hours by 16 employees. Eight quarts of varnish were used, on average, for each table. The standard amount of varnish per table is nine quarts. The cost of inspection for September was equal to the budgeted amount of $76,000.

    The $76,000 represents
    a. an activity cost pool.
    b. a possible cost allocation base.
    c. an internal failure cost.
    d. a work-in-process control.

    Answer: a   *Difficulty:* 2   *Objective:* 1

31. Mount Vernon Furniture manufactures expensive tables. Its varnishing department is fully automated and requires substantial inspection to keep the machines operating properly. An improperly varnished table is very expensive to correct. Inspection hours for the 10,000 tables varnished in September totaled 2,500 hours by 16 employees. Eight quarts of varnish were used, on average, for each table. The standard amount of paint per table is ten quarts. The cost of inspection for September was equal to the budgeted amount of $76,000.

    What is the inspection cost per unit?
    a. $30.40
    b. $7.60
    c. $3,800
    d. $4,000

    Answer: b   *Difficulty:* 3   *Objective:* 1
    Rate per unit = $76,000/10,000 units = $7.60 per unit

32. Cost of quality reports usually do not consider
    a. external failure costs.
    b. opportunity costs.
    c. internal failure costs.
    d. appraisal costs.

    Answer: b   *Difficulty:* 2   *Objective:* 1

33. Examples of opportunity costs include
    a. lost sales.
    b. forgone contribution margin.
    c. lower production.
    d. all of the above.

    Answer: d   *Difficulty:* 2   *Objective:* 1

34. A graph of a series of successive observations of a particular step, procedure, or operation taken at regular intervals of time is a
    a. control chart.
    b. Pareto diagram.
    c. cause-and-effect diagram.
    d. fishbone diagrams.

    Answer: a   *Difficulty:* 2   *Objective:* 2

35. Statistical quality control includes a control chart that
    a. graphs a series of random events of a process.
    b. plots each observation relative to specified ranges that represent the expected distribution.
    c. plots control observations over various periods of time.
    d. plots only those observations outside specified limits.

    Answer: b   *Difficulty:* 2   *Objective:* 2

36. When using a control chart, a manager does not investigate the activity when
    a. all observations are outside the preset range.
    b. some observations are outside the preset range.
    c. all observations are within the range of preset standard deviations.
    d. almost all observations are within the range of two standard deviations.

    Answer: c   *Difficulty:* 2   *Objective:* 2

37. A tool which indicates how frequently each type of defect occurs is a
    a. control chart.
    b. Pareto diagram.
    c. cause-and-effect diagram.
    d. fishbone diagrams.

    Answer: b   *Difficulty:* 2   *Objective:* 2

38. A tool which identifies potential causes of failures or defects is
    a. a control chart.
    b. a Pareto diagram.
    c. a cause-and-effect diagram.
    d. none of the above.

    Answer: c   *Difficulty:* 2   *Objective:* 2

THE FOLLOWING INFORMATION APPLIES TO QUESTIONS 39 THROUGH 41.
Metropolitan Manufacturing expects to spend $400,000 in 20x4 in appraisal costs if it does not change its incoming materials inspection method. If it decides to implement a new receiving method, it will save $40,000 in fixed appraisal costs and variable costs of $0.40 per unit of finished product. The new method involves $60,000 in training costs and an additional $160,000 in annual equipment rental. It takes two units of material for each finished product.

Internal failure costs average $80 per failed unit of finished goods. During 20x3, 5% of all completed items had to be reworked. External failure costs average $200 per failed unit. The company's average external failures are 1% of units sold. The company carries no ending inventories, because all jobs are on a per order basis and a just-in-time inventory ordering method is used.

39. What is the net effect on appraisal costs for 20x4, assuming the new receiving method is implemented and that 800,000 material units are received?
    a. $20,000 increase
    b. $20,000 decrease
    c. $200,000 decrease
    d. $220,000 increase

    Answer: a   *Difficulty:*   2   *Objective:*   3

Current costs			$400,000	
Savings:	Fixed	$ 40,000		
	Variable	160,000	($200,000)	
New method:	Training cost	$ 60,000		
	Equipment cost	160,000	220,000	20,000
New costs of method				420,000
Net change - Increase				$ 20,000

40. How much will internal failure costs change, assuming 800,000 units of materials are received and that the new receiving method reduces the amount of unacceptable product units in the manufacturing process by 10%?
    a. $ 20,000 increase
    b. $ 25,000 decrease
    c. $80,000 decrease
    d. $160,000 decrease

    Answer: c   *Difficulty:*   3   *Objective:*   3

Internal failure costs [(800,000/4) x 0.05 x $80]	$800,000
10% reduction from new method	x 0.10
Savings	$ 80,000

41. How much will external failure costs change assuming 800,000 units of materials are received and that product failures with customers are cut in half with the new receiving method?
    a. $10,000 increase
    b. $200,000 decrease
    c. $320,000 decrease
    d. $400,000 decrease

    Answer: b   *Difficulty:* 3   *Objective:* 3

    External failure ((800,000/4) x 1% x $200) $400,000
    Failure reduction of 50%   x   0.50
        Savings $200,000

THE FOLLOWING INFORMATION APPLIES TO QUESTIONS 42 THROUGH 46.
Regal Products has a budget of $900,000 in 20x3 for prevention costs. If it decides to automate a portion of its prevention activities, it will save $60,000 in variable costs. The new method will require $18,000 in training costs and $120,000 in annual equipment costs. Management is willing to adjust the budget for an amount up to the cost of the new equipment. The budgeted production level is 150,000 units.

Appraisal costs for the year are budgeted at $600,000. The new prevention procedures will save appraisal costs of $30,000. Internal failure costs average $15 per failed unit of finished goods. The internal failure rate is expected to be 3% of all completed items. The proposed changes will cut the internal failure rate by one-third. Internal failure units are destroyed. External failure costs average $54 per failed unit. The company's average external failures average 3% of units sold. The new proposal will reduce this rate by 50%. Assume all units produced are sold and there are no ending inventories.

42. What is the net change in the budget of prevention costs if the procedures are automated in 20x4? Will management agree with the changes?
   a. $60,000 decrease, yes
   b. $78,000 increase, yes
   c. $60,000 increase, no
   d. $138,000 increase, no

   Answer: b   *Difficulty:* 3   *Objective:* 3

New costs:	Training	$ 18,000	
	New equipment	120,000	$138,000
Savings			60,000
	Net increase in budget		$ 78,000

43. How much will appraisal costs change assuming the new prevention methods reduce material failures by 40% in the appraisal phase?
   a. $240,000 decrease
   b. $60,000 increase
   c. $30,000 decrease
   d. $12,000 decrease

   Answer: c   *Difficulty:* 2   *Objective:* 3
   The new prevention procedures will save appraisal costs of $30,000.

44. How much will internal failure costs change if the internal product failures are reduced by 50% with the new procedures?
    a. $33,750 decrease
    b. $67,500 decrease
    c. $500,000 decrease
    d. $750,000 decrease

    Answer: a   *Difficulty:* 3   *Objective:* 3

Internal failure rate (150,000 x 0.03)	4,500
Cost per unit	x $15
Total	$67,500
Savings rate	x 0.50
Savings	$33,750

45. How much does external failure costs change if all changes are as anticipated with the new prevention procedures? Assume all units produced are sold and there are no ending inventories.
    a. $121,500 decrease
    b. $121,500 increase
    c. $243,000 decrease
    d. None of the above

    Answer: a   *Difficulty:* 3   *Objective:* 3

External failure costs (150,000 x 0.03 x $54)	$243,000
Savings rate	x 0.50
Savings	$121,500

46. Management has offered to allow the prevention changes if all changes take place as anticipated and the amounts netted are less than the cost of the equipment. What is the net impact of all the changes created by the preventive changes?
    a. $78,000
    b. $(33,750)
    c. $(93,570)
    d. $(119,070)

    Answer: c   *Difficulty:* 3   *Objective:* 3

Prevention changes, net	$ 78,000
Appraisal changes, net	(30,000)
Internal failure changes, net	(22,500)
External failure changes, net	(119,070)
Net of all changes	$ (93,570)

47. An important difference between financial measures of quality and nonfinancial measures of quality is
    a. financial measures of quality tend to be useful indicators of future long-term performance, while nonfinancial measures have more of a short-term focus.
    b. nonfinancial measures of quality tend to be useful indicators of future long-term performance, while financial measures of quality have more of a short-term focus
    c. nonfinancial measures are generally too subjective to have any long-term value.
    d. there is no substantive difference between the financial and nonfinancial measures of quality.

    Answer: b   *Difficulty:* 3   *Objective:* 4

48. Examples of nonfinancial measures of quality include
    a. percentage of defective units shipped to customers as a percentage of total units shipped.
    b. the number of customer complaints.
    c. percent of products that experience early or excessive failure.
    d. all of the above are nonfinancial measures of quality.

    Answer: d   *Difficulty:* 1   *Objective:* 4

49. The ratio of good output to total output is referred to as
    a. cause and effect.
    b. process yield.
    c. conformance quality.
    d. quality of design.

    Answer: b   *Difficulty:* 2   *Objective:* 4

50. The ratio of the number of processes where employees have rights to make decisions without consulting supervisors to the total number of processes is
    a. employee satisfaction.
    b. employee empowerment.
    c. employee turnover.
    d. process yield.

    Answer: b   *Difficulty:* 2   *Objective:* 4

51. Nonfinancial measures of quality are of limited use by themselves. They are more informative when
    a. combined with trend analysis.
    b. used with the half-life depreciation method.
    c. used with nonroutine financial data.
    d. used alone.

    Answer: a   *Difficulty:* 2   *Objective:* 5

52. The cost of quality measure has all of the following advantages EXCEPT
    a. being a useful measure of comparing different quality improvement projects.
    b. serving as a common denominator for evaluating trade-offs among prevention and failure costs.
    c. focusing on how costly poor quality can be.
    d. being in existence in almost every production circumstance.

    Answer: d   *Difficulty:* 2   *Objective:* 5

53. A disadvantage of nonfinancial measures of quality include
    a. often difficult to quantify.
    b. often difficult to understand.
    c. they are not useful indicators of future long-run performance.
    d. none of the above are disadvantages of nonfinancial measures of quality.

    Answer: d   *Difficulty:* 2   *Objective:* 5

54. The amount of time from when a customer places an order for a product or requests a service to when the product or service is delivered to the customer is referred to as
    a. manufacturing lead time.
    b. bottleneck.
    c. customer-response time.
    d. time driver.

    Answer: c   *Difficulty:* 2   *Objective:* 6

55. The amount of time from when an order is ready to start on the production line to when it becomes a finished good is referred to as
    a. manufacturing lead time.
    b. bottlcneck.
    c. customer-response time.
    d. time driver.

    Answer: a   *Difficulty:* 2   *Objective:* 6

56. Companies that use manufacturing lead time as the base for allocating manufacturing costs to products consider that it has the following benefit(s):
    a. Managers are motivated to reduce the time taken to manufacture products.
    b. Total overhead costs decrease.
    c. Operating income rises.
    d. All of the above are benefits.

    Answer: d   *Difficulty:* 1   *Objective:* 6

57. Any factor where change in the factor causes a change in the speed with which an activity is undertaken is referred to as
   a.   time driver.
   b.   bottleneck.
   c.   manufacturing lead time.
   d.   customer-response time.

   Answer: a   *Difficulty:*   2   *Objective:*   6

58. _____ is an operation where the work to be performed approaches or exceeds the available capacity.
   a.   A bottleneck
   b.   A time driver
   c.   Customer-response time
   d.   Manufacturing lead time

   Answer: a   *Difficulty:*   1   *Objective:*   6

59. In the formula to calculate the average waiting time, the manufacturing time is squared. The reason is
   a.   the shorter the manufacturing time, the less the chance that the machine will be in use when an order arrives.
   b.   the shorter the manufacturing time, the greater the chance that the machine will be in use when an order arrives.
   c.   the longer the manufacturing time, the greater the chance that the machine will be in use when an order arrives.
   d.   the longer the manufacturing time, the less the chance the machine will be in use when an order arrives.

   Answer: c   *Difficulty:*   3   *Objective:*   6

60. For a fast-food restaurant, the average waiting time might be formulated as
   a. $\dfrac{[(\text{average number of customers}) \times (\text{average serving time})^2]}{2 \times [\text{serving capacity} - (\text{avg. \# of customers} \times \text{avg. serving time})]}$
   b. $[(\text{average number of customers}) \times (\text{average serving time})^2] / \text{capacity}$
   c. $\dfrac{[(\text{average customers per hour}) \times (\text{average serving time})^2]}{60 \text{ minutes}}$
   d. $\dfrac{[(\text{average customers per hour}) \times (\text{average serving time})^2]}{(60 \text{ minutes}) \times (\text{number of workers})}$

   Answer: a   *Difficulty:*   3   *Objective:*   6

THE FOLLOWING INFORMATION APPLIES TO QUESTIONS 61 THROUGH 63.
Ballard's Glass Company has a variable demand. Historically, its demand has ranged from 10 to 20 windows per day with an average of 15. John Ballard works eight hours a day, five days a week. Each order is one window and each window takes 26 minutes.

61. What is the average waiting time, in minutes?
   a. 1.6
   b. 4.4
   c. 28.2
   d. 56.3

   Answer: d   *Difficulty:* 3   *Objective:* 6

   Waiting minutes = [15 x (26 squared)] / {[2 x [480 minutes per day- (15 x 26)]} =56.33 minutes

62. What is the cycle time for an order?
   a. 26 minutes per window
   b. 56.4 minutes per window
   c. 82.3 minutes per window
   d. 520 minutes per day

   Answer: c   *Difficulty:* 3   *Objective:* 6
   Cycle time = waiting time + manufacturing time = 56.33 + 26 = 82.33

63. Ballard plans to add doors to its product line and anticipates that they will average 5 doors per day. Each door takes 12 minutes to install.

   What is the average waiting time, in minutes, if Ballard continues to be the only worker?
   a. 38.0 minutes
   b. 112.4 minutes
   c. 181.0 minutes
   d. 410.0 minutes

   Answer: c   *Difficulty:* 3   *Objective:* 6
   $$WT = \frac{(15 \times (26)^2) + (5 \times (12)^2)}{\{2 \times [480 - (15 \times 26) - (5 \times 12)]\}} = 10,860/60 = 181 \text{ minutes}$$

64. The theory of constraints is used for cost analysis when
   a. a manufacturing company produces multiple products and uses multiple manufacturing facilities and /or machines.
   b. using a long-term time horizon.
   c. operating costs are assumed fixed.
   d. all of the above are correct.

   Answer: a   *Difficulty:* 2   *Objective:* 7

65. Throughput contribution equals
    a. revenues minus direct material and direct labor costs.
    b. revenues minus direct material costs and minus operating costs.
    c. revenues minus direct material costs of goods sold.
    d. revenues minus operating costs.

    Answer: c   *Difficulty:* 2   *Objective:* 7

66. Keeping the bottleneck operation busy and subordinating all nonbottleneck operations to the bottleneck operation involves
    a. maximizing the contribution margin of the nonbottleneck operation.
    b. keeping the bottleneck resource busy at least 90% of the time.
    c. having the workers at the nonbottleneck operation or machine improving their productivity.
    d. none of the above.

    Answer: d   *Difficulty:* 2   *Objective:* 8

67. Producing more nonbottleneck output
    a. creates more inventory, but does not increase throughput contribution.
    b. creates more inventory and increases throughput contribution.
    c. creates less pressure for the bottleneck workstations.
    d. allows for the maximization of overall contribution.

    Answer: a   *Difficulty:* 2   *Objective:* 8

THE FOLLOWING INFORMATION APPLIES TO QUESTIONS 68 AND 69.
Speedy Dress Manufacturing has two workstations, cutting and finishing. The cutting station is limited by the speed of operating the cutting machine. Finishing is limited by the speed of the workers. Finishing normally waits for work from cutting. Each department works an eight-hour day. If cutting begins work two hours earlier than finishing each day, the two departments generally finish their work at about the same time. Not only does this eliminate the bottleneck, but also it increases finished units produced each day by 160 units. All units produced can be sold even though the change increases inventory stock by 20% from 400 units. The cost of operating the cutting department two more hours each day is $1,600. The contribution margin of the finished products is $6 each. Inventory carrying costs are $0.40 per unit per day.

68. What is the total production per day if the change is made?
     a.   6400 units
     b.   800 units
     c.   880 units
     d.   1600 units

     Answer: b   *Difficulty:*   1   *Objective:*   8
     Units per hour = 160/2 = 80 units per day = 80 x 10 = 800 units

69. What is the change in the daily contribution margin if the change is made?
     a. $(608)
     b. $(634)
     c. $(672)
     d. $800

     Answer: c   *Difficulty:*   3   *Objective:*   8
     Total contribution margin (160 x $6) $ 960
     Carrying cost   (32)
     Increased costs   (1,600)
         Net change in contribution margin $ (672)

70. The Glass Shop, a manufacturer of large windows, is experiencing a bottleneck in its plant. Setup time at one of its workstations has been identified as the culprit. A manager has proposed a plan to reduce setup time at a cost of $72,000. The change will result in 8,000 additional windows. The selling price per window is $18, direct labor costs are $3 per window, and the cost of direct materials is $5 per window. Assume all units produced can be sold. The change will result in an increase in the throughput contribution of

     a. $104,000.
     b. $80,000.
     c. $32,000.
     d. $8,000.

     Answer: a   *Difficulty:*   3   *Objective:*   8
     8,000 x (18-5) = $104,000

EXERCISES AND PROBLEMS

71. Write a paragraph outlining how a manufacturer of personal computers such as Dell Computer can benefit from the introduction of a quality improvement program.

    Answer: (Answers may vary)

    A quality improvement program for Dell would result in substantial savings in operating costs and higher revenues. Operating costs would be reduced since fewer funds would be spent checking output and correcting defective products. Higher revenues would result since existing customers would likely increase their orders and the higher quality output would attract additional customers. In addition, a number of competitors will likely be implementing quality programs. Dell must meet the competition.

    Difficulty: 1   *Objective*:   1

72. The two basic aspects of quality are quality of design and conformance quality. Define and give an example of each.

    Answer:

    Quality of design measures how closely the characteristics of products or services meet the needs and wants of customers. For example, customers of photocopying machines want copiers that combine copying, faxing, scanning, and electronic printing. If the photocopy machines fail to meet these customer needs, sales will fall.

    Conformance quality refers to the performance of a product or service according to design and product specifications. For example, if a photocopy machine constantly has paper jams or breaks down, it fails to satisfy conformance quality.

    Difficulty: 1   *Objective*:   1

73. The Door Company manufactures doors. Classify each of the following quality costs as prevention costs, appraisal costs, internal failure costs, or external failure costs.

a. Retesting of reworked products
b. Downtime due to quality problems
c. Analysis of the cause of defects in production
d. Depreciation of test equipment
e. Warranty repairs
f. Lost sales arising from a reputation for poor quality
g. Quality circles
h. Rework direct manufacturing labor and overhead
i. Net cost of spoilage
j. Technical support provided to suppliers
k. Audits of the effectiveness of the quality system
l. Plant utilities in the inspection area
m. Reentering of data because of keypunch errors

_____   Prevention costs

_____   Appraisal costs

_____   Internal failure costs

_____   External failure costs

Answer:

g, j _____   Prevention costs

d, l, k _____   Appraisal costs

a, b, c, h, i, m _____   Internal failure costs

e, f, m _____   External failure costs

Difficulty: 3   *Objective*:   1

74. Dawn and Kim just bought a bed and breakfast inn at a very attractive price. The business had been doing poorly. Before they reopened the inn for business, they attended a seminar on operating a high quality business. Now that they are ready to open the inn, they need some advice on quality costs and management.

Required:

Identify four categories of quality costs. In addition, identify three items that would be classified in each of the categories.

Answer: (Answers will vary)

Prevention:	Hiring employees with good references
	Training of owners and employees
	Good security
	Good reservation system
	Purchasing quality furniture
Appraisal:	Verifying accuracy of reservation and registration procedures
	Inspecting rooms, facilities, building and grounds regularly
	Observing activities of employees
	Testing furniture and fixtures
	Taste testing food
Internal failure:	Recleaning rooms and facilities
	Restocking rooms with linens, glasses, etc.
	Out of stock supplies
	Reinspection
	Failure to bill on a timely basis
External failure:	Responding to complaints about rooms and food
	Responding to complaints about reservations
	Emergency cleaning of rooms when not ready on time
	Customer refunds because of unsatisfactory conditions
	Opportunity cost of lost revenue resulting from unhappy customers

Difficulty: 3   *Objective*:   1

75. Discuss the methods used to identify quality problems.

   Answer:

   1. A *control chart* is a graph of a series of successive observations of a particular step, procedure, or operation taken at regular intervals of time.

   2. A *Pareto diagram* indicates how frequently each type of failure (defect) occurs.

   3. A *cause-and-effect* diagram helps to identify potential causes of failures or defects.

   Difficulty: 2   *Objective*:   2

76. A corporation can measure its quality performance by utilizing financial or nonfinancial measures of quality. Discuss the merits of each method and whether the use of one precludes the use of the other.

   Answer:

   Financial measures of quality are quantifiable. The business can calculate the costs of setting up quality control systems, the costs of noncompliance with quality in terms of the internal and external costs (rework, warranty costs etc.), and estimate the revenues lost as a result of quality problems.

   Nonfinancial measures of quality are useful indicators of future long-run performance. They are helpful in revealing future needs and preferences of customers and in indicating the specific areas that need improvement.

   The use of one does not preclude the use of the other. Financial measures tend to be short term in nature (what is happening now). Nonfinancial measures tend to be long term and are useful in terms of estimating trends.

   Financial performance measures are more readily available than nonfinancial measures, but are no more important to the overall goals of the organization. By considering nonfinancial measures, the organization can improve operational control. Superior financial performance usually follows from superior nonfinancial performance.

   Difficulty: 2   *Objective*:   5

77. Design Products is committed to its quality program. It works with all areas of the company to establish sound quality programs within reasonable budget guidelines. For 20x3, it has budgeted $1,000,000 for prevention costs and $800,000 for appraisal costs. Internal failure has a budget of $100 per failed item, while external failure has a total budget of $600,000.

Product Testing has proposed to management a change in the 20x3 budget for a new method of testing products. If management decides to implement the new method, $2 per unit of appraisal costs will be saved, up to a level of 200,000 tests. No additional savings are expected past the 200,000 level. The new method involves $110,000 in training costs and $60,000 in yearly testing supplies.

Traditionally, 3% of all completed items have to be reworked. External failure costs average $120 per failed unit. The company's average external failures are 1% of units sold. The company carries no ending inventories.

Required:

a. What is the adjusted budget for appraisal costs, assuming the new method is implemented and 800,000 units are tested during the manufacturing process in 20x3?

b. How much do internal failure costs change, assuming 600,000 units are tested under the new method and it reduces the amount of unacceptable units in the manufacturing process by 40%?

c. What would be the change in the external failure budget, assuming external failures are reduced by 60% and the same facts as in part (b)?

Answer:

a.

Current Budget		$ 800,000
Additions: Training	$110,000	
Additions: Supplies	60,000	170,000
Savings: 200,000 x $2		(400,000)
Adjusted budget		$ 570,000

b.

Current budget $100 x 0.03 x 600,000 =	$1,800,000
Savings rate	x 0.40
Net savings (reduction in internal failure costs)	$ 720,000

c.

Current budget $120 x 0.01 x 600,000 =	$ 720,000
Savings rate	x 0.60
Net savings (reduction in external failure budget)	$ 432,000

Difficulty: 2   *Objective*:   3

78. Brown Laundry has a variable demand. The daily demand ranges from 100 to 140 customers a day with an average of 5 items. The average daily demand is 110 customers. The laundry operates 10 hours a day. Each order takes approximately 5 minutes.

Required:
a. What is the average customer waiting time, in minutes?

b. What is the cycle time for an order?

c. The manager has decided that the waiting time is too long and has increased the workday to 11 hours. What is the waiting time now? Will the customers be any happier?

Answer:
a. Waiting minutes = $[110 \times (5)^2]/\{2 \times [600$ minutes per day - $(110 \times 5)]\}$
   = 27.5 minutes

b. Cycle time = waiting time + processing time = 27.5 + 5
   = 32.5 minutes

c. Waiting minutes = $[110 \times (5)^2] / \{2 \times [660$ minutes per day - $(110 \times 5)]\}$
   = 12.5 minutes

   The customers are probably not much happier unless they change the time when they stop by the laundry. If the customers now fill the 11-hour day, the new reduced waiting time will be a definite improvement.

Difficulty: 2   *Objective*:   6

79. Little Dog Unlimited makes small motorcycles. The monthly demand ranges from 80 to 100 motorcycles. The average demand is 92 motorcycles. The plant operates 300 hours a month. Each cycle takes approximately 1.5 hours.

If the company adds a new line of scooters, initial demand will be 20 per month. Each scooter will take 1 hour to make. To offset approaching production capacity, expanding the assembly line is possible. This will decrease manufacturing time for all products by 20%. However, this will increase the costs of cycles from $400 to $500 and scooters from $200 to $240. The change will also cause increases in prices from $700 to $750 for cycles and from $450 to $500 for scooters.

Required:
a. What is the average waiting time for cycles if they are the only item manufactured?

b. What are the average waiting times if both cycles and scooters are produced and the assembly line is not enlarged?

c. What are the average waiting times if both cycles and scooters are produced and the assembly line is enlarged?

79. (continued)

d.   What is the expected monthly margin without scooters if the company sells all 92 cycles it manufactures?

e.   What are the expected monthly contribution margins if scooters are made with the current assembly line and with the new assembly line? Assume average sales and that sales equal production.

f.   What action do you recommend?

Answer:

a.   Waiting time= $[92 \times (1.5)^2] / \{[2 \times [300 \text{ hr. a month} - (92 \times 1.5)]\}$
    = 0.639 hours

b.   WT = $92 \times (1.5)^2 + (20 \times 1) / \{2 \times [300 - (92 \times 1.5) - (20 \times 1)]\}$
    = 227/284 = 0.799 hours

c.   WT = $92 \times (1.2)^2 + (20 \times (0.8)^2) / \{2 \times [300 - (92 \times 1.2) - (20 \times 0.8)]\}$
    = 145.28/347.2 = 0.418 hours

d.   *Expected monthly margin without scooters:*

Motorcycle sales (92 x $700)	$64,400
Manufacturing costs (92 x $400)	36,800
Expected margin	$27,600

e.   *Without changing assembly line:*

Motorcycle sales (92 x $700)		$64,400
Scooter sales (20 x $450)		9,000
Total expected sales		73,400
Manufacturing costs:		
Motorcycles (92 x $400)	$36,800	
Scooters (20 x $200)	4,000	40,800
Expected margin		$32,600

With new assembly line:

Motorcycle sales (92 x $750)		$69,000
Scooter sales (20 x $500)		10,000
Total expected sales		79,000
Manufacturing costs:		
Motorcycles (92 x $500)	$46,000	
Scooters (20 x $240)	4,800	50,800
Expected margin		$28,200

f.   Unless there are critical customer relation problems with a slower response time, the scooters should be added without changing the assembly line. The expected margin is $4,400 higher without the new assembly line.

Difficulty: 3   *Objective:*   6

80. Brix, Inc., prepares frozen food for fast-food restaurants. It has two workstations, cooking and assembly. The cooking station is limited by the cooking time of the food. Assembly is limited by the speed of the workers. Assembly normally waits on food from cooking. Because the demand has increased in recent months to 2,800 dozen units, management is considering adding another cooking station or else having the cooks start to work earlier. The monthly cost of operating the cooking station one more hour each day is $2,400. The cost of adding another cooking station would add an average of $10 per hour. The current operating hours total eight hours a day, 22 days a month. The contribution margin of the finished products is currently $8 per dozen. Inventory carrying costs average $2.00 per dozen per month. Either the extra hour or the new cooking station would increase production by 20 dozen a day, with a long-run increase of 80 dozen units in finished goods inventory to 280 dozen.

Required:

a. What is the total production per month if the change is made?

b. What is the increase in the expected monthly product contribution for each of the possible changes? Assume long-run production equals sales.

Answer:

a. Total dozen per month = 2,800 + (22 x 20) = 3,240

b.

Current product contribution margin (2,800 x $8)		$22,400
Carrying costs (200 x $2)		400
Current net contribution		$22,000
More hours:		
Expected product contribution margin (3,240 x $8)		$25,920
Carrying costs (280 x $2)	$ 560	
Increased costs	2,400	2,960
Expected net product contribution		$22,960
Increase = $22,960 - $22,000 =		$ 960
New cooking station:		
Expected product contribution margin (3,240 x $8)		$25,920
Carrying costs (280 x $2)	$ 560	
Increased costs ($10 x 22 x 8)	1,760	2,320
Expected net product contribution		$23,600
Increase = $23,600 - $22,000 =		$1,600

Difficulty: 2   *Objective*: 7

81. Baby Care Products has just completed a very successful program of improving quality in its manufacturing operations. The next step is to improve the operations of its administrative functions, starting with the accounting information system. As the manager of the accounting operations, you are requested to begin a quality improvement program.

Required:
What are some possibilities of finding out about the current status of quality in the accounting system?

Answer:
The manager might begin by identifying "customer" needs. Then the manager might use one of the methods of identifying quality problems. Statistical quality control helps to distinguish between random variation and nonrandom variation. A control chart of observations usually accompanies this. Another method is the use of a Pareto diagram. This indicates how frequently each type of failure occurs. Also, cause-and-effect diagrams help to identify potential causes of failure. A fishbone diagram is often used here to identify multiple causes of failure. Quality of design could potentially be the biggest problem.

Difficulty: 2 *Objective*: 2

82. The Custom Shirt House is concerned about its declining sales, especially the reduction in the number of customers. For the last two years, its shirts have won industry awards for high quality and trend-setting styles. At the latest executive managers' meeting, everyone was blaming everyone else for the decline. After much discussion and the presenting of some fact-finding information, it was determined that sales relationships were the cause of most of the problems.

Required:
What may be some of the causes and how can the causes be detected if product quality is not an issue?

Answer:
The causes may be customer satisfaction with sales staff (poor sales skills), delivery problems (not on time), accounting problems (poor billing and collection procedures), or poor returns and allowance policies.

The causes may be detected by comparing nonfinancial measures of the company with those found in the industry. These might include measures of: number of shipments incorrect or not on time, number of customer complaints about certain areas (billing, shipping, etc.), response time to customer complaints, or a questionnaire about why former customers quit buying from the company.

Difficulty: 2 *Objective*: 3

83. Acme Janitor Service has always taken pride in the fact that it had one of the highest customer response times in the home cleaning service industry. However, as the products manufactured for this industry have become more complex, the company's customer response time has declined.

Required:

Why do you think that response time declined if all other quality factors have remained the same?

Answer:

If quality production was one of the other control factors, and the products became more complex, it probably takes more time to inspect and verify the quality of the finished products. Therefore, to maintain the same level of quality, additional time had to be put into the product cycle. Apparently this was not allowed for in the setting of the production times of the newer, more complex products.

Difficulty: 2   *Objective*:   6

84. The Alpha Beta Corporation experiences numerous instances of constraints hindering the effective operation of their manufacturing process. Identify the methods that might be utilized to maximize operating income, and minimize the effect of the constraints.

Answer:

A manager's objective should be to increase throughput contribution (revenues minus direct material costs) while decreasing investments and operating costs. The manager should consider adjusting the product mix to maximize the total contribution margin. Another possibility is subcontracting out part of the production process. Quality considerations should be paramount, since a defective unit, or one that has to be reworked, is in effect replacing a unit that could be sold.

Difficulty: 1   *Objective*:   7

85.	A machine has been identified as a bottleneck and the source of the constraint for a manufacturing company that has multiple products and multiple machines. Discuss ways the company can overcome the bottleneck.

Answer:

The ways include:

a.	Eliminating idle time at the bottleneck operation. Extra staffing at the bottleneck would be a possibility, particularly if numerous manual type tasks were involved.

b.	Concentrate on processing those parts or products that increase throughput contribution, not parts or products that remain in finished goods or spare parts inventories.

c.	Shift a part of the products produced at the bottleneck machine to other machines or outsource part of the production.

d.	Solicit the opinions of the factory workers for ideas as to how the design of the manufacturing process can be simplified.

e.	Improve the quality of the production process. Poor quality is especially costly at a bottleneck operation.

Difficulty:	3	*Objective:*	8

CHAPTER 20: INVENTORY MANAGEMENT, JUST-IN-TIME, AND BACKFLUSH COSTING

TRUE/FALSE

1. Retailers generally have a high percentage of net income to revenues.

    Answer: False   *Difficulty:* 2   *Objective:* 1
    Retailers have a low percentage of net income to revenues.

2. Inventory management is the planning, organizing, and controlling activities that focus on the flow of materials into, through, and from the organization.

    Answer: True   *Difficulty:* 2   *Objective:* 1

3. Purchasing costs generally include the freight and transportation costs on goods acquired from suppliers.

    Answer: True   *Difficulty:* 2   *Objective:* 1

4. Expediting costs of a stockout include the additional ordering costs, plus any associated transportation costs.

    Answer: True   *Difficulty:* 2   *Objective:* 1
    Expediting costs include the associated transportation costs.

5. Carrying costs arise when an organization experiences an ability to deliver its goods to its customers.

    Answer: False   *Difficulty:* 2   *Objective:* 1
    Carrying costs arise when an organization holds its goods for sale.

6. The simplest version of the Economic Order Quantity model incorporates only ordering costs, carrying costs, and purchasing costs into the calculation.

    Answer: False   *Difficulty:* 2   *Objective:* 2
    Purchasing costs are ignored in the Economic Order Quantity.

7. To determine the Economic Order Quantity, the relevant ordering costs are minimized and the relevant carrying costs are maximized.

    Answer: False   *Difficulty:* 2   *Objective:* 2
    We minimize both the relevant ordering costs and the relevant carrying costs.

8. The Economic Order Quantity increases with demand and ordering costs and decreases with carrying costs.

    Answer: True   *Difficulty:* 2   *Objective:* 2

9. The annual relevant total costs are at a minimum where relevant ordering costs and their relevant carrying costs are equal.

Answer: True   *Difficulty*: 2   *Objective*: 2

10. The annual relevant carrying costs of inventory consist of incremental costs plus the opportunity cost of capital.

Answer: True   *Difficulty*: 3   *Objective*: 3

11. Just-in-time purchasing requires organizations to place smaller purchase orders with their suppliers.

Answer: True   *Difficulty*: 2   *Objective*: 3

12. Just-in-time purchasing is guided solely by the economic order quantity.

Answer: False   *Difficulty*: 2   *Objective*: 3
Inventory management also includes purchasing costs, stockout costs, and quality costs.

13. The higher level of variability at manufacturers rather than suppliers, and at retailers rather than rather than manufacturers is called the "bullwhip effect."

Answer: False   *Difficulty*: 3   *Objective*: 3
The higher level of variability is at suppliers rather than manufacturers, and at manufacturers rather than at suppliers.

14. A "push-through" system, often described as a just-in-time system, emphasizes simplicity and close coordination among work centers.

Answer: False   *Difficulty*: 2   *Objective*: 5
The narrative describes a Materials Requirement Planning system.

15. A "demand-pull" system, often described as a materials requirement planning system, focuses first on the forecasted amount and timing of finished goods and then determines the demand for materials components and subassemblies at each of the prior stages of production.

Answer: False   *Difficulty*: 2   *Objective*: 5
The narrative describes a push-through system.

16. In a just-in-time inventory system, there is less emphasis on the need to eliminate scrap and rework problems.

Answer: False   *Difficulty*: 2   *Objective*: 5
There is more emphasis on the need to eliminate scrap and rework problems.

17. In a backflush-costing system, no record of work in process appears in the accounting records.

Answer: True   *Difficulty:* 3   *Objective:* 7

18. Companies that have fast manufacturing lead times usually find that a version of backflush costing will report cost numbers similar to what a sequential costing approach would report.

Answer: True   *Difficulty:* 3   *Objective:* 8

19. Backflush costing is usually restricted to companies adopting JIT production methods.

Answer: False   *Difficulty:* 3   *Objective:* 8
Backflush costing is also helpful in companies that have fast manufacturing times, and that have very stable inventory.

20. A positive aspect of backflush costing is the presence of the visible audit trail.

Answer: False   *Difficulty:* 3   *Objective:* 8
In backflush costing, the visible audit trail diminishes.

21. Which of the following industries would have the highest cost of goods sold percentage relative to sales?
    a. Computer manufacturers
    b. Retail organizations
    c. Drug manufacturers
    d. The percentage will usually depend on the success of a particular company.

    Answer: b   *Difficulty*: 2   *Objective*: 1

22. The costs of goods acquired from suppliers including incoming freight or transportation costs are
    a. purchasing costs.
    b. ordering costs.
    c. stockout costs.
    d. carrying costs.

    Answer: a   *Difficulty*: 2   *Objective*: 1

23. The costs of preparing, issuing, and paying purchase orders, plus receiving and inspecting the items included in orders is
    a. purchasing costs.
    b. ordering costs.
    c. stockout costs.
    d. carrying costs.

    Answer: b   *Difficulty*: 2   *Objective*: 1

24. Quality costs include
    a. purchasing costs.
    b. ordering costs.
    c. stockout costs.
    d. prevention costs.

    Answer: d   *Difficulty*: 2   *Objective*: 1

25. Obsolescence is an example of which cost category?
    a. Carrying costs
    b. Labor costs
    c. Ordering costs
    d. Quality costs

    Answer: a   *Difficulty*: 2   *Objective*: 2

26. The costs associated with storage are an example of which cost category?
    a. Quality costs
    b. Labor costs
    c. Ordering costs
    d. Carrying costs

    Answer: d   *Difficulty:* 2   *Objective:* 2

27. Which of the following is an assumption of the economic-order-quantity decision model?
    a. The quantity ordered can vary at each reorder point.
    b. Demand ordering costs and carrying costs fluctuate.
    c. Timely labor costs.
    d. No stockouts occur.

    Answer: d   *Difficulty:* 2   *Objective:* 2

28. The economic order quantity ignores
    a. purchasing costs.
    b. relevant ordering costs.
    c. stockout costs.
    d. both (a) and (c).

    Answer: d   *Difficulty:* 3   *Objective:* 2

29. The purchase-order lead time is
    a. the difference between the times an order is placed and delivered.
    b. the difference between the products ordered and the products received.
    c. the discrepancies in purchase orders.
    d. the time required to correct errors in the products received.

    Answer: a   *Difficulty:* 2   *Objective:* 2

30. Which of the following statements about the economic-order-quantity decision model is FALSE?
    a. It assumes purchasing costs are relevant when the cost per unit changes due to the quantity ordered.
    b. It assumes quality costs are irrelevant if quality is unaffected by the number of units purchased.
    c. It assumes stockout costs are irrelevant if no stockouts occur.
    d. It assumes ordering costs and carrying costs are relevant.

    Answer: a   *Difficulty:* 3   *Objective:* 2

31. Relevant total costs in the economic-order-quantity decision model equal
   a. relevant ordering costs plus relevant carrying costs.
   b. relevant ordering costs plus relevant stockout costs.
   c. relevant ordering costs plus relevant quality costs.
   d. relevant ordering costs plus relevant purchasing costs.

   Answer: a   *Difficulty*: 2   *Objective*: 2

32. Phonic Goods is a distributor of videotapes. Tape-Disk Mart is a local retail outlet which sells blank and recorded videos. Tape-Disk Mart purchases tapes from Phonic Goods at $3.00 per tape; tapes are shipped in packages of 20. Phonic Goods pays all incoming freight, and Tape-Disk Mart does not inspect the tapes due to Phonic Goods' reputation for high quality. Annual demand is 104,000 tapes at a rate of 4,000 tapes per week. Tape-Disk Mart earns 20% on its cash investments. The purchase-order lead time is two weeks. The following cost data are available:

Relevant ordering costs per purchase order	$90.50
Carrying costs per package per year:	
Relevant insurance, materials handling,	
breakage, etc., per year	$ 4.50

   What is the required annual return on investment per package?
   a. $60.00
   b. $2.50
   c. $12.00
   d. $0.60

   Answer: c   *Difficulty*: 3   *Objective*: 3
   20 tapes x $3.00 = $60.00
   $60.00 x 0.2 = $12.00

THE FOLLOWING INFORMATION APPLIES TO QUESTIONS 33 THROUGH 35.
Stereo Goods is a distributor of videotapes. Video Mart is a local retail outlet which sells blank and recorded videos. Video Mart purchases tapes from Stereo Goods at $5.00 per tape; tapes are shipped in packages of 25. Stereo Goods pays all incoming freight, and Video Mart does not inspect the tapes due to Stereo Goods' reputation for high quality. Annual demand is 104,000 tapes at a rate of 2,000 tapes per week. Video Mart earns 15% on its cash investments. The purchase-order lead time is one week. The following cost data are available:

> *Relevant ordering costs* per purchase order $94.50
> *Carrying costs* per package per year:
>   Relevant insurance, materials handling,
>   breakage, etc., per year $ 3.50

33. What is the economic order quantity?
    a.   874 packages
    b.   652 packages
    c.   200 packages
    d.   188 packages

    Answer: d   *Difficulty*:   2   *Objective*:   3
    EOQ = The square root of [(2 x (104,000/25) x $94.50) / ($18.75 + $3.50)]
    EOQ = 188 packages

34. What are the relevant total costs?
    a. $6,150.50
    b. $4,182.56
    c. $2,560.20
    d. $1,951.70

    Answer: b   *Difficulty*:   3   *Objective*:   3
    RTC = [(104,000 / 25) x $94.50] + [188 x ($18.75 + $3.50)] = $4,182.56
                188   2

35. How many deliveries will be made during each time period?
    a.   22.1 deliveries
    b.   26.0 deliveries
    c.   29.4 deliveries
    d.   32.0 deliveries

    Answer: a   *Difficulty*:   3   *Objective*:   3
    [(104,000 / 25) / 188] = 22.1 deliveries

THE FOLLOWING INFORMATION APPLIES TO QUESTIONS 36 THROUGH 39.
The Wood Furniture company produces a specialty wood furniture product, and has the following information available concerning its inventory items:

Relevant ordering costs per purchase order $150
Relevant carrying costs per year:
    Required annual return on investment   10%
    Required other costs per year $1.40

Annual demand is 10,000 packages per year. The purchase price per package is $16.

36. What is the economic order quantity?
    a.   150,000 units
    b.   1,000 units
    c.   75,000 units
    d.   5,000 units

Answer: b   *Difficulty:*   3   *Objective:*   2
EOQ = The square root of $[(2 \times 10,000 \times \$150) / \$3] = 1,000$ units
Unit carrying costs $= \$16 (0.10) + \$1.40 = \$3$

37. What are the relevant total costs at the economic order quantity?
    a. $1,000
    b. $1,500
    c. $3,000
    d. $3,500

Answer: c   *Difficulty:*   3   *Objective:*   2
$$RTC = \left[\frac{(10,000 \times \$150)}{1,000} + \frac{(1,000 \times \$3)}{2}\right] = \$3,000$$

38. What are the total relevant costs, assuming the quantity ordered equals 500 units?
    a. $3,500
    b. $500
    c. $4,000
    d. $3,750

Answer: d   *Difficulty:*   3   *Objective:*   2
$$RTC = \left[\frac{(10,000 \times \$150)}{500} + \frac{(500 \times \$3)}{2}\right] = \$3,750$$

39. How many deliveries will be required at the economic order quantity?
    a.   1.0 delivery
    b.   5.1 deliveries
    c.   8.2 deliveries
    d.   10.0 deliveries

Answer: d   *Difficulty:*   3   *Objective:*   2
$10,000 / 1,000 = 10$ deliveries

40. The annual relevant total costs are at a minimum when
    a. relevant ordering costs are greater than the relevant carrying costs.
    b. relevant carrying costs are greater than the relevant ordering costs.
    c. relevant carrying costs are equal to relevant ordering costs.
    d. none of the above.

    Answer: c   *Difficulty:* 3   *Objective:* 2

41. The reorder point is simplest to compute when
    a. both demand and purchase-order lead times are known with certainty.
    b. the number of units sold varies.
    c. the safety stock amount never varies.
    d. the relevant ordering costs and the relevant carrying costs are equal.

    Answer: a   *Difficulty:* 2   *Objective:* 3

42. Diskette Company sells 200 discs per week. Purchase-order lead time is 1 1/2 weeks and the economic-order quantity is 450 units. What is the reorder point?
    a. 200 units
    b. 300 units
    c. 750 units
    d. 1,125 units

    Answer: b   *Difficulty:* 2   *Objective:* 4
    200 x 1.5= 300 units

THE FOLLOWING INFORMATION APPLIES TO QUESTIONS 43 AND 44.
Owen-King Company sells optical equipment. Lens Company manufactures special glass lenses. Owen-King Company orders 5,200 lenses per year, 100 per week, at $20 per lens. Lens Company covers all shipping costs. Owen-King Company earns 30% on its cash investments. The purchase-order lead time is 2.5 weeks. Owen-King Company sells 125 lenses per week. The following data are available:

Relevant ordering costs per purchase order	$21.25
Relevant insurance, materials handling, breakage, and so on, per year	$ 2.50

43. What is the economic order quantity for Owen-King Company?
    a. 325 lenses
    b. 297 lenses
    c. 210 lenses
    d. 161 lenses

    Answer: d   *Difficulty:* 2   *Objective:* 4
    EOQ = The square root of [(2 x 5,200 x $21.25) / (($20 x 30%) + $2.50)]
    EOQ = 161 lenses

44. What is the reorder point?
    a. 220.5 lenses
    b. 312.5 lenses
    c. 397.5 lenses
    d. 415.5 lenses

    Answer: b   *Difficulty:* 2   *Objective:* 4
    125 lens x 2.5 weeks = 312.5 lenses

THE FOLLOWING INFORMATION APPLIES TO QUESTIONS 45 THROUGH 47.
The following information applies to Labs Plus, which supplies microscopes to laboratories throughout the country. Labs Plus purchases the microscopes from a manufacturer which has a reputation for very high quality in its manufacturing operation.

Annual demand (weekly demand= 1/52 of annual demand)	15,600 units
Orders per year	20
Lead time in days	15 days
Cost of placing an order	$100

45. What are the annual relevant carrying costs, assuming each order was made at the economic-order-quantity amount?
    a. $200
    b. $1,000
    c. $2,000
    d. $6,000

    Answer: c   *Difficulty:* 2   *Objective:* 2
    Annual carrying costs = annual ordering costs = $100 x 20 = $2,000

46. What is the economic order quantity assuming each order was made at the economic-order-quantity amount?
    a. 15 units
    b. 20 units
    c. 780 units
    d. 1,040 units

    Answer: c   *Difficulty:* 2   *Objective:* 2
    15,600/20 = 780

47. What is the reorder point?
    a. 780 units
    b. 643 units
    c. 1,560 units
    d. 1,680 units

    Answer: b   *Difficulty:* 2   *Objective:* 1
    15,600/52= 300/7= 42.86 daily demand x 15 = 643

48. What are the major relevant costs in maintaining safety stock?
    a.   Carrying costs and purchasing costs
    b.   Ordering costs and purchasing costs
    c.   Ordering costs and stockout costs
    d.   Stockout costs and carrying costs

    Answer: d   *Difficulty:*   2   *Objective:*   3

49. If Ferry Company has a safety stock of 160 units and the average daily demand is 20 units, how many days can be covered if the shipment from the supplier is delayed by 12 days?
    a.   12.0 days
    b.   10.0 days
    c.   8.0 days
    d.   6.7 days

    Answer: c   *Difficulty:*   3   *Objective:*   2
    160/20 = 8 units

50. The optimal safety stock level is the quantity of safety stock that minimizes the
    a.   sum of the annual relevant stockout costs and carrying costs.
    b.   sum of the annual relevant ordering costs and carrying costs.
    c.   sum of the annual relevant ordering costs and stockout costs.
    d.   sum of the annual relevant ordering costs and purchasing costs.

    Answer: a   *Difficulty:*   2   *Objective:*   2

51. The annual relevant carrying costs of inventory consists of
    a.   the sum of the ordering costs and carrying costs.
    b.   the sum of the stockout costs and carrying costs.
    c.   the sum of the incremental costs plus the opportunity costs of capital.
    d.   the sum of the incremental costs plus the carrying costs.

    Answer: c   *Difficulty:*   2   *Objective:*   3

52. Party Animals sells stuffed tigers. Products, Inc. manufactures all sorts of stuffed animals. Party Animals orders 10,400 tigers per year, 200 per week, at $10 per tiger. The manufacturer covers all shipping costs. Party Animals earns 12% on its cash investments. The purchase-order lead time is 3 weeks. Party Animals sells 210 tigers per week. The following data are available (based on management's estimates):

Estimated ordering costs per purchase order	$10
Estimated insurance, materials handling, breakage, and so on, per year	$ 3
Actual ordering costs per order	$15

What is the economic order quantity using the estimated amounts?
a. 119 stuffed tigers
b. 223 stuffed tigers
c. 273 stuffed tigers
d. 325 stuffed tigers

Answer: b   *Difficulty*: 3   *Objective*: 3
EOQ = The square root of [(2 x 10,400 x $10) / ($3 + (0.12 x $10))]
EOQ = 223 units

53. A conflict between the EOQ model's optimal order quantity and the order quantity the purchasing manager, evaluated on conventional accounting numbers, regards as optimal is considered
a. a problem for the chief financial officer to resolve.
b. a problem for the performance evaluation system to resolve.
c. goal congruence.
d. an opportunity cost.

Answer: b   *Difficulty*: 2   *Objective*: 3

54. Just-in-time purchasing requires
a. larger and less frequent purchase orders.
b. smaller and less frequent purchase orders.
c. smaller and more frequent purchase orders.
d. larger and more frequent purchase orders.

Answer: c   *Difficulty*: 2   *Objective*: 3

55. Increases in the carrying cost and decreases in the ordering cost per purchase order result in
a. smaller EOQ amounts.
b. larger EOQ amounts.
c. larger relevant total costs.
d. smaller relevant total costs.

Answer: a   *Difficulty*: 2   *Objective*: 3

56. A push-through system that manufactures finished goods for inventory on the basis of demand forecasts is referred to as
    a. just-in-time purchasing.
    b. materials requirements planning.
    c. relevant total costs.
    d. economic order quantity.

    Answer: b   *Difficulty*: 1   *Objective*: 5

57. A demand-pull system in which each component in a production line is produced immediately as needed by the next step in the production line is referred to as
    a. just-in-time purchasing.
    b. materials requirements planning.
    c. relevant total costs.
    d. economic order quantity.

    Answer: a   *Difficulty*: 1   *Objective*: 5

58. A grouping of all the different types of equipment used to make a given product is referred to as
    a. total quality management.
    b. materials requirements planning.
    c. manufacturing cells.
    d. economic order quantity.

    Answer: c   *Difficulty*: 1   *Objective*: 5

59. The time required to get equipment, tools, and materials ready to start production is referred to as
    a. setup time.
    b. manufacturing lead time.
    c. pass-through time.
    d. none of the above.

    Answer: a   *Difficulty*: 1   *Objective*: 6

60. All of the following are potential financial benefits of just in time EXCEPT
    a. lower investments in inventories.
    b. lower investments in plant space for inventories.
    c. reducing the risk of obsolescence.
    d. reducing manufacturing lead time.

    Answer: c   *Difficulty*: 1   *Objective*: 6

61. Traditional normal and standard costing systems use
    a. backflush costing.
    b. delayed costing.
    c. post-deduct costing.
    d. sequential tracking.

    Answer: d   *Difficulty*: 2   *Objective*: 7

62. A costing system that omits recording some or all of the journal entries relating to the cycle from purchase of direct materials to the sale of finished goods is called
    a. dependent costing.
    b. synchronous costing.
    c. sequential costing.
    d. backflush costing.

    Answer: d   *Difficulty*: 2   *Objective*: 7

THE FOLLOWING INFORMATION APPLIES TO QUESTIONS 63 THROUGH 65.
Games R Us manufactures various games. For March, there were no beginning inventories of direct materials and no beginning or ending work in process. Conversion costs is the only indirect manufacturing cost category currently used. Journal entries are recorded when materials are purchased and when conversion costs are allocated under backflush costing.

Conversion costs - March	$ 800,000
Direct materials purchased - March	$2,140,000
Units produced - March	117,600
Units sold - March	83,600

63. Which of the following journal entries properly records the purchase of direct materials?

    a.   Accounts Payable Control $2,140,000
            Inventory: Raw and In-Process Control $2,140,000

    b.   Inventory: Raw and In-Process Control $2,140,000
            Accounts Payable Control $2,140,000

    c.   Inventory: Raw and In-Process Control $2,140,000
            Conversion Costs $2,140,000

    d.   Conversion Costs $2,140,000
            Inventory: Raw and In-Process Control $2,140,000

Answer: b   *Difficulty:* 3   *Objective:* 7

64. Which of the journal entries properly records conversion costs?

    a.   Conversion Costs $800,000
            Various Accounts $800,000

    b.   Various Accounts $800,000
            Conversion Costs $800,000

    c.   Conversion Costs $800,000
            Inventory: Direct Materials $800,000

    d.   Inventory: Direct Materials $800,000
            Conversion Costs $800,000

Answer: a   *Difficulty:* 2   *Objective:* 7

65. Which of the following entries properly records the cost of goods sold for the month?

    a.   Finished Goods $2,090,000
            Work in Process $2,090,000

    b.   Cost of Goods Sold $2,090,000
            Finished Goods $2,090,000

    c.   Finished Goods $2,090,000
            Cost of Goods Sold $2,090,000

    d.   Cost of Goods Sold $2,090,000
            Work in Process $2,090,000

Answer: b   *Difficulty:* 3   *Objective:* 7

Complete Microfilm Products manufactures microfilm cameras. For October, there were no beginning inventories of direct materials and no beginning or ending work in process. Conversion costs is the only indirect manufacturing cost category currently used. Journal entries are recorded when materials are purchased and when units are sold.

Conversion costs - October	$ 90,400
Direct materials purchased - October	$250,400
Units produced - October	80,000 units
Units sold - October	75,000 units
Selling price	$10 each

66. Which of the following journal entries properly reflects the purchase of materials in a JIT environment?

a.	Inventory: Raw and In-Process		$250,400	
	Accounts Payable Control			$250,400
b.	Accounts Payable Control		$250,400	
	Allocated Costs: Direct Materials			$250,400
c.	Accounts Payable Control		$250,400	
	Materials Inventory			$250,400
d.	Allocated Costs: Direct Materials		$250,400	
	Inventory: Raw and Material			$250,400

Answer: a *Difficulty*: 3 *Objective*: 7

67. Which of the following journal entries would be recorded when units are sold for the month?

a.	Cost of Goods Sold	$319,500	
	Inventory: Raw and In-Process		$319,500
b.	Cost of Goods Sold	$319,500	
	Inventory: Raw and In-Process		$234,750
	Conversion Costs Allocated		$ 84,750
c.	Inventory: Raw and In-Process	$234,750	
	Conversion Costs Allocated	$ 84,750	
	Cost of Goods Sold		$319,500
d.	Cost of Goods Sold	$319,500	
	Inventory: Raw and In-Process		$229,500
	Conversion Costs Allocated		$ 90,000

Answer: b *Difficulty*: 3 *Objective*: 7

Direct materials ($250,400/80,000)	$3.13
Conversion costs ($90,400/80,000)	1.13
Total	$4.26

75,000 x $4.26= $319,500
75,000 x $3.13= $234,750
75,000 x $1.13= $ 84,750

68. Which of the following entries would occur if the only trigger point is the production of finished units?

    a.   Cost of Goods Sold $319,500

             Inventory: Raw and In-Process Control $229,500

             Conversion Costs Allocated $ 90,000

    b.   Inventory: Raw and In-Process Control $234,750

             Conversion Costs Allocated $ 84,750

             Cost of Goods Sold $319,500

    c.   Finished Goods $340,800

             Accounts Payable Control $250,400

             Conversion Costs Allocated $ 90,400

    d.   Accounts Payable Control $250,400

             Conversion Costs Allocated $ 90,400

             Finished Goods $340,800

Answer: c   *Difficulty*: 3   *Objective*: 7

80,000 x $4.26= $340,800

80,000 x $3.13= $250,400

80,000 x $1.13 = $90,400

69. Companies that would benefit from backflush costing include companies
    a.   which have fast manufacturing lead times.
    b.   whose inventories vary from period to period.
    c.   companies that require audit trails.
    d.   both (a) and (b).

Answer: a   *Difficulty*: 2   *Objective*: 8

70. The implications of JIT and backflush costing systems for activity-based costing systems include
    a.   more of the costs are direct.
    b.   overhead cost allocations are reduced.
    c.   neither (a) nor (b).
    d.   both (a) and (b).

Answer: d   *Difficulty*: 2   *Objective*: 8

71. Due to unprecedented growth during the year, Flowers by Kelly decided to use some of its surplus cash to increase the size of several inventory order quantities that had been previously determined using an EOQ model.

    Required:

    Identify whether increasing the size of inventory orders will increase, decrease, or have no effect on each of the following items.

    _____ a. Average inventory

    _____ b. Cost of goods sold

    _____ c. Number of orders per year

    _____ d. Total annual carrying costs

    _____ e. Total annual carrying and ordering costs

    _____ f. Total annual ordering costs

    Answer:

    a. Increase
    b. No effect
    c. Decrease
    d. Increase
    e. Depends which costs increase/decrease more
    f. Decrease

    Difficulty: 2   *Objective*: 2

72. Products' only product has an annual demand of 2,000 units. The cost of placing an order is $40 and the cost of carrying one unit in inventory for one year is $16.

    Required:

    Determine the economic order quantity.

    Answer:

    The square root of [(2 x 2,000 x $40) / $16] – 100 units

    Difficulty: 1   *Objective*: 2

73. Video Boy has one particular product that has an annual demand of 1,000 units. Total manufacturing costs per unit total $40 and setup costs per batch are $15. Direct material ordering costs for the product total $10 per order. Currently, the carrying costs per unit are 25% of manufacturing costs.

Required:

Determine the economic manufacturing order quantity.

Answer:

The square root of [(2 x 1,000 x $25) / $10] = 70.71 units

Difficulty: 2   *Objective*:   3

74. Ralph was in the process of completing the quarterly planning for the purchasing department when a major computer malfunction lost most of his data. For direct material XXX he was able to recover the following:

Average inventory level of XXX	200
Orders per year	40
Average daily demand	48
Working days per year	250
Annual ordering costs	$4,000
Annual carrying costs	$6,000

Ralph purchases at the EOQ quantity level.

Required:

Determine the annual demand, the cost of placing an order, the annual carrying cost of one unit, and the economic order quantity.

Answer:

Annual demand	= 48 x 250 = 12,000
Cost of placing an order	= $4,000/40 = $100 per order
Carrying cost of one unit	= $6,000/200 = $30 per unit
EOQ	= The square root of (2 x 12,000 x $100)/30 = 283 units

Difficulty: 3   *Objective*:   2

75. Clothes, Inc., has an average annual demand for red, medium polo shirts of 25,000 units. The cost of placing an order is $80 and the cost of carrying one unit in inventory for one year is $25.

Required:

a. Use the economic-order-quantity model to determine the optimal order size.

b. Determine the reorder point assuming a lead time of 10 days and a work year of 250 days.

c. Determine the safety stock required to prevent stockouts assuming the maximum lead time is 20 days and the maximum daily demand is 125 units.

Answer:

a. The square root of [(2 x 25,000 x $80) / $25] = 400 units

b. Daily demand = 25,000/250 = 100 units
   Reorder point = 100 units per day x 10 days = 1,000 units

c.

Maximum demand per day	125 units
Maximum lead time	x 20 days
Maximum lead time demand	2,500 units
Reorder point without safety stocks	1,000 units
Safety stock	1,500 units

Difficulty: 2   *Objective*:   2

76. An inventory item of XYZ Manufacturing has an average daily demand of 10 units with a maximum daily demand of 12 units. The economic order quantity is 200 units. Without safety stocks, the reorder point is 50 units. Safety stocks are set at 94 units.

Required:

a.   Determine the reorder point with safety stocks.
b.   Determine the maximum inventory level.
c.   Determine the average lead time.
d.   Determine the maximum lead time.

Answer:

a.

Reorder point without safety stocks	50 units
Safety stock	94 units
Reorder point with safety stocks	144 units

b.

Economic-order quantity	200 units
Safety stocks	94 units
Maximum inventory level	294 units

c.   Average lead time = 50 units at reorder point/10 units a day = 5 days

d.   Reorder point with safety stocks is 144
     Maximum demand is 12
     Maximum lead time = 144/12 = 12 days

Difficulty: 2   *Objective*:   2

77. For supply item ABC, Andrews Company has been ordering 125 units based on the recommendation of the salesperson who calls on the company monthly. A new purchasing agent has been hired by the company who wants to start using the economic-order-quantity method and its supporting decision elements. She has gathered the following information:

Annual demand in units	250
Days used per year	250
Lead time, in days	10
Ordering costs	$100
Annual unit carrying costs	$20

Required:

Determine the EOQ, average inventory, orders per year, average daily demand, reorder point, annual ordering costs, and annual carrying costs.

Answer:

EOQ = The square root of [(2 x 250 x $100) / $20] = 50

Average inventory = 50/2 = 25

Orders per year = 250/50 = 5

Average daily demand = 250/250 = 1 unit

Reorder point = 10/1 = 10 units

Annual ordering costs = 5 x $100 = $500

Annual carrying costs = 25 x $20 = $500

Difficulty: 2   *Objective*: 2

78. The IBP Grocery orders most of its items in lot sizes of 10 units. Average annual demand per side of beef is 720 units per year. Ordering costs are $25 per order with an average purchasing price of $100. Annual inventory carrying costs are estimated to be 40% of the unit cost.

Required:

a. Determine the economic order quantity.

b. Determine the annual cost savings if the shop changes from an order size of 10 units to the economic order quantity.

c. Since the shelf life is limited, the IBP Grocery must keep the inventory moving. Assuming a 360-day year, determine the optimal lot size under each of the following: (1) a 20-day shelf life and (2) a 10-day shelf life.

Answer:

a. The square root of [(2 x 720 x $25) / $40] = 30 units

b.

Current 10-unit order:
Ordering costs ($25 x 720/10)	$1,800	
Carrying costs ($100 x 0.40 x 10/2)	200	$2,000

EOQ 30-unit order:
Ordering costs ($25 x 720/30)	600	
Carrying costs ($100 x 0.40 x 30/2)	600	1,200
Annual savings		$ 800

c. Average daily demand = 720 / 360 = 2 per day

Average days' supply in EOQ = 30/2 = 15 days
(1) 20-day shelf life allows for up to 40 units (20 x 2), EOQ is acceptable.
(2) 10-day shelf life allows for up to 20 units (10 x 2), EOQ is not acceptable

Difficulty: 3   *Objective*: 3

79. Tornado Electronics manufactures stereos. All processing is initiated when an order is received. For April there were no beginning inventories. Conversion Costs and Direct Materials are the only manufacturing cost accounts. Direct Materials are purchased under a just-in-time system. Backflush costing is used with a finished goods trigger point. Additional information is as follows:

Actual conversion costs	$232,000
Standard materials costs per unit	60
Standard conversion cost per unit	140
Units produced	3,200
Units sold	2,800

Required:

Record all journal entries for the monthly activities related to the above transactions if backflush costing is used.

Answer:

To record actual conversion costs:

Conversion Costs	$232,000	
Various Accounts		$232,000

To record finished goods:

Finished Goods (3,200 x $200)	$640,000	
Accounts Payable Control (3,200x 60)		$192,000
Conversion Costs Allocated (3,200 x 140)		448,000

To record sale of 2,800 units:

Cost of Finished Goods Sold (2,800 x 200)	$560,000	
Finished Goods		$560,000

Difficulty: 2   *Objective*:   7

80. Corry Corporation manufactures filters for cars, vans, and trucks. A backflush costing system is used and standard costs for a filter are as follows:

Direct materials	$2.60
Conversion costs	4.20
Total	$6.80

Filters are scheduled for production only after orders are received, and are shipped immediately upon completion. This results in product costs being charged directly to cost of goods sold. In December, 3,000 filters were produced and shipped. Materials were purchased at a cost of $8,450 and actual conversion costs of $13,650 were recorded.

Required:

Prepare journal entries to record December's costs for the production of the filters.

Answer:

Materials Inventory	$ 8,450	
Accounts Payable		$ 8,450
Conversion Costs	$13,650	
Various Credits		$13,650
Cost of Goods Sold	$22,100	
Materials Inventory		$ 8,450
Conversion Costs		$13,650

Difficulty: 2   *Objective*:   7

CRITICAL THINKING

81. The executive vice president of Robotics, Inc., is concerned because the cost of materials has not been in line with the budget for several periods, even after implementing an EOQ model. The company has the normal direct material variance computations of price and efficiency at the end of each month. The price variance of the direct materials used is usually near expectations. The vice president does not understand how the budget differences are always larger than the material price variances.

Required:

What explanation can you give for the evaluation problems presented?

Answer

An EOQ model does not solve all inventory related problems. The first problem is the timing of material price variance computations. They should be at the time of purchase, not at the time of usage. By changing when the variance is computed, the responsibility is placed where it should be, in purchasing, not in production. Also, the timing of when materials are used could explain the difference between the budget variances and the material price variances. Materials may be purchased in one period and not used until another period. Also, material usage may include items purchased during several previous periods.

Difficulty: 2   *Objective*: 3

82. The manufacturing manager of New Technology Company is concerned about the company's newest plant. When the plant began operations three years ago, it had the best of everything. It had modern equipment, well-trained employees, engineered work and assembly stations, and a controlled environment. During the first two years, the evaluation results were very good with almost all cost variances being favorable. However, recently, things have turned negative.

In recent months, everything seems to be operating in a crisis management mode. Although most cost variances remain favorable, the plant's segment contribution is declining and customers are complaining about poor quality and slow delivery. Several customers have suggested that they may take their business elsewhere if things do not improve.

The shop floor is in continual turmoil. In-process inventory is everywhere, production employees have difficulty finding jobs that need to be worked on, and scheduling has requested a larger computer to keep track of work in process.

The vice president of sales does not know where to begin with solving the customers' problems. It seems that everyone is working very hard and the plant has the best facilities and trained employees in the industry.

Required:

What is the nature of the plant's problems? What recommendation would you make to help improve the situation?

Answer:

The basic problem appears to be too much work-in-process inventory and a lack of control over the flow of this inventory. Since the plant had two good years of production, it may be that increased demands are pushing the plant near its capacity and management has lost control of how to manage a near-capacity situation. Although the employees are well trained and skilled in what they do, that is not enough to ensure the production process runs smoothly. All activities must be organized to be efficient.

A beginning recommendation is to implement a materials required planning system where each work station controls what it produces, and pushes it to the next workstation. This can be accomplished by tighter controls over the scheduling of production units by workstation. This would be incorporated with a master production schedule, bill of materials, and timely inventory system.

Difficulty: 2   *Objective*:   4

83. Kretzinger Company makes extensive use of financial performance reports for each of its departments. Although most departments have been reporting favorable cost variances with the company's current inventory system, management is concerned about the overall performance of the purchasing department. For example, the following information is for the purchasing of materials for a product the company has been manufacturing for several years:

Purchase Year	Quantity Used	Average Inventory	Price Variance
20x1	40,000	8,000	$ 1,000 F
20x2	60,000	15,000	10,000 F
20x3	60,000	20,000	12,000 F
20x4	50,000	12,500	20,000 U
20x5	54,000	18,000	8,000 F
20x6	58,000	23,200	9,500 F

Required:

a. Compute the inventory turnover for each year. Can any conclusions be drawn for a yearly comparison of the purchase price variance and the inventory turnover?

b. Identify problems likely to be caused by evaluating purchasing only on the basis of the purchase price variance.

c. What recommendations will improve the evaluation process?

Answer:

a.

Year	Quantity used		Average inventory	Turnover
20x1	40,000	divided by	8,000	5.0
20x2	60,000	divided by	15,000	4.0
20x3	60,000	divided by	20,000	3.0
20x4	50,000	divided by	12,500	4.0
20x5	54,000	divided by	18,000	3.0
20x6	58,000	divided by	23,200	2.5

Favorable purchase prices appear to be associated with decreases in inventory turnover and increases in average inventory levels. Decreases in inventory turnover are a possible signal of the buildup of excess inventory. Excess inventory will reduce return on investment of the company and the above information indicates a need for a just-in-time inventory system.

83.   (continued)

b.   To achieve quantity discounts and favorable materials price variances, purchasing may be ordering excess inventory, thereby increasing subsequent storage, obsolescence, and handling costs. To obtain a low price, purchasing may be ordering from a supplier whose goods have inferior quality which may, in turn, lead to increased inspection, rework, and, perhaps, dissatisfied customers.

c.   It appears that two items may help improve the situation. First, consider the change to a just-in-time inventory system that would greatly improve the inventory turnover and reduce the amount of inventory carried. Second, additional measures should be used in the evaluation of the purchasing department. Either other financial measures should be used or the addition of nonfinancial measures should be implemented.

Difficulty: 3   *Objective*:   5

84.   Minnesota Ore Company mines iron ore for production into various metal products. During recent years, the company has had large fluctuations in its inventories of metal ingots. Much of the volatility of the inventory levels is due to the variability of demand by the company's largest customers, automobile manufacturers. For large orders, the company has the technology to quickly shift production from one product to another.

Required:

Explain how the company can improve its inventory control system and give the advantages of whatever you recommend.

Answer:

The company can probably benefit from changing to a just-in-time system for inventory control. This would allow the company to be responsive to actual needs rather than finished goods inventory building. The advantages would be:

1.   Lower inventory requirements
2.   Reductions in carrying and handling costs of inventories
3.   Reduction in risks of obsolete inventories
4.   Reduction in total manufacturing costs
5.   Reductions in paperwork.

Difficulty: 2   *Objective*:   5

85. Backflush costing does not strictly adhere to generally accepted accounting principles. Explain why. Also, describe the types of businesses that might use backflush costing.

Answer:

The principal reason why backflush costing does not strictly adhere to GAAP is that the work-in-process accounts are not recognized in the accounting records. Work in process consists of unfinished goods. Substantial business resources were dedicated to their production, and should be recognized in the accounts as an asset. This approach to costing is usually used by companies that adopt JIT production methods. While not totally devoid of inventories, such companies seek to minimize inventories thus minimizing the problems associated with no work-in-process accounts.

The type of business which would use backflush costing would be firms that use JIT production, have fast manufacturing lead times, or have very stable inventory levels from period to period. For these companies, backflush costing will report cost numbers similar to what a sequential costing approach would report.

Difficulty: 3   *Objective*:   8

CHAPTER 21: CAPITAL BUDGETING AND COST ANALYSIS

TRUE/FALSE

1. Capital budgeting focuses on projects over their entire lives in order to consider all the cash flows or cash savings from investing in a single project.

    Answer: True   *Difficulty:* 2   *Objective:* 1

2. The identification stage of capital budgeting explores alternative capital investments that will achieve the objectives of the organization.

    Answer: False   *Difficulty:* 1   *Objective:* 2
    This is the definition of the search stage.

3. The information-acquisition stage of capital budgeting considers the expected costs and the expected benefits of alternative capital investments.

    Answer: True   *Difficulty:* 1   *Objective:* 2

4. The selection stage of the capital budgeting process consists of choosing projects for possible implementation.

    Answer: True   *Difficulty:* 1   *Objective:* 2

5. Discounted cash flow methods measure all the expected future cash inflows and outflows of a project as if they occurred at equal intervals over the life of the project.

    Answer: False   *Difficulty:* 2   *Objective:* 3
    As if they occurred at a single point in time.

6. Discounted cash flow methods focus on operating income.

    Answer: False   *Difficulty:* 2   *Objective:* 3
    Discounted cash flow method focus on cash inflows and cash outflows.

7. The net present value method calculates the expected monetary gain or loss from a project by discounting all expected future cash inflows and outflows to the present point in time using the hurdle rate.

    Answer: True   *Difficulty:* 2   *Objective:* 3

8. Internal rate of return is a method of calculating the expected net monetary gain or loss from a project by discounting all expected future cash inflows and outflows to the present point in time.

    Answer: False   *Difficulty*: 2   *Objective*: 3
    The internal rate of return calculates the discount rate at which the present value of expected cash inflows from a project equals the present value of expected cash outflows.

9. A capital budgeting project is accepted if the required rate of return equals or exceeds the internal rate of return.

    Answer: False   *Difficulty*: 2   *Objective*: 3
    A capital budgeting project is accepted if the internal rate of return equals or exceeds the required internal rate of return.

10. The net present value method can be used in situations where the required rate of return varies over the life of the project.

    Answer: True   *Difficulty*: 2   *Objective*: 3

11. Relevant cash flows are expected future cash flows that differ among the alternative uses of investment funds.

    Answer: True   *Difficulty*: 2   *Objective*: 4

12. Deducting depreciation from operating cash flows would result in counting the initial investment twice, in the discounted cash flow analysis.

    Answer: True   *Difficulty*: 2   *Objective*: 4

13. Unlike the net present value method and the internal rate-of-return method, the payback method does not distinguish between the origins of the cash flows.

    Answer: False   *Difficulty*: 2   *Objective*: 5
    None of the three capital budgeting methods distinguish between the origins of the cash flows.

14. The payback method is only useful when the expected cash flows in the later years of the project are highly uncertain.

    Answer: False   *Difficulty*: 3   *Objective*: 5
    The payback method is only useful when the expected cash flows in the later years are highly certain.

15. The accrual accounting rate-of-return method is similar to the internal rate-of-return method in that both methods calculate a rate-of-return percentage.

Answer: True   *Difficulty*:   2   *Objective*:   6

16. A manager who uses discounted cash flow methods to make capital budgeting decisions does not face goal-congruence issues if the accrual accounting rate of return is used for performance evaluation.

Answer: False   *Difficulty*:   2   *Objective*:   7
The manager does face goal-congruence issues.

17. Depreciation tax deductions result in tax savings that partially offset the cost of acquiring the capital asset.

Answer: True   *Difficulty*:   2   *Objective*:   8

18. The use of an accelerated method of depreciation for tax purposes would usually increase the present value of the investment.

Answer: True   *Difficulty*:   3   *Objective*:   8

19. An example of an intangible asset would be a corporation's customer base.

Answer: True   *Difficulty*:   2   *Objective*:   8

20. The nominal approach to incorporating inflation into the net present value method predicts cash inflows in real monetary units and uses a real rate as the required rate of return.

Answer: False   *Difficulty*:   2   *Objective*:   A
This is the definition of the real approach.

21. Which of the following involves significant financial investments in projects to develop new products, expand production capacity, or remodel current production facilities?
    a. Capital budgeting
    b. Working capital
    c. Master budgeting
    d. Project-cost budgeting

    Answer: a   *Difficulty*: 1   *Objective*: 1

22. The accounting system that corresponds to the project dimension in capital budgeting is the
    a. net present value method.
    b. internal rate of return.
    c. accrual accounting rate of return.
    d. life-cycle costing.

    Answer: d   *Difficulty*: 1   *Objective*: 1

23. The stage of the capital budgeting process which distinguishes which types of capital expenditure projects are necessary to accomplish organization objectives is the
    a. identification stage.
    b. search stage.
    c. information-acquisition stage.
    d. selection stage.

    Answer: a   *Difficulty*: 1   *Objective*: 2

24. The stage of the capital budgeting process which explores alternative capital investments that will achieve organization objectives is the
    a. identification stage.
    b. search stage.
    c. information-acquisition stage.
    d. selection stage.

    Answer: b   *Difficulty*: 1   *Objective*: 2

25. The stage of the capital budgeting process which considers the expected costs and the expected benefits of alternative capital investments is the
    a. identification stage.
    b. search stage.
    c. information-acquisition stage.
    d. selection stage.

    Answer: c   *Difficulty*: 1   *Objective*: 2

26. The stage of the capital budgeting process which chooses projects for implementation is the
    a. selection stage.
    b. search stage.
    c. identification stage.
    d. management-control stage.

    Answer: a   *Difficulty*: 1   *Objective*: 2

27. The stage of the capital-budgeting process in which projects get underway and performance is monitored is the
    a. implementation and control stage.
    b. search stage.
    c. identification stage.
    d. management-control stage.

    Answer: a   *Difficulty*: 1   *Objective*: 2

28. Capital budgeting emphasizes two factors
    a. qualitative and nonfinancial.
    b. quantitative and nonfinancial.
    c. quantitative and financial
    d. qualitative and financial.

    Answer: c   *Difficulty*: 1   *Objective*: 2

29. Which of the following are NOT included in the formal financial analysis of a capital budgeting program?
    a. Quality of the output
    b. Safety of employees
    c. Cash flow
    d. Neither (a) nor (b) are included

    Answer: d   *Difficulty*: 2   *Objective*: 2

30. Which capital budgeting technique(s) measure all expected future cash inflows and outflows as if they occurred at a single point in time?
    a. Net present value
    b. Internal rate of return
    c. Payback
    d. Both (a) and (b).

    Answer: d   *Difficulty*: 2   *Objective*: 3

31. Discounted cash flow methods for capital budgeting focus on
    a. cash inflows.
    b. operating income.
    c. cash outflows.
    d. both (a) and (c).

    Answer: d   *Difficulty:* 2   *Objective:* 3

32. Net present value is calculated using
    a. the internal rate of return.
    b. the required rate of return.
    c. the rate of return required by the investment bankers.
    d. none of the above.

    Answer: b   *Difficulty:* 2   *Objective:* 3

33. All of the following are methods that aid management in analyzing the expected results of capital budgeting decisions EXCEPT
    a. accrual accounting rate-of-return method.
    b. discounted cash-flow method.
    c. future-value cash-flow method.
    d. payback method.

    Answer: c   *Difficulty:* 2   *Objective:* 3

34. The capital budgeting method which calculates the expected monetary gain or loss from a project by discounting all expected future cash inflows and outflows to the present point in time using the required rate of return is the
    a. payback method.
    b. accrual accounting rate-of-return method.
    c. sensitivity method.
    d. net present value method.

    Answer: d   *Difficulty:* 2   *Objective:* 3

35. Assume your goal in life is to retire with one million dollars. How much would you need to save at the end of each year if interest rates average 6% and you have a 20-year work life?
    a. $14,565
    b. $27,184
    c. $120,102
    d. $376,476

    Answer: b   *Difficulty:* 3   *Objective:* 3
    S (36.786) = $1,000,000
    S = $ 27,184.25

36. Hawkeye Cleaners has been considering the purchase of an industrial dry-cleaning machine. The existing machine is operable for three more years and will have a zero disposal price. If the machine is disposed of now, it may be sold for $60,000. The new machine will cost $200,000 and an additional cash investment in working capital of $60,000 will be required. The new machine will reduce the average amount of time required to wash clothing and will decrease labor costs. The investment is expected to net $50,000 in additional cash inflows during the year of acquisition and $150,000 each additional year of use. The new machine has a three-year life, and zero disposal value. These cash flows will generally occur throughout the year and are recognized at the end of each year. Income taxes are not considered in this problem. The working capital investment will not be recovered at the end of the asset's life.

What is the net present value of the investment, assuming the required rate of return is 10%? Would the company want to purchase the new machine?
  a. $82,000; yes
  b. $50,000; no
  c. $(50,000); yes
  d. $(82,000); no

Answer: a   *Difficulty:*   3   *Objective:*   3
Yr. 0 ($60,000 - $200,000 - $60,000) x 1.000 = $(200,000)
Yr. 1 $50,000 x 0.909 =   45,450
Yr. 2 $150,000 x 0.826 =   123,900
Yr. 3 $150,000 x 0.751 =   112,650
                                                      $ 82,000

37. Hawkeye Cleaners has been considering the purchase of an industrial dry-cleaning machine. The existing machine is operable for three more years and will have a zero disposal price. If the machine is disposed of now, it may be sold for $60,000. The new machine will cost $200,000 and an additional cash investment in working capital of $60,000 will be required. The new machine will reduce the average amount of time required to wash clothing and will decrease labor costs. The investment is expected to net $50,000 in additional cash inflows during the year of acquisition and $150,000 each additional year of use. The new machine has a three-year life. These cash flows will generally occur throughout the year and are recognized at the end of each year. Income taxes are not considered in this problem. The working capital investment will not be recovered at the end of the asset's life.

What is the net present value of the investment, assuming the required rate of return is 24%? Would the company want to purchase the new machine?
   a. $(32,800); yes
   b. $(16,400); no
   c. $16,400; yes
   d. $32,800; no

Answer: c   *Difficulty:*   3   *Objective:*   3
Yr. 0 ($60,000 - $200,000 - $60,000) x 1.000 = $(200,000)
Yr. 1 $ 50,000 x 0.806 =   40,300
Yr. 2 $150,000 x .0.650 =   97,500
Yr. 3 $150,000 x 0.524 =   78,600
                                                    $ 16,400

38. In using the net present value method, only projects with a zero or positive net present value are acceptable because
   a.   the return from these projects equals or exceeds the cost of capital.
   b.   a positive net present value on a particular project guarantees company profitability.
   c.   the company will be able to pay the necessary payments on any loans secured to finance the project.
   d.   of both (a) and (b).

Answer: a   *Difficulty:*   2   *Objective:*   3

39. Which of the following is NOT an appropriate term for the required rate of return?
   a.   Discount rate
   b.   Hurdle rate
   c.   Cost of capital
   d.   All of the above are appropriate terms

Answer: d   *Difficulty:*   2   *Objective:*   3

40. Which of the following results of the net present value method in capital budgeting is the LEAST acceptable?
   a. $(10,000)
   b. $(7,000)
   c. $(18,000)
   d. $0

   Answer: c   *Difficulty:* 2   *Objective:* 3

41. The definition of an annuity is
   a. similar to the definition of a life insurance policy.
   b. a series of equal cash flows at intervals.
   c. an investment product whose funds are invested in the stock market.
   d. both (a) and (b) are correct.

   Answer: b   *Difficulty:* 2   *Objective:* 3

42. The net present value method focuses on
   a. cash inflows.
   b. accrual-accounting net income.
   c. cash outflows.
   d. both (a) and (c).

   Answer: d   *Difficulty:* 2   *Objective:* 3

43. If the net present value for a project is zero or positive, this means
   a. the project should be accepted.
   b. the project should not be accepted.
   c. the expected rate of return is below the required rate of return.
   d. both (a) and (c).

   Answer: a   *Difficulty:* 2   *Objective:* 3

44. Shirt Company wants to purchase a new cutting machine for its sewing plant. The investment is expected to generate annual cash inflows of $300,000. The required rate of return is 12% and the current machine is expected to last for four years. What is the maximum dollar amount Shirt Company would be willing to spend for the machine, assuming its life is also four years? Income taxes are not considered.
   a. $507,000
   b. $720,600
   c. $791,740
   d. $911,100

   Answer: d   *Difficulty:* 3   *Objective:* 3
   X = $300,000 x PV Ann 4 (12%) = $300,000 x 3.037
   X = $911,100

45. The Zeron Corporation wants to purchase a new machine for its factory operations at a cost of $950,000. The investment is expected to generate $350,000 in annual cash flows for a period of four years. The required rate of return is 14%. The old machine can be sold for $50,000. The machine is expected to have zero value at the end of the four-year period. What is the net present value of the investment? Would the company want to purchase the new machine? Income taxes are not considered.
   a. $119,550; yes
   b. $69,550; no
   c. $1,019,550; yes
   d. $326,750; no

Answer: a   Difficulty: 3   Objective: 3
Year 0 = ($50,000 - $950,000) = $(900,000)
Year 1 = $350,000 x 0.877 =   306,950
Year 2 = $350,000 x 0.769 =   269,150
Year 3 = $350,000 x 0.675 =   236,250
Year 4 = $350,000 x 0.592 =   207,200
                                       $ 119,550

46. Wet and Wild Water Company drills small commercial water wells. The company is in the process of analyzing the purchase of a new drill. Information on the proposal is provided below.

Initial investment:	
Asset	$160,000
Working capital	$ 32,000
Operations (per year for four years):	
Cash receipts	$160,000
Cash expenditures	$ 88,000
Disinvestment:	
Salvage value of drill (existing)	$ 16,000
Discount rate	20%

What is the net present value of the investment? Assume there is no recovery of working capital.
   a. $(62,140)
   b. $10,336
   c. $42,362
   d. $186,336

Answer: b   Difficulty: 3   Objective: 3
- $32,000 - $160,000 + $16,000= $(176,000)
     Yr 1 = $72,000 x 0.833=   59,976
     Yr 2 = $72,000 x 0.694=   49,968
     Yr 3 = $72,000 x 0.579=   41,688
     Yr 4 = $72,000 x 0.482=   34,704
                                     $ 10,336

47. The capital budgeting method that calculates the discount rate at which the present value of expected cash inflows from a project equals the present value of expected cash outflows is the
   a.   net present value method.
   b.   accrual accounting rate-of-return method.
   c.   payback method.
   d.   internal rate of return.

   Answer: d   *Difficulty:*   2   *Objective:*   3

48. In capital budgeting, a project is accepted only if the internal rate of return
   a.   equals or exceeds the required rate of return.
   b.   equals or is less than the required rate of return.
   c.   equals or exceeds the net present value.
   d.   equals or exceeds the accrual accounting rate of return.

   Answer: a   *Difficulty:*   2   *Objective:*   3

49. The Zeron Corporation recently purchased a new machine for its factory operations at a cost of $921,250. The investment is expected to generate $250,000 in annual cash flows for a period of six years. The required rate of return is 14%. The old machine has a remaining life of six years. The new machine is expected to have zero value at the end of the six-year period. The disposal value of the old machine at the time of replacement is zero. What is the internal rate of return?
   a.   15%
   b.   16%
   c.   17%
   d.   18%

   Answer: b   *Difficulty:*   3   *Objective:*   3
   $921,250= $250,000 F
   F = 3.685
   Chart criteria for six years is 3.685 = 16%

50. Brown Corporation recently purchased a new machine for $339,013.20 with a ten-year life. The old equipment has a remaining life of ten years and no disposal value at the time of replacement. Net cash flows will be $60,000 per year. What is the internal rate of return?
   a.   12%
   b.   16%
   c.   20%
   d.   24%

   Answer: a   *Difficulty:*   2   *Objective:*   3
   $339,013.20 = $60,000F
   F = 5.65022
   Chart criteria for 10 years is 5.65022 = 12%

51. Soda Manufacturing Company provides vending machines for soft-drink manufacturers. The company has been investigating a new piece of machinery for its production department. The old equipment has a remaining life of three years and the new equipment has a value of $52,650 with a three-year life. The expected additional cash inflows are $25,000 per year. What is the internal rate of return?
   a. 20%
   b. 16%
   c. 10%
   d. 8%

   Answer: a   *Difficulty:* 2   *Objective:* 3
   $52,650 = $25,000F
   F = 2.106
   Chart criteria for 3 years is 2.106 = 20%

52. An important advantage of the net present value method of capital budgeting over the internal rate-of-return method is
   a. the net present value method is expressed as a percentage.
   b. the net present values of individual projects can be added to determine the effects of accepting a combination of projects.
   c. no advantage.
   d. both (a) and (b).

   Answer: b   *Difficulty:* 2   *Objective:* 3

53. In situations where the required rate of return is not constant for each year of the project, it is advantageous to use
   a. the adjusted rate-of-return method.
   b. the internal rate-of-return method.
   c. the net present value method.
   d. sensitivity analysis.

   Answer: c   *Difficulty:* 2   *Objective:* 3

54. A "what-if" technique that examines how a result will change if the original predicted data are not achieved or if an underlying assumption changes is called
   a. sensitivity analysis.
   b. net present value analysis.
   c. internal rate-of-return analysis.
   d. adjusted rate-of-return analysis.

   Answer: a   *Difficulty:* 1   *Objective:* 3

55. Investment A requires a net investment of $800,000. The required rate of return is 12% for the four-year annuity. What are the annual cash inflows if the net present value equals 0? (rounded)
    a. $189,483
    b. $263,418
    c. $274,848
    d. $ 295,733

    Answer: b   *Difficulty:* 3   *Objective:* 3
    3.037 x ACI - $800,000 = $0
     = $ 263,418

56. The focus in capital budgeting should be on
    a. the tax consequences of different investment strategies.
    b. the internal rate of return of different strategies.
    c. expected future cash flows that differ between alternatives.
    d. none of the above.

    Answer: c   *Difficulty:* 2   *Objective:* 4

57. All of the following are major categories of cash flows in capital investment decisions EXCEPT
    a. the initial investment in machines and working capital.
    b. recurring operating cash flows.
    c. the initial working capital investment
    d. depreciation expense reported on the income statement.

    Answer: d   *Difficulty:* 2   *Objective:* 4

58. An example of a sunk cost in a capital budgeting decision for new equipment is
    a. increase in working capital required by a particular investment choice.
    b. the book value of the old equipment.
    c. the necessary transportation costs on the new equipment.
    d. all of the above are examples of sunk costs.

    Answer: b   *Difficulty:* 2   *Objective:* 4

59. Depreciation is usually not considered an operating cash flow in capital budgeting because
    a. depreciation is usually a constant amount each year over the life of the capital investment.
    b. deducting depreciation from operating cash flows would be counting the lump-sum amount twice.
    c. depreciation usually does not result in an increase in working capital.
    d. depreciation usually has no effect on the disposal price of the machine.

    Answer: b   *Difficulty:* 1   *Objective:* 4

60. The relevant terminal disposal price of a machine equals
    a. the difference between the salvage value of the old machine and the ultimate salvage value of the new machine.
    b. the total of the salvage values of the old machine and the new machine.
    c. the salvage value of the old machine.
    d. the salvage value of the new machine.

    Answer: a   *Difficulty:* 3   *Objective:* 4

61. The method that measures the time it will take to recoup, in the form of future cash inflows, the total dollars invested in a project is called
    a. the accrued accounting rate-of-return method.
    b. payback method.
    c. internal rate-of-return method.
    d. the book-value method.

    Answer: b   *Difficulty:* 1   *Objective:* 5

62. The net initial investment for a piece of construction equipment is $1,000,000. Annual cash inflows are expected to increase by $200,000 per year. The equipment has an 8-year useful life. What is the payback period?
    a. 8.00 years
    b. 7.00 years
    c. 6.00 years
    d. 5.00 years

    Answer: d   *Difficulty:* 2   *Objective:* 5
    $1,000,000/$200,000 = 5.0 years

63. The payback method of capital budgeting approach to the investment decision highlights
    a. cash flow over the life of the investment.
    b. the liquidity of the investment.
    c. the tax savings of the depreciation amounts.
    d. having as lengthy payback time as possible.

    Answer: b   *Difficulty:* 2   *Objective:* 5

64. The approach to capital budgeting which divides an accounting measure of income by an accounting measure of investment is
    a. net present value.
    b. internal rate of return.
    c. payback method.
    d. accrual accounting rate of return.

    Answer: d   *Difficulty:* 1   *Objective:* 6

65. For capital budgeting decisions, the use of the accrual accounting rate of return for evaluating performance is often a stumbling block to the implementation of the
    a. net cash flow.
    b. most effective goal-congruence choice.
    c. discounted cash flow method for capital budgeting.
    d. most effective tax strategy.

    Answer: d   *Difficulty:* 2   *Objective:* 7

66. In the analysis of a capital budgeting proposal, for which of the following items are there no after-tax consequences?
    a. Cash flow from operations
    b. Gain or loss on the disposal of the asset
    c. Reduction of working capital balances at the end of the useful life of the capital asset
    d. There are no after-tax consequences of any of the above.

    Answer: c   *Difficulty:* 2   *Objective:* 8

67. The Alpha Beta Corporation disposes of a capital asset with an original cost of $85,000 and accumulated depreciation of $54,500 for $25,000. Alpha Beta's tax rate is 40%. Calculate the after-tax cash inflow from the disposal of the capital asset.
    a. $2,200
    b. ($2,200)
    c. $27,200
    d. $31,500

    Answer: c   *Difficulty:* 3   *Objective:* 8
    ($85,000 - 54,500) = $30,500 - $25,000 = $5,500 loss x 0.4 = $2,200 tax savings from loss plus $25,000 proceeds = $27,200.

68. The Phenom Corporation has an annual cash inflow from operations from its investment in a capital asset of $50,000 for five years. The corporation's income tax rate is 40%. Calculate the five years total after-tax cash inflow from operations.
    a. $250,000
    b. $175,000
    c. $150,000
    d. $50,000

    Answer: c   *Difficulty:* 3   *Objective:* 8
    $50,000 x 5 = $250,000 x (1- 0.4) = $150,000 net cash flow

69. Comparison of the actual results for a project to the costs and benefits expected at the time the project was selected is referred to as
    a. the audit trail.
    b. management control.
    c. a postinvestment audit.
    d. a cost-benefit analysis.

    Answer: c   *Difficulty:* 2   *Objective:* 8

70. A capital budgeting tool management can use to summarize the difference in the future net cash inflows from an intangible asset at two different points in time is referred to as
    a. the accrual accounting rate-of-return method.
    b. the net present value method.
    c. sensitivity analysis
    d. the payback method.

    Answer: b   *Difficulty:* 2   *Objective:* 8

EXERCISES AND PROBLEMS

71. Match each one of the examples below with one of the stages of the capital budgeting decision model.

Stages:
1. Identification
2. Search
3. Information-acquisition
4. Selection
5. Financing
6. Implementation and control

_____   a.   Issuing corporate stock in order to supply the funds to purchase new equipment

_____   b.   Learning how to effectively operate Machine #8 only takes 15 minutes

_____   c.   The need to reduce the costs to process the vegetables used in producing goulash

_____   d.   Monitoring the costs to operate a new machine

_____   e.   Percentage of defective merchandise considered too high

_____   f.   Will introducing the new product substantially upgrade our image as a producer of quality products

_____   g.   Research indicates there are five machines on the market capable of producing our product at a competitive cost

_____   h.   Utilization of the internal rate of return for each alternative

Answer:

a. Financing
b. Information-acquisition
c. Identification
d. Implementation and control
e. Identification
f. Information-acquisition
g. Search
h. Selection

Difficulty: 2   *Objective*:   2

72. The Zero Machine Company is evaluating a capital expenditure proposal that requires an initial investment of $20,960 and has predicted cash inflows of $5,000 per year for 10 years. It will have no salvage value.

Required:

a. Using a required rate of return of 16%, determine the net present value of the investment proposal.

b. Determine the proposal's internal rate of return.

Answer:

a.

	Predicted Cash Flows	Year(s)	PV Factor	PV of Cash Flows
Initial investment	$(20,960)	0	1.000	$(20,960)
Annual operations	5,000	10	4.833	24,165
Net present value				$ 3,205

b. Present value factor of an annuity of $1.00 = $20,960/$5,000 = 4.192.

From annuity table, the 4.192 factor is closest to the 10-year row at the 20% column. Therefore, the IRR is 20%.

Difficulty: 2   *Objective:* 3

73. Network Service Center is considering purchasing a new computer network for $82,000. It will require additional working capital of $13,000. Its anticipated eight-year life will generate additional client revenue of $33,000 annually with operating costs, excluding depreciation, of $15,000. At the end of eight years, it will have a salvage value of $9,500 and return $5,000 in working capital. Taxes are not considered.

Required:

a. If the company has a required rate of return of 14%, what is the net present value of the proposed investment?

b. What is the internal rate of return?

Answer:

a.

	Predicted Cash Flows	**Year(s)**	**PV Factor**	**PV of Cash Flows**
Initial investment	$(95,000)	0	1.000	$(95,000)
Annual operations, net	18,000	1 - 8	4.639	83,502
Salvage value, work cap	14,500	8	0.351	5,090
Net present value				$ (6,408)

b. Trial and error is necessary. You know it is below 14% because the answer to Part A was negative and, therefore, less than the discount rate. Therefore, let's try 12%.

	Predicted Cash Flows	**Year(s)**	**PV Factor**	**PV Of Cash Flows**
Initial investment	$(95,000)	0	1.000	$(95,000)
Annual operations, net	18,000	1 - 8	4.968	89,424
Salvage value, work cap	14,500	8	0.404	5,858
Net present value				$ 282

The (almost) zero net present value indicates an internal rate of return of approximately 12%.

Difficulty: 3   *Objective:* 3

74. EIF Manufacturing Company needs to overhaul its drill press or buy a new one. The facts have been gathered, and are as follows:

	Current Machine	New Machine
Purchase Price, New	$80,000	$100,000
Current book value	30,000	
Overhaul needed now	40,000	
Annual cash operating costs	70,000	40,000
Current salvage value	20,000	
Salvage value in five years	5,000	20,000

Required:

Which alternative is the most desirable with a current required rate of return of 20%? Show computations, and assume no taxes.

Answer:

Present value of keeping current system:

	Predicted Cash Flows	Year(s)	PV Factor	PV of Cash Flows
Overhaul	$(40,000)	0	1.000	$ (40,000)
Annual operations	(70,000)	1-5	2.991	(209,370)
Salvage value	5,000	5	0.402	2,010
Net present value				$(247,360)

Present value of new system:

	Predicted Cash Flows	Year(s)	PV Factor	PV of Cash Flows
Investment	$(100,000)	0	1.000	$(100,000)
Salvage value, old	20,000	0	1.000	20,000
Annual operations	(40,000)	1-5	2.991	(119,640)
Salvage value	20,000	5	0.402	8,040
Net present value				$(191,600)

Buying the new equipment is the most desirable by $55,760 ($247,360 - $191,600).

Difficulty: 3   *Objective:* 4

75. ABC Boat Company is interested in replacing a molding machine with a new improved model. The old machine has a salvage value of $20,000 now and a predicted salvage value of $4,000 in six years, if rebuilt. If the old machine is kept, it must be rebuilt in one year at a predicted cost of $40,000.

The new machine costs $160,000 and has a predicted salvage value of $24,000 at the end of six years. If purchased, the new machine will allow cash savings of $40,000 for each of the first three years, and $20,000 for each year of its remaining six-year life.

Required:

What is the net present value of purchasing the new machine if the company has a required rate of return of 14%?

Answer:

	Predicted Cash Flows	Year(s)	PV Factor	PV of Cash Flows
Initial Investment	$(160,000)	0	1.000	$(160,000)
Salvage of old	20,000	0	1.000	20,000
Annual operations	40,000	1-3	2.322	92,880
Annual operations	20,000	4-6	(3.889-2.322)	31,340
Save by not rebuilding	40,000	1	0.877	35,080
Salvage of new	24,000	6	0.456	10,944
Net present value				$ 30,244

Difficulty: 3   *Objective:*   4

76.   Supply the missing data for each of the following proposals.

	Proposal A	Proposal B	Proposal C
Initial investment	(a)	$62,900	$226,000
Annual net cash inflow	$60,000	(c)	(e)
Life, in years	10	6	10
Salvage value	$0	$10,000	$0
Payback period in year	(b)	(d)	5.65
Internal rate of return	12%	24%	(f)

Answer:

a.

Annual cash inflow	$ 60,000
Present value factor for 10 years	x 5.650
Initial investment	$339,000

b.   Payback period = $339,000/$60,000 = 5.65 years

c.

Initial investment	$62,900
PV of salvage value ($10,000 x 0.275)	(2,750)
Net PV of annual net cash inflow	$60,150

Annual cash inflow = $60,150/3.020 = $19,917.22

d.   Payback = $62,900/$19,917.22 = 3.158

e.   Annual net cash inflow = $226,000/5.650 = $40,000

f.   PV factor for 10 years = $226,000/$40,000 = 5.650

Look up value 5.650 in PV of annuity table under 10 years and the internal rate of return is 12%.

Difficulty: 3   *Objectives*: 3, 5

77. Terrain Vehicle has received three proposals for its new vehicle-painting machine. Information on each proposal is as follows:

	Proposal X	Proposal Y	Proposal Z
Initial investment in equipment	$180,000	$120,000	$190,000
Working capital needed	0	0	10,000
Annual cash saved by operations:			
Year 1	75,000	50,000	80,000
Year 2	75,000	48,000	80,000
Year 3	75,000	44,000	80,000
Year 4	75,000	8,000	80,000
Salvage value end of year:			
Year 1	100,000	80,000	60,000
Year 2	80,000	60,000	50,000
Year 3	40,000	40,000	30,000
Year 4	10,000	20,000	15,000
Working capital returned	0	0	10,000

Required:

Determine each proposal's payback.

Answer:

Proposal X payback = $180,000/75,000 = 2.4 years

Proposal Y	Cash Savings	Savings Accumulated	To Be Recovered
Year 0			$120,000
Year 1	$50,000	$ 50,000	70,000
Year 2	48,000	98,000	22,000
Year 3	44,000	142,000	0

Proposal Y payback = 2 years plus $22,000/$44,000 or 2.5 years.

Proposal Z payback = ($190,000 + $10,000)/80,000 = 2.5 years

Difficulty: 3   *Objective:* 5

78. Book & Bible Bookstore desires to buy a new coding machine to help control book inventories. The machine sells for $36,586 and requires working capital of $4,000. Its estimated useful life is five years and will have a salvage value of $4,000. Recovery of working capital will be $4,000 at the end of its useful life. Annual cash savings from the purchase of the machine will be $10,000.

Required:

a.   Compute the net present value at a 14% required rate of return.
b.   Compute the internal rate of return.
c.   Determine the payback period of the investment.

Answer:

a.

	Predicted Cash Flows	Year(s)	PV Factor	PV of Cash Flows
Investment	$(36,586)	0	1.000	$(36,586)
Working capital needed	(4,000)	0	1.000	(4,000)
Annual operations	10,000	1-5	3.433	34,330
Working capital returned	4,000	5	0.519	2,076
Salvage value	4,000	5	0.519	2,076
Net present value				$(2,104)

b.   Trial and error is required. Because net present value is negative in part a, the internal rate of return is less than 14%. Start by trying 12%.

	Predicted Cash Flows	Year(s)	PV Factor	PV of Cash Flows
Investment	$(36,586)	0	1.000	$(36,586)
Working capital needed	(4,000)	0	1.000	(4,000)
Annual operations	10,000	1-5	3.605	36,050
Working capital returned	4,000	5	0.567	2,268
Salvage value	4,000	5	0.567	2,268
Net present value				$-0-

With a zero net present value, the internal rate of return is 12%.

c.   Payback period = ($36,586 + $4,000)/$10,000 = 4.06 years.

Difficulty: 3   *Objectives:*   3, 5

79. Jensen Manufacturing is considering buying an automated machine that costs $250,000. It requires working capital of $25,000. Annual cash savings are anticipated to be $103,000 for five years. The company uses straight-line depreciation. The salvage value at the end of five years is expected to be $10,000. The working capital will be recovered at the end of the machine's life.

Required:

Compute the accrual accounting rate of return based on the initial investment.

Answer:

Accrual accounting income	= $103,000 - (($250,000 - $10,000)/5)
	= $103,000 - $48,000
	= $ 55,000

AARR with initial investment	= $55,000/($250,000 + $25,000)
	= $55,000/$275,000
	= 0.20

Difficulty: 2   *Objective:* 6

80. Gavin and Alex, baseball consultants, are in need of a microcomputer network for their staff. They have received three proposals, with related facts as follows:

	Proposal A	**Proposal B**	**Proposal C**
Initial investment in equipment	$90,000	$90,000	$90,000
Annual cash increase in operations:			
Year 1	80,000	45,000	90,000
Year 2	10,000	45,000	0
Year 3	45,000	45,000	0
Salvage value	0	0	0
Estimated life	3 yrs	3 yrs	1 yr

The company uses straight-line depreciation for all capital assets.

Required:

a. Compute the payback period, net present value, and accrual accounting rate of return with initial investment, for each proposal. Use a required rate of return of 14%.

b. Rank each proposal 1, 2, and 3 using each method separately. Which proposal is best? Why?

80. **Answer:**

a. *Payback Method*

Payback for Proposal A:	Year 1	$80,000
	Year 2	10,000
Payback is 2 years		$90,000

Payback for Proposal B:	Year 1	$45,000
	Year 2	45,000
Payback is 2 years		$90,000

Payback for proposal C:	Year 1	$90,000
Payback is 1 year		

Net Present Value:

Proposal A:	Predicted Cash Flows	Year(s)	PV Factor	PV of Cash Flows
Investment	$(90,000)	0	1.000	$(90,000)
Annual operations:				
Year 1	80,000	1	0.877	70,160
Year 2	10,000	2	0.769	7,690
Year 3	45,000	3	0.675	30,375
Net present value				$ 18,225

Proposal B:	Predicted Cash Flows	Year(s)	PV Factor	PV of Cash Flows
Investment	$(90,000)	0	1.000	$(90,000)
Annual operations:				
Year 1	45,000	1	0.877	39,465
Year 2	45,000	2	0.769	34,605
Year 3	45,000	3	0.675	30,375
Net present value				$ 14,445

Proposal C:	Predicted Cash Flows	Year(s)	PV Factor	PV Of Cash Flows
Investment	$(90,000)	0	1.000	$(90,000)
Annual operations:				
Year 1	90,000	1	0.877	78,930
Net present value				$ 11,070

80. (continued)

Accrual Accounting Rate of Return:

Proposal A: $\dfrac{(80{,}000 + 10{,}000 + 45{,}000)/3 - (90{,}000/3)}{90{,}000} = 0.167$

Proposal B: $(45{,}000 - 30{,}000)/90{,}000 = 0.167$

Proposal C: $(90{,}000 - 90{,}000)/90{,}000 = 0.0$

b. ***Summary:***

Method	Proposal A	Proposal B	Proposal C
Payback method ranks	2.5	2.5	1.0
Net present value	1.0	2.0	3.0
AARR	1.5	1.5	3.0

Even though Proposal C is Number 1 for payback, it comes in last with the other two methods. Because the net present value method takes into account the time value of money and the other proposals are less comprehensive, Proposal A would be the best alternative.

Difficulty: 3   *Objectives*:   3, 5, 6

CRITICAL THINKING

81. Explain why a corporation's customer base is considered an intangible asset.

    Answer:

    A corporation's customer base is considered an intangible asset because if it is handled properly, a corporation's existing customers will be a source of revenues for an indefinite time period. One could make the case that the customer base is like an annuity -- a steady source of revenues and earnings. Thus it is an asset, although an intangible one.

    An existing customer usually will stay with your corporation if he or she is handled properly. Usually there is minimal marginal cost in retaining a customer other than producing a satisfactory product. In contrast, attracting new customers takes time, effort, and most times substantial marketing dollars. Thus, it is much easier to retain a current customer than to obtain a new one. This is why the existing customer base is considered an asset.

    Difficulty: 2   *Objective*:   1

82. Cast Iron Stove Company wants to buy a molding machine that can be integrated into its computerized manufacturing process. It has received three bids for the machine and related manufacturer's specifications. The bids range from $3,500,000 to $3,550,000. The estimated annual savings of the machines range from $260,000 to $270,000. The payback periods are almost identical and the net present values are all within $8,000 of each other. The president just doesn't know what to do about which vendor to choose since all of the selection criteria are so close together.

    Required:

    What suggestions do you have for the president?

    Answer:

    The president needs to consider nonfinancial and qualitative factors between the three vendors. Quality of output units, manufacturing flexibility, and cycle time are all additional factors that can be considered about the machines. Other items might include worker safety, ease of learning and using, and ease of maintenance.

    Difficulty: 2   *Objective*:   2

83. Retail Outlet is looking for a new location near a shopping mall. It is considering purchasing a building rather than leasing, as it has done in the past. Three retail buildings near a new mall are available but each has its own advantages and disadvantages. The owner of the company has completed an analysis of each location that includes considerations for the time value of money. The information is as follows:

	Location A	Location B	Location C
Internal rate of return	13%	17%	20%
Net present value	$25,000	$40,000	$20,000

The owner does not understand how the location with the highest percentage return has the lowest net present value.

Required:

Explain to the owner what is (are) the probable cause(s) of the comparable differences.

Answer:

The highest probability is that location C has a much lower initial investment than the other two. Therefore, it can show a higher rate of return with fewer dollars of inflow. Unfortunately, this may cause it to have the lowest net present value since this model is presented in dollar terms. Location C could also have a shorter life which could give it a higher percentage return during its life but fewer dollars overall.

Difficulty: 2   *Objective:* 3

84. Explain why the term tax shield is used in conjunction with depreciation.

Answer:

Depreciation tax deductions result in tax savings, which offset the cost of acquiring the capital equipment. The more rapid for tax purposes an asset's costs can be written off for tax purposes, the earlier the reductions in taxes can be realized. The term tax shield refers to the reduction in the tax payments owed. Thus the faster the depreciation, the earlier the reductions in taxes and the greater the net present value of the tax shield.

Difficulty: 2   *Objective:* 8

85. Bock Construction Company is considering four proposals for the construction of new loading facilities that will include the latest in ship loading/unloading equipment. After careful analysis, the company's accountant has developed the following information about the four proposals:

	Proposal 1	Proposal 2	Proposal 3	Proposal 4
Payback period	4 years	4.5 years	6 years	7 years
Net present value	$80,000	$178,000	$166,000	$308,000
Internal rate of return	12%	14%	11%	13%
Accrual accounting rate of return	8%	6%	4%	7%

Required:

How can this information be used in the decision-making process for the new loading facilities? Does it cause any confusion?

Answer:

The managers can use the information to determine which proposal is best under the various alternatives. This may be accomplished by ranking each alternative. Also, the managers must determine the factors that are the most important to the company. For example, if short-run risk is high, a short payback period may be highly desirable. In this case, Proposal 1 is best. However, if total cash returned is critical to the company's operations, then Proposal 4 is probably best.

Any time that multiple measures are used there may be confusion because very seldom will one proposal appear to be the best with all models. In this case, payback ranks Proposal 1 the best, NPV ranks Proposal 4 the best, IRR ranks Proposal 2 the best, and AARR ranks Proposal 1 the best. The importance of each ranking will depend upon the circumstances of the organization and the managers must be attuned as to what is most favorable.

The net present value and the internal rate-of-return methods are superior because they consider the time value of money.

Difficulty: 2   *Objectives:* 3-6

CHAPTER 22: MANAGEMENT CONTROL SYSTEMS, TRANSFER PRICING, AND MULTINATIONAL CONSIDERATIONS

TRUE/FALSE

1. The goal of a management control system is to improve the collective decisions in an organization in an economically feasible way.

    Answer: True   *Difficulty:* 1   *Objective:* 1

2. Management control systems reflect only financial data.

    Answer: False   *Difficulty:* 1   *Objective:* 1
    Management control systems also reflect nonfinancial data.

3. Information in a management control system report at the individual-facility level would include information on employee absenteeism.

    Answer: True   *Difficulty:* 1   *Objective:* 1

4. Presenting financial and nonfinancial information in a single report is called the unified reporting method.

    Answer: False   *Difficulty:* 1   *Objective:* 1
    This is called the balanced scorecard.

5. Motivation is the desire to attain a selected goal combined with the resulting drive or pursuit towards that goal.

    Answer: True   *Difficulty:* 1   *Objective:* 1

6. The essence of decentralization is the freedom for managers at lower levels of the organization to make decisions.

    Answer: True   *Difficulty:* 1   *Objective:* 1

7. Suboptimal decision making is also called congruent decision making.

    Answer: False   *Difficulty:* 2   *Objective:* 2
    It's also called incongruent decision making.

8. Surveys indicate that decisions made most frequently at the corporate level are related to sources of supplies and products to manufacture.

    Answer: False   *Difficulty:* 2   *Objective:* 2
    These decisions are made at a decentralized level.

9. An important advantage of decentralized operations is that it improves corporate control.

   Answer: False   *Difficulty:* 1   *Objective:* 2
   Decentralized operations weaken controls.

10. Products transferred between subunits within an organization are considered intermediate products.

    Answer: True   *Difficulty:* 1   *Objective:* 3

11. The costs used in cost-based transfer prices can only be actual costs.

    Answer: False   *Difficulty:* 2   *Objective:* 4
    The costs can also be budgeted costs.

12. The choice of a transfer-pricing method has minimal effect on the allocation of company-wide operating income among divisions.

    Answer: False   *Difficulty:* 2   *Objective:* 3
    The choice of a transfer-pricing method has a large effect.

13. No matter how low the transfer price, the manager of the selling division should sell the division's product to other company divisions in the interests of overall company profitability.

    Answer: False   *Difficulty:* 2   *Objective:* 3
    The manager of the selling division should maximize overall company profitability by selling the product at the highest possible price.

14. A major disadvantage of using budgeted costs for transfer prices is that often inefficiencies in actual costs are passed along to the receiving division.

    Answer: False   *Difficulty:* 2   *Objective:* 6
    When actual costs are used inefficiencies are passed along to the receiving division.

15. Dual pricing reduces the goal-congruence problem associated with a pure cost-based transfer-pricing method.

    Answer: True   *Difficulty:* 2   *Objective:* 6

16. The prices negotiated by two divisions of the same company usually have no specific relationship to either costs or market price.

    Answer: True   *Difficulty:* 2   *Objective:* 7

17. Opportunity costs represent the cash flows directly associated with the production and transfer of the products and services.

Answer: False   *Difficulty:* 2   *Objective:* 8

Opportunity costs are the maximum contribution forgone by the selling division if the products or services are transferred internally.

18. Market-based transfer prices are ideal in perfectly competitive markets when there is idle capacity in the selling division.

Answer: False   *Difficulty:* 2   *Objective:* 8

Market-based transfer prices are ideal when there is no idle capacity.

19. If the product sold between divisions has no intermediate market, the opportunity cost of supplying the product internally is the variable cost of the product.

Answer: False   *Difficulty:* 2   *Objective:* 8

The opportunity cost of supplying the product internally is zero.

20. Additional factors that arise in multinational transfer pricing include tariffs and customs duties levied on imports of products into a country.

Answer: True   *Difficulty:* 2   *Objective:* 9

21. Which of the following is NOT a characteristic of a management control system?
    a. It aids and coordinates the process of making decisions.
    b. It encourages short-term profitability.
    c. It motivates individuals throughout the organization to act in concert.
    d. It coordinates forecasting sales and cost-driver activities, budgeting, and measuring and evaluating performance.

    Answer: b   *Difficulty:* 2   *Objective:* 1

22. Stock price information would be an example of management control information at the
    a. total organization level.
    b. customer/market level.
    c. individual-facility level.
    d. individual-activity level.

    Answer: a   *Difficulty:* 1   *Objective:* 1

23. Cost of competitors' products information would be an example of management control information at the
    a. total organization level.
    b. customer/market level.
    c. individual-facility level.
    d. individual-activity level.

    Answer: b   *Difficulty:* 1   *Objective:* 1

24. Employee absenteeism information would be an example of management control information at the
    a. total organization level.
    b. customer/market level.
    c. individual-facility level.
    d. individual-activity level.

    Answer: c   *Difficulty:* 1   *Objective:* 1

25. Labor costs information would be an example of management control information at the
    a. total organization level.
    b. customer/market level.
    c. individual-facility level.
    d. individual-activity level.

    Answer: c   *Difficulty:* 2   *Objective:* 1

26. A report which contains both financial and nonfinancial management control information is referred to as the
    a.   total-organization report.
    b.   unified management information system report.
    c.   balanced scorecard.
    d.   none of the above.

    Answer: c   *Difficulty:*   1   *Objective:*   1

27. The formal management control system includes
    a.   performance measures.
    b.   mutual commitments.
    c.   incentive plans.
    d.   both (a) and (c).

    Answer: d   *Difficulty:*   1   *Objective:*   1

28. Exertion towards a goal is
    a.   motivation.
    b.   effort.
    c.   goal congruence.
    d.   incentive.

    Answer: b   *Difficulty:*   1   *Objective:*   1

29. The degree of freedom to make decisions is
    a.   decentralization.
    b.   autonomy.
    c.   centralization.
    d.   motivation.

    Answer: b   *Difficulty:*   1   *Objective:*   1

30. An advantage of decentralization is that it
    a.   creates greater responsiveness to local needs.
    b.   focuses manager's attention on the organization as a whole.
    c.   does not result in a duplication of activities.
    d.   reduces the cost of gathering information.

    Answer: a   *Difficulty:*   1   *Objective:*   2

31. A disadvantage of decentralization is that it
    a.   creates greater responsiveness to local needs.
    b.   focuses manager's attention on the organization as a whole.
    c.   does not result in a duplication of activities.
    d.   encourages suboptimal decision making

    Answer: d   *Difficulty:*   1   *Objective:*   2

32. All of the following are benefits of decentralization EXCEPT that
    a.   it creates greater responsiveness to local needs.
    b.   it decreases management and worker morale.
    c.   it leads to quicker decision making.
    d.   it sharpens the focus of managers.

    Answer: b   *Difficulty:*   2   *Objective:*   2

33. What is the term used to describe the situation when a manager's decision which benefits one subunit is more than offset by the costs to the organization as a whole?
    a.   Suboptimal decision making
    b.   Dysfunctional decision making
    c.   Congruent decision making
    d.   Both (a) and (b)

    Answer: d   *Difficulty:*   2   *Objective:*   2

34. Which of the following statements is FALSE?
    a.   A centralized structure does not empower employees to handle customer complaints directly.
    b.   A decentralized structure forces top management to lose some control over the organization.
    c.   Decentralization slows responsiveness to local needs for decision making.
    d.   The extent to which decisions are pushed downward and the types of decisions that are pushed down provide a measure of the level of centralization/decentralization in an organization.

    Answer: c   *Difficulty:*   2   *Objective:*   2

35. An area which is usually appropriate for decentralized decision making is
    a.   sources of supplies and materials.
    b.   long-term financing.
    c.   product advertising.
    d.   both (a) and (c).

    Answer: d   *Difficulty:*   2   *Objective:*   2

36. The benefits of a decentralized organization are greater when a company
    a.   is large and unregulated.
    b.   is facing great uncertainties in their environment.
    c.   has few interdependencies among division.
    d.   is all of the above.

    Answer: d   *Difficulty:*   1   *Objective:*   2

37. A product may be passed from one subunit to another subunit in the same organization. The product is known as
   a. an interdepartmental product.
   b. an intermediate product.
   c. a subunit product.
   d. a transfer product.

   Answer: b   *Difficulty:* 1   *Objective:* 3

38. Transfer prices should be judged by
   a. whether they promote goal congruence.
   b. whether they promote the balanced scorecard method.
   c. whether they promote a high level of subunit autonomy in decision making.
   d. both (a) and (c).

   Answer: d   *Difficulty:* 2   *Objective:* 3

39. A transfer-pricing method leads to goal congruence when
   a. managers always act in their own best interest.
   b. managers act in their own best interest and the decision is in the long-term best interest of the manager's subunit.
   c. managers act in their own best interest and the decision is in the long-term best interest of the company.
   d. managers act in their own best interest and the decision is in the short-term best interest of the company.

   Answer: c   *Difficulty:* 3   *Objective:* 3

40. Negotiated transfer prices are often employed when
   a. market prices are stable.
   b. market prices are volatile.
   c. market prices change by a regular percentage each year.
   d. goal congruence is not a major objective.

   Answer: b   *Difficulty:* 2   *Objective:* 4

THE FOLLOWING INFORMATION APPLIES TO QUESTIONS 41 THROUGH 43.
Dakoil Corporation has two divisions, Refining and Production. The company's primary product is Enkoil Oil. Each division's costs are provided below:

Production:	Variable costs per barrel of oil	$ 3
	Fixed costs per barrel of oil	$ 2
Refining:	Variable costs per barrel of oil	$10
	Fixed costs per barrel of oil	$12

The Refining Division has been operating at a capacity of 40,000 barrels a day and usually purchases 25,000 barrels of oil from the Production Division and 15,000 barrels from other suppliers at $20 per barrel.

41. What is the transfer price per barrel from the Production Division to the Refining Division, assuming the method used to place a value on each barrel of oil is 180% of variable costs?
    a. $5.40
    b. $9.00
    c. $18.00
    d. $23.40

Answer: a   *Difficulty*: 2   *Objective*: 4
1.8 x $3 = $5.40

42. What is the transfer price per barrel from the Production Division to the Refining Division, assuming the method used to place a value on each barrel of oil is 110% of full costs?
    a. $5.50
    b. $22.00
    c. $24.20
    d. $29.70

Answer: a   *Difficulty*: 2   *Objective*: 4
1.10 x ($3 + $2) = $5.50

43. Assume 200 barrels are transferred from the Production Division to the Refining Division for a transfer price of $6 per barrel. The Refining Division sells the 200 barrels at a price of $40 each to customers. What is the operating income of both divisions together?
    a. $2,400
    b. $2,600
    c. $3,600
    d. $6,800

Answer: b   *Difficulty*: 3   *Objective*: 4
Revenues = ($40 x 200)= $8,000
Cost = ($3 + $2 + $10 + $12) x 200 =   5,400
    Operating income $2,600

THE FOLLOWING INFORMATION APPLIES TO QUESTIONS 44 THROUGH 49.
Calculate the Division operating income for the BetaShoe Company which manufacturers only one type of shoe and has two divisions, the Sole Division, and the Assembly Division. The Sole Division manufactures soles for the Assembly Division, which completes the shoe and sells it to retailers. The Sole Division "sells" soles to the Assembly Division. The market price for the Assembly Division to purchase a pair of soles is $20. (Ignore changes in inventory.) The fixed costs for the Sole Division are assumed to be the same over the range of 40,000-100,000 units. The fixed costs for the Assembly Division are assumed to be $7 per pair at 100,000 units.

Sole's costs per pair of soles are:
Direct materials	$4
Direct labor	$3
Variable overhead	$2
Division fixed costs	$1

Assembly's costs per completed pair of shoes are:
Direct materials	$6
Direct labor	$2
Variable overhead	$1
Division fixed costs	$7

44. What is the market-based transfer price per pair of soles from the Sole Division to the Assembly Division?
     a. $10
     b. $16
     c. $20
     d. $26

     Answer: c   *Difficulty:*   2   *Objective:*   4
     $20 as given in the problem.

45. What is the transfer price per pair of soles from the Sole Division to the Assembly Division if the method used to place a value on each pair of soles is 180% of variable costs?
     a. $14.40
     b. $12.60
     c. $16.20
     d. $28.80

     Answer: c   *Difficulty:*   2   *Objective:*   4
     $9 x 1.8 = $16.20

46. What is the transfer price per pair of shoes from the Sole Division to the Assembly Division per pair of soles if the transfer price per pair of soles is 125% of full costs?
   a. $10
   b. $12.50
   c. $13
   d. $15

   Answer: b   *Difficulty:*   2   *Objective:*   4
   $10 x 1.25 = $12.50

47. Calculate and compare the difference in overall corporate net income between Scenario A and Scenario B if the Assembly Division sells 100,000 pairs of shoes for $60 per pair to customers.

   Scenario A: Negotiated transfer price of $15 per pair of soles
   Scenario B: Market-based transfer price

   a. $500,000 more net income under Scenario A
   b. $500,000 of net income using Scenario B
   c. $100,000 of net income using Scenario A.
   d. none of the above

   Answer: d   *Difficulty:*   3   *Objective:*   4
   The net income would be the same under both scenarios.

48. Assume the transfer price for a pair of soles is 180% of total costs of the Sole Division and 40,000 of soles are produced and transferred to the Assembly Division. The Sole Division's operating income is
   a. $320,000
   b. $360,000
   c. $400,000
   d. $440,000

   Answer: a   *Difficulty:*   3   *Objective:*   4
   Revenue ($18 x 40,000) = $720,000
   Costs ($10 x 40,000) =   400,000
   Operating income $320,000

49. If the Assembly Division sells 100,000 pairs of shoes at a price of $60 a pair to customers, what is the operating income of both divisions together?
   a. $4,400,000
   b. $3,400,000
   c. $3,000,000
   d. $2,600,000

   Answer: b   *Difficulty:*   3   *Objective:*   4
   Revenues = ($60x 100,000)= $6,000,000
   Cost = ($26 x 100,000)=   2,600,000
   Operating income = $3,400,000

THE FOLLOWING INFORMATION APPLIES TO QUESTIONS 50 AND 51.
Division A sells soybean paste internally to Division B, which in turn, produces soybean burgers that sell for $5 per pound. Division A incurs costs of $0.75 per pound while Division B incurs additional costs of $2.50 per pound.

50. What is Division A's operating income per pound, assuming the transfer price of the soybean paste is set at $1.25 per pound?
    a. $0.500
    b. $0.875
    c. $1.250
    d. $1.625

    Answer: a   *Difficulty:* 2   *Objective:* 4
    $1.25 - 0.75 = $0.50

51. Which of the following formulas correctly reflects the company's operating income?
    a. $5.00 - ($0.75 + $2.50) = $1.75
    b. $5.00 - ($1.25 + $2.50) = $1.25
    c. $5.00 - ($0.75 + $3.75) = $0.50
    d. $5.00 - ($0.25 + $1.25 + $3.50) = 0

    Answer: a   *Difficulty:* 2   *Objective:* 4
    $5.00- ($.75 + $2.50)= $1.75

52. Transferring products or services at market prices generally leads to optimal decisions when
    a. the market for the intermediate product is perfectly competitive.
    b. the interdependencies of the subunits are minimal.
    c. there are no additional costs or benefits to the company in buying or selling in the external market.
    d. all of the above are needed for optimal decisions.

    Answer: d   *Difficulty:* 2   *Objective:* 5

53. A benefit of using a market-based transfer price is
    a. the profits of the transferring division are sacrificed for the overall good of the corporation.
    b. the profits of the division receiving the products are sacrificed for the overall good of the corporation.
    c. the economic viability and profitability of each division can be evaluated individually.
    d. none of the above.

    Answer: c   *Difficulty:* 2   *Objective:* 5

54. Optimal corporate decisions do NOT result
    a. when goods or services are transferred at market prices.
    b. when goods or services are transferred at full-cost prices.
    c. when goods or services are transferred at variable-cost prices.
    d. for either (b) or (c).

    Answer: d   *Difficulty*: 2   *Objective*: 6

55. When an industry has excess capacity, market prices may drop well below their historical average. If this drop is temporary, it is called
    a. distress prices.
    b. dropped prices.
    c. low-average prices.
    d. substitute prices.

    Answer: a   *Difficulty*: 1   *Objective*: 5

56. Cost-based transfer prices are helpful
    a. when a market exists for the product.
    b. when a price is easy to obtain.
    c. when the product is unique.
    d. for all of the above.

    Answer: c   *Difficulty*: 2   *Objective*: 5

57. When companies do not want to use market prices or find it too costly, they typically use _____ prices, even though suboptimal decisions may occur.
    a. average-cost
    b. full-cost
    c. long-run cost
    d. short-run average cost

    Answer: b   *Difficulty*: 2   *Objective*: 6

58. Crush Company makes internal transfers at 180% of full cost. The Soda Refining Division purchases 30,000 containers of carbonated water per day, on average, from a local supplier, who delivers the water for $30 per container via an external shipper. In order to reduce costs, the company located an independent supplier in Missouri who is willing to sell 30,000 containers at $20 each, delivered to Crush Company's Shipping Division in Missouri. The company's Shipping Division in Missouri has excess capacity and can ship the 30,000 containers at a variable cost of $2.50 per container. What is the total cost to Crush Company if the carbonated water is purchased from the local supplier?
    a. $ 900,000
    b. $1,200,000
    c. $1,501,000
    d. $1,620,000

    Answer: a   *Difficulty*:   2   *Objective*:   6
    30,000 containers x $30 = $900,000

59. Crush Company makes internal transfers at 160% of full cost. The Soda Refining Division purchases 40,000 containers of carbonated water per day, on average, from a local supplier, who delivers the water for $40 per container via an external shipper. In order to reduce costs, the company located an independent supplier in Illinois who is willing to sell 40,000 containers at $30 each, delivered to Crush Company's Shipping Division in Missouri. The company's Shipping Division in Missouri has excess capacity and can ship the 40,000 containers at a variable cost of $4.50 per container. What is the total cost of purchasing the water from the Illinois supplier and shipping it to the Soda Division?
    a. $1,200,000
    b. $1,380,000
    c. $1,600,000
    d. $180,000

    Answer: b   *Difficulty*:   2   *Objective*:   6
    40,000 containers x ($4.50 + $30.00) = $1,380,000

60. An advantage of using budgeted costs for transfer pricing among divisions is
    a.   overall corporate profitability is usually higher.
    b.   it usually provides a basis for optimal decision making.
    c.   the divisions know the transfer price in advance.
    d.   it promotes subunit autonomy.

    Answer: c   *Difficulty*:   2   *Objective*:   6

61. In analyzing transfer prices,
    a. the buyer will not willingly purchase a product for less than the incremental costs incurred to manufacture the product internally.
    b. the seller will not willingly sell a product for less than the incremental costs incurred to make the product.
    c. the buyer will willingly pay more than the ceiling transfer price.
    d. the buyer will not pay less than the ceiling transfer price.

    Answer: b   *Difficulty:* 3   *Objective:* 8

62. The transfer-pricing method that reduces the goal-congruence problems associated with a pure cost-plus-based transfer-pricing method is
    a. dual pricing.
    b. market pricing.
    c. single pricing.
    d. both (a) and (b).

    Answer: a   *Difficulty:* 2   *Objective:* 6

63. Dual pricing is not widely used in practice because
    a. the manager of the supplying division does not have sufficient incentive to control costs.
    b. it increases goal congruence.
    c. managers are not insulated from the frictions of the market place.
    d. of both (b) and (c).

    Answer: a   *Difficulty:* 2   *Objective:* 6

64. An advantage of a negotiated transfer price is
    a. the close relationship between the negotiated price and the market price.
    b. the negotiated transfer price preserves divisional autonomy.
    c. the negotiations usually do not require much time and energy.
    d. both (b) and (c).

    Answer: b   *Difficulty:* 2   *Objective:* 7

65. Which of the following transfer-pricing methods always achieves goal congruence?
    a. A market-based transfer price
    b. A cost-based transfer price
    c. A negotiated transfer price
    d. Full-cost plus a standard profit margin

    Answer: c   *Difficulty:* 2   *Objective:* 8

66. Which of the different transfer-pricing methods preserves sub-unit autonomy?
   a.   Market-based transfer pricing
   b.   Cost-based transfer pricing
   c.   Negotiated transfer pricing
   d.   Both (a) and (c)

   Answer: d   *Difficulty:*   2   *Objective:*   8

67. The minimum transfer price equals
   a.   opportunity costs less the additional outlay costs.
   b.   opportunity costs times 125% plus the additional outlay costs.
   c.   opportunity costs divided by the additional outlay costs.
   d.   incremental costs plus opportunity costs.

   Answer: d   *Difficulty:*   1   *Objective:*   8

68. The seller of Product A has no idle capacity and can sell all it can produce at $20 per unit. Outlay cost is $4. What is the opportunity cost, assuming the seller sells internally?
   a. $4
   b. $16
   c. $20
   d. $24

   Answer: b   *Difficulty:*   2   *Objective:*   8
   $20 - $4 = $16

69. Section 482 of the U.S. Internal Revenue Code governing the taxation of multinational transfer pricing recognizes that transfer prices can be
   a.   market based.
   b.   negotiated.
   c.   cost-plus based.
   d.   both (a) and (c).

   Answer: d   *Difficulty:*   1   *Objective:*   9

70. Soft Cushion Company is highly decentralized. Each division is empowered to make its own sales decisions. The Assembly Division can purchase stuffing, a key component, from the Production Division or from external suppliers. The Production Division has been the major supplier of stuffing in recent years. The Assembly Division has announced that two external suppliers will be used to purchase the stuffing at $20 per pound for the next year. The Production Division recently increased its unit price to $40. The manager of the Production Division presented the following information -- variable cost $32 and fixed cost $8 -- to top management in order to attempt to force the Assembly Division to purchase the stuffing internally. The Assembly Division purchases 20,000 pounds of stuffing per month.

What would be the monthly operating advantage (disadvantage) of purchasing the goods internally, assuming the external supplier increased its price to $50 per pound and the Production Division is able to utilize the facilities for other operations, resulting in a monthly cash-operating savings of $30 per pound?
   a. $1,000,000
   b. $360,000
   c. $(240,000)
   d. $(400,000)

Answer: c   *Difficulty*:   2   *Objective*:   9
Purchase cost: (20,000 lbs. x $50) $1,000,000
Outlay cost: (20,000 lbs. x $32)   (640,000)
Opportunity cost: (20,000 lbs. x $30)   (600,000)
      Advantage/(Disadvantage) $ (240,000)

EXERCISES AND PROBLEMS

71. Your textbook reports that the General Electric Company 's management control system gathers and reports information for management control at various levels. For each of the following levels list examples of the information needed:
   a. Total-organization level
   b. Customer/market level
   c. Individual-facility level
   d. Individual-activity level

   Answer: (The following is a partial list)

   a. *Total-organization level* Stock price, net income, return on investment, cash flow from operations, total employment, pollution control.
   b. *Customer/market level* Customer satisfaction, time taken to respond to customer requests for products, and cost of competitor's products.
   c. *Individual-facility level* Materials costs, labor costs, absenteeism, and accidents in various divisions or business functions.
   d. *Individual-activity level* The time taken and the costs incurred for receiving, storing, assembling, and dispatching goods in a warehouse; scrap rates, defects, and units reworked on a manufacturing line; and the number of sales transactions and revenue dollars per salesperson.

   Difficulty: 1   *Objective:* 1

72. For each of the following activities, characteristics, and applications, identify whether they can be found in a centralized organization, a decentralized organization, or both types of organizations.

   _____ a. Freedom for managers at lower organizational levels to make decisions
   _____ b. Gathering information may be very expensive
   _____ c. Greater responsiveness to user needs
   _____ d. Have few interdependencies among divisions
   _____ e. Maximum constraints and minimum freedom for managers at lowest levels
   _____ f. Maximization of benefits over costs
   _____ g. Minimization of duplicate functions
   _____ h. Minimum of suboptimization
   _____ i. Multiple responsibility centers with various reporting units
   _____ j. Profit centers

72. **Answer:**

    a.   Decentralization
    b.   Decentralization
    c.   Decentralization
    d.   Decentralization
    e.   Centralization
    f.   Both
    g.   Centralization
    h.   Centralization
    i.   Both
    j.   Both

Difficulty: 2   *Objective:* 2

73. For each of the following, identify whether it BEST relates to market-based, cost-based, negotiated, or all types of transfer pricing.

   _____   a.   Bargaining between selling and buying units
   _____   b.   Budgeted costs
   _____   c.   145% of full costs
   _____   d.   Internal product transfers are required if goods are available internally
   _____   e.   Manufacturing costs plus marketing costs plus distribution costs plus customer service costs
   _____   f.   Prices listed in a trade journal
   _____   g.   Selling price less normal sales commissions
   _____   h.   Variable manufacturing cost plus a markup

Answer:

    a.   Negotiated
    b.   Cost-based
    c.   Cost-based
    d.   Any method
    e.   Cost-based
    f.   Market-based
    g.   Market-based
    h.   Cost-based

Difficulty: 2   *Objective:* 4

74. The Mill Flow Company has two divisions. The Cutting Division prepares timber at its sawmills. The Assembly Division prepares the cut lumber into finished wood for the furniture industry. No inventories exist in either division at the beginning of 20x3. During the year, the Cutting Division prepared 60,000 cords of wood at a cost of $660,000. All the lumber was transferred to the Assembly Division, where additional operating costs of $6 per cord were incurred. The 600,000 boardfeet of finished wood were sold for $2,500,000.

Required:

a. Determine the operating income for each division if the transfer price from Cutting to Assembly is at cost, $11 a cord.

b. Determine the operating income for each division if the transfer price is $9 per cord.

c. Since the Cutting Division sells all of its wood internally to the Assembly Division, does the manager care what price is selected? Why? Should the Cutting Division be a cost center or a profit center under the circumstances?

Answer:

a.

	Cutting	Assembly
Revenue	$660,000*	$2,500,000
Cost of services:		
Incurred	$ 660,000	$ 360,000
Transferred-in	0	660,000
Total	$ 660,000	$1,020,000
Operating income	$ 0	$1,480,000

* 60,000 cords x $11 = $660,000

b.

	Cutting	Assembly
Revenue	$540,000*	$2,500,000
Cost of service		
Incurred	$ 660,000	$ 360,000
Transferred-in	0	540,000
Total	$ 660,000	$ 900,000
Operating income	$(120,000)	$1,600,000

* 60,000 cords x $9 = $540,000

74.	(continued)

c.	The manager of Cutting cares about the transfer price if the division is a profit center but not if it is a cost center. Under the circumstances, the division probably should be a cost center and not worry about the profit it pretends to make by selling to another division.

Difficulty:	2	*Objective:*	4

75.	Bedtime Bedding Company manufactures pillows. The Cover Division makes covers and the Assembly Division makes the finished products. The covers can be sold separately for $5.00. The pillows sell for $6.00. The information related to manufacturing for the most recent year is as follows:

Cover Division manufacturing costs	$6,000,000
Sales of covers by Cover Division	4,000,000
Market value of covers transferred to Assembly	6,000,000
Sales of pillows by Assembly Division	7,200,000
Additional manufacturing costs of Assembly Division	1,500,000

Required:

Compute the operating income for each division and the company as a whole. Use market value as the transfer price. Are all managers happy with this concept? Explain.

Answer:

	Cover	**Assembly**	**Company**
Revenue:			
External	$ 4,000,000	$7,200,000	$11,200,000
Internal	6,000,000	0	0
Total	$10,000,000	$7,200,000	$11,200,000
Cost of goods:			
Incurred	$ 6,000,000	$1,500,000	$ 7,500,000
Transferred-in	0	6,000,000	0
Total	$ 6,000,000	$7,500,000	$ 7,500,000
Operating income	$ 4,000,000	$ (300,000)	$ 3,700,000

The Assembly manager is probably not happy because the division is showing a loss. The manager would probably argue for a transfer price at something less than market price. However, since the market is open and competitive, the market price can be justified. The division needs to either increase its price or reduce its costs if it expects to show a profit.

Difficulty:	3	*Objective:*	4

76. DesMoines Valley Company has two divisions, Computer Services and Management Advisory Services. In addition to their external customers, each division performs work for the other division. The external fees earned by each division in 20x3 were $200,000 for Computer Services and $350,000 for Management Advisory Services. Computer Services worked 3,000 hours for Management Advisory Services, who, in turn, worked 1,200 hours for Computer Services. The total costs of external services performed by Computer Services were $110,000 and $240,000 by Management Advisory Services.

Required:

a. Determine the operating income for each division and for the company as a whole if the transfer price from Computer Services to Management Advisory Services is $15 per hour and the transfer price from Management Advisory Services to Computer Services is $12.50 per hour.

b. Determine the operating income for each division and for the company as a whole if the transfer price between divisions is $15 per hour.

c. What are the operating income results for each division and for the company as a whole if the two divisions net the hours worked for each other and charge $12.50 per hour for the one with the excess? Which division manager prefers this arrangement?

Answer:

a.

	Computer	Management	Company
Revenue:			
External	$200,000	$350,000	$550,000
Internal*	45,000	15,000	0
Total	$245,000	$365,000	$550,000
Cost of services:			
Incurred	$110,000	$240,000	$350,000
Transferred-in	15,000	45,000	0
Total	$125,000	$285,000	$350,000
Operating income	$120,000	$ 80,000	$200,000

* Computer Services = 3,000 hours x $15 = $45,000
Management Advisory Services = 1,200 hours x $12.50 = $15,000
Revenue for one is an expense of the other.

76. (continued)

b.

	Computer	Management	Company
Revenue:			
External	$200,000	$350,000	$550,000
Internal*	45,000	18,000	0
Total	$245,000	$368,000	$550,000
Cost of services:			
Incurred	$110,000	$240,000	$350,000
Transferred-in	18,000	45,000	0
Total	$128,000	$285,000	$350,000
Operating income	$117,000	$ 83,000	$200,000

* Computer Services = 3,000 hours x $15 = $45,000
Management Advisory Services = 1,200 hours x $15 = $18,000
Revenue for one is an expense of the other.

c.

	Computer	Management	Company
Revenue:			
External	$200,000	$350,000	$550,000
Internal*	22,500	0	0
Total	$222,500	$350,000	$550,000
Cost of services:			
Incurred	$110,000	$240,000	$350,000
Transferred-in	0	22,500	0
Total	$110,000	$262,500	$350,000
Operating income	$112,500	$ 87,500	$200,000

* Computer Services net = (3,000 - 1,200) x $12.50 = $22,500
Revenue for one is an expense of the other.

The manager of Computer Services favors this procedure for the current year. If the hours are always in favor of Computer Services, the manager of Computer Services will favor this procedure.

Difficulty: 2   *Objective*: 4

77. Better Food Company recently acquired an olive oil processing company that has an annual capacity of 2,000,000 liters and that processed and sold 1,400,000 liters last year at a market price of $4 per liter. The purpose of the acquisition was to furnish oil for the Cooking Division. The Cooking Division needs 800,000 liters of oil per year. It has been purchasing oil from suppliers at the market price. Production costs at capacity of the olive oil company, now a division, are as follows:

Direct materials per liter	$1.00
Direct processing labor	0.50
Variable processing overhead	0.24
Fixed processing overhead	0.40
Total	$2.14

Management is trying to decide what transfer price to use for sales from the newly acquired company to the Cooking Division. The manager of the Olive Oil Division argues that $4, the market price, is appropriate. The manager of the Cooking Division argues that the cost of $2.14 should be used, or perhaps a lower price, since fixed overhead cost should be recomputed with the larger volume. Any output of the Olive Oil Division not sold to the Cooking Division can be sold to outsiders for $4 per liter.

Required:

a. Compute the operating income for the Olive Oil Division using a transfer price of $4.

b. Compute the operating income for the Olive Oil Division using a transfer price of $2.14.

c. What transfer price(s) do you recommend? Compute the operating income for the Olive Oil Division using your recommendation.

Answer:

a.

Sales:		
External (1,200,000 x $4)	$4,800,000	
Internal (800,000 x $4)	3,200,000	$8,000,000
Cost of goods sold:		
Variable (2,000,000 x $1.74)	$3,480,000	
Fixed (2,000,000 x $0.40)	800,000	4,280,000
Operating income		$3,720,000

77. (continued)

b.

Sales:		
External (1,200,000 x $4)	$4,800,000	
Internal (800,000 x $2.14)	1,712,000	$6,512,000
Cost of goods sold:		
Variable (2,000,000 x $1.74)	$3,480,000	
Fixed (2,000,000 x $0.40)	800,000	4,280,000
Operating income		$2,232,000

c. Due to current demand in excess of the capacity, the Olive Oil Division should not be penalized by having to sell inside. All sales equivalent to the current external demand of 1,400,000 should be at the market price.

Current external demand	1,400,000
Current internal demand	800,000
Total demand	2,200,000
Capacity	2,000,000
Excess demand	200,000
Internal demand	800,000
Noncompetitive internal demand	600,000

Sales:		
External (1,200,000 x $4)	$4,800,000	
Internal (200,000 x $4)	800,000	
Internal (600,000 x $2.14)	1,284,000	$6,884,000
Cost of goods sold:		
Variable (2,000,000 x $1.74)	$3,480,000	
Fixed (2,000,000 x $0.40)	800,000	4,280,000
Operating income		$2,604,000

Difficulty: 3   *Objective*:   4

78. Sportswear Company manufactures socks. The Athletic Division sells its socks for $6 a pair to outsiders. Socks have manufacturing costs of $2.50 each for variable and $1.50 for fixed. The division's total fixed manufacturing costs are $105,000 at the normal volume of 70,000 units.

The European Division has offered to buy 15,000 socks at the full cost of $4. The Athletic Division has excess capacity and the 15,000 units can be produced without interfering with the current outside sales of 70,000. The 85,000 volume is within the division's relevant operating range.

Explain whether the Athletic Division should accept the offer.

Answer:

Sales	$4.00
Variable costs	2.50
Contribution margin	$1.50

The proposal should be accepted because it makes a contribution to fixed costs and profits of $1.50 per unit. This would increase the division's operating income by $22,500 ($1.50 x 15,000 units).

Difficulty: 2   *Objective*:   6

79. Copperstone Company has two divisions. The Bottle Division produces products that have variable costs of $3 per unit. Its 20x3 sales were 150,000 to outsiders at $5 per unit and 40,000 units to the Mixing Division at 140% of variable costs. Under a dual transfer-pricing system, the Mixing Division pays only the variable cost per unit. The fixed costs of the Bottle Division are $125,000 per year.

Mixing sells its finished products to outside customers for $11.50 per unit. Mixing has variable costs of $2.50 per unit in addition to the costs from the Bottle Division. The annual fixed costs of Mixing were $85,000. There were no beginning or ending inventories during the year.

Required:

What are the operating incomes of the two divisions and the company as a whole for the year? Explain why the company's operating income is less than the sum of the two divisions' total income.

Answer:

	Bottle	**Mixing**	**Company**
Revenue:			
External	$750,000	$460,000	$1,210,000
Internal*	168,000	0	0
Total	$918,000	$460,000	$1,210,000
Variable costs:			
Incurred	$570,000	$100,000	$670,000
Transferred-in	0	120,000	0
Total	$570,000	$220,000	$670,000
Contribution margin	$348,000	$240,000	$540,000
Fixed Costs	125,000	85,000	210,000
Operating income	$223,000	$155,000	$330,000

* 40,000 x $3 x 1.40 = $168,000

The internal sales are not included in the company's statement because the company cannot sell to itself. Therefore, it has to exclude $48,000 of dual pricing.

Difficulty: 2   *Objective:* 6

80. The Home Office Company makes all types of office desks. The Computer Desk Division is currently producing 10,000 desks per year with a capacity of 15,000. The variable costs assigned to each desk are $300 and annual fixed costs of the division are $900,000. The computer desk sells for $400.

The Executive Division wants to buy 5,000 desks at $280 for its custom office design business. The Computer Desk manager refused the order because the price is below variable cost. The executive manager argues that the order should be accepted because it will lower the fixed cost per desk from $90 to $60 and will take the division to its capacity, thereby causing operations to be at their most efficient level.

Required:

a. Should the order from the Executive Division be accepted by the Computer Desk Division? Why?

b. From the perspective of the Computer Desk Division and the company, should the order be accepted if the Executive Division plans on selling the desks in the outside market for $420 after incurring additional costs of $100 per desk?

c. What action should the company president take?

Answer:

a.

Sales	$280
Variable costs	300
Contribution margin	$(20)

The manager should not accept the order because it is below variable costs. It will generate a loss of $100,000 [5,000 units x $(20)]. This is a losing proposition in both the short run and long run.

b. What the Executive Division does with the desks after receiving them is of no consequence to the Computer Desk Division. However, the division will still object to the transfer price of $280. The company, on the other hand, will encourage the offer because it increases total company operating income by $100,000 = 5,000 x [$420 - ($300 + $100)].

c. If the company president wants the Executive Division to have the new business, it should arrange a dual-pricing system or else have negotiated prices between divisions. Dual pricing would allow the selling division to get a market value for the transfer and the buying division to get some type of cost-plus transfer price. The negotiated price would allow the buying and selling divisions to feel like they had a part in the final pricing decision.

Difficulty: 3   *Objectives:* 6, 7

81. The president of Silicon Company has just returned from a week of professional development courses and is very excited that she will not have to change the organization from a centralized structure to a decentralized structure just to have responsibility centers. However, she is somewhat confused about how responsibility centers relate to centralized organizations where a few managers have most of the authority.

   Required:

   Explain how a centralized organization might allow for responsibility centers.

   Answer:

   It does not make any difference what type of organizational structure exists when it comes to defining responsibility centers. If a centralized organization desires to hold its managers responsible for their actions, it can design a reporting system that assigns all costs and revenues to their controllable managers. It's just that, in a centralized organization, each manager may have more items to control than are reasonably possible.

   Difficulty: 2   *Objective*: 2

82. Discuss the possible problems a corporation might have if its operations are totally decentralized.

   Answer: (Answers may vary)

   Senior management has the ultimate responsibility for the business. In a totally decentralized operation, senior executive management has little say about the conduct of the business. Another problem could be caused by the appointment of managers who are not capable of running their business. The lack of senior management control might result in problems developing and resulting in even bigger problems before anyone was aware of the incompetent managers.

   Certain types of activities belong centralized such as gathering information and certain human resource functions.

   Difficulty: 2   *Objective*: 1

83. If a company has a plant in a high tax jurisdiction that produces products for a facility in a low tax jurisdiction - suggest a strategy that will result in the lowest tax for the overall corporation.

Answer:

The overall corporate objective would be to report high costs and low revenue in the high tax jurisdiction, and low costs and high revenue in the low tax jurisdiction.

Difficulty: 1   *Objective*:   9

84. The Micro Division of Silicon Computers produces computer chips that are sold to the Personal Computer Division and to outsiders. Operating data for the Micro Division for 20x3 are as follows:

	Internal Sales	External Sales
Sales:		
300,000 chips at $10	$3,000,000	
200,000 chips at $12		$2,400,000
Variable expenses at $4	1,200,000	800,000
Contribution margin	$1,800,000	$1,600,000
Fixed cost (allocated in units)	1,500,000	1,000,000
Operating income	$ 300,000	$ 600,000

The Personal Computer Division has just received an offer from an outside supplier to furnish chips at $8.60 each. The manager of Micro Division is not willing to meet the $8.60 price. She argues that it costs her $9.00 to produce and sell each chip. Sales to outside customers are at a maximum of 200,000 chips.

Required:

a.   Verify the Micro Division's $9.00 unit cost figure.

b.   Should the Micro Division meet the outside price of $8.60? Explain.

c.   Could the $8.60 price be met and still show a profit for the Micro Division sales to the Personal Computer Division? Show computations.

84. **Answer**:

a.

Variable costs	$4.00
Fixed costs [($1,500,000 + $1,000,000)/500,000 units]	5.00
Total unit costs	$9.00

b. Yes, because the contribution margin is positive ($8.60 - $4.00 = $4.60). If it loses the internal business, the other sales would have to absorb the fixed costs, which would force even higher external prices. The Micro Division manager does not have much bargaining power since the external sales are already at a maximum.

c.

Sales (300,000 x $8.60)	$2,580,000
Variable costs (300,000 x $4)	1,200,000
Contribution margin	$1,380,000
Fixed costs (300,000 x $5.00)	1,500,000
Operating income	$ (120,000)

Internal sales will not show a profit. This assumes the fixed costs are still allocated at $5.00 per unit.

Difficulty: 2 *Objective*: 7

85. The Assembly Division of American Car Company has offered to purchase 90,000 batteries from the Electrical Division for $104 per unit. At a normal volume of 250,000 batteries per year, production costs per battery are as follows:

Direct materials	$ 40
Direct manufacturing labor	20
Variable factory overhead	12
Fixed factory overhead	40
Total	$112

The Electrical Division has been selling 250,000 batteries per year to outside buyers at $136 each; capacity is 350,000 batteries per year. The Assembly Division has been buying batteries from outside sources for $130 each.

Required:

a. Should the Electrical Division manager accept the offer? Explain.

b. From the company's perspective, will the internal sales be of any benefit? Explain.

Answer:

a. Variable cost per battery = $40 + $20 + $12 = $72

Sales to Assembly	$104
Variable costs	72
Contribution margin	$ 32

Because the Electrical Division is not at capacity, it should sell to the Assembly Division up to 100,000 units at $104. This will add $2,880,000 (90,000 x $32) at the current level to its operating income without reducing its outside sales.

b. The internal sales would be beneficial to the company because the internal variable manufacturing costs of $72 per battery are less than the external price of $130 currently being paid by the Assembly Division. The company would be saving $5,220,000 [90,000 x ($130 - $72)] per year.

Difficulty: 3   *Objective*:   8

CHAPTER 23: PERFORMANCE MEASUREMENT, COMPENSATION, AND MULTINATIONAL CONSIDERATIONS

TRUE/FALSE

1. Many common performance measures, such as customer satisfaction, rely on internal financial accounting information.

   Answer: False   *Difficulty:* 1   *Objective:* 1
   Customer satisfaction would be obtained by surveys that are not in the financial accounting records.

2. Some companies present financial and nonfinancial performance measures for various organization units in a single report called the " balanced scorecard."

   Answer: True   *Difficulty:* 1   *Objective:* 1

3. A major weakness of comparing two companies using only operating incomes as the basis of comparison is this method ignores differences in the size of the investment required to earn the operating income.

   Answer: True   *Difficulty:* 1   *Objective:* 2

4. Return on investment is also called the accrual accounting rate of return.

   Answer: True   *Difficulty:* 1   *Objective:* 3

5. Investment turnover is calculated by dividing investments by revenues.

   Answer: False   *Difficulty:* 1   *Objective:* 3
   Investment turnover is calculated by dividing revenues by investments.

6. The three alternatives for increasing return on investment include increasing assets such as receivables, increasing revenues, and decreasing costs. (In all cases assume that all other items stay the same.)

   Answer: False   *Difficulty:* 2   *Objective:* 3
   Increasing receivables does not increase return on investment.

7. Imputed costs are costs recognized in particular situations that are not usually recognized by accrual accounting procedures.

   Answer: True   *Difficulty:* 2   *Objective:* 4

8. The objective of maximizing return on investment may induce managers of highly profitable divisions to reject projects that from the viewpoint of the overall organization should be accepted.

    Answer: True   *Difficulty*: 2   *Objective*: 4

9. Goal congruence is more likely to be promoted by using return on investment rather than residual income as a measure of a subunit's managerial performance.

    Answer: False   *Difficulty*: 2   *Objective*: 4
    Goal congruence is more likely to be promoted by using residual income rather than return on investment.

10. Economic value added, unlike residual income, charges managers for the costs of their investments in long-term assets and working capital.

    Answer: False   *Difficulty*: 2   *Objective*: 5
    Both economic value added and residual income charge managers for the costs of their investments in long-term capital.

11. To evaluate overall aggregate performance, return on investment and residual income measures are more appropriate than return on sales.

    Answer: True   *Difficulty*: 2   *Objective*: 5
    Return on investment and residual income are better measures of overall aggregate performance because they both consider income earned and investments made.

12. Companies that adopt economic value added define investment as total assets employed minus current liabilities.

    Answer: False   *Difficulty*: 2   *Objective*: 5

13. Current cost return on investment is a better measure of the current economic returns from an investment than historical cost return on investment.

    Answer: True   *Difficulty*: 2   *Objective*: 6

14. Comparing the performance of divisions of a multinational company operating in different countries is difficult due to the differences in economic, legal, political, social, and cultural environments.

    Answer: True   *Difficulty*: 1   *Objective*: 7

15. One way to achieve greater comparability of historical cost-based ROIs for a company's foreign division is to restate performance in dollars.

    Answer: True   *Difficulty*: 2   *Objective*: 7

16. An important consideration in designing compensation arrangements is the tradeoff between creating incentives and imposing risks.

   Answer: True   *Difficulty*:   1   *Objective*:   8

17. Moral hazard describes contexts in which an employee prefers to exert less effort than the effort that the owner wants because the employee's effort cannot be accurately monitored and enforced.

   Answer: True   *Difficulty*:   1   *Objective*:   8

18. Another term for benchmarking is a relative performance evaluation.

   Answer: True   *Difficulty*:   1   *Objective*:   9

19. Evaluating an executive's performance using the annual return on investment would sharpen an executive's long-run focus.

   Answer: False   *Difficulty*:   2   *Objective*:   9
   Using return on investment is a short-run tool.

20. Examples of "cooking the books" are understated assets and overstated liabilities.

   Answer: False   *Difficulty*:   1   *Objective*:   9
   Cooking the books is *overstating* assets and *understating* liabilities.

MULTIPLE CHOICE

21. A report that measures financial and nonfinancial performance measures for various organization units in a single report is called a(n)
    a. balanced scorecard.
    b. financial report scorecard.
    c. imbalanced scorecard.
    d. unbalanced scorecard.

    Answer: a   *Difficulty:* 1   *Objective:* 1

22. Customer-satisfaction measures are an example of
    a. goal-congruence approach.
    b. balanced scorecard approach.
    c. financial report scorecard approach.
    d. investment success approach.

    Answer: b   *Difficulty:* 1   *Objective:* 1

23. An example of a performance measure with a long-run time horizon
    a. is direct materials efficiency variances.
    b. is overhead spending variances.
    c. is number of new patents developed.
    d. include all of the above measures.

    Answer: c   *Difficulty:* 2   *Objective:* 1

24. Does operating income best measure a subunit's financial performance? This question is considered part of which step in designing an accounting-based performance measure?
    a. Choose performance measures that align with top management's financial goals.
    b. Choose the time horizon of each performance measure.
    c. Choose a definition for each performance measure.
    d. Choose a measurement alternative for each performance measure.

    Answer: a   *Difficulty:* 2   *Objective:* 2

25. Should assets be defined as total assets or net assets? This question is considered part of which step in designing an accounting-based performance measure?
    a. Choose performance measures that align with top management's financial goals.
    b. Choose the time horizon of each performance measure.
    c. Choose a definition for each performance measure.
    d. Choose a measurement alternative for each performance measure.

    Answer: c   *Difficulty:* 2   *Objective:* 2

26. Should assets be measured at historical cost or current cost? This question is considered part of which step in designing an accounting-based performance measure?
    a. Choose performance measures that align with top management's financial goals
    b. Choose the time horizon of each performance measure
    c. Choose a definition for each performance measure
    d. Choose a measurement alternative for each performance measure

    Answer: d   *Difficulty:* 2   *Objective:* 2

27. Which of the following statements about designing an accounting-based performance measure is FALSE?
    a. The steps may be followed in a random order.
    b. The issues considered in each step are independent.
    c. Management's beliefs are present during the analyses.
    d. Behavioral criteria are important when evaluating the steps.

    Answer: b   *Difficulty:* 2   *Objective:* 2

28. Managers usually use the term return on investment to evaluate
    a. the performance of a subdivision.
    b. a potential project.
    c. the performance of a subunit.
    d. both (a) and (c).

    Answer: d   *Difficulty:* 2   *Objective:* 3

29. The return on investment is usually considered the most popular approach to incorporating the investment base into a performance measure because
    a. it blends all the ingredients of profitability into a single percentage.
    b. once determined, there is no need to use it with other measures of performance.
    c. it is similar to the company's price earnings ratio in that a corporation's return on investment appears every day in *The Wall Street Journal*.
    d. of both (a) and (c).

    Answer: a   *Difficulty:* 2   *Objective:* 3

30. Return on investment can be increased by
    a. increasing operating assets.
    b. decreasing operating assets.
    c. decreasing revenues.
    d. both (b) and (c).

    Answer: b   *Difficulty:* 2   *Objective:* 3

31. During the past twelve months, the Aaron Corporation had a net income of $50,000. What is the amount of the investment if the return on investment is 20%?
    a. $100,000
    b. $200,000
    c. $250,000
    d. $500,000

    Answer: c   *Difficulty:* 2   *Objective:* 3
    0.20 = $50,000/x;   x = $250,000

32. During the past twelve months, the Zenith Corporation had a net income of $39,200. What is the return on investment if the amount of the investment is $280,000?
    a. 10%
    b. 12%
    c. 14%
    d. 16%

    Answer: c   *Difficulty:* 1   *Objective:* 3
    $39,200/$280,000 = 14%

33. The Alpha Beta Corporation had the following information for 20x3:
Revenue	$ 900,000
Operating expenses	670,000
Total assets	1,150,000

    What is the return on investment?
    a. 10%
    b. 20%
    c. 25%
    d. 78.2%

    Answer: b   *Difficulty:* 2   *Objective:* 3
    $230,000/$1,150,000 = 20%

34. Wacker Company has two regional offices. The data for each is as follows:
	Maryland	New York
Revenues	$ 580,000	$ 596,000
Operating assets	4,800,000	9,000,000
Net operating income	2,016,000	2,400,000

    What is the Maryland Division's return on investment?
    a. 0.42
    b. 0.54.
    c. 0.96.
    d. 4.12.

    Answer: a   *Difficulty:* 1   *Objective:* 3
    $2,016/$4,800 = 0.42%

35. Thacker Company has two regional offices. The data for each is as follows:

	Maryland	New York
Revenues	$ 580,000	$ 596,000
Operating assets	4,800,000	9,000,000
Net operating income	2,016,000	4,860,000

What is the return on investment for the New York Division?
a. 0.42.
b. 0.54
c. 0.96
d. 4.12

Answer: b   *Difficulty:* 1   *Objective:* 3
$4,860/$9,0000= 54%

THE FOLLOWING INFORMATION APPLIES TO QUESTIONS 36 THROUGH 38.
The Cybertronics Corporation reported the following information for its Cyclotron Division:

Revenues	$1,000,000
Operating costs	600,000
Taxable income	200,000
Operating assets	500,000

Income is defined as operating income.

36. What is the Cyclotron Division's investment turnover ratio?
a. 2.00
b. 3.33
c. 2.50
d. 0.80

Answer: a   *Difficulty:* 2   *Objective:* 3
$1,000,000/$500,000 = 2

37. What is the Cyclotron Division's return on sales?
a. 0.2
b. 0.4
c. 0.5
d. 0.6

Answer: b   *Difficulty:* 2   *Objective:* 3
$1,000,000 - $600,000 = $400,000; $400,000/$1,000,000 = 0.40

38. What is the Cyclotron Division's return on investment?
a. 0.2
b. 0.4
c. 0.5
d. 0.8

Answer: d   *Difficulty:* 2   *Objective:* 3
$400,000 / $500,000 = 0.8

THE FOLLOWING INFORMATION APPLIES TO QUESTIONS 39 THROUGH 43.
The top management at Munchie Company, a manufacturer of computer games, is attempting to recover from a flood that destroyed some of their accounting records. The main computer system was also severely damaged. The following information was salvaged:

	Alpha Division	Beta Division	Gamma Division
Sales	$2,500,000	(a)	$1,150,000
Net operating income	$1,500,000	$650,000	$ 575,000
Operating assets	(b)	(c)	$ 766,667
Return on investment	0.25	0.15	(d)
Return on sales	(e)	0.10	0.5
Investment turnover	(f)	(g)	1.5

39. What were the sales for the Beta Division?
    a. $4,333,333
    b. $5,952,380
    c. $6,500,000
    d. $7,151,800

    Answer: c   *Difficulty:* 2   *Objective:* 3
    0.10 = $650,000/x;   x = $6,500,000

40. What is the value of the operating assets belonging to the Alpha Division?
    a. $4,333,333
    b. $6,000,000
    c. $6,500,000
    d. $7,151,800

    Answer: b   *Difficulty:* 2   *Objective:* 3
    $1,500,000/0.25 = $6,000,000

41. What is the value of the operating assets belonging to the Beta Division?
    a. $4,333,333
    b. $5,952,380
    c. $6,500,000
    d. $7,151,800

    Answer: a   *Difficulty:* 2   *Objective:* 3
    1.5 = $6,500,000/x;   x = $4,333,333

42. What is the Gamma Division's return on investment?
    a. 0.25
    b. 0.42
    c. 0.60
    d. 0.75

    Answer: d   *Difficulty:* 2   *Objective:* 3
    0.5 x 1.5 = 0.75

43. What is the Alpha Division's return on sales?
    a. 0.25
    b. 0.42
    c. 0.60
    d. 0.75

    Answer: c   *Difficulty:* 2   *Objective:* 3
    $1,500,000/$2,500,000 = 0.60

44. Costs recognized in particular situations that are not recognized by accrual accounting procedures are
    a. opportunity costs.
    b. imputed costs.
    c. cash accounting costs.
    d. none of the above.

    Answer: b   *Difficulty:* 1   *Objective:* 4

45. A problem with utilizing residual income is that
    a. a corporation with a high investment turnover ratio always has a higher residual income than a corporation with a smaller investment turnover ratio.
    b. a corporation with a high return on sales always has a higher residual income than a corporation with a smaller return on sales.
    c. A corporation with a larger dollar amount of assets is likely to have a higher residual income than a corporation with a smaller dollar amount of assets.
    d. none of the above are correct.

    Answer: c   *Difficulty:* 2   *Objective:* 4

46. A company which favors the residual income approach
    a. wants managers to concentrate on maximizing an absolute amount of dollars.
    b. wants managers to concentrate on maximizing a percentage return.
    c. wants managers to maximize the investment turnover ratio.
    d. wants managers to maximize return on sales.

    Answer: a   *Difficulty:* 2   *Objective:* 4

47. Using residual income as a measure of performance rather than return on investment promotes goal congruence because
    a.   residual income places importance on the reduction of underperforming assets.
    b.   residual income calculates a percentage return rather than an absolute return.
    c.   residual income concentrates on maximizing an absolute amount of dollars.
    d.   residual income concentrates on maximizing the return on sales.

    Answer: c   *Difficulty:*   2   *Objective:*   4

THE FOLLOWING INFORMATION APPLIES TO QUESTIONS 48 THROUGH 50.
The Bandage Medical Supply Company has two divisions that operate independently of one another. The financial data for the year 20x3 reported the following results:

	North	South
Sales	$3,000,000	$2,500,000
Operating income	750,000	550,000
Taxable income	650,000	375,000
Investment	6,000,000	5,000,000

The company's desired rate of return is 10%. Income is defined as operating income.

48. What are the respective return-on-investment ratios for the North and South Divisions?
    a.   0.110 and 0.125
    b.   0.108 and 0.075
    c.   0.125 and 0.110
    d.   0.050 and 0.150

    Answer: c   *Difficulty:*   2   *Objective:*   3
    North = $750,000/$6,000,000 = 12.5%
    South = $550,000/$5,000,000 = 11.0%

49. What are the respective residual incomes for the North and South Divisions?
    a. $30,000 and $50,000
    b. $150,000 and $30,000
    c. $150,000 and $50,000
    d. $50,000 and a negative $150,000

    Answer: c   *Difficulty:*   2   *Objective:*   4
    North = $750,000 - (0.1) $6,000,000 = $150,000
    South = $550,000- (0.1) $5,000,000 = $50,000

50. Which division has the best return on investment and which division has the best residual income figure, respectively?
    a.   North, North
    b.   South, South
    c.   North, South
    d.   South, North

    Answer: a   *Difficulty:*   2   *Objective:*   4

51. After-tax operating income minus the after-tax weighted-average cost of capital multiplied by total assets minus current liabilities equals
    a. return on investment.
    b. residual income.
    c. economic value added.
    d. weighted-average cost of capital.

    Answer: c   *Difficulty:* 1   *Objective:* 5

52. The after-tax average cost of all the long-term funds used by a corporation equals
    a. economic value added.
    b. return on investment.
    c. return on equity.
    d. weighted-average cost of capital.

    Answer: d   *Difficulty:* 1   *Objective:* 5

53. A negative feature of defining investment by excluding the portion of total assets employed that are financed by short-term creditors is
    a. current liabilities are sometimes difficult to define.
    b. short-term debt is always more expensive to finance than long-term debt.
    c. this method encourages managers to use an excessive amount of short-term debt.
    d. this method encourages managers to use an excessive amount of long-term debt.

    Answer: c   *Difficulty:* 2   *Objective:* 5

THE FOLLOWING INFORMATION APPLIES TO QUESTIONS 54 THROUGH 56.
Waldorf Company has two sources of funds: long-term debt with a market and book value of $10 million issued at an interest rate of 12%, and equity capital that has a market value of $8 million (book value of $4 million). Waldorf Company has profit centers in the following locations with the following operating incomes, total assets, and total liabilities. The cost of equity capital is 12%, while the tax rate is 25%.

	Operating Income	Assets	Current Liabilities
St. Louis	$ 960,000	$ 4,000,000	$ 200,000
Cedar Rapids	$1,200,000	$ 8,000,000	$ 600,000
Wichita	$2,040,000	$12,000,000	$1,200,000

54. What is the EVA for St. Louis?
   a. $255,740
   b. $327,460
   c. $392,540
   d. $720,000

Answer: b   *Difficulty:* 3   *Objective:* 5
WACC = [(0.09 x $10,000,000) + (0.12 x $8,000,000)]/$18,000,000 = 0.1033
St. Louis (EVA) = ($960,000 x 0.75) – [0.1033 x (4,000,000 - $200,000)]
= $720,000 - $392,540= $327,460

55. What is the EVA for Cedar Rapids?
   a. $135,580
   b. $220,000
   c. $234,000
   d. $305,000

Answer: a   *Difficulty:* 3   *Objective:* 5
Cedar Rapids (EVA) = ($1,200,000 x 0.75) - [0.1033 x ($8,000,000 - $600,000)]
= $900,000 - $764,420= $135,580

56. What is the EVA for Wichita?
   a. $450,000
   b. $1,530,000
   c. $414,360
   d. $1,115,640

Answer: c   *Difficulty:* 3   *Objective:* 5
Wichita (EVA) = ($2,040,000 x.75) – [(0.1033 x ($12,000,000 - 1,200,000)]
= $1,530,000 - $1,115,640= $414,360

THE FOLLOWING INFORMATION APPLIES TO QUESTIONS 57 THROUGH 59.

Ruth Cleaning Products manufactures home cleaning products. The company has two divisions, Bleach and Cleanser. Because of different accounting methods and inflation rates, the company is considering multiple evaluation measures. The following information is provided for 20x3:

	ASSETS		INCOME	
	Book value	Current value	Book value	Current value
Bleach	$225,000	$300,000	$150,000	$155,000
Cleanser	$450,000	$250,000	$100,000	$105,000

The company is currently using a 15% required rate of return.

57. What are Bleach's and Cleanser's return on investment based on book values, respectively?
   a. 0.22; 0.67
   b. 0.42; 0.52
   c. 0.52; 0.42
   d. 0.67; 0.22

   Answer: d   *Difficulty:* 2   *Objective:* 6
   Book value ROI:
         Bleach: $150,000/$225,000 = 0.67
         Cleanser: $100,000/$450,000 = 0.22

58. What are Bleach's and Cleanser's return on investment based on current values, respectively?
   a. 0.22; 0.67
   b. 0.42; 0.52
   c. 0.52; 0.42
   d. 0.67; 0.22

   Answer: c   *Difficulty:* 2   *Objective:* 6
   Current ROI:
         Bleach: $155,000 / $300,000 = 0.52
         Cleanser: $105,000 / $250,000 = 0.42

59. What are Bleach's and Cleanser's residual incomes based on book values, respectively?
   a. $116,250; $32,500
   b. $110,000; $67,500
   c. $67,500; $110,000
   d. $37,500; $116,250

   Answer: a   *Difficulty:* 2   *Objective:* 6
   Book value RI:
         Bleach: $150,000 - ($225,000 x 0.15) = $116,250
         Cleanser: $100,000 - ($450,000 x 0.15) = $32,500

60. The cost today of purchasing an asset identical to the one currently held is called
   a. an actual cost.
   b. a current cost.
   c. a dual cost.
   d. a fixed cost.

   Answer: b   *Difficulty:* 2   *Objective:* 6

61. If a company is a multinational company with operations in several different countries, one way to achieve comparability of historical-cost based ROIs for facilities in different countries is
   a. restate the results of operations using the cash basis method of accounting.
   b. use GAAP for all reporting and calculations.
   c. restate the results of all operations in dollars.
   d. all of the above would achieve comparability.

   Answer: c   *Difficulty:* 2   *Objective:* 7

62. Which of the following statements is true?
   a. The economic, legal, political, social, and cultural environments differ across countries.
   b. Governments in some countries may impose controls and limit selling prices of a company's products.
   c. Because of advances in telecommunications and transportation, the availability of materials and skilled labor does not differ significantly across countries.
   d. Both (a) and (b) are correct.

   Answer: d   *Difficulty:* 2   *Objective:* 7

63. In performance evaluations
   a. the performance of the division prior to the manager assuming control should be considered.
   b. economic conditions for the specific industry should not be considered.
   c. to have an effective and fair evaluation, a manager should be evaluated over several time periods.
   d. both (a) and (c) are correct.

   Answer: d   *Difficulty:* 2   *Objective:* 8

64. A problem with rewarding managers only on the basis of residual income
   a. is that residual income is difficult to measure.
   b. is that on occasion the items in the residual income calculation are not quantifiable.
   c. is that residual income can depend on items over which the manager has little control.
   d. include all of the above.

   Answer: c   *Difficulty:* 2   *Objective:* 8

65. _____ describes contexts in which an employee prefers to exert less effort than the effort that the owner wants because the employee's effort cannot be accurately monitored and enforced.
   a. Goal congruence
   b. Moral hazard
   c. Management compensation
   d. Incentive compensation

   Answer: b   *Difficulty*: 1   *Objective*: 8

66. Tying performance measures more closely to a manager's efforts
   a. encourages the use of nonfinancial measures.
   b. results in a strict use of financial ratios.
   c. results in the salary component of compensation dominating the total compensation package.
   d. includes both (a) and (c).

   Answer: a   *Difficulty*: 2   *Objective*: 9

67. Relative performance evaluation
   a. is called benchmarking.
   b. filters out the effect of common noncontrollable factors.
   c. results in managers having no incentive to help one another.
   d. include all of the above.

   Answer: d   *Difficulty*: 2   *Objective*: 9

68. Team incentives encourage cooperation by
   a. forcing people to work together on difficult tasks.
   b. improving morale.
   c. letting individuals help one another as they strive toward a common goal.
   d. rewarding all teams the same amount.

   Answer: c   *Difficulty*: 1   *Objective*: 9

69. Many manufacturing, marketing, and design problems require employees with multiple skills; therefore, teams are used and the members have the added encouragement of
   a. individual incentives.
   b. management incentives.
   c. morale incentives.
   d. team incentives.

   Answer: d   *Difficulty*: 1   *Objective*: 9

70. Designers of executive compensation plans emphasize which of the following factors?
   a. Achievement of organizational goals
   b. Administrative ease
   c. The probability that the executives affected by the plan will perceive the plan as fair
   d. All of the above are emphasized.

   Answer: d   *Difficulty*: 2   *Objective*: 9

EXERCISES AND PROBLEMS

71. Assume you are evaluating a manufacturing company. Match the various organizational activities and concepts with the performance measures listed. Some items may have more than one match.

Activities:
1. Change in revenues
2. Cycle time
3. Economic order quantity
4. Manufacturing defects
5. Market share
6. New products
7. On-time delivery
8. Operating income
9. Product reliability
10. Time-to-market

Performance measure:

_____ a. Profitability

_____ b. Customer satisfaction

_____ c. Innovation

_____ d. Efficiency, quality, and time

Answer:

1, 8 _____ a. Profitability

5, 7, 9 _____ b. Customer satisfaction

6, 10 _____ c. Innovation

2, 3, 4, 7, 9, 10 _____ d. Efficiency, quality, and time

Difficulty: 2   *Objective*: 1

72. Designing an accounting based performance measure requires six steps. List each step. For three of the steps, describe a question that must be resolved as part of the implementation process.

Answer:
1. *Choose performance measures that align with top management's goals.*
   Does operating income, return on assets, or revenues best measure a subunit's financial goals?
2. *Choose the time horizon of each performance measure.*
   Should the performance measures be calculated for one year or a multi-year time horizon?
3. *Choose a definition for each performance measure.*
   Should assets be defined as total assets or net assets?
4. *Choose a measurement alternative for each performance measure.*
   Should assets be measured at historical cost or current cost?
5. *Choose a target level of performance.*
   Should all subunits have the same targets such as the same required rate of return on assets?
6. *Choose the timing of the feedback.*
   How often should manufacturing performance reports be sent to management?

Difficulty: 2   *Objective:* 2

73. Museum Corporation uses the investment center concept for the museums that it manages. Select operating data for three of its museums for 20x3 are as follows:

	St. Louis	Dallas	Miami
Revenue	$600,000	$750,000	$900,000
Operating assets	300,000	250,000	350,000
Net operating income	51,000	56,000	59,000

Required:
a. Compute the return on investment for each division.
b. Which museum manager is doing best based only on ROI? Why?
c. What other factors should be included when evaluating the managers?

Answer:
a. St. Louis = $51,000/$300,000 = 0.170
   Dallas   = $56,000/$250,000 = 0.224
   Miami   = $59,000/$350,000 = 0.169

b. Dallas was doing the best because the ROI was the highest, and compared to Miami, was doing better with fewer assets.

c. At a minimum, the company should consider examining the DuPont method, residual income, and the age of operating assets.

Difficulty: 2   *Objective:* 3

74. Kase Tractor Company allows its divisions to operate as autonomous units. The operating data for 20x3 follow:

	Plows	Tractors	Combines
Revenues	$2,250,000	$500,000	$4,800,000
Accounts receivable	800,000	152,500	1,435,000
Operating assets	1,000,000	400,000	1,750,000
Net operating income	220,000	60,000	480,000
Taxable income	165,000	90,000	385,000

Required:

a. Compute the investment turnover for each division.
b. Compute the return on sales for each division
c. Compute the return on investment for each division.
d. Which division manager is doing best? Why?
e. What other factors should be included when evaluating the managers?

For parts (b) and (c) income is defined as operating income.

Answer:

a. *Investment turnover*:
  Plows   = $2,250,000/$1,000,000   = 2.25
  Tractors = $500,000/$400,000   = 1.25
  Combines = $4,800,000/$1,750,000   = 2.74

b. *Return on Sales*:
  Plows   = $220,000/$2,250,000   = 0.10
  Tractors = $60,000/$500,000   = 0.12
  Combines = $480,000/$4,800,000   = 0.10

c. *ROI*:
  Plows   = 2.25 x 0.10   = 0.225
  Tractors = 1.25 x 0.12   = 0.150
  Combines = 2.74 x 0.10   = 0.274

d. Combines' manager had the best performance because he had the highest investment turnover, which offset his second-best return on sales.

e. Residual income should be considered and noncontrollable factors such as the age of the assets.

Difficulty: 2   *Objective:* 3

75. Provide the missing data for the following situations:

	Red Division	White Division	Blue Division
Sales	$?	$10,000,000	$?
Net operating income	$200,000	$400,000	$288,000
Operating assets	$?	$?	$1,600,000
Return on investment	0.16	0.10	?
Return on sales	0.04	?	0.12
Investment turnover	?	?	1.5

Answer:

Red Division:

ROI	= ROS x IT	
0.16	= 0.04 x IT	
IT	= 4.0	

ROS	= Income/Sales	
0.04	= $200,000/Sales	
Sales	= $5,000,000	

IT	= Sales/OA	
4	= $5,000,000/OA	
OA	= $1,250,000	

White Division:

ROS	= $400,000/$10,000,000		= 0.04
IT	= ROI/ROS	= 0.10/0.04	= 2.5
OA	= S/IT	= $10,000,000/2.5	= $4,000,000

Blue Division:

Sales	= IT x OA	= 1.5 x $1,600,000	= $2,400,000
ROI	= 0.12 x 1.5	= 0.18	

Difficulty: 3   *Objective*: 3

76. Hargrave Products has three divisions, which operate autonomously. Their results for 20x3 were as follows:

	East	West	International
Sales	$30,000,000	$40,000,000	$50,000,000
Cost of goods sold	15,000,000	25,000,000	37,000,000
Operating income	4,500,000	4,750,000	5,000,000
Investment base	30,000,000	30,500,000	31,000,000

The company's desired rate of return is 15%.

Required:

a. Compute each division's ROI. Round to three decimal places.
b. Compute each division's residual income.

Answer:

a. East ROI = $4,500,000/$30,000,000 = 0.150
   West ROI = $4,750,000/$30,500,000 = 0.156
   International = $5,000,000/$31,000,000 = 0.161

b.

	East	West	International
Investment base	$30,000,000	$30,500,000	$31,000,000
Minimum rate	x 0.15	x 0.15	x 0.15
Minimum return	$ 4,500,000	$ 4,575,000	$ 4,650,000
Operating Income	$4,500,000	$4,750,000	$5,000,000
Minimum return	4,500,000	4,575,000	4,650,000
Residual income	$ 0	$ 175,000	$ 350,000

Difficulty: 2   *Objectives:*   3, 4

77. Batman Abstract Company has three divisions that operate autonomously. Their results for 20x3 are as follows:

	Riddler	Joker	Penguin
Sales	$5,000,000	$7,000,000	$10,000,000
Contribution margin	1,440,000	1,700,000	3,500,000
Operating income	1,000,000	1,750,000	2,520,000
Investment base	9,000,000	10,000,000	14,000,000

The company's desired rate of return is 20%.

Required:

a. Compute each division's ROI.
b. Compute each division's residual income.
c. Rank each division by both ROI and residual income.
d. Which division had the best performance in 20x3? Why?

Answer:

a.
Riddler ROI	= $1,000,000/$9,000,000	= 0.111
Joker ROI	= $1,750,000/$10,000,000	= 0.175
Penguin ROI	= $2,520,000/$14,000,000	= 0.180

b.

	Riddler	Joker	Penguin
Investment base	$9,000,000	$10,000,000	$14,000,000
Minimum rate	x 0.20	x 0.20	x 0.20
Minimum return	$1,800,000	$2,000,000	$2,800,000
Income	$1,000,000	$1,750,000	$2,520,000
Minimum return	1,800,000	2,000,000	2,800,000
Residual income	$(800,000)	$ (250,000)	$(280,000)

c. *ROI Rank:*
Penguin # 1
Joker # 2
Riddler # 3

RI Rank:
Joker #1
Penguin #2
Riddler #3

77. (continued)

    d.   As to which division was the best, it is difficult to determine without knowing what the results are being used to evaluate. If management is measuring only the return of capital, the Penguin Division has the highest ranking, although not much ahead of Joker. However, Penguin does have a substantially higher income level. As to meeting management's expectations of residual income, all divisions fall short of the goal with Joker being slightly ahead of Penguin.

Difficulty: 3   *Objectives:* 3, 4

78. The Coffee Division of American Products is planning the 20x3 operating budget. Average operating assets of $1,500,000 will be used during the year and unit selling prices are expected to average $100 each. Variable costs of the division are budgeted at $400,000, while fixed costs are set at $250,000. The company's required rate of return is 18%.

Required:

a. Compute the sales volume necessary to achieve a 20% ROI.

b. The division manager receives a bonus of 50% of residual income. What is his anticipated bonus for 20x3, assuming he achieves the 20% ROI from part (a)?

Answer:

a. Target operating income = 0.20 x $1,500,000 = $300,000

Operating income	$300,000
Variable costs	400,000
Fixed costs	250,000
Target revenues	$950,000

Sales volume = $950,000/$100 = 9,500 units

b.

Asset base	$1,500,000
Minimum rate	x 0.18
Required return	$ 270,000
Target operating income	$ 300,000
Required return	270,000
Residual income	$ 30,000

Bonus = $30,000 x 0.50 = $15,000

Difficulty: 3   *Objectives:* 3, 8, 9

79. LaserLife Printer Cartridge Company is a decentralized organization with several autonomous divisions. The division managers are evaluated, in part, on the basis of the change in their return on invested assets. Operating results for the Packer Division for 20x3 are budgeted as follows:

Sales	$5,000,000
Less variable costs	2,500,000
Contribution margin	2,500,000
Less fixed expenses	1,800,000
Net operating income	$ 700,000

Operating assets for the division are currently $3,600,000. For 20x3, the division can add a new product line for an investment of $600,000. The new product line will generate sales of $1,600,000 and will incur fixed expenses of $600,000 annually. Variable costs of the new product will average 60% of the selling price.

Required:
a. What is the effect on ROI of accepting the new product line?
b. If the company's required rate of return is 6% and residual income is used to evaluate managers, would this encourage the division to accept the new product line? Explain and show computations.

Answer:

a.

New investment:		
Sales		$1,600,000
Variable costs	$960,000	
Fixed costs	600,000	1,560,000
Operating income		$ 40,000

Current ROI = $700,000/$3,600,000 = 0.194
New investment ROI = $40,000/$600,000 = 0.067
Combined ROI = $740,000/$4,200,000 = 0.176

Accepting the new product line will reduce the division's ROI. This would make the manager reluctant to make the investment.

b.

Investment	$600,000
Minimum return	x 0.06
Required amount	$ 36,000

Income	$ 40,000
Required amount	36,000
Residual income	$ 4,000

Manager would accept the investment because income is increased by $4,000.

Difficulty: 2   *Objectives:* 3, 4, 8, 9

80. Capital Investments has three divisions. Each division's required rate of return is 15%. Planned operating results for 20x3 are as follows:

Division	Operating income	Investment
A	$15,000,000	$100,000,000
B	$25,000,000	$125,000,000
C	$11,000,000	$ 50,000,000

The company is planning an expansion, which is requiring each division to increase its investments by $25,000,000 and its income by $4,500,000.

Required:

a.   Compute the current ROI for each division.

b.   Compute the current residual income for each division.

c.   Rank the divisions according to their current ROIs and residual incomes.

d.   Determine the effects after adding the new project to each division's ROI and residual income.

e.   Assuming the managers are evaluated on either ROI or residual income, which divisions are pleased with the expansion and which ones are unhappy?

Answer:

a.   A ROI   = $15,000,000/$100,000,000   = 0.15
     B ROI   = $25,000,000/$125,000,000   = 0.20
     C ROI   = $11,000,000/$50,000,000   = 0.22

b.   A RI   = $15,000,000 - ($100,000,000 x 0.15)   = $ 0
     B RI   = $25,000,000 - ($125,000,000 x 0.15)   = $6,250,000
     C RI   = $11,000,000 - ($50,000,000 x 0.15)   = $3,500,000

c.   *ROI Rank*:   1. C   *RI Rank*:   1. B
                   2. B   2. C
                   3. A   3. A

80. (continued)

d. A ROI = $19,500,000/$125,000,000   = 0.156
    B ROI = $29,500,000/$150,000,000   = 0.197
    C ROI = $15,500,000/$75,000,000   = 0.207

    A RI   = $19,500,000 - ($125,000,000 x 0.15)   = $ 750,000
    B RI   = $29,500,000 - ($150,000,000 x 0.15)   = $7,000,000
    C RI   = $15,500,000 - ($75,000,000 x 0.15)   = $4,250,000

e. Everyone would be pleased if residual income was used because residual incomes increase with the expansion. However, it would be difficult to evaluate each division on a comparative basis because each division's investment base is different.

Only the manager of Division A is pleased with the new investment if ROI is used because that is the only division with an increased ROI. In the case of additional investments that are required by corporate management, residual income may be the best to use for evaluating each manager individually, but not collectively.

Difficulty: 3   *Objectives*: 3, 4, 9

81. The executive vice president of Wicker Pen Company wants to establish an accounting-based performance measurement system for the company's new plant. The company has an accounting information system sufficient to support a fairly sophisticated performance measurement system. The new plant is going to be considered an investment center since its products will be markedly different from others the company currently sells. The new plant will have no internal dealings with other plants within the company.

    Required:
    What are some of the key steps that should be undertaken in the establishment of an accounting-based performance measurement system?

    Answer:
    Key steps include:

    1. Choose variables that represent the company's financial goals for the plant. They would include those that relate to the plant as an investment center.

    2. Define the variables in terms of the company's general goals.

    3. Determine how the variables will be measured.

    4. Select benchmarks against which the variables will be measured.

    5. Select periodicity of reporting for each variable to be measured.

    Difficulty: 2   *Objective:* 2

82. Companies are increasingly using nonfinancial measures to evaluate performance. Why? Since these numbers do not come from the company's financial records, why are they used?

    Answer:
    The correct answer will revolve around the objective of providing quality goods to the corporation's customers. Quality goods bring repeat business and satisfied customers are a business' best advertisement.

    The idea is that these nonfinancial measures concentrate on areas and questions that indicate the quality of a particular corporation's products. While some of these items do not come from a companies' financial records, such as defect rates, they are quantifiable and can be verified.

    Difficulty: 3   *Objective:* 1

83. Bob Cellular Phone uses ROI to measure divisional performance. Annual ROI calculations for each division have traditionally employed the ending amount of invested capital along with annual operating income and net revenue. The Dupont method is generally used. The company's Phone Accessories Division had the following results for the last two years:

20x3 ROI = ($2,000,000/$20,000,000) x ($20,000,000/$10,000,000) = 0.20
20x4 ROI = ($2,400,000/$25,000,000) x ($25,000,000/$15,000,000) = 0.16

Corporate management was disappointed in the performance of the division for 20x4, since it had made an additional investment in the division that was budgeted for a 23% ROI.

Required:

a. Discuss some factors that may have contributed to the decrease in ROI for 20x4.

b. Would there have been any substantial difference if average capital had been used?

Answer:

a. While sales increased by 25%, net income only increased by 20%. This may indicate that expenses increased more than they should have. Apparently, the expected marginal net income from the new investment was $1,150,000 ($5,000,000 x 0.23), and either sales were too low or expenses too high for the new products. But this calculation is somewhat hypothetical since we do not know expected sales. Start-up costs may have also contributed to the increased expenses of the first year's operations. An increase in investment also contributed to the decline in return on investment.

b. Using average capital: = ($10,000,000 + $15,000,000)/2 = $12,500,000

ROI = $2,400,000/$12,500,000 = 0.192

Using average capital would have improved the ROI from 16 to over 19%. This would still have been a disappointment to management because the total ROI fell below expectations. Perhaps it is unreasonable to expect a new investment to achieve its target ROI in the first year of operations.

Difficulty: 3   *Objective:* 3

84. The economic value added concept has attracted considerable attention in recent years. Explain the attractiveness of this number as a measure of performance.

Answer:
The attractiveness of economic value added at the divisional level is primarily the fact that it allows managers to incorporate the cost of capital in decisions at the divisional level.

Difficulty: 3   *Objective:* 5

85. R&D Storage is a small, but diversified, moving and storage company. In recent years, its corporate income has declined to unacceptable levels. To change the direction of the company, the board of directors hired a new chief executive officer. She is currently considering three alternative ways to reward division managers for performance. They are:

1. Give each manager a competitive salary with no bonus for performance.

2. Give each manager a base salary with the largest portion being a bonus based on performance, ROI being the yardstick.

3. Give each manager a base salary with a bonus based on comparative performance with the other divisions.

Required:
Evaluate each of the ideas, giving strengths and weaknesses.

Answer:
1. Opportunities for salary increases might be decided via other means such as improvements in employee motivation, cost savings ideas, or improved management skills. This method will fit some types of situations and managers better than the bonus methods, but should not be used in situations where a high degree of motivation is desired.

2. The second idea is good for motivating a manager to improve the performance of each given division. A weakness in this method occurs when managers make decisions that maximize return on investment in the short run because they have no intent to stay with the company over a long period of time.

3. The third method is great for motivating managers to compete with each other. However, some reward should be available for the lowest rated manager if that manager's performance is, in fact, above the company's standard for performance. Suboptimization is a potential problem with this approach if the winning manager's bonus is substantially above everyone else's bonus.

Difficulty: 2   *Objectives:* 8, 9